The Collected Works of

Langston Hughes

Volume 9

Essays on Art, Race, Politics, and World Affairs

Projected Volumes in the Collected Works

The Poems: 1921–1940

The Poems: 1941–1950

The Poems: 1951–1967

The Novels: *Not without Laughter* and *Tambourines to Glory*

The Plays to 1942: *Mulatto* to *The Sun Do Move*

The Gospel Plays, Operas, and Other Late Dramatic Work

The Early Simple Stories

The Later Simple Stories

Essays on Art, Race, Politics, and World Affairs

Fight for Freedom and Other Writings on Civil Rights

Works for Children and Young Adults: Poetry, Fiction, and Other Writing

Works for Children and Young Adults: Biographies

Autobiography: *The Big Sea*

Autobiography: *I Wonder As I Wander*

The Short Stories

The Translations

An Annotated Bibliography of the Works of Langston Hughes

Publication of

The Collected Works of Langston Hughes

has been generously assisted by

Landon and Sarah Rowland

and

Morton and Estelle Sosland

Editorial Board

The Collected Works of

Langston Hughes

Volume 9

Essays on Art, Race, Politics, and World Affairs

Edited with an Introduction by Christopher C. De Santis

University of Missouri Press
Columbia and London

University of Missouri Press, Columbia, Missouri 65201
Printed and bound in the United States of America

5 4 3 2 1 06 05 04 03 02

Library of Congress Cataloging-in-Publication Data

Hughes, Langston, 1902–1967
[Works. 2001]
The collected works of Langston Hughes / edited with an introduction by Christopher C. De Santis
p. cm.
Includes bibliographical references and indexes.
ISBN 0-8262-1394-4 (v. 9 : alk. paper)
1. African Americans—Literary collections. I. De Santis, Christopher C. II. Title.
PS3515 .U274 2001
818'.5209—dc21 00066601

∞™This paper meets the requirements of the American National Standard for Permanence of Paper for Printed Library Materials, Z39.48, 1984.

Designer: Kristie Lee
Typesetter: BOOKCOMP, Inc.
Printer and binder: Thomson-Shore, Inc.
Typefaces: Galliard, Optima

Contents

Acknowledgments

I would like to gratefully acknowledge the Department of English and the College of Arts and Sciences at Illinois State University for providing research grants and additional funding that helped in the completion of this volume. Ron Fortune, Chair of the Department of English, has been particularly supportive of faculty research and deserves special recognition and thanks. Beverly Jarrett and Jane Lago of the University of Missouri Press expertly guided this volume to completion. They fielded endless questions with patience and enthusiasm, and their advice about the final contents of the book was invaluable. I would also like to thank Karen Chachere for her research assistance and those teachers and scholars who have inspired my work on Langston Hughes over the years: Sandra Adell, William L. Andrews, John Callahan, Nellie McKay, Arnold Rampersad, and Craig Werner. Finally, I thank Stacey Gottlieb and Julie Jung for the generosity of spirit and humor that sustained me while working on this book.

The University of Missouri Press is grateful for assistance from the following individuals and institutions in locating and making available copies of the original editions used in the preparation of this edition: Anne Barker and June DeWeese, Ellis Library, University of Missouri–Columbia; Teresa Gipson, Miller Nichols Library, University of Missouri–Kansas City; Ruth Carruth and Patricia C. Willis, Beinecke Rare Book and Manuscript Library, Yale University; Ann Pathega, Washington University.

The *Collected Works* would not have been possible without the support and assistance of Patricia Powell, Chris Byrne, and Wendy Schmalz of Harold Ober Associates, representing the estate of Langston Hughes, and of Arnold Rampersad and Ramona Bass, co-executors of the estate of Langston Hughes.

Chronology
By Arnold Rampersad

1902 James Langston Hughes is born February 1 in Joplin, Missouri, to James Nathaniel Hughes, a stenographer for a mining company, and Carrie Mercer Langston Hughes, a former government clerk.

1903 After his father immigrates to Mexico, Langston's mother takes him to Lawrence, Kansas, the home of Mary Langston, her twice-widowed mother. Mary Langston's first husband, Lewis Sheridan Leary, died fighting alongside John Brown at Harpers Ferry. Her second, Hughes's grandfather, was Charles Langston, a former abolitionist, Republican politician, and businessman.

1907 After a failed attempt at a reconciliation in Mexico, Langston and his mother return to Lawrence.

1909 Langston starts school in Topeka, Kansas, where he lives for a while with his mother before returning to his grandmother's home in Lawrence.

1915 Following Mary Langston's death, Hughes leaves Lawrence for Lincoln, Illinois, where his mother lives with her second husband, Homer Clark, and Homer Clark's young son by another union, Gwyn "Kit" Clark.

1916 Langston, elected class poet, graduates from the eighth grade. Moves to Cleveland, Ohio, and starts at Central High School there.

1918 Publishes early poems and short stories in his school's monthly magazine.

1919 Spends the summer in Toluca, Mexico, with his father.

1920 Graduates from Central High as class poet and editor of the school annual. Returns to Mexico to live with his father.

1921 In June, Hughes publishes "The Negro Speaks of Rivers" in *Crisis* magazine. In September, sponsored by his father, he enrolls at Columbia University in New York. Meets W. E. B. Du Bois, Jessie Fauset, and Countee Cullen.

1922 Unhappy at Columbia, Hughes withdraws from school and breaks with his father.

1923 Sailing in June to western Africa on the crew of a freighter, he visits Senegal, the Gold Coast, Nigeria, the Congo, and other countries.

1924 Spends several months in Paris working in the kitchen of a nightclub.

1925 Lives in Washington for a year with his mother. His poem "The Weary Blues" wins first prize in a contest sponsored by *Opportunity* magazine, which leads to a book contract with Knopf through Carl Van Vechten. Becomes friends with several other young artists of the Harlem Renaissance, including Zora Neale Hurston, Wallace Thurman, and Arna Bontemps.

1926 In January his first book, *The Weary Blues*, appears. He enrolls at historically black Lincoln University, Pennsylvania. In June, the *Nation* weekly magazine publishes his landmark essay "The Negro Artist and the Racial Mountain."

1927 Knopf publishes his second book of verse, *Fine Clothes to the Jew*, which is condemned in the black press. Hughes meets his powerful patron Mrs. Charlotte Osgood Mason. Travels in the South with Hurston, who is also taken up by Mrs. Mason.

1929 Hughes graduates from Lincoln University.

1930 Publishes his first novel, *Not without Laughter* (Knopf). Visits Cuba and meets fellow poet Nicolás Guillén. Hughes is dismissed by Mrs. Mason in a painful break made worse by false charges of dishonesty leveled by Hurston over their play *Mule Bone*.

1931 Demoralized, he travels to Haiti. Publishes work in the communist magazine *New Masses*. Supported by the Rosenwald Foundation, he tours the South taking his poetry to the people. In Alabama, he visits some of the Scottsboro Boys in prison. His brief collection of poems *Dear Lovely Death* is privately printed in Amenia, New York. Hughes and the illustrator Prentiss Taylor publish a verse pamphlet, *The Negro Mother*.

1932 With Taylor, he publishes *Scottsboro, Limited*, a short play and four poems. From Knopf comes *The Dream Keeper*, a book of previously published poems selected for young people. Later, Macmillan brings out *Popo and Fifina*, a children's story about Haiti written with Arna Bontemps, his closest friend. In June, Hughes sails to Russia in a band of twenty-two young African

Americans to make a film about race relations in the United States. After the project collapses, he lives for a year in the Soviet Union. Publishes his most radical verse, including "Good Morning Revolution" and "Goodbye Christ."

1933 Returns home at midyear via China and Japan. Supported by a patron, Noël Sullivan of San Francisco, Hughes spends a year in Carmel writing short stories.

1934 Knopf publishes his first short story collection, *The Ways of White Folks.* After labor unrest in California threatens his safety, he leaves for Mexico following news of his father's death.

1935 Spends several months in Mexico, mainly translating short stories by local leftist writers. Lives for some time with the photographer Henri Cartier-Bresson. Returning almost destitute to the United States, he joins his mother in Oberlin, Ohio. Visits New York for the Broadway production of his play *Mulatto* and clashes with its producer over changes in the script. Unhappy, he writes the poem "Let America Be America Again."

1936 Wins a Guggenheim Foundation fellowship for work on a novel but soon turns mainly to writing plays in association with the Karamu Theater in Cleveland. Karamu stages his farce *Little Ham* and his historical drama about Haiti, *Troubled Island.*

1937 Karamu stages *Joy to My Soul,* another comedy. In July, he visits Paris for the League of American Writers. He then travels to Spain, where he spends the rest of the year reporting on the civil war for the *Baltimore Afro-American.*

1938 In New York, Hughes founds the radical Harlem Suitcase Theater, which stages his agitprop play *Don't You Want to Be Free?* The leftist International Workers Order publishes *A New Song,* a pamphlet of radical verse. Karamu stages his play *Front Porch.* His mother dies.

1939 In Hollywood he writes the script for the movie *Way Down South,* which is criticized for stereotyping black life. Hughes goes for an extended stay in Carmel, California, again as the guest of Noël Sullivan.

1940 His autobiography *The Big Sea* appears (Knopf). He is picketed by a religious group for his poem "Goodbye Christ," which he publicly renounces.

1941 With a Rosenwald Fund fellowship for playwriting, he leaves California for Chicago, where he founds the Skyloft Players. Moves on to New York in December.

1942 Knopf publishes his book of verse *Shakespeare in Harlem.* The Skyloft Players stage his play *The Sun Do Move.* In the summer he resides at the Yaddo writers' and artists' colony, New York. Hughes also works as a writer in support of the war effort. In November he starts "Here to Yonder," a weekly column in the Chicago *Defender* newspaper.

1943 "Here to Yonder" introduces Jesse B. Semple, or Simple, a comic Harlem character who quickly becomes its most popular feature. Hughes publishes *Jim Crow's Last Stand* (Negro Publication Society of America), a pamphlet of verse about the struggle for civil rights.

1944 Comes under surveillance by the FBI because of his former radicalism.

1945 With Mercer Cook, translates and later publishes *Masters of the Dew* (Reynal and Hitchcock), a novel by Jacques Roumain of Haiti.

1947 His work as librettist with Kurt Weill and Elmer Rice on the Broadway musical play *Street Scene* brings Hughes a financial windfall. He vacations in Jamaica. Knopf publishes *Fields of Wonder,* his only book composed mainly of lyric poems on nonracial topics.

1948 Hughes is denounced (erroneously) as a communist in the U.S. Senate. He buys a townhouse in Harlem and moves in with his longtime friends Toy and Emerson Harper.

1949 Doubleday publishes *Poetry of the Negro, 1746–1949,* an anthology edited with Arna Bontemps. Also published are *One-Way Ticket* (Knopf), a book of poems, and *Cuba Libre: Poems of Nicolás Guillén* (Anderson and Ritchie), translated by Hughes and Ben Frederic Carruthers. Hughes teaches for three months at the University of Chicago Lab School for children. His opera about Haiti with William Grant Still, *Troubled Island,* is presented in New York.

1950 Another opera, *The Barrier,* with music by Jan Meyerowitz, is hailed in New York but later fails on Broadway. Simon and Schuster publishes *Simple Speaks His Mind,* the first of five books based on his newspaper columns.

1951 Hughes's book of poems about life in Harlem, *Montage of a Dream Deferred,* appears (Henry Holt).

1952 His second collection of short stories, *Laughing to Keep from Crying,* is published by Henry Holt. In its "First Book" series for children, Franklin Watts publishes Hughes's *The First Book of Negroes.*

1953 In March, forced to testify before Senator Joseph McCarthy's subcommittee on subversive activities, Hughes is exonerated after repudiating his past radicalism. *Simple Takes a Wife* appears.

1954 Mainly for young readers, he publishes *Famous American Negroes* (Dodd, Mead) and *The First Book of Rhythms.*

1955 Publishes *The First Book of Jazz* and finishes *Famous Negro Music Makers* (Dodd, Mead). In November, Simon and Schuster publishes *The Sweet Flypaper of Life,* a narrative of Harlem with photographs by Roy DeCarava.

1956 Hughes's second volume of autobiography, *I Wonder As I Wander* (Rinehart), appears, as well as *A Pictorial History of the Negro* (Crown), coedited with Milton Meltzer, and *The First Book of the West Indies.*

1957 *Esther,* an opera with composer Jan Meyerowitz, has its premiere in Illinois. Rinehart publishes *Simple Stakes a Claim* as a novel. Hughes's musical play *Simply Heavenly,* based on his Simple character, runs for several weeks off and then on Broadway. Hughes translates and publishes *Selected Poems of Gabriela Mistral* (Indiana University Press).

1958 *The Langston Hughes Reader* (George Braziller) appears, as well as *The Book of Negro Folklore* (Dodd, Mead), coedited with Arna Bontemps, and another juvenile, *Famous Negro Heroes of America* (Dodd, Mead). John Day publishes a short novel, *Tambourines to Glory,* based on a Hughes gospel musical play.

1959 Hughes's *Selected Poems* published (Knopf).

1960 *The First Book of Africa* appears, along with *An African Treasury: Articles, Essays, Stories, Poems by Black Africans,* edited by Hughes (Crown).

1961 Inducted into the National Institute of Arts and Letters. Knopf publishes his book-length poem *Ask Your Mama: 12 Moods for Jazz. The Best of Simple,* drawn from the columns, appears (Hill and Wang). Hughes writes his gospel musical plays *Black Nativity* and *The Prodigal Son.* He visits Africa again.

1962 Begins a weekly column for the *New York Post.* Attends a writers' conference in Uganda. Publishes *Fight for Freedom: The Story of the NAACP,* commissioned by the organization.

1963 His third collection of short stories, *Something in Common,* appears from Hill and Wang. Indiana University Press publishes

Five Plays by Langston Hughes, edited by Webster Smalley, as well as Hughes's anthology *Poems from Black Africa, Ethiopia, and Other Countries.*

1964 His musical play *Jericho–Jim Crow,* a tribute to the civil rights movement, is staged in Greenwich Village. Indiana University Press brings out his anthology *New Negro Poets: U.S.A.,* with a foreword by Gwendolyn Brooks.

1965 With novelists Paule Marshall and William Melvin Kelley, Hughes visits Europe for the U.S. State Department. His gospel play *The Prodigal Son* and his cantata with music by David Amram, *Let Us Remember,* are staged.

1966 After twenty-three years, Hughes ends his depiction of Simple in his Chicago *Defender* column. Publishes *The Book of Negro Humor* (Dodd, Mead). In a visit sponsored by the U.S. government, he is honored in Dakar, Senegal, at the First World Festival of Negro Arts.

1967 His *The Best Short Stories by Negro Writers: An Anthology from 1899 to the Present* (Little, Brown) includes the first published story by Alice Walker. On May 22, Hughes dies at New York Polyclinic Hospital in Manhattan from complications following prostate surgery. Later that year, two books appear: *The Panther and the Lash: Poems of Our Times* (Knopf) and, with Milton Meltzer, *Black Magic: A Pictorial History of the Negro in American Entertainment* (Prentice Hall).

The Collected Works of

Langston Hughes

Volume 9

Essays on Art, Race, Politics, and World Affairs

Introduction

Among the most prolific of American writers, Langston Hughes gained international attention and acclaim in nearly every genre of writing, including poetry, the short story, drama, the novel, history, autobiography, journalistic prose, works for children and adolescents, the libretto, and song lyrics. While scholars and general readers have enjoyed relatively easy access to most of these writings, however, one genre in Hughes's vast oeuvre—the essay—has gone largely unnoticed. From his radical pieces praising revolutionary socialist ideology in the 1930s to the more conservative, previously unpublished "Black Writers in a Troubled World," which he wrote especially for a 1966 writers' colloquium at Dakar, Senegal, a year before his death, Hughes used the essay form as a vehicle through which to comment on the contemporary issues he found most pressing at various stages of his career. Although Hughes is best known as a poet, he generated some of his most powerful critiques of economic and racial exploitation and oppression through the genre of the essay. It was also the essay as a literary form that allowed Hughes to document the essential contributions of African Americans to U.S. literature, music, film, and theater and to chronicle the immense difficulties that black artists faced in gaining recognition, fair remuneration, and professional advancement for these contributions. Finally, it was in his essays that Hughes most fully represented the unique and endearing persona of the blues-poet-in-exile. While never literally forced out of the United States, Hughes nevertheless sought temporary refuge from American class prejudice and racial discrimination in locales that, for various reasons, seemed more conducive to the spirit and ideals of democracy than his own nation.

Many of the essays and other pieces of short nonfiction included in this volume of *The Collected Works of Langston Hughes* have long been out of print and will be new to most readers. Surprisingly, though, it was the genre of the essay that helped launch Hughes's long writing career. At the age of only eighteen, he had gained the attention of Jessie Redmon Fauset, the literary editor of the youth-oriented *Brownies' Book* and the NAACP's prestigious *Crisis* magazine, with several poems written for children that he submitted for publication in the fall of 1920. Fauset was impressed with the submissions, promised to publish one poem in an upcoming issue of *Brownies' Book,* and inquired whether Hughes had written any children's articles or stories about Mexico (he was living with his father in Toluca at this time). Hughes responded by sending a brief piece on Mexican games, an essay about daily life in Toluca, and a third article about a Mexican volcano, all of which Fauset accepted and published, respectively, in the January, April, and December 1921 issues of *Brownies' Book.*[1] Fauset published a fourth Hughes essay, "The Virgin of Guadalupe," in the *Crisis* that same year. Thus, at the very beginning of his writing career, Hughes demonstrated promise both as an essayist and as a poet.

This initial promise was further substantiated with two additional essays Hughes contributed to the *Crisis* while still in his early twenties, both reflective of the wanderlust that would compel him to travel and live in numerous places throughout the United States and abroad over the course of his writing career. The first, "Ships, Sea and Africa" (1923), is an impressionistic series of brief, vivid images that Hughes recorded while a crew member aboard the *West Hesseltine,* a freighter bound for the west coast of Africa from New York, where he had taken up residence. Arriving at the port of Dakar in Senegal on July 3, 1923, Hughes would remain in Africa for nearly three months. There, poetic and essayistic inspiration coalesced, resulting in a lovely essay that reads at times like a prose poem: "Evening . . . The copper-gold of the Congo sunset . . . Blue-green twilight . . . The hot, heavy African night studded with stars."

If Africa impressed Hughes with its abundance of new sights, sounds, and smells, equally provocative to the young writer were his experiences in the great cities of the United States, Mexico, and France, which he recollected in an essay that won second prize in a *Crisis*-sponsored literary contest. "The Fascination of Cities" (1926), like the earlier "Ships, Sea and Africa," is impressionistic in technique, as when Hughes describes Chicago as a "vast, ugly, brutal, monotonous city, checker-boarded, hard," or Paris as "a sorceress-city making herself beautiful with jewels."

1. See Arnold Rampersad, *The Life of Langston Hughes,* 2 vols. (New York: Oxford University Press, 1986, 1988), 1:45–48. Hughes's early essays for children—"Mexican Games," "In a Mexican City," and "Up to the Crater of an Old Volcano"—are included in *Works for Children and Young Adults: Poetry, Fiction, and Other Writing,* vol. 11 of *The Collected Works of Langston Hughes* (Columbia: University of Missouri Press, forthcoming).

Hughes beautifully evokes the childlike wonder of discovery in this essay, softening the harsher aspects of city life behind a veil of grandeur: "New York is then truly the dream-city, city of the towers near to God, city of hopes and visions, of spires seeking in the windy air loveliness and perfection." Evident here as well, however, are the brutal instances of racial injustice that would become central to so much of Hughes's nonfiction. Marveling at Chicago's cultural diversity, the writer is interrupted in his romantic reverie by a simple, blunt statement: " 'We don't 'low no niggers in this street.' "

"The Fascination of Cities" hinted both at the major themes Hughes would pursue and at his maturing talent in creative nonfiction. It was the publication of "The Negro Artist and the Racial Mountain" (1926) in the *Nation,* however, that signaled Hughes's transformation from a promising writer of nonfictional prose to one of America's most engaging essayists. At stake in the essay was no less than the very existence of a distinct African American aesthetic, an art originating in the confluence of African folk culture and the black experience of the Middle Passage, slavery, Reconstruction, and the long era of segregation. Hughes had touched on this subject implicitly in his most famous poem, "The Negro Speaks of Rivers" (1921), but it would take a controversial essay by another African American writing for the *Nation,* George S. Schuyler, to provoke a more explicit articulation of a distinct black art. Schuyler's "The Negro-Art Hokum" challenged the very premise that art produced in the United States is in any way influenced by race. In the midst of the intense excitement surrounding the publication of Alain Locke's anthology *The New Negro* (1925), which heralded an awakening in African American visual arts, literature, music, and scholarship, Schuyler registered strong and bitingly sarcastic skepticism that the movement that has come to be known as the Harlem Renaissance was anything more than racial propaganda and the self-promotion of an elite few:

> Negro art "made in America" is as non-existent as the widely advertised profundity of Cal Coolidge, the "seven years of progress" of Mayor Hylan, or the reported sophistication of New Yorkers. Negro art there has been, is, and will be among the numerous black nations of Africa; but to suggest the possibility of any such development among the ten million colored people in this republic is self-evident foolishness. Eager apostles from Greenwich Village, Harlem, and environs proclaim a great renaissance of Negro art just around the corner waiting to be ushered on the scene by those whose hobby is taking races, nations, peoples and movements under their wing. New art forms expressing the "peculiar" psychology of

> the Negro were about to flood the market. In short, the art of Homo Africanus was about to electrify the waiting world. Skeptics patiently waited. They still wait.[2]

Central to Schuyler's argument is the idea that "race" is a cultural construct, a product of social class, caste, and physical environment rather than a biological determinant. Schuyler correctly points out that the concept of fundamental differences among the races was historically used in the United States to erect a white supremacist ideology that cast African Americans as inherently inferior to white Americans. Schuyler insisted that celebrations of a distinct African American art—which might be translated by whites as a "peculiar art"—could only serve to legitimize such an ideology.

Hughes understood the merits of Schuyler's argument concerning "fundamental differences" among races, but he was incensed by Schuyler's suggestion that "the Aframerican is merely a lampblacked Anglo-Saxon." In a letter to the editor of the *Nation* that appeared shortly after Schuyler's essay was published, Hughes made his own position clear: "For Mr. Schuyler to say that 'the Negro masses . . . are no different from the white masses' in America seems to me obviously absurd. Fundamentally, perhaps, all peoples are the same. But as long as the Negro remains a segregated group in this country he must reflect certain racial and environmental differences which are his own." Hughes had enumerated these differences two months prior to this letter in "The Negro Artist and the Racial Mountain," his finest essay and a virtual declaration of independence for the younger artists and writers of the Harlem Renaissance. Troubled by what he perceived as a reliance on dominant white standards of art and culture among the African American middle classes and intelligentsia, Hughes challenged black artists and writers to embrace a racial aesthetic and a source of creativity generated from within the black communities in the United States rather than from without. In creating a truly racial art, the black artist could not be swayed by critiques of his or her subject matter or techniques, nor could fears of revealing aspects of black life that dominant standard-bearers of propriety frowned upon stand in the way of artistic inspiration. "An artist must be free to choose what he does," Hughes insisted, "but he must also never be afraid to do what he might choose." In this respect, Hughes believed

2. George S. Schuyler, "The Negro-Art Hokum," *Nation* 122 (June 16, 1926): 662–63.

that a vast storehouse of largely untapped artistic material resided within the culture of the African American working masses. Jazz, the spirituals, and the blues offered the artist a wealth of resources for the creation of a distinct black aesthetic, and the often conflicted relations between black and white people in the United States furnished "an inexhaustible supply of themes" for the writer and dramatist. In utilizing these resources, the black artist could—indeed, *must*—begin to challenge and overturn dominant white standards of beauty that limited the representation of blackness to minstrel-show stereotypes. Hughes dismissed Schuyler's argument that environment and economics had transformed African Americans into darker Anglo-Saxons, issuing in its place a code of responsibility to the artists of his generation: "It is the duty of the younger Negro artist, if he accepts any duties at all from outsiders, to change through the force of his art that old whispering 'I want to be white,' hidden in the aspirations of his people, to 'Why should I want to be white? I am a Negro—and beautiful!' "

"The Negro Artist and the Racial Mountain" anticipated the themes Hughes would pursue in his essays for the next decade, particularly in its strong critique of white racial prejudice but also in its condemnation of the black bourgeoisie's complicity in perpetuating racist attitudes. Uncompromising in his belief that the younger generation of African American artists and writers was being held back by timeworn attitudes, Hughes chastised "the best Negroes" in "These Bad New Negroes: A Critique on Critics" (1927) for rejecting the work of writers such as Jean Toomer and Rudolph Fisher on the basis of their representations of conflict and violence within African American communities. He also took a controversial stance in the essay on the issue of Carl Van Vechten's sensationalistic novel, *Nigger Heaven* (1926), which had caused a firestorm among the black literati and intelligentsia for its grossly stereotypical depictions of Harlem society and nightlife. A combination of his friendship with Van Vechten, a desire to shock the black bourgeoisie, and perhaps a sincere conviction that he was correct compelled Hughes to pronounce the novel "true to the life it pictures." Addressing charges by critics that his own work was mired in the lives of the lowest classes of African America, Hughes posed an honest question: "Is life among the better classes any cleaner or any more worthy of a poet's consideration?" He answered this question in the ironically titled "Our Wonderful Society: Washington" (1927), an essay that appeared in the National Urban League's *Opportunity* magazine. Eager to experience the " 'wonderful society life' among Negroes in Washington" that he remembered hearing about even as a child, Hughes found only small-minded snobbery and intraracial prejudice among many of the black elite of the nation's capital to whom he was introduced: "Speaking of a fraternity dance, one in a group of five college men said proudly, 'There was nothing but pinks there,—looked just like 'fay women. Boy, you'd have thought it was an o'fay dance!' "

Concerned as he was with issues affecting the black communities in the United States, Hughes was no provincial; as many of the essays in this volume make clear, his increasing engagement with the political Left was fueled as much by an active awareness of global class and racial oppression as it was by his commitment to represent the voices of the African American working masses. A trip to Haiti in 1931 confirmed for Hughes the extent to which U.S. imperialism had cast an ugly net of racism and economic exploitation over a once proud people—a people descended from Toussaint L'Ouverture, Jean-Jacques Dessalines, and Henri Christophe, heroic leaders who freed their land from slavery and established the first independent black republic. When Hughes arrived in the small country, signs of the American occupation were everywhere. U.S. military intervention, purportedly arranged on humanitarian grounds after a 1915 coup d'etat resulted in the overthrow and death of the Haitian president and the execution of political prisoners, had stripped the Haitian government of all vestiges of independence; the Haitian military, finances, and legislative powers were firmly under U.S. control. Hughes discovered that the occupation affected far more than the daily workings of the country, however. In "A Letter from Haiti" (1931), sent to *New Masses,* a radical magazine to which he contributed poems and essays frequently in the 1930s, Hughes reported, "Haiti is a hot, tropical little country, all mountains and sea; a lot of marines, mulatto politicians, and a world of black people without shoes—who catch hell." Searching in vain for signs of Haiti's heroic past—Christophe's great Citadel "stands in futile ruin now"—Hughes found only extreme poverty and illiteracy among the Haitian masses, and corruption and greed among the ruling elite. In "People without Shoes" (1931), an impassioned essay also published in *New Masses,* Hughes noted that the "barefooted ones care for the rice and cane fields under the hot sun. They climb high mountains picking coffee beans, and wade through surf to fishing boats in the blue sea. All of the work that keeps Haiti alive, pays for the American Occupation, and enriches foreign traders—that vast and basic work—is done there by Negroes without shoes." By contrast, Hughes discovered that the cultural and political elite of Haiti—those fortunate enough to have shoes—seemed largely unconcerned with the squalid huts and shops near the waterfront, the ragged child beggars, or the lack of adequate roads, factories, and schools in the country. Rather than working toward agricultural or commercial development, they contented themselves with luxury items acquired through government loans from abroad while drawing sharp class lines between themselves and the poverty-stricken masses.

Hughes's love of foreign travel was fed in part by a desire to temporarily escape the racial prejudice and discrimination of the United States. Learning of the color line in Haiti between the mulattoes and the blacks, and that the Haitian ruling class segregated itself from the workers, was thus a painful blow to the young writer, reminding him again of the ways in which class lines and color lines often intersect. The discovery that soldiers of the American occupation enforced Jim Crow customs in Haiti, however, did not surprise Hughes in the least. Signs of the white American presence—and its negative influence—abounded in Haiti. Having strayed from its supposedly humanitarian purpose, Hughes pointed out in "White Shadows in a Black Land" (1932), an essay published in *Crisis,* the American occupation had touched on nearly every aspect of life in Haiti:

> Before you can go ashore, a white American Marine has been on board ship to examine your passport, and maybe you will see a U.S. gunboat at anchor in the harbor. Ashore, you are likely to soon run into groups of Marines in the little cafes, talking in "Cracker" accents, and drinking in the usual boisterous American manner. You will discover that the Banque d'Haiti, with its Negro cashiers and tellers, is really under the control of the National City Bank of New York. You will become informed that all the money collected by the Haitian customs passes through the hands of an American comptroller. . . . The dark-skinned little Republic, then, has its hair caught in the white fingers of unsympathetic foreigners, and the Haitian people live today under a sort of military dictatorship backed by American guns. They are not free.

Hughes returned from Haiti to an equally troubled United States. The Great Depression had brought to an abrupt halt the sense of joy and hope with which he had proclaimed in the 1920s a new and shining moment in African American art. The gaiety of the Harlem Renaissance had given way to the stark reality of economic crisis, and African Americans all over the nation were facing record levels of unemployment. Having exposed in his essays of the mid-1920s the effects of white racial prejudice on African American artists—and the ways in which the valuation of whiteness among blacks contributed to an often impassable color line within African America—Hughes focused in the early 1930s on the broader racist and classist attitudes that seemed to be increasing as the nation moved further into economic depression. The 1931 Scottsboro trials especially reinforced in Hughes's mind the connections between race and class, further convincing the young writer that conservative thinking among blacks and whites alike was leading the nation—and particularly its millions of black citizens—toward disaster.

The Scottsboro case involved nine African American youths who had been arrested in Alabama in 1931 and charged with the rape of two young white women on an open railroad freight car. Eight of the youths were quickly convicted by all-white juries and sentenced to death, while the ninth of the "Scottsboro boys," as they were called in the media, received life imprisonment.[3] From the outset, reaction to the Scottsboro case took on sensational dimensions. To many white southerners, the alleged rapes represented crimes not merely against two women who happened to be in the wrong place at the wrong time, but against white womanhood in general. In this racist context, the youths involved in the incident came to be seen as representatives of the moral dissipation among African Americans in the South that had resulted from the collapse of slavery. Indeed, one Alabama newspaper reporter referred to the Scottsboro boys as "beasts unfit to be called human," and mobs of white townspeople, intent on seeing the youths lynched for their alleged crimes, were held back only by the Scottsboro sheriff's foresight to ensure the security of the jail by calling in the National Guard.[4] Contributing to the sensationalism that tended to shift the nation's focus away from the young African Americans themselves was the legal atmosphere surrounding the incident. Immediately after the case broke, the Communist Party's International Labor Defense offered to represent the

3. In March 1932 the Alabama Supreme Court reversed the conviction of the youngest of the nine youths, and in November 1932 the U.S. Supreme Court overturned guilty verdicts against the other seven. The next four years brought a series of retrials, appeals—some of which reached the U.S. Supreme Court again—and more retrials, even though Ruby Bates, one of the alleged victims, recanted her charges of rape on the witness stand and admitted that she had fabricated the entire story. In the end, none of the youths was put to death for the alleged crime. See Dan T. Carter, *Scottsboro: A Tragedy of the American South* (1969; Baton Rouge: Louisiana State University Press, 1990), and James Goodman, *Stories of Scottsboro* (New York: Vintage, 1995).

4. Quoted in Goodman, *Stories of Scottsboro,* 13.

nine youths, convinced that its participation in the case would not only help the defendants but also bring both recognition to its antilynching crusade and new members to the party. The NAACP, by contrast, was slow to act on the defendants' behalf, fearful that its association with nine poor, barely literate black youths charged with raping two white women would bring the nation's premier civil rights organization bad publicity.

For Hughes, the NAACP's hesitancy to act represented an alarming trend among conservative black leaders to place status and fears of white reprisal before the welfare of the race. The Scottsboro case thus further strengthened Hughes's embrace of the radical Left, a political commitment that had been building at least since high school, when he had immersed himself in Max Eastman's *The Liberator.* As he journeyed through the South in the winter of 1931–1932, reading his poems at schools and colleges and visiting with students, professors, and administrators, the connections between the nine youths imprisoned at the Kilby State Penitentiary in Montgomery, Alabama, the fear of some black leaders to take a vocal stand against injustice, and the broader issues of southern racial intolerance and violence became brutally clear to him.

During his reading tour, two additional incidents reminded Hughes that he was in a land of racial bigotry and violence. Juliette Derricotte, the dean of women at Fisk University and a renowned speaker on issues relating to black colleges and education, died from injuries sustained in a car accident after being refused admission to the nearest hospital, which treated whites only. That same weekend, a recent graduate of Hampton Institute, en route to watch the football team he coached play its first game of the season, was beaten to death by a white mob. Outraged by the incidents, students at Hampton, where Hughes was lecturing at the time, attempted to band together and protest the racial violence. Hughes agreed to speak at their meeting, but soon discovered that school administrators, both white and black, refused to allow the students to stage a protest. Hampton Institute, he and the students were told, was an educational institution, not a site for protests.

The refusal of Hampton's administrators to allow students an outlet for the anger and pain caused by southern white bigotry was one of several serious problems Hughes discovered in the black schools and colleges he visited on his tour through the South. While he himself was universally received with kindness and hospitality by students, faculty, and administrators alike, behind the genial facade were attitudes and practices that compromised both the educational mission and the struggle for civil rights and racial justice. Hughes found that Victorian codes of conduct prevailed on many campuses, with administrators doing their best to prevent students from smoking, playing cards, dancing, and engaging in sexual activities. Committed as he was to speaking out against racial intolerance, Hughes was shocked to find that many students and teachers at Tuskegee Institute knew nothing (or pretended to know nothing) about the Scottsboro trials, despite the fact that Tuskegee was only a short drive from Scottsboro. Additionally, he discovered colleges that expelled students for organizing protests against Jim Crow theaters, black campuses that maintained "whites only" guest houses, teachers afraid to discuss communism with their students, and administrators who consistently acquiesced to the wishes of white trustees and the customs of the color line.

Hughes's personal experiences with white patronage during the Harlem Renaissance certainly contributed to the honest conviction with which he criticized white philanthropy in the 1930s. He had been well supported by a wealthy white woman, Charlotte Mason, while writing his first novel, thoroughly enjoying the opportunity to focus on his art without having to worry about where his next paycheck would come from. The moment Hughes's work took on a radical edge of social critique, however, Mason withdrew her patronage. This kind of hypocrisy, which seemed to fester behind philanthropic fronts, troubled Hughes long after the end of the Harlem Renaissance and the largesse of wealthy patrons who supported it. In 1935, addressing in absentia the first American Writers' Congress—organized by politically committed writers on the Left and out of which grew the radical League of American Writers—Hughes called on African American writers to reveal through their art "the lovely grinning face of Philanthropy—which gives a million dollars to a Jim Crow school, but not one job to a graduate of that school; which builds a Negro hospital with second-rate equipment, then commands black patients and student-doctors to go there whether they will or no; or which, out of the kindness of its heart, erects yet another separate, segregated, shut-off, Jim Crow Y.M.C.A." In this radical statement, which was published in essay form under the title "To Negro Writers," Hughes championed the transformative powers of the written word and urged writers to use their art to effect social change. Black writers *must* use their talents, Hughes argued, to overturn minstrel stereotypes and establish racial unity "on the *solid* ground of the daily working-class struggle to wipe out . . . all the old inequalities of the past." They *must* reveal, he continued, "the sick-sweet smile of organized religion" and the false leaders within black communities who fear speaking out against injustice.

Three years prior to the first American Writers' Congress, Hughes had made a trip to the Soviet Union that would substantially shape many of the ideas expressed in "To Negro Writers" and other radical essays that he wrote in the 1930s. Traveling with a group of twenty-two young African Americans to make *Black and White,* a film about American race relations commissioned by the Meschrabpom Film Corporation of the Worker's International Relief, Hughes arrived in Moscow on June 26, 1932. In "Moscow and Me" (1933), the first of many essayistic pieces to come out of this trip, Hughes wrote of the city with an exuberance matched only by that with which he had described his arrival in New York in "The Fascination of Cities" six years earlier: "Moscow and freedom! The Soviet Union! The dream of all the poor and oppressed—like us—come true." The contrast between the Soviet Union and the American South, where Hughes had just spent over four months on his speaking tour, could not have been more pronounced. Warmly greeted, hugged, and kissed by the white Muscovites gathered at the train station to meet them, Hughes and the other African American travelers were whisked across Red Square in luxury sedans to the Grand Hotel, where they found courteous attendants and clean, comfortable rooms. "Everything that a hotel for white folks at home would have," Hughes remarked in "Moscow and Me," "except that, quite truthfully, there was no toilet paper. And no Jim Crow." In this essay and "Negroes in Moscow" (1933), both published in *International Literature,* Hughes emphasized the courtesy with which African Americans were treated in the city and elsewhere in the Soviet Union. Sympathetic with oppressed groups throughout the world, Russians were especially so with black Americans. Hughes discovered that the exploitation of black workers in the United States was a topic discussed frequently in Moscow newspapers, schools, and theaters, and always with a great deal of respect.

The relative lack of racial distinctions was one of many aspects of life in the Soviet Union that intrigued Hughes. Although the production of *Black and White* was called off due to artistic disagreements among the many people involved with the film, he chose to remain in the Soviet Union for a year and write about his experiences. Hughes discovered that in the Soviet Union, unlike the United States, he *could* make a living entirely from writing, and many of the cultural activities denied him at home because of his race were now open to him. This served him well when he accepted an assignment to write a series of articles about Soviet Central Asia for the newspaper *Izvestia,* several of which concerned transformations in theater and dance since the Bolshevik Revolution of 1917.

Published as a small book, *A Negro Looks at Soviet Central Asia,* in 1934, the *Izvestia* pieces constituted at this point in his career Hughes's most sustained treatment of (and support for) revolutionary socialist ideology. While Hughes would maintain later in his career that he had never been a member of the Communist Party, he wrote about Soviet life after the Revolution with unabashed—and, as biographer Arnold Rampersad has pointed out, with *uncritical*—admiration.[5] As he headed south on a train in Russia, painful memories of verbal insults and inferior accommodations on Jim Crow modes of travel in the United States were juxtaposed with the pleasure he felt at being surrounded by people of various shades of skin color, all sharing a camaraderie based on a fundamental respect for human beings and a recognition of the importance of the common worker. Life had certainly not always been this way, however. Soviet Central Asia, Hughes was told by a new friend, was "truly a land of Before and After." Before the Revolution, emirs, khans, mullahs, and beys had ruled. Now, power was in the hands of the workers. Rampant illiteracy had begun to be addressed, and education was no longer limited to the wealthy elite. Factories now existed in Asia itself, its raw materials no longer pillaged by capitalists. Hughes was told, moreover, that racial persecution and segregation had been banished—"Russian and native, Jew and gentile, white and brown, live and work together." The Revolution had transformed nearly every aspect of life in Soviet Asia, but most remarkable to Hughes were the changes it brought about in the status of women. In the *Izvestia* pieces and in two essays that he published in *Woman's Home Companion* and *Travel*—"In an Emir's Harem" (1934) and "Farewell to Mahomet" (1935), respectively—Hughes wrote passionately of the women who suffered persecution for daring to lift their veils and those who escaped the stultifying atmosphere of the harem to lead meaningful, politically committed lives after the Revolution. "Today the torch of liberated womanhood burns throughout Soviet Asia," Hughes concluded in "Farewell to Mahomet," "and the whisper of its brightness sweeps across the frontiers into Persia, India, even into China where strange and barbaric customs still prevail."

Hughes wrote essays on an eclectic range of subjects upon returning from the Soviet Union in 1933, including the International Longshoremen's Association strike of 1934 (he himself came under fire from right-wing reactionaries for supporting the strike through participation in the radical John Reed Club), the photography of Henri Cartier-Bresson and

5. See Rampersad, *Life,* 1:265.

Manuel Alvarez Bravo, tourist attractions in Paris, and the Russian writer Alexander Pushkin. His sheer productivity as an essayist during his stay in the Soviet Union, however, would not be matched until 1937, when he traveled to Madrid on assignment to cover the Spanish Civil War for the Baltimore *Afro-American*. Blending journalistic reportage with the conversational quality of memoir to give readers back home a sense of both the politics of the war and day-to-day life in a besieged city, the articles he wrote touched on subjects ranging from his own experience in an air raid to the heroic acts of black soldiers who had left the United States to join the International Brigades. Like his writings for *Izvestia*, the *Afro-American* pieces were anything but nonpartisan. As Arnold Rampersad notes, "the articles viewed the war from a perspective that merged the narrowly racial *Afro-American* view with Hughes's proletarianism and anti-fascism. The result was excellent propaganda for the left, aimed directly at the black American world."[6]

Hughes's political passions were nowhere more apparent than when addressing the subject of Franco's Moorish troops, brought over from Morocco. "As usually happens with colored troops in the service of white imperialists," Hughes pointed out, "the Moors have been put in the front lines of the Franco offensive in Spain—and shot down like flies." As horrifying as the destruction and bloodshed of the war were to him, however, Hughes found among the people gathered at the headquarters of the Alianza de Intelectuales Antifascistas, where he stayed while in Madrid, a good deal of hope. The alliance, an outgrowth of the first International Writers' Congress in Paris, was an organization composed of artists and intellectuals who used their various talents to disseminate pro-Loyalist information throughout Spain. In a radio speech on September 3, 1937, Hughes spoke lyrically of the work done by these people and the broader importance of the center that housed the alliance: "It is a place where now, today, art becomes life and life is art, and there is no longer any need of a bridge between the artists and the people—for the thing created becomes immediately a part of those for whom, and from whom, it was created. The poem, the picture, the song is only water drawn from the well of the people and given back to them in a cup of beauty so that they may drink—and in drinking, understand themselves."

Themes of economic and racial oppression remained central to Hughes's essays in the years following his departure from Madrid in November 1937, as did his belief that artists must maintain politically

6. Ibid., 1:351.

committed perspectives if their creations are to have social significance. Addressing the Paris meeting of the International Writers Association for the Defense of Culture on July 25, 1938, he was adamant that to be a good writer, one could not afford to ignore global events. Because of the interrelatedness of international politics, Hughes argued, "a creative writer has no right to neglect to understand clearly the social and economic forces that control our world." The revolutionary zeal with which Hughes addressed these themes in his writings on the Soviet Union and the Spanish Civil War, however, was somewhat tempered in his later nonfiction. Hesitant to champion his radical socialism after the announcement of the Nazi-Soviet Nonaggression Pact of 1939, Hughes offered instead a measured essayistic voice that framed social critique in the rhetoric of American democratic idealism. Nowhere was this shift more evident than in a series of articles he wrote in the early 1940s about the status of blacks in American society, including "What Shall We Do about the South?" (1943), "The Future of Black America" (1943), and "My America" (1944). Unafraid to voice his position on Jim Crow customs and other forms of racial prejudice, Hughes did so with a good deal of rhetorical savvy, almost always emphasizing during this period of his career that the status of African Americans was a barometer for the progress and future of America itself.

Hughes perhaps had good reason to create in his essays of the 1940s the persona of the dedicated American citizen committed to the ideals of democracy, for he was increasingly under attack by organizations and individuals on the right that threatened to compromise his position as one of African America's most respected writers. Hoping to publicize the first volume of his autobiography, *The Big Sea,* at a 1940 "Book and Author" luncheon in California, Hughes instead was greeted by an angry crowd of protesters. Aimee Semple McPherson, the head of the fundamentalist Temple of the Four Square Gospel in Los Angeles, had arranged for a contingent of picketers to spread awareness of Hughes's impious poem "Goodbye Christ" (1932), in which he had sarcastically mentioned the evangelist. Shaken by the protest, Hughes was mortified to discover a month later that the *Saturday Evening Post,* which also came under fire in the poem, had reprinted "Goodbye Christ" without his permission.[7] Rather than revel in the spotlight on his radicalism, Hughes immediately sent a statement, "Concerning 'Goodbye, Christ' " (1941), to friends,

7. See ibid., 1:390–92.

publishers, and foundations. In this piece he reaffirmed his opposition to the systems of global oppression that had prompted his satirical words in the early 1930s. Nevertheless, he ultimately dismissed the poem as a product of the political fervor of his youth: "Now, in the year 1941, having left the terrain of 'the radical at twenty' to approach the 'conservative of forty,' I would not and could not write 'Goodbye, Christ,' desiring no longer to *épater le bourgeois.*"

Yet the fact that the ongoing struggle of African Americans was far from over was especially apparent to Hughes as he considered the many ironies inherent in the nation's fight against fascism in World War II. African American soldiers, both overseas and in U.S. training camps, found themselves treated with the same humiliating disrespect as their fellow black civilians. Separate and less desirable living and eating quarters, little opportunity for advancement, and even segregated latrines, made life for the African American soldier quite unbearable. Moreover, the separation of "white" and "Negro" blood by the American Red Cross blood banks was an act that at once infuriated Hughes and caused him to chuckle at the lengths whites would go to maintain the illusion of racial supremacy. In "White Folks Do the Funniest Things" (1944), an article published in *Common Ground,* Hughes explored the tragicomic nature of the racial jokes popular during the war years. Humor was an integral tool for survival, Hughes believed, but he was all too aware that those who perpetuated racial prejudice and discrimination were utterly blind to the absurdities of their practices. "I suppose the greatest killers cannot afford to laugh," he mused. "Those most determined to Jim Crow me are grimly killing America."

Despite the segregated troops, discrimination in the U.S. war industries, and the daily racial insults suffered by black civilians, Hughes believed in and supported the war effort as a necessary measure toward the realization of true democracy in his nation and the obliteration of fascism worldwide. In one of his most inspired essays of this period, "Negro Writers and the War" (1942), Hughes revisited his position from the 1930s on the responsibility of writers to use their art for social change. Published three months prior to Hughes's inaugural column in one of African America's most influential newspapers, the *Chicago Defender,* this essay recognized members of the black press for their leadership in bringing the war effort—and its meaning to African Americans in particular—to the masses. African American writers in general needed to follow their lead, Hughes maintained, taking it upon themselves as a basic duty to demonstrate in their writing the international dimensions of American racism. Racial conflicts at home were, after all, "part of the great problem of world freedom everywhere." It was thus the duty of black writers

> to show how our local fascists are blood brothers of the Japanese fascists—though they speak with a Dixie drawl, to show how on the great battle front of the world we must join hands with the crushed common people of Europe, the Soviet Union, the Chinese, and unite our efforts—else we who are American Negroes will have not only the Klan on our necks in intensified fashion, but the Gestapo, as well. (And the Nazis, I am sure, could teach the Klan a few things, for the Germans do not bother with silly crosses and childish nightshirts. Death and the concentration camps are more effective.)

Hughes continued to write passionately about the war effort and its aftermath in his *Chicago Defender* columns, championing once again the Soviet Union and drawing connections between reactionary Cold War propaganda and the continued oppression of minority groups in the United States. His nonjournalistic essays of the late 1940s and early 1950s, however, evidenced less of the radical young troublemaker and more of the reflective, middle-aged writer beginning to take stock of his life and career. This was particularly apparent in the increasingly reminiscent and autobiographical nature of his essays. Recounting his brushes with censorship and his conflicts with the reactionary right in "My Adventures as a Social Poet" (1947), an essay published in Atlanta University's *Phylon* magazine, Hughes charmingly compared himself to poets whose lyrics of love, roses, and moonlight enabled them to float above the earth with their heads in the clouds. "Unfortunately, having been born poor—and also colored—in Missouri," he quipped, "I was stuck in the mud from the beginning. Try as I might to float off into the clouds, poverty and Jim Crow would grab me by the heels, and right back on earth I would land." While Hughes made it clear in this essay that he was proud of his past work as a social poet, the reminiscent tone suggests a distance between the radicalism of his younger years and how he chose to define himself as an increasingly public figure in his middle age.

This distance would become more pronounced a few years later, when he sat for an interview with the editors of *Phylon* to discuss the current state of African American literature. In "Some Practical Observations: A Colloquy" (1950), Hughes charted the many positive advances made by African American writers since the Harlem Renaissance, noting in particular a publishing industry and reading public more "willing to accept

Negro problems and Negro art" than they had been in the past. There was a cost to this acceptance, of course. Taking a position that would contradict his earlier advice to black writers to expose systems of oppression through their art, Hughes argued that "the Negro writer has to work especially hard to avoid the appearance of propaganda."

Despite his attempts to position himself as politically moderate, individuals and organizations on the right refused to allow Hughes to forget his radicalism of the recent past. The FBI had targeted him as a subversive after the incident in 1940 with Aimee Semple McPherson, maintaining a file that listed him as a member of the Communist Party and a potential threat to the white race. He was also denounced by the House Un-American Activities Committee (HUAC)—established in 1938 to investigate subversive political groups and individuals in the United States—for his membership in radical organizations. Right-wing reaction to Hughes came to a head in 1953, when he was subpoenaed by a U.S. marshal to appear before Senator Joseph McCarthy's Senate Permanent Sub-Committee on Investigations to explain and account for his "un-American," radical past. Understandably fearful of McCarthy's witch-hunts for communists, Hughes prepared a statement that effectively repudiated his radical writings and saved him from serious charges by the committee.[8] Nonetheless, he did not abandon his commitment to writing critically about issues affecting African America.

That commitment was especially apparent when Hughes addressed the National Assembly of Authors and Dramatists at a symposium in May 1957. Speaking on the subject of "The Writer's Position in America," Hughes explained that African American writers "have been on the blacklist all our lives." Facing constant censorship, denied publication and opportunities on the lecture circuit, and barred from jobs in Hollywood and the publishing industry, Hughes suggested, the black writer works against overwhelming obstacles in attempting to make a living. Coupled with these realities, recent violence against African Americans drove many of the best black writers to live and work in other countries: "Why? Because the stones thrown at Autherine Lucy at the University of Alabama are thrown at them, too. Because the shadow of Montgomery

8. For information on Hughes's troubles with HUAC and his involvement in the McCarthy hearings, see ibid., 2:90–98, 209–22. Hughes's statement, "Langston Hughes Speaks," is included in *"Fight for Freedom" and Other Writings on Civil Rights*, vol. 10 of *The Collected Works of Langston Hughes* (Columbia: University of Missouri Press, 2001), 245–46.

and the bombs under Rev. King's house, shadow them and shatter them, too. Because the body of little Emmett Till drowned in a Mississippi river and no one brought to justice, haunts them, too."

If the violence surrounding the Civil Rights Movement was an extreme reminder of the difficulties African American writers faced on a daily basis, the victories won by Rosa Parks and Martin Luther King Jr., the Little Rock Nine, the Freedom Riders, and other individuals and groups at the forefront of the struggle for civil rights reinvigorated in Hughes a sense of the writer's importance in helping people make sense of their world. They also compelled him to reexamine his earlier beliefs about the duty of the black writer. In the "Negro Artist and the Racial Mountain" he had boldly stated that "we younger Negro artists who create now intend to express our individual dark-skinned selves without fear or shame," at whatever cost to one's "respectability" in the eyes of black or white America. In the 1950s and 1960s, however, Hughes grew increasingly uncomfortable with some of the literature being produced by the younger generation of African America writers. "Pride, nobility, sacrifice, and decency," he argued in "The Task of the Negro Writer as Artist" (1965), a brief statement published in the *Negro Digest,* "are qualities strangely lacking in some of the most talented outpourings by or about Negroes these days." Surrounded by the heroism of men and women committed to making full equality a reality for African Americans, Hughes reminded black writers, "There is today no lack within the Negro people of beauty, strength and power—world shaking power. If I were a young writer, I would try to put some of these qualities on paper and on stage."

Thus, almost forty years after his stunning manifesto of the Harlem Renaissance, Hughes found himself in the very position occupied by those members of the black intelligentsia in 1926 who worried that the younger artists and writers were not doing justice to the positive qualities of African American culture. In concluding "The Task of the Negro Writer as Artist," however, Hughes would reaffirm a belief in the political potential of African American writers that remained consistent throughout his forty-six-year professional writing career: "Ours is a social as well as a literary responsibility." Such a belief resounds everywhere in this volume of *The Collected Works of Langston Hughes,* which represents the testament of a man committed to the possibilities of language to generate social awareness and, ultimately, to compel social change.

A Note on the Text

This is not the first collection of Hughes's essayistic nonfiction, nor does it make the claim of being a "complete" volume. It is, however, the most comprehensive volume published to date. Three prior edited collections both set precedents for and reaffirmed the need for an edition of Hughes's nonfictional, essayistic writings that would be as close to complete as possible in a single volume. Faith Berry's *Good Morning Revolution: Uncollected Social Protest Writings by Langston Hughes* (1973), a multigenre collection, includes thirteen essays and ten newspaper columns, many of the former written by Hughes during the radical phase of his career in the 1930s. As Berry's title makes clear, the focus of the volume is relatively narrow and therefore limited in its representation of Hughes's nonfiction. Edward J. Mullen's *Langston Hughes in the Hispanic World and Haiti* (1977), also a multigenre collection, is limited to Hughes's writings on Mexico, Cuba, Haiti, and Spain. Mullen includes eleven essays as well as the series of thirteen journalistic articles that Hughes wrote as a correspondent for the Baltimore *Afro-American* during the Spanish Civil War. Unfortunately, these important volumes are no longer in print as of this writing. More recently, Christopher C. De Santis brought together the best of Hughes's writings from his long-running *Chicago Defender* column in *Langston Hughes and the* Chicago Defender: *Essays on Race, Politics, and Culture, 1942–62* (1995). Each of these volumes made available specific components of Hughes's writings, but none of them attempted to represent the vast range of the essayistic nonfiction Hughes produced between 1921 and 1967.

The present volume rectifies the limited access to Hughes's short nonfiction by reprinting most of the essays, speeches, introductions to edited volumes, book reviews, published letters to editors, and brief miscellaneous pieces that he wrote over the course of his long career. Every attempt has been made to catalog and locate all of the essays Hughes published during his lifetime and include them in this volume or in the companion volume on civil rights. Because of space and cost limitations, however, omissions were inevitable. Hughes was a weekly contributor to the *Chicago Defender* for more than twenty years, writing hundreds of columns on disparate topics. These journalistic writings have not been included in this volume. Several important essays by Hughes—"Southern Gentlemen, White Prostitutes, Mill-Owners, and Negroes" (1931), "Brown America in Jail: Kilby" (1932), "Cowards from the Colleges" (1934), "Too Much of Race" (1937), "The Need for Heroes" (1941), "What the Negro Wants" (1941), and "Langston Hughes Speaks" (1953)—are included in *"Fight for Freedom" and Other Writings on Civil Rights* (volume 10 of *The Collected Works of Langston Hughes*) and have not been reprinted here. Other material appears in other volumes of *The Collected Works of Langston Hughes:* essays for children in volume 11, *Works for Children and Young Adults: Poetry, Fiction, and Other Writing,* and volume 12, *Works for Children and Young Adults: Biographies;* and essays that formed part of Hughes's two autobiographical volumes in volume 13, *Autobiography: The Big Sea,* and volume 14, *Autobiography: I Wonder as I Wander.* On occasion Hughes published multiple versions of the same essay under different titles. In these instances, the fullest version of the essay has been included, and alternate titles and places of publication are documented in the annotations.

With a few exceptions, the texts of Hughes's essays are based on the original published versions. In the case of previously unpublished essays, again with a few exceptions noted in the annotations, the texts used are Hughes's file copies, which incorporate his most recent revisions. These manuscripts are housed in the James Weldon Johnson Memorial Collection at the Beinecke Rare Book and Manuscript Library, Yale University, and are identified in the headnotes as LHP, for Langston Hughes Papers, with the date and location indicated on the manuscript copy.

In preparing this volume, I have made silent corrections of obvious misspellings and typographical errors, unless Hughes intentionally altered standard spelling and usage to convey African American folk vernacular. These corrections are not substantive, but are rather attempts to regularize inconsistent typesetting in the originals. Stylistic inconsistencies among the various works included have been allowed to stand.

In order to facilitate study of Hughes's development as an essayist, the changes in his essayistic style over time, and the vacillations in his political ideology, theories on art and aesthetics, and beliefs about the duties and responsibilities of artists, the essays in this volume are arranged chronologically by decade. Hughes's introductions to edited volumes, book reviews, and miscellaneous pieces, also arranged by date of publication, follow the essays in distinct sections of this volume.

Essays on Art, Race, Politics, and World Affairs

1

Essays, 1921–1929

"The Virgin of Guadalupe," *Crisis* 23 (December 1921): 77

After the coming of the Spaniards, who brought priests and missionaries, as well as soldiers to conquer Mexico, most of the subdued Indians were converted to the faith of the Catholics. The ancient Indian temples to barbaric gods were torn down by the Europeans who built new Christian churches in their stead. Thus it came about that the brown men learned to worship the saints and idols brought by the invaders and so forgot their old gods.

One day a pious follower of the Spaniards' faith, Juan Diego by name, was returning from mass across the hill of Guadalupe, when suddenly a veiled figure, all light and beauty, appeared before him. The poor Indian was much astonished and filled with surprise when the woman spoke to him and commanded in a soft voice that he go to the bishop and tell His Excellence to construct a church on the hill where the figure was standing. This Juan did, or attempted to do, but the bishop's servants, thinking the man a common ignorant Indian, would not give him admission to the house, so Juan Diego went back.

For a second time the vision appeared before him, issuing the same command in her beautiful voice, so the Indian returned in search of the bishop. Each time, however, he was refused an entry but the vision told him to persevere. Finally, after many days, he was admitted and the old father asked him what he wished. When Juan Diego told of the beautiful spirit and her message, the bishop could not believe such a tale and thought perhaps that the poor fellow was demented. At last he told the Indian that he would have to bring some sign or token of proof in support of his strange words.

Once more the man returned to the hill and there at its foot the bright vision reappeared. Hearing the message that the bishop had sent, she said, "Pluck those flowers there at your feet." But Juan Diego, standing on the bare and rocky earth, asked, "What flowers?" Then suddenly looking down he saw the ground covered with white blossoms which he began to pick and with which he filled his small woven *tilma* or mantle, used to wrap about his shoulders on cold mornings.

Then he went to the bishop and said, "Here is your sign." Opening the mantle the white flowers rolled out at their feet. The bishop looked, but still more marvellous than the flowers, the surprised priest saw, painted on the mantle where the blossoms had been, the figure of the Virgin surrounded by a halo of light. "This," he said, "is surely the proof." So they proceeded to erect the church on the top of the hill. Later a magnificent cathedral was built at its foot where the *tilma* bearing the picture of the Virgin is preserved to this day above the altar and on the spot where the vision first appeared, a spring of water gushed forth and is now covered by a pretty shrine where people may stop to drink.

Once a year a great *fiesta* is held in honor of this patron saint of Mexico and many people come from far away to visit her. Any day when one cares to take a trip out to the stately church where she is housed near Mexico City, her faithful worshippers may be seen going on their knees the long distance from the outside door to the high altar carrying white candles in their hands, crawling up to place them before her—La Virgin de Guadalupe—whose name is known and loved by all Mexico.

"Ships, Sea and Africa: Random Impressions of a Sailor on His First Trip Down the West Coast of the Motherland," *Crisis* 26 (December 1923): 69–71

I. Senegal to the Congo

The East River . . . The Battery half veiled in fog . . . The Statue of Liberty dim to starboard as our ship glides past headed for the open sea . . . Sandy Hook . . . Grey green water . . . Darkness . . . In the lighted fo'c'sle sailors unpack sea bags . . . We are off for five months to Africa.

Long days of sea and sun . . . The last of June the mountains of the Azores float on the sky-line . . . High volcanic islands rise sharply from the water . . . We anchor in the harbor of Horta, a picture-book town . . . Houses painted like toy Noah's arks, palm trees, nuns in flaring bonnets, oxen pulling wooden-wheeled carts, scores of brown-white children begging for cigarettes and pennies.

We unload all night . . . The winches rattle, bags of wheat rise in the air, swing over and out, drop down into the harbor boats . . . At dawn we sail.

The Canary Islands . . . Teneriffe . . . Las Palmas, a breath of Spain in a city of palms.

Tomorrow,—Dakar . . . The Motherland.

Dawn . . . The coast of Africa, long, low, bare and rocky, backed by a curtain of light and then a red sun that rises like a ball of fire.

The port of Dakar, Senegal . . . The wharf crowded with black Muhammadans in billowing robes . . . The strange costumes seen . . . The thermometer at ninety . . . Women in scant clothes . . . Little naked children . . . The fierce sun.

Portuguese Bissao, lost in a maze of islands . . . The old Negro pilot who guides our ship . . . The wild, fierce boatmen who take the mail-bag.

Conakry from the sea . . . Groves aflame with vermillion flowers . . . White houses hidden in trees and foliage.

Freetown . . . The hills of Sierra Leone . . . The fine young Negro policemen and harbor officials . . . Rain, all day rain.

The Ivory Coast . . . The Gold Coast . . . Towns with strange names,—Grand Bassam, Assinie, Accra, Lome, Cotonou . . . No harbors, the ship anchors in the sea . . . A sand-white, perfectly straight coast-line . . . Towns hidden in deep coconut groves . . . The soft boom of the surf on the beach.

The lagoon behind Grand Bassam . . . Streets shaded with palm and almond trees . . . French cafés . . . Clean, delightful natives.

Secondee . . . The market flashing with colors, the piles of fruit, the dark girls in bright bandannas, gay strips of cloth twined about their bodies . . . The African princesses with gold coins in their hair.

The roar of the surf at Assinie . . . Always the surf . . . The surf boats with their crew of eight black naked paddlers, their superbly muscled bodies, damp with sea-spray, glistening in the sunshine.

Lagos, a fascinating, half-oriental town . . . Indian bazaars . . . Muhammadan traders . . . Goats, dogs, pigs in the streets . . . Life, movement, crowds, dashing horses, rich Negroes driving expensive cars, a harbor full of ships . . . Seven days in port . . . Shore leave and money for the crew whose pounds, like Villon's francs, go "*tous aux tavernes et aux filles.*"

II. The Delta of the Niger

Port Harcourt up a jungle-walled river . . . Ostriches walking in the streets . . . The small, stark naked cane-bearer following his master . . . The date-palms . . . The boy with the bananas . . . The little black girls with henna-dyed nails and bare feet . . . The one with the Peruvian gold which she displays so proudly and guards so jealously . . . The monkeys . . . The young boy from the customs, brown with dreams in his eyes . . . "America, is it a wonderful place?" . . . The policeman whose salary is four pounds a month . . . Rain, swift, cool rain.

Calabar among the hills . . . The descent of the Bonny River in the late afternoon, the steamer keeping near to the left bank . . . Impassable forests on either side . . . Swampland of snakes and monkeys . . . Yellow leaves like hidden stars . . . Smoldering crimson blossoms . . . The slender canoes of the wood-cutters . . . The palm-like bushes . . . Sunset . . . The river, broken by islands, dividing into vast alleyways of water . . . The little boats lost in the twilight—a twilight of violet merging to purple dusk . . . The islands hidden in darkness . . . The impossibility of reaching open sea . . . We drop anchor for the night.

With pious homage to Father Neptune, we cross the Equator, the young sailors, according to ancient custom, being properly doused and shaved . . . At night we run through a sea aglow with phosphorescent fire . . . A million fallen stars foam in the wake of the ship and streaks of light move where fish swim near the surface.

Banana, the point of land that stretches into the sea at the mouth of the Congo . . . Sailor's chanteys on deck—

"They sailed us down the Congo River,
Blow, boy, boys! Blow!"

The ninety mile ascent to Boma and Matadi . . . Forests, but not so thick or tropical as those of the Niger . . . Then wide, arid plains, parched palms, dry yellow grass . . . Boma . . . The river narrows, runs swiftly between high hills, fantastic, bare . . . A strong and dangerous current . . . A sudden, broad, cañon-like curve and the white houses of Matadi rise before us . . . A town of hills . . . A busy wharf piled with drums of palm oil . . . Native villages scattered about, each on its own highland . . . Streets bordered by mango trees . . . The dirtiest, saddest lot of Negro workers seen in Africa . . . Black soldiers with bayoneted guns pacing the docks . . . Evening . . . The copper-gold of the Congo sunset . . . Blue-green twilight . . . The hot, heavy African night studded with stars.

"The Fascination of Cities,"

Crisis 31.3 (January 1926): 138–40

The First City

Dawn is sodden, grey. The stubble of wheat fields, the hills and bluffs of the Kansas River. The clack, clack, clack of the train running between long lines of freight cars, the railroad yards. "Union Station!" "Kansas City!"

The bellowing voice of the brakesman, a jar and a curve, houses high on a bluff, a tiny street car running way up there. The old station in the bottoms. Hustle, hurry. "Cab, mom, cab?"—*This way to the street cars*—. "Bus to your hotel! Take your baggage!" Mother holds me tightly by the hand. I am five years old. I am in the city for the first time.

I remember well. Night. My uncle's house. Spare ribs and corn and sweet potatoes and a can of beer. A gala occasion. The Williams and Walker company in town.[1] The greatest colored show in the world is in town.

"O Bon Bon Buddie,
"My chocolate drop,
"My chocolate drop
"Dat's me!"

George Walker, the beautiful brown girls, the crowded theatre, the applause, the laughter. I am five years old. The cool night air, the autos, the streets, the lights, the people affect me. "Look, mother! Oh, mother, look!" The fascination of cities seizes me, burning like a fever in the blood. "I don't want to leave this city, mamma. When I get to be a big man, I am going to live forever in this city!"

Chicago

I am fourteen. I work in a hat store in the loop. The crush of the city is all about me. The vast, ugly, brutal, monotonous city, checker-boarded, hard. The L trains circle in a crazy loop. The L trains rattle and roar behind Wabash Avenue, shaking the houses, houses, houses on Wabash Avenue. The tiny second-story room I sleep in has a window opening onto the tracks of the L trains. The red and green lights of the passing cars whiz and flash in my sleep, dreams. The approaching dull rumble, the loud rattle and roar fading to the dying dull rumble, punctuate my hours of sleep. I take long rides on the L trains, Evanston, Oak Park, Englewood. I cover the monotonous miles of Chicago delivering hats. On Sundays I walk on State Street,—glittering Broadway of the Black Belt. Lighted theatre fronts. The Whitman Sisters at the Grand.[2] *The first colored movie ever shown*. Street stands. "Sweet watermillion right here!" The fish sandwich man. The girls with too much powder, beckoning eyes, red, red lips. "You love me, don't you, honey!" "Ah, Cora, leave him alone. He's only a kid." Crap games in the vacant lots. "Cheese it, the cop!" The medicine man, the corner preacher. The dark, throbbing life of the streets.

Long afternoons on the lake shore, the Ghetto's strange old Jews, the foreign quarters, Polish, Irish, until—

"We don't 'low no niggers in this street."

"I'm not bothering you."

"Makes no difference. We don't 'low no niggers in this street." And the lanky boy stuns me with a blow to the jaw. A shrill whistle brings the gang. Blows and counter-blows, oaths and kicks. We butt and fight and scratch. I would run but someone knocks my cap on the ground. My old dirty cap on the ground. I'll get my cap. It becomes life, death, God, everything,—my cap.

"Let me get my cap! Fight fair, you poor white cowards! Ganging a fellow like this!" We sway and grunt and pant, a mass of fists, arms, bodies. I grab someone's legs, kick, shove, reach down, grab my cap, turn, push, run. Escape! A whizzing of stones. Street corner, head out, body safe.

"Bastards!"
"Nigger!"

Chicago before the riots.[3] Power and brutality, strength. Ugly, sprawling, mighty city.

Mexico

I have come from far up in the mountains to the capital for this Feast-Sunday. It is the bull-ring in Mexico. Juan Luis de la Rosa, youngest and most graceful of Spanish matadors, places the banderillos. With one gay, paper-covered, sharp steel-pointed dart held high above his head in each hand, the young fighter, in a suit of silk and silver, moves in a circle about the angry bull. The animal paws the ground, bellows, rushes toward him. Quick as a flash, the hooked darts are fastened in his torn skin. The fighter leaps aside. The surprised bull roars, turns. The colored, cruel instruments of the fight decorate his bloody neck, making him seem like some garlanded festival animal ready for the sacrifice. It has been a perfect placement. "*Bravo, los hombres!*" The crowd goes mad. Hats, scarves, jeweled combs, fans are thrown in the arena at his feet as the young fighter receives the acclamations of his public.

The bull has killed four horses, goring them till their entrails spill on the ground. The bull has wounded one man. Now the youthful fighter, ready for the kill, receives his sword and cape. The vast crowd about the great ring is silent almost to the point of breathlessness. The supreme moment has arrived, the crisis in that savage drama, that old, old drama of youth against odds, youth against evil, death, the beast. The bull, tired by the exertions of the fight, stands still in the center of the arena, panting, but his stillness is pregnant with unused strength. Will he rush toward the young man, gore him through, lift him high on his horns as he did the bodies of the bleeding horses? Will the drama end in human death?

It is late afternoon and the quick, tropical darkness is approaching. Already dusk is gathered over the arena. Hurry, oh, hurry! The nervous stillness of the crowd is like a scream. The fighter advances slowly, his red cape before him, his sword held high. The bull paws the ground, seems to moan deeply, gathers his waning strength and rushes forward. The sword goes straight and deep into his neck. The fighter, in his suit of silk and silver, is lifted high in the air between the horns of the bull. He springs back. The mighty moment of the drama is over. The dying animal stops, takes one, two steps toward his human slayer, trembles, then slowly and in a manner of great state, like some ponderous animal god, topples down in the sand to death.

Already it is dark. The crowd, making for the exits, fills narrow steps, pushes in enclosed corridors. A great number of men and boys climb the high barrier into the arena and carry the young triumphant fighter off on their shoulders. I follow shouting, pushing with the rest, trying to get near, to touch this hero of the day and dusk. Through the dark stone arches of the plaza, through the toreadores' quarters, out to the waiting long powerful car with head-lights softly glowing, they carry him. In the car, with much cheering, they place the young matador. One of his friends throws a ring-cape of pale grey silk broidered in gold about him. The flash of a match shows me his face as he lights a cigarette,—a hard, sun-browned boy-face, scarred, shadowed. Tomorrow the newspapers will headline his name and in all the little bars and cafés, theatres and great restaurants of the capital, they will talk about him. The people will idolize him. The loveliest of courtesans will offer him their bodies, and the international news reels will flash his picture on the screen in Canton, China, and Kenosha, Wisconsin. He has fought the good fight and brought to a triumphant end the drama of youth against odds, youth against evil, death, the beast. He has played his part well in the afternoon's savage and primordial spectacle.

Down the narrow street, through the talking crowds, out into the wide Avenida, his car glides silently. The space it leaves in passing fills with moving crowds as a mud-rut fills with water after the passing of a wagon wheel. I am lost in the moving crowds, lost with my two friends speaking rapid Spanish on the brilliantly lighted sidewalks of the avenue, lost in a maze of wild, beautiful people. Oh, the ecstasy of crowds; the joy of lights; the fascination of cities!

New York

The sea brought me to Manhattan. Days and nights at sea. Sultry days, starry nights, and then suddenly, rising from the very waters themselves, the living cliffs and towers of New York. There is no thrill in all the world like that of entering, for the first time, New York harbor,—coming in from the flat monotony of the sea to this rise of dreams and beauty. New York is then truly the dream-city, city of the towers near to God, city of hopes and visions, of spires seeking in the windy air loveliness and perfection.

I am anxious to disembark. Quickly I want to be ashore, to touch its life, to mingle with the crowds in its deep canyons, to walk in the shadow of its strong towers. I want to be one of the many millions, one of the many moving living beings in the swirling greatness of the city.

I go. Manhattan takes me, is glad, holds me tightly. Like a vampire sucking my blood from my body, sucking my very breath from my lungs, she holds me. Broadway and its million lights. Harlem and its love-nights, its cabarets and casinos, its dark, warm bodies. The thundering subways, the arch of the bridges, the mighty rivers hold me. I am amazed at the tremendousness of the city, at its diverseness, its many, many things, its spiritual and physical playthings, its work things, its joy things. I cannot tell the city how much I love it. I have not enough kisses in my mouth for the avid lips of the city. I become dizzy dancing to the jazz-tuned nights, ecstasy-wearied in the towered days.

The sea takes me away again. I am glad. But I come back. Always I come back. The fascination of this city is upon me, burning like a fire in the blood.

Paris

Springtime—Paris—Dusk, opalescent, pale, purpling to night—Montmartre. The double windows of my high little attic room open to the evening charm of the city.

"C'est très grand, ce Paris," Sonia says. "Vois-tu Notre Dame là bas, et le Tour?"[4] And we search for the things we know in the darkening panorama of the vast town. We search for the things we know and watch the lights come out beneath us and the stars above.

"C'est très beau," says Sonia. "Oui, c'est très beau,—this old, old queen of cities."[5] And I think of the many illustrious ones who, through the centuries, have been her lovers,—Dante, the exile; Villon of the ragged heart; Molière and the great Lecouvreur; Heine, Napoleon, the little corporal; the strange, satanic Baudelaire; Wilde, and the gorgeous Bernhardt.[6] And I think of the seeking wandering ones she has drawn from all the world,—poets, students, adventurers and lovers. And I think of her as the center in the great wheel of cities circling around her,—New York, London, Berlin, Vienna, Rome, Madrid. And in the darkening day she becomes like an enchantress-city adorning herself with lights. She becomes like a sorceress-city making herself beautiful with jewels.

"Allons," says Sonia, who all the while has been standing quiet in the shadows. "Oui, allons," I answer.[7] And we go together down the winding stairs, out into the living streets, eagerly into the moving life of the Paris night.

"The Negro Artist and the Racial Mountain," *Nation* 122 (June 23, 1926): 692–94

One of the most promising of the young Negro poets said to me once, "I want to be a poet—not a Negro poet," meaning, I believe, "I want to write like a white poet"; meaning subconsciously, "I would like to be a white poet"; meaning behind that, "I would like to be white."[8]

And I was sorry the young man said that, for no great poet has ever been afraid of being himself. And I doubted then that, with his desire to run away spiritually from his race, this boy would ever be a great poet. But this is the mountain standing in the way of any true Negro art in America—this urge within the race toward whiteness, the desire to pour racial individuality into the mold of American standardization, and to be as little Negro and as much American as possible.

But let us look at the immediate background of this young poet. His family is of what I suppose one would call the Negro middle class: people who are by no means rich yet never uncomfortable nor hungry—smug, contented, respectable folk, members of the Baptist church. The father goes to work every morning. He is a chief steward at a large white club. The mother sometimes does fancy sewing or supervises parties for the rich families of the town. The children go to a mixed school. In the home they read white papers and magazines. And the mother often says "Don't be like niggers" when the children are bad. A frequent phrase from the father is, "Look how well a white man does things." And so the word white comes to be unconsciously a symbol of all the virtues. It holds for the children beauty, morality, and money. The whisper of "I want to be white" runs silently through their minds. This young poet's home is, I believe, a fairly typical home of the colored middle class. One sees immediately how difficult it would be for an artist born in such a home to interest himself in interpreting the beauty of his own people. He is never taught to see that beauty. He is taught rather not to see it, or if he does, to be ashamed of it when it is not according to Caucasian patterns.

For racial culture the home of a self-styled "high-class" Negro has nothing better to offer. Instead there will perhaps be more aping of things white than in a less cultured or less wealthy home. The father is perhaps a doctor, lawyer, landowner, or politician. The mother may be a social worker, or a teacher, or she may do nothing and have a maid. Father is often dark but he has usually married the lightest woman he could find. The family attend a fashionable church where few really colored faces are to be found. And they themselves draw a color line. In the North they go to white theaters and white movies. And in the South they have at least two cars and a house "like white folks." Nordic manners, Nordic faces, Nordic hair, Nordic art (if any), and an Episcopal heaven. A very high mountain indeed for the would-be racial artist to climb in order to discover himself and his people.

But then there are the low-down folks, the so-called common element, and they are the majority—may the Lord be praised! The people who have their nip of gin on Saturday nights and are not too important to themselves or the community, or too well fed, or too learned to watch the lazy world go round. They live on Seventh Street in Washington or State Street in Chicago and they do not particularly care whether they are like white folks or anybody else. Their joy runs, bang! into ecstasy. Their religion soars to a shout. Work maybe a little today, rest a little tomorrow. Play awhile. Sing awhile. O, let's dance! These common people are not afraid of spirituals, as for a long time their more intellectual brethren were, and jazz is their child. They furnish a wealth of colorful, distinctive material for any artist because they still hold their own individuality in the face of American standardizations. And perhaps these common people will give to the world its truly great Negro artist, the one who is not afraid to be himself. Whereas the better-class Negro would tell the artist what to do, the people at least let him alone when he does appear. And they are not ashamed of him—if they know he exists at all. And they accept what beauty is their own without question.

Certainly there is, for the American Negro artist who can escape the restrictions the more advanced among his own group would put upon him, a great field of unused material ready for his art. Without going outside his race, and even among the better classes with their "white" culture and conscious American manners, but still Negro enough to be different, there is sufficient matter to furnish a black artist with a lifetime of creative work. And when he chooses to touch on the relations between Negroes and whites in this country with their innumerable overtones and undertones, surely, and especially for literature and the drama, there is an inexhaustible supply of themes at hand. To these the Negro artist can give his racial individuality, his heritage of rhythm and warmth, and his incongruous humor that so often, as in the Blues, becomes ironic laughter mixed with tears. But let us look again at the mountain.

A prominent Negro clubwoman in Philadelphia paid eleven dollars to hear Raquel Meller sing Andalusian popular songs. But she told me a few weeks before she would not think of going to hear "that woman," Clara Smith, a great black artist, sing Negro folksongs.[9] And many an upper-class Negro church, even now, would not dream of employing a spiritual in its services. The drab melodies in white folks' hymnbooks are much to be preferred. "We want to worship the Lord correctly and quietly. We don't believe in 'shouting.' Let's be dull like the Nordics," they say, in effect.

The road for the serious black artist, then, who would produce a racial art is most certainly rocky and the mountain is high. Until recently he received almost no encouragement for his work from either white or colored people. The fine novels of Chesnutt go out of print with neither race noticing their passing. The quaint charm and humor of Dunbar's dialect verse brought to him, in his day, largely the same kind of encouragement one would give a sideshow freak (A colored man writing poetry! How odd!) or a clown (How amusing!).[10]

The present vogue in things Negro, although it may do as much harm as good for the budding colored artist, has at least done this: it has brought him forcibly to the attention of his own people among whom for so long, unless the other race had noticed him beforehand, he was a prophet with little honor.[11] I understand that Charles Gilpin acted for years in Negro theaters without any special acclaim from his own, but when Broadway gave him eight curtain calls, Negroes, too, began to beat a tin pan in his honor.[12] I know a young colored writer, a manual worker by day, who had been writing well for the colored magazines for some years, but it was not until he recently broke into the white publications and his first book was accepted by a prominent New York publisher that the "best" Negroes in his city took the trouble to discover that he lived there. Then almost immediately they decided to give a grand dinner for him. But the society ladies were careful to whisper to his mother that perhaps she'd better not come. They were not sure she would have an evening gown.[13]

The Negro artist works against an undertow of sharp criticism and misunderstanding from his own group and unintentional bribes from the whites. "O, be respectable, write about nice people, show how good we are," say the Negroes. "Be stereotyped, don't go too far, don't shatter our illusions about you, don't amuse us too seriously. We will pay you," say the whites. Both would have told Jean Toomer not to write "Cane." The colored people did not praise it. The white people did not buy it. Most of the colored people who did read "Cane" hate it. They are afraid of it. Although the critics gave it good reviews the public remained indifferent. Yet (excepting the work of Du Bois) "Cane" contains the finest prose written by a Negro in America. And like the singing of Robeson, it is truly racial.[14]

But in spite of the Nordicized Negro intelligentsia and the desires of some white editors we have an honest American Negro literature already with us. Now I await the rise of the Negro theater. Our folk music, having achieved world-wide fame, offers itself to the genius of the great individual American Negro composer who is to come. And within the next decade I expect to see the work of a growing school of colored artists who paint and model the beauty of dark faces and create with new technique the expressions of their own soul-world. And the Negro dancers who will dance like flame and the singers who will continue to carry our songs to all who listen—they will be with us in even greater numbers tomorrow.

Most of my own poems are racial in theme and treatment, derived from the life I know. In many of them I try to grasp and hold some of the meanings and rhythms of jazz. I am sincere as I know how to be in these poems and yet after every reading I answer questions like these from my own people: Do you think Negroes should always write about Negroes? I wish you wouldn't read some of your poems to white folks. How do you find anything interesting in a place like a cabaret? Why do you write about black people? You aren't black. What makes you do so many jazz poems?

But jazz to me is one of the inherent expressions of Negro life in America: the eternal tom-tom beating in the Negro soul—the tom-tom of revolt against weariness in a white world, a world of subway trains, and work, work, work; the tom-tom of joy and laughter, and pain swallowed in a smile. Yet the Philadelphia clubwoman is ashamed to say that her race created it and she does not like me to write about it. The old subconscious "white is best" runs through her mind. Years of study under white teachers, a lifetime of white books, pictures, and papers, and white manners, morals, and Puritan standards made her dislike the spirituals. And now she turns up her nose at jazz and all its manifestations—likewise almost everything else distinctly racial. She doesn't care for the Winold Reiss portraits of Negroes because they are "too Negro."[15] She does not want a true picture of herself from anybody. She wants the artist to flatter her, to make the white world believe that all Negroes are as smug and as near white in soul as she wants to be. But, to my mind, it is the duty of the younger Negro artist, if he accepts any duties at all from outsiders, to change through the force of his art that old whispering "I want to be white," hidden in the aspirations of his people, to "Why should I want to be white? I am a Negro—and beautiful!"

So I am ashamed for the black poet who says, "I want to be a poet, not a Negro poet," as though his own racial world were not as interesting as any other world. I am ashamed, too, for the colored artist who runs from the painting of Negro faces to the painting of sunsets after the manner of the academicians because he fears the strange un-whiteness of his own features. An artist must be free to choose what he does, certainly, but he must also never be afraid to do what he might choose.

Let the blare of Negro Jazz bands and the bellowing voice of Bessie Smith singing Blues penetrate the closed ears of the colored near-intellectuals until they listen and perhaps understand. Let Paul Robeson singing Water Boy, and Rudolph Fisher writing about the streets of Harlem, and Jean Toomer holding the heart of Georgia in his hands, and Aaron Douglas drawing strange black fantasies cause the smug Negro middle class to turn from their white, respectable, ordinary books and papers to catch a glimmer of their own beauty.[16] We younger Negro artists who create now intend to express our individual dark-skinned selves without fear or shame. If white people are pleased we are glad. If they are not, it doesn't matter. We know we are beautiful. And ugly too. The tom-tom cries and the tom-tom laughs. If colored people are pleased we are glad. If they are not, their displeasure doesn't matter either. We build our temples for tomorrow, strong as we know how, and we stand on top of the mountain, free within ourselves.

"These Bad New Negroes: A Critique on Critics," LHP 3773 (March 22, 1927)

Tired of living penniless on bread and figs in Genoa, I found myself a job on a ship bound for New York in the fall, 1924.[17] When, after many days of scrubbing decks on my part, the boat reached Manhattan there was a letter waiting for me from my mother saying, "We're living in Washington now. Come home." And I went.

I'd never been in Washington before but I found it a city as beautiful as Paris and full of nice colored people, many of them nice looking and living in nice houses. For my mother and me, the city was a sort of ancestral shrine of which I had heard much. The great John M. Langston, senator, educator, and grand-uncle of mine had once lived there.[18] Indeed, I was to stop with descendants of his and, of course, I would meet the best people. And I did.

But since this is to be an article on literature and art, I must get on into the subject. For two years, working at sea and travelling, I had been away from books. Many of my own I had thrown into the ocean because I found life more attractive than the printed word.[19] But now I wanted to read again and talk about literature so I set out to borrow, in good Negro fashion, a copy of Jean Toomer's *Cane*. "What!" said the well-bred Washington folk. "*Cane*?" they repeated, not many having heard of it. Then I was soon given to understand by the female heads of several nice families that *Cane* was a vulgar book and that no one read it. "Why do you young folks write that way?" they asked. I offered no protest for I had not heard the question before and I am not much at answering questions quickly. But, amazed, I thought how a prophet is without honor in his own country, since Jean Toomer was born and had lived in Washington. *Cane* had received critical recognition all over America, and even in Europe, as a beautiful book, yet in the society of the author's own home-town it was almost unknown. And those who knew it thought it something low and indecent. Whenever *Cane* was mentioned the best Washingtonians posed this question: "Why doesn't Jean Toomer write about nice people?" And I began to think they wanted to add, "Like ourselves."

When Rudolph Fisher's *City of Refuge* appeared in the *Atlantic Monthly* (Washington is Fisher's home-town, too) the best persons again asked the same thing: "Why can't you young folks write about nice people? Rudolph Fisher knows decent folks." And then I knew the "nicer people" meant themselves.[20]

Then Alain Locke's *New Negro* appeared on the scene with stories by Toomer, Fisher, Eric Walrond, Zora Hurston, Matheus, and none of them were nice stories in the Washington sense of the word. "Too bad," they said. But the storm broke on the Reiss drawings. They were terrible! And anyone defending them had to answer questions like these: "Why does he make his subjects so colored?" (As though they weren't colored.) And of the two school teachers pictured in the book: "Couldn't he find any better looking school teachers to paint than these two women?" (As though all teachers should resemble the high-yellow ladies dominating the Washington school system.) And always: "Does he call this art?" I said it was art and that the dark-skinned school teachers were beautiful. But one day a nice old grandmother, with whom I disliked to disagree, summed up everybody's aversion to Fisher, Toomer, Walrond, and the Reiss drawings in one indefinite but pregnant remark, "Lord help these bad New Negroes!"[21]

Now that there has appeared in the colored press a definite but rather uncritical aversion to much of the work of the younger Negro writers and particularly myself; and because the Negro press reflects to a certain extent the minds of its readers, it is time to attempt to uncover the reasons for this dislike toward the "New Negro." I present these as possible solutions:

1. The best Negroes, including the newspaper critics, still think white people are better than colored people. It follows, in their minds, that

since the drawings of Negroes do not look like the drawings of white people they are bad art.

2. The best Negroes believe that what white people think about Negroes is more important than what Negroes think about themselves. Then it follows that because a story by Zora Hurston does not tend to make white people think all Negroes good, then said story by Zora Hurston is a bad story.

3. Many of the so-called best Negroes are in a sort of *nouveau riche* class, so from the snobbishness of their positions they hold the false belief that if the stories of Fisher were only about better-class people they would be better stories.

4. Again, many of the best Negroes, including the newspaper critics, are not really cultured Negroes after all and, therefore, have little appreciation of any art and no background from which to view either their own or the white man's books or pictures.

Perhaps none of these reasons are true reasons but I offer them for consideration. Now I shall proceed to the defense.

Art is a reflection of life or an individual's comment on life. No one has labeled the work of the better known younger Negro writers as untrue to life. It may be largely about humble people, but three-fourths of the Negroes are humble people. Yet I understand these "best" colored folks when they say that little has been written about them. I am sorry and I wish some one would put them into a nice story or a nice novel. But I fear for them if ever a really powerful work is done about their lives. Such a story would show not only their excellencies but their pseudo-culture as well, their slavish devotion to Nordic standards, their snobbishness, their detachment from the Negro masses, and their vast sense of importance to themselves. A book like that from a Negro writer, even though true and beautiful, would be more thoroughly disliked than the stories of low-class Negroes now being written. And it would be more wrathfully damned than *Nigger Heaven,* at present vibrating throughout the land in its eleventh edition.

It seems to me too bad that the discussions of Mr. Van Vechten's novel in the colored press finally became hysterical and absurd. No book could possibly be as bad as *Nigger Heaven* has been painted. And no book has ever been better advertised by those who wished to damn it. Because it was declared obscene everybody wanted to read it and I'll venture to say that more Negroes bought it than ever purchased a book by a Negro author. Which is all very fine because *Nigger Heaven* is not a bad book. It will do nice people good to read it and maybe it will broaden their minds a bit. Certainly the book is true to the life it pictures. There are cabarets in Harlem and both white and colored people who are nationally known and respected can be found almost any night at Smalls'.[22] I've seen ministers there,—nobody considers cabaret-going indecent any longer. And college boys, as you know, do have affairs with loose women. Some are even given allowances and put through medical school by such generous females. But nowhere in the novel does the author represent his college boy as a typical Negro college boy. And nowhere does he say he is writing about the whole Negro race. I admit I am still at a loss to understand the yelps of the colored critics and the reason for their ill-mannered onslaught against Mr. Van Vechten. The sincere, friendly, and helpful interest in things Negro of this sophisticated author, as shown in his published reviews and magazine articles, should at least have commanded serious, rather than vulgar, reviews of his book.

That many of the Negro write-ups of my own new collection of poems, *Fine Clothes to the Jew,* were unfavorable was not surprising to me.[23] And to be charged with painting the whole Negro race in my poems did not amaze me either. Colored critics are given to accusing all works of art touching on the Negro of portraying and representing *all* Negro life. *Porgy,* about a beggar in Charleston, is said by them to picture all Negroes as beggars, yet nowhere does DuBose Heyward imply such a thing.[24] Newspaper critics, of course, came to the same amazing conclusion about *Nigger Heaven* picturing all Negroes as cabaret goers. And now *Fine Clothes to the Jew* "low-rates" everybody of color, in their opinion.

In analyzing their reviews of my book their main objections against my work seem to be based on the reasons I am listing below with my own comments following:

1. White people will gain a bad impression of Negroes from my poems. This then implies that a Negro artist should create largely for the benefit of and for the approval of white people. In answering this I ask these questions: Does George Bernard Shaw write his plays to show Englishmen how good the Irish are? Do any of the great Russian writers write novels for the purpose of showing the perfections of the Russians? Does any true artist anywhere work for the sake of what a limited group of people will think rather than for the sake of what he himself loves and wishes to interpret? It seems to me that there are plenty of propagandists for the Negro, but too few artists, too few poets, too few interpreters and recorders of racial life, whether of the masses or of the best people.

2. My poems are indelicate. But so is life.

3. I write about "harlots and gin-bibers." But they are human. Solomon, Homer, Shakespeare, and Walt Whitman were not afraid or ashamed to include them.

4. "Red Silk Stockings." An ironical poem deploring the fact that in certain southern rural communities there is little work for a beautiful colored girl to do other than the selling of her body,—a fact for one to weep over rather than disdain to recognize.[25]

5. I do not write in the conventional forms of Keats, Poe, Dunbar, or McKay. But I do not write chiefly because I'm interested in forms,—in making a sonnet or a rondeau. I write because I want to say what I have to say. And I choose the form which seems to me best to express my thoughts. I fail to see why I should be expected to copy someone else's modes of expression when it amuses me to attempt to create forms of my own. Certainly the Shakespearean sonnet would be no mould in which to express the life of Beale Street or Lenox Avenue. Nor could the emotions of State Street be captured in rondeau.[26] I am not interested in doing tricks with rhymes. I am interested in reproducing the human soul, if I can.

6. I am prostituting my talent. But even the income from a very successful book of poems is not worth the prostitution of one's talent. I make much more money as a bell-hop than as a poet.

7. I deal with low life. But I ask this: Is life among the better classes any cleaner or any more worthy of a poet's consideration?

8. Blues are not poetry. Those who have made a more thorough study of Negro folk verse than I, and who are authorities in this field, say that many Blues are excellent poetry. I refer to James Weldon Johnson, Dorothy Scarborough, Carl Van Vechten and H. O. Osgood in their published writings.[27]

9. I am "supposed to be representative of Negro progress in the literary arts." To which I can only answer that I do not pretend, or ask anyone to suppose, that I officially represent anybody or anything other than myself. My poems are my own personal comments on life and represent me alone. I claim nothing more for them.

If the colored newspaper critics (excepting Dewey Jones and Alice Dunbar Nelson) choose to read only the words I write and not their meaning, if they choose to see only what they call the ugliness of my verse and not the protest against ugliness which my poems contain, what can I do? Such obtuse critics existed in the days of Wordsworth, Shelley, Burns, and Dunbar,—great poets with whose work I dare not compare my own. Burns was maligned because he did not write of Scottish nobles.

And as Miss Nannie Burroughs says, "to come down to the nasty now," Jean Toomer is without honor in Washington.[28] But certainly my life has been enlivened by the gentle critics who called me a "gutter-rat" and "sewer-dweller" right out in print! Variety, even in the weekly press, is the spice of criticism.

Since I am said to be the "baddest" of the bad New Negroes, I may as well express my own humble opinion on my young contemporaries, although I may vary with the race newspapers and the best Negroes. To me the stories of Rudolph Fisher are beautiful although he deals with common folks. To me it seems absurd to say that they are not elevating to the race. The stories of Sherwood Anderson deal largely with people of the same classes but white America calls him one of the greatest of the moderns. If Rudolph Fisher can write beautifully about a poor Negro migrant from the South, more power to him. A well-written story, no matter what its subject, is a contribution to the art of the Negro and I am amazed at the educated prudes who say it isn't. Jean Toomer is an artist to be proud of. Wallace Thurman, Countee Cullen with his marvellous command of technique and his poems of passion and free love, Zora Hurston with her fine handling of Negro dialect, Edward Silvera and the newer poets, all are contributing something worthwhile to the literature of the race.[29] To me it seems that we have much to be proud of in the work of these younger colored writers whom the old lady in Washington so disapprovingly called the "bad New Negroes."

"Our Wonderful Society: Washington," *Opportunity* 5.8 (August 1927): 226–27

As long as I have been colored I have heard of Washington society. Even as a little boy in Kansas vague ideas of the grandeur of Negro life in the capital found their way into my head. A grand-uncle, John M. Langston, had lived there during and after the time of colored congressmen and of him I heard much from my grandmother. Later, when I went to Cleveland, some nice mulatto friends of ours spoke of the "wonderful society life" among Negroes in Washington. And some darker friends of ours hinted at "pink teas" and the color line that was drawn there. I wanted to see the town. "It must be rich and amusing and fine," I thought.

Four or five years passed. Then by way of Mexico and New York, Paris and Italy, through a season of teaching, a year at college, and a period of travel, I arrived at Washington. "Of course, you must meet the best people," were almost the first words I heard after greetings had been exchanged. "That is very important." And I was reminded of my noble family ties and connections. But a few days later I found myself a job in a laundry, carrying bags of wet-wash. The dignity of one's family background doesn't keep a fellow who's penniless from getting hungry.

It was not long, however, before I found a better place in the office of a national Negro organization. There I opened up in the morning, did clerical work, took care of the furnace, and scrubbed the floors. This was termed a "position," not a "job." And I began to meet some of the best people. The people themselves assured me that they were the best people,—and they seemed to know. Never before, anywhere, had I seen persons of influence,—men with some money, women with some beauty, teachers with some education,—quite so audibly sure of their own importance and their high places in the community. So many pompous gentlemen never before did I meet. Nor so many ladies with chests swelled like pouter-pigeons whose mouths uttered formal sentences in frightfully correct English. I admit I was awed by these best people.

Negro society in Washington, they assured me, was the finest in the country, the richest, the most cultured, the most worthy. In no other city were there so many splendid homes, so many cars, so many A. B. degrees, or so many persons with "family background." Descendants of distinguished Negroes were numerous, but there were also those who could do better and trace their ancestry right on back to George Washington and his colored concubines: "How lucky I am to have a congressman for grand-uncle," I thought in the presence of these well-ancestored people.

She is a graduate of this . . . or, he is a graduate of that . . . frequently followed introductions. So I met many men and women who had been to college,—and seemed not to have recovered from it. Almost all of them appeared to be deeply affected by education in one way or another, and they, too, had very grand manners. "Surely," I thought when I saw them, "I'll never be important unless I get a degree." So I began to spend ten cents for lunch instead of fifteen,—putting the other nickel away for college.

Then I met some of the younger colored people, sons and daughters of the pompous gentlemen and pouter-pigeons ladies, some of them students at Northern colleges or at Howard. They were not unlike youth everywhere today,—jazzy and loud. But, "They are the hope of the race," I was told. Yet I found that their ideals seemed most Nordic and un-Negro and that they appeared to be moving away from the masses of the race rather than holding an identity with them. Speaking of a fraternity dance, one in a group of five college men said proudly, "There was nothing but pinks there,—looked just like 'fay women. Boy, you'd have thought it was an o'fay dance!"[30] And several of the light young ladies I knew were not above passing a dark classmate or acquaintance with only the coolest of nods, and sometimes not even that. "She's a dark girl but nice," or similar apologies were made by the young men for the less than coffee-and-cream ladies they happened to know. These best young people had, too, it seemed, an excessive admiration for fur coats and automobiles. Boasts like this were often to be heard! "There were more fur coats in our box at the Thanksgiving game than in anybody else's." Or concerning the social standing of a young lady: "Her father owns two cars." Or of a sporty new-comer in town: "He's got a racoon coat just like a 'fay boy." Or as the criterion of success: "He's one of our leading men. He has a Packard and a chauffeur."

But cars or fur coats or fine houses were not more talked about, however, than was culture. And the members of Washington society *were* cultured. They themselves assured me frequently that they were. Some of those who could pass for white even attended down-town theatres when "The Scandals" or Earl Carrol's "Vanities" came to town. But when a concert series of Negro artists including Abbie Mitchell and other excellent musicians was put on at a colored theatre, the audiences were very small and most of the members of cultured society were absent.

I knew that Jean Toomer's home was Washington and I had read his book *Cane* and talked about it with other readers in New York and Paris and Venice. I wanted to talk about it in Washington, too, because I had found it beautiful and real. But the cultured colored society of the capital, I mean those persons who always insisted that they were cultured, seemed to know little about the book and cared less. And when the stories of Rudolph Fisher (also a colored Washingtonian) appeared in *The Atlantic Monthly,* what I heard most was, "Why didn't he write about nice people like us? Why didn't he write about cultured folks?" I thought it amazing, too, that a young playwright of ability and three or four poets of promise were living in Washington unknown to the best society. At least, I saw nothing being done to encourage these young writers, for the leading women's clubs appeared to be founded solely for the purpose of playing cards, and the cultured doctors and lawyers and caterers and butlers and government messengers had little concern for poets or playwrights. In supposedly intellectual gatherings I listened to conversations as arid as the sides of the Washington monument.

There appeared, also, to be the same love of scandal among the best folks as among the lower classes. Sometimes I heard how such-and-such a pompous gentleman had struck his wife or how this or that refined couple had indulged in physical combat,—all of which was very amusing but hardly compatible with a society which boasted of its gentility. Such consciously nice people ought never to let down the bars, I thought, but they did.

Washington is one of the most beautiful cities in the world. For that I remember it with pleasure. Georgia Douglass Johnson conversed with charm and poured tea on Saturday nights for young writers and artists and intellectuals.[31] That, too, I remember with pleasure. Seventh Street was always teemingly alive with dark working people who hadn't yet acquired "culture" and the manners of stage ambassadors, and pinks and blacks and yellows were still friends without apologies. That street I remember with pleasure. And the few fine and outstanding men and women I met who had seemingly outgrown "society" as a boy outgrows his first long trousers,—those men and women I remember with pleasure. But Washington society itself,—perhaps I am prejudiced toward it. Perhaps I had heard too much about it before hand and was disappointed. Or perhaps I didn't really meet the best society after all. Maybe I met only the snobs, and the high-yellows, and the lovers of fur coats and automobiles and fraternity pins and A. B. degrees. Maybe I'm all wrong about everything.—Maybe those who said they were the best people had me fooled.—Perhaps they weren't the best people,—but they looked tremendously important. Or, perhaps they *were* the best people and it's my standard of values that's awry . . . Well, be that as it may, I have seen Washington, of which city I had heard much, and I have looked at something called "society" of which I had heard much, too. Now I can live in Harlem where people are not quite so ostentatiously proud of themselves, and where one's family background is not of such great concern. Now I can live contentedly in Harlem.

2

Essays, 1930–1939

"A Cuban Sculptor,"
Opportunity 8.11 (November 1930): 334

Among the sculptors of the darker world, Ramos Blanco is most certainly deserving of your sincere attention.[1] He is a Cuban Negro, formerly a policeman in the city of Havana where, during his spare hours off duty, he moulded the forms and figures that have lately attracted interest to the amazing promise of this young artist.

He is twenty-nine years old—but already within the last few years his work has been exhibited in France, Italy, and Spain, as well as in his own Cuban island. And in October of this year his monumental statue to heroic black motherhood, *Maternal Heroism,* will be erected in the Parque Medina at Havana, one of the public gardens of the city. This master work of the young Negro sculptor represents, in white marble, the figure of one of the noblest women of the Cuban Revolution, Mariana Granjales, sending her last and youngest son out to die for freedom, after all the other members of her family had been killed by the enemy.

Ramos Blanco spent fourteen months in Italy working on his gigantic monument, for there only could he find the necessary marble for his creation. While in Rome last spring, a successful exhibition of his work was held in the main galleries of the Casa de España, eliciting much favorable comment from the press of the Italian capital. In no way is this young man's work undeserving of the praise it has received. Its great dignity and simple strength indicate the arrival of a new and interesting personality in the field of American art. And the fact that the first great figure by this dark Cuban sculptor is that of a Negro heroine makes it not without significance to the readers of this magazine—we who have so few memorials to our own racial heroes in this country, so few monuments to Sojourner Truth or Frederick Douglass or Booker Washington or any of the great figures in our own perilous history.[2] Is it that we have no artists—or no pride?

"Negro Art and Claude McKay,"
LHP 755 (1931)

In spite of the devastating criticisms which the Negro press gave to *Home to Harlem* and *Banjo* when they appeared on the book market, I have always believed Claude McKay to be the greatest living Negro writer in creative literature today. His single book of poems, *Harlem Shadows,* contains some of the finest sonnets any member of our race has ever written, including the famous one, "If We Must Die."[3] And there is about his poetry a singing beauty and depth of emotion that I find in no one else. Negroes did not like Mr. McKay's novels because they are about the so-called "lower classes." And most Negro book reviewers seem to feel that authors should write only about mulatto doctors, school teachers, or lawyers; and then only about such phases of our life as would do us no harm in the eyes of white people—as though poor Negroes were not human, and as though all Negroes, unlike other races, had no faults; and as though, even in art, we must forever consider white people first. Claude McKay, however, writes of life as he knows it, and as he first saw it in America when he came here, a young man, from the West Indies. He was not received by the "best colored society" because they had never heard of him. He earned his living as a dishwasher, train servant, and in many other poor ways. In his novels he writes about the life he knew here, the way he lived. He writes about it truthfully, beautifully, in swiftly moving prose, passionate and warm.

Home to Harlem exposes the terrible conditions under which certain classes of Negroes must live and work today. It should have awakened sympathy and pity, instead of the scorn which the Negro press gave it. True, it was not about the "best people." But why is it that, with all their pretensions to culture, their money, and their degrees, the "best Negroes" have not yet produced a single writer who can write about the upper classes with anything remotely approaching the artistry of Claude McKay? Somebody please tell me. I'd like to know.

"People without Shoes,"
New Masses 12 (October 1931): 12

Haiti is a land of people without shoes—black people, whose bare feet tread the dusty roads to market in the early morning, or pat softly on the bare floors of hotels, serving foreign guests. These barefooted ones care for the rice and cane fields under the hot sun. They climb high mountains picking coffee beans, and wade through surf to fishing boats in the blue sea. All of the work that keeps Haiti alive, pays for the American Occupation, and enriches foreign traders—that vast and basic work—is done there by Negroes without shoes.

Yet shoes are things of great importance in Haiti. Everyone of any social or business position must wear them. To be seen in the streets barefooted marks one as a low-caste person of no standing in the community. Coats, too, are of an importance equal to footwear. In a country where the climate would permit everybody to go naked with ease, officials, professional men, clerks, and teachers swelter in dignity with coats buttoned about their bellies on the hottest days.

Strange, bourgeois, and a little pathetic is this accent on clothes and shoes in an undeveloped land where the average wage is thirty cents a day, and where the sun blazes like fury. It is something carried over, perhaps, from the white masters who wore coats and shoes long ago, and then had force and power; or something remembered, maybe, as infinitely desirable—like leisure and rest and freedom. But articles of clothing for the black masses in Haiti are not cheap. Cloth is imported, as are most of the shoes. Taxes are high, jobs are scarce, wages are low, so the doubtful step upward to the dignity of leather between one's feet and the earth, and a coat between one's body and the sun, is a step not easily to be achieved in this island of the Caribbean.

Practically all business there is in the hands of white foreigners, so one must buy one's shoes from a Frenchman or a Syrian who pays as little money as possible back into Haitian hands. Imports and exports are in charge of foreigners, too, German often, or American, or Italian. Haiti has no foreign credit, no steamships, few commercial representatives abroad. And the government, Occupation controlled, puts a tax on almost everything. There are no factories of any consequence in the land, and what few there are are largely under non-Haitian control. Every ship brings loads of imported goods from the white countries. Even Haitian postage stamps are made abroad. The laws are dictated from Washington. American controllers count their money. And the military Occupation extracts fat salaries for its own civilian experts and officials.

What then, pray, have the dignified native citizens with shoes been doing all the while—those Haitians, mulattoes largely, who have dominated the politics of the country for decades, and who have drawn almost as sharp a class line between themselves and their shoeless black brothers as have the Americans with their imported color line dividing the Occupation from *all* Haitians? How have these super-class citizens of this once-Republic been occupying themselves? Living for years on under-paid peasant labor and lazy government jobs, is one answer. Writing flowery poetry in the manner of the French academicians, is another. Creating bloody civil wars and wasteful political-party revolutions, and making lovely speeches on holidays. Borrowing government money abroad to spend on themselves—and doing nothing for the people without shoes, building no schools, no factories, creating no advancements for the masses, no new agricultural developments, no opportunities—too busy feeding their own pride and their own acquisitiveness. The result: a country poor, ignorant, and hungry at the bottom, corrupt and greedy at the top—a wide open way for the equally greedy Yankees of the North to step in, with a corruption more powerful than Paris-cultured mulattoes had the gall to muster.

Haiti today: a fruit tree for Wall Street, a mango for the Occupation, coffee for foreign cups, and poverty for its own black workers and peasants. The recently elected Chamber of Deputies (the Haitian Senate) has just voted to increase its salaries to $250.00 a month. The workers on the public roads receive 30¢ a day, and the members of the gendarmerie $2.50 a week. A great difference in income. But then—the deputies must wear shoes. They have dignity to maintain. They govern.

As to the Occupation, after fifteen years, about all for which one can give the Marines credit are a few decent hospitals and a rural health service. The roads of the country are still impassable, and schools continue to be lacking. The need for economic reform is greater than ever.

The people without shoes cannot read or write. Most of them have never seen a movie, have never seen a train. They live in thatched huts or rickety houses; rise with the sun; sleep with the dark. They wash their clothes in running streams with lathery weeds—too poor to buy soap. They move slowly, appear lazy because of generations of undernourishment and constant lack of incentive to ambition. On Saturdays they dance to the Congo drums; and on Sundays go to mass,—for they believe in the Saints and the Voodoo gods, all mixed. They grow old and die, and are buried the following day after an all-night wake where their friends drink, sing, and play games, like a party. The rulers of the land never miss them. More black infants are born to grow up and work. Foreign ships continue to come into Haitian harbors, dump goods, and sail away with the products of black labor—cocoa beans, coffee, sugar, dyewoods, fruits, and rice. The mulatto upper classes continue to send their children to Europe for an education. The American Occupation lives in the best houses. The officials of the National City Bank, New York, keep their heavy-jawed portraits in the offices of the Banque d'Haiti. And because black hands have touched the earth, gathered in the fruits, and loaded ships, somebody—across the class and color lines—many somebodies become richer and wiser, educate their children to read and write, to travel, to be ambitious, to be superior, to create armies, and to build banks. Somebody wears coats and shoes.

On Sunday evening in the Champs de Mars, before the Capitol at Port au Prince, the palace band plays immortally out-worn music while genteel people stroll round and round the brilliance of the lighted bandstand. Lovely brown and yellow girls in cool dresses, and dark men in white suits, pass and repass.

I asked a friend of mine, my first night there, "Where are all the people without shoes? I don't see any."

"They can't walk here," he said. "The police would drive them away."

"Books and the Negro Child," *Children's Library Yearbook* 4 (1932): 108–10; LHP 209

Albert Einstein, in his message to American Negroes in *The Crisis* for January 1932, says, "It seems to be a universal fact that minorities, especially when their individuals are recognizable because of physical differences, are treated by the majorities among whom they live as an inferior class. The tragic part of such a fate, however, lies not only in the automatically realized disadvantages suffered by these minorities in economic and social relations, but also in the fact that those who meet such treatment themselves, for the most part, acquiesce in this prejudiced estimate because of the suggestive influence of the majority, and come to regard people like themselves as inferior."

Overcoming this racial inferiority complex is, undoubtedly, one of the greatest tasks of the teachers of Negro children. To make their little charges feel that they will be men and women, not "just niggers," is a none too easy problem when textbooks are all written from a white standpoint. Geographies picturing the African natives as bushy headed savages with no culture of their own; civics describing Negro neighborhoods as the worst quarters in our cities; histories that note the backwardness of the Negro South but none of its amazing progress in only three score years of freedom; all of the bad, depressing phases of racial life set before the black child—none of the achievements; these are what the school books usually give. A Negro pilot with Columbus; black Crispus Attucks, first citizen to fall in the American Revolution; a colored Benjamin Banneker creating the first clock made in this country—none of these is mentioned.[4]

Only when one is no longer ashamed of one's self can one feel fully American, and capable of contributing proudly to the progress of America. To drive out false shame, then, with its companions, timidity and fear, is one of the duties of all grown-ups toward the Negro child. Teachers, authors, and librarians can help greatly in this, once they understand the problem and books are made available.

For so long, the Negro folk-tales, often in difficult dialect even for Negroes, have been the only kind of stories directly appealing to the life-background of the colored child. So far, the children's booklets on Negro themes, other than the folk-tales have been of the pickaninny variety, poking fun (however innocently) at the little youngsters whose skins are not white, and holding up to laughter the symbol of the watermelon and the chicken. Perhaps Topsy set the pattern; Sambo and the others came along—amusing undoubtedly to the white child, but like an unkind word to one who has known too many hurts to enjoy the additional pain of being laughed at.[5]

The need today is for books that Negro parents and teachers can read to their children without hesitancy as to the psychological effect on the growing mind, books whose dark characters are not all clowns and whose illustrations are not merely caricatures.

There are a few volumes on Negro life that librarians can recommend to colored children without apology. For older youngsters, Vandercook's *Black Majesty,* a tale of the Haitian kings, is excellent. Elizabeth Ross Haynes' *Unsung Heroes,* and Arthur Fauset's *For Freedom* can teach the achievements of black character. Mary White Ovington's *Hazel* and her more recent *Zeke* are two stories for dark youth by a white woman of sympathy and understanding.[6] But there is a need for many more books still unwritten in this field; and after the books are written, a need for Negro library facilities throughout the South where most dark people still live.

The main public libraries in the cities of the South, are not open to Negro readers. Some of the larger towns (but far too few) have branch libraries for their colored citizens, but these branches are understaffed, often with only a single librarian who is sometimes janitress as well, and usually poorly supplied with books, perhaps a collection of dog-eared volumes turned over to the Negro branch when too badly worn for further use by the whites.

Few of these Negro branch libraries in the South can afford or have the books or space to allow separate children's departments. Many of the libraries in the Negro schools and colleges are pitifully lacking in books, too. Fortunately, the Rosenwald Fund has done something to remedy this for the schools—but much more needs to be done, in both schools and cities, for through the written word a people may find themselves.[7]

Faced too often by the segregation and scorn of a surrounding white world, America's Negro children are in pressing need of books that will give them back their souls. They do not know the beauty they possess.

"White Shadows in a Black Land," *Crisis* 39 (May 1932): 157

Imagine a country where the entire national population is colored, and you will have Haiti—the first of the black republics, and that much discussed little land to the South of us. To a Negro coming directly from New York by steamer and landing at Port au Prince, the capital, it is like stepping into a new world, a darker world, a world where the white shadows are apparently missing, a world of his own people. The custom officials who examine his baggage will be Negroes, the taxi drivers will be black or brown, his hotel keeper will probably be mulatto. In the shops, clerks of color will wait on him. At the banks, Negroes will cash his travellers' checks and explain the currency of the country to him. Should he visit the Chamber of Deputies, he will find the governing body filled with dark faces, and even the president of the Republic will have a touch of color in his blood. In the country districts, the peasants who make up the bulk of the population will smile at him from kind black faces, and the dark visitor from America will feel at home and unafraid.

It is doubly disappointing then, to discover, if you have not already known, how the white shadows have fallen on this land of color. Before you can go ashore, a white American Marine has been on board ship to examine your passport, and maybe you will see a U.S. gunboat at anchor in the harbor. Ashore, you are likely to soon run into groups of Marines in the little cafes, talking in "Cracker" accents, and drinking in the usual boisterous American manner. You will discover that the Banque d'Haiti, with its Negro cashiers and tellers, is really under control of the National City Bank of New York. You will become informed that all the money collected by the Haitian customs passes through the hands of an American comptroller. And regretfully, you will gradually learn that most of the larger stores with their colored clerks are really owned by Frenchmen, Germans, or Assyrian Jews. And if you read the Haitian newspapers, you will soon realize from the heated complaints there, that even in the Chamber of Deputies the strings of government are pulled by white politicians in far-off Washington—and that the American Marines are kept in the country through an illegal treaty thrust upon Haiti by force and never yet ratified by the United States senate. The dark-skinned little Republic, then, has its hair caught in the white fingers of unsympathetic foreigners, and the Haitian people live today under a sort of military dictatorship backed by American guns. They are not free.

But Haiti glories in a splendid history studded with the names of heroes like Toussaint L'Ouverture, Dessalines, and Christophe—great black men who freed their land from slavery and began to work out their own national destinies a full half-century before American Negroes were freed by the Civil War.[8] Under the powerful leadership mentioned above, the French slave-owners were driven from the island, and Haiti became a free country of dark-skinned peoples. Then Christophe built roads and schools, factories and mills. He established laws and constructed a great Citadel on top of a mountain to defend the land and to create a monument in stone that could be seen for many miles away, so that his subjects might look upon it and be proud. That Citadel today, standing in lonely majesty against the clouds twenty miles from the city of Cape Haitien, is still one of the wonders of the New World, and one of the most amazing structures ever built by man. The story of its building, of how thousands of blacks labored at the task of dragging material and heavy bronze cannons up the steep mountain slopes for years, and how the walls gradually began to tower against the sky is most beautifully told in Vandercook's *Black Majesty*, a record of Christophe's life.

But after Christophe's death in 1820, misfortune set in. Revolution after revolution kept the country in turmoil. Politicians and grafters gained control. The Citadel, the palaces, the schools, the roads were left to rack and ruin. The mulattoes and the few blacks with money set themselves apart as an aristocracy, exploited the peasantry, did little to improve the land, and held their heads high in a proud and snobbish manner, not unlike the French masters of old. They sent their children abroad to be educated in the futile upper-class patterns of European culture. Practical work became distasteful to them, physical labor undignified. If one wore shoes, one should not even be seen in the streets carrying a package. Business and commerce were left to foreign initiative. The white shadows began to fall across the land as the dark aristocracy became cultured, and careless, conceited, and quite "high hat." Today, the Marines are there.

"Claude McKay: The Best,"
LHP 29 (1933?)

Claude McKay is the outstanding living Negro writer.[9] In both quality and quantity he leads all others. He is a creator of poetry and of prose. Some of his sonnets are among the finest in contemporary English. His novels have more color, depth, and social force than any others being written about the Negro peoples today. He has now to his credit three books of poems, three novels, and one volume of short stories. Besides America, his books have appeared in England, France, Germany, and the Soviet Union. He is forty-two years old.

McKay is the only one of the famous Negro writers with whom I am not personally acquainted. Our friendship has been entirely by letter. He has written me from France, Spain, and North Africa, in the more than ten years he has been away from America.[10] I have sent him my books and he has commented upon then, criticized and advised me. I have admired him greatly and feel that, to some extent, my own work has been influenced by his.

McKay, with Max Eastman, Floyd Dell, and Mike Gold, was one of the editors of the old *Liberator.*[11] I read every copy of that magazine I could get my hands on during my high school days. I learned from it the revolutionary attitude toward Negroes. Was there not a Negro on its staff—and what other "white" American magazine would have a colored editorial member? I sent my own earliest poems (young and very bad) to the *Liberator.* Of course, they were returned to me. But I kept on sending others. And when the *Liberator* became the *Workers Monthly* I sent poetry there, too, some of which was published. Now I am happy to be one of the contributing editors of the *New Masses.* It was Claude McKay's example that started me on this track.

Before I reached New York, McKay had gone to Soviet Russia. He never came back to the States. Folks say that although he had lived in America for some time, he had never become a naturalized citizen. (He is a British colonial subject from the island of Jamaica.) So the United

States immigration authorities would not permit him to return to New York after his months in Moscow. I guess they were afraid of him. So Claude went to London, Paris, Berlin, Barcelona. And now he lives in Tangiers.

His early life is interesting. Before he was twenty, he belonged to the Jamaican constabulary, the island police force. He wrote poems, too, in the island dialect. And for his first book, *Songs of Jamaica,* he received the gold medal of the Institute of Arts and Sciences of the island—the first Negro to ever be accorded that honor. They called him the Robert Burns of Jamaica.[12] His verse was the essence of the folk-life of the Negro peoples there.

Then he was sent away by the government to study in the States—not to study literature—but agriculture. He went to Tuskegee, a reactionary Negro school in Alabama.[13] He couldn't stand it. He came north to the State University of Kansas. But in a short time he drifted away to Chicago and New York. He lived in Harlem, the Negro quarter, and later in Greenwich Village, the artists' center of Manhattan a decade ago. This was shortly after the War. He wore a red shirt and mingled with the white radicals and writers of the town—a thing that shocked both Negroes and whites who were not used to seeing a big black boy breaking away from the color line.

He wrote a poem called "The Harlem Dance" that attracted attention among the literati. And after the wide-spread race riots of 1919, he wrote a sonnet, "If We Must Die," defiant and, for that time, most revolutionary in tone, in which he advised the hunted Negroes to fight back against the white mobs.[14] This poem became famous in Negro America, and has since been widely quoted. In 1922 his first book in literary English, *Harlem Shadows,* appeared and was favorably received by both the critics and the public. Here at last was a really fine Negro poet.

And then his name began to appear often in the papers. When the police broke up a ball of artists and radicals in Greenwich Village, they gave as the reason that they objected to Negroes dancing with white women—the Negroes being namely one Claude McKay. Shortly thereafter, pictures began to arrive from the Soviet Union showing McKay in the midst of workers' gatherings, showing him speaking from the tribunals draped in red, showing him surrounded by revolutionaries. The "best" Negroes and the "best" white folks shook their heads doubtfully. A Negro had stepped too far (for their safety) over the traditional American color line. He had even gone abroad to Red Russia. Little wonder then that he was never permitted to come back to New York.

In London McKay published a book of poems called *Spring in New Hampshire*. And in 1928 his initial novel, *Home to Harlem*, appeared. This book became the first Negro "best-seller." The verve and color of its prose, the singing movement of its adventurous tale, made everybody want to read it. It told the story of a simple black worker come back from the War, trying to adjust himself to the jobs black boys are limited to in America, trying to enjoy life, and laugh and dance and love, in spite of the daily grind of earning a living. That the laughter and dancing and loving appear more joyous than is usually true in reality is the book's chief fault as a proletarian novel. But it contains some fine chapters showing in realistic fashion the exploitation of certain classes of black workers in wealthy post-war America. And to my mind, it is the most alive and vivid novel yet written by a Negro in the wide world.

After *Home to Harlem*, came *Banjo*, a heavier and more seriously patterned book about the black and white dock-rats of Marseilles. This novel moved with less verve and life than did McKay's first volume, perhaps because it attempted to probe deeper beneath the surface of civilized existence to the cancers at the core. It shows the lumpenproletariat, ironically enough, as the happy sores of civilization. It contains pages of slow-moving conversations that are really the author's own philosophical dissertations on the ways of our age. And here I was intensely disappointed. The book is deadly serious, but one puts it down at the end with an impression of mingled back to Africa, pagan, O-how-joyous-Negroes-are-even-as-dock-rats stuff, mixed with the conclusion that the strong almost always win out, therefore let the individual fight for his own life in no matter what the social order. It is Claude McKay turned pagan and individualist, vagabond and race-chauvinist; Claude McKay talking like a colored Greenwich Villager, serious over cocktails, with an artist's tie and a Harry Kemp temperament.[15] There is nothing of the revolution in *Banjo;* nothing of the spirit of the Moscow from which McKay had but shortly returned to Europe; and nothing of the workers of the world uniting to break their chains.

What happened to Claude McKay? Don't ask me. I don't know. But then what happened to most of the old *Liberator* crowd—Floyd Dell and Max Eastman and Arturo Giovannitti?[16] Well, they're old and fairly well-off and as revolutionary as kittens now. And the latest news from North Africa is that McKay is thinking seriously of taking up the Mohammedan faith!

All of which doesn't keep his *Gingertown* from being an excellently readable volume of short stories, mostly of West Indian life; or his new novel *Banana Bottom* from being a book which I hear is well worth having; for McKay is a literary artist, knowing the magic of poetry and story-telling, even if he is [a] revolutionary backslider. As a person, those who know him say that he lives from city to city with a simple, primitive gusto that shows that he hasn't yet had the need of the Internationale knocked into him—like, for instance, the colored share-croppers of Alabama, or the black workers of the capital of McKay's Jamaica where the British soldiers recently mobbed Negro subjects in the streets.

"Moscow and Me,"
International Literature 3 (July 1933): 61–66

"If you can't carry from New York, then buy in Berlin. Everything: Canned goods, sugar, soap, toilet paper, pencils, ink, winter clothes, can openers, toothbrushes, shoestrings, and so on, and so on, and so on. Otherwise you will go hungry, dirty and ragged in Moscow," thus good friends earnestly advised me.

"You will be guided, guarded and watched all the time in Moscow—the G.P.U.," they warned me.[17]

"The peasants and poor folks have control and they're the stupidest people on earth. You will be sadly disappointed in Moscow," estimable gentlemen who had especially studied the "Russian experiment" told me.

"Oh, and what might happen to your poetry! There's only propaganda in Moscow," charming ladies with artistic souls exclaimed.

"They only want to make Communists out of you-all, you and the rest of these Negroes going in that group—and get you slaughtered when you come back home—if the American government lets you come back," genteel colored people told me. "You'd better stay home."

"Can't," I said. "I want to see Moscow."

So when the Europa sailed from New York on June 14 in the year of our one-time Lord 1932, there I was in a group of 22 Negroes going to the Soviet Union to make a film, *Black and White!*

Moscow met us at Leningrad—in the persons of some of the officials of the Meschrabpom for whom we were to work. And among them was a Negro! None of these men from Moscow appeared pale and undernourished or in need of the canned goods we had brought. And certainly colored Comrade Whiteman didn't look anything like

A motherless chile
A long ways from home.

And he has lived in Moscow for years.

The banquet they spread for us at the October Hotel in Leningrad ran all the way from soup on through roast chicken and vegetables right down to ice cream and black coffee. And an orchestra playing dinner music. All of which was

Better, better, than I gets at home.

The speeches were short and warm with proletarian greetings and the orchestra played the *Internationale:*

Arise, ye prisoners of starvation.

But we were all a little too full of good food at the moment to give that line its real meaning.

Arise, ye slaves no more in thrall.

We did better on that; we Negroes: Moscow and freedom! The Soviet Union! The dream of all the poor and oppressed—like us—come true.

You have been naught,
You shall be all.

We slept on the Express roaring through the night toward Moscow. In the morning we emerged from the train to the clicking of a battery of newspaper cameras and the greetings of a group of Moscovites come to meet us. And among them were two more Negroes! One was Emma Harris who's lived in Russia for thirty years, sings, and makes the best apple pies in the world. And the other was a grandly black boy whom we thought was from Africa—but who turned out to be from Chicago. His name was Bob.

Our hands were shaken. We were hugged and kissed. We were carried along in the crowd to the bright sunshine of the street outside. And there a flock of long shiny cars waited for us—Buicks and Lincolns—that swept us through the Moscow boulevards making as much time as the taxis in

Central Park. We drove across the Red Square past Lenin's Mausoleum and the towers and domes of the Kremlin—and stopped a block away at the Grand Hotel.

Our rooms were ready for us—clean and comfortable, with hot and cold water, homelike settees and deep roomy chairs. Courteous attendants there were, baths and elevator, a book shop and two restaurants. Everything that a hotel for white folks at home would have—except that, quite truthfully, there was no toilet paper. And no Jim Crow.

Of course, we knew that one of the basic principles of the Soviet Union is the end of all racial distinctions. That's the main reason we had come to Moscow.

That afternoon another long table was spread in the hotel dining room, and we ate again. Around this welcoming board we met our first Russian friends. And learned to say, "Tovarish."[18] And thus began our life in Moscow, the Red Capital.

Here there should follow several pages about how we made the movie that we had come to take part in—except that the movie was not made! Why? Well, here's the inside dope. A few days after I got here, I was contracted to revise the dialogue so, with an interpreter, I sat in at most of the conferences. I listened to Pudovkin, Eck, and other famous kino experts analyze and dissect the proposed script for *Black and White* as prepared for filming. There were heated discussions on every scene and every line of dialogue. There were a dozen different disagreements. The defects of the plot and continuity were mercilessly exposed. And finally the production of a picture based on the scenario at hand was called off.

Moving picture studios all over the world are, after all, more or less alike. Pictures are listed and cancelled. Directors are hired and fired. Films are made and shelved. What happened to *Black and White* in Moscow, happens to many films in Hollywood. But between the studios of Hollywood and those of Moscow there is this difference: In Hollywood the production of films is quite frankly a business for the making of money. In Moscow the production of films is quite frankly an art for the advancement of certain ideas of social betterment. In Hollywood, too, writers, directors, and producers will squabble over a scenario for weeks, but in the end, if the artistic ideals of the writers are opposed to the money-making ideals of the producers, the artistic ideals go and box-office appeal takes their place. In Moscow, on the other hand, the profit-making motif is entirely absent. It has no need for being, as the films do not necessarily depend on the box office for their funds. And the endless arguments that go on between scenario writers, directors, and producers center rather around how to present with the greatest artistic force the ideals that will make for the betterment of the Soviet people. In Moscow, the aim is to create a socially important film. In Hollywood, it is to make money.

So when the best minds of the Soviet film industry declared the scenario of *Black and White* artistically weak and unsound; and when they said that they felt it could not do justice to the oppressed and segregated Negroes of the world, or serve to further enlighten Soviet movie audiences, there could hardly have been a better reason for the postponement of the film until a more effective scenario could be prepared. Nevertheless, a few of the members of the group, loath to leave the comforts of the Grand Hotel and return to Harlem, shouted loudly that the black race of the whole world had been betrayed, and they themselves had been cheated and disillusioned. Even after they had been paid in full for the four months of our contract, fare in dollars reimbursed, and sent home via Paris, some few still continued to weep in the Harlem papers about the evils of Moscow which housed a film company that would not make a bad picture from a weak scenario—so they could act in it. One can understand that attitude, however, so great is the urge to go in the movies, even among us Negroes. Many an aspirant has left Hollywood cursing Metro-Goldwyn-Mayer. But between leaving Hollywood and Moscow there is this difference: Many disappointed would-be screen stars depart from Hollywood hungry. Our Negro artists left Moscow well-fed, well paid, and well entertained, having been given free excursions that included Odessa, the Black Sea, Central Asia, Tiflis, and Dnieprostroy. They went home via London, Paris, or Berlin. Or they could have stayed (and several did) with offers of parts in other films or jobs in Moscow. But I hear from New York that a few are still mad because they could not immediately star in *Black and White,* be the scenario good or bad.

O, Movies. Temperaments. Artists. Ambitions. Scenarios. Directors, producers, advisors, actors, censors, changes, revisions, conferences. It's a complicated art—the cinema. I'm glad I write poems.

After three months of the movies, I was delighted to pack my bags and go off on a plain prose writing assignment to Central Asia for a study of the new life there around Bukhara and Samarkand—socialism tearing down the customs of ages: veiled women, concubines, mosques, Allah-worship, and illiteracy disappearing. When I came back to Moscow in the winter, those of our Negro group who had remained, seven in all, had settled down comfortably to life in the Soviet capital. Dorothy West was writing, Mildred Jones taking screen tests for a new picture. Long, tall Patterson who paints houses had married a girl who paints pictures, and together they have executed some of the finest decorations for the May Day celebration. Wayland Rudd was studying singing, fencing, and dancing, and taking a role in a new Meyerhold play. McKenzie stayed in the films, working for Meschrabpom. And Homer Smith, as a special consultant in the Central Post Office, was supervising the installation of an American special delivery system for Moscow mail. So the Negroes made themselves at home. Some were getting fat.[19]

After five months in Asia, I was glad to be back in Moscow again—great bustling city comparable in some ways to Chicago, Cleveland or New York. But very different, too. For instance, in the American cities money is the powerful and respected thing. In Moscow, work is powerful —and not money. One can have ever so many rubles and still find many places and pleasures closed to him. Food, lodging, theatre tickets, medical service, all the things that dollars buy at home, are easily available in Moscow only if one is a worker and has the proper papers from one's factory, shop, office or trade union. I was glad I belonged to the International Union of Revolutionary Writers. Credentials were far more important than rubles.

And another thing that makes Moscow different from Chicago or Cleveland, or New York, is that in the cities at home Negroes—like me—must stay away from a great many places—hotels, clubs, parks, theatres, factories, offices, and union halls—because they are not white. And in Moscow, all the doors are open to us just the same, of course, and I find myself forgetting that the Russians are white folks. They're too damn decent and polite. To walk into a big hotel without the doorman yelling at me (at my age), "Hey, boy, where're you going?" Or to sit at the table in any public restaurant and not be told, "We don't serve Negroes here." Or to have the right of seeking a job at any factory or in any office where I am qualified to work and never be turned down on account of color or a WHITE ONLY sign at the door. To dance with a white woman in the dining room of a fine restaurant and not be dragged out by the neck—is to wonder if you're really living in a city full of white folks (as is like Moscow).

But then the papers of the other lands are always calling the Muscovites red. I guess it's the red that makes the difference. I'll be glad when Chicago gets that way, and Birmingham.

For me, as a writer, Moscow is certainly different, too. It's the first city I've ever lived in where I could make my living entirely from writing. Not that I write more here than I do elsewhere, but I am paid better, and there is a wider market. In America the magazines in which one can frequently publish stories or poems about Negroes are very few, and most of these do not pay, since they are of a social service or proletarian nature. The big American bourgeois publications are very careful about what they publish by or about colored people. Exotic or humorous tales they will occasionally use. Stories that show Negroes as savages, fools, or clowns, they will often print. And once in a blue moon there may be a really sound and serious literary picture of black life in a big magazine—but it doesn't happen often enough to feed an author. They can't live on blue moons. Most colored writers find their work turned down with a note that the files are already full of "Negro material," or that the subject is not suitable, or, as happened to me recently when I submitted a story about a more or less common situation in American inter-racial life—the manuscript was returned with regrets since the story was "excellently written, but it would shock our good middle-class audience to death." And thus our American publications shy away from the Negro problem and the work of Negro writers.

In Moscow, on the other hand, the editors welcome frank stories of American Negro life. They print them and pay for them. Book publishers welcome volumes by black writers, and, in spite of the paper shortage, a great many books of Negro life have appeared in translation in Moscow. Large audiences come to hear colored writers lecture on their work, and dinners and testimonials are given in their honor. There is no segregated Harlem of literature in Moscow.

As to writers in general, I feel safe in saying that members of the literary craft, on the whole, live better in the Soviet Union than they do in America. In the first place there is a tremendous reading public buying millions of books, papers, and magazines, in dozens of different languages. Translation rights of a Soviet writer's work here within the Union alone may bring in thousands of rubles. And there are, in Moscow and other cities, cooperative dining rooms for writers, specially built modern apartments with very low rents, excellent clubs and tennis courts and libraries—all for the workers in words.

As for me, I received for one edition of my poems in translation more money in actual living value than I have yet made from the several editions of my various volumes of poetry in America. For an edition in Uzbek, a minority language that most Americans never heard of (nor I either till I came here), I was paid enough to live in grand style for a year or modestly for two years—which is more than poetry alone ever did for me at home.

There is in Moscow a great curiosity for things American, and a great sympathy for things Negro. So, being both an American and a Negro, I am met everywhere with friendly questions from children and adults as to how we live at home. Is there really a crisis, with people hungry and ragged when there are in America so many factories, so much technique, so much wheat, and cotton and livestock? How can that be? Do they actually kill people in electric chairs? Actually lynch Negroes? Why?

The children in the Moscow streets, wise little city children, will ofttimes gather around you if you are waiting for a street car, or looking into a shop window. They will take your hand and ask you about the Scottsboro boys, or if you like the Soviet Union and are going to stay forever. Sometimes as you pass a group of children playing, they will stop and exclaim, "Negro!" But in wonder and surprise a long way from the insulting derision of the word "Nigger" in the mouths of America's white children. Here, the youth in the schools are taught to respect all races. And at the Children's Theatre there is a sympathetic play being given of how a little Negro girl found her way from Africa to Moscow, and lived happily ever after.

Strangers in general meet with widespread curiosity from the citizens of Moscow. *Inastranyetz,* they will say, and let you go to the head of the line, if there is a crowd waiting at the stamp window in the post office, or standing in the queue for an auto bus, or buying tickets to the theatre. If you go alone to the movies, someone is sure to offer to translate for you, should they happen to know a little German or English. If you hand a written address to a citizen on a Moscow street, often said citizen will go out of his way to lead you to the place you are seeking. I have never lived in a more truly courteous city. True, there is not here anywhere in public places the swift and efficient directness of America. Neither is there the servile, tip-chasing, bowing and scraping service of Paris. But here there is friendliness. In Moscow there are often mountains and swamps of red tape that would drive you crazy, were it not for the gentle patience and kindness of the ordinary citizens and simple workers anxious to offer to strangers their comradely help and extend their services as hosts of the city. So in spite of the entirely new routine of life which Moscow offers it does not take one long to feel at home.

Of course, there is the room problem, for the city is the most overcrowded in the world. A foreigner coming to Moscow (unless as a tourist) should really bring a room with him. The great Eisenstein, maker of marvellous movies, lives in only one room. In spite of hundreds of new apartments that have been built, the growth of housing has not been able to keep up with the growth of the populace. A Moscow apartment is as crowded as a Harlem flat at the height of the great Negro migration from the South. Yet, with all their own housing difficulties, the Muscovite can listen patiently to irate foreign workers who are indignant at not immediately receiving on arrival a three room apartment with kitchenette and bath.

The Negroes whom I know in Moscow are all housed comfortably and are not as much given to complaints as certain other nationalities who come to the workers' capital with a greater superiority complex as to their world importance. The colored people in Moscow move easily in Russian circles, are well received, and cordially welcomed in private homes, in workers' clubs, and at demonstrations. There are always dark faces in the tremendous May Day demonstrations that move for hours through the Red Square. A great many Negroes took part in the gigantic Scottsboro Demonstration in the summer of 1932 at the Park of Rest and Culture. The pictures of Negro workers are often displayed in the windows of shops on the main Moscow streets. During the recent May holidays there was a huge picture of Robinson, the colored udarnik[20] at the Ball Bearing Plant, on display in a busy part of Gorky Street. Moscow's black residents are well woven into the life of this big proletarian city, and they are received as comrades.

As for me, I've had a swell time. I've spoken at demonstrations, read poems at workers' clubs, met lots of poets and writers and artists and actors, attended all the leading theatres from the Opera to Ohlopkov's Realistic Theatre where the stage is all around the audience and you sit in the middle. I've seen the finest Gauguins and Cézannes in the world, have eaten soup with the Red Army, danced with the Gypsies, and lived excitingly well, and have done a great deal of writing.

I shall go back to America just as clean (there is soap here), just as fat (and food), just as safe and sound (and the G.P.U.) as I was when I left New York. And once there, I'm thinking that I'll probably be homesick for Moscow. There's an old song that says:

You never miss the water till the well runs dry. Those who ought to know, tell me that you never really appreciate Moscow until you get back again to the land of the bread lines, unemployment, Jim Crow cars and crooked politicians, brutal bankers and overbearing police, three per cent beer and the Scottsboro case.

Well, the Russian workers and peasants were awfully patient with the Tsar, but when they got rid of him—they really *got rid* of him. Now they have a right to be proud of their red flags flying over the Kremlin. They put them there. And don't let anybody in America kid you into believing what with talking about lack of soap and food and the G.P.U., that Moscow isn't the greatest city in the world today. Athens used to be. Then Rome. And more recently, Paris. Now they'll put you in jail in Alabama for even mentioning Moscow! That's one way of recognizing its leadership.

"Negroes Speak of War," *Fight against War and Fascism* 1.1 (November 1933): 4

When the time comes for the next war, I'm asking you, remember the last war. I'm asking you, what you fought for, and what you would be fighting for again? I'm asking you, how many of the lies you were told, do you still believe? Does any Negro believe, for instance, that the world was actually saved for Democracy? Does any Negro believe, any more, in closing ranks with the war makers? Maybe a few Negro soldiers believed Dr. Moton when he came over to France talking about, "Be nice and fight for the nice white folks. Be meek and shoot some Germans." But do any Negroes believe him now, with lynched black workers hanging on trees all around Tuskegee? I'm asking you?[21]

And after the Chicago riots and the Washington riots and the East St. Louis riots, and more recently the Bonus March, is it some foreign army needs to be fought?

And listen, I'm asking you, with all the war ships and marines and officers and Secretary of the Navy going to Cuba, can't they send even one sergeant after Sheriff Shamblin in Alabama?[22]

And with all the money they get to buy bombing planes, why in the hell can't they pay the teachers for my kids to go to school?

And even if I was studying about fighting (which I ain't) why couldn't I do a little killing in the navy without wrassling with pots and pans, or join the marines (the lily white marines) and see the world, or go in the air force where you never admitted Negroes yet? I'd like to be above the battle too. Or do you think you gonna use me for stevedoring again?

And speaking of France, our once beloved ally, where Negroes can still eat in the restaurants in spite of Woodrow Wilson—don't let that fool you. Somebody ought to put the French black Africans wise to the fact that they *ought* to treat them well in Paris when they are drilling them by the hundreds of thousands to stop bullets with their breasts and bombs with their heads and fill the front line trenches for dear old France (that only a handful of them have ever seen) in the next war. Or have they got a French Dr. Moton to lie to black Africans, too, I'm asking you?

And when the next war comes, I want to know whose war and why. For instance, if it's the Japanese we're speaking of—there's plenty of perils for me right here at home that needs attending to: what about them labor unions that won't admit Negroes? And what about all them factories where I can't work, even if there was work? And what about the schools I can't go to, and the states I can't vote in, and the juries I can't sit on? And what about all them sheriffs that can never find out who did the lynching? And what about something to eat without putting on a uniform and going out and killing folks I never saw to get it? And what about some work? And what about them "separate colored" codes in the NRA?[23] And what about a voice in who's running this country and why—before I even think about crossing the water and fighting again?

Who said I want to go to war? If I do, it ain't the same war the President wants to go to. No, sir. I been hanging on a rope in Alabama too long.

"Negroes in Moscow: In a Land Where There Is No Jim Crow," *International Literature* 4 (1933): 78–81

In the very heart of Moscow, for a great many years now, day and night, night and day, a tall curly-headed Negro stands looking down on the moving life of Russia's greatest city. Autos and tram cars cross the square, and crowds of people. Overhead airplanes fly. And soon, under his feet, there will be a subway. At night, the lights blaze, electric signs flash and theatre crowds merge. By day, mothers with kids come and sit on the park benches around the square and often say to their children, "Look, there is Pushkin." And sometimes the children walk up the steps to the foot of the statue and learn to spell out, among their first words, the name of the greatest of the Russian poets.

Pushkin! Pride of the Negroes, too, standing in the central square of Moscow. I first read about him years ago as a child in the Negro magazine, *The Crisis*. The *Negro Year Book* contains a sketch of his life, as well. And recently, on my long tour of the South, I saw his picture in many schools and colleges in the American Black Belt. I heard colored teachers in Mississippi and Georgia point to him as an inspiration for their oppressed and exploited pupils. And in their graduating orations, black students laud him every year as one of the great persons of Negro blood in the cultural past of the world.

Pushkin! Dead nearly a hundred years. Standing now in bronze in the heart of the Red Capital, looking down on the workers who own the earth; standing with his long black cape thrown about his shoulders, an equal of Shakespeare, Dante, Goethe, in the literature of all time; Pushkin, his books sold and read and studied everywhere by more people than ever before because the Russian masses now are literate; his poems loved and recited by the sons and daughters of workers and peasants; his memory honored by the Soviets even more than it could have been honored by the Tsars.

Pushkin, a great grandson of the Negro of Peter the Great.[24] Of course, by the time the black blood got down to the poet, two generations removed, it was pretty well mixed with the blood of the Slavs and Tartars, too. But Pushkin's mother was a beautiful mulatto. And Pushkin himself was dark enough to show, in hair and skin, traces of Africa. There is an anecdote current in Russia that Poe, the famous American poet from Baltimore, refused to shake hands with Pushkin when he looked into his face upon meeting and saw how much it resembled the faces of some of the light slaves in Maryland. Pushkin, however, being a member of the nobility, deemed it beneath his dignity to be insulted by a mere white American—otherwise there might have been a duel of historical and literary importance.

Pushkin died in 1837. Before the end of the century, another Negro of purer blood, a black actor from America, was attracting the greatest of attention and receiving high praise for his art from the Russian public. This man, Aldridge, played Shakespeare with great force and power.[25] He specialized in Othello, but also performed King Lear and other roles most successfully and for his performances he was made a member of the famous Imperial Academy of Arts and Sciences in St. Petersburg. In several old books on the Russian theatre, Ira Aldridge is written on at length and his photographs displayed.

From the more recent past, indeed since the October Revolution, two other famous Negroes have crossed the Russian scene.[26] One is Claude McKay, the poet and novelist, who lived for a time in Moscow, and whose books have been published in Russian. The other is Roland Hayes, the singer, who was invited to sing in the largest Soviet cities.[27] He sang to immense audiences in the Big Hall of the Conservatory at Moscow, leaving a most favorable impression on the crowds of music lovers who came to hear him.

Claude McKay is well remembered in the Moscow literary world. His picture and one of his poems may be seen in a text book of the Russian language for foreigners. It is said that McKay wrote a book in Moscow about the American Negroes, too, a very rare book that appeared only in Russian (now out of print) and is the only factual book he ever wrote. Claude McKay was one of the first of the Negro intellectuals to come to Moscow after the Revolution. He came as a friend and a comrade, and his visit evidently made a great impression, as many people in Moscow still ask visiting Negroes for news of him.

There are, among permanent foreign working residents of Moscow, perhaps two dozen Negroes, several of whom I have not met as there is no Negro colony; and colored people mix so thoroughly in the life of the big capital that you cannot find them merely by seeking out their color. Like the Indians and Uzbeks and Chinese, the Negro workers are so well absorbed by Soviet life that most of them seldom remember that they are Negroes in the old oppressive sense that black people are always forced to be conscious of in America or the British colonies. In Moscow there are no color bars, and the very nature of the Soviet system can never admit any sort of discriminatory racial separation, or the setting apart from the general worker's life of Negroes or any other minority groups.

Indeed, in Moscow, the balance is all in favor of the Negro. The Russian people know that he comes from one of the most oppressed groups in the world, so the Soviet citizen receives the black worker with even greater interest and courtesy than is paid to most other foreigners coming to the capital. In the Moscow papers and magazines, schools and theatres there is frequent and sympathetic attention paid by writers, teachers and playwrights to the widespread and difficult struggle of the black peoples in the capitalist lands where they are subjected to exploitation and oppression as serfs and colonials. Negroes in Moscow sense at once this great Soviet sympathy for them. Black workers soon feel at home. And most of them resident at present in Moscow have no thought of returning soon to the countries where Jim Crow rules.

Among the foreign specialists in the factories of the Moscow district, Robert N. Robinson is one of the best known. His picture is frequently seen among the udarnik groups (shock brigade workers) whose photos are often displayed in the windows of the Moscow shops. His dark face is thus known to thousands of Muskovites who pass in the city streets. Some two years ago his name flashed across the press of the world as the Negro who was attacked by white Americans in the dining room of the Stalingrad Tractor Plant, said Americans being expelled from the Soviet Union immediately on a charge of racial chauvinism. Thus the Union protects its darker workers from imported prejudice.

Robinson came to Russia in a group of more than a hundred American specialists brought over to work at Stalingrad in 1930. He was the only Negro in the group. Seven other Negro specialists had been contracted, but at the last moment backed out, with the characteristic reluctance of most North American Negroes to pioneer abroad. (Robinson himself is a Jamaican, B. W. I.) He formerly worked as a gauge grinder at the Ford Plant in Detroit. There, being the only Negro in his department, he has many tales to tell of how his fellow workers attempted to drive him off the job, even putting a short circuit into his machine so that upon touching his tools he would receive a severe shock.

In the Soviet Union no such things have happened. After two years at Stalingrad, Robinson is now working as general tool maker and instructor in the gauge grinding department of the Moscow Ball Bearing Plant. His work, of all in the tool room, requires the most exact precision, demanding an accuracy of up to one-thousandth of a millimeter.

In his spare time, Robinson is a lover of the theatre, especially the opera. He has seen the best of the theatres abroad, London, Paris, New York, and Berlin, but he insists that none of them compare with the Soviet productions, and that the music at the Bolshoi is the finest he has ever heard. And in Moscow there are no Jim Crow galleries.

There are other Negro workers in Moscow factories who, unfortunately, I have not been able to interview. And in far away Tashkent, there is a group of American Negroes employed at the Machine-Tractor Station and Seed Selection Station of the State Cotton Trust. Members of this group may be seen occasionally on vacations in Moscow, bringing their Russian wives to the shops and theatres.

Among the oldest Negro residents of the capital are two artists of the theatre and concert stage. Emma Harris and Coretti Arle-Titz. Emma Harris has been in Russia for more than thirty years and is well known by the resident American workers and journalists. Among other things, she is famous for her apple pies. But these pies are among the least of her achievements. Her life story would make a colorful and exciting book.

She came to Europe in 1901 as a member of the "Louisiana Amazon Gods," a singing group which included Fannie Wise and Ollie Burgoyne, now old and well known artists in the States. After a tour of Germany, a smaller group, the "Six Creole Belles," invaded Russia and Poland with great success. When this group disbanded, Emma Harris formed a singing trio of her own which performed in the large cities for a number of years. Finally, stranded in Siberia, Mrs. Harris taught English for a livelihood. Upon her return to Russia proper, she appeared as a concert soloist. And during the early days of the war she conducted a motion picture theatre in Kharkov. Later she owned an American Pension in Moscow. During the days of the Civil War she served as a nurse for the revolutionary forces in the Ukraine. Then under Colonel Haskell she worked with the American Relief Association. And after the establishment of the Bolshevik power, she continued active as a speaker and propagandist for the International Red Aid.

One of my first memories of Moscow is Emma Harris speaking at a huge Scottsboro meeting one July night in the Park of Rest and Culture, her dark face glowing in the blaze of the gigantic flood lights, her voice magnified by loud speakers so that thousands of people could hear. She is more than sixty years old now, but no one would think so. She is full of life and fire. And she has come a long ways from Augusta, Georgia, through the days of the revolution to the red freedom of Moscow.

Coretti Arle-Titz has been in Russia for more than twenty years. She thinks in Russian, and often English words come hard for her now. For a time, she sang with the Emma Harris trio, then she took up the serious study of voice at the St. Petersburg Conservatory, and later with Madame Vladimirova at the famous studio in Moscow founded by Ipolite-Ivanov. She has sung the role of Aida at the Kharkov Opera, and has toured the whole Soviet Union in concert with great success. Her scrap books are full of critiques and testimonials from workers and Red Army men. She has known many of the leading revolutionists and is a friend of Maxim Gorky's.

At the Moscow school for children of English speaking parents there is a Negro teacher, Lovett Forte Whiteman of Chicago. His field is chemistry, physics and biology. He has lived in Moscow for more than five years, is married and intends to be a permanent resident.

Of those Negroes who came with the Meschrabpom film group in 1932, three have remained as workers. Wayland Rudd, the actor, is a member of the famous Meyerhold Theatre. He acts a small role in Russian in one of the new productions. At the same time, he is taking full advantage of the opportunities which the theatre offers for the study of singing, dancing, fencing and allied theatrical arts.

Homer Smith, a former postal employee of Minneapolis, is now a special consultant in the rationalization of the Soviet postal system. He is credited with the planning and supervision of Moscow's first special delivery service recently introduced. He is the only American, Negro or white, in a position of high responsibility in the Soviet Post Offices, and as such, is being frequently written about in the press.

The youngest member of the film group, Lloyd Patterson, came directly from his graduation at Hampton Institute in Virginia to the Soviet Union. He is an expert painter, and whereas in America he could work only at simple jobs of house painting, he is employed in Moscow on the interior decorations of the de luxe tourist hotel, Metropole. Patterson is married to a talented Komsomolka[28] who is a painter of pictures, and together they executed some of the best street decorations for the last May Day demonstration.

Although the actual number of Negroes in Moscow is not large, the Muscovites, from reading and from the theatre if not from direct contact, are well-informed on the various phases of Negro life. Each year, a number of books by or about Negroes are published. At present *Georgia Nigger* has appeared in both Russian and English.[29] The Moscow papers follow the Scottsboro case closely. In the theatre, Muscovites have started with *Uncle Tom's Cabin* and have lately come down to a very modernistic production of Eugene O'Neill's worst play, *All God's Chillun Got Wings*, called in Moscow, *Negro*. At the Children's Theatre there is a playlet called, *The Good Little Negro Girl*. And recently the manuscript of a new play has been completed by a Russian playwright, Ronn, depicting the struggles of a black boxer in America whose career is hampered by prejudice, and who is exploited by his managers for all the money they can get out of him.

Negro music is popular in Moscow, too. Irma Yunzen, the great folk singer, uses southern melodies on her programs. Sergei Radamsky of New York sang [with] a Negro group during the past season. And it is rumored this fall Paul Robeson is expected to appear in concert. In the Museum of Western Art there is a bust of the American Negro musician and composer, Hall Johnson, done by Minna Harkovy, of the New York John Reed Club.[30]

So modern Negro art, both literature and music, is well represented in the Soviet capital. The music is kept alive not only by Coretti Arle-Titz and visiting Negro artists but by the Russian singers, also. And as to the workers, the great task of building socialism and the labor it entails has given work of importance to the competent black hands of Robinson,

Patterson, Homer Smith, and other Negroes in Moscow, where specialists from all countries in the world are employed.

A Moscow poet, Julian Anissimov (translator of a forthcoming anthology of Negro poetry), has written a little poem which begins like this article with Pushkin; but which ends, not like this article, with today, but with tomorrow.

It is called:

Kinship

The blood of Pushkin
Unites
The Russian and the Negro
In art.
Tomorrow
We will be united anew
In the International.

So merge past facts and present prophecy.

A Negro Looks at Soviet Central Asia (Moscow: Co-Operative Publishing Society of Foreign Workers in the U.S.S.R., 1934)

1. Going South

To an American Negro living in the United States the word *South* has an unpleasant sound, an overtone of horror and of fear.[31] For it is in the South that our ancestors were slaves for three hundred years, bought and sold like cattle. It is in the South today that we suffer the worst forms of racial persecution and economic exploitation—segregation, peonage, and lynching. It is in the southern states that the colour line is hard and fast, Jim Crow rules, and I am treated like a dog. Yet it is in the South that two-thirds of my people live: a great Black Belt stretching from Virginia to Texas, across the cotton plantations of Georgia and Alabama and Mississippi, down into the orange groves of Florida and the sugar cane lands of Louisiana. It is in the South that black hands create the wealth that supports the great cities—Atlanta, Memphis, New Orleans where the rich whites live in fine houses on magnolia-shaded streets and the Negroes live in slums restricted by law. It is in the South that what the Americans call the "race problem" rears its ugly head the highest and, like a snake with its eyes on a bird, holds the whole land in its power. It is in the South that hate and terror walk the streets and roads by day, sometimes quiet, sometimes violent, and sleep in the beds with the citizens at night.

Last spring I came almost directly out of this American South to the Soviet Union. You can imagine the contrast. No need for me to write about it. And after a summer in Moscow, last September I found myself packing up to go South again—but, this time, South under the red flag. I was starting out from Moscow, capital of the new world, bound for Central Asia to discover how the people live and work there. I wanted to compare their existence with that of the coloured and oppressed peoples I had known under capitalism in Cuba, Haiti, Mexico, and my own United States of America. I wanted to study the life of these people in the Soviet Union, and write a book about them for the dark races of the capitalist world.

On the train I had a lot of time to think. I thought how in the thirty years of my life I had never gotten on a train in America without being conscious of my colour. In the South, there are Jim Crow cars and Negroes must ride separate from the whites, usually in a filthy antiquated coach next to the engine, getting all the smoke and bumps and dirt. In the South, we cannot buy sleeping car tickets. Such comforts are only for white folks. And in the North where segregated travel is not the law, coloured people have, nevertheless, many difficulties. In auto buses they must take the last seats in the rear, over the wheels. On boats they must occupy the worst cabins. The ticket agents always say that all other accommodations are sold. On trains, if one sits down by a white person, the white person will often get up, flinging back an insult at the Negro who has dared to take a seat beside him. Thus it is that in America, if you are yellow, brown, or black, you can never travel anywhere without being reminded of your colour, and oft-times suffering great inconveniences.

I sat in the comfortable International car[32] on my first day out of Moscow and remembered many things about trips I had taken in America. I remembered how, once as a youngster going alone to see my father who was working in Mexico, I went into the dining car of the train to eat. I sat down at a table with a white man. The man looked at me and said, "You're a nigger, ain't you?" and left the table. It was beneath his dignity to eat with a Negro. At St. Louis I went onto the station platform to buy a glass of milk. The clerk behind the counter said, "We don't serve niggers," and he refused to sell me anything. As I grew older I learned to expect this kind of happenings when travelling. So when I later went South to lecture on my poetry at Negro universities, I carried my own food because I knew I could not go into the dining cars. Once from Washington to New Orleans, I lived all the way in the train on cold food. I remembered this miserable trip as I sat eating my hot dinner on the diner of the Moscow-Tashkent express.

Traveling South from New York, at Washington, the capital of our country, the official Jim Crow begins. There the conductor comes through the train and, if you are a Negro, touches you on the shoulder and says, "The last coach forward is the car for coloured people." Then you must move your baggage and yourself up near the engine, because when the train crosses the Potomac River into Virginia, and the dome of the Capitol disappears, it is illegal any longer for white people and coloured people to ride together. (Or to eat together, or sleep together, or in some places even to work together. But we will speak about these things later.) Now I am riding South from Moscow and am not Jim-Crowed, and none of the darker people on the train with me are Jim-Crowed, so I make a happy mental note in the back of my mind to write home to the Negro papers: "There is no Jim Crow on the trains of the Soviet Union."

In the car ahead of mine there is a man almost as brown as I am. A young man dressed quite ordinarily in a pair of tan trousers and a nondescript grey coat. Some Asiatic factory worker who has been to Moscow on a vacation, I think. We talk a little. He asks me what I do for a living, and I ask him what he does. I am a writer. He is the mayor of Bukhara, the Chairman of the City Soviet! I make a note in the back of my mind: "In the Soviet Union dark men are also the mayors of cities." And here is a man who is the head of a very famous city, old Bukhara, romantic Bukhara known in stories and legends the world over. I must write about this for the Negro papers in America. But I learned in the course of our conversation, that there were many cities in Central Asia where dark men and women were in control of the government—many, many such cities. And I thought about Mississippi where more than half of the population is Negro, but one never hears of a Negro mayor, or of any coloured person in the government. In fact, in that state Negroes cannot even vote. And you will never meet them riding in the sleeping car.

Here, there were twelve of us going South from Moscow, for I was travelling with a Negro group from Mezhrabpom[33] Film on a tour of the Soviet Union. Later they left me in Central Asia, while they returned to

Moscow by way of the Caspian Sea, Tiflis and Dnieprostroy. And then went back to America.

Kurbanov, for that was the name of the young Uzbek from the Bukhara Soviet, came often to talk to us. He was a mine of information about the liberation of Central Asia and the vast changes that have come about there after the revolution. Truly a land of Before and After—as we listened to him talk: Before the Revolution, emirs and khans, mullahs and beys. After the Revolution, the workers in power. Before, one half of one per cent of the people literate. Now, fifty per cent read and write. Before, education solely for the rich, mostly in religious schools; and no schools in the villages. Now, free schools everywhere. Before, the land was robbed of its raw materials for the factories of the Russian capitalists. Now, there are factories in Asia itself, big plants, electric stations, and textile mills. Before, no theatres, no movies, no modern culture. Now, national art encouraged and developed everywhere. Before, Kurbanov said, racial persecution and segregation, the natives treated like dogs. Now, that is finished, and Russian and native, Jew and gentile, white and brown, live and work together. Before, no intermarriages of white and dark, now there are many. Before, Kurbanov himself was a herd-boy in the mountains. Now, he is a member of the Party and the Chairman of a city soviet. Truly, Soviet Asia is a land of Before and After, and the Revolution, with tremendous strides, is creating a new life that is changing the history of the East, as Comrade Kurbanov talked.

We gathered these things not only from our Uzbek comrade, but from many other passengers we met on the long train during the five days and nights south-east to Central Asia. There was a woman librarian from Leningrad, who had been home on a vacation going back to the work of which she spoke with pride—the growth of the library at Tashkent, the large number of books in the native languages with the new Latin alphabet that were now being published, and the corresponding growth of native readers. There was a young Red Army man who told us of the camaraderie and understanding growing up between lads of widely different and environmental backgrounds in the Red Army School at Tashkent. There was a Russian merchant privileged to help in the building of new industries in an ancient and once backward, but now awakening Asia. And there were two young Komsomol poets going from Moscow to work on new publications for the encouragement of national literature in the young writers of Soviet Asia.

One night, we held a meeting with the members of the train crew not then on duty. Our Negro group and the workers of the express exchanged information and ideas. They told us about their work and their part in the building of socialism. We told them about the conditions of Negro labour in America, about the crisis abroad, about Al Capone and the Chicago bandits, and the bootleggers and bankers of Broadway. We found that they knew, as their comments and questions indicated, a great deal more about America than the average American knows about the Soviet Union. And we learned that their working conditions are superior to those of American railway workers—particularly in regard to the train porters. Here, in each coach, there is a compartment with berths where the crew might rest. The Negro porters on American trains have no such conveniences. Here, on the sleeping cars, there are two attendants. In the U.S.A. a single man takes care of a car, working throughout a long trip, and perhaps managing to catch a little sleep on the bench in the men's toilet. Our porters depend on tips for a living, their wages being extremely low. In 1925 they organized a union but, under a compromising bourgeois leadership, so they have gained nothing save occasional threats of wholesale dismissal from the company and their replacement by Filipinos. The American Federation of Labour refused to receive them (the various white railway unions do not admit Negroes).[34] These things we told the crew of the Moscow-Tashkent express and they, in turn, sent back through us their revolutionary greetings to the Negro railway workers of America.

So, with our many new and interesting comrades of the train, the days on the road passed quickly. First, the rich farm lands slid by outside our windows; stations where peasant women from the kolkhozes[35] sold chickens and cheese and eggs; then the Volga at sunset, famous old river of song and story; a day or so later, Orenburg where Asia begins and camels are in the streets; then the vast reaches of the Kirghiz steppes and the bright tip of the Aral Sea like silver in the sun.

On the day when we passed through the Kazakstan desert, the Fortieth Anniversary of Gorky's literary life was being celebrated throughout the Union. The Komsomol poets and the train crew organized a meeting, too. At a little station where the train stopped in late afternoon, we all went onto the platform and short speeches were given in honor of Gorky and his tremendous work. (Even in the heart of the desert, this writer whose words throb with the lives of the common people, was not forgotten.) Nomad Kazaks, the men in great coats of skins, the women in their white headdresses, gathered around, milling with the passengers. One of the young poets spoke; then a representative of the train crew, and someone from the station. My speech in English was translated into

Russian, and again into the Kazak tongue. Then the meeting closed. We sent a telegram to Comrade Gorky from the passengers of the train, and another from our Negro group. And as the whistle blew, we climbed back into our coaches, and the engine steamed on through the desert pulling the long train deeper into Asia. It was sunset, and there was a great vastness of sky and sand before the first stars came.

Late the following afternoon, we saw a fertile oasis of water and greenery, cotton growing and trees in fruit, then crowds of yellow faces and bright robes at the now frequent stations. At evening we came to the big city of Tashkent, the new center of the East.[36]

2. A Visit to Turkmenia

In the autumn, if you step off the train almost anywhere in the fertile parts of Central Asia, you step into a cotton field, or into a city or town whose streets are filled with evidences of cotton nearby.[37] On all the dusty roads, camels, carts, and trucks loaded with the white fibre go toward the gins and warehouses. Outside the towns, oft-times as far as the eye can see, the white balls lift their precious heads.

The same thing is true of the southern part of the United States. In Georgia and Mississippi and Alabama, you ride for hundreds of miles through fields of cotton bursting white in the sun. Except that on our roads there are no camels. Mules and wagons bear the burdens. And at home, cotton is not so valuable any more with the crisis and the factories closed. And, too, whereas here the textile mills now run full blast, in America many of them are closed or working part time. There's really a vast difference between Turkmenistan and Alabama. And a world between.[38]

About a year ago, when I was in the South all winter, I spent some time in Alabama, fifty miles or so from the now famous Scottsboro. I wanted to visit a village in the big cotton plantations there. "It's dangerous," my friends said. "The white folks don't like strange Negroes around. You can't do it." But I did finally manage to do it—and this is how: During the December holidays, I went with a section of the Red Cross (a Negro section, of course, as everything is segregated in the South) to distribute fruit to the poor—the *poor* meaning in this case the black workers on a rich plantation nearby.

We set out in a rickety Ford and drove for miles through the brown fields where the cotton had been picked. We came to a gate in a strong wire fence. This passed, some distance further on, we came to another fence. And then, far back from the road, huddled together beneath the trees, we came upon the cabins of the Negro workers—cheerless one-room shacks, built of logs. A group of ragged children came running out to meet us.

The man with the Red Cross button descended from the car and spoke to them in a Sunday-school manner. He asked them if they had been good, and if they had gotten any presents for the holidays. Yes, the children said, they had been good, but they hadn't got any presents. They reached out eager little hands for the apples and oranges of charity we offered them.

We went into several of the huts, and while the Red Cross man talked about the Lord, I asked a few earthly questions. I asked an old man if the cotton had been sold. He answered listlessly, "I don't know. The boss took it. And even if it has been sold, it don't make no difference to me. I never see none of the money nohow." He shrugged his shoulders helplessly and sucked at his pipe. A woman I spoke to said she hadn't been to town for four years. Yet the town was less than fifteen miles away. "It's hard to get off," she said, "and I never has nothing to spend." She gave her dreary testimony without emotion. The Red Cross man assured her that God would help her and that she shouldn't worry.

A broken-down bed, a stove, and a few chairs were all she had in her house. Her children were among those stretching out their skinny arms to us for charity fruit. Yet the man who owned the big plantation lived in a great house with white pillars in the town. His children went to private schools in the North and travelled abroad. And these black hands working in white cotton created the wealth that built his fine house and supported his children in their travels. A woman who couldn't travel fifteen miles to town was sending somebody else's child to Paris. Thus the base of culture in the South.

Economists call it the share-crop system, this mass robbery and exploitation of the southern Negro workers in the American cotton fields. Ironical name—for cotton is a crop that the Negro never shares. This is how the planters arrange it: The black peasant signs a contract (which often he cannot read) for a year's work for himself and his family. His pay is to be a portion of the crop that he raises on shares. He moves into a cabin on the white man's lands. The plantation owner advances him the seed to plant, and every month a little corn meal and salt meat from the commissary. These advances are charged to the peasant's account by the plantation bookkeeper. At the end of the year when the cotton is picked, the plantation owner takes the whole crop, tells the worker his share is not large enough to cover the rent of the cabin, the cost of the seed, the price of the corn meal and fat meat, and the other figures in the book. "You owe me," says the planter. So the Negro is automatically in debt, and must work another year to pay what he owes the landlord. If he wishes to take his family and leave, he is threatened with the chain gang or lynch-terror. Thus the black field-hands are kept in slavery on the big plantations of America. A beautiful system for getting free labour, white cotton, and culture. A modern legal substitute slavery—this share-crop system. And yet American capitalists have the nerve to accuse the Soviet Union of forced labour.

How different are the cotton lands of Soviet Central Asia! The beys are gone, the landlords done with forever. I have spoken to the peasants and I know. They are not afraid like the farm-hands of the South. "We were afraid once," they said, "but not now. The beys are gone."

It was the height of the picking season when I visited the Aitakov Kolkhoz near Merv. The Turkmen director took us to the fields where, in the bright morning sun, a brigade of women were picking cotton, moving rapidly through the waist-high rows, some stuffing the white bolls into the bosoms of their gowns until they were fat with cotton, others into sacks tied across one shoulder. Thirty-two kilos of picked cotton was counted a working day, but the udarniks picked sixty-four kilos or more a day. And many of the women I was watching were udarniks. This brigade had fulfilled 165 per cent of its plan. In their beautiful native dresses of red and green with their tall headdresses surmounting moon-coloured faces, these women moved like witches of work in a sweeping line down the length of the broad field, taking the whiteness and leaving the green-brown stalks, stuffing into their sacks and bosoms all the richness of the earth.

On this particular day, while the women worked in the fields, the men were repairing the irrigation canals near the main stream, the director told us. But the men also pick cotton when there is no heavy work to do.

I remarked at the absence of children in the fields. In the American South they would be picking along with the parents. "Here they are in school," the director said. "Our kolkhoz has a four-year school. And in the village nearby there is a school for five hundred pupils where the older students go. There is a teacher here for the grown-ups, too. You will see during the rest period."

The director went away and left us with the time-keeper and assistant, a young student learning to keep the books. They were both Turkmen with marvellously high black *telpeks*[39] of shaggy lamb's skin towering above their heads. With them I could not speak a word. My bad Russian did not work. But Shali Kekilov, the poet of the Turkmen Proletarian Writer's Union, translated. We sat on the grass under the fruit trees bordering a dry canal and learned the facts about their kolkhoz, and the success of collectivization in their districts. Within the village radius of eight kilometres, out of a population of 2,700 people, only twenty individual farmers remained. On the Kolkhoz Aitakova itself there were 230 workers, ten of them members of the Party, and eleven candidates. Two of the Party members were women, and two women were candidates. There were twenty-eight Komsomols.

When the rest period came, a boy brought tea and bread to the fields. The women sat in a group on the grass and, as they ate, a girl moved among them with a book, helping each woman to read aloud a passage—thus they were learning to read, a thing that in all the long centuries before, women in Central Asia had never done.

The men sitting on the grass with us were proud. "Before the Revolution there weren't twenty-five women in the whole of Turkmenia who could read. Now look!" A woman peasant sat on the edge of the cotton field reading out of a book. Something to cry with joy about! Something to unfurl red banners over! Something to shout in the face of the capitalist world's colonial oppressor. Something to whisper over the borders of India and Persia.

In the afternoon, I helped pick cotton, too. Then the young man came to take us to the tea-house for dinner. There I answered many questions concerning the Negroes in America. It was dusk when we walked across the fields to the cluster of buildings that formed the centre of the kolkhoz. They were preparing the nursery as a guest-room for us, moving back the little chairs and tables of the children and spreading beautiful rugs on the floor that we might sit down.

Soon guests began to arrive, teachers from the village school came, and then the men who had been out on the irrigation works all day, and among them musicians. They came in twos and threes and larger groups until the room was full. One oil lamp on the floor was the only light, and as they sat around it, their tall hats cast tremendous shadows on the walls. *Chainiks*[40] of tea were brought, and a half-dozen bowls that were shared by all. As the tea-pots emptied, they were passed continually back and forth from hand to hand to the door where a man replenished them from the water boiling over an open fire outside in the dark.

Many stories were told to us there in the nursery by the men who shared with us their little bowls of tea; stories of the days when women were purchased for sheep or camels or gold—if you were rich enough—young women; or, if you were poor, you worked three to five years in the field to receive an old wife that some rich man had tired of. Stories were told of the boys who controlled the water, and whose land you must till in order to water your own poor crops. Stories were told of feuds, and tribal wars, tsarist oppression, and mass misery. And all this *not* a hundred years ago, but *only* ten or fifteen years past. These men in the tall hats had not read about it in history books. It had been their life. And now they were free.

Then the boys began to sing to the notes of their two-string lutes. The high monotonous music of the East filled the room. The two singers sat crossed legged on the floor, face to face, rocking to and fro. One was the young man who, during the day, learned to be a time-keeper. The other, a peasant, between verses threw back his head and made strange clucking sounds with his throat. They sang of the triumphs of the Revolution. Then they sang old songs of the power of love and the beauties of women with faces like the moon. Sometimes they played, without singing, music that was like a breeze over the desert, a quiet breeze coming out of the night to the cotton fields.

A sheep had been killed and, from the fire outside, great steaming platters of mutton were brought which we ate with our hands. Most of the men left at midnight, but several remained to keep us company, and slept on the floor with us.

In the morning, Shura, the little son of the Russian woman who runs the nursery, and his playmate, a golden-faced Turkmen lad, came to show me the new cat that had just been born in the stables. They took me with great pride all over the barnyard. We saw the oxen being driven out to work, yoked in pairs; the camels in the long line loaded with cotton starting off for town. We saw the brick kiln, and the two children and I climbed to the top of it, and looked at the gay fields of cotton in the morning sun, stretching away toward the desert.

Shura, the little white boy, and the darker Turkmen boy took me by the hands and insisted that I see the oven for making bread. I went, but I was not thinking particularly about the oven. I was thinking, as I looked at the two small boys, "This would never happen in Alabama where white children and coloured children do not grow up together. I am glad that here, in the Soviet Union, all the ugly artificial barriers of race have been broken down. Little Russian boy and little Turkmen boy, you will never know the distorted lives full of distrust and hate and fear that we know in America, or that strangle the Indians and the British over the mountains to the South."

"Look where we bake our bread," the children said. I put my head into the big brick oven. Then I heard Kekilov calling that it was time to start for the irrigation ditches. And the children had to go to school.[41]

I visited several other cotton kolkhozes in Turkmenia and Uzbekistan, and one sovkhoz.[42] I filled two note books with figures and data: the number of hectares under cultivation, the yield per hectare, the percentages fulfilled according to the plan—some not always good—the method of irrigation, the amount the state pays for cotton in rubles and wheat and cloth and tea. All these things will be of great interest for American readers who are not familiar with the basic details. I stayed for two days at the mechanization station for farm machinery near Tashkent; and another day at the seed selection station where a number of American Negro chemists are employed at work they would seldom be allowed to do in the United States. I saw the cotton college. I visited the big building of the Cotton Trust at Tashkent. I looked at statistics. I studied charts.

The figures, sooner or later (important as they are) I shall forget. Maybe I will lose the note book in my travels. But these things I shall always remember the peasants themselves have told me: "Before, there were no schools for our children; now there are. Before, we lived in debt and fear; now we are free. Before, women were bought and sold; but that is gone. Before, the water belonged to the beys; today it's ours. Before, life was never certain—now it is!"

3. Palaces, Priests and Power

Throughout the centuries, the biggest and most successful robbers have always lived in palaces. The sweat and blood of the masses have always furnished the moisture to cement the stones of plunder for the walls, and the hands of thousands of hunger-driven women have woven the rugs and tapestries of comfort for the masters and mistresses of the great houses of splendour. To look back a bit: The Pharaohs in Egypt and the Medicis in Florence; the Doges of Venice and the Tsars of St. Petersburg; the Rajahs at Delhi and the Emperors at Peiking. Or, to be strictly contemporary: the Pope at Rome and the Rockefellers at Pocantico Hills.

And always, throughout the centuries, close to the palaces have been the temples. It's happened so much that it surely could not have been by chance. Remember the temples at Karnac, and St. Mark's at Venice. The Taj Mahal, and the golden domes along the Neva. St. Peter's at Rome, and the Rockefeller Baptist Church on Riverside Drive in New York. And in London, Buckingham Palace and Westminster Abbey. How religious are the great who live in palaces!

The Emir of Bukhara, too, was a holy man. His city was a shrine for all true believers in its day. His best friends were the mullahs. And his town palace, a walled citadel, rose high on an artificial eminence above the city. The only thing the Emir allowed to rise higher was the tall tower beside the official mosque of Mejid-halyan. But this tower had much more than a religious meaning. Not only here did the muezzins call to prayer, but from it, the Emir threw his enemies to their death on the stones of the dusty road beneath. O, most high and holy tower of Bukhara. Religion and power. Power and death.

In the very front of the Emir's palace was a bazaar, and in the street leading to his chief mosque, also, there was buying and bargaining. The Emir collected taxes from the traders and tribute from the mullahs—a dealer in both goods and holiness. The Emir. He lived well. And loved Allah. And put fifty million gold rubles in an English bank.

He had some two or three hundred wives, off and on, did the Emir Alum-Khan of Bukhara. Four of them were the official wives permitted by the Koran. The others were of lesser standing. At his palace in the country outside the walls of the city, he kept a permanent harem of about a hundred veiled girls in residence. This harem was consistently replenished with lovely young maidens. The women he tired of were given as presents to his court officials and military officers. When the revolution came, and the Emir fled to Afghanistan, he left most of his women behind, taking instead boys and gold and jewels.

One of his former wives works now in the Tea House of the Red Partisans at Bukhara. I went to see her one day. She is still beautiful, with skin like ivory, and soft grey eyes. She is married now to a workman, uncovers her face, and is much happier, she says, than she was in the Emir's palace. With strangers she is a shy little woman who does not talk much. But she recounted how, when she was only twelve, she was given to the Emir. Then began three monotonous years in the palace harem, which was little more than a prison, guarded by old women and eunuchs. At fifteen, the Emir gave her away to his prime minister. She went from one harem to another till the Revolution set her free. Now she walks the streets without a veil, she belongs to herself, and she earns her own living.

One day, at the Emir's former estate in the country, I saw the women's quarters in which she once lived. They were some distance removed from the palace proper, behind double doors and thick walls of their own. A series of rooms around small court-yards, the walls and the narrowness shutting out the breeze, making them stifling hot in summer. The girls were illiterates, the servants did all the work, and the doors to the outer world were locked. No wonder the death rate for women was high in Bukhara. Many of them must have died of sheer ennui. The Emir's dogs at least had the freedom of the entire court, the orchards, and the grape arbours. The women were always shut up in one place—except when one or two of them might be called to the Emir's bed-chamber. Or when, on occasions, he might allow them all to bathe in the great square pool behind his summer house. Then he would sit on a screened balcony and gaze down upon the beauty of a hundred wives in the water.

The Emir's summer house had modern plumbing, and is built like a European villa. The official palace itself, within the same double-walled enclosure, is a huge and ornate building around a court where a fountain played. Inside, each room was decorated by a noted Eastern artist. But some of the artists must have been pretty bad. Their taste was atrocious. The walls are gaudy and confused with shelves, niches, gilt, and too many colours. The ceilings are patterned indentations of many hues. In the niches hundreds of vases and knick-knacks and marble clocks sit. There are gigantic lacquered vases, too, brought by special escort from China. On the walls there are pictures of the Emir himself, his staff, and the Russian embassies that came to visit him. The floors are of inlaid wood. The window panes are multi-coloured.

Only one room is really beautiful. That is the reception hall. It is done entirely of mirrors and white plaster. Both walls and ceiling are pure white with bits of patterned mirrors beneath the plaster; everywhere live flowers. There is a great silver chandelier hanging in the centre. When this was lighted, so the present caretaker said, the room blazed with such light, the white walls and their hundreds of tiny mirrors glowed so brightly that, through the long French windows, the reflection could be seen on the night sky for miles around.

Here in this room, the Emir received only the most special guests. All others, he would allow to stand in the courtyard outside, while they addressed him through the tall windows. Such careful differentiation was not due entirely to a sense of honour and dignity. It was due somewhat to fear also. The Emir had a thousand enemies—so it was not wise to allow too many people near him. Better that folks stood in the courtyard outside.

As to the peasants and common people, the Emir never received them within the walls of the palace. Sometimes in the road, he would allow them to bow their heads in the dust and present him with a petition. But during the last years of his reign, these petitions became so numerous, and the demands of the people so insistent, that the Emir could not sleep well in his brass bed in the palace, nor hold pleasant courts. So he applied measures of great repression to the populace. Prison, beatings, death.

Haji Mir-baba and Ata Hajaiv, two of the old revolutionists of Bukhara, told me about it. Shishkin, the historian, told me, too. In those days, one ruble out of every six had to be given to the Emir as taxes. From the peasants the officials took two-thirds of their crops, leaving scarcely enough to eat. (These officials received no salary, only a commission on what they collected, so their greed knew no bounds.) Young wives then cost six thousands rubles—no poor man could buy. Rooms in the medress, where one had to go for religious training if one wanted to rise in the world, were sold for fabulous prices. Cotton, wool, caracul, cocoons, tea, went to the markets of Europe and tsarist Russia, enriching the court but leaving the masses of Central Asia hungry.

Life was too hard. Revolt came, as in Russia. Kerensky told the Emir to make a few reforms, so a ministry of mullahs and merchants was created.[43] The masses soon learned that this meant nothing. In Bukhara, they demonstrated against it. Troops and religious elements attacked. Many were arrested. Prison. Seventy-five strokes on the back. Some died. (Haji Mir-baba, who lived to tell the tale, showed me a picture of himself in the Emir's jail with the striped wounds across his back.)

This did not stop the revolutionaries. The struggle went on. To tell it quickly: The young Bukharians sent a committee to Tashkent to confer with the leaders there on tactics. They returned with other revolutionary workers, and comrades from Baku and Samara. From Kazan, they sent an ultimatum to the Emir. The Emir requested that a committee come to see him. Twelve comrades went. They were killed.

In the city, armed revolt broke out. It was crushed. The Emir killed three thousand comrades. Tortured and burned others. Rewards were offered for each head of a revolutionist. The Emir still slept in his brass bed in the country palace. But not for long.

Faisula Hajaiv (now President of the Council of Peoples Commissars of Uzbekistan) and two others were selected to go to Comrade Lenin at Moscow. Captured by the White Army at Samara. Sentenced to death. Escape. Moscow at last. Plans and organization. In March, 1920, a well-planned attack on the Emir began. After five days, he was forced to flee to Afghanistan. Then the beginning of the end of terror and persecution, an opening of doors to women, and the death of Allah. In 1925 the workers and peasants organized the People's Republic of Bukhara and asked to be allowed to join the Soviet Union. In 1925 the First Soviet Congress of Uzbekistan was held. Now the brass bed of the Emir still stands in the summer palace, but the wives are free from the harem, the Emir is gone, and the whole estate is shortly to become a rest home for the workers of the sovkhozes. Peasants will sleep where they could not enter before, and women will stroll unveiled beneath the grape arbours where once they walked only in paranjas[44] guarded by eunuchs. And the fountains will play for the workers.

In the citadel in Bukhara, the Emir's castle high on a fortified mound overlooking the city, guess who lives there now? Behind the walls of this town palace, where the great officials resided, where the mint was, and the prison, and the best water cisterns, guess who lives there now? Students from the technicums, sons and daughters of poor peasants and workers, whose fore-parents for ages and ages bowed in the dust in front of rulers and beys. And what are these students doing? For one thing, they are learning to read and write by the new Latin alphabet which the mullahs who formerly controlled education declared unholy. Only the Arabic script of the Koran had the sanction of Allah, the priests said. Cursed be all those who learn the new letters!

But the new letters are learnt, now, and nobody is cursed. Everybody lives better than they did before. The great mosques of the once holy Bukhara are nearly empty of worshippers. The many towers where the muezzins called to prayer are only play-places for children. The twisted turbans that once had a religious significance no longer mean anything, and pilgrimages to Mecca are no more.

In the courtyard of a once famous religious medress whose cold little cells were filled with students stupidly learning by rote the books of the Koran, the Soviets have built a new museum. Here there are many beautiful things, old books and jewels and rugs and hangings. And here too are the cudgels of the dervishes, the horses tails of the saints, and other holy relics of the past. Religion has gone into a museum and out of the world. And a new alphabet has come into the people's life, an alphabet that brings knowledge to poor peasants and women, to workers and all those who before knew only the lies of the priests and the threats of the tax collectors.

The wisest of the priests went with the Emir when he fled. Priests love palaces and gold and power. When Ibrahim Bek, the bandit, tried to organize the counter-revolution, the greatest of the mullahs were behind him crying a holy war. And still there are men, I am told, in Bukhara who bow toward the East and pray for the Emir and his soldiers to come back. But they don't pray out loud. The young workers and students laugh at them—their heads in the dust—for holy Bukhara is no more. Even its physical aspects will soon disappear since the city soviet has a plan for a brand new town. All the old minarets and walls and hovels will be torn down, and within the next ten years a new modern city will be built. The Tower of Death will be left standing as a historical curiosity—like the cudgels of the dervishes in the museum.

Two years ago I was in Haiti, the little black island of Toussaint L'Ouverture, that is now a colony under the rule of the American marines. There, too, the towers of churches rise everywhere, Catholic churches. And the puppet governments that aid in American exploitation are made up of most religious gentlemen faithful to the holy mass. In Cuba, too, where the *universities* have been closed for three years because the students were revolutionaries, the *churches* are wide open. Read Mayakovsky's poems, *Black and White,* or *Syphilis,* if you don't know what life is like in Cuba.[45] In both Haiti and Cuba terror and repression, hunger and fear predominate, like those last years of the rule of the Emir in Bukhara. Uprisings are crushed, youths are killed, women prostituted, American gunboats circle the Caribbean waters. Shark fishing is prohibited off the harbour of Havana, say the newspapers. It seems that the gentlemen who go to holy mass and run the government are afraid that dead bodies will be pulled up from the waves instead of fish—the military prisons overlook the ocean at Havana.

Across the water, on the mainland of America, the god worshippers are legion. Mencken, America's literary clown, calls the South "The Bible Belt" because there are so many churches, preachers, and prayers there.[46] And it is in this Bible Belt that hundreds of Negroes are lynched, race riots are staged, peonage and chain gangs and forced labour of all forms are found, women are exploited in the cotton mills, and farces of justice like the Scottsboro trial are staged. The rich live in modern palaces with white columns, the ministers grow fat, and the air is full of sermons every Sunday night—out-smelling the magnolias—for the radio belongs to the rich in the big houses.

In New York, priests, ministers, and fortune tellers ply their trade by the thousands. And tourists go to see the stained-glass windows in the big church with elevators that the Rockefellers of Standard Oil have built to the glory of God. From New York and Boston and Chicago the religious rich stretch out their fingers to the black South in the guise of missionary philanthropy, endowing Negro church schools, buying the brains of the dark youth in the ghettos and cotton fields and stuffing them with meekness and humbleness and "the opium of the people."

In the Northern industrial cities hundreds of thousands of Negro and white workers, unemployed, walk the streets in the shadows of the skyscrapers, hungry. Ford turns his machine guns on them in Detroit; and in Washington the army is called out against them. And in the churches, the bosses pray and the ministers are one in denouncing communism—and calling on God—like the mullahs of Bukhara when the Emir ruled.

I walk through the streets of Bukhara, eastern city of song and story, place of legend. I walk through the crumbling walls of sun-dried brick, beneath the empty towers and minarets, past the palaces and mosques. I remember how, as a boy in far-away Kansas, I dreamed of seeing this fabulous city of Bukhara—as distant then as a fantasy of the *Thousand and One Nights*. And now, in 1932, here I am (dreams come true) travelling through the courtesy of a Soviet newspaper throughout Central Asia, and seeing for myself all the dusty and wonderful horrors that feudalism and religion created in the dark past, and that have now been taken over by socialism. Great changes there have been in ten years. Greater changes there will be, certainly. Yesterday, the inaccessible Emir and his walled palaces. And today . . .

Well, today I am going to dinner with Kurbanov, the former herd boy, who is now chairman of the city soviet of the fabulous town of Bukhara.

4. Youth and Learning in Turkmenia

In the United States a year or more ago, a well-known beloved Negro woman, a teacher, was severely injured in an automobile wreck when her car turned over, throwing the passengers into a field beside a country road. The teacher's name was Juliette Derricotte.[47] She was motoring with three of her students from Fisk University in Nashville, where she was Dean of Women, to the home of her parents in the state of Georgia. Suddenly an approaching car, in order to pass a slower vehicle, swerved toward the centre of the road. Miss Derricotte, to avoid a collision, turned quickly to the side of the highway. Her wheels sank into a ditch, and her car turned over. The Negro teacher and the three students accompanying her were all badly injured. Passing motorists carried them into the nearest town, a small southern farming centre. Here the white hospital refused point blank to give treatment to Negroes, so the bruised and bleeding victims were not admitted. Instead, they were taken to the house of a poor black woman of the town and there white doctors gave them attention, but without the necessary instruments and anaesthetics that the hospital could have furnished. Three of them were suffering intensely, but the least injured of the four, a young student, was able to find a telephone. He called the nearest city in which a Negro hospital was located, and asked that an ambulance be sent for them. Late in the night the ambulance arrived, but on the way to the distant Negro hospital Juliette Derricotte, the teacher, died. Thus one of the most brilliant of the younger coloured women was lost to America. Had not a white hospital refused to treat black people—even in so grave an emergency as this serious automobile accident—her life might have been saved.

That same day in Birmingham, Alabama, another young teacher, a man but recently graduated from Hampton Institute, was beaten to death by a white mob, lynched in broad daylight in the streets of a big city.

That week-end I was lecturing at Hampton, one of the largest and best known of the schools for Negroes in the South. The students there, learning of the circumstances of Juliette Derricotte's death and of the lynching in Birmingham, were full of grief and anger—one of the finest Negro teachers refused treatment in a white village hospital or an ambulance to carry her to the city, and one of their own graduates beaten to death.

"We will organize a protest meeting," said the students. "Not even dogs would be treated like that."

So a committee was formed and plans were made. I was asked to help with the organization, to speak at the protest meeting, and to aid in formulating telegrams to the newspapers. But word of the students' plans soon reached the faculty, and when we met in the evening for a final talk, a representative of the President's office was there. This Negro teacher immediately began to throw cold water on the students' plans. He said that perhaps the newspaper reports of Miss Derricotte's death were not true. That the students should wait and investigate first. That even if the reports were true, the students could go quietly about writing a letter of condolence to the parents of the victims, and not hold an open protest meeting.

"Hampton," he said, "never protests. That is not our kind of a word. We go slowly and carefully and investigate."

When this teacher had finished speaking, the students were afraid to go ahead with their plans for a protest meeting. They knew that they would surely be expelled from the school. They knew that it would be difficult for them to get into other schools. They would be blacklisted as agitators. That had happened at Hampton before when there had been a student strike against oppressive and inhuman rules and regulations over campus life. So now, almost without argument, the students abandoned the idea of having a meeting. One or two of them were bitter and defiant, but the rest were afraid so the meeting was not held. A teacher for whom the word *protest* was too strong, had killed the spontaneous and healthy desire of his students to speak against a system that lets injured Negroes die before it will open its white hospitals to them, and that lets white mobs beat black men to death in the streets.

What kind of school is this Hampton staffed by meek teachers educating spineless students? A religious school, of course, a Christian charity school supported by the philanthropy of rich and kind-hearted white capitalists who are willing for them to know how to work, but not to protest; and who are willing for black children to go to a black school, but not to a free white state school; and who therefore support and condone with their philanthropy the vicious colour-caste system of America.

The famous industrial school for Negroes, Tuskegee, in Alabama (founded by Booker T. Washington) has an endowment of over a million dollars gained by begging from rich white folks. Here the president and all the teachers are Negroes—yet there is on the grounds of Tuskegee a guest house where black people may not eat or sleep! This guest house is for white visitors only. Against this the teachers say nothing. But this indicates to what an extent capitalist philanthropy has bought the pride and manhood of the "intellectuals" of the black South. Behold how the education of Negro youth is controlled and demeaned by capitalist charity!

And with these charity dollars go preachers and prayers and hymns. Most of the presidents of the Negro schools are ministers, and a large part of the education is religious. Many harmless amusements are forbidden the students on religious grounds. A rigorous and unnatural separation is enforced between boys and girls. Modern and scientific attitudes of study are discouraged. A mid-Victorian atmosphere prevails.

The reason, of course, for the prevalence of these Negro philanthropic schools and colleges is this: The free public school system in the southern cotton regions extends only partially to Negroes. Throughout this section laws separate Negroes from whites in all public places—trains, street cars, theatres, hospitals, and schools. Most southern cities have excellent school buildings for whites, but small and inadequate shacks for Negroes, with oft-times no institutions of higher learning for them at all. For example, the average annual expenditure per child of school age in Alabama is as follows: For white children, $23.57; for Negro children, $3.81. A startling difference! In South Carolina the state spends for each white child an average of $27.88 per school year; but on each Negro child only $2.74 is spent. With such discriminatory odds against him, the Negro child has a difficult time getting an education. Thus, without the religious philanthropic schools, in many localities Negro children would remain utterly illiterate.

In Kazakstan and Turkestan, before the Revolution when they were colonies of tsarist Russia, the native children were utterly illiterate. Conditions were even worse than they are now in Alabama. In Asia the tsar supplied no schools for the education of the conquered peoples. And in the cells of the established Mohammedan medresses practically nothing except religion was taught, the Koran being the main text book, and seeking for Allah the main reason for learning. And even this meagre knowledge was open only to boys and men, not to girls and women.

Now, of course, in Soviet Central Asia all that is changed. The world knows of this change. But the surprising thing to a visitor from abroad, coming to Uzbekistan or Turkmenia, is the rapidity with which this change has been brought about. In less than ten years a new system of education has been introduced—and not only introduced but put into amazing working order. Teachers have been developed; students have been graduated; and illiteracy, not only of children but of adults, has been greatly reduced. The cells of the medresses are empty, and the schools of the state are overcrowded. New books in a new alphabet have come into being. Already, to the youth today, Allah is only a legend, and the Koran is forgotten. Marx, Lenin, Stalin, chemistry, economics, scientific agriculture, mathematics, electricity, and hygiene are the new realities to millions who once knew only the sleepy teachings of the priestcraft.

"How have you done this?" I asked in wonder when I visited the office of the Commissariat of Education in Ashkhabad, capital of the Turkomen Soviet Socialist Republic in the heart of Asia. "How in so short a time have you developed this new Soviet educational system, created teachers, built schools, and taught thousands of students, awakening the minds of the masses?"

They told me how it had been done. It had not been easy—building this path to education in a region where illiteracy had been so great.

In the early years many teachers came down from Russia to help. Bright young Turkmen workers were chosen and sent away to normal schools in Russia with all expenses paid. They returned bringing the new light. Textbooks were translated from the Russian and other languages. New texts were written in the Turkmen tongue. Sometimes they were copied by hand when printing processes were unavailable. Students taught one another, taught their parents, taught the peasants and workers. There was a comradely exchange of knowledge. What would have been a tremendously hard task was made easier by the great eagerness of all the people to learn—the hunger for knowledge that tsarism had starved. Thousands of new books, magazines, and newspapers in the national languages, but in the new universal Latin alphabet, were published, thus encouraging the desire to read. And now in 1933 in Turkmenia, this once most backward of the tsarist colonies, there are 6,100 teachers (85 per cent of them native people) and 75,000 pupils and students!

This information came to me from the group of officials in the Turkomen Narcompros (Commissariat of Education)—a group that included Turkmen, Russian, Tartar, and Tyurk nationalities—all working for the common aim of enlightening the masses. Each man spoke with great enthusiasm of his work, one telling of the creation of text books, another of the village schools, another of the kindergartens, another of the theatres and art classes. I was told how teachers study in summer and are paid while studying. (And I thought of America where teachers must spend their own hard earned money to get further educational advantages for themselves; and of Chicago where teachers have not been paid at all for months.) I was told of the excursions and rest-homes provided for educational workers in Turkmenia. I was told, too, how children here in Soviet Asia stay in school during the cotton gathering season. (And I contrasted in my mind Alabama where school bells may ring—but black children remain in the fields when cotton needs picking.) I was told how at present seven years' schooling is required for all Turkmen children but that, beginning next year, ten years will be the minimum. And I was told that the struggle now is for quality in teaching, and that all forces are being pushed toward that end—for the broad basis of education is already established. Today the task is to make education as excellent as possible.

During the weeks that followed, I visited nearly all of the scholastic institutions of Ashkhabad and several of the surrounding villages. I was under the guidance of a most enthusiastic Soviet teacher and MOPR worker,[48] Comrade Stephan, a political exile many years ago from Belgium, who threw in his lot with the workers' Revolution and now teaches in one of the large seven-year schools at Ashkhabad. Every morning before his teaching duties began, Comrade Stephan would call at the *Dom Sovietov* for me to visit with him a school, a museum, a library, or a factory.

I met many teachers and students and had a chance to talk to them. How different, I discovered, was the Soviet students' attitude from the American students'. At home, with most students, football and other sports occupy a leading place in their conversations. Here in Turkmenia, students held passionate conversations about the progress of life under the First Five-Year Plan,[49] the growth of literature under the Soviets, the plans of the imperialists beyond the borders. Here in a remote corner of Asia, I found young people asking intelligent and penetrating questions about happenings in France, Cuba, Mexico, and other countries where I had been.

And everywhere in Ashkhabad there are schools—an amazing number! There are schools for Turkmen children, for Farci children, for Russian children, and other nationalities, with the teaching in each case in their own language. There are high schools. There are colleges of pedagogy, commerce, science, transport, veterinary treatment. There are special research institutes, with laboratories of bacteriology, mineralogy and botany for graduate students. There is a library school every summer for village librarians held under the guidance of the Turkmen Central Library. And besides all these, there are night schools for workers, schools in clubs, schools in the Red Army barracks, and schools in factories. For instance, attached to the Eighth of March Silk Mill there is not only a seven-year school, but a silk high school, a liquidation of illiteracy school and a Communist Party school for candidates to the Party. Children and grown-ups all go to school. All this, mind you, in the comparatively small city of Ashkhabad in the heart of the Turkmenian desert where once, under the tsar, Turkmens were not even allowed on certain streets of the towns, let alone in the classrooms of the Russian schools; and as recently as 1920 not more than 1 per cent of the whole country's population could read or write!

But now the masses are making up for lost time. Even in the dusty little villages of the desert, new school buildings are being built, larger and better than the small ones that served in the early years immediately after the Revolution. To these new rural schools will come new young Turkmen teachers from the normal schools at Ashkhabad; some even from the larger institutions at Tashkent; and others who have been to far-away Moscow for their education. The light of learning is pouring in an intense blaze over Soviet Asia. Turkmenia welcomes this light with open arms.

I spent a day at the First Turkmenian Normal School at Kishi. This is attached to a modern combinat containing within itself all grades from kindergarten through the normal courses. It is located in a sandy plain a short distance from the city of Ashkhabad. On one side the desert stretches away to the horizon, and on the other the mountains rise like a wall. Beyond is Persia.

The director of the First Turkmenian Normal School is a political immigrant from Persia. There he was a shoemaker. Here he has under his guidance three hundred and fifty students and thirty-eight teachers. He received his training at the Communist University in Tashkent. He is a dark, firm man who impresses one well. He did not talk a great deal, but he showed me through the wide halls and well-lighted class rooms of the main normal building—and what I saw was better than words. I saw the splendidly equipped laboratories, the museum of biological and geological specimens and charts, and the room where the live animals for student study are kept: white rats, turtles, frogs, and fish, and great lizards that swell their bodies with air to ferocious size. I listened to some of the classes being conducted. I remarked on the various nationalities among both teachers and students. The students were largely local Turkmen, Farci, Beluchi, and Berberi, but there were a few Russians, some Tartars and Armenians. The teachers were Russian, Turkmen, and Farci. Among them were five women, one an assistant professor. This is a remarkable thing in a land where a decade ago women neither taught nor received teaching.

I was interested in the social origin of the students. The greater number, the director explained to me, are from poor peasant parentage, one hundred and forty-one in actual figures. Sixty-six are from the kolkhozes, forty-six are workers, twenty-nine are from the militia, and the rest are from hired farm labour and small proprietor stock. One hundred and twenty-six students are Komsomols, and thirty-seven are either in the Party or are candidates for membership.

The students who gathered to greet me were interested in learning of student life in America. I spoke to them in English, which Comrade Stephan translated into Russian, which was then re-translated into Turkmen. But even with these double translations we succeeded in effecting some interesting exchanges of background and opinion. I told them of the difficulties for poor students, especially of minority groups in America. And they in turn told me of their new life and gave me their revolutionary greetings to carry back to the proletarian youth in the United States who still live under capitalism, and to the Negro students caught in the tangled web of religious philanthropy and racial oppression.

But the little children of the seven-year school to whom I spoke later were not satisfied with sending mere verbal greetings so far away as America. When they gathered in the open yard in the sunshine about the steps of their building, they brought with them a beautiful wall newspaper that they had made themselves in the Turkmen language for me to carry back to the Young Pioneers of America.[50]

I shall not soon forget that sea of little faces below me as I stood on the steps—yellow, brown, white faces of these children of the Turkmen Socialist Soviet Republic as represented in this school on the edge of the desert. I shall not forget the eager questions that they put to me for more than an hour about life in those utterly different lands abroad where workers' children may suffer from hunger and cold and lack of schooling, while other children have everything. And how can there be enough food, they asked, and yet people do not eat? And do they actually burn wheat in America to keep from selling it cheaply? Why are Negroes lynched? And why striking workers imprisoned? And is there really an electric chair?

And when the questions were finished, a little fellow came forward with the wall newspaper with its bright picture of a revolutionary sun at the top, which they entrusted to my care—for the Pioneers of America. Then I went away. Their lusty young voices rang out in farewell. A horse and cart belonging to the school carried me back to Ashkhabad.

5. Dances and Music of Uzbekistan

In Samarkand and Bukhara the trade union arranged concerts of the old folk dances and folk music for our Negro delegation. In Tashkent we saw *Farhar Va Shirin,* an Uzbek opera woven of the oldest tunes and dance patterns of Central Asia, retelling on the stage an ancient legend.

After our delegation left for America, I, remaining in Central Asia, saw many of the new plays in the national minorities' theatres. In Ashkhabad I saw an exciting drama about the struggle against the counter-revolutionary forces. In Tashkent I attended vivid and thought-provoking plays about the taking off of the veil from the faces of the women, about the bandits (basmachi) of the hills, and other very modern subjects growing out of the growth and triumph of the Revolution. These new plays were well written and well acted, straightforward and direct, sometimes crudely melodramatic, but certainly not turgid or dull or unimportant.

On the other hand, these new plays of Soviet Asia were not very different in intent and construction from many dramas I had seen in Moscow about the struggles for the new life in this land of socialist construction. In America we have many articles, and even books, about the Soviet theatres of Moscow and the themes of their plays. To repeat much the same information with Asiatic coloring would not be giving anything new to my readers. "I will find out instead about the folk-art and the ways in which it is being carried over into the new era," I said to myself. So I went to some of the official people of the Tashkent theatre world and began to ask about the history of their theatre and especially about the survival of the folk-arts therein.

Strangely enough, I could get very little information about the old art. Maybe they didn't know. Whatever the reason, they would talk only about the new dramas and their political importance and Soviet meaning.

"I appreciate all that," I said, "But I want to know about the old, too. Of course, the new drama is tremendously important, but the old music and dances are still of use, aren't they? In all the chai-khanas[51] the old music is still being played. To many old tunes, new Soviet songs are sung. At *subbotniks,*[52] Pioneers and Komsomols still dance the old Uzbek dances. And *Farhar Va Shirin,* one of the loveliest theatrical spectacles I have ever seen anywhere, is built from the folk art."

To no avail. No one would talk about the past. I thought about Lenin and Lunacharsky, among others, warning young artists of the dangers of being too scornful of the culture of yesterday.[53]

"O.K." I said to myself. "I will go to folk artists themselves and find out about their work."

Some days later, I sought out the greatest of the Uzbek dancers, Tamara Khanum. And she in turn found for me two of the oldest and most famous of the musicians, Austa Alim Kamilov, player of hand-drums, and Achmedjean Umozazov, player of flutes. And from them I learned many things.

The history of the Uzbek dance is the history of the breaking down of traditions. Tamara Khanum herself is a breaker down of traditions. She was the first woman in the history of the peoples of Uzbekistan to perform on a public stage. And that was only ten years ago. Tamara Khanum's appearance on the stage, unveiled and unashamed, marks the opening of the Uzbek theatre to women artists. Before that time all the performers had been men.

And so with the dancers, both public and private—they had all been men. At festivals and weddings the men danced—and the women looked, if they were allowed. In the public squares and folk theatres the men danced—and often the women did not even look. In the old days, dancing, like most of the other joys of life, belonged only to the males. Now since Tamara Khanum, with a bravery that is worth noting, smashed past traditions, women dance, too.

Before the Revolution, the professional dancers began as boys, and some of them became very famous—to their world what Nijinski was to the world of the classical ballet. Their names were known in all the tea-houses, and great crowds often would come to see them dance. Often these boy-dancers were bought outright by the rich beys, and thus became exclusive entertainers to the bey's invited guests at private feasts. At certain times of the year there would be a sort of dancer's fair, when prospective buyers of boy-dancers would gather to select their entertainers. At these colourful dance-markets, the best and most handsome of the youthful dancers would display their steps before a vast gathering seated around an enormous space in the open air.

The old men of Tashkent and Andizhan still speak of a certain male dancer, Ata Haja, who could circle this great open exhibition area three times doing the most delicate and complicated patterns with his body. The old men recall one competition of boy-dancers at which four thousand men were gathered, including many rich beys who had come for miles around to the dance market. In their turbans and silken gowns, they had come to buy dancers.

The traditional Uzbek dances are not vigorous and boisterous exercises as many of the folk dances of the West are. Nor are they artificially acrobatic in the manner of the ballet and the theatre. Uzbek dances, typical of the dances of the East, are delicately patterned movements and graceful body-rhythms, often weaving a story in plastics that the uninitiated would not understand. Each of the old dances had their own traditional beginning, middle, and end—the forms being a mould only for the grace of the individual performer. Like the classical sonatas for the piano in Europe, the traditional Uzbek dances might vary only in so far as the subtlety and interpretive skill of different performers gave them shaded variations within the mould of the pattern.

Of course, many famous dancers originated marvellous variations on traditional themes. Extremely subtle and extremely delicate movements of the wrists and of the hands, the fingers and the head, the mouth and the eyes might come into play. Certain dancers of the past were able to execute a very famous movement of the eyebrows as they danced: one eyebrow up, the other down, continuously, like the two sides of a balance. This particular movement is said to have come from the way in which a rice-mill is propelled by a flowing stream. And all over Uzbekistan people said, "How good it is that we have rice-mills, because from them we have been given a dance."

As the water and the rice mill enters in the Uzbek dance, so the native folk music makes use, too, of sounds from the daily life of the country. The *carnai,* that long horn often of greater length than the man is tall who plays it, reproduces the cry of the tiger in the steppes. The little flutes of bamboo trill like a bird of the forest in an oasis of sweet water. These things the old musicians told me.

"In the silence of the steppes, there are a thousand sounds," Achmedjean, player of reeds, said. "Our instruments know them all."

To most Westerners, however, the music of the East is unbearably monotonous. At first in Central Asia, all the tunes sounded alike to me. But after hearing much native music, I could finally distinguish many subtle variations of melody that a piece might display, variations of tone so shaded and delicate that the ear of a New Yorker, used to the blare of jazz bands, or the marked patterns of European symphonies, would never catch at first hearing.

With rhythms, however, I felt more at home. In America, the Negro players of the jazz bands achieve a variety of rhythmic effect that white players, no matter how competent, somehow never master. Deep and subtle rhythms that never lose themselves in tangled inaccuracies can often be heard in the humblest little band of Negro musicians in a backwoods Mississippi village. So in Uzbekistan, the folk musicians are capable of infinite rhythmic variations defying notation by the conventional trained musicians of the conservatories.

The two old and famous Uzbek musicians whom I came to know are very simple people, not proud and puffed up about their art. The player of flutes was a shepherd in his youth. He began to play in the fields on reeds that he would cut and tune himself. Then he became a weaver of silk. Only since the Revolution has he been a professional musician, playing at great concerts in the workers' clubs and theatres. He still makes his own instruments from the shoots of the young bamboo, and in order to hasten their mellowness, he takes them with him into the steaming caverns of the Uzbek baths—and there he plays on them for hours.

Kamilov, the player of drums, was a maker of *arbas* (high-wheeled carts) until very recently. He was the best maker of *arbas* in the whole city of Margelan. Everybody with goods to haul wanted a Kamilov *arba.* But now the old man spends a great deal of time in Tashkent playing drums as only he can play them. Tamara Khanum will not dance unless he is in the orchestra.

I asked Kamilov about his life and his music. He told me that in his youth music was not a special or highly paid art. Almost all the boys learned to play and sing and dance for their own amusement and that of their friends. By the time he was eighteen, Kamilov was known all over Margelan as especially good at fingering out compelling rhythms on the round single Eastern drum-head, like a huge tambourine, that is held in one hand and played with the fingers of the other. He was often asked to play at the *gaps*, or friendly entertainments in the men's quarters on Fridays, the day of rest in the Mahommedan world. Sometimes Kamilov and his fellow musicians would be invited to come and play for the rich beys, especially when there were wedding feasts lasting for ten or fifteen days. For these occasions in the homes of the rich, the musicians would be paid well in gold, food, and clothing. But mostly Kamilov played for nothing for himself and his companions in the tea-houses and the court yards of private dwellings where the men came together.

He knows now sixty sets of traditional folk-rhythms, and has developed from them more than two hundred variants. His old teacher, the musician whom he listened to and played with in his youth, is still alive, and knows all the rhythms, too, but Kamilov is considered the greatest artist and is more beloved by the native public. He is one of the mainstays of the orchestra of the National Uzbek Musical Theatre at Tashkent.

He has done his share in the upbuilding of modern Uzbek stage. And there has been in his life, in this connection, one great tragedy. His sister-in-law who, like Tamara Khanum, was after the Revolution one of the earliest women actresses, went against the will of her husband's family in appearing as a public artist. For this she was stabbed one night twenty-seven times by her brother, with the connivance of her husband. Thus they avenged what her family considered a disgrace.

In the history of the Uzbek theatre under the Soviets, there are several other such cases of women artists suffering death from irate relatives. Tamara Khanum, however, had no trouble from her father about going into the theatre because, before her professional appearance, her father was killed by basmachi in Fergana. The bandits had come to carry away the young girls, his daughters, including Tamara, but it happened that week the girls were in Tashkent, and the old man was alone. The bandits killed him and robbed the house.

In the early days of Tamara Khanum's appearances on the stage, there was danger that the basmachi might invade the theatres and steal the women from the stage. More than once she has danced under guard, and has been afraid to leave the theatre.

In 1925 Tamara Khanum was in Paris with a group of Uzbek musical and dance artists. While there, however, she was seriously ill, so the Parisians did not get to enjoy the beauty of her art, nor was she able to see much of the Parisian theatres. She went once to the music hall, but did not care for the art of the nude ladies performing therein—for she herself dances in the full robes and heavy jewels of an Uzbek woman of pre-revolutionary times.

She is a specialist in the dances to barabans and cymbals. She has taken over the best of the old dances of the former boy-dancers and has created new patterns of her own. In the opera *Farhar Va Shirin,* to a great burst of music in which the percussion instruments predominate, she comes across the stage straight and tall like some young animal of the steppes. Then with lithe and vigorous movements, she begins one of those patterned and posed, yet vibrant dances that have in their simple precisions something of the clear sharpness of the mountains and plains of Central Asia. To the steady heart-like beat of the drums, the tempo of her dance never slackens, and finally she whirls away only to be called back by the applause of her audience, invariably, until she repeats the dance. Her appearance in this opera is one of the high spots in an evening of general excellence.

In the early years of the new Uzbek theatre, Tamara Khanum danced, acted, and sang, playing in many productions from their repertory. In several of the revolutionary plays she originated the leading feminine role. Now, however, her appearances are, as a rule, confined to dance numbers alone in some of the plays, occasional concerts, and many hours of teaching young pupils to whom she is greatly devoted. From one woman—herself—in company with a group of men, she has seen the Uzbek musical theatre grow until now it numbers twenty-six women in the Tashkent company alone, not counting the dozens of women playing in affiliated groups of this theatre in other cities.

Tamara Khanum has been married twice, her first husband being a famous folk-singer, Musafar Muhamid. Her present husband is a young musician. She has two children. The oldest is a little girl called Vanzetta because she was born on the day of the Sacco-Vanzetti execution.[54] When her mother dances, she watches with bright eyes of admiration.

"What is happening to the old folk dances and music nowadays?" I asked Tamara Khanum. "Are steps being taken to preserve them?"

In reply, she told me that even then a special series of concerts were being arranged at which the best of the folk artists from the whole of Uzbekistan would perform at Tashkent; that all the young artists would be there to see and to learn; and that a conference would be held as how best to preserve the heritage of music and of dance that has come down to the October Revolution.

"Faisula Hajaiv himself is greatly interested," she said, "and will help us." Then I knew that the folk arts of the Uzbek Republic were assured of serious attention—I had met Faisula Hajaiv and found him to be, as many citizens affirmed, a man of great culture and intelligence.

In parting, Tamara Khanum gave me, very shyly, one of her own records. Later, a friend translated its words for me. It was an old tune, but the words were filled with a new spirit. The song was about a father who wanted to sell his daughter in marriage. Well, daughters in Uzbekistan have rapidly become acquainted with the new laws which prohibit the selling of women. And they are not afraid to sing about it either.

6. New People

New times demand new people. This saying one has heard before. But in Soviet Asia, as elsewhere in the Soviet Union, new people are coming into being. And they are not all just newly born babies either. Or only Pioneers. Or Komsomols. No indeed.

For instance, in the old city of Tashkent: Halima Kasakova didn't learn to read and write until she was forty. She is a middle-aged woman now, but for only eight years of her life has she walked in the streets without a thick horse-hair veil hiding her face. In 1925, with the Revolution still young in her part of the world, she took off the veil, went to school—and now? Well, now she is an important figure in the management of the Women's Club in the old part of the town where for the first time in remembered history women sit on terraces open to the street and drink tea! Furthermore, she is a member of the City Soviet.

But don't think that at the Women's Club in Tashkent they only drink tea. Much, much more is done there than that. Under the active guidance of Halima Kasakova and other women like her, classes are held in reading, writing, the care of the house and of babies; clinics are held; health work is centered. Old habits and customs are broken down, and other new women are being made.

Not all those, by any means, who are being made over for the better in Central Asia are former people of the working class, either. There is in Tashkent a woman, no longer young, of the once-aristocracy, who lived a life of easy culture and well-fed leisure. Now she goes to work every morning as a translator in an office. In her spare time she aids a German specialist. She is happy. She has found a life of active usefulness under the Soviets. And as a translator, she has been for months on some of the most important construction works—dams and electrical projects—working on highly technical material with foreign engineers. To me, also, her services were of great help in gathering information and interviewing people for my articles and book. Never once did she speak, or even hint by the slightest shade or tone, dislike of the workers' republic that is the new Uzbekistan. Never, in her conversations nor in her translations did she intrude (as some old translators are not averse to doing) slimy insinuations against the Soviet power. Her speech and her work indicated always only a respect for the new and a great interest in being able to help in its development. "My child will grow up under this new life," she said. "It is better than the old."

Children under the new life, well, there's no comparing them with children in Europe or America. In Uzbekistan, many youngsters seemed to know world politics better than I did. They could ask me questions I didn't know how to answer. And at their Pioneer meetings, they stand on their strong little legs, independent and confident, and give intelligent opinions on subjects as big as war and world revolution—things a New York child has not even heard of before adolescence.

And in the Komsomols, here are the sturdy young men and women: new workers with udarnik zeal; new journalists knowing how to interpret a modern world to the people; new poets writing not the old songs of religion and love, but the new songs of growth and construction under socialism. And in positions of trust as official representatives of the people there are many new young men, graduates of the Komsomols. Kurbanov, chairman of the city soviet of Bukhara, is only twenty-eight years old. Fifteen years ago, he was a herd-boy in the mountains who didn't know his letters.

But of all the new citizens I met in Central Asia, I think I shall remember as long as any a simple young worker at Chirchikstroy. I am not even sure of his name. I think he said Tajaiv. I didn't take notes, and I wasn't speaking with him over five minutes. But the glow in his face, the pride in his voice, as he told me about the building of the first Komsomol barracks—somehow that sticks in my head to this moment.

I had driven out with the manager of construction and some newspaper men to the site of the dam that is to be, about an hour's ride from Tashkent. Here at Chirchikstroy will rise an enormous electrical and chemical development. But it is only just beginning now. Until 1933 they had not even barracks for the workmen on the site. The

Komsomols working there said, "We will build our own barracks." And they did. That is why I was motoring through the snowy dusk one January evening, along a rough country road across the steppe, to attend the opening of these barracks the Komsomols had built.

Tajaiv, the lad I'm writing of, didn't meet us at the door or anything like that. He was not one of the official people. Nor did he speak on the program. But once inside the big warm barracks with its many cots in a row like a Red Army dormitory, it wasn't long before I saw him. He had an udarnik's badge, and a very clean shirt, and a big smile. He wasn't a big person. He was shorter than the other young workers about the room. Just a little hard Uzbek or Tadjik boy of perhaps fifteen or sixteen or seventeen. A youngster who hadn't ever seen a bed of roses. But now he was very happy. As one of our hosts he came near the stove to greet us. . . . Look what we have built—our Komsomols here—the first barracks at Chirchikstroy. Here we will live while the dam is made. Before we built this, there was nothing on this land. This is the first building—our work!

His dark round young face was aglow with their big achievement, and with the much bigger achievements to follow at this place: Chirchikstroy—light and power and chemicals for all that section of Asia. Tajaiv would build it. His hard young hands. They had the power to transform the whole future. To build, to build, to build.

Now I know why the near-by Indian Empire trembles and Africa stirs in a wretched sleep. Chirchikstroy will throw such a light on the southern sky! In Soviet Asia there are a million Tajaivs with strong hands and young hearts proud of new buildings on new land in a new world. A million Tajaivs who will build and build and build! And the light will shine not only on their sky alone.

"Swords over Asia,"
Fight against War and Fascism
1:8 (June 1934): 3

Recently, I took a Japanese boat from Vladivostok. At our first port of call in Korea, I heard the rattle of swords coming up the gangplank. The Japanese military came on board to inspect passports. They lined up the passengers, and looked us over. In each Korean port there was some form of inspection, whether you landed or not. If you went ashore for a walk, someone tailed a respectable distance behind you, always there.

At Tsuruga, where the boat docks in Japan, scarcely had I gotten to my hotel, before a representative of the military came to call to ask me about Soviet Russia, and to demand why I came to Japan.

Japan is covered with fortified zones, zones where you can't take pictures and where a foreigner shouldn't be. Upon checking out of a hotel, you must inform your hotel keeper where you are going. To alight from any train at any station is dependent upon whether the military wish to allow your presence there or not. Foreigners living in Japan have permanent spies attached to them. Travelers have their temporary spies. The Japanese militarists are quite open about all this. They make no secret that they are shadowing you, and that they are suspicious of everyone.

Imperialist Dictatorship

In Tokio, my second night there, I thought I heard tractors going through the streets but they were tanks, more than a dozen of them. Where they were going down a big city street in the middle of the night, I do not know. But I read in the papers that day that three young men of Tokio had committed suicide rather than become a part of the yearly draft for the imperial army—for more than 11,000 young fellows have come back maimed for life from the recent wars in Manchuria. The three who killed themselves the day the tanks came by did not want to fight. In Japan there are thousands of other young men who do not want to fight either—but the present military dictatorship imprisons them, shames them through the press, drives them to suicide, or forces them at the point of a gun to shoulder arms.

In Shanghai, that vast international powder-keg of a city, the Japanese marines patrol the streets in fives, marching slowly and gravely, armed, swinging little sticks on constant patrol.

Guns, Guns Everywhere

Arms bristle everywhere, on everybody, on all nationalities—except the Chinese whose land the foreigners have taken. In Shanghai, the British are armed, guarding shops and banks. The French are armed, and their gendarmes, the Annamites. The Sikh police are armed. The White Russian mercenaries are armed. The American marines are armed. They all guard banks, important corners, consulates, and steel gates at the end of the foreign quarter's streets.

All kinds of gunboats mass in the harbor of Shanghai, too, facing one another, taking the best buoys away from commercial shipping. Up and down the Chinese rivers these foreign gunboats travel protecting investments and missionaries, shooting down Chinese who rebel against the graft and rapine going on in their own land.

Our American gunboats protect Standard Oil. They trail Standard Oil tankers like enormous flunkies. Our Admirals bow down to Standard Oil—shooting at Communists and letting opium runners pass, for opium is not dangerous to Standard Oil. Communists are dangerous. Hungry people are, too.

On the edge of Shanghai is Chapei, in blackened ruins, empty wall to wall, charred stone on stone, destroyed by the Japanese. In the canals of Shanghai, the bodies of babies dead from hunger float and rot. And in the poor streets of Tokio, young men drink poison rather than go to a stupid War. In the prisons of Nanking, students are slowly tortured to death for protesting against War, hunger, and foreign battleships. The President of China and the Emperor of Japan are one in killing and torturing the young and fearless.

Imperialists vs. Workers

In Asia the rich international bandits fight for spoils: England, France, Japan, America, and the traitors of the Kuomintang. If you don't own warships and bombing planes, you're out of luck. The fighting is crude and cruel—and the masses get their heads smashed and their hearts shot out.

Over Asia the swords rattle. Over Shanghai, over Tokio, over Nanking. The military dictators of China and Japan snarl and shake their bloody sticks. Meanwhile, the British guns prepare to bark, snarling, too. The French are oiling their pistols. The American cruisers maneuver. Everywhere steel prepares to point, to ram, to shoot, to cut, to kill. And overhead the airplanes zoom, steel bombs in their bodies.

WAR IN THE FAR EAST
FLEET MASSES AT HAWAII
PATRIOTS PREPARE

Mr. Rockefeller is our brother. Fight for Standard Oil! Carry civilization to the Orient! Swing another sword over Asia! Burn down another Chapei! The Japanese imperialists shall rule the world! Boom!

The white race shall rule the world! Boom! Guns shall rule the world! Boom! Unless the workers pull down the War-makers—destroy their governments—and turn their battleships into yachts to use on summer holidays.

"In an Emir's Harem," *Woman's Home Companion* (September 1934): 12, 91–92

"Bring them to the pool," said the Emir.

The chief steward bowed very, very low, bumped his head upon the ground and turned and ran. Leaving His All Holy Highness, despotic ruler of the realm of Bukhara, on the balcony of the summerhouse with only a boy to brush the flies away, the steward ran through the room where the big brass bed with its silken covers was, ran through the hall with its European bath, ran down the steps and out past the swarthy guard at the door.

"Bring them to the pool," said the Emir, "to bathe in the sun. Let me behold them white and yellow and brown in the sun. Bring them to the pool."

Whereupon through the long grape arbors heavy with tiny red-gold globes of sweetness and zooming with bees, past the fountains that splashed and sang in the courtyard, way down past the fruit trees and the flowers blooming in a riot of color at the edge of the garden, down to the low wooden doors of the harem went the steward. Faced by the guards beneath the portico, the steward stopped. The guards smiled. They let the steward knock upon the door. He delivered his message to a wraith of a woman within, who in spite of the long black veil covering her face you knew was old because she was bent and stooped and her voice quavered. She shut the door in the steward's face. He turned and hurried back the long way to the summerhouse.

Suddenly the guards let out loud bray-like cries of wooing. The paths of the palace gardens were cleared. Ministers and courtiers and attendants stood stock-still at a proper distance from the walks. Then beneath the fruit trees, spreading, spreading, flowing along the graveled ways, rippling from beneath the green grape arbors, sweeter than the bees zooming and the fountains splashing, there rose the tiny birdlike sounds of young and lovely girls laughing and chattering.

The Emir's young wives were passing, scores of them. Guarded by old women, the Emir's wives went toward the high-walled pool of the summerhouse—dozens and dozens of them with gay silks flowing behind them and heavy veils from head to knees hiding their faces, quite covering their faces. Anklets and amulets clinking, bright slippers flying, between the guards and the old women, the Emir's wives passed.

They did not turn into the summerhouse. They kept on along the high wall that surrounded the pool until they came to a tall wooden doorway. The old women tugged and pulled at the heavy doors and when they were opened, through into the sunlight of the pool's wide edge streamed more than a hundred veiled young girls. And when the doors were closed, there in the sunlight against the high wall they began to disrobe with the aid of the old women.

Beyond the square of the bathing pool was the summerhouse, and on its spacious balcony sat the Emir, alone, gazing at the warm feminine loveliness just across the pool. No one else dared look as his lovely houris went down into the water.

The young bodies of some of the girls were milk-white and fair but most of them were a little golden like the grapes in the arbor, or like peaches in the fall. Others were brown as russet pears and one or two were dark as chocolate. The Emir sat in his great soft chair and looked at this luxury of a hundred pretty wives moving up and down the steps of the sunshiny pool. By and by he stood up and leaned over the railing of the balcony. He beckoned to one. Several old women scooted along the edge of the pool to identify his choice.

That was a dozen years ago. As, recently, I stood beside the pool, only in my mind's eye could I see the lovely houris bathing—for the pool is empty even of water today.

The Emir is gone. Over the gates of his former country palace there are a hammer and sickle. The City Soviet of Bukhara has just decided to make the estate into a rest-home for farm workers. And nobody in all of Central Asia can have a hundred wives now. In fact you can have only one.

Zevar Razik, a former wife of the Emir's and once one of the bathers in the summer palace pool, is now a cashier in a red tea house in the center of Bukhara. Quite without a veil today, free and self-reliant, Zevar has almost forgotten the Emir's harem. At least she says she seldom thinks of it and only speaks about it occasionally to satisfy the curious.

During my first week in Bukhara I had been twice to the former estate of the Emir outside the city walls. There I had seen the big square pool with its flight of steps. I had seen too the brass bed the Emir occupied; most of his courtiers slept on the floor. I saw the famous all-white and mirrored reception room with its huge French windows, a room that, at night when the chandeliers were lighted, cast its glow on the sky for miles around as its looking-glass walls and ceiling gave back the brilliance. I saw the gardens and the barns and the horse stables too. And not far from the stables I saw the royal harem.

One entered the harem by a small unimposing door, then passed through a sort of outer court, narrow as a corridor. Then you found yourself in a large courtyard open to the sky with a score or more rooms about it on two sides. The opposite sides of the court were merely very high walls. There was a narrow upper balcony along the second story rooms. Within the chambers there appeared no mirrored splendor, no brass beds, no gorgeous chandeliers. About these women's quarters there was none of the apparent luxury of the palace. But because of my curiosity concerning the one-time inhabitants of this royal harem I looked up Zevar Razik, known now as Comrade Razikova.

We sat talking together, Comrade Razikova and I, as the dusk came down into the dusty crooked streets of that ancient city that was once, next to Mecca, the most important religious center of all Mohammedan Asia. Donkeys and camels and motor buses passed. There were laughter and child-cries and murmur of voices as all of Bukhara seemed to come into the cool streets when the hot sun sank. But inside where we sat talking, today's day seemed to fade away, to go back with Zevar Razik to her years at the court of the Emir.

In her early thirties now, still beautiful with ivory skin and gray-green eyes, Zevar, in a flow of musical Arabic-like syllables, began to tell me about her past. An interpreter put her words into English.

"Before the revolution," she said, "everybody was afraid of the Emir. He was ruler and he took what he wanted. People had to give him their sons and daughters if he wanted them. He had old women who went about the city taking notice of all the pretty girls in the houses they visited and carrying word back to the Emir.

"The Emir was always getting fresh young wives. When he sent for me I was only twelve. After my father's death the servant of the Emir came and carried me away from my house in the night. They took me to his palace and put me in the women's quarters. But it was many weeks, maybe months, I don't know, before I saw the Emir. Then one night he sent for me. I cried and cried. He never sent for me again.

"He had so many wives," Zevar said.

Always new ones coming, younger ones. Sometimes more than a hundred at once were in the women's quarters. It was not very often he sent for a girl more than once or twice. Frequently he gave wives away as presents to his ministers and courtiers or to his military officers. For the girls in his harem, this was their one hope of escape—to be given away. All of them waited for that to happen. It would be a change. Locked always in the same harem they were, to say the least, extremely bored.

The Emir's four official wives, sanctioned by the Koran, may have had a bit more freedom, an occasional feast or a trip, but it was hardly likely. Certainly for the dozens of others life was almost always monotonous. Zevar recounted for me the prosaic details of a harem day.

The old women woke them with the sun. The young wives washed their faces and cleaned their rooms where they slept, five or six girls together. Then they had tea and bread to eat, and maybe a little fruit. Zevar said they almost never got enough food. At midday and evening there would be pilaff, the stand-by of all Central Asia, a dish of steaming rice with bits of mutton and sometimes carrots, sometimes raisins.

They were not happy. They had nothing to do. The old women did all the work. For the girls—three times a day to eat, four times to pray—that was all, day after day after day. There was nobody to amuse them, no visitors were allowed (except one's mother at childbirth) and there were not even enough contacts with the outside world to supply gossip. You could only tell and retell old stories. Not one of the girls could read or write. That was unheard of for a Bukharan woman before the coming of the Soviet State. So in this large official harem there was nothing to do but be bored. Sometimes in sheer desperation they would wash their hair.

Once in a blue moon a favored few might be taken on a little trip into the city, the great near-by city of Bukhara with its mosques and minarets, its dusty streets and crowded bazaars. For such a trip they would be heavily guarded by the old women and beardless men and they would put on their heavy black veils, the *paranja*, down to their very ankles. Maybe a few coins for sweets would be in their childish hands. Thus lived the wives of the great Emir Alim-Khan, whom Zevar said the girls called Zara, but of whom some of them were so frightened that they had never looked into his face.

For Zevar after five years escape came. One day the Emir presented her as a gift to one of his favorites, a minister of the court named Astanakol who was seventy-five years old and had ninety other wives. This was in 1917, the year that the revolution broke out in far-off Moscow and rumbled its slow way toward Asia.

In Bukhara itself, under the very nose of the Emir, the youths in 1917 were joining an association called the Young Bukharans, intending to overthrow the tyranny of Alim-Khan. Zevar's brother joined and was killed. In the face of the gathering storm aged Astanakol fled with all his wives to Hatirji, a city near Tashkent. There in 1922 he died, shortly after the fall of the Emir and just before the historic formation of the People's Republic of Bukhara.

For to Central Asia—Khiva, Turkestan, Bukhara—those distant, wild and semi-independent colonies of the Tzar, the Russian revolution of 1917 did not arrive until 1922, 1923, 1924. But when it did, suddenly the doors of the harem were broken. For Zevar a new world began. The revolution had come!

That strange Bolshevik revolution commenced at once smashing the customs of hundreds and hundreds of years, shattering the oldest traditions of the Orient, deposing beys and emirs, unfrocking mullahs, educating children and freeing women. Everywhere—in Bukhara, in Samarkand, in Ferghana, in Osh—women were leaving the harems, casting off their veils, walking alone in the streets, working in factories and going to school. Of all things hitherto reserved for men—going to school!

Zevar learned to read and write at twenty-six. She learned to count money and figure. She got a job. She no longer hid her face from the world. She belonged to herself. She was free to do as she chose.

"It's better than the Emir's harem," she said to me.

Zevar, after her freedom began, not only married again but she did something much more amazing for the east—she got a divorce! It was unheard of in the old days, impossible for a woman to get rid of a man. Always then it was the husband who had the privilege of getting rid of her. But the young man that Zevar married would not learn to read and write, she told me, would not learn to improve himself, so she divorced him.

Now she lives alone with the child she bore. She works in the red tea house with its posters of Lenin and its slogans of Stalin on the wall. She has a little home. She comes and goes as she chooses. She doesn't often think of the Emir and his harem. If she does, she probably calls him an old "bourgeois," which is as insulting a term as one can use in a Soviet State.

"The Vigilantes Knock at My Door," LHP 3811 (September 28, 1934)

They were having a strike in San Francisco and all along the West Coast.[55] The longshoremen went out. Then the seamen. They wanted a living wage, control over the hiring and firing of themselves, and the recognition of their unions.

Where I lived in Carmel, on the Monterey Peninsula, a pretty little village of cypresses and sea (where Robinson Jeffers lives too and a grand old man named Lincoln Steffens), nobody at first was very much excited about the strike except the members of the John Reed Club. We were excited because some of us knew the physical meanings of hunger and insecurity; others of us understood what happens to labor when capital calls on the police department; and some of us had gone to the San Joaquin Valley during the cotton strike of 1933 and had seen there the cost of profits in terms of blood and terror. We had also experienced the fisherman's strike in Monterey four miles from our doors.

So when the longshoremen and the sailors went out, we wanted to help them. We were a hundred and twenty-five miles away from San Francisco, mostly artists and writers, and pretty poor. But some of us in the John Reed Club were able to give money, and others of us were able to beg it. So we sent cash and food and clothing to the strikers. We sent telegrams to Mayor Rossi, Governor Merriam, Frances Perkins, and the President asking them to protect the strikers.[56] And we got other people to send telegrams or write letters requesting the officials not to use tear gas and guns against workers seeking to make their lives a little better.

There were no answers from Mayor Rossi, the Governor, Frances Perkins, or the President. (And very shortly the President went on his vacation to Hawaii that year.) And the police, having a hard time because the dockmen and sailors wanted security, were presently joined by three thousand patriotic young men in the uniforms of the National Guard, and machine guns were pointed at the strikers. In Carmel, a hundred and twenty-five miles away, we felt them pointing at us, too. Nobody said they were pointing at us, but perhaps being artists and writers, and therefore oversensitive, we felt them pointing *at us.*

Meanwhile, the John Reed Club secured the Greenroom of the Community Theatre for our public meetings. Our first meeting was a successful strike program at which Lloyd Stroud spoke, an organizer directly from the strikers' front. We had a big crowd, interested and sympathetic. Summer vacationists, clerks, old ladies, Negro maids and working men, little merchants, artists, and college graduates without jobs. They asked questions; we took up a good collection. There was a spirited discussion. Some were against the strikers, of course, and it was obvious that a number of Carmelites believed the newspapers when they called the strikers thugs, hoodlums, aliens and traitors. Lots of people talked about the strike, and some understood it better. At the close, we announced another public meeting for the following week.

In the meantime, the American Legion had organized a post in Carmel and, in conjunction with nearby Peninsula cities (according to the papers), they began to practice getting together in a hurry. About that time, too, in San Francisco, the police ordered on gas masks—although only the police had gas to throw. Presently they threw it at the strikers and, of course, *themselves* wore the masks.

Our second strike meeting, where Delaney Shoemaker and Sam Telford spoke, was crowded. This time even more people were interested; more people sympathetic. They gave us a good collection. *But more people were antagonistic, too.* Questions and comments were sharper. In the streets of Carmel that week, smelling of cypresses and sea wind, people stood and discussed the strike, heatedly for or against. The newspapers screamed, all of them, against strikers who dared demand better wages, control of hiring and firing, and recognition of their unions. Such demands would cause the foundations of America to fall! Many Carmelites believed the papers.

About that time, a city councilman of Carmel (who was also the Police Commissioner) began to inquire among the few Negroes of the village, mostly domestics, just which ones had been at the John Reed Club strike meetings? Didn't they know it was dangerous to associate with Communists? And a business man of Carmel (secure and not hungry himself) is reported to have said to a poor old man in charge of a little cooperative food exchange, "I hear you are sympathizing with those strikers and going to John Reed Club rallies. Well, I want to warn yon that if I had my way, I'd drag everyone of you out in Ocean Avenue and shoot you."

Clearly, the good Americans were starting to intimidate the weakest first—the Negroes and the very poor. They were working up their courage.

Just before July Fourth, with patriotism running high, the San Francisco Industrial Association declared that it would move trucks off the docks in spite of the strikers. The Mayor agreed, the Governor, too. The guns barked, the police clubs fell, the gas bombs flew. Two men were dead.

There was a mass funeral. And the National Guard put snipers on top of the piers to pick off more workers.

"Shoot to kill," said Lieutenant Colonel Mittelstaedt.

The Industrial Association brought in professional strikebreakers from the East, gangsters and thugs. But strangely enough, the papers called them true Americans, and praised them for what they were hired to do. In our charming village by the sea (where Robinson Jeffers lives and a by now suspicious character named Lincoln Steffens who favored the strikers) lots of Carmelites kept on believing the papers. And they began to agree with the man who would like to shoot all the members of the John Reed Club. Surely we could not be Americans. We had not yet killed anybody.

In San Francisco the workers called a general strike. They SEEK TO OVERTURN AMERICA, yelled the California papers. And in Pebble Beach, a hundred and twenty-four miles from the strike centre (the rich district of homes and castles next to Carmel, where the banker Mr. Crocker keeps one of his residences) some folks thought the Revolution had come. A butler in one of the wealthy houses reported that his mistress had stored in great quantities of food and had warned the keeper at her gate to let pass no strangers.

Ultra-patriotic Citizens' Committees were formed in San Francisco and nearby towns to protect the government and the Constitution. Sympathizing greatly with the imported thugs and hired strikebreakers, these committees were praised by the newspapers and urged to commence upholding law and order. So they immediately began—under the protection of the police department—to smash workers' halls, the Western Worker offices, the Marine Workers' Union headquarters, the Finnish Workers' Hall, the Workers' School. They began to break furniture and crack heads. They began to throw bricks through windows, to frighten radicals, intimidate liberals, and dare anybody to take the side of the strikers. And more than ever they began to talk about America, Americanism, the Constitution, and the Flag.

Following in their wake, the police smashed, too, broke heads, and made in one day, four hundred arrests of people poor enough to be vagrants even if they were employed, or sympathetic enough to favor the strikers.

In fear of arrest or violence, a number of liberals fled from San Francisco. They were middle and upper class liberals who had helped all along, had given money or sent telegrams of protest to Frances Perkins and the far-off President. Now, if they were able, they fled. They went to the mountains, to the seashore, to summer homes, to Indian dances in the desert. Some of them had been threatened by the Citizens' Committees; some by anonymous telephone calls; some by bricks through their windows. Some had been browbeaten by the newspapers and called reds. Some had relatives who were too close to the Industrial Association to stand for family whims that included helping strikers. Others had positions they *couldn't* lose. And so the liberals fled the city, or else were silent, or retired under fire. From then on Frances Perkins didn't get nearly so many telegrams.

The General Strike was crushed.

In Carmel, when the extras brought news of the San Francisco vigilante raids following the crushing of the strike, of the head-breaking and the terror, the police aid and official praise, the John Reed Club met to plan an immediate meeting of protest, and to re-affirm what to us were Constitutional liberties. This was in the early afternoon, and we were doubtful of securing an audience of any size for that evening on so short a notice but we felt that an immediate public meeting would be of some effect regardless. We announced the meeting by telephone, and by hurriedly painted posters on the backs of cars.

Within an hour, threats and rumors began to fly through Carmel. Under the cypresses beside the sea, through the quaint streets and charming bypaths, ominous rumors began to fly: *The patriotic citizens will not allow the John Reed Club to meet tonight. The hall will be raided. The Legion will get together! The protest will be broken up.*

When I got to the meeting about eight the street before the theatre was blocked with cars, and the hall was crowded. A police car focussed its headlights on the door, and the Chief of Police stood at the entrance. Inside the Legion *had* gotten together. Rows of them in front, at the sides, around the meeting. A stenographer was taking down everything that was said: Ella Winter's speech on 1776 and the right to strike; Dan James' talk on eye-witness views of the raids; every word the chairman uttered. Some of the citizens applauded the speeches, and some were silent. The hall was divided. The vigilant Legionnaires sat grim and unsmiling:

one's laundry man and one's druggist, real estate men and hotel keepers, and the young man who sold papers in front of the Post Office and probably believed what the papers said—there they sat, gathered together to protect America. They were against the John Reed Club, and against the strikers.

I was the only Negro there.

CLASH THREATENED AS WAR VETERANS ATTEND REED CLUB MEETING, said the local paper the following day. And the next morning the town seethed. Vile names were flung at the John Reed Club, traitors, agitators, un-American.

Had we not helped the strikers?

The Carmel Council ordered tear gas and began to drill citizens with riot guns on the polo grounds. A Citizens' Committee, Sons of the Legion, Company A, a group of Special Deputies, and other auxiliaries to aid the police in combating radicals were organized. Two or three hundred villagers got together to fight the John Reed Club. (We had twenty members.) Our hall was taken away from us, its owner, a leading Carmel citizen, was threatened with boycott, destruction of his property, and possible personal violence. Threatening letters were sent through the mails by devoted but anonymous Americans. (An unsigned postcard demanded why Lincoln Steffens had been christened Lincoln!) and wilder than ever, ominous rumors began to fly through Carmel as the papers announced new vigilante raids on workers' homes and headquarters in nearby cities and towns. Headlines told of groups of workers being driven South from one county line to another. And editorials in our leading papers praised the vigilantes and called for destruction to those speaking out against them.

In Carmel (our charming village by the sea where lives the poet Robinson Jeffers and a subversive old gentleman named Steffens who abetted the strikers) the vigilantes began to speak. Mr. Jo Mora, a sculptor, headed Company A, a group of 107 sworn enemies of the John Reed Club. Mr. Byington Ford, a realtor and a neighbor of the banker, Mr. Crocker, took charge of the Citizens' Committee. Mayor Thoburn spoke against freedom of speech. The city council took its stand—but hardly on the American Constitution. The papers poured out editorial attacks on the John Reeders as a group and as individuals. Monterey Peninsula began to take on the color and tone of Hitler's Germany.

The Carmel Pine Cone stooped to the vilest piece of journalism I have ever seen—a sneering attack on a nine-year-old boy, Pete Steffens, because his parents are Lincoln Steffens and Ella Winter. (The

Heywood Broun column commenting on this bit of scurvy writing appeared in the Eastern papers, but was dropped, as are his daily syndicated pieces, in the *San Francisco News* out here.[57] Similarly, a column of Mr. Broun's sympathetic to the strike some weeks earlier appeared in only one edition of the *News* and was cut out of all the later editions that day.)

In Carmel there was no actual physical violence, but there were anonymous letters, open threats, "warnings," and verbal and printed attacks against the John Reed Club and persons known to have been sympathetic to the strike.

I, as a Negro member of the Club, seemed to be singled out as especially worthy of attack. Rumors of malicious intent filled the town: that I was frequently seen on the beach and in cars in company of white women, that I called them by their first names, that I was a bad influence on the Negroes of the town, that I aspired to social equality with the white race, that I ought to be run out of the village, tarred and feathered. On the basis of these rumors, irresponsible youths and street corner cowboys were aroused.

Very early one morning an excited young artist hurried to the house of one of the John Reed Club members with the information that certain of us were marked for physical violence by the patriots of the town, and that for our own safety, we should leave at once. All day Carmel bubbled with a kind of hysteria. Telephones of John Reeders kept ringing and friends inquiring for their safety. Writers were advised to hide manuscripts in case houses were stoned and raided. The papers were bellowing for the good citizens to rid the Peninsula of reds and all others not sympathetic to the American Constitution—meaning all who had sided with the San Francisco strikers.

In New York, Mr. Crocker, the banker, said to the press: "The strike is the best thing that ever happened in San Francisco. It's costing us money, certainly, but it's solving the labor problem for years to come, perhaps forever. Mark my words. When this nonsense is out of the way and the men have been driven back to their jobs, we won't have to worry anymore. They'll have learned their lesson. Labor is licked."

In Carmel, Mr. Byington Ford, a neighbor of Mr. Crocker's, began to make extremely patriotic speeches in which he called upon all persons in the name of his one-hundred percent American Citizens' Protective Committee to sign pledges of loyalty to the government and constitution "and make this town one-hundred percent American." He also approved the council's buying of tear gas.

Whereupon, a member of one of Carmel's newly formed vigilante organizations came to a Negro employed on the main street of the town and told him to quietly advise me to leave the village, that I *was* in physical danger, and that there was no way of assuring anyone safety during the hysteria. Unable to write under such conditions, I went away for a month.

I am back in Carmel now, however. (Charming little village by the sea where Robinson Jeffers lives and an utterly seditious American alien named Lincoln Steffens—for during the hysteria he stated to the press, "If communism is a crime, I'll plead guilty. I'd rather have them send me to jail than to the White House. It's more honorable.") The John Reed Club has not stopped meeting, although, being denied a hall, we can no longer host public lectures. We are limited at the moment to a printed bulletin—whereas the vigilantes, protected by the police department, and praised by the Mayor, hold all the public meetings they choose, and continue to interest themselves greatly in the technique of throwing gas and promulgating their own kind of Americanism. For Negroes, according to *The Carmel Sun,* this means: "free, unhindered social intercourse between the races is a very difficult subject. So difficult as to have been in the past odorous, to say the least."

A week earlier the *Sun* had stated in a long attack on me:

> "Langston Hughes has been a very 'distinguished' guest in Carmel—not that the town is proud of it. He has been the guest of 'honor' at parties. Whites were invited—a 'select' few—to bask in his wisdom. White girls have ridden down the street with him, have walked with him smiling into his face. . . . Russia would be a good place for Hughes."

In spite of those deliberate appeals to race hatred, it is interesting to note that on the Peninsula Citizens' Committees there are four Negro members—political opportunists hoping for a rake-off from somebody after elections—who solemnly declare it a crime to associate with white folks, or to take the side of the strikers. In spite of the fact that our John Reed Club raised several hundred dollars for Scottsboro, and that one of the express objectives of the San Francisco strike was the opening of the longshoreman's union to Negroes without discrimination, these four colored citizens eagerly and boastfully side with the most reactionary elements in the community—which must make even the vigilantes laugh—contemptuously.

"The Soviet Theater in Central Asia," *Asia* (October 1934): 590–93

In Samarkand, Bokhara, Tashkent, Askhabad and many other cities in Central Asia north of the Persian and Afghan borders, the people's theater has become a vital and exciting force since the Soviet régime established its flow of life through that once backward part of the Orient. The flutes and *barabans* still play in the tea houses as of old, but they play also in the modern theaters, where their music has been woven, as have the other folk arts, into the patterns of new plays that picture the struggles and triumphs of socialism in a world of ancient ways. The Soviet theaters could hardly wish for more dramatic material with which to work than they find here in old cities amid green oases where reactionary Mohammedans, not long ago united with mountain bandits against the Red army, and veiled women are still fleeing from husbands who want harems despite new laws. The revolutionary history of Central Asia is filled with conflict, change and startling contrast between the present and the past.

In Tashkent I sat in the little hotel room where Ismailov, leading dramatist of Soviet Uzbekistan and chairman of the Writers' Union, lives. On an oil stove in one corner, his wife, in a red *khalat,* was busy making *plov,* a dish of mutton and rice, which she soon brought to the table in my honor. There were tea and sweet wine, too. As we talked, somebody was continually pouring me something to drink.

Ismailov was telling me about the history of the Uzbek theater, a history so scant—before the Revolution—that it did not take long in the telling. In the Czar's day, there had been practically no native theater. Tashkent had a small Tartar theater and also a poor provincial Russian playhouse, Ismailov said, for the entertainment of the military and colonial families. But the Uzbek masses, unlettered as they were, contented themselves with folk music and jugglers, magicians and other outdoor performers. These wandering folk-performers are rapidly disappearing, some of them being absorbed into the State circuses and others into the modern theater. Some have gone even as far as Odessa and Leningrad to perform for distant audiences in indoor circuses.

It is too bad that the old Uzbek marionette theater is seldom seen these days. Gone, too, are the *dorvos,* native ropewalkers who used to perform in the public squares. Uzmozaif, an old musician whom I met, told me that he had never heard of any European ropewalkers as skillful as these dorvos. They worked on high ropes with no protecting nets and crowds of people below them. Among them were accomplished dancers, doing graceful steps in mid-air. There was a celebrated one, Mardarzum-dorvos, who performed a dangerous and beautiful stunt which is still talked about—although he himself has long been dead. He used to stretch his rope, so Uzmozaif said, at the height of four poplars above the crowd. He would then take two hollow pumpkins, placing in each a half dozen white doves. These pumpkins he would tie, one to each ankle, with a silk cord. Out he would go, dancing on his high taut rope. At the very center of the rope he would suddenly spring whirling into the air, cracking his heels together, breaking the pumpkins and letting the white doves fly free. In the Soviet circuses touring Asia there are still some splendid oriental stunt artists, but none so great as Mardarzum-dorvos.

The native drama, before the Revolution, was most meager, and, as in the Chinese theater, only men acted. Among the upper-class Uzbeks in Tashkent (only a few, even among them, could read or write twelve years ago), some attempt was made to develop a native theater modeled after the Russian stage. In 1912 they put on a play in the Uzbek language called *The Murder of the Father.* In this play, inspired by a group of young *jedigi* (reformers among the aristocracy), a wealthy Mohammedan merchant who has opposed a modern education for his son is killed by the boy.

Among these radical jedigi, a number of Uzbek youths who had connections with Russian revolutionaries then living in Asia wrote poems and plays treating of their oppressive life under the khans and emirs and the Czar. But in those days nothing could be performed or published without permission of the Czar's Governor-General, who exercised a strict censorship over the native peoples as part of his military rule. The Mohammedan *mullahs,* too, opposed any liberalizing influences emanating from the jedigi, who retaliated with broadsides against the immoralities of the priesthood—which never got published. These little groups of amateur literati made no headway in founding a theater in the Uzbek language. They did, however, develop a few native writers like Zasaidov and Esaparov who, when the Bolshevik Revolution came, had already written plays of oppression interesting enough to be produced by the newly established Soviet theaters.

It was only after the Revolution that women appeared on the native stage. The ice was broken by Tamara Khanum, now a famous dancer, who first dared to perform in public—under guard. After her, other women, newly liberated from their harems, went into the theater. Some continued to wear their veils at home, although they took them off on the stage. Several actresses were murdered by reactionary relatives. At Bokhara, Tucson-oi, a talented native woman who had studied in Moscow, was killed by her husband for refusing to desert the theater; and in Samarkand, as recently as 1930, another young actress, Nurhan, was put to death by her parents for appearing unveiled on the stage. Her funeral was made the occasion for a stirring appeal to all women to take off their veils, to refuse to remain in harems or to submit to the slavelike customs of the past. Today there are a great many women in the theaters of Soviet Asia, and they are an important factor in freeing others from the chains of the old life.

At Ismailov's invitation I attended a national congress of playwrights who came together in Tashkent to discuss the problems of the Uzbek stage and its relation to the second Five-Year Plan.[58] Ways and means of devising plays and pageants that would further the plans for industrializing the land and pushing on to complete socialism were taken up by the assembled young men and women interested in creating a theater to meet the specific needs of the day.

Ismailov's own famous play, *The Spoilers of Cotton,* reflects the new social order. It is important not only because it is an excellent drama but because it shows clearly the value of cotton, Central Asia's main crop, to the economics of socialism. It pictures vividly the fight that had to be waged against the counterrevolutionary elements that sought to destroy and sabotage cotton production, in an effort to break down the first Central Asian workers' republic.

Halima, another drama popular with Uzbek audiences, has for its theme the closing of the harems and the unveiling of the women—one of the most amazing transformations since the Revolution. Countless Mussulman women had to face the violent opposition of their orthodox parents, husbands and brothers when they sought to take advantage of the new freedom to remove the veil, attend school and choose their own husbands. *Halima* has been presented for a number of years and at each performance fewer veiled faces are seen. At the production of *Halima* which I attended in Tashkent I counted only twelve veiled women among the two or three hundred in the audience—many of them school girls who have never been and never will be veiled now.

Not all the plays of the Uzbek theater are concerned with the treatment of contemporary problems. The most beautiful theatrical production I saw in Tashkent was the native opera *Farhar Va Shirin,* based on the old folk tale of a Chinese prince who wandered across the great mountains from Cathay seeking a girl whose face he had seen but once in a magic mirror. Centuries ago a river near Ferghana was named Shirin, after the girl, and a mountain, Farhar, after the boy. This legend, recently set to the old folk music of Central Asia, is played and sung by a group of more than one hundred actors trained in the folk songs and dances of Uzbekistan. They are accompanied by a large orchestra of folk musicians who play the five-hour score without written notes. Nazira Aleava, loveliest of Uzbek actresses, sings the part of Shirin; and in the third act Tamara Khanum does one of her amazing dances.

I also saw, at the Uzbek theater, a musical comedy imported from Baku and sung and danced in modern European clothes to Azerbaijan tunes. The production, however, was far less beautiful than *Farhar Va Shirin,* with its gorgeous Chinese costumes and lacquered settings. A number of plays from European languages, especially from the Russian, have been translated and staged in the modern Uzbek theater. Furmanov's *Revolt* and Gogol's *Inspector General,* for instance, have proved popular.

The Uzbek theaters, like all theaters in the Soviet Union, are under the supervision of the People's Commissariat of Education. They are now on a solid financial basis, supported by their audiences. Entrance fees are moderate, and most workers secure tickets in advance from their factory, club or trade union. Many of the actors, especially those in small parts, are workers during the day. All performers take active part in the social tasks connected with the theater, such as organizing dramatic circles in factories and workers' clubs, staging pageants and demonstrations on holidays or special occasions and aiding in the campaign for the liquidation of illiteracy and the popularization of the Latinized alphabet, which is replacing the old Arabic script.

Under the Czar, folk art was discouraged and even suppressed. Since the Revolution, however, there has been a great renaissance of folk art in Central Asia—ruled by the iron hand of the Cossack generals. Now the theater, the radio and the motion picture are utilizing the best of folk expression, and all the leading folk musicians make records for the phonograph. On rest days in the larger cities, there are sometimes two or three concerts of folk music with dancing. At these concerts the best of the old and the new artists appear, and the wailing strains of the native flutes, the beat of horsehide drums and the sway of booted dancers enthrall the audiences. Under Kari Yabubov, National Singer of the Republic, the Uzbek Musical Theater has developed into an important institution, with branches in several cities. The leading company divides its time between Tashkent and Samarkand. Sometimes the players go to Moscow and Leningrad as guests of the theater publics. The native drama theaters, as well as the musical companies, occasionally go on tour.

Moscow theater-goers (and that includes practically the entire population) continually delight in the exotic productions which the various national minorities of the Soviet Union bring to the stages of the "center." Last spring when the Rustavelli players from the famous Georgian State Theater at Tiflis came to town, not a seat could be had for days in advance. The Uzbeks draw equally crowded houses.

The Mongolian players at the International Olympiad of Workers Theaters (non-professional) held in Moscow a year ago last June created the greatest interest of any group present. For eight or nine days they had traveled from Ulan Bator, in Outer Mongolia, to the Red Capital, bringing their silken costumes and exotic musical instruments via the Trans-Siberian. When the curtains of Moscow's vast music hall parted to the low monotone of Chinese pipes and fiddles, the Mongolian actors were welcomed with a prolonged burst of applause by the Russian public. Their play, *Dark Power,* pictured the sufferings of the Mongols under their former princes of the golden tents and the lamas of the corrupt temples. It was a revolutionary play acted to native music in the formal Chinese tradition, except that women took the feminine rôles in the cast, not men, as in the old Chinese theater.

In the minority nations of the Soviet Union, every form of art expression is being utilized as a weapon to show up the faults and evils of the old régime. As Ismailov, the Uzbek playwright, said, "We must use the theater to teach our people how terrible and dangerous the beys and the priests and the Cossacks were in the past, and how beautiful life can be in the future when all workers get together."

The campaign against provincialism and racial intolerance has been greatly aided by the theaters and motion pictures of the Soviet Union. To its varied nationalities, the modern playhouses in the distant corners of the Union are of tremendous value, too, in presenting the problems of socialism in terms of local cultures. Aside from their social importance, these racial theaters are fascinating. No one interested in studying the Soviet drama should content himself with visits to the Russian playhouses of Moscow. The Gypsy theater should be seen, the Jewish theater and the Ukrainian. Outside of Moscow, one should see the Georgian theater at Tiflis, the Turkish theater at Baku and the Uzbek theater at Tashkent or Samarkand. The development of the Uzbek theater in ten short years, since the establishment of the Republic, is one of the miracles of art.

"Tamara Khanum: Soviet Asia's Greatest Dancer," *Theater Arts Monthly* (November 1934): 829–35

On the evening of my second day in Tashkent, that ancient city of Central Asia, now an administrative centre for the Soviets, I went to the Uzbek Musical Theatre to see the *Farhar Va Shirin,* sung by a cast of native actors in the Uzbek language.[59] It was an astonishingly beautiful production, mimed with such expertness that even one like myself, a total stranger to the tongue, could follow its story.

Before the Bolshevik revolution in Uzbekistan (that country between Afghanistan and the Hungry Steppe), there had been no native theatre other than that of jugglers and magicians, wandering singers and boy-dancers performing mostly in the open air. Since 1924, however, the year of the final establishment of the Soviets in that part of the world, there has been an amazing development in the arts of the drama. From the great theatres of Moscow and Leningrad, experts have come down into Asia to direct and aid the development of the native stage. Today in Samarkand, Bokhara, Tashkent, and other large cities of the Uzbek Republic one may see excellent productions of full-length plays by young playwrights who, ten years ago, scarcely knew what a theatre was.

There are now many plays about the new Soviet life—the winning over of the people from the antiquities of religion, Allah and the mullahs; the dramatic unveiling of the women and the breaking down of the harems; the conflicts between the peasants and the counter-revolutionary bandits who once menaced the new red state.

Most popular, however, of all the varied productions of the Uzbek theatre has been the opera *Farhar Va Shirin,* which retells on the stage in terms of folk-poetry and folk-music one of the oldest legends of Central Asia. It is a singing version of that famous folk-poem about the Chinese prince, Farhar, who centuries ago looked into a forbidden mirror and saw the face of a girl so beautiful that he knew he could not live without her. He spent his life wandering the world to find her, crossing the Gobi Desert and the ranges of the Tian Shan, even into what is now Uzbekistan—and finally came upon Shirin.

It was in the third act of this picturesque musical drama that I first saw Tamara Khanum. As a dancer at some wild mountain court where the queen's throne was set among the rocks, to a deafening whir of drums and wail of flutes, suddenly from the wings in a velvet coat and soft high leather boots, straight across the stage there came a human vibrance like an electric magnet, instantly pulling the whole audience into the dynamic stride of her dancing feet. Had Gertrude Stein been there, surely a bell would have rung—for that vibrance, stamping out a swiftly postured rhythm before the queen, was Tamara Khanum, Eastern genius of the dance.

Primitive and strong like the wind that sweeps across the Kizil Kum and roars in the passes of the Pamirs; clean-cut and sharp as the sky-peaks of the Hindu Kush; neither male nor female, but wind-like, torrent-like, sand-like, suddenly her dance ended. Whirling into the wings, the electric magnet released a thousand hands into a roar of applause. To appease the shouting audience, the drums and cymbals, the flutes and barabans suddenly began for the second time their cloud-burst of rhythm and the dance was repeated, ending with the same dynamic disappearance and the same roar of hands. They say it is like that every time Tamara Khanum appears. She does something to her audience that no other dancer in Central Asia can do, and her name is known in all the cities of the Soviet East from the Caspian to the Chinese border.

Weeks later, upon my return to Tashkent after a long stay in Turkmenia, I went to call on Tamara Khanum at her house. I could not imagine the little woman in carpet slippers who greeted me with children about her feet as being the human dynamo of the dance that had electrified a huge theatre. That is, I could not reconcile the two people—the housewife and the dancer—until I had spent an evening listening to her talk; then they came together again, the wife at home and the artist of *Farhar Va Shirin,* the human being and the dancer, the flesh and the god—remade from the story she told me of her brave and fascinating life.

The night my interpreter came to the hotel to accompany me to Tamara Khanum's it was snowing in Tashkent. The interpreter, a Russian woman of aristocratic birth, had been born there in Central Asia in the days when it was a Tzarist colony and her father was an officer of the military overlordship. She knew, of course, both Uzbek and Russian; and spoke, besides, beautiful English, French and German. She was quite as excited as I to be calling on so famous a dancer.

Tamara Khanum greeted us at the door, a child beside her. Within it was warm and comfortable. There were lovely hand-embroidered *suzané* on the walls, and on the floor a rug that was probably from Bokhara. But about the other furnishings of the room there was nothing rich or unusual—except that there were a few simple chairs and a table, European style—furnishings not used in an ordinary Uzbek home where the Oriental custom of sitting on the floor still prevails. Little bowls and pots of tea were brought and plates of candy and cakes. Her sister, a young writer, joined us. And by and by, two old men, famous folk-musicians, came—Austa Alim Kamilov, player of hand drums, and Achmedjean Aca Uzmozaif, player of flutes. From this little gathering of artists that night (and at subsequent meetings), I learned many things about the age-old folk-music and dancing of Uzbekistan, and its new use in the modern Soviet theatres.

I learned that the history of the Uzbek dance since the revolution, like almost everything else in that once Mohammedan world, is the history of the breaking down of timeless Asiatic traditions. Tamara Khanum herself is a mighty breaker of these traditions, for she was the first woman in the annals of Uzbekistan to dare perform on a public stage. And that was only ten years ago—for, prior to the revolution, women were kept locked in harems and were never seen without the *paranja,* a long black veil from head to foot. Tamara Khanum's appearance on the stage, unveiled and unashamed, marks the opening of the Uzbek theatre to women artists.

Before the revolution, the professional dancers began as boys, and some of them became very famous—to their world what Nijinsky was to the world of the classical ballet. Their names were known in all the tea-houses, and great crowds of men would come to see them dance. Often these boy-dancers were bought outright by the rich beys, and thus became exclusive entertainers to the bey's invited guests at private feasts. At certain times of the year there would be a sort of dancer's fair, when prospective buyers of boy-dancers would gather to select entertainers. At these colorful dance-markets, the best and most handsome of the youthful performers would display their steps before a vast gathering seated around an enormous space in the open air.

The old men of Tashkent and Andizhan still speak of a certain male dancer, Ata Haja, who could circle an open exhibition area three times doing the most delicate and complicated patterns with his body. The old men recall one competition of boy-dancers at which four thousand men gathered, including many rich beys who had come for miles around to the dance market. In their turbans and silken gowns, the rich men bargained for the dancers.

The traditional Uzbek dances, so I learned from watching them, are not vigorous and boisterous exercises as many of the folk dances of the West are. Nor are they artificially acrobatic in the manner of the ballet and the theatre. Uzbek dances, typical of the dances of the East, are delicately patterned, graceful body-rhythms, often weaving a subtle story in plastics that the uninitiated would not understand. Each of the old dances had its own traditional beginning, middle and end—the strict forms, always respected and observed, being a mold for the grace of the individual performer.

These traditional dances, handed down by generations of dance-makers out of the past, might be varied only in so far as the subtlety and interpretive skill of different performers give them shaded variations within the accepted mold of the pattern.

Of course, in the old days many famous boy-dancers originated marvelous variations on traditional themes. Extremely subtle and extremely delicate movements of the wrists and of the hands, the fingers and the head, the mouth and the eyes might come into play. Certain great dancers of the past were able to execute a very famous movement of the eyebrows as they danced; one eyebrow up, the other down, continuously, like the two sides of a balance. This particular movement is said to have come from the way in which a rice-mill is propelled by a flowing stream. So all over Uzbekistan people said, "How good it is that we have rice-mills, because from them we have been given a dance."

As the water and the rice-mill enter in the Uzbek dance, so the native folk-music makes use, too, of sounds from the daily life of the country. The *carnai,* that long horn of greater length than man is tall, reproduces the ear-splitting cry of the tiger in the steppes. The little flutes of bamboo trill like a bird in an oasis of sweet water. These things the old men in their gentle voices told me.

Speaking of the native music, Uzmozaif, player of reeds, said, "In the silence of the steppes, there are a thousand sounds. Our instruments know them all."

The two old and very famous Uzbek musicians, whom I came to know that night at Tamara Khanum's, are simple people, not proud and puffed up about their art. The player of flutes was a shepherd in his youth. He began to play in the fields on reeds that he would cut and tune himself. Then he became a weaver of silk. Only since the revolution has he been a professional musician, playing at great concerts in the workers' clubs and theatres. He still makes his own instruments from the shoots of the young bamboo, and in order to hasten their mellowness he takes them with him into the steaming caverns of the Uzbek baths—and there he plays on them for hours.

Kamilov, the player of drums, was a maker of *arbas* (high-wheeled carts) until very recently. He was the best maker of *arbas* in the whole city of Margelan. Everybody with goods to haul wanted a Kamilov *arba.*

But now the old man spends a great deal of time in Tashkent playing drums as only he can play them, and Tamara Khanum will not dance unless he is in the orchestra.

These old men have many pupils now, for in Uzbekistan it is only from the elderly musicians that the young may learn the music of the past—since none of it is written down. Even the orchestra of some forty pieces at the native opera plays the complete scores of four- to five-hour performances like *Farhar Va Shirin* entirely without notes, and without the benefit of a conductor's baton.

Kamilov, the old drummer, has had, in connection with the stage, one great tragedy in his life. His sister-in-law, following in the footsteps of Tamara Khanum, was, after the revolution, one of the earliest women actresses; but she went against the will of her family in appearing as a public artist. For this, in the dead of night, she was stabbed twenty-seven times by her brother, with the connivance of her own husband. Thus was formally avenged what the family considered a terrible disgrace. But for this counter-revolutionary crime (interference with the freedom and development of women), Kamilov's brother and brother-in-law were put to death.

In the history of the Soviet theatre in Uzbekistan, there are several such cases of women artists suffering death from irate relatives who thought it bad enough for them to take off the veil—let alone to go on the stage. Tamara Khanum, however, had no trouble from her father about the theatre because, a year before her first professional appearance, he was killed by *basmachi* in Fergana. Late at night the bandits came to carry off his several daughters, including Tamara, but that week the girls were in Tashkent, and the old man was alone. The bandits killed him, robbed the house, and rode away without the women they were seeking.

During the revolution, Tamara Khanum told me, she began as a young dancer at weddings in Fergana. Then, in 1923, she first appeared in a theatre—making and breaking history—at a concert in Tashkent. Later, when a few of the leading male musicians gathered the best of the native artists of the wedding feasts and tea-houses to form the first group of the Uzbek Musical Theatre, Tamara Khanum was the only woman. In a land where men still believed in veils and harems in spite of Soviet decrees, her participation was extremely dangerous. But she stuck—and today there are women in every theatrical company in Soviet Asia.

Tamara Khanum's fame as a dancer began to spread and grow until, in 1925, she was in Paris with a group of Uzbek musical artists. While there, however, she became seriously ill, so the Parisians could not enjoy the beauty of her performances, nor was she able to see much of the French theatres. She went once to a music hall, but did not care for the art of the nude ladies performing therein—for she herself dances in the full robes and heavy jewels of an Uzbek woman of pre-revolutionary times.

She is a specialist in the dances to barabans and cymbals. She has taken over the best of the old steps of the former boy-dancers. And she has studied in Samarkand the now-forbidden dances of the dervishes with their four basic rhythms and wild fanatic frenzy. From them she has created patterns of her own.

Far and wide, this dancer is known for her artistry and her bravery. Everywhere she is a great drawing card in the theatres of Central Asia. You may see her name on the bill-boards of many ancient cities along the golden road to Samarkand. Sometimes she goes across the Caspian to Baku and Tiflis, and up to Moscow. But it is in her own home land that she is both an artist and a symbol—a living symbol of that new freedom that has come to the women of Soviet Asia.

There are some who have not yet taken off their veils in Uzbekistan for fear of husbands or fathers. But they have all heard of Tamara Khanum. And veiled women are always in her audiences, peering at her through their heavy *paranjas* of horse-hair. After seeing her dance, some have been known to go home and definitely throw their veils forever into the fire, in spite of conservative and dangerous men-folk about the house.

This dancer of Soviet Asia, Tamara Khanum, illustrates very clearly what Soviet critics continually speak of—art that is also a social force, that changes life, that makes it better. She is such an artist, brave and creative, breaking down old taboos, and, through her example, helping others to break them down. Had she grown up fifteen years ago, she would have been locked in a harem, and only her husband would have known about her dancing. Today she is famous throughout Central Asia.

"The Boy Dancers of Uzbekistan," *Travel* 64 (December 1934): 36–37

The Central Asiatic Republic of Uzbekistan lies in that portion of the map where Afghanistan curves toward China. Before the Communist revolution, the cult of boy dancers permitted any handsome young man skilled in the subtle steps of the dance to achieve the kind of fame that in the West attends a Greta Garbo or a Clark Gable. From Ferghana to Bokhara, from Osh to Samarkand the great boy dancers, before Stalin came, were known and loved by the men who crowded the tea houses and dance fairs to see them perform.

As in the orthodox theaters of China and Japan, so in Central Asia formerly only men took part in public performances of any sort. No women were allowed to act or dance. Nor did the men in Uzbekistan ever take women to public spectacles. Woman's place was very much in the home—locked up.

Those boys who danced as women put on wigs and dresses and cultivated the delicate gestures of rhythmic pantomime. Some became great artists, but many were only common entertainers in tea houses, the centers of masculine life in Central Asia—particularly in Uzbekistan, where the *chai-khana* is as common as a soda fountain in America.

To these tea houses only men came. In sunny weather they sat outside on raised platforms squatting on soft Oriental rugs from Merv or Bokhara, little bowls of tea in front of them and gourds of powdered tobacco in their laps. Their padded gowns, their turbans and their bright round caps were gay against the mud walls of the *chai-khana* as they sat on the shaded platforms, a bit removed from the dust of the road and the passing camels and asses.

At night, long-necked instruments with one or two strings and the *hashnigh,* a kind of double flute, would send up their curiously wailing music. The boy dancers would be there shaking curly black heads in the courtyard, stamping out their patterned rhythms. Allah and the Prophet forbade the drinking of wines and liquors, but on nights of revelry the tea bowls did not always contain tea. Through the dark streets in these Oriental cities, shouts of merriment would echo from the frequent pools of light that were the tea houses.

I learned most about the boy dancers from Achmedjean Aca-Uzmozaif, to whom I was introduced in Tashkent by that amazing woman, Tamara Khanum, leading dancer of the Uzbek National Theater. Aca-Uzmozaif is an old man of great gentleness and fine musicianship. His memories go back far beyond the recent Bolshevik revolution, back to the days when both the British and the Russians were seeking control of that vast territory east of the Caspian—and he was a flute player for the wedding feasts of the rich beys. Now he is an honored member of the National Orchestra of the Uzbek Republic and one of the finest makers of reed instruments in all Soviet Asia.

Seated with tea and cakes and candy in the modern home of Tamara Khanum, with chairs and tables instead of rugs and cushions on the floor, Aca-Uzmozaif told me about the boy dancers of the past. None of the younger members of the present theater, Soviet educated boys and girls, would talk with me about this particular phase of the old native life. Even those men who once were boy dancers before the revolution would not speak of it. They knew it was something visitors from the West might not approve of, or understand. Besides, the young people were full of the present, full of excitement about the Second Five Year Plan and the latest plays from Moscow on the triumphs of Communism that were being translated for their native theater. Not that Aca-Uzmozaif was uninterested in these things but he remembered the past, too, and spoke of it.

Through an interpreter (a member of the former Russian nobility at Tashkent), he told me about the great dance fairs that used to be held years ago throughout Uzbekistan. To those fairs the rich beys came from mountains and desert to buy the boy dancers, or employ them as semi-permanent entertainers in the great walled gardens of their remote estates.

At those widely heralded dance fairs, great crowds of men would gather in their robes and bright sashes, turbans and round little caps, their gourds of tobacco tasseled to their waists. They squatted or stood, their yellow-brown faces in a tight packed circle, about a vast cleared space in the open air. (Tamara Khanum had an old photograph of such a fair in one of her albums.) There would be an orchestra of strings, flutes, and drums to play the traditional tunes. The sun would blaze down. The dust would fly.

From the four corners of Uzbekistan, all the boy dancers, *bacha,* who were free and could travel and knew about it would come to perform. They would put on their wigs with the girlish curls, their silken robes and bright boots. Then each one in turn would begin to circle to the music in the vast outdoor space, recreating in his own way the patterned movements, the delicate turning of the head and wrists, that characterize the Uzbek dance. The huge male audience would shout their approval as each especially beautiful traditional movement revealed itself anew, expertly developed by the boy in the dusty ring.

Aca-Uzmozaif told me of one very famous boy dancer called Ata Haja whom he had once seen circle an enormous area three times repeating with each step the intricate and delicate pattern of a difficult traditional movement, repeating it so beautifully that the four thousand onlookers at the fair broke into roar after roar of shouts and cheers.

About these dances there was nothing vulgar or uncouth. They were ancient gestured rhythms and plastic pantomimes moulded into traditional patterns, handed down by generations of dance-makers out of the past. The spectators knew the movements of many of them by heart, and loved them for their beauty. To Western eyes nothing would have seemed unduly strange—except that the dancers with their long curls, smiling and beckoning with their eyes, were boys, not girls.

As each boy finished dancing, he would leave the circle and go with his father or guardian to bargain with the merchants, the beys and the tea house proprietors. Only the very rich few could secure for themselves the services of a great dancer like Ata Haja. Only the rich, anyway, were able to maintain on a grand scale the use of numerous boy dancers for the entertainment of themselves and their male guests and, at the same time, to keep the large harems that went with position in the East.

The less expert of the dancing boys at the festivals, finding no favor in the sight of the wealthy, would have to pass their time performing in the roadside tea houses until another dance fair came around. But the lucky ones who secured a good master would be well cared for. They would dance before his company in luxurious courtyards with music and fountains and silken rugs and food aplenty, and would no longer have to go about the land from tea house to tea house, dance fair to dance fair.

All this, however, was yesterday—fifteen years ago, twenty, thirty; then on back into the past, far, far back into the past as long as man can remember. Suddenly, one year there were no more dance fairs, there were no more boys in the tea houses!

Why? How could that be?

What could have happened to change the customs of a thousand years—to start women pouring out of harems, tearing off their veils, and beys fleeing to Afghanistan?

"The revolution," said Aca-Uzmozaif. "All is changed! Changed! Today, a woman, Tamara Khanum, does the steps the *bacha* used to do. Today the young boys have jobs. They go to school. They belong to the Komsomols."

For Asia's youths, the old man told me (as I already knew), there are now many schools, compulsory up to a certain age, filled with brown and yellow boys and girls. There are illustrated text books for them in all the Oriental languages of that part of the world, Uzbek, Farci, Tartar, and even in languages that had no alphabet before 1922. Since the revolution, athletic activities of all sorts have been introduced to Central Asia. Football, boxing, tennis, and track events. In Samarkand, Kokand, and Tashkent several large stadiums and many tennis courts are built, or are being built. Huge crowds gather at rugby games on rest days—cheering native boys fighting for a goal.

Those days when men crowded about the dusty circles of the dance fairs are over. Healthier, if less traditional, amusements now hold the popular fancy, and every youth is anxious to be a *fisculturnik*, and wear the badge given by the state to those who are physically perfect.

The days of the boy dancers in the tea houses—those youngsters who whirled in silks and wigs at the fairs and sold themselves to the rich—those days are over. The Soviets forbid the buying and selling of anybody, male or female.

However, the old dance steps are still preserved in the Uzbek theaters. They are danced at festivals and taught to young theater workers—but these workers get a salary from the state. They belong to a union. And the art of dancing in public is no longer limited to men, either as participants or spectators. Indeed, the dancer most famous today—from Ferghana to Bokhara, Khiva to Kokand—whose every move across the stage brings shouts of approval, is this same little woman with dark eyes and long black hair, Tamara Khanum, my hostess of the evening.

Aca-Uzmozaif says she knows almost all the steps the great boy dancers once knew. They say in Tashkent that she will soon be made a People's Artist of the Republic of Uzbekistan, the highest honor the government can give to one who creates beauty. Had she grown up twenty year ago, she would have been locked in a harem. Now, when she goes on tour you may see her name TAMARA KHANUM on the bill boards of many ancient cities along the golden road to Samarkand. Already, she has traveled further than any of the boy dancers, even those belonging to the richest beys, ever traveled. As a Soviet artist, Tamara Khanum has been to Moscow and even to Paris.

"To Negro Writers," *American Writer's Congress*, ed. Henry Holt (New York: International Publishers, 1935), 139–41

There are certain practical things American Negro writers can do through their work.[60]

We can reveal to the Negro masses, from which we come, our potential power to transform the now ugly face of the Southland into a region of peace and plenty.

We can reveal to the white masses those Negro qualities which go beyond the mere ability to laugh and sing and dance and make music, and which are a part of the useful heritage that we place at the disposal of a future free America.

Negro writers can seek to unite blacks and whites in our country, not on the nebulous basis of an inter-racial meeting, or the shifting sands of religious brotherhood, but on the *solid* ground of the daily working-class struggle to wipe out, now and forever, all the old inequalities of the past.

Furthermore, by way of exposure, Negro writers can reveal in their novels, stories, poems, and articles:

The lovely grinning face of Philanthropy—which gives a million dollars to a Jim Crow school, but not one job to a graduate of that school; which builds a Negro hospital with second-rate equipment, then commands black patients and student-doctors to go there whether they will or no; or which, out of the kindness of its heart, erects yet another separate, segregated, shut-off, Jim Crow Y.M.C.A.

Negro writers can expose those white labor leaders who keep their unions closed against Negro workers and prevent the betterment of all workers.

We can expose, too, the sick-sweet smile of organized religion—which lies about what it doesn't know, and about what it *does* know. And the half-voodoo, half-clown, face of revivalism, dulling the mind with the clap of its empty hands.

Expose, also, the false leadership that besets the Negro people—bought and paid for leadership, owned by capital, afraid to open its mouth except in the old conciliatory way so advantageous to the exploiters.

And all the economic roots of race hatred and race fear.

And the Contentment Tradition of the O-lovely-Negroes school of American fiction, which makes an ignorant black face and Carolina head filled with superstition appear more desirable than a crown of gold; the jazz-band; and the O-so-gay writers who make of the Negro's poverty and misery a dusky funny paper.

And expose war. And the old My-Country-'Tis-of-Thee lie. And the colored American Legion posts strutting around talking about the privilege of dying for the noble Red, White and Blue, when they aren't even permitted the privilege of living for it. Or voting for it in Texas. Or working for it in the diplomatic service. Or even rising, like every other good little boy, from the log cabin to the White House.

White House is right!

Dear colored American Legion, you can swing from a lynching tree, uniform and all, with pleasure—and nobody'll fight for you. Don't you know that? Nobody even salutes you down South, dead or alive, medals or no medals, chevrons or not, no matter how many wars you've fought in.

Let Negro writers write about the irony and pathos of the *colored* American Legion.

> "*Salute, Mr. White Man!*"
> "Salute, hell! . . . You're a nigger."

Or would you rather write about the moon?

Sure, the moon still shines over Harlem. Shines over Scottsboro. Shines over Birmingham, too, I reckon. Shines over Cordie Cheek's grave, down South.[61]

Write about the moon if you want to. Go ahead. This is a free country.

But there are certain very practical things American Negro writers can do. And must do. There's a song that says, "the time ain't long." That song is right. Something has got to change in America—and change soon. We must help that change to come.

The moon's still shining as poetically as ever, but all the stars on the flag are dull. (And the stripes, too.)

We want a new and better America, where there won't be any poor, where there won't be any more Jim Crow, where there won't be any lynchings, where there won't be any munition makers, where we won't need philanthropy, nor charity, nor the New Deal, nor Home Relief.

We want an America that will be ours, a world that will be ours—we Negro workers and white workers! Black writers and white! We'll make that world!

"Farewell to Mahomet,"
Travel 64 (February 1935): 28–31

The Vice-President of the Uzbek Socialist Soviet Republic, north of Afghanistan, is a woman, Jahan Abinova. The day that I saw her in the offices of the vast new government building at Tashkent, she was dressed in a plain black skirt and a sweater pulled over a high-necked Russian blouse. She looked not unlike a woman clerk in a cooperative food store.

Jahan Abinova is thirty-five years old. She is short and dark. Her olive complexion is not unlike that of an American mulatto. Her face is plain and strong. Her hair is bobbed and very black. She is slight and dynamic. She spoke rapidly and simply, and seldom smiled.

She was born of poor peasants in a Kazakstan village, she said. When she was eleven years old, she was sold for one hundred and fifty rubles as the fourth wife of a rich bey. He was not kind to her. On the eve of the 1917 revolution, her husband moved with his four wives to Tashkent. In October Lenin and the Bolsheviks triumphed in far-away St. Petersburg and Moscow. Abinova learned that the Tsar had fallen and that soldiers and beys would no longer rule Central Asia. Sensing the unrest of the times, she ran away from her husband and never came back.

She was one of the very first women in Uzbekistan to dare take off her veil. In those days hundreds of thousands of women were locked in harems, not daring to remove the heavy black *paranjas* over their faces. But Abinova went bravely ahead, creating for herself a new life in the big Oriental city of Tashkent that no longer belonged to the Tzar and the mullahs.

She had no friends but she found a job as a kitchen helper in a Tartar household. When the first schools were opened for native women, she went to them and learned to read and write. In 1920 she went into the women's department of the Young Communist League, and in 1921 she was admitted to the Party. At that time, it was not easy to find Uzbek women brave enough to join the Communist Party or take an active part in any kind of public life. For thousands of years women in Uzbekistan had been only the pretty prisoners of men and, among the poor, the beasts of burden, as well. They did not know what it meant to be free.

But Jahan Abinova must have been made for freedom. She was made, too, with an ardent zeal for inspiring a desire for freedom in others. It was her mission to spread the new life among the veiled women of Uzbekistan, to arouse the timid ones to come out of their harems, to cast off their veils, and take advantage of the new Soviet laws. It was a brave and dangerous business. Women were daily being killed by irate fathers and husbands of the old school for merely lifting their veils, to say nothing of agitating as Abinova was doing.

In her book, *Red Star in Samarkand,* Anna Louise Strong describes the mob murders and lynchings of women that went on in those days.[62] One girl agitator was killed, her body cut into little bits, and her remains sent back to the Party as a warning. The religious and reactionary males were determined to keep their harems and their female underlings. All the mosques of Allah were on the men's aide, and the mullahs preached against the liberation of women. Religious warnings were broadcast that if women so much as thought of lifting their veils or leaving their many-wived husbands, Allah would be furious.

There were hundreds of murders of women; there were beatings and tortures; but gradually veils came off and harem doors opened until today the majority are at least partially freed of the old male dominations of the past. Certainly this liberation of the women is one of the great epics of Soviet Asia. It will be celebrated in song and story for many generations to come. Its historical significance is tremendous.

Even in the Communist Party ten years ago there were female members still wearing the veil. But in 1923 the Party made a rule that all Communist women must unveil, and that no Party man could keep a woman of his household veiled. By that time, however, many women of Uzbekistan had already taken off the long hideous black *paranja*. The heroic work of pioneers like the now famous Abinova had begun to bear fruit. In 1929 at the Second Uzbek Congress of Soviets, this courageous little woman was elected Vice-President of the Republic! Strangely enough, many of those voting for her were men who, ten years before, would never have dreamed of tolerating the existence of an unveiled native woman.

In addition to the story of Jahan Abinova, there are many thrilling tales of the difficult rise of women to freedom in this once backward Soviet Asia. There is the dramatic story of Tamara Khanum, the dancer, defying the traditions of a thousand years to appear on a public stage; or that of old Annagol Jumaieva in Turkmenia who learned to read after fifty and is now a member of the Party and the head of a Children's Garden; or the amazing tale of Shadiva, a young Communist leader, who was a girl-wife at ten, but who is now a student in the university at Moscow.

But even more thrilling than these tales of individual development are the accomplished facts in the mass development of the women of Central Asia.

Listen to the tale of the building of the Women's Club of Tashkent now benefiting thousands of mothers and girls. This club was erected under the supervision of the Women's Department of the Communist Party. But at first it was very difficult to get any cooperation from the men of the city, even as laborers. One reason: the women announced in advance that they intended to have connected with the club a tea house where they might sit in the open like men and drink tea.

Immediately the irate males of Tashkent rose in opposition. What! Women gathering in a public tea house unveiled, drinking tea! By the head of the Prophet, NO! It should never happen. That was too much. Not a man would turn a spade to help them.

Perhaps the male Party members were all too active doing other things. Anyhow, according to the story, the women bravely set forth digging the foundations and carting material. The men, finally realizing they were determined to have a club with a tea house attached—and that good wages were paid to workers, too—joined in and helped them. Result: today in the heart of the Old Town (the former native quarter of Tashkent as distinguished from the Russian section under the colonial regime) there stands a large modern club house—and across the street on a raised terrace is a courtyard where tea is served to parties of women, that all the passing world may see and marvel. Another tradition of the centuries is broken!

Halima Kasakova, a member of the Tashkent City Soviet, conducted us through the club building the first day I visited there in company with a delegation of American workers.

Comrade Kasakova is a middle aged woman. She did not take off her veil until 1925. She was forty years old when she learned to read and write. But her eagerness to learn and her energy in fighting for the cause of women's freedom in a city of veils and harems has won for her a high executive position in the management of the Women's Club and an elective post in the City Soviet.

A tall, hardy, pleasantly wrinkled woman, Halima Kasakova talked to us with a glowing pride of the tremendous importance of the club to the women of Tashkent.

"You see," she said (we were standing in a class for the liquidation of illiteracy where reading was being taught to adults), "there are veiled women in this class, even now. Some of them are afraid of their husbands, their fathers. But when they learn to read and write, when they realize how useful they can be, when they understand that they can get work if they choose and earn their own living, they will no longer be afraid to take off that ugly veil. Some of them are still religious, too," she whispered. "They think Allah wants them to keep a veil on."

We smiled. In the class of some fifteen women four were veiled. But one or two others had their veils thrown back over their heads, ready to pull them down when they went into the street on their way home. They sat at their desks like children, learning the new Latin alphabet from simple books. One girl had a baby lying on the desk in front of her. Others had left their children in the nursery provided for them. They were a strange mixture of old and young, veiled and unveiled, this class learning the once forbidden mystery of letters. Another age-long Mussulman tradition broken—women learning to read and write.

While mothers are studying in their classes or away at work in the new factories, the children in the kindergartens and nurseries of the Women's Club are not left in idleness. There are teachers for them, too. Indeed the whole Club seemed to me like one vast school. In a large sunny room thirty little children of varied Asiatic races and tribes were taking the first steps in a modern Soviet education. There were simple charts and bright pictures on the walls, little models of houses and theaters and tractors. The children, very clean and cute with their little brown and yellow faces, black hair and almond eyes, stood before their big sand pit and gave a loud greeting in unison for the visitors, raising their small fists in solidarity with the international proletariat. Then they sang us a song about cotton growing and the way people work on collective farms. Thus Soviet education is proceeding in Central Asia.

In the nursery we visited next, we saw how younger ones are taught to dress and undress before taking a nap, to place their clothes in a box at the foot of the bed and put their shoes in order. We saw their wash room with towel, cup, and toothbrush for each child under a simple little colored symbol.

On the same floor, across from the nurseries, there is an excellent exhibit of wax models and charts on child care. There is a graduated display of the proper food for children of different ages. There are several cases of frightening things out of the past on exhibit, too: charms, dangerous herbs, fake medicines, and feather shakers used on sick children by the witch doctors. Vigorous warnings are posted against them.

The Women's Club has a visiting nurse service, and a consultant for pre-natal care connected with the Institute for Mother and Child. In the old days the mortality rate for Uzbek babies was very great. Then a mother often bore ten children—and raised but one. Improper feeding, bad water, no sense of sanitation contributed to their early deaths. Mothers in childbirth used to say with Eastern fatalism, "If this one dies Allah will send another in due time."

A bad custom which the Soviet health services have to some extent succeeded in destroying is that of using the old style Uzbek baby bed or cradle. This little wooden box, usually on rockers and gaily painted, has a round hole for the child's buttocks cut in the center of it. The child was tied in this cradle in a more or less rigid position for hours, even days at a time. In a land where water is scarce, this device saved washing linen, but what it did to the children is another story. Many Uzbeks today have flat heads. These beds are the cause. Many babies died or were permanently affected by the cramped position. Flies crawled into their mouths, and insects stung them. They grew inactive. Now in every child clinic and health exhibit these cruel beds are on display with attendants to explain to mothers what dangerous devices they are.

As we left the Club and walked across the street to the famous tea terrace, Backli Gulan, a bobbed-haired, golden-skinned girl, walked along beside me. Minus any of the timid shyness that Oriental women in non-Soviet countries might have displayed with a strange man, this girl walked calmly beside me like a woman of the West. She spoke to me in simple Russian that, limited as my knowledge was, I could occasionally understand. Yes, she was an Uzbek, she said. Of course, a Komsomol. No, she had never worn a *paranja*. (I realized then that she had grown up since the revolution.) Yes, she was married. Her husband was a Party man. (And I learned later that her brother was Gafur Gulan, the famous proletarian poet.) Her work? Cultural worker at the Women's Club.

We sat on the open terrace and had tea. We could see the passing crowds in the Oriental street: turbaned men, high-wheeled carts loaded with goods, camels, women and girls—occasionally a veiled woman. And directly across from us, the tall square front of the Women's Club.

"You know," one of our translators said, "there are women in this town who have never seen street cars, women who married long before the revolution and have never been out of their harems. Do not think that we communists have reached everyone yet, by any means. You see how some in the streets are still veiled. Well, there are others like them behind the grey walls of all Uzbek villages and towns, others who are not even allowed to walk in the streets. But very few young ones are veiled any more. They are mostly the old and religious."

I looked at the colored murals about us on the three walls of the tea house: unveiled women working in the factories, girls standing beside airplanes, students learning to fire rifles. "Those are the women that are increasingly being developed here in the Soviet East," said our translator. I could not doubt but that she was right. Slowly but surely the new world would transform the old.

The next day I went to the New Woman's Hospital on the edge of the Old Town. It was opened in 1930—a large plain building from without, towering above the trees that surrounded it. The chief doctor, who conducted us through the hospital, was a Russian woman in spotless white except for a string of amber beads about her neck.

We went first to the sun-porch where convalescent patients have their meals. We sat down for a half-hour while the Chief Doctor told us about the hospital and its work. Then she took us through several of the departments, later turning us over to an assistant.

At first, native women were very backward about availing themselves of the facilities of the hospital. They were shy and afraid. They had never seen such a house for the sick before. They did not know what would happen to them there. Gradually their prejudices are being overcome, but even this year native women coming for treatment are only forty per cent of the cases received, the others being Russian residents of the town.

"For the native women," said the Chief Doctor, "our hospital is not just a place for medical treatment. It is a school, too. Before our patients go back to their families, we teach them how to take care of their bodies, safeguard their health, and bring sanitation into their homes. In this respect we pay special attention to expectant mothers, for Uzbek women have suffered greatly in the past through loss of children. So many babies died. Now all our maternity cases are carefully followed up by a visiting nurse service. Everything is done to make and keep the child healthy."

The staff of this New Women's Hospital consists of eleven doctors—ten women and one man. Three of the women physicians are of Asiatic nationality, the others are Russian. There are thirty-eight nurses and twenty-four midwives. Thirteen of the nurses are Uzbek.

I was struck by the apparent devotion of the Russian women, both nurses and doctors, to the work of the hospital. During the months that followed in Central Asia, I frequently met Russian women—physicians, dentists, librarians, teachers, clerks, Party workers—who were devoting the best years of their lives to the development of their darker and more backward sisters in this newly liberated Asia.

I once heard a foreigner object to what he termed the possible Russification of Central Asia. Very quickly the answer came back to him, "Not Russification, but modernization." And it was pointed out how, under the Tsar, the term Russification might have been just. Then, it was a definite colonial policy to stamp out native cultures and instill Russian ways of thinking. The schools, if any, were always taught in Russian.

Now, the Soviet policy is to preserve whatever of native life has value, to encourage native culture, and to destroy those things that tend to hold the masses in ignorance and darkness.

Certainly in the matter of dress, the majority of Uzbeks continue to wear colorful native clothes, suitable to their customs and climate. (Minus, of course, the veils for women.) The old music, too, is still played and sung, although oft-times the words are entirely new. The Uzbek language is taught, but with a new Latin, instead of Arabic, alphabet.

But the most substantial contribution coming into being for the women of Soviet Asia is that of the opportunity for economic independence. The building of cotton mills and silk mills for the employment of women workers, the great need for teachers, the demand for clerks, dancers, doctors, dentists, nurses and journalists—and the education which is being given to fit native women for these demands—will create in another decade or so an independent mass of women workers who can never again, by any power, be brought back to the old male-dominated, harem-enclosed patterns of the past.

All this has not been and will not be easy to sustain and develop. More women undoubtedly will be beaten and killed by the religious fanatics and old-fashioned husbands who still exist. But the foundations have been laid for an ever-accelerating progress.

In the Soviet Union, March 8th is International Woman's Day. Last year, for *The Moscow Daily News,* Anne Louise Strong wrote an article on the heroines of the East. In it she spoke of one Zulfia Khan, early Uzbek rebel against the veil and the harem, about whose violent death a folk-song has been made.

Because Zulfia wanted to be free, her husband, sided by the mullahs, poured kerosene on the house where she was sleeping and burned her in it; so the women of the village made a lament for her saying:

"The flame in which you burned
Is a torch in our hands."

Today the torch of liberated womanhood burns throughout Soviet Asia—and the whisper of its brightness sweeps across the frontiers into Persia, India, even into China where strange and barbaric customs still prevail. Lenin said, "Every housewife must learn to rule the State." In Uzbekistan several are already Chairmen of their village Soviets. And Jahan Abinova, from a harem, is Vice-President of the Republic.

"Pictures More Than Pictures: The Work of Manuel Bravo and Cartier-Bresson," LHP 871 (Mexico, March 6, 1935)

A picture, to be an interesting picture, must be more than a picture, otherwise it is only a reproduction of an object, and not an object of value in itself.[63]

Anyday, one can walk down the street in a big city and see a thousand people. Any photographer can photograph these people—but very few photographers can make their prints not only reproductions of the people taken, but a comment upon them—or more, a comment upon their lives—or more still, a comment upon the social order that creates their lives.

It is the same with objects as with people. A wall can be merely a wall—but in some of Henri Cartier-Bresson's photographs the walls are painfully human, and live and talk about themselves. There is that vulgar wall behind the man in the brass bed; that great lonesome wall of broken paint and plaster along which some child is wandering; there is a huge sun-bright wall of a prison or an apartment house with a boy who is like a shadow at its base. In other photos there are the tumble-down walls of demolished dwellings in Spain where children are playing in a tumble-down world; in others, the worn-bright gestures of prostitutes against doors that are also walls.

There is the clash of sun and shadow, like modern music, in a Cartier-Bresson picture.

In Bravo, the sun is a quiet veil making the shadows like velvet. The shadows are endlessly deep and full, holding more—and more there—and more. Whereas the sun in a Bravo photo almost always has a sense of humor, one cannot be sure about the shadows.

In a cheap little restaurant where the stools are chained to the counter—the whole open to the street—Bravo's camera shows the stools in the sunshine and a row of Charlie Chaplin feet belonging to the ragged customers dining there. The iron curtain is partly down, and the heads of the customers are in shadow—so one can laugh about the feet!

That is what I mean concerning Bravo.

He photographs the doorway of a casket shop with the adult coffins inside in the shadows. Outside on display in the sun is a child's coffin for such a little death.

He photographs shop windows on fashionable streets, catching through the glass the fine things exhibited therein, and further back things less clear, and behind them all the interior of the shop too deep in shadow for one to see if life is equally fine there.

In one of the most beautiful of Bravo's prints, out of the shadows of a canvas covering dash four motionless wooden horses—part of a merry-go-round—to break your heart.

Manuel Alvarez Bravo, Mexican, and Henri Cartier-Bresson of Paris have succeeded in making pictures that are more than pictures—even when they are less.

"Just Traveling," LHP 600 (May 1941)

I like to travel.[64] Just travel. The urge first came upon me at the age of four. I left home in a play-wagon, my own. But I did not leave alone. I took a neighbor's child with me. Once past the corner and across the forbidden street, we went on, then on, myself pulling the wagon. We traveled a good mile from home and up a hill where K. U. (Kansas State University) gazed down upon miles of wheat fields surrounding Lawrence.[65] From our hill we looked upon the wide world, and longed to go further. But, unfortunately, before we could descend the hill on the other side where the real country began, my grandmother hove in sight with a switch in her hand. She discovered our path and came prepared to teach us a lesson—namely, to stay at home. I never learned that lesson very well.

The wanderlust came from my mother, I guess. She liked to travel, too. Or maybe it came from my father. He also liked to travel. Both parents liked traveling so well that they almost always traveled in opposite directions. As a small child I knew what it was to go back and forth across the country, from New York to the Rockies, from Mexico City to Cleveland. When my mother left Mexico she said she was never going back. Too many earthquakes. And shortly came the revolutions, one after another. Several years later, my father took me right down into a revolution—and ever since I've been revolutionary.

When my father and mother were divorced, I was much too big to ride on a half-fare ticket (let alone free) so they went their various ways without me, leaving me at school to learn about the world from maps. I never liked such printed knowledge. After high school in Cleveland, my father again called me to Mexico, where he had taken up permanent residence. His object in sending for me this time was to divine, at close range, whether I had sense enough to go to college or not. He finally decided to send me to Columbia. I set out by boat from Vera Cruz to New York. The anticipated thrill of college was as nothing to the reality of seeing for the first time the towers of Manhattan rising out of the sea. If you've never seen New York, any of you inland travelers, it's worth your while to go hundreds of miles out of your way via Boston, Norfolk or New Orleans (even Vera Cruz) and there take a boat and wait on deck for those magic towers to rise white and shining from the water. Such a view of the tallest city in the world is the greatest sight of modern times.

At Columbia there were too many maps and too many books. I quit and went to sea. That trip from Vera Cruz had put a spell on me, Neptune's spell. And I couldn't shake it off. I wanted to travel by water, to see waves, not logarithms. I didn't do so well in college, so I got a job on a boat. But I was too excited to ask for its destination before I left the shipping office. Once aboard, to my amazement I discovered that it wasn't going anywhere. It belonged to the United States Shipping Board, and was consigned to a large fleet of boats left over from the war to be tied up all winter, and maybe forever, at Jones Point on the Hudson. A skeleton crew was employed to keep the engines oiled that they wouldn't rust to pieces. So for several months I was just "anchored in the stream."

But the following spring, I came back to New York looking for a real trip. I found one—to Africa. Six months. And then to Europe. And ever since, I have been traveling. Sometimes working my way, sometimes paying—but always going. The typewriter, on which I am now hammering forth this article, has journeyed with me hundreds of thousands of miles—not only back and forth across America, but from Leningrad to Soviet Turkestan, Quebec to the West Indies, Helsinfors to China, Japan, and around the world.

The nice thing about my typewriter is that it's always ready to go. It never says, "Stay home," as friends (and relatives) are often in the habit of advising. The result it that we usually travel alone—me and my portable.

Sometimes I feel alone, too, and lonely. But not often. The time that I felt most alone, I guess, was when I first went to Paris. I had quit my ship in Rotterdam because the chef wouldn't give me a piece of chicken one Sunday. All the officers were eating chicken. And I, the cabin boy, was only permitted to gaze upon the empty platters. There was chicken left in the oven, but the chef said it wasn't intended for the members of the crew. We could eat stew. So I quit and went to Paris.

It was in the middle of the winter. The Dutch canals were frozen, the streets of Rotterdam covered with snow. I had only twenty-five dollars. A French visa cost ten. My fare took most of the rest. I got to the Gare du Nord in Paris one February morning with $7.00 and a single bag containing all I owned in the world. The French I heard around me sounded nothing like the French we spoke in high school. Strange, too strange! And here am I, a stranger!

I didn't know a soul in all of Europe. But I wanted to see the Champs-Elysées and the Folies Bergères, so I checked my bag and started out. I boarded a bus that went to the Opera. I emerged across the street from the Café de la Paix! Heart stand still! I looked around—and there were the famous Boulevards running every which away. Dog bite my soul! Who says dreams never come true? I went down a street—and there was the Place de la Concorde—and the Seine just beyond! To my right, as far as eyes could see, stretched the tree-bordered Champs-Elysées! Oh, memories of Maupassant! I hadn't had any breakfast. I felt dizzy, so I went and leaned on the bridge and looked down at the soft white snowdrops melting in the Seine.

How *do* dreams come true? I don't know. You make them come true, if you want to bad enough. I always wanted to see Paris.

Wondering where I was going to sleep that night, I looked around for someone I could talk to, in a language we both understood. In a doorway, clad in a bright blue uniform, I saw a Negro. A real American Negro! He advised me to go to Montmartre! (And the word fell right out of *La Vie de Boheme*!)[66]

The Negroes of Montmartre were almost all musicians and dancers—people of the theatre and the night-clubs. As I climbed that hill (more famous than K. U. in Kansas) it was late afternoon. Most of the people were just getting out of bed and having their breakfasts. Some of them drank cognac for breakfast—and then had coffee and croissants. I sat down in a little cafe and drank coffee.

I said, "I've just come to Paris and I'm looking for a job."

They said, "What instrument do you play?"

I said, "None."

They said, "You're a tap dancer then?"

I said, "No, I just want a job—any job."

They said, "Boy, you'd better go back home."

I said, "I can't—with only seven dollars."

They laughed, thinking I was fooling, and went on drinking their cognac and coffee. The snow kept falling. Night came. I didn't have any place to go. That's when I felt lonely.

But that was, by no means, the last time I've had no place to go. Then and there, I learned that if one *just must* travel, one must learn to look out for one's self, and not depend on others. (I mean, if you are a *poor* person—and just must travel.) So I stopped asking people anything and went and got myself a room in a tourist hotel. It cost me $1.00 a night. I knew it was too much, but I said, I'll sleep here first and then tomorrow I'll find a room in France, outside the night-life section, away from the places tourists go to. And that is what I did. I got a room for 35 francs a week in rue Nollet (less than two dollars) where I lived seven months, and had a swell time, except that in Paris it rains too often.

I worked as a dishwasher in a night club, the Grand Duc, where the then well-known entertainer, Florence, sang. When she quit to open her famous Ches Florence, Bricktop was called from New York to take her place.[67] Bricktop was unknown then. Somebody had stolen her pocketbook on the pier at Havre, so she arrived in Paris broke. Today she is probably the most famous night-club hostess on the continent. But the night she got there, traveling alone, she cried and cried. She came out in the kitchen of the club and cried because there were no customers and the jazz band was silent, there being nobody to dance.

By summer, I'd saved enough to go third class to Italy. I wanted to see Venice—so I went. I saw Milan, too (but I had no card to drop in Juliette's tomb), and Verona.[68] On the way back to France in September, I went to sleep in a crowded coach and somebody stole my passport, my pocket book, and everything out of my pocket. I had to get off the train at Genoa with no means of going further. Thus I missed seeing Nice and Monte Carlo.

In Genoa I got hungrier and hungrier. I lived in a municipal flophouse, where you could stay ten nights for nothing in a bed, ten more nights for nothing on the floor—then you had to get out. Or go to jail. I never reached the jail. I got one or two jobs painting boats in the harbor when sailors wanted a day off to get drunk—or sober up. I didn't know how to use a stage to pull myself up and down, so I usually just sat swinging over the side of the vessel all day in one place, painting the same five feet over and over again. But I earned enough to pay for a nightly corner to sleep in and a daily bowl of *pasta* with red wine. The Italians were swell, but I didn't like the ones who wore black shirts, and beat people's heads. Neither did most of the Italians.

I worked my way back to New York as a sailor without pay, but I still had a quarter left when I reached my native shore. I'd had (as you know) $7.00 when I got to the Gare du Nord in Paris, months before. Twenty-five cents still remained when I reached Manhattan again as a work-away. A winter in Paris and a summer in Italy on $6.75! I bought two hot-dogs with my last quarter and took the subway to Harlem.

Don't let anybody tell you it's expensive to travel. It isn't—if you just like traveling. And traveling is my dish. Yeah, bo!

"The Paris of the Tourists," LHP 842 (ca. 1937?)

In so many ways and to so many people Paris is a paradise, a dream-city, a travel goal, and an ultimate achievement, but most of all for tourists it is an ideal town.[69] The phrase "a tourist paradise" is, of all cities, most applied to Paris. Why?

Is it because Paris is to the scholar one great depository of wisdom with its Sorbonne, its Trocadero, its libraries and its world-renowned teachers? Is it because to the artist it is one vast treasure-trove: the Louvre, the Tuilleries, the Luxembourg, the famous art schools? Or to the gourmet simply one excellent restaurant after another? Or to women, the center of fashion and the rue de la Paix? Maybe all these things put together, but I think there are other reasons, too, why every summer thousands and thousands of tourists from all over the world come to Paris.

One reason, and by no means a minor one, is that in Paris are to be found the most delightful sidewalk cafes in the entire universe. And the sidewalk cafe provides about the most pleasant way of doing nothing to be found anywhere. When you stop to think, you Frenchmen, that in many parts of the world there are no sidewalk cafes whatsoever, then perhaps you can realize what France has that many tourists miss at home. For a few francs a good drink, a long rest, and a sight of the world going by. The French world, the foreign world, the shoppers, the soldiers, the diplomats, the adventuresses—all those mixed and wonderful unknown people who fill the streets of Paris. And if one sits long enough, one is almost sure to see some near neighbor or friend from one's own home town stroll past, let us say from Kansas City, Kansas. Some one whom you knew in high school and haven't seen for years. Paris is like that, a meeting place for all travellers.

In Paris there are so many exciting things to see with the eyes. The Grand Boulevards are a show in themselves with their trees, their neon lights, and the crowds. Then there is the justly famous Champs-Elysées, a street and a park combined such as few cities have. And especially for Americans accustomed to only perfectly straight avenues with right-angle corners, the slanting, curving, and crooked streets of Montmartre and the Quartier Latin have an unending charm. When you come from Detroit where everything is new, the oldness of the Paris buildings, quads, bridges, and fountains, the lovely Ile de la Cité, do something to you, awaken romance, nostalgia, and human love for all the dead but living builders of the past.

Then there are the Paris people of today, too, of never ending interest to visitors from abroad. The chic and lovely women of the Grand Boulevards, the working women of the voluminous skirts behind market stalls, the old women who pass sometimes in the caps of their native villages, the boys and girls riding tandems, the delivery boys with the bicycle-carts almost never seen in America, the amazing variety of uniforms the French military men wear! All those things fill the eyes of the tourists with sights to remember. Sometimes they never get over a Spahi passing in his cape. Or a Légionnaire going by just as if he'd stepped out of the films of one's youth.

And then when a tourist has passed a day of active sight-seeing, or passive looking-on from the terasse of a cafe, in the evening with no trouble at all he can repair to a dinner such as he often never finds at home, especially in a restaurant. France must be very proud of its cooks, even the ones in the littlest and most modest of restaurants. Foreign visitors continually comment on the tastiness of the food to be found at reasonable prices in Paris. And those who are wealthy, well, if they can they often take French chefs back to the lands of their origin with them!

And I guess French pastry-makers must be artists as well as bakers, because the windows full of éclairs, tarts, and cakes, are sometimes worthy of permanent exhibition in a state museum! To a new-comer to Paris, there seem to be so many different kinds of pastries that a course at the Elycée Française or the Berlitz School seems in order just to learn their various names.

Then when the day's eating is done, Paris at night begins. The theatre, the cinema, the cafe-concert, all have their attractions to offer. And here opinion varies greatly among the travellers. To many, the drama is taken as a duty. The Comédie-Française and the Odéon are world-famous, and so one goes as a necessary part of one's travel-education, even if not a word is understood. The Opera is different. Music is music everywhere, so you can shut your eyes and listen, and when the ballet comes on, sit up and look. At the Opéra Comique, usually, one both looks and listens. Or if it's the Folies Bergère, you look all the time, of course! These are the five theatres the tourist almost always wants to visit. Some like them, some don't. Some make no comment.

But the cinema is never taken as a duty, or as part of a planned itinerary. It's something for fun. And here's where many travellers start using the word American, even when they're not American themselves. Is the picture American? The French pictures are too slow. Well, maybe it's because we don't understand the dialogue. Aren't there any cowboys, or Tarzans, or gangsters, or Eddie Cantors in France? Something like that their comment goes. And if they are from the United States, they always object to tipping in a theatre. They don't like fumbling in the dark trying to find (and figure out the correct 10%) change for the usher.

But once back on a cafe terrace, little things like that are forgotten. The Dome and the Rontonde will be remembered long after the movies are forgotten. And if the night is still young (or the tourists, at any rate, young themselves in body or spirit) the cabarets will see them dancing and listening to entertainers into the wee hours of the morning. Paris night life is as well-managed and as amusing as any night life anywhere in the world. Better than most places from the standpoint both of safety and of entertainment. Although the prices are high (as always every place on earth after midnight in such places) the champagne is good, and with [it] comes anything from a lovely Parisienne walking beautifully to string music to a Russian Cossack dancing like a dervish with knives in his mouth and yelling like a cowboy at the same time.

That's the charm of Paris: so many different things to see, so much to do. And now of late, to the great delight of the Americans especially, the new MILK BARS, with ham and eggs for breakfast—on the sidewalk, if you wish. Quite a pleasant combination of France and Kansas City!

"Negroes and Pushkin," LHP 776 (January 14, 1937)

To the Negroes of America the name Alexander Pushkin is a proud name and we have long claimed him as our own, because in America the least amount of Negro blood causes one to be classed with the poorest and most oppressed group in the western world—and in our oppression we have need of names to be proud of.[70] Under the heading, "The Negro As Poet," the *Negro Year Book* contains a biography of Pushkin along with those of Juan Latino, Antar, and the two Dumas—*père* and *fils*.[71] Often in Negro schools Pushkin's name is mentioned with that of Shakespeare, Goethe, and Cervantes as an example of what literary greatness can be, and of how far the blood of Africa has gone.

Unfortunately, the work of Pushkin is known scarcely at all to Americans, although his name is like a legend. One of the great values of the present world centenary is that it has already encouraged the further translation and publication of Pushkin's writings in English in America. In line with the centenary, the celebrated Gilpin Players of Cleveland, the finest Negro Little Theatre group in the country, are planning a special presentation of one of Pushkin's plays.[72] Various Negro schools and colleges will also observe the centenary with fitting programs. So out of the past the greatest of Russian writers whose warmth, humanity, and beauty ignore time and space, today stretches forth his hand to his black brothers in the land of Scottsboro.

A few years ago, during my sojourn in the Soviet Union, I was privileged to translate from the Russian a short poem by Julian Annisimov called "Kinship" which reads as follows:

> The blood of Pushkin
> Unites the Russian and the Negro
> In art.
>
> Tomorrow
> We will be united anew
> Through the International.

Pushkin belongs to the world. May the world soon belong to the people.

"The Alliance of Antifascist Intellectuals, Madrid," radio speech, LHP 20 (Madrid, September 1937)

One of the liveliest artistic and intellectual centers in the world at the moment is, without doubt, the house of the Alianza de Intelectuales Antifascistas in Madrid.[73] In English, the Alliance of Antifascist Intellectuals. It is a large house, in fact a palace, belonging to a former gentleman of title who fled from Spain to devote his riches and his aid to the cause of those who are trying to overturn the government and force the people back into feudalism again. The Marquis, for that was his title, took with him all the gold he could carry, but he left his palace, his Sorollas and El Greco,[74] his hand-carved furniture, and his enormous library behind him. Now his mansion has been taken over by the State. And the State has given it into the care of the artists and writers as the headquarters and meeting place of all these men and women in Madrid who are devoting their pens, paint brushes, and talents to the Spanish Republic and its welfare.

The Alianza de Intelectuales Antifascistas itself, as an organization, is an outgrowth of the First International Writers Congress held in Paris in 1935. But, in Spain, it has been enlarged to include not only writers, but painters, sculptors, composers, and all others who, through the arts, are contributing to a better and more beautiful world. It now has centers, or affiliates, in Valencia, Barcelona, and Alicante. When the Fascist rebellion broke out,[75] the Alianza immediately aligned itself with the government, and began to devote all its resources to the preservation of the Republic—for who could know better than artists and writers what happens to creative efforts under a Fascist regime? Many of the members of the Alianza had experienced censorship and suppression of thought under the monarchy, and the dictatorship of the late Primo de Rivera.[76] And all of them know what happens to books and theatres and science in Italy and Germany. They do not want that to happen here now. That is why, last November when Franco and his Italians and Moors were at the gates of Madrid, many writers and artists and musicians died on the barricades defending their city against the burners of books and the assassins of culture. At present, many members of the Alianza are at the front, some as soldiers, some as teachers in the campaign against illiteracy, others as editors of brigade newspapers or as makers of posters, some reading their poems to the troops, others playing their music in the trenches.

Here in Madrid, the house is a hive of intense and varied intellectual activities. Its president is José Bergamín, the Catholic writer. Its Executive Secretary is the poet, Rafael Alberti. (Alberti and his wife, María Teresa León, writer of short stories, are known in New York and in Latin America, having lectured there a few years ago.) In and out of this Madrid house, formerly a palace for the idle rich, now pour the best of the Spanish writers and artists and thinkers, as well as the visiting foreigners resident in Spain or here gathering material for articles and books: famous foreigners like Ernest Hemingway, like André Malraux, like Ludwig Renn, Egon Erwin Kisch, Jef Last, and Michael Kolsov. Sometimes these writers, Spanish or foreign, leave the house to continue their work as fighters or thinkers or artists at the front and they do not come back again. Pablo de la Torriente, the Cuban, went away a few months ago, never to return. He was killed on the front at Majada Honda. One of Spain's great sculptors, Francisco Pérez Mateo, died in the defense of Madrid. The poet, Federico García Lorca, was executed in rebel territory at Granada. And in the recent battle of Brunete, that excellent woman photographer, Gerda Taro, was killed by a tank at the front while making pictures of the soldiers of the People's Army for the papers and magazines she represented in Paris. You see, the artists and writers who frequent the Alianza in Madrid are not of the ivory tower school. In fact, there couldn't possibly be an ivory tower in Madrid. The Fascist cannons would blast it to pieces.[77]

In time of war, what can writers and artists do that is useful, entertaining, and beautiful in a living, vital way? Here are some of the things the Alianza did—and does. At the beginning of the War, members of the Alianza went into the trenches and the villages near the front explaining to the fighters the basic meaning of this Civil War and why a group of industrialists and military men has chosen to rise against the majority of the voters of Spain. They made posters, they gave speeches, they read poems, they worked with and under the direction of the Ministry of Public Instruction. From Paris, the French writers sent them as a present to Spain, a school on wheels, a truck equipped with a motion picture machine and a printing press, brought to Spain by a committee headed by Louis Aragon, famous poet and novelist.[78] Last August, a year ago, the Alianza founded its paper, *El Mono Azul* (Overalls), and began to publish stories, poems, and chronicles of the war. When the People's Army was formed, members of the Alianza helped to establish, and several of them still edit, the brigade newspapers that are such an important part of the cultural work carried on among the men in camp and at the front. The Alianza now has its own publishing activities, too, and has edited and printed a number of books, including a concise historical record of the first year of the war called *The General Chronicle of the Civil War,* and also that valuable anthology, *Poets in Loyalist Spain.* There are now in preparation two volumes of short stories about the war, one to include the work of Spanish writers, the other the work of foreign writers familiar with democratic Spain such as Gustav Regler,[79] André Malraux, and Kisch. In Valencia, a new and beautiful magazine, *Hora de España,* has many Alianza members on its editorial board.

In the field of the theatre, the Alianza has been most active, too. Its members established the first serious dramatic theatre of the war, presenting plays by Ramón Sender and Rafael Dieste. And now in Madrid, María Teresa León, the first woman in Spain to direct a playhouse, has in rehearsal Schnitzler's *Green Cockatoo* and a hitherto unproduced play by García Lorca, as her first bill. At the front, one of the most popular entertainments with the soldiers has been the satirical puppet show, *La Tarumba,* directed by Miguel Prieto with the assistance of several other members of the Alianza, and picturing by means of gesturing dolls the fantastic boastings and struttings of those grandiose generals on the rebel side, from Franco on down.[80]

But, from every standpoint, one of the most important achievements of the Alianza in recent months has been the bringing to Spain in July the Second International Writers Congress which held sessions in Madrid, Valencia, and Barcelona, all cities within the range of either Franco's shell fire or the bombs of Fascist aviation. This Congress, certainly of great historic importance, brought together more than a hundred men and women of letters from all over the world, of all races and colors, meeting in the very front line trenches for the defense of world culture and the preservation of the integrity of the arts against Fascist aggression. These men and woman, many of them of international fame, are of those who do not wish to write books to be burned in public squares by international gangsters, or blown to bits on library shelves by bombs dropped from the air, or censored until all their meaning is drained away. And so they came together in Spain, famous and busy writers, to show their solidarity with, and their faith in, the Spanish workers and intellectuals who are now battling against those forces that would kill all culture and send the human race back to the dark ages.

The Alliance of Anti-Fascist Intellectuals is Madrid's center for such men and women. It is a center for every writer and artist who opposes the return to barbarism. It is a center for today's work and tomorrow's dream. It is a place where creative miracles continually happen. It is a place where now, today, art becomes life and life is art, and there is no longer any need of a bridge between the artists and the people—for the thing created becomes immediately a part of those for whom, from whom, it was created. The poem, the picture, the song is only water drawn from the well of the people and given back to them in a cup of beauty so that they may drink—and in drinking, understand themselves.

That is art in Loyalist Spain. And that is the function of Madrid's Alianza, the Alianza de Intelectuales Antifascistas.

"Enrique Lister: An Immigrant Comes Home," LHP (Madrid, September 1937)

When the Civil War in Spain broke out, only four regiments of the regular army remained loyal to the government. All the rest of the troops went over to the side of the Fascist rebels. The result was that the Spanish people had to create their own army, and develop their own military leaders. From squads of workers, many of them without guns, who went out from Madrid in taxicabs to stave off the enemy advance, from such non-military elements, in fourteen months the government has built up a well-organized and disciplined People's Army. And from the people themselves have come leaders to guide and direct this army. El Campesino, Modesto, Lister, Duran, are all important commanders. And none of them were military men a year and a half ago. Duran was a musician writing ballet-scores for the dancer, Argentina. Modesto was a carpenter. El Campesino worked among the peasants. And Enrique Lister, of whom I write, used to be a grocery boy and a stone-cutter in Cuba.

No, Lister is not a Cuban, but he is one of the thousands of Spaniards who immigrated to the Americas looking for a pot of gold at the foot of a foreign rainbow. Like thousands of these thousands, Lister did not find gold. In Cuba he found only hard work, low pay, and dreams that didn't come true. Like the Spanish immigrants in New York, or in the steel mills of Gary and Youngstown, Lister discovered in Havana that the main use which America has for foreigners is to make of them a reserve of cheap labor to do the hardest and dirtiest work for the lowest pay. So, very early in life, Lister learned the difference between those who have nothing and must work for a living, and those who have money and property and can afford to hire others.

Lister went to Cuba as a child of twelve with his father and his brothers. He was put to work as a grocery boy in a Havana store. He worked fourteen hours a day, wrapping packages, cleaning up, delivering orders. He did not know how to read and write. When he was fifteen years old he decided to learn. He went to night classes at the Galician Center. For two hours every night, after his long day's work, he studied spelling and grammar, and struggled to form letters in a copy book.

Being a strong boy, he decided to take up the trade of his father and become a stone-cutter. There was a great deal of building going on in Havana in the 1920's. Lister worked on various constructions then underway. But the stone-cutters had no union. They needed one, so Lister took part in the issuing of the first call to form a stone-cutter's union in Cuba, and he became one of the charter members. This was in 1925 when he was eighteen years old. The following year, already experienced in union organization, he went back to Spain, to his native Galicia. Here he was immediately arrested as a dangerous character with advanced ideas. For the next three or four years, he was continually in and out of prison—and always in great disfavor with the officers of the Spanish monarchy, who had no desire to see Spanish workers organized into effective unions.

When the Republic was declared in 1931, and Lister was released from a thirteen month's prison term, he was elected President of one of the most important trade unions of Coruna. Shortly after he took office, there was a strike in which fighting broke out and, in the struggle, a reactionary worker was killed. As President of the union, Lister was again arrested, and sentenced to thirty years in prison. He escaped and went abroad. But he could not keep out of the struggle and ferment for democracy that was then sweeping through all Spain, so he returned to live illegally from town to town in his own country. When the People's Front came to power in February, 1936, he was in Madrid. And when in July the generals and big industrialists rose up against this people's government and ordered their soldiers to fire from the Montana Barracks on the citizens of Madrid, Lister was in the crowd that stormed those barracks and took them over for the government. A few days later he was in the Guadarrama Mountains fighting against the Fascist foes. But not only fighting. Lister realized at once Spain's need for disciplined forces, and he began immediately to help organize what was to become the new army of the republic.

From untrained men to disciplined soldiers. From workers, many of whom never handled a gun before, to the army which now efficiently defends all loyalist Spain. That is an achievement in which Lister has played a great part. He himself rose rapidly in the ranks of the army. In the early days of the war, he was made a lieutenant. And with the formation of the now famous Fifth Regiment (really the first regiment of the new loyalist army) Lister was raised to captain and given two companies of shock troops to direct. In his first skirmish with the enemy, he took seven prisoners and two machine guns. Shortly thereafter, he was made a Commander. And in the early autumn of last year, the Fifth Regiment elected him Commander-in-Chief. Then the government ordered him to organize the first brigade of the People's Army, a job which meant making soldiers of men with no previous experience in warfare. The glorious history of this brigade and the way it took part in the defense of Madrid during the dark days of November, 1936, is now one of the flaming epics of the Spanish Republic. The Fascists did not pass! Madrid held its own. Now its citizens feel that their city will never be taken.

During the last year, Lister and his men have passed over half the war-map of Spain: Jarama, Guadalajara, Garabitas, Toledo, Valdemoros, Brunete, Aragon. And Lister's name itself has become a symbol of bravery and leadership in Spain.

When I interviewed him, he was in Valencia on his way from one front to another. He is a young man, only thirty. Heavy-set. Strong determined face. A quick mind. A great memory for dates and places. It was after ten o'clock at night when Lister and his aides came into the building where I had been waiting to interview him.

"Too late," I thought. "I'll merely make an appointment for another time."

But when I asked him when I might have an interview, Lister's reply was, "Now!"

No hesitation, no postponement. And as he talked, there was no boasting, no pompousness. Quite simply, he told me the story of his life, and of the dramatic incidents of the war months. He spoke of four brothers killed by the fascists in the North, and of the bewilderment of his father at a world in which sons grew up only to be killed.

"We must end this war quickly," Lister said. "I do not doubt that the victory is ours. We have a million men in reserve. The enemy lacks men. But what we must do now is organize *all* our forces, military and industrial, so as to end this war soon."

He spoke like a man who does not relish warfare and killing, but who is a lover of work and life. Someday, he says he would like to go back to Cuba. He remembers that it was there that he learned to read and write, having been denied schooling as a child in Spain. But he remembers, too, that in Cuba he worked fourteen hours a day—and his employers were Spaniards like himself, not Cubans. What he learned from that is that one's own people will exploit you just as much as foreigners will—that it's not racial differences that count, but class differences! So in Cuba, Lister joined his first union, and took his first steps toward the defense of the rights of the common working people. Today, in Spain, he is one of the great commanders of the People's Army. Enrique Lister—the immigrant boy who came home bringing not a pot of gold from the foot of a foreign rainbow, but instead a mind and a heart full of the strength which working people pour into the channels of unionization and into organized action for the creation of a democracy where Fascism cannot exist. Lister is helping Spain maintain and strengthen such a democracy.

"Negroes in Spain," *Volunteer for Liberty* 1.14 (September 1937): 4

In July, on the boat with me coming from New York, there was a Negro from the far West on his way to Spain as a member of the 9th Ambulance Corps of the American Medical Bureau. He was one of a dozen in his unit of American doctors, nurses, and ambulance drivers offering their services to Spanish democracy.

When I reached Barcelona a few weeks later, in time for my first air-raid and the sound of bombs falling on a big city, one of the first people I met was a young Porto Rican of color acting as interpreter for the Loyalist troops.

A few days later in Valencia, I came across two intelligent young colored men from the West Indies, aviators, who had come to give their services to the fight against Fascism.

All Fight Fascism

And now, in Madrid, Spain's besieged capital, I've met wide-awake Negroes from various parts of the world—New York, our Middle West, the French West Indies, Cuba, Africa—some stationed here, others on leave from their battalions—all of them here because they know that if Fascism creeps across Spain, across Europe, and then across the world, there will be no place left for intelligent young Negroes at all. In fact, no decent place for any Negroes—because Fascism preaches the creed of Nordic supremacy and a world for whites alone.

In Spain, there is no color prejudice. Here in Madrid, heroic and bravest of cities, Madrid where the shells of Franco plow through the roof-tops at night, Madrid where you can take a street car to the trenches, this Madrid to whose defense lovers of freedom and democracy all over the world have sent food and money and men—here to this Madrid have come Negroes from all the world to offer their help.

"Deluded Moors"

On the opposite side of the trenches with Franco, in the company of the professional soldiers of Germany, and the illiterate troops of Italy, are the deluded and driven Moors of North Africa. An oppressed colonial people of color being used by Fascism to make a colony of Spain. And they are being used ruthlessly, without pity. Young boys, men from the desert, old men, and even women, compose the Moorish hordes brought by the reactionaries from Africa to Europe in their attempt to crush the Spanish people.

I did not know about the Moorish women until, a few days ago I went to visit a prison hospital here in Madrid filled with wounded prisoners. There were German aviators that bombarded the peaceful village of Colmenar Viejo and machine-gunned helpless women as they fled along the road. One of these aviators spoke English. I asked him why he fired on women and children. He said he was a professional soldier who did what he was told. In another ward, there were Italians who joined the invasion of Spain because they had no jobs at home.

What They Said

But of all the prisoners, I was most interested in the Moors, who are my own color. Some of them, convalescent, in their white wrappings and their bandages, moved silently like dark shadows down the hall. Others lay quietly suffering in their beds. It was difficult to carry on any sort of conversation with them because they spoke little or no Spanish. But finally, we came across a small boy who had been wounded at the battle of Brunete—he looked to be a child of ten or eleven, a bright smiling child who spoke some Spanish.

"Where did you come from?" I said.

He named a town I could not understand in Morocco.

"And how old are you?"

"Thirteen," he said.

"And how did you happen to be fighting in Spain?"

Bring Moorish Women

Then I learned from this child that Franco had brought Moorish women into Spain as well as men—women to wash and cook for the troops.

"What happened to your mother?" I said.

The child closed his eyes. "She was killed at Brunete," he answered slowly.

Thus the Moors die in Spain, men, women, and children, victims of Fascism, fighting not for freedom—but against freedom—under a banner that holds only terror and segregation for all the darker peoples of the earth.

A great many Negroes know better. Someday the Moors will know better, too. All the Francos in the world cannot blow out the light of human freedom.

"Hughes Bombed in Spain,"
Afro-American, October 23, 1937

I came down from Paris by train.[81] We reached Barcelona at night. The day before there had been a terrific air raid in the city, killing almost a hundred persons in their houses and wounding a great many more. We read about it in the papers at the border: AIR RAID OVER BARCELONA.

"Last night!" I thought, "Well, tonight I'll be there."

There's a tunnel between France and Spain, a long stretch of darkness through which the trains pass. Then you come out into the sunlight again directly into the village of Port Bou on the Spanish side of the mountain, with a shining blue bay below where children are swimming.

But as you leave the train, you notice that the windows of the station are almost all broken. Several nearby houses are in ruins, gutted by bombs. And in the winding streets of the village there are signs, REFUGIO, pointing to holes in the mountains in case of air-raids. That is wartime Spain. A little town by the blue Mediterranean where travellers change trains.

In the country they were harvesting the wheat land; as we rode southward, we saw men and women working with their scythes in the fields. The Barcelona train was very crowded. I was travelling with Nicolás Guillén, the colored poet from Havana, and a Mexican writer and his wife.

They kept up a rapid fire of Spanish in various accents all around me. Guillén and I were the only colored on the train, so I thought, until at one of the stations when we got out to buy fruit, we noticed a dark face leaning from the window of the coach ahead of us. When the train started again, we went forward to investigate.

He was a young brown-skin boy from the Canary Islands. He wore a red shirt and blue beret. He had escaped from the fascists who now control his island by the simple expedient of getting into his fishing boat with the rest of her crew and sailing toward Africa.

The Canary Islands belong to Spain, but the fishermen do not like the fascists who have usurped power there, and so many of them sail their boats away and come to fight on the mainland with the Spanish government. This young man had come to fight.

He spoke a strange Spanish dialect which was hard for us to understand, but he made it clear to us that he did not like fascism with its crushing of the labor unions and the rights of working people like himself. He told us that a great many folks who live in the Canary Islands are colored, mixed with African and Spanish blood.

It was almost midnight when we got to Barcelona. There were no lights in the town, and we came out of the station into pitch darkness. A bus took us to the hotel. It was a large hotel several stories high which, before the Civil War, had been a fashionable stopping place for tourists.

We had rooms on an upper floor. The desk clerk said that in case of air-raids we might come down into the lobby, but that a few floors more or less wouldn't make much difference. The raids were announced by a siren, but guests would be warned by telephone as well. That night there was no bombing, so we slept in peace.

The next day Guillén and I were sitting in a sidewalk cafe on the tree-lined boulevard called Las Ramblas, when a dark young colored man came by.

He looked at us, then turned and spoke. He recognized me, he said, because he had heard me speak in New York. He was a Puerto Rican who had come from Harlem to serve as interpreter in Spain. His name was Roldan. He invited us to go with him to the Mella Club where Cubans and West Indians gather in Barcelona.

The Mella Club, named after Julio Antonio Mella, famous Cuban student leader assassinated in Mexico, occupies the whole second floor of a large building near the center of the town. It has a beautiful courtyard for games and dancing, and a little bar where Cuban drinks are mixed. We were invited to a dance that afternoon given in honor of the soldiers on leave, and here we met a number of Cubans, both colored and white, and a colored Portuguese, all taking an active part in the Spanish struggle against the fascists.

And all of them finding in loyalist Spain more freedom than they had known at home—for most of the West Indian Islands are burdened by colonial or semi-fascistic types of dictatorships such as Batista's in Cuba, and Vincent's in Haiti. And all of them draw the color-line between colored and whites.

In Spain, as one could see at the dance that afternoon, there is no color line, and Catalonian girls and their escorts mingled gaily with the colored guests.

That night, back at the hotel, one knew that it was war-time because, in the luxurious dining room with its tuxedoed waiters, there was only one fixed dinner menu, no choice of food. It was a good dinner of soup, fish, meat, one vegetable, and fruit, but nothing elaborate. Later, as one often does in Europe, we went to a sidewalk cafe for coffee.

Until midnight, we sat at our table watching the crowd strolling up and down the broad Ramblas. The fact that Barcelona was lightless did not seem to keep people home on a warm evening. A few wan bulbs from the interior of the cafes cast a dull glow on the sidewalks, but that was the only visible light, save for the stars shining brightly above.

The buildings were great grey shadows towering in the night, with windows shuttered and curtains drawn. There must be no light on any upper floors to guide enemy aviators.

At midnight, the public radios began to blare forth the war-news, and people gathered in large groups on corners to hear it. Then the cafe closed and we went to the hotel. I had just barely gotten to my room and had begun to undress when the low extended wail of the siren began, letting us know that the fascist planes were coming. (They come from Mallorca across the sea at a terrific speed, drop their bombs, and circle away into the night again.)

Quickly, I put on my shirt, passed Guillén's room, and together we started downstairs. Suddenly all the lights went out in the hotel, but we heard people rushing down the halls and stairways in the dark. A few had flashlights with them to find the way. Some were visibly frightened. In the lobby two candles were burning, casting weird, giantlike shadows on the walls.

In an ever increasing wail the siren sounded louder and louder, droning its deathly warning. Suddenly it stopped. By then the lobby was full of people, men, women, and children, speaking in Spanish, English, and French. In the distance we heard a series of quick explosives.

"Bombs?" I asked.

"No, anti-aircraft gun," a man explained.

Everyone was very quiet. Then we heard the guns go off again.

"Come here," the man called, leading the way. Several of us went out on the balcony where, in the dark, we could see the searchlights playing across the sky. Little round puffs of smoke from the anti-aircraft shells floated against the stars. In the street a few women hurried along to public bomb-proof cellars.

Then for a long while nothing happened. After about an hour, the lights suddenly came on in the hotel again as a signal that the danger had ended. Evidently, the enemy planes had been driven away without having dropped any bombs. Everyone went back upstairs to bed. The night was quiet again. I put out my light, opened the window, and went to sleep.

Being very tired, I slept soundly without dreaming. The next thing I knew, the telephone was ringing violently in the dark, the siren screaming its long blood-curdling cry again, and the walls of the building shaking.

BOOM! Then the dull roar of a dying vibration. And another BOOM! Through my window I saw a flash of light. I didn't stay to look again. Down the hall I went, clothes in my arms, sensing my way toward the staircase in the dark.

This time the air-raid was on for sure. When I got to the lobby, the same people as before were gathered there in various stages of dress and undress. Children crying, women talking hysterically, men very quiet. Nobody went out on the balcony now.

In the street an ambulance passed, its bell ringing into the distance. The anti-aircraft guns kept up their rapid fire. The last BOOM of the enemy bombs was a long way off. The planes, with their cargo of death partially emptied, were driven away. But for a long time nobody left the lobby.

When I went back to bed, dawn was coming in at my open window. Below, in the cool light, the rooftops of Barcelona were grey and lonely. Soon a little breeze blew in from the sea and the red of the rising sun stained the sky. I covered up my head to keep out the light, but I couldn't go to sleep for a long time.

"Hughes Finds Moors Being Used as Pawns by Fascists in Spain," *Afro-American,* October 30, 1937

Down through the Catalonian country-side our car went speeding, through villages as old as the Romans, and out along the Mediterranean, bright and blue as the morning sky. Straight across the Mediterranean, Italy. To the North, France. And here, Spain. The Latin lands, Italy, fascist. France, democratic. Spain torn between fascism and democracy.

Why had I come to Spain? To write for the colored press. I knew that Spain once belonged to the Moors, a colored people ranging from light dark to dark white. Now the Moors have come again to Spain with the fascist armies as cannon fodder for Franco. But, on the loyalist side there are many colored people of various nationalities in the International Brigades. I want to write about both Moors and colored people.

I sat comfortably in the back seat of the car beside that excellent colored writer, Nicolás Guillén, who had come from Cuba, representing *Mediodia,* of which he is the editor. We were headed South to Valencia on the way from Barcelona, the night after an air-raid, driving through fields of wheat and groves of olives and oranges, and cities that recently had been bombed from the air or shelled from the sea. And as the tragic and beautiful landscape went by, I began to think back over the first stages of my trip to Spain.

I came from California and the writing of an opera with Grant Still. I sailed alone on the *Aquitania* from New York, but once on board, I found several people that I knew. Among them, Mary Church Terrell from Washington, who was sailing for London to deliver a speech on "The Progress and Problems of Colored Women" before the International Assembly of the World Fellowship of Faith.[82]

She presented me to Bishop J. A. Hamlett and his wife, of Kansas City, who were going to Oxford to attend the World Conference of the Universal Christian Council where, they said, other colored churchmen in attendance would include Dr. Mays of Howard University, Dr. King of Gammon, Bishop Ransom, and Bishop Kyles.[83]

Washington was indeed well represented on shipboard. Mrs. Lorenzo Turner was London bound to join her husband, Dr. Turner of the English Department at Fisk. Mrs. Marie B. Schanks, engaged in juvenile work for the District of Columbia Police Department, was vacationing in England, France, Holland, and Belgium, with Mrs. Kathryn Cameron Brown, teacher of sciences in Washington, and Mrs. E. T. Fields of Chattanooga. Miss Catherine Grigsby, also of the capital, was bound for a summer course at the University of Paris.

Altogether, a large and representative group of colored people—some sailing for cultural and Christian missions, some for study, some for pleasure.

But, in addition, there were four of us going to Spain: myself as a writer; two young men in third class who did not announce their destination, but whom I later met in Spain—aviators from one of the Caribbean Islands; and finally, C. G. Carter, formerly a student in the School of Medicine at the University of Minnesota.

He was the only colored person among the members of the Ninth Medical Unit of the American Medical Bureau to Aid Spanish Democracy, also sailing on the *Aquitania.* The twelve members of the unit, in their trim uniforms, made an attractive and interesting group.

The American Medical Bureau has sent to Spain more than a hundred doctors and nurses, five hundred beds, great quantities of hospital material, and over thirty ambulances. In their selection of doctors, nurses, and assistants, they have not drawn the color-line, and at least one colored nurse, Salaria Kee of Harlem, has come to Spain under their auspices. And there are several colored ambulance drivers.

So far, I believe, there are no colored doctors in Spain, but the bureau would welcome the participation of colored physicians in their work, so the doctor in charge of the Ninth Unit assured me.

Carter, who hails from Ogden, Utah, attracted a great deal of attention on the boat, dressed in his khaki-colored uniform. The nurses wore long blue capes and blue caps. Carter told me that he found them a fine group of people to travel with and that, although one of the nurses was from the South, she proved to be a splendid and friendly person.

This Ninth American Medical Unit was in the charge of Dr. S. N. Franklin of Milwaukee and was composed, besides Dr. Franklin, of one x-ray man, one dental technician, six graduate nurses, two ambulance drivers, and one mechanic. They had sent ahead of them four ambulances, two trucks, and a large supply of blankets, sheets, surgical instruments, and canned goods, as well as automatic washing-machines, dryers, and other apparatus for the establishment of a modern hospital laundry.

Their unit included two Catholics, as well as members of the Protestant and Jewish faiths. They were going to Spain for humanitarian work in government territory, and seemed to be delighted to have a colored person among them as a co-worker.

When I saw Carter a few weeks later in Spain, he told me that he had learned more in the short time he had been abroad than he had in all the thirty-odd years of his life in the States put together.

"Spain is a fine country," he said. "I hope these people win their war. Mussolini wants to take over Spain just as he did Ethiopia, but the way these people feel, I don't think he's going to do it. Who wants to be a slave to Mussolini?"

As our car sped southward toward Valencia that sunny morning, when I stopped thinking back over my trip to look out the window, I could see quite plainly for myself that the Spanish people didn't want to be enslaved to anyone, native or foreign.

As we passed, peasants in the fields lifted their clenched fists in the government salute. On walls ruined by fascist bombardments, slogans were freshly painted hailing the People's Army. In the villages, young men were drilling to go to the front.

The beautiful landscapes of Spain rolled by as our car went down the road, the Spain that now for more than a year has occupied the headlines on the front pages of the world. The Spain of the huge meetings I had attended at home, with three and four thousand dollar collections given for food and medical supplies, and milk for babies.

The new democratic Spain that I had seen placarded in the main streets of cities like Denver and Salt Lake City when I lectured there. AID REPUBLICAN SPAIN! MILK FOR THE BABIES OF SPANISH DEMOCRACY! The Spain for which Josephine Baker in Paris had danced at a benefit for child refugees; and for which Paul Robeson had sung in London.

A colored band, too, from the Paris Moulin Rouge had played in honor of the Second International Writers Congress just returned to France from Madrid, having in attendance the French African writer, René Maran, the French West Indian poet, Leon Damas, and the Haitian poet, Jacques Roumain, as well as Nicolás Guillén and myself—five colored writers, each from a different part of the world.

Within the last year, colored people from many different countries have sent men, money, and sympathy to Spain in her fight against the forces that have raped Ethiopia, and that clearly hold no good for any poor and defenseless people anywhere. Not only artists and writers with well-known names, the Paul Robesons and René Marans of international fame, but ordinary colored people like those I met in the Cuban club in Barcelona, and like Carter, the ambulance driver, or the nurse from Harlem! These especially are the people I want to write about in Spain.

Naturally, I am interested in the Moors, too, and what I can find out about them. As usually happens with colored troops in the service of white imperialists, the Moors have been put in the front lines of the Franco offensive in Spain—and shot down like flies. They have been brought by the thousands from Spanish Morocco where the fascists took over power in the early days of their uprising.

First, the regular Moorish cavalry and guard units came to Spain, then civilian conscripts forced into the army, or deceived by false promises of loot and high pay. When they got to Spain, as reputable newspaper correspondents have already written, they were often paid off in worthless German marks which they were told would be good to spend when they got back to Africa.

But most of the Moors never live to get back to Africa. Now, in the second year of the war, they are no longer a potent force in Franco's army. Too many of them have been killed!

What I sought to find out in Spain was what effect, if any, this bringing of dark troops to Europe had had on the Spanish people in regard to their racial feelings. Had prejudice and hatred been created in a land that did not know it before? What has been the treatment of Moorish prisoners by the loyalists? Are they segregated and ill-treated? Are there any Moors on the government side?

As I thought of these things, our car began to slow down and I noticed that the traffic had grown heavier on the road. Burros, trucks, and ox-carts mingled in long lines of dust. Fords and oxen, the old and the new! Peasants on mule-back, soldiers in enormous American-made trucks. On either side of us there were orange groves as far as one could see. And in the distance, tall medieval towers mingled with modern structures. We were approaching a city, a big city. "Valencia," the chauffeur said.

Valencia, ancient Mediterranean seaport, and now the seat of the Spanish government. I had been there twelve years ago as a sailor in the days when there was a king on the throne in Spain. Now, the people themselves are in power and democracy prevails—except that the rich, the generals, and the former friends of the king are trying to smash this democracy and have hired Franco to put the country back in chains again.

To help them do this, they called in professional soldiers, Italians, Germans, and Moors, to crush the duly elected government. Only four regiments of the regular army remained with the government, so the government had to form its own army, the People's Army, made up of farmers and working men.

To help this People's Army, and to fight fascism before it makes any further gains in the world, men came to Spain from all over the earth. They formed the International Brigades. In these brigades there are many colored people. To learn about them, I came to Spain.

"'Organ Grinder's Swing' Heard above Gunfire in Spain," *Afro-American,* November 6, 1937

Colored people are not strange to Spain, nor do they attract an undue amount of attention.

In small villages, they may or may not be the center of friendly curiosity for a while, depending on whether or not the villagers have seen a colored face before. But most Spaniards have seen colored faces. In the first place, many Spaniards are quite dark themselves, particularly those from the South, where the sun is hot and Africa not far away. Distinct traces of Moorish blood still remain.

Copper-colored gypsies, too, are common everywhere. In Mexico, I once saw a Spanish bullfighter who was what Harlem would call brownskin. And since I've been in Spain, I've seen plenty of Spanish Spaniards who couldn't possibly pass for white in the States—except that their hair is usually straight.

There seem to be quite a number of colored Portuguese living in Spain. I've met them in both Valencia and Madrid. And in both cities, too, I've seen pure-blooded Africans from the Spanish colonies. Not to mention the Cubans who, especially since the oppressive dictatorships in their homeland, have migrated to the Iberian peninsula.

All the colored people of whatever nationality to whom I've talked in Spain agree that there is not the slightest trace of color-prejudice to be found. In that respect, Spain is even better than France, because in Paris, charming city that it is, some of the big hotels catering to American and English tourists are a bit snooty about receiving dark-skinned guests.

In Valencia I talked to a young medical student from Spanish Guinea. He was a pure African, educated in Spain. I saw him at the beach one Sunday afternoon bathing with a group of Spanish friends, young men and women. Thinking perhaps he was an American or West Indian from one of the International Brigades, I went up to him to inquire.

When he learned that I came from the United States he immediately asked me about Harlem. He said he had heard a great deal about Harlem, and he hoped to go there to visit sometime.

"To stay?" I asked him.

"I don't think I want to stay," he said. "I like Spain, but I want to see Harlem."

He told me that he was a member of the People's Army and because he had been a university student, he was studying for an officership. He said he had not heard from his parents in Africa for more than a year, since the Fascists were in control of the Spanish colonies, and no mail came through any more.

I asked him what he thought about the war and Spain's People's Front government.

He said:

"I really want the government to win the war. They stand for a liberal colonial policy with a chance for the people in Africa to develop and become educated. On the other side with the Fascists are all the old dukes and counts and traders who have exploited the colonies so long for their own benefit, without giving anything back to the people.

"The generals on Franco's side don't even want their own Spanish peasants to escape from serfdom, let alone us in Africa. The same Italians who dropped bombs on Ethiopia have come over here to help Franco bomb the Spaniards!"

"That's right," I said. "I wish I had some paper, I'd interview you for the colored readers in America."

But we were in our bathing suits on the crowded Valencia beach on a Sunday afternoon—which is like Coney Island, and not a very convenient place for an extended conversation. The African student-soldier promised to come to my hotel later in the week for my requested interview, but before the appointed day, I left for Madrid.

Transportation being difficult to find, since there are no trains to the interior, I had to take the first chance opportunity offered me. I would've liked to talk more with the Spanish African boy, and perhaps I can when I return to Valencia.

In Madrid, as I learned shortly after my arrival, one of the most popular of theatrical stars in the city is El Negro Aquilino, now in his third month at the Calderon Theatre, a leading Spanish vaudeville house. Colored jazz bands and performers both from Cuba and the United States have always been very well received in Spain, and colored performers whom I met in Paris told me that in normal times they enjoyed playing in Spain, and that they found the audiences most cordial.

Aquilino, a Cuban, has been here for some time, right through the worst of the war days, and is a great favorite with the soldiers for whom he often performs at the front.

As for jazz in Spain as in all Europe, it is very well liked, and Spanish orchestras do better at playing hot music in the true style than do most bands of other European nations. In normal times, records by Duke Ellington and Cab Calloway sell in large numbers here.

Now, they are exhausted and no new ones are arriving, but they are to be heard frequently by transcription on the air. In fact, during one of the heavy shellings of Madrid a few nights ago, a shell from one of Franco's cannons fell crashing into the street at our corner just as our radio in the dining room began to play Jimmie Lunceford's version of "Organ Grinder's Swing!"[84]

Paul Robeson's British-made picture, *Song of Freedom*, with Nina Mae McKinney,[85] has been playing lately at the neighborhood theatres, and the Madrileños are hoping he will come to loyalist Spain to sing in person. They like him.

As for books, the least representative of the books on colored people seem to be the only ones translated into Spanish—or rather perhaps I should say, the most sensational and exotic. Seabrook's *Magic Island,* Peterkin's *Scarlet Sister Mary,* Paul Morand's bad short stories of stavism. And nothing by colored writers themselves.[86]

Walter White's *Fire in the Flint,* for instance, or James Weldon Johnson's *Along This Way,* would be of greatest interest to Spanish readers just now, struggling as they are with tremendous social problems of their own.[87] However, because of the war, very few books are being published at present in Spain, and the old ones still sold in the shops are typical of the money-making commercialism of former days.

The People's Front government will, no doubt, now that the publishing houses belong to the unions themselves in most cases, improve the selection of foreign books chosen for publication in Spain.

The only representative books on colored people to be found in Madrid now are Blaise Cendrars's African anthology, and an excellent anthology of Spanish-American Negro poetry edited by the Cuban poet, Emilio Ballagas of Havana. It is called *Antologia de Poesía Negra,* and contains the best of the poems written by or about colored people in the Spanish language.

Tap-dancing is quite popular, and whenever colored dancers are seen in the movies, Spanish youngsters try their best to imitate their steps—and do pretty well, too, because the Spanish sense of rhythm is not at all bad.

Among Madrid sports lovers, talk of the last Olympic games and the exploits of Jesse Owens and the other dark stars therein has not yet died down.[88] Their amazing performances in that most Aryan of all lands—Germany—cause the Spaniards to continue to laugh with glee—since Hitler is none too popular here anyway, considering all the bombing planes he has sent to the Spanish Fascists to be used against the working people.

Old-timers still remember Jack Johnson and his exhibition bouts in Madrid years ago.[89] And they say that a colored fighter who once boxed with him is still living here but, so far, I've been unable to locate him. If I do, he's in for an interview and a picture.

But in Spain, the most interesting colored people one meets—at the front or on Madrid's Gran Via—are not prizefighters, or writers, or performers in the theatres.

They're men with uniforms on, khaki-colored uniforms, and the insignia of various regiments. Men from St. Louis, Chicago, Harlem,

Panama City, Havana. Those you never heard of in any book. (But you will, in due time, no doubt.) They're in the International Brigade.

And they're just people from the various corners of the world who've come to help the "just people" of Spain in their fight with the folks with the big names—folks like the Duke of Alba, General Francisco Franco, and Il Duce.[90]

"Madrid Getting Used to Bombs; It's Food Shortage That Hurts," *Afro-American,* November 20, 1937

Today the Fascists are shelling Madrid again. The shells from their big guns exploding as they strike and the sound of crumbling plaster can be heard quite clearly as I write. In fact, "clearly" is not the word. Loud and near would be a better description of their sounds.

The house where I live has only been struck once, and then not by a direct hit. A shell fell one night just across the street, killing two lovers who were standing in a doorway, and the shrapnel broke our windows and nicked the brick of our walls—so that now our house looks as if it had had smallpox.

Today the shells sound as if they might be falling in the midtown region, which means that street cars crowded with people (for it is the afternoon rush hour) may be hit, and dozens killed and wounded.

The street car men of Madrid, by the way, have often been written of as splendid examples of civilian bravery under fire. Their cars continue to run, bombardments or not. There is no way of telling where the shells are going to fall—in the street or on the houses, on the east side of town or on the west side, in the suburbs or in the heart of the city—so why stop the street cars?

Sometimes a car is struck, yes, but if one took to shelter, the shelter might be hit, too. Besides, most Madrileños have become so used to shellings that they seldom alter their plans on account of cannon fire, and if they have some place to go at a time when shells are falling, they start, anyway—although on the road they may have to take sudden refuge in a courtyard, or a subway station.

Mothers in the more dangerous sections of town usually call their children at the sound of the first boom of the cannon. But the children are often more expert than the grown-ups in recognizing the sounds of artillery and from which direction the shells are coming.

"Aw, those are our cannons, ma. The Fascists haven't started firing yet." I heard a small boy yell from the street to his mother in the window one day, as he kept on playing.

Frequently, late at night or rather very early in the morning for three or four o'clock seems to be the favorite hours for Franco, the crash of shells on nearby pavements or roof-tops will cause you to open your eyes, forget all about sleep, and wonder whether the next shell intends to fall in your bedroom. That is, if you haven't been in Madrid very long.

The Madrileños, however, unless the shelling is very heavy, seldom even wake up any more. If the bombardment is a long one, and several guns are dropping missiles of death on the town, then people may get out of bed and seek the basement, particularly if the aim is directed toward one's own neighborhood.

There are certain sections of Madrid, so they say, that are more dangerous than the actual trenches, for they are wide open to artillery fire. Between the Fascist cannons and the aviation, whole districts of Madrid have been quite destroyed, and people can no longer live in them.

The beautiful Arguelles section of modern apartment houses is nothing but a shambles of broken walls and floorless houses. One enormous apartment house, covering a whole city block, and known as the House of Flowers, because in the planning of it each balcony had its window-box or row of potted vines and plants—this formerly lovely dwelling place is empty and desolate, its tenants dead or scattered, great shell holes in its walls, and the huge rents of aviation bombs in its roofs.

In the center of the city, scarcely a store or office building has not, at one time or another during the past year, been hit by either aviation or shell fire. The world-famous Telefónica, American built center of Spain's telephones (and Madrid's main switchboard) has more than a hundred shell holes in the walls of its twelve stories—yet the telephone service continues to function.

The upper floors, however, are no longer in use, as its tower still serves as a target for Franco's gunners. Since Madrid sits on a raised plateau, and the Telefónica is the highest building in Madrid, it can be seen easily from any of the surrounding Fascist positions.

The hotel where the famous American writer Ernest Hemingway lives, has also been the object of frequent shelling. Its lower floor is well-protected by sandbags, but it is impossible to sandbag a whole building. From its upper floors, one can look through shell holes on a bird's-eye view of Madrid and the nearby Fascist territory.

To a stranger arriving in Spain's capital city for the first time, it seems strange and amazing to see people going calmly about their business in the streets, the theatres and cafes open, the street car lines running right up to the barricades and the trenches.

But then when night comes and no street lights are lighted as dusk falls, the visiting stranger begins to realize that he is in a war zone. Then if a battle begins in one of the sectors of the city, he realizes that not only is he in a war zone, but at the very front itself. The crack of rifle fire, the staccato run of the machine-guns, and the boom of trench mortars and hand-grenades can be heard so clearly that one finally realizes the war is only a few blocks away.

But no doubt before the night is over, Fascist artillery will begin to drop shells on the town, and then the visitor to Madrid is not only near the war, but in it. Madrid is a city under fire, itself a front-line trench.

But not only shells and the sound of shells make one know that Madrid is at war. There are other signs. In the hotels there is no choice of food at meals, only one menu. In the streets, one notices long lines in front of certain food stores, particularly those for milk and meat.

Sometimes a restaurant will have no bread, or a cafe no sugar for the coffee. Cigars and cigarettes are impossible to buy. A great deal of the shortage of food in Madrid is due to the fact that there is no train service of any kind into the city.

In spite of the difficulties of living in Madrid at present, and those difficulties are many: war and death at one's door, a monotonous and limited diet, soap and cigarettes impossible to find, no heat in the houses—in spite of all this, the people of Madrid are calm, serene, even gay at times with flashes of the old gaiety for which Madrid was noted among the capitals of Europe before the war.

Every day the streets are crowded with soldiers in from the trenches on leave. Sundays, the town-folks, too, are walking on the Gran Via, or up and down the tree-lined boulevards.

Cafes are lively. Long lines wait in front of the theatres for tickets. Special meetings in honor of some brigade, or to report on some phase of the country's problems, are crowded to the doors. Concerts and exhibits are packed. During a shelling, the streets become less crowded for awhile, but as soon as the big guns stop, people are out again.

To foreigners, the Spaniards are most hospitable and helpful. They often turn and accompany a stranger to his destination, if he stops bewildered to ask the way. Their precious cigarettes, when they have them, they will share on the shortest acquaintance. Generosity seems to be a national characteristic.

One day I stopped at a shoe shop to get a loose sole sewn on. The shoemaker fixed the shoe for me, a ten-minute job, and when I asked him how much it would be, his reply was, "Nothing! That's all right! Nothing."

Another day, I passed a family eating long slices of Persian melon in their doorway. They had seen me pass before and knew that I was a stranger. This time, the old grandmother called me and held out a slice of melon. "We're poor, but we have good hearts," she said. "Take this with you."

For those foreigners who've remained in Spain helping the people during the war, or for those who approach their problems with sympathy, nothing is too good. In this respect, the Spanish common people are like those of Russia, where the average worker seems proud to be able to show hospitality to any visitor to the workers' republic.

To colored visitors, the Spaniards are just as hospitable as to any others. And many of them are interested in discussing the problems of colored people in America, having read so often of the lynchings held in our country. They do not, however, realize the extent of the economic and social discrimination which we have to face, and when I tell them about jim-crow theatres, trains, jobs, and schools, they wonder, since there are fifteen million of us, why we don't do something radical about it.

They often ask me, too, concerning the labor movement in America, and whether the colored people are a part of the CIO that is now so often mentioned in the European papers.[91]

Then I ask about their war and whether they think they will win. And, of course, they do. That is what makes Madrid so entirely calm and brave in the face of the guns, and the almost daily bombardments. They say that Franco has no men who believe in him—only hired troops, conscripted Moors, and borrowed Germans and Italians.

They say that he holds his conquered territory only by terror, by the execution of all the workers and intellectuals who oppose him, and by the forming of huge concentration camps. They know that the international situation is becoming more and more favorable to loyalist Spain. And that the government forces are now stronger and better than ever, with greater supplies of material and thousands of well-disciplined men at their command.

Time is with the people of Spain. Time, and the moral consciousness of the world.

The Fascists who bomb women and children, who have put to death García Lorca, Spain's greatest poet, who deliberately rained explosives on the art museum of El Prado and on the National Library with its priceless books and manuscripts, who use churches for arsenals and bring Mohammedans to battle for a "Christian ideal," and who fight for no cause at all except the forcing of the Spanish people back into economic and spiritual slavery for the sake of a handful of rich men and outworn nobles—these Fascists, Madrid feels, cannot win.

Let them pour a million foreign-made shells into the city, they cannot win! Even a great many of the workers of the countries that make the shells for Franco do not want Franco to win.

Sometimes a shell falls that does not explode. And sometimes in such a shell a note is found: This shell will not go off! Greetings! Signed: A German Worker.

"Madrid's Flowers Hoist Blooms to Meet Raining Fascist Bombs," *Afro-American,* November 27, 1937

A few days ago, I went to visit a section of the trenches of Madrid that runs through one of the formerly populous working-class suburbs of the city. Ordinarily, from the center of the town, one can walk to the trenches, but this particular sector was a bit far, so we went in a car, myself and two other foreign writers.

In less than five minutes from the Puerta del Sol, we passed the first barricades built across the road. And soon another set of barricades.

Then we entered a section of the city that had been evacuated where nobody lived any longer. Here the houses, most of them, were in various stages of destruction. Some of the buildings had been completely gutted by bombs from the fascist planes. Others had great ragged holes in their front walls from shell fire.

In third- and fourth-floor tenements, one could see the humble furniture of the former inhabitants still there: a bed with weather-stained mattress, a washstand with the mirror broken by bullets, a bath tub still clinging to the wall although the door is gone.

On the railings of some of the balconies, flowers still bloomed in red pots that the guns had missed.

Ruined and lifeless cities are very sad. I've seen them in Mexico. And I've seen what remained of Chapai after the Japanese bombarded it in their attack on Chinese Shanghai some years ago. And lately I've seen Arguelles, that ruined section of Madrid proper which faces the fascist cannon and was the target of so much foreign aviation last fall and winter.

The district through which I passed on my way to the trenches was not unlike Arguelles in appearance, or Chapai: roofless houses, wall-less buildings, peopleless homes.

Here there had been hand to hand fighting in those November days when the fascists had entered the very city of Madrid itself, only to be thrown back—never, so the people say now, to enter again. The ruins through which I passed remain as a reminder of the death and destruction which the fascists created during their attack, an attack repelled by working people, many of them armed only with courage, because a year ago Madrid itself did not have the arms or the trained soldiers which it now has to defend itself.

Nevertheless, the traitorous army of Franco, with its Italian and Moorish mercenaries, met with one of the most heroic examples of mass resistance in the history of modern warfare, and were forced to retreat beyond the edges of the city. Now I was going to see a section of those trenches which serve as Madrid's present line of defense.

The tall ruined buildings gave way to smaller buildings, and then to brick and stucco houses with yards about them and what had once been gardens. We were approaching the open country. But here our car stopped because it was dangerous to drive any further.

We got out and went to staff headquarters and presented our papers. The commandant was most cordial, and sent an officer and an aide to guide us through the trenches. Here began one of the strangest and most fantastic tours I have ever made in my life.

For awhile we walked down what would have been in normal times a suburban street, but now nobody lived in the houses we passed. Empty and shell-scarred, they stood in the afternoon sunlight.

Many of the walls were chipped by the marks of recent bullets, because we were now in range of enemy machine-gun and rifle fire. The trunks of the trees were broken and scarred by bullets.

Shells and trench-mortars had made deep holes in some of the lawns where scanty grass still tried to grow. No birds sang in the trees. They had all been frightened away months ago.

We came to the beginning of our rear line of trenches which started modestly enough in a slight rise of land and deepened as the slope went upward.

But the strange thing to me about these trenches was that they were not long straight lines such as we see in the war-movies.

Instead they curved and zig-zagged through gardens, under fences, and beneath houses. Or sometimes they passed right through the wall and living room of a cottage, or maybe through the whole house, past the stove in the kitchen and then on out of doors to become an open trench again.

Like frightful modernistic drawings, the mangled houses lifted their broken walls and torn roofs to the cool blue sky, and trenches cut through rooms where once families had lived and children had played. In one house, or rather a portion of a house—for one whole side had been blown away—we paused and were shown up a broken staircase to the second floor.

Here, through a sand-bagged window, we could get an excellent view of the fascist lines a few hundred yards away. The scattered houses on the furthest edge of the suburb were in fascist territory. Like as not, I thought, newspaper men from Rome and Berlin come down here to this fascist front and peer out of those houses at us in Madrid!

But we went even closer to rebel territory! Our own front-line trenches were nearer yet. And because it was a quiet afternoon, with practically no firing going on, we were allowed to visit them. There was a cold wind blowing, and the soldiers were, many of them, wrapped in blankets as they stood at their posts.

They gave us a courteous "Salud!" Not salute, but s-a-l-u-d, spoken in a friendly voice. Sometimes they let us look through their gun-sights toward the enemy. Sometimes we stopped to talk with a group of them in their dugouts, men off duty and at rest.

The trenches were very clean, and the men we talked with were the soldiers of Spain's new People's Army—disciplined, well-trained, and wise in the knowledge that their country must belong to the people, and not to a handful of generals, counts, and wealthy landowners and industrialists.

These men of Spain's new People's Army know that in the old days nobody cared whether they lived and worked and ate or not; that always they were paid as little as possible; that when they went to vote, their vote counted for nothing so long as the dictator, Primo de Rivera, was in power.

When Primo fell and the people elected a popular democratic government, the fascist elements rose up against them and tried to force them back into political darkness at the point of guns. Nobody cared, either, in the old days whether the people learned to read and write or not. Spain's percentage of illiteracy was enormous.

Now, even in the trenches themselves schools have been set up, and these very soldiers to whom I talked were learning to read and write, and to escape from the darkness of ignorance.

The old days were dark days indeed—and the fascists want those old days back. The soldiers in the trenches of Madrid say, NO! And that is why the fascists do not pass. That is why, for months now, with all the modern implements of warfare, Franco hammers away at the gates of Madrid, but he does not pass. The People's Army says, NO!

When we left the trenches, the sun was sinking in the West over behind the hills which belong to the enemy. With evening, and the coming darkness, the quiet was broken and the crack of rifle and machine-gun fire began to echo through the empty houses. We heard the sharp hiss of bullets above our heads.

Occasionally, a stray shot would hit a wall nearby with a sharp crack. We followed a path back to our car that was more or less out of range of direct fire—but much too near the bullets for a pleasant stroll.

Through the dark and ruined streets of the war zone, back to the equally dark city of Madrid we drove, our headlights dim. And somehow, as I rode through the night now increasingly loud with gun-fire, I kept thinking about the flowers I had seen on the balcony railings of those empty and shell-torn houses.

And I thought that perhaps those flowers might well symbolize the whole struggle in Spain—those flowers blooming so bravely there in the face of fascist fire; those flowers like the brave and beautiful books of Thomas Mann and others that Hitler burned in his bonfire in Berlin;

Those flowers like the brave and hopeful Chinese students the Japanese put before the firing squads in Pekin; those flowers like the young Ethiopians from the hills massacred in Addis Ababa; those flowers like the wonderful old paintings in the museum of the Prado which the fascist shells sought to destroy before they could be carried to safety by the government;

Those flowers like the strong and beautiful working men and women who poured, unarmed, into the streets of Madrid on July 19, and defied the reactionaries in the attempt to seize the city; those flowers blooming in the face of shell fire like the copy-books of the soldiers learning to read and write today in the front-line trenches of Spain.

The fascist guns are turned against the simple words in copy books that for the first time the men of the new army are learning to spell.

The fascists do not like living flowers. That is why the people of Madrid say, NO—and close their city with a ring of human trenches against the enemy.

"N.Y. Nurse Weds Irish Fighter in Spain's War," *Afro-American,* December 11, 1937

Miss Salaria Kee of Harlem, charming nurse at one of the American hospitals in Spain, was married on October 2 to John Joseph O'Reilly, ambulance driver from Thurles, County Tipperary, Ireland.

Her husband was one of the first international volunteers to come to fight on the loyalist side in Spain, and was for several months in the trenches. Recently he was transferred to hospital service.

A letter from a fellow-worker in their hospital, written to Joe North, and in turn passed on to Thyra Edwards and myself, gives a graphic description of the wedding of these two internationals from distinct parts of the world mating in Spain. An extract from the letter follows.

"They were married at Villa Paz and the marriage was celebrated with music and dancing. Speeches were made by various American and Spanish guests including the blind soldier, Raven, who spoke for the patients of the hospital, and Dr. Arnold Donawa, member of the staff, who spoke for the hospital.

"Salaria came to Spain in April and has worked at Villa Paz. She is known to hundreds of American boys for her patience, her smile, and her wit. She is a very charming person, and the bridegroom, known as Pat, discovered that as soon as he landed in Villa Paz. He was so much in love with her that he began writing poetry about her, but being a shy Irishman, he was afraid to tell her about it. The other nurses, however, read the poetry and told Salaria.

"Instead of the usual wedding march, a chorus of young Spanish girls sang 'Joven Guardia' and other songs. The old judge from Salices, who sports large handlebar moustaches, performed the ceremony. The three-piece band from Salices supplied the music and it seems to me that although they may not know it, they dished out pretty good swing. The American and Spanish guests gave the bride and bridegroom numerous presents. The affair broke up late, but no one staggered.

"The bride, Salaria, is 26, a graduate of Harlem Hospital, and has been a nurse there. She has also nursed at Sea View Hospital in Staten Island. She is considered by her colleagues to be very efficient and capable. Hemingway and Martha Gellhorn were here October 2, but could not stay for the wedding.[92] They took the story, however."

Other social notes from Spain this week might include the visit of Miss Thyra Edwards of Chicago, the "social" in this case meaning a delegate from the Social Workers' Committee for the Aid of Spanish Democracy.

Miss Edwards has just returned to Valencia from Madrid where she was received by the famous loyalist commander, El Campesino, and shown about his headquarters and encampments, where she met various colored officers and soldiers from Cuba who volunteered for service in his ranks.

Miss Edwards is especially interested in the problems of the women and children in war-torn Spain and is bringing back to America a report of her investigations here.

"Soldiers from Many Lands United in Spanish Fight," *Afro-American,* December 18, 1937

They come from all over the world, the members of the International Brigades in Spain. Officially, they say, there are thirty-seven nationalities represented. But I think there are more. All the countries of Europe have sons here in Spain. All the countries of America, too, both the English and Spanish-speaking lands.

Far off Australia is here. China and Japan. Negroes are here from the States, the Islands, Africa. I have seen and talked to them, white, and black, and yellow, and brown. In the trenches, in the cities on leave, wounded in the hospitals. Regiments predominantly English, or predominantly French, or German, understanding and speaking each its own language.

Or individuals scattered in Spanish units, alone in a group that does not know one's tongue or tradition—united only in their antifascist ideal: freedom for workers. These are the Internationals! Men who've come from far away of their own free will, to fight in Spain:

Of their own free will. And it is that quality of will which differentiates the international fighters on the side of Spanish democracy from those Germans and Italians and Moors who support the Fascists. In the first place, regular German and Italian soldiers are with Franco because their governments sent them there.

Many of the Germans are professional soldiers, anyway, who fight for a living, like hired gangsters. Many of the Italians are poor peasants whose only way of earning a living wage is in the army—and once there, to blindly obey its orders is their only choice. Abyssinia or Spain as Mussolini chooses, to fight against and kill whom Mussolini chooses.

Even sadder and more ironic than with the others, is the position of the Moors who fight in favor of Fascism. They are illiterate African colonials forced to obey the commands of the Fascist generals in power. To keep up their morale, they are spurred on by promises of loot, rape, and the doubtful pleasure of killing some of those Spaniards who in the past have taken so many shots at them.

But unfortunately, the Moors are shooting the wrong way. In pointing their guns against the workers and farmers of democratic Spain, they are only further aiding the rebel generals to tighten more surely their grip of despotism on Africa as well as on Spain.

Germans, Italians, and Moors fighting for Fascism! But on the side of the Spanish government, there are also Germans, Italians, and Moors fighting for a new democracy; economic democracy. A different kind of soldier and a different kind of man. The members of the International Brigades.

In the first place, they know why they are fighting, and that why is made up of very definite reasons. For instance, Germans fighting on the loyalist side in Spain do so because they recognize in Franco the shadow and extension of Hitler and all that Nazism stands for: rigid control of the rights of workers and the suppression of their labor unions; suppression of experimentation in science, and freedom of thought in writing, art, and the theatre, suppression and segregation of racial minorities that happen not to be Nordic, but are instead Jewish or colored.

In other words, Hitler means Jew-baiting, Nordic supremacy, the burning of books and company unions. No decent German likes those things.

Italians are in the International Brigades because they see in Franco the shadow and extension of Mussolini with his cry of eternal war, war, war; his love of oppression in its most savage forms such as the bombing of the helpless natives of Ethiopia and the women and children of Spain; his creation of a land in which all political parties are banned, all workers' organizations are subjected to State control, all books to censorship, and where all male children are taken over by the army as soon as they can walk, to make of them future killers. No decent Italian likes those things.

And so they come to help Spain fight against them, because they know that Franco means a spreading of Fascism and Hitlerism to yet another part of the world. And no good man wishes Fascism to go any further.

As for the Moors who managed to avoid Franco's ranks and instead take up arms for the people's cause—and there are a considerable number—they know that the generals who now control North Africa and support Franco are the same generals who in the old days kept the Moors down by force, sent the Spanish army against them, and shot and starved them into submission.

Now these generals use Moors against the workers and peasants of Spain in order to crush the new bloom of Spanish democracy, deceiving the Moors into believing that it was the workers who oppressed them in the first place. (A very dangerous way, to be sure, of playing with one's colonies—and a way which the common people of England and France had best quickly understand, lest they wake up some morning to find that the ruling class of their own lands also has called in African natives to shoot London or Paris in the back.

In fact, those lands that now talk so much about democracy had better do a little something about it quickly in regard to their colored subjects, lest their colored subjects, confused like the Moors, may not know quite which side to fight on when the struggle comes to a head.)

Fortunately, some Moors and some Africans realize that Fascism can never be, under any guise, a friend of colonial freedom. Those colored colonials who have joined the International Brigades against Franco, understand this.

But colored people are not the only oppressed folks in the world, by any means. From Ireland, that has known oppression for so long, many good fighters have come to republican Spain. Why? Because one of the great enemies of the Spanish people is that same Bank of England that helps starve and exploit Ireland.

France has contributed thousands of men to loyalist Spain, too, because the French workers know that another Fascist border, like Germany's, on the edge of France will so greatly strengthen the Fascist elements within France that no working man will any longer be secure in his right to vote for working class representation in the Chamber of Deputies, if he chooses, or organize a strike for higher wages, or read a book or paper not approved by the wealthy reactionaries that control French finance capital, and that seek to control as well, French men and women, and their labor.

From these countries that I've named and from others all over the world, class-conscious workers come to fight in Spain because they realize that the enemy now firing from the Fascist trenches is the same old enemy they have at home—except that at home he still wears a mask, as a rule, whereas in Spain he has not only dropped his mask, but has let his pants down as well.

Give Franco a hood and he would be a member of the Ku Klux Klan, a kleagle. Fascism is what the Ku Klux Klan will be when it combines with the Liberty League and starts using machine guns and airplanes instead of a few yards of rope. Fascism is oppression, terror, and brutality on a big scale.

The colored group must fight it wherever it is found. Opposing it in Spain now as members of the international brigades are colored men in every branch of the military service, as officers, as soldiers, as scouts, as transport workers, as teachers in the Brigade training schools.

In the Medical Aid as ambulance drivers, one doctor, and a nurse. On a recent visit to the Aragon front I met a dozen men from Harlem, seven colored boys from Los Angeles, a half-dozen from Chicago, and several from my own State of Ohio.

"Milt Herndon Died Trying to Rescue Wounded Pal," *Afro-American,* January 1, 1938

It was quiet on the front. No action. Our attack was over. Silence in the blanket of a rainy night in a valley where perhaps twenty thousand men lie in trenches, behind barricades in ruined villages, squatting beside machine-guns spitting a row of bullets into space. Then, long blanks of silence again.

Afar off, the boom of cannon, steady for maybe half an hour. Perhaps the government guns trained on Zaragossa, as the enemy guns are trained on Madrid. Then silence again. And the rain coming down in a soft, steady drizzle.

Where the tent sags, water drips down and spatters on the table. Two candles burn. Men come in and out with messages for members of the General Staff, papers to sign, calls to the field telephone in a dugout on the side of the hill. The pop of a motorcycle. A courier arriving or departing for the lines.

When the tent flap is lifted, you see the sentry with his gun on his shoulder outside, scarcely visible in the darkness, his capelike coat touching the ground. He stands there silent, on guard in the rain.

Dave Doran comes in, the Political Commissar of the 15th Brigade.

"Sorry," he says, "but we can't go to the Mac-Pap's tonight. Too much rain. Too difficult for you to see the men on a night like this. Besides, his battalion's the furthest away, a couple of miles or more through the trenches, the last in our lines. Instead of your going, I've telephoned for two of the members of Herndon's section to come in and talk to you."

The rain seemed to come down harder than ever. Rain and the dull boom of artillery. It was cold so I went out, and into the next tent to look for an overcoat. One of my tent-mates was spreading down the groundcloth, with a flashlight, preparatory to making our pallets on the damp earth.

"They've just dug a little trench around our tent so the water'll run off," he said. "You know, this is the first night the Estado Mayor's been located here."

"Yes," I said, because I knew that the day before the Fascists had discovered the site of the International's field headquarters and had blasted them with artillery shells, killing three and wounding seven in the bombardment. I'd have been there myself if we hadn't been delayed a day on the road waiting for a truck.

This was my first visit to the Internationals in action. They were on the Aragon front, specifically Fuentes de Ebro—which means the village of Fuentes, located on the River Ebro. The loyalist troops, including the English-speaking battalions of the brigades, had taken Belchite and Quinto a short time before, important victories for the government.

Now our lines lay just outside the town of Fuentes de Ebro. In an attack on Fuentes, Milton Herndon was killed. To learn how Herndon died, I wished to visit the trenches in which his battalion was lying that rainy October night. But my trip had been countermanded. Instead, two of his comrades were coming to field headquarters behind the lines to talk with me.

I put on my heavy coat and went back to the busy tent to wait. Two or three hours passed. They did not come. Meanwhile, there was a meeting of the Political Commissars from the various International companies, English, American, Irish and Spanish-speaking, on the front.

I was invited to sit in and listen to the problems and daily interests of the men in the trenches whom the Commissars were commissioned to look after, to keep in shape physically and mentally.

Nine o'clock came, ten, eleven. Still the men hadn't come from the Mackenzie-Papineau Battalion where Herndon served. The meeting of Commissars broke up. It was raining very hard, so Doran decided to telephone for a truck to carry them back to the trenches where, even then, some of them would have an hour, or two hours' walk to reach their companies.

"Something must have happened that they couldn't leave," Doran said to me regarding the men from the Mac-Pap's. "But I'll phone again and see."

I followed him out into the rain. On our way to the communications dugout, we ran into two men, dark shapes in the dark on the side of the hill.

"Johnson! Sankari!" they said.

"What happened to you?" Doran asked. "We had given you up."

"Snipers must have seen us coming out," one of them answered, "so they kept picking at us all around until we had to stop."

"So many bullets kept whizzing by for a while that we had to lie down in a ditch and stay there more'n an hour."

"Then when we did get out, in the rain, we couldn't find the path up here since you've moved."

But they had finally arrived. Two men from the 4th Company of the Mackenzie-Papineau Battalion who had served under Sergeant Herndon in his machine-gun section. They were big American fellows, standing there in the dark. Dave Doran introduced me: Aaron Johnson of Los Angeles, Hjalmar Sankari of New York.

Back in the candle-lighted tent, I saw that one was a colored boy, dark-brown skin, young—Johnson. And the other was a Scandinavian-American, blond, light-skinned, and strong.

"You'd better go back in the truck I'm sending for," Dave Doran advised them as he started out to phone, "so there won't be much time to talk."

The two men wiped the rain from their faces and we sat down on a bank of earth that had been dug out like a hollow square around the table. The others left us alone in the tent. I began to ask questions about Herndon and his life in Spain but, at first, it was a rather halting interview. No fighter likes to talk much about a comrade who's just been killed. But these men were his friends. They had come to tell me about him.

"Milt Herndon! He died like this," they said. Sometimes one talked, sometimes the other. One answered a question, another added a phrase. Two voices in the night, a colored voice and a white voice. Two American voices telling how Milton Herndon died.

"He died like this," they said. "He was taking the second machine-gun over the top. He was the sergeant, the section leader. He had three guns under him. He was taking the second gun over the top with his men. We went about three hundred meters up a little rise—when all of a sudden the Fascists opened up on us. We had to stop. A regular rain of bullets.

"They got one of our comrades, Irving, and he fell just ahead of us on top of the ridge in full view of the Fascist fire. He was wounded in the leg and couldn't move. The man nearest to him, Smitty, raised up to drag him back aways, and a bullet got Smitty in the heart. Got him right in the heart. Then Herndon crawled on up the slope to rescue the wounded boy. They got Herndon, too.

"Through the head, through the mouth—two bullets, just like that! And Herndon and Smitty both died. The other boy lived. He's in the hospital now. But Herndon and Smitty were killed right there. It was October thirteenth, our first day in the lines. At one o'clock we went over the top."

The rain came down in torrents on the little tent where we were sitting. A motor truck drew up outside. We heard the fellows piling in for their return to the trenches. Someone came to say that they would wait for us to finish our conversation. But I did not like to keep a whole truck full of men standing in the rain.

"Tell me a little of what he was like," I said, "before you go. I know Angelo, but I never knew Milton."[93]

"He used to talk a lot about Angelo," Sankari said. "He was proud of his brother. But Milton was smart, too, and he knew what lies behind this war. He was always politically alert. He worked hard in the company and in his section. The men liked him. He had both Americans and English under him, and we all liked him."

"Two of us are colored in the company besides Herndon," Johnson said. "Myself and Charlie Lewis from New York. We all liked Herndon. He worked hard. He was good natured. He was a good card player, too. A good fellow."

"He wanted to be a dynamiter," the Scandinavian added. "He was a big tall fellow, used to be a miner, and he would have been in one of the Spanish companies as a dynamiter if he could've spoken Spanish. He was a good singer, too. Everybody liked him."

"He and Smitty were both fine fellows," Johnson said. "They were good friends, too. Smitty was white. They're buried together."

"Out in No-Man's Land by Fuentes, we buried them that night," Sankari said.

"You know, our machine-gun company was named after Frederick Douglass," Johnson added as they left the tent. "Herndon suggested the name, and when we named it the Frederick Douglass Machine-Gun

Company, he made a speech on the connections between our rights at home in America and the fight here in Spain. He said, 'Yesterday, Ethiopia. Today, Spain. Tomorrow, maybe America. Fascism won't stop anywhere—until we stop it.' That's what he said."

The truck rumbled away in the blackness of the downpour, its headlights out. With it went the two young Americans, one dark with the blood of Africa, and the other light-haired and Scandinavian. Together they had come an hour earlier through the rain, stooping in the trenches, hiding in roadside ditches away from the bullets, in order to tell me how two others, Americans, one black and one white, had died to stop Fascism. And how, at the moment of their death, they saved a wounded comrade from the bullets.

I remembered long ago it was written, "Greater love hath no man than this, that he lay down his life for another." And I thought how Milton Herndon had died not only to save another comrade, or another country, Spain, but for all of us in America, as well. You see, he understood the connections between the enemy at home and the enemy in Spain: They are the same enemy.

"Fighters from Other Lands Look to Ohio Man for Food," *Afro-American,* January 8, 1938

He was about to start out with two trucks, several helpers, and several thousand pesetas on a food purchasing tour for the various kitchens at the Anglo-American Training Base of the International Brigades in the heart of Spain. He was a heavy-set, dark brownskin fellow of perhaps 35, snappy and efficient-looking in his well-kept officer's uniform.

He had little time to talk to me, as the trucks were about to get under way, but while the chauffeurs were getting their gas for the journey, he told me something of himself and his work in Spain.

Abraham Lewis is his name. He comes from Cleveland, Ohio, where he was one of the most active workers in the Future Outlook League, a leading colored organization there. He has been in Spain almost a year. At first he was attached to a transport regiment and after two months of service he was made a sergeant.

Now he is a lieutenant, and the quartermaster in charge at the English-speaking training base with a large staff of various nationalities under him, American, English, and Spanish. His responsibilities include the feeding, clothing, sanitary, and recreational facilities of the entire base. No small job for one man.

Abraham Lewis, however, is not without experience in such work. He was formerly a steward on an American government boat and there acquired the knowledge of handling food and preparing menus. Here in Spain though, the feeding of Internationals is no simple problem. In the first place, the Spaniards cook with olive oil, a procedure not agreeable to the palate of most foreigners.

Lewis had to find various available substitutes for this oil, substitutes that would appeal to the International mouths at his tables in a land where lard and butter are not easily to be gotten. Then there was the problem of cooks. Very few of the International Brigaders who came to Spain wanted to serve as cooks. They wanted to fight.

So Lewis had to train Spanish cooks in American ways of cooking, stressing as well sanitation and efficiency, especially in the matter of time—having food ready exactly at the hour when it should be served.

For Lewis who speaks little Spanish, this has been a double task. He has, of course, an interpreter. But because many of his Spanish kitchen workers could neither read nor write, written orders and listed menus were at first impossible.

Out of twenty-seven cooks and helpers, only seven were literate. So Lewis organized classes for them. Now, after five months, seventeen have learned to read their own language, Spanish. For this achievement the U.G.T. Trade Unions, to which the kitchen employees belong, have complimented Lewis in an official letter.

But Lewis's job includes much more than food. As Quartermaster, he is in charge of all distribution of clothing and bedding at the camp, and has installed a modern American filing system to keep track of things. He has set up a tailoring repair service, employing women of the village. He has modernized greatly the camp laundry.

He has set up a shoe-repair shop which was badly needed, but lacking before Lewis came. At present, through the various services of which Lewis is in charge, more than a hundred thousand pesetas a month pass through his hands for purchases and expenses.

Abraham Lewis is deeply interested in and proud of his job. He is proud of the opportunity which the International Brigades have given him to make use of his full capacities for organizational and administrative work. He knows that in America such opportunities come too seldom to members of the darker race. Here he has done well in the responsible position which he occupies.

Just before the trucks returned to staff headquarters to pick him up for their buying expedition, I asked Lewis what he thought of Spain and the Spanish people. His answer was an enthusiastic one, and a very racial one. He said, "Here nobody sneers at a colored person because he has a position of authority. Everybody tries to help him. Everybody salutes him.

"A colored person has a chance to develop here. Spain is all right! And in the International Brigades, people of all races, even if they can't speak your language, help you and work with you. That's the kind of comradeship that gets things done!"

The trucks came, and he was notified that they were waiting. Lewis shook my hand warmly and went away. It was midnight. At dawn they would be in the distant city where the wholesale houses and supply bases were. With him on the first truck were two white helpers. On the second truck also, his co-workers were white.

When will we learn to work together like that in America? I wondered. In Spain now the Internationals of all races stand against Fascism and its barbarous theories of white supremacy and working-class oppression. When the black and white workers of America learn to stand together in the same fashion, no oppressive forces in the world can hurt them.

When Abraham Lewis comes home, he can no doubt help America achieve that unity. That is what I thought as I watched his trucks drive away through the Spanish night across La Mancha where centuries ago Don Quixote wandered with his lance.

"Pittsburgh Soldier Hero, but Too Bashful to Talk," *Afro-American,* January 15, 1938

We sat in the improvised office of the daily mimeographed bulletin of the Washington-Lincoln Battalion in the middle of the ruined city of Quinto shortly after the loyalist forces took it away from the Fascists.

Artillery and air-bombs had left few buildings standing whole. The Brigade library, post-office, and bulletin had taken possession of one of the more or less whole houses left standing. Ralph Thornton was acting as a clerk there when I saw him.

We sat in the sunlight near the door, and I tried to get him to tell me why he had just been cited for bravery beyond the ordinary call of duty, and why the brigade had presented him a gold watch.

Thornton, light-brown skin fellow from the smoky city of Pittsburgh, was loathe to talk about himself. "Oh, it wasn't much," he insisted. "We just took four prisoners in Belchite; that's all. Me and two other boys captured them."

Luckily, two other members of Thornton's outfit were sitting there with us. They weren't at all bashful in talking about Thornton, even if he wouldn't talk much about himself.

The story was that at the taking of Belchite by the Spanish People's Army including the American units of the International Brigades, one of the largest buildings in the city, filled with Fascists, held out even after our troops had entered the town.

At dawn a group of Internationals were ordered to take it. Ralph Thornton was in that group. They stormed the building with hand grenades and took it for the government in the face of heavy resistance.

That same morning, Thornton and two white comrades, Ben Findley and Carl Geiser, were given several blocks of houses to inspect in the captured city. Many of the houses were in ruins, but some stood intact. From upper windows, snipers still operated.

Behind barred doors and closed blinds Fascists who had been unable to escape crouched in hiding. Inspecting these ominously quiet houses was no gentle task. You could easily get a hand grenade in the face.

They went up the narrow stone stairs of an ancient old house with walls three feet thick. Dark cold silence everywhere. But on the top floor, the third, when Thornton opened the door to the front bedroom, the silence was suddenly perfumed with the scent of powder and acrid smoke stung him in the eyes and burned his throat.

Someone moved in the dark, turned and cried out, then jumped to his feet crying, "Salud!" At the same time he threw a rifle from him. The gun was still hot when Thornton picked it up.

The man was a Fascist who had been lying there sniping on the government soldiers. Now he cowered in a corner crying "Salud!" The word with which the loyalists greet one another. But he didn't look like a man who would say "Salud," naturally.

The captured sniper turned out to be the vice president of the local Falangists, the town's Fascist organization (like our Ku Klux Klan) and one of the most active enemies of republicanism in that section of Aragon.

Further inspection revealed several cupboards in the house filled with gold and hidden jewels.

Nearby, in another house whose inhabitants had been unable to flee, the three Americans found an old woman sitting at a window. They asked her whether there was anyone hiding in the house. She said, "No."

A careful search of the premises revealed a hidden opening leading to a tunnel dug beneath the dwelling. Down there in the dark, at the end of the tunnel, an Italian soldier was hiding—one of Mussolini's contributions to the conquering of Spain.

He probably thought he was in Ethiopia by mistake when he saw Thornton's dark face inviting him to come out and surrender.

Before they went back to staff headquarters that morning, Thornton and his comrades had taken two other Fascist prisoners and had made sure that there were no more snipers in the blocks of houses they had been sent out to inspect.

Because of Thornton's valor at Belchite, his part in the storming of the Fascist-held building, and the importance of the prisoners he took, the whole brigade united in the presentation of a watch to him on the day when his citation for bravery arrived.

No doubt Thornton was pleased, but he was too modest to talk about it to a writer.

Thornton says he used to be a newsboy in Pittsburgh. And more recently he worked for the Center Printing Company. He says the skies of Spain are the most beautiful he's ever seen—after Pittsburgh—but that there's too much olive oil in the cooking. When the war is over, he's coming home.

"St. Louis Man's Spanish Helped Him Cheat Death," *Afro-American,* January 22, 1938

The first time I met Walter Cobb was in the Puerta del Sol, that big and busy square that is the heart of Madrid. An American in town on leave and I were looking for a place to have luncheon. Across the square came three internationals in their uniforms, two of them white and one colored.

The colored fellow had his pack on his back and his rifle on his shoulder, fully equipped to do battle. The three of them were talking French in the heat of a summer afternoon.

"That must be a French West African," I said to the fellow with me.

"No, it isn't either," he answered. "That's Walter Cobb."

And Walter Cobb it was, from St. Louis. He happened at that time to be the only American with an all-French Battalion. How he got there I was never able to find out, but there he was.

The next time I saw Cobb, it was three months later on the Aragon front. In the fall he had been transferred to an American brigade, one of the transport units, and this time he was talking Spanish to a girl who worked at the camp kitchen!

"I have to keep in practice with my languages," he explained. "Why, if I hadn't known Spanish, a week or so ago here, they would've taken me for a Moor, and made me a prisoner, sure."

"Who, our own soldiers?" I asked.

"Right! You see, I was driving a captured Fascist truck that we took at Belchite. I was bringing it back behind the lines to be repaired, and we hadn't had a chance yet to paint out the Fascist markings on it. It was night, and in the dark between a place called Todo and El Varade some Spanish soldiers on control-duty stopped me at the cross-roads and threw their flashlights on the truck.

"When they saw me, colored as I am, and saw that truck with the Fascist signs on it, they thought sure I was a Moor who had got lost and had accidentally run across the line somewhere. They yelled at me to come down, and held their guns on me until I got off the truck. But by that time, they saw that I was an international, and when I showed them my papers and told them we had captured that big truck from the Fascists, and that it belonged to our side now, they almost hugged me!

"But suppose I hadn't been able to speak a little Spanish and explain what I was doing driving a Fascist truck in Loyalist territory so near the front!"

Then Cobb went on to tell me that in the smaller villages, being quite dark in color, he is often the center of an interested and friendly crowd. In the cities of Spain, a dark person attracts no attention, but in some of the smaller towns they may never have seen a real colored man before.

Their curiosity, however, is always friendly, and village families often vie with one another in offers of hospitality should their colored visitor wish to eat a meal or spend a night there.

Walter Cobb has been in Spain for eight months. At first in the infantry on the mountainous Guadarrama front with a French company, now he is back with the Americans again where the laughter of this young and jolly boy from St. Louis helps to keep his whole regiment in good humor.

"Laughter in Madrid," *Nation* 146 (January 29, 1938): 123–24

The thing about living in Madrid these days is that you never know when a shell is going to fall. Or where. Any time is firing time for Franco. Imagine yourself sitting calmly in the front room of your third-floor apartment carefully polishing your eyeglasses when all of a sudden, without the least warning, a shell decides to come through the wall—paying no attention to the open window—and explodes like a thunderclap beneath the sofa. If you are sitting on the sofa, you are out of luck. If you are at the other side of the room and good at dodging shrapnel you may not be killed. Maybe nobody will even be injured in your apartment. Perhaps the shell will simply go on through the floor and kill somebody else in apartment 27, downstairs. (People across the hall have been killed.)

Who next? Where? When? Today all the shells may fall in the Puerta del Sol. Tomorrow Franco's big guns on the hills outside Madrid may decide to change their range-finders and bombard the city fan-wise, sending *quince-y-medios* from one side of the town to the other. No matter in what section of the city you live, a shell may land in the kitchen of the sixth-floor apartment (whose inhabitants you've often passed on the stairs), penetrate several floors, and make its way to the street via your front room on the third floor.

That explains why nobody in Madrid bothers to move when the big guns are heard. If you move, you may as likely as not move into the wrong place. A few days ago four shells went through the walls of the Hotel Florida, making twenty that have fallen there. The entrance to the hotel is well protected with sandbags, but they couldn't sandbag nine stories. All this the desk clerk carefully explains to guests who wish to register. But most of the other hotels have been severely bombed, too. And one has to stay somewhere.

The Hotel Alfonso a few blocks away has several large holes through each of its four walls but is still receiving guests. One of the halls on an upper floor leads straight out into space—door and balcony have been shot away. In one of the unused bedrooms you can look slantingly down three floors into the street through the holes made by a shell that struck the roof and plowed its way down, then out by a side wall into the road. Walking up to your room, you pass a point where the marble stairs are splintered and the wall pitted by scraps of iron; here two people were killed. Yet the Hotel Alfonso maintains its staff, and those of its rooms that still have walls and windows are occupied by paying guests.

The now world-famous Telefónica, Madrid's riddled skyscraper in the center of the city, is still standing, proud but ragged, its telephone girls at work inside. The Madrid Post Office has no window-panes left what-so-ever, but the mail still goes out. Around the Cibeles Fountain in front of the Post Office the street cars still pass, although the fountain itself with its lovely goddess is now concealed by a specially built housing of bricks and sandbags, so that the good-natured Madrileños have nicknamed it "Beauty Under Covers," laughing at their own wit.

Yes, people still laugh in Madrid. In this astonishing city of bravery and death, where the houses run right up to the trenches and some of the street-car lines stop only at the barricades, people still laugh, children play in the streets, and men buy comic papers as well as war news. The shell holes of the night before are often filled in by dawn, so efficient is the wrecking service and so valiantly do the Madrileños struggle to patch up their city.

A million people living on the front lines of a nation at war! The citizens of Madrid—what are they like? Not long ago a small shell fell in the study of a bearded professor of ancient languages. Frantically his wife and daughter came running to see if anything had happened to him. They found him standing in the center of the floor, holding the shell and shaking his head quizzically. "This little thing," he said, "this inanimate object, can't do us much damage. It's the philosophy that lies behind it, wife, the philosophy that lies behind it."

In the Arguelles quarter to the north, nearest to the rebel lines—the neighborhood that has suffered most from bombardments and air raids—many of the taller apartment houses, conspicuous targets that they are, have been abandoned. But in the smaller houses of one and two stories people still live and go about their tasks. The Cuban poet, Alejo Carpentier, told me that one morning after a heavy shelling he passed a house of which part of the front wall was lying in the yard.[94] A shell had passed through the roof, torn away part of the wall, carried with it the top of the family piano, and buried itself in the garden. Nevertheless, there at the piano sat the young daughter of the house, very clean and starched, her hair brushed and braided, her face shining. Diligently she was beating out a little waltz from a music book in front of her. The fact that the top of the piano had been shot away in the night did not seem to affect the chords. When passers-by asked about it, calling through the shell hole, the child said, "Yes, an *obús* came right through here last night. I'm going to help clean up the yard after a while, but I have to practice my lessons now. My music teacher'll be here at eleven."

The will to live and laugh in Madrid is the thing that constantly amazes a stranger. At the house where I am staying, sometimes a meal consists largely of bread and of soup made with bread. Everybody tightens his belt and grins, and somebody is sure to repeat good-naturedly an old Spanish saying, "Bread with bread—food for fools!" Then we all laugh.

One of Franco's ways of getting back at Madrid is to broadcast daily from his radio stations at Burgos and Seville the luncheon and dinner menus of the big hotels, the fine food that the Fascists are eating and the excellent wines they drink. (Rioja and the best of wine areas are in Fascist hands.) But Madrid has her ways of getting even with the Fascists, too. Mola, a lover of cafes, said at the very beginning of the war that he would soon be drinking coffee in Madrid.[95] He was mistaken. Then he said he would enter Madrid by the first of November. He didn't. Then he swore he would enter the city on the eighth of December. He didn't. But on the evening of the eighth some wag remembered, and the crowds passing that night in Madrid's darkened Puerta del Sol saw by moonlight in the very center of the square a coffee table, carefully set, the coffee poured, and neatly pinned to the white cloth a large sign reading "For Mola."

Bread and coffee are scarce in Madrid, and so are cigarettes. The only cigarettes offered for sale more or less regularly are small, hard, and very bad. They are so bad that though they cost thirty centimos before the war they bring only twenty now despite their comparative scarcity. The soldiers call them "recruit-killers," jocularly asserting that they are as dangerous to the new men in the army as are bombs and bullets.

Bad cigarettes, poor wine, little bread, no soap, no sugar! Madrid, dressed in bravery and laughter; knowing death and the sound of guns by day and night, but resolved to live, not die!

The moving-picture theaters are crowded. Opening late in the afternoon and compelled to close at nine, they give only one or two showings a day. One evening an audience was following with great interest an American film. Suddenly an *obús* fell in the street outside. There was a tremendous detonation, but nobody moved from his seat. The film went on. Soon another fell, nearer and louder than before, shaking the whole building. The manager went out into the lobby and looked up and down the Gran Via. Overhead he heard the whine of shells. He went inside and mounted the stage to say that, in view of the shelling, he thought it best to stop the picture. Before he had got all the words out of his mouth he was greeted with such a hissing and booing and stamping of feet and calls for the show to go on that he shrugged his shoulders in resignation and signaled the operator to continue. The house was darkened. The magic of Hollywood resumed its spell. While Franco's shells whistled dangerously over the theater, the film went its make-believe way to a thrilling denouement. The picture was called "Terror in Chicago."

"Howard Man Fighting as Spanish Loyalist," *Afro-American,* February 5, 1938

When the 1st Regiment de Train of the 15th Brigade was at rest not far from Madrid last fall, its camp was near a road. The tents were so cleverly camouflaged (painted a zig-zag green and brown), and so carefully hidden under trees that, from the highway, it was difficult to know there was a camp there.

Once the enemy bombers came over and dropped a few bombs, but they landed in the woods and did no damage. The Madrid front, a few kilometers away, was not dangerously near, but still near enough for the wind to bring with it the sound of heavy artillery and exploding mines. The first day I visited the camp, there was a steady rumble in the air.

Thaddeus Battle, one of the two colored members of the regiment, was a student at Howard University. He intended to major in political science before he came to Spain, and will resume his studies in Washington when he returns.

He is a mild-mannered, quiet young man, wears glasses, and busies himself studying Spanish and French during his spare time when the regiment is not in service, or the Fascist planes are not zooming overhead.

Battle came originally from North Carolina. At Howard he was on the freshman football team. His main off-campus activity was helping with the Washington work of the National Negro Congress. And he was very happy to read in copies of the *Afro-American* that reached Madrid about the successful Philadelphia meeting of the congress in October. He wondered if there were many colored students taking part in the sessions.

"Our students must take a more active interest in labor problems, in the efforts of colored workers to better their conditions," Battle said as we sat smoking in his tent one chilly autumn afternoon.

"At home in America the forces of reaction can so easily use colored workers as a decoy to keep labor from achieving unity. That makes it easier for them to bring about a regime of repression in real Fascist style at home."

"Can colored college students help prevent this?" I asked.

"Of course they can," Battle replied. "Student movements in America are beginning to carry some weight as a serious force in our national life.

"Colored students must be a part of these movements whenever they are directed against the spread of reactionary tendencies, against war, and toward the strengthening of real democracy. I mean economic as well as political democracy!"

Outside we heard what seemed to be the hum of planes. We stuck our heads out of the tent and looked up, but nothing was in sight, so we went on with our conversation.

"Colored college students must realize, too, the connection between the international situation and our problems at home," Battle continued.

"When we see certain things happening in Europe and Asia that may involve America in another world war, then, and only then do we see clearly the need for combating such tendencies at home and abroad.

"Right here in Madrid I've seen how Fascists destroy schools and libraries. University City, a million-dollar educational center, is in ruins!

"Why gain culture only to see it destroyed? Franco destroys what it has taken people years to build. He burns books and closes schools and stifles education.

"In America our students, colored and white, must take a stand against all factors that even point toward a Fascist type of social order. And our colored campuses should play a much more vital role in national, and even international affairs, than they have done in the past."

I agreed with Battle, and made notes of what he said.

We talked until the big gong for supper sounded and we went to get in line before the cook tent. Three Spanish women were ladling out a delicious rabbit stew.

The long line of men forming there were a typical section of the English-speaking units of the International Brigades in Spain. There were Irish lads, English and American Jews, a Southern father and son from Oklahoma, two cousins from a wealthy old family in California, an Australian school teacher, and two colored men.

One was Bernard Rucker, a worker from Columbus, O., the other Thaddeus Battle of Howard University, taking time out from books to learn from life.

"Harlem Ball Player Now Captain in Spain," *Afro-American,* February 12, 1938

Basilio Cueria, well-known colored Cuban baseball player and resident of Harlem, is now the captain of a machine gun company in loyalist Spain. More than a year ago, Cueria went to Spain to enlist in the International Brigades.

For five months he was with the Lincoln Battalion on the Jarrama front during the hardest of the battles there, holding off the Italian and Moorish troops of Franco's Fascist legions who sought to enter Madrid.

At present Cueria is with an all Spanish brigade under the leadership of the famous peasant general, "El Campesino." While this brigade was training new recruits at Alcalá de Henares, ancient birthplace of Cervantes, I often visited them and talked frequently with the tall fine looking young captain who was immensely popular with the officers and men under his command.

Campesino himself told me that Cueria was one of the best of the officers in his brigade, the 1st Shock Brigade, 4th Battalion, 46th Division of the Spanish People's Army. Even when General Miaja, heroic defender of Madrid and member of the Spanish general staff, inspected the Campesino troops, Cueria and his company were singled out for special attention.

On the field, they gave a lightning demonstration of how quickly a machine gun may be assembled. Cueria and his men put their machine guns together with such rapidity, from the various parts which each man carries, that they were declared a model unit.

Back home in America, old baseball fans often speak of Cueria. A baseball player in Havana before he moved to the United States ten years ago, Cueria has long been associated with the game. He was a catcher with the Cuban Stars. Then in 1929 he became manager of the Miami Red Sox. And later he was with the Cuban Giants.

He has also played with a number of other clubs, and in New York he formed the Julio Antonio Melia Baseball Club in the Latin-American section of Harlem. Cueria is now interested in developing baseball as a recreational sport for the Spanish soldiers.

A year in Spain, and Cueria is already a veteran of many battles. In the early days, the Jarrama front was one of the most active in Spain. Transferred from there, Cueria took part in the great battles at Quijorna and Brunete last spring. For days he was under one of the most terrific artillery and air bombardments known in history.

At Brunete, near Madrid, the rebels put into action the largest air force yet used in modern warfare up to that time. Trenches, troop concentrations, convoys, roads, all were bombed hour after hour, day after day. From Brunete the government was forced to retreat, leaving a ruined city that Fascist explosives had destroyed.

Today Brunete is no-man's land, the government lines being just outside the town. But the offensive gained important objectives for the government, including the town of Quijorna, and Cueria came through it all unscathed. Now his division is reported in action at Teruel.

Captain Cueria says that his men are fine fellows to lead, and that all of them are proud to be fighting under Campesino, who is a worker-peasant commander right up from the ranks of the people. Campesino is indeed Spain's most colorful military man and in a year and a half of warfare has become almost a folk hero.

The people say that he rides into battle with his men, often mounted on a tank in full view of the enemy. And another story is that once badly wounded, he was carried behind the lines to a dressing station where his wounds were given emergency bandaging and placed in an ambulance to be rushed to a hospital at the rear. The ambulance started off. But the next thing the attendant knew was that there was no Campesino. He had opened the door, stepped out, and was shortly back in the midst of the battle with his men, bandages and all.

The soldiers laugh at him and love him, and follow him without question, so I could easily believe Cueria when he told me that everybody wants to fight with Campesino.

Since there are a large number of Cubans fighting in Spain on the government side, many of them colored Cubans, I asked Cueria how they were received, and whether any of them had ever been taken for Moors, or had encountered any color prejudice. Cueria laughed and said that sometimes dark Cubans were asked by Spaniards whether they were Moorish, but never in an unfriendly way, since the Spaniards have no color feeling about the Moors. (And there are Moors on the loyal side, as well as with Franco.)

But toward Cubans, who are a Spanish speaking people themselves, Spain has always been most hospitable. Before the revolt many Cubans lived in Spain.

And Cubans, of color especially, who sought another homeland often preferred Spain to the United States where they might run into difficulties on the basis of complexion. But Cueria himself insured me that he liked Harlem and would be coming back to America when the war is over. His family is in New York.

"Our side is sure to win," he said. "We can't let the Fascists put it over on us. They'd put all the worst old prejudices back in to force and probably even introduce new ones, like Hitler and his Aryanism in Germany. No, we're not going to let them win!"

"Anything else you'd like to say to the folks back home?" I asked as I said goodbye just before the Teruel offensive.

"Well, tell all the baseball players hello for me," Cueria said. "And tell the Melia Club to keep up that team in Harlem, so I can play with them when I get back. Tell all those Harlem baseball players hello!"

"Writers, Words and the World," speech made at the Paris Meeting of the International Writers Association for the Defense of Culture, July 25, 1938, LHP 2995

Words have been used too much to make people doubt and fear. Words must now be used to make people *believe and do*. Writers who have the power to use words in terms of belief and action are responsible to that power *not* to make people believe in the wrong things. And the wrong things are, as surely everyone will agree, death instead of life, suffering instead of joy, oppression instead of freedom, whether it be freedom of the body or of the mind.

Words put together beautifully, with rhythm and meaning, are as the branches and roots of a tree—if that meaning be a life meaning—such words can be of more value to humanity than food to the hungry or garments to the cold. For words big with the building of life rather than its destruction, filled with *faith* in life rather than doubt and distress, such words entering into the minds of men last much longer than today's dinner in the belly or next year's overcoat on the back. And such words, even when forgotten, may still be reflected in terms of motives and actions, and so go out from the reader to many people who have never seen the original words themselves.

Writers have power. The better the writer the greater that power to impel people toward the creation of a good life. We know that words may be put together in many ways: in beautiful but weak ways having meaning only for the few, worldly-wise and capable of understanding; or in strong and sweeping ways, large and simple in form, like yesterday's Walt Whitman or today's Theodore Dreiser.

The best ways of word-weaving, of course, are those that combine music, meaning and clarity in a pattern of social force.

One's own creative talents must supply the music of the words, one's background and experience, the meaning, and one's ability to study, simplify and understand, the clarity. To understand being the chief of these.

To understand! In one way the whole world situation today is very simple: greed against need. But within that simplicity there are many complexities and apparent contradictions. The complexities of race, of capital and labour, of supply and demand, of the stock exchange and the bowl of rice, of treaties that lie and bombs that tell the truth. And all these things are related to creative writing, and to the man or woman who writes. The shortest poem or story—let us say about a child playing quietly alone in a courtyard—and such a poem or story will be a better one if the author understands the relationship of his child to the Tokio war-machine moving against China. Why? Because the Tokio war-machine—if its lines be traced clearly back to Paris or London or Berlin or New York—the Tokio war-machine touches that very child in our simple little story, no matter in whose yard the child may be playing.

Because our world is like that today, so related and inter-related, a creative writer has no right to neglect to understand clearly the social and economic forces that control our world. No matter what his country or what his language, a writer, to be a good writer, cannot remain unaware of Spain and China, of India and Africa, of Rome and Berlin. Not only do the near places and the far places influence, even without his knowledge, the very subjects and material of his books, but they affect their physical life as well, their actual existence and being. For there are two depositories for books today: on democratic shelves or in reactionary bonfires. That is very simple. Books may live and be read, or be burned and blown away.

So there may still be those who use words to make people doubt and wonder, to remain inactive, unsure of the good in life, and afraid to struggle for it. But we must use words to make them believe in life, to understand and attempt to make life better. To use words otherwise, as decent members of society, we have no right.

"Around the Clock in Madrid: Daily Life in a Besieged City," LHP 45 (August 1938)

I happened to come up out of the subway into the Puerta del Sol just as a shell from one of Franco's cannons fell nearby. The Puerta del Sol is Madrid's busiest square, full of traffic, streetcars, and people. It was the first time I had ever been in the square during a shelling. I discovered that the world is seemingly divided into two kinds of human beings: those who run when a shelling starts and those who simply go calmly on about their business; those who get off of streetcars and dart into doorways and subway stations for safety, and those who get on the cars and go where they are going.

The Madrid streetcars, by the way, keep right on running, shells or no shells, and their motormen and conductors have an amazing record of bravery under fire. But not only in Madrid, for the streetcar men, too, have sent a whole company of their own to the front.

Well, I could hear the shells falling somewhere up the street as I stood there in the Puerta del Sol, but I, too, got on a streetcar and went on where I had started. I was going to the theatre to see *La Copla Andaluza*, a play built around the flamenco folk-songs of Andalucia. It was playing in a little neighborhood house a few blocks from the front. To reach it, you had to pass the first barricades that block the roads to the enemy.

The theatre was well-filled with neighborhood families: fathers and mothers and children, and a great many soldiers. The play, *La Copla Andaluza*, is a simple love story about the rivalry between two peasants for a girl. But the novelty of the piece is that the two men do most of their fighting in song, flamenco song, singing dire threats back and forth at one another to the accompaniment of guitars—stopping after each verse for the applause of an audience made up largely of enthusiastic lovers of flamenco.

Flamenco is to Spain, I suppose, what the blues are to America—I mean the real Negro folk blues. And the flamencos seem to have the same effect on their audiences as blues do when sung in the Negro theatres of the deep South. People yell and cry out and stamp their feet. Flamencos are the kind of Spanish songs that make folks shout, *Ole!*

They are very simple songs, each verse an entire song in itself, consisting of only three or four lines sung in a long-drawn-out wail that must have come up from Africa with the Moors centuries ago—a high rhythmic wail that some people say does violence to the art of song. For flamenco has its enemies, as well as its friends. A great many Spaniards do not like such songs, but the ones who do like them, *love* them. And they will gather with a guitar in groups and remember or improvise verse after verse for hours, in a kind of contest as to who can wail the loudest and longest. The flamencos are like blues in that they are sad songs, with a kind of triumphant sadness, a vital earthiness about them from which life itself springs.

When I came out of the theatre, it was quite dark. And night in Madrid is very dark indeed, for all the lights are out on account of the bombardments. Nights when there is no moon, you cannot see your hand before you in the Madrid streets. You have to find your home by instinct, avoiding people, trees, and buildings as best you can. A city of a million people without lights is something you cannot imagine unless you have lived in such a city.

The theatres and cafes close, at the latest, by nine o'clock every night. Shortly thereafter, the streetcars stop running. At eleven, only people on special missions are allowed in the streets, and the guards have a right to stop everyone for their credentials. If you are in a car, you must know the password for the night—and the password is changed everyday.

Midnight in Madrid, one can walk for blocks and not meet a soul save perhaps an occasional guard on the corner. When the moon is shining, the great buildings in the center of the city loom up like silver shadows against the sky. Like shadows in a city in a dream, an unearthly city, where nobody lives. If it is a quiet night for the troops holding the rebels at bay on the edge of Madrid, then you hear only an occasional rifle shot, or a quick run of machine-gun fire from trench to trench. Then silence again. But if it is a night of battle, you hear quite loudly and plainly the medley of bullets, hand-grenades, and trench mortars. And maybe before the night is out, the boom of cannons and the crack of shells falling, not at the front at all, but in the very street where you live. (You see, in quiet moments one forgets all Madrid is the front.)

Often enough, the firing keeps up all night. For strangers, this is not so pleasant. But the Madrileños are used to it, and they sleep, unless the shells are falling in their immediate neighborhood, in which case some people go to the cellar, if there is one, but other people simply stay in bed.

People whose work requires them to be out late, such as newspaper men and radio employees, all carry permits to use the streets after eleven. When they come home they find, of course, the doors of their apartment house locked, so they clap their hands and call for the *sereno*. The *sereno* is an old Spanish custom dating back to nobody knows when. He is the man who acts as guard for a whole block, or several blocks of houses—usually an old man with a heavy stick, which he uses both for walking and for protection. Sometimes it takes him a long time to arrive and open the door for you with his heavy bunch of keys. And sometimes he can't find the key to your door. But eventually he does. Then you go in and climb up innumerable stairs in the dark to the apartment where you live.

Since the war, there has been a rushing business in the sale of flashlights in all Spanish cities. But flashlights are like umbrellas—one almost always forgets to carry one. Besides the batteries have a way of sometimes going dead on the darkest nights—and leaving you lightless.

If Madrid streets are quiet after ten o'clock, and all the houses are shuttered and sleepy-looking, that does not mean everyone has gone to bed within. Madrid, before the war, had the reputation of living the clock around. Even now, in many families the supper hour is nine or ten o'clock, and sometimes later. At midnight, the war news comes over the radio. Everyone stays up to hear that. From within darkened houses, you suddenly hear an enormous voice blaring out the latest happenings on the front that day, how many towns were taken, how many enemy planes brought down. Just as in America, so in Spain, nobody seems to think of playing their radios softly. At midnight in Madrid, there is war news on all sides of me. And then dance music into the small hours of the morning.

Dawn in Madrid (as in all the cities of the world) brings out the early workers, the truckmen and market folks, the street cleaners and streetcar men. And a little later (just as though there were no war and the trenches are not on the edge of town) the clerks and store-keepers, office workers and professional men pour into the streets and crowd the cars and subways. In front of food stores lines begin to form for bread, and milk, and meat. And the life of the town begins.

Madrid works until one o'clock, then the siesta starts. Time out to rest and eat. Four o'clock and everything opens up once more, until seven. Behind sandbagged entrances and protected window panes, business goes on. The streets are crowded with shoppers and soldiers. The movie shows and theatres are packed. Beer-time in the cafes, from ten to eleven in the morning, you can't get a table. Coffee-time, or cocktail-time in the afternoon, crowded again. And outside in the streets, children coming home from school, soldiers on leave from the front.

Life goes on! Even though there is war in Madrid, its material and cultural life goes on. People eat and sleep, work and play, study, shop, go to concerts and theatres, listen to the radio, buy newspapers, live and die while the hands of the clocks go around. Except that many of the clocks in the towers of Madrid's main buildings are smashed and broken by shell fire, and no longer run. And at night, there are no lights with which to see the clocks, anyhow. There is very little to eat. And almost all the time, everyday, the crackle of guns on one side of the city or another. Or else, in the city itself, the loud sound of shells exploding, and the dusty thunder of walls crumbling in bombardments. Often there is blood on the sidewalks—so often it isn't news any more. But Madrid goes on! Life goes on!

"Democracy and Me," speech made at the public session of the Third American Writers' Congress, Carnegie Hall, New York City, June 1939

Twice now I have had the honor and the pleasure of representing the League of American Writers at Congresses held abroad in Paris and in Spain. In Europe I spoke first as an American and as a writer, and secondarily as a Negro. Tonight, here in New York at the Third American Writers' Congress, I feel it wise in the interest of democracy to reverse the order, and to speak first as a Negro and a writer, and secondarily as an American—because Negroes are secondary Americans. All the problems known to the Jews today in Hitler's Germany, we who are Negroes know here in America—with one difference. Here we may speak openly about our problems, write about them, protest, and seek to better our conditions. In Germany the Jews may do none of these things. Democracy permits us the freedom of a hope, and some action towards the realization of that hope. Because we live in a democracy, tonight I may stand here and talk to you about our common problem, the problem of democracy and me.

Since this [is] a Writers' Congress, I shall approach that problem as a writer. I shall speak of the color-line as it affects writers, as it affects me—and when I say me, I do not mean me, myself, alone. By me, I mean all those Negro writers who are seeking to put on paper today in the form of verse, or prose, or drama, life in America as we know it.

Here are our problems: In the first place, Negro books are considered by editors and publishers as *exotic*. Negro material is placed, like Chinese material or Bali material or East Indian material, into a certain classification. Magazine editors will tell you, "We can use but so many Negro stories a year." (That "so many" meaning very few.) Publishers will say, "We already have one Negro novel on our list this fall."

The market for Negro writers, then, is definitely limited as long as we write about ourselves. And the more truthfully we write about ourselves, the more limited our market becomes. Those novels about Negroes that sell best, by Negroes or whites, those novels that make the best-seller lists and receive the leading prizes, are almost always books that touch very lightly upon the facts of Negro life, books that make our black ghettos in the big cities seem very happy places indeed, and our plantations in the deep South idyllic in their pastoral loveliness. In such books there is no hunger and no segregation, no lynchings and no tears, no intimidations and no Jim Crow. The exotic is the quaint and the happy—the pathetic or melodramatic, perhaps, but not the tragic. We are considered exotic. When we cease to be exotic, we do not sell well.

I know, of course, that very few writers of any race make a living directly from their writing. You must be very lucky and very famous to do that. But a great many American writers—who are not Negroes—may make a living in fields more or less connected with writing. They may thus be professional writers living on or from their literary reputations and able, from their earnings, to afford some leisure time for personal creation. Whether their books are good or bad, they may work in editorial offices, on publishers' staffs, in publicity firms, in radio, or in motion pictures. Practically never is such employment granted to a Negro writer though he be as famous as the late James Weldon Johnson or as excellent a craftsman as the living Richard Wright. Perhaps an occasional prize or a fellowship may come a Negro writer's way—but not a job. It is very hard for a Negro to become a professional writer. Magazine offices, daily newspapers, publishers' offices are as tightly closed to us in America as if we were pure non-Aryans in Berlin.

Of course, Negro novelists do not sell their novels to motion pictures. No motion picture studio in America, in all the history of motion pictures, has yet dared make one single picture using any of the fundamental dramatic values of Negro life—not one. Not one picture. On the screen we are servants, clowns, or fools. Comedy relief. Droll and very funny. Such Negro material as is used by the studios is very rarely written by Negroes.

I speak first of this problem of earning a living because it is basic. Most undernourished writers die young—or cease to be writers, because they are forced to do something else.

Let us turn to the lecture field, a source of income for many Nordic and non-Nordic writers who are white. The leading lecture bureaus do not handle Negro speakers. Thousands of women's clubs and forums have never had—and will not have—a Negro speaker. Since tea is often served, the factor of social equality, of course, enters into the arrangements. In a number of states of our American republic, it is prohibited by law for whites and Negroes to drink tea together in public places.

On lecture tour, the Negro writer, if a tour he has, runs into all the difficulties that beset colored travellers everywhere in this country: in the South the Jim Crow coach and the segregated waiting room. If travelling by car, no tourist camps for Negroes, few restaurants that will serve a meal. Everywhere lack of hotel accommodations. This week the press reports that Marian Anderson was refused accommodations in the Hotel Lincoln at Springfield [Illinois] where she went to sing at the premiere of *Young Mr. Lincoln*. Negro writers and artists on tour in this country, if greeted with acclaim on the platform, are often rudely received outside the hall as human beings. They are expected, I suppose, to sleep in stables, if there happen to be no colored families in the town to accommodate them.

Ten days ago, a friend of mine, a well-known Negro novelist whose third novel has just come from the press, was invited to talk about his book before a large women's club at their clubhouse. At the hour of the lecture, the novelist could not get past the attendant at the outer door. He was forced to go to the corner drugstore and telephone the ladies that he was on the sidewalk waiting to appear before them. Doormen, you see, and elevator operators accustomed to our segregation patterns, will often not admit Negroes to hotels and clubs even when they say they are specifically invited there as guests. Negroes, in America, whether they be authors or not, are still expected to use the servant's entrance.

When these things are put into a story or book, they are not exotic or charming. There is about them no sweet southern humor—even when told in dialect—so they do not sell well. One of our oldest and most cultural of American magazines once, in turning down a story of mine—which they had a perfect right to turn down on literary grounds—wrote me a quaint little note with it. The editor said, "We believe our readers still read for pleasure."

So, in summary: The market for Negro writers is very limited. Jobs as professional writers, editorial assistants, publisher's readers, etc., are almost non-existent. Hollywood insofar as Negroes are concerned, might just as well be controlled by Hitler. The common courtesies of decent travel, hotel and restaurant accommodations, politeness from doormen, elevatormen, and hired attendants in public places is practically everywhere in America denied Negroes, whether they be writers or not. Black authors, too, must ride in Jim Crow cars.

These are some of our problems. What can you who are writers do to help us solve them? What can you, our public, do to help us solve them? My problem, your problem. No, I'm wrong! It is not a matter of *mine* and *yours.* It is a matter of *ours.* We are all Americans. We want to create the American dream, a finer and more democratic America. I cannot do it without you. You cannot do it omitting me. Can we march together then?

But perhaps the word *march* is the wrong word—suggesting soldiers and armies. Can we not put our heads together and think and plan—not merely dream—the future America? And then create it with our hands? A land where even a Negro writer can make a living, if he is a good writer. And where, being a Negro, he need not be a secondary American.

We do not want any secondary Americans. We do not want a weak and imperfect democracy. We do not want poverty and hunger and prejudice and fear on the part of any portion of our population. We want America to really be America for everybody. Let us make it so!

3

Essays, 1940–1949

"Concerning 'Goodbye, Christ,'"
LHP 262 (January 1, 1941)

Almost ten years ago now, I wrote a poem in the form of a dramatic monologue entitled "Goodbye, Christ" with the intention in mind of shocking into being in religious people a consciousness of the admitted shortcomings of the church in regard to the condition of the poor and oppressed of the world, particularly the Negro people.

Just previous to the writing of the poem, in 1931 I had made a tour through the heart of our American Southland. For the first time I saw peonage, million-dollar high schools for white children and shacks for Negro children (both of whose parents work and pay taxes and are Americans). I saw vast areas in which Negro citizens were not permitted to vote, I saw the Scottsboro boys in prison in Alabama and colored citizens of the state afraid to utter a word in their defense, I crossed rivers by ferry where the Negro drivers of cars had to wait until all the white cars behind them had been accommodated before boarding the ferry even if it meant missing the boat. I motored as far North as Seattle and back across America to New York through towns and cities where neither bed nor board was to be had if you were colored, cafes, hotels, and tourist camps were closed to all non-whites. I saw the horrors of hunger and unemployment among my people in the segregated ghettos of our great cities. I saw lecture halls and public cultural institutions closed to them. I saw the Hollywood caricatures of what pass for Negroes on the screens that condition the attitudes of a nation. I visited state and religious colleges to which no Negroes were admitted. To me these things appeared unbelievable in a Christian country. Had not Christ said, "Such as ye do unto the least of these, ye do it unto Me"? But almost nobody seemed to care. Sincere Christians seeking to combat this condition were greatly in the minority.

Directly from this extensive tour of America, I went to the Soviet Union. There it seemed to me that Marxism had put into practical being many of the precepts which our own Christian America had not yet been able to bring to life, for, in the Soviet Union, meagre as the resources of the country were, white and black, Asiatic and European, Jew and Gentile stood alike as citizens on an equal footing protected from racial inequalities by the law. There were no pogroms, no lynchings, no Jim Crow cars as there had once been in Tzarist Asia, nor were the newspapers or movies permitted to ridicule or malign any people because of race. I was deeply impressed by these things.

It was then that I wrote "Goodbye, Christ." In the poem I contrasted what seemed to me the declared and forthright position of those who, on the religious side in America (in apparent actions toward my people) had said to Christ and the Christian principles, "Goodbye, beat it on away from here now, you're done for." I gave to such religionists what seemed to me to be their own words merged with the words of the orthodox Marxist who declared he had no further use nor need for religion.

I couched the poem in the language of the first person, I, as many poets have done in the past in writing of various characters other than themselves. The *I* which I pictured was the newly liberated peasant of the state collectives I had seen in Russia merged with those American Negro workers of the depression period who believed in the Soviet dream and the hope it held out for a solution of their racial and economic difficulties. (Just as the *I* pictured in many of my blues poems is the poor and uneducated Negro of the South—and not myself who grew up in Kansas.) At the time that "Goodbye, Christ" first appeared, many persons seemed to think I was the characterized *I* of the poem. Then, as now, they failed to see the poem in connection with my other work, including many verses most sympathetic to the true Christian spirit for which I have always had great respect—such as that section of poems, "Feet Of Jesus," in my book, *The Dream Keeper,* or the chapters on religion in my novel, *Not Without Laughter,* which received the Harmon Gold Award from the Federated Council of Churches. They failed to consider "Goodbye, Christ" in the light of various of my other poems in the ironic or satirical vein, such as "Red Silk Stockings"—which some of my critics once took to be literal advice.

Today, accompanied by a sound truck playing "God Bless America" and bearing pickets from the Aimee Semple McPherson Temple of the Four Square Gospel in Los Angeles, my poem of ten years ago is resurrected without my permission and distributed on handbills before a Pasadena Hotel where I was to speak on Negro folk songs. Some weeks later it was reprinted in *The Saturday Evening Post,* a magazine whose columns, like the doors of many of our churches, has been until recently entirely closed to Negroes, and whose chief contribution in the past to a better understanding of Negro life in America has been the Octavus Roy Cohen stories with which most colored people have been utterly disgusted.[1]

Now, in the year 1941, having left the terrain of "the radical at twenty" to approach the "conservative of forty," I would not and could not write "Goodbye, Christ," desiring no longer to *épater le bourgeois.* However, since those at present engaged in distributing my poem do not date it, nor say how long ago it was written, I feel impelled for the benefit of persons reading the poem for the first time, to make the following statement:

"Goodbye, Christ" does not represent my personal viewpoint. It was long ago withdrawn from circulation and has been reprinted recently without my knowledge or consent. I would not now use such a technique of approach since I feel that a mere poem is quite unable to compete in power to shock with the current horrors of war and oppression abroad in the greater part of the world. I have never been a member of the Communist party. Furthermore, I have come to believe that no system of ethics, religion, morals, or government is of permanent value which does not first start with and change the human heart. Mortal frailty, greed, and error, know no boundary lines. The explosives of war do not care whose hands fashion them. Certainly, both Marxists and Christians can be cruel. Would that Christ came back to save us all. We do not know how to save ourselves.

"Jeffers: Man, Sea, and Poetry," LHP 559 (January 10, 1941)

Not merely because his house is by the sea and the sound and sight of waves are always without his windows and the smell and salt of sea air always within his dooryard, does Robinson Jeffers seem to belong to and be a part of the sea. Not merely because his house is built of grey stones that are but an extension of, and tower above the cliffs of Carmel's ocean front, does Jeffers seem to belong to the sea. But even more because of a quality in the man himself and in his work, a quality of great depth and great strength, and calm, and immense power, does Robinson Jeffers seem to belong to the sea that is his dooryard and his horizon.

The ever clean quality of the sea to absorb and transfigure all the mud and silt and earth-wash of all the rivers in the world that empty into it, and still remain salt and clean and foam tinged and beautiful, is the quality of the sea that has always held and intrigued me. There is that same quality about the poems of the man Jeffers, and about the man himself. All of human terror and frailty, and all the mud of mankind's earth-rooted feet and the sea-wind and sky-wind in men's hair, and their hands that would find a star, and the shock of rock here and star there through the human body—absorbing and transfiguring and changing the chemicals that are ours and the earth's and the sea's—these things come to rest in Jeffers, are there on the pages of his books, are clean and clear in his noble friendly face and the strong clasp of his hand.

English poetry and American Carmel and the sea road that curves past Tor House salute him this January tenth in honor of his birthday, which is the birthday, too, of the earth-songs and the wave-songs that are his books.

"Democracy, Negroes, and Writers," LHP 286 (May 13, 1941)

Writing is the urge to tell folks about it. About what? About what hurts you inside. Colored folks, through the sheer fact of being colored, have got plenty hurting them inside. You see, we, too, are one of those minority races the newspapers are always talking about. Except that we are here in America, not in Europe, fourteen million of us—a rather large minority, but still a minority.

Now, what's hurting us? Well, Jim Crow is hurting us. Ghettos, and segregation, and lack of jobs is hurting us. Signs up: COLORED TRADE NOT DESIRED, and dirty names such as the Jews know under Hitler hurt us. So those of us who are writers have plenty to tell the world about.

To us democracy is a paradox, full of contradictions. Sure, in the North Negroes can vote, but we can't work in airplane factories and various other defense industries supported with *our* tax money as well as that of other citizens. In the South we can't vote, but we can howl to high heaven about it in our newspapers—and run the risk of lynching and the Ku Klux Klan for howling. In Mississippi the state spends nine times as much for the education of each white child as it does to educate a Negro child, yet the Negro population equals the white, and the wealth of the state is based on the labor of Negroes in the sun of the cotton fields. We give and others take. That's what makes us mad. So we feel bad and have to write about it.

The color line runs right on down from capital through labor, although labor is waking up a bit. But in many industries today the factories won't hire us because they say the unions won't admit us, and the unions won't admit us because they say the factories won't hire us: a vicious circle into which a swastika fits perfectly. We can sweep a floor almost anywhere if a white man doesn't need the job, but even if we graduate from Massachusetts Institute of Technology, we still are not permitted to run a machine in the average American Factory. A great many Negroes work, study, and learn, and then are frustrated by the blind alley of color-segregation in American industry. That color line runs all the way through culture and the arts, as well. There are world-famous and very great American Negro singers, some of whom have appeared in opera abroad, but not one had been asked to appear at the Metropolitan. And in many cities where they sing, their own people, the Negro concert goers, are Jim Crowed and segregated. There are some excellent Negro writers in this country, too, but, to my knowledge, none is employed at present in Hollywood where the real money for writers lies. All along the line, we suffer economic discrimination of a discouraging and arbitrary sort, be we artisan or artist.

The League of American Writers, meeting in their Fourth Writer's Congress in New York on June 6th, has been one of the few cultural organizations to take up the fight for the artistic and economic equality of the Negro writer. Another stand of equal importance to Negro, and all writers, is the League's position on freedom of speech and publication. To colored people in the United States this is of particular importance as the trend toward suppression and censorship is growing and already there is a tendency to attempt to prevent Negro newspapers, with their editorials against discrimination in defense industries and the Jim Crow set-up of our army and navy, from being read by Negro soldiers and draftees in the army camps. From this it is but a step to the actual suppression of Negro papers, or else the censorship of their articles and editorials.

Negroes, like all other Americans, are being asked at the moment to prepare to defend democracy. But Negroes would very much like to have a little more democracy to defend. And democracy is achieved only through constant vigilance, struggle, and the educational processes of the written and spoken word. For Negro writers it is vital that the channels of free press and publication be kept open. It is necessary to the well-being of the creative soul that the harsh and ugly aspects of our life be exposed to public view in order that they might be changed and remedied in accordance with the democratic ideals for which we are urged to be ready to die. But ideals on paper mean very little. They must be put into practice. Writers must be free to call for and work toward the realization of full democracy in regard to peoples of all colors, else the light will rapidly go out for everyone of us, white or Negro, gentile or Jew, for if we wish to preserve democracy, we must not only defend it but *extend* it.

"Ancient Contemporaries in the Forest Theatre," LHP 35 (June 1941)

It is fitting that Robinson Jeffers' modern version in play form of the ancient Greek legend of Clytemnestra, Agamemnon, and Electra should be performed in the Forest Theatre in the open air as were performed the dramas of the Greeks.[2] Down the stairs of a palace built in the Carmel Woods next week the ancient passions brought alive again in *The Tower beyond Tragedy* will circle and cry their tender pain and conflict old as the first yesterday and new as tomorrow. Jeffers' poem echoes eternal tragedies—as the same passions still flare in the human heart as flared in the days when daggers not pistols were the best weapons for settling private quarrels, and spears instead of dive bombers for wars. But a mere change in weapons makes little difference in what people or nations fight about. The trials and tribulations of Jeffers' dim and distant kings and queens become no less contemporary than those of California's recent front-page duchess of gangdom. And Agamemnon's soldiers fallen before the walls of some ancient city no less real than the Australian dead on the cliffs of Crete[3]—for words and legends have kept the Greeks of centuries ago alive.

In Carmel there lives a great weaver of words and legends, Robinson Jeffers. Fortunate indeed are we to have him here. And fortunate that the city fathers have seen fit to grant the town's lovely outdoor theatre to a production for the first time in a professional manner of one of Jeffers' plays with a great actress, Judith Anderson, appearing therein—thus Carmel herself writes a new page in the mighty history of the theatre. And that vital lady, Clytemnestra, comes to life again just off Ocean Avenue.

"Songs Called the Blues," *Phylon* 2 (summer 1941): 143–45

The blues are folk-songs born out of heartache. They are songs of the black South, particularly the city South. Songs of the poor streets and back alleys of Memphis and Birmingham, Atlanta and Galveston, out of black, beaten, but unbeatable throats, from the strings of pawn-shop guitars, and the chords of pianos with no ivory on the keys.

The Blues and the Spirituals are two great Negro gifts to American music. The Spirituals are group songs, but the Blues are songs you sing alone. The Spirituals are religious songs, born in camp meetings and remote plantation districts. But the Blues are *city* songs rising from the crowded streets of big towns, or beating against the lonely walls of hall bed-rooms where you can't sleep at night. The Spirituals are escape songs, looking toward heaven, tomorrow, and God. But the Blues are *today* songs, here and now, broke and broken-hearted, when you're troubled in mind and don't know what to do, and nobody cares.

There are many kinds of Blues. There are the family Blues, when a man and woman have quarreled, and the quarrel can't be patched up. There's the loveless Blues, when you haven't even got anybody to quarrel with. And there's the left-lonesome Blues, when the one you care for's gone away. Then there's also the broke-and-hungry Blues, a stranger in a strange town. And, the desperate going-to-the-river Blues that say:

> I'm goin' down to de river
> And take ma rockin' chair—
> If the Blues overcome me,
> I'm gonna rock on away from here!

But it's not always as bad as that, because there's another verse that declares:

> Goin' down to de railroad,
> Lay ma head on de track.
> I'm goin' to de railroad,
> Lay ma head on the track—
> But if I see de train a-comin'
> I'm gonna jerk it back!

For sad as Blues may be, there's almost always something humorous about them—even if it's the kind of humor that laughs to keep from crying. You know,

> I went to de gypsy's
> To get ma fortune told.
> Went to de gypsy's

To get ma fortune told,
But the gypsy said, dog-gone
Your un-hard-lucky soul!

In America, during the last quarter of a century, there have been many great singers of the Blues, but the finest of all were the three famous Smiths—no relation, one to another—Mamie Smith, Clara Smith, and the astonishing Bessie Smith. Clara and Bessie are both dead now, and Mamie no longer sings, but thousands of Blues collectors in the United States and abroad prize their records. Today a girl named Georgia White carries on the old tradition of the Blues in the folk manner. And Midge Williams, of the Louis Armstrong band, sings them in a more polished, but effective way. Of the men, Lonnie Johnson is perhaps the finest living male singer of the Blues, although that portly fellow Jimmy Rushing in Count Basie's orchestra is a runner-up. And Lead Belly, of course, is in a class by himself.[4]

The most famous Blues, as everybody knows, is the *St. Louis Blues,* that Mr. W. C. Handy wrote down one night on the corner of a bar on a levee street in St. Louis thirty years ago, and which has since gone all over the world. The *St. Louis Blues* is sung more than any other song on the air waves, is known in Shanghai and Buenos Aires, Paris and Berlin—in fact, is heard so often in Europe that a great many Europeans think it must be the American National Anthem.

Less popular, but equally beautiful are the Blues, *Troubled In Mind, Memphis Blues, Yellow Dog Blues,* and the never to be surpassed *Gulf Coast Blues,* which begins with one of the loneliest lines in all the realm of song:

The mail man passed but
He didn't leave no news . . .

Blues are still being made. One of the newest authentic Blues to come up out of the South, by way of the colored boys in the government work camps, is the *DuPree Blues,* that sad story of a man who wanted to give his girl a diamond ring, but had none to give her, so he took his gun and went to the jewelry store where, instead of getting the diamond ring, he got the jewelry man, jail, and the noose.

The real Negro Blues are as fine as any folk music we have, and I'm hoping that the day will come when famous concert singers like Marian Anderson and Paul Robeson will include a group of Blues on their programs as well as the Spirituals which they now sing so effectively.

A young dancer in New York, Felicia Sorel, is already using the Blues as a background for the creation of new dance forms. I see no reason why great dances could not be born of the Blues. Great American dances containing all the laughter and pain, hunger and heartaches, search and reality of the contemporary scenes—for the Blues have something that goes beyond race or sectional limits, that appeals to the ear and heart of people everywhere—otherwise, how could it be that in a Tokio restaurant one night I heard a Louis Armstrong record of the *St. Louis Blues* played over and over for a crowd of Japanese diners there? You don't have to understand the words to know the meaning of the Blues, or to feel their sadness, or to hope their hopes:

Troubled in mind, I'm blue!
But I won't be blue always:
De sun's gonna shine
In my back door someday!

"Negro Writers and the War,"
LHP 773 (August 24, 1942)

There is an old story almost everyone has heard.[5] The version I remember is this:

During slavery time on a certain big plantation, the slaves were very meagrely fed. Although master's bins and smoke-houses were bursting with food, the field hands had only cow peas, corn pone, and bitter molasses day after day. One night, sitting in her cabin, an old slave woman said, "Huh! I *do* wish I had some ham!"

From his pallet in the corner, her grandson commented, "Old Massa's smoke-house is just full of hams. I could sneak in there some evening and steal one, Granny—then we all could eat."

"Un-huh!" cried the old woman sternly. "That's wicked! Satan done put that thought in your head. Wouldn't nobody but the Devil steal a ham. Stop that talk and go to sleep, boy!"

The boy went to sleep, but he dreamed about a great big juicy ham, dozens of great big old juicy hams hanging from the rafters in Massa's well-stocked smoke-house. Grandma dreamed about hams, too, perhaps. When the good things of life are consistently denied folks, they often think about them over much, even in their sleep.

A few nights later, as Granny bent above the fireplace putting together a meagre supper—a hoe-cake in the ashes, two tin plates of molasses—

she heard bare feet running toward the house in the darkness. Suddenly, as the feet went past, through the open window a ham sailed, a great big old juicy ham. It fell ker-plunk in the front of the fire as her grandson fled in the dusk. The old woman stooped down and picked up the ham.

"Halleluiah!" she cried, shouting. "Thank God for this ham—even if the Devil did bring it!"

That is the way a lot of colored people feel about democratic gains and the war. They feel that Executive Order 8802 opening defense plants to all without discrimination, the abolition of Jim Crow seating on the Washington-Virginia busses, and other similar advances are a kind of ham that indirectly the Japanese and the Germans have thrown them—by forcing democracy to recognize belatedly some of its own failings in regard to the Negro people.[6] The trouble is that many colored folks do not think as strongly as they should that the Germans and the Japanese are *really* devils, and very dangerous ones, at that. Some colored people mistakenly think Talmadge, Rankin, and Dixon are more devilish because they are closer at hand and holler so loud. The truth of the matter is, of course, that they are *all* devils—Hitler, Mussolini, and Hirohito abroad, plus their Klan-minded followers at home.[7] It is the duty of Negro writers to point out this fact. But since all Negroes recognize deviltry at home, the stress should be laid on those devils abroad whom we are now engaged in fighting—so that our race will fully realize how dangerous they are and how, in triumph, they would merely back up the worst of our enemies at home.

That in large areas of this country deplorable racial conditions exist, nobody can deny. But that some attempts at improvement have been set in motion by our government since the war is also true. Also that great newspapers like *PM* in New York, great Americans like Vice-President Wallace, Eleanor Roosevelt, Paul Robeson, and Pearl Buck openly fight our battles as part of democracy's, and that even in the traditionally Jim Crow city of Washington, Jim Crowism has begun ever so slowly and weakly, but slightly, to crack—these are facts of great importance.[8] That huge pro-democracy, anti-Jim Crow meetings of Negroes have been held from New York to Los Angeles in recent weeks is of great importance. And the fact that the Negro press, our several hundred valiant colored newspapers have been clearer on the war aims and the real meaning of world democracy than any similar number of white newspapers is also of very great importance. Negro editors know what democracy is about because they haven't got much of it—and they want it.

But we do have in America freedom of press and of speech denied, for instance, to Jews—and Negroes—in Germany. In Berlin now a Negro can no longer even blow a trumpet in a jazz band—silenced musically as well as verbally. In Japan under the current militarist regime nobody, no matter what color they are, can speak out for any liberal cause. It's the same in Italy. The Axis is out to crush the little people all over the world, to dominate by force of arms everything from labor to radio, from women in kitchens (where the Axis likes them) to jazz bands. The fact that the Japanese have slapped a few white faces in Hong Kong to the delight of American Negroes who have been maltreated by Jim Crow, does not mean that the Japanese are friends of ours. The Japanese militarists are more nearly friends of Dixon and Talmadge. They use the same tactics to keep down subject peoples under them—and to submerge their own liberals and intellectuals, as well. Japanese militarism is a reactionary force, like the German, that respects nobody else's face, white or colored.

Therefore, it is the duty of Negro writers to point out quite clearly that it is an error to think of World War II in terms of race—in spite of the apparent determination of the British imperialists in India to force people to think that way. We have to remember that English imperialism, for as long as it could, treated the Irish about the same as they do the Indians—and the Irish are white. Imperialism does not run by color. Korea under Japan has today a kind of Asiatic Jim Crow. Imperialism everywhere dies hard. Africa is still enchained and needn't even read the Atlantic Charter. But the pro-democratic forces who are fighting this war for the Allies will have to consider the freedom of Africa at the peace table—or go right back where they started to economic chaos and further war.

It is the duty of Negro writers to reveal the international aspects of our problems at home, to show how these problems are merely a part of the great problem of world freedom everywhere, to show how our local fascists are blood brothers of the Japanese fascists—though they speak with a Dixie drawl, to show how on the great battle front of the world we must join hands with the crushed common people of Europe, the Soviet Union, the Chinese, and unite our efforts—else we who are American Negroes will have not only the Klan on our necks in intensified fashion, but the Gestapo, as well.[9] (And the Nazis, I am sure, could teach the Klan a few things, for the Germans do not bother with silly crosses and childish nightshirts. Death and the concentration camp are more effective.)

But for Negro writers to point out merely the negative reasons for full Negro co-operation in the war effort—merely that we should fight because, although Alabama is bad, the Axis is worse, is to throw out of perspective the basic reasons why all oppressed peoples must take part in the current struggle to overcome the devils of the world. The reasons are that Hitlerism, Fascism, and Japanese imperialism are but intensifications and buttresses of all that is bad, indeed all the *worst,* left over from barbarism in world politics and government today. They represent the old techniques of force and robbery carried out in their boldest form without even lip service to decency. They represent racial oppression as a means of economic oppression without even pretending to do otherwise. The Axis represents organized gangsterism lifted to government. Against their bombs and machine guns—their frank and deadly Jim Crow—the darker millions of the world, including ourselves, could be for generations helpless.

Negro journalists have so far been the best writers among us since December 7th. They have been clear, brave, and hard-hitting. They have sometimes written movingly and with great effect—their articles on the death of Waller, the slugging of Roland Hayes.[10] The journalists have beaten the creative writers, poets, essayists, and novelists all hollow of late. They have pleaded, cajoled, explained the need of, and demanded democracy for the fourteen million sub-citizens of this country week by week. They deserve great praise. If creative writers, during the course of the war, get into their poems, stories, novels, and plays half the hard-hitting fire of Negro weekly journalism, very likely *the* great novel, or great poem of World War II—like a flaming dream of democracy—will come from the pen of a Negro—a Richard Wright, a Sterling Brown, or a Margaret Walker.[11]

Unfortunately, however, our journalists have written almost entirely for publications read exclusively by Negroes. The creative writers then, who publish in the general American magazines, have a task before them of great positive value to carry out. It is their duty to explain to our white American brothers why it is urgently necessary that we now and immediately take steps in this country—for *all* our sakes—to wipe out all forms of public discrimination against minorities within our borders. Great masses of white people are even yet only vaguely aware of the enormous discrimination against Negroes. They do not realize how difficult it is for us to earn a decent living, nor how essential it is that Order 8802 really be carried out ALL over America. They do not realize the indignities of the Jim Crow car on Southern railways, nor how hungry—not to speak of angry—a Negro soldier can get coming home on furlough penned up in the black coach and denied service in the public dining cars of Dixie trains. They do not realize how, when Negro soldiers march through a colored community with all white officers at their head, Negroes mutter, "The white man's always boss. Won't even let us lead our own troops out to die."

A great many white people still accept the false grinning caricatures of the movies as being true of colored people—Negroes are happy-go-lucky, they always smile, they always sing, they don't care what happens to them, they're not sensitive about persecution or segregation. Probably the British and the Dutch thought that about the Malayans, too—but the Malayans welcomed the Japanese when they came. Maybe now the British think the Indians do not mind a declaration of war in which they have no part—but they do mind. Just as maybe our Southern whites think Negroes do not mind being unable to vote in most of the South—but they do mind. Fear and intimidation may keep them from saying so. It is the duty of our writers to express what these voiceless people cannot say, and to relate their longings for decency and fairness to the world aims of the President's Four Freedoms for everybody.[12]

Furthermore, we must study methods for the practical working out of these democratic aims at home now, and present concrete plans to our white brothers with whom we have to work as to how we may create a fully democratic America. We must show them that it will not injure them to be fair to us. It will instead help them. We must stress the fact that in this coming world of international co-operation, no one group within a country or without, can work alone. That all of us might live, let's be decent to one another. Our white fellow citizens must be made to realize that Jim Crow and all it symbolizes—meagre educational facilities, discrimination in industries, lynchings—is not decent. It is an anachronism in American life that, especially for the sake of the war effort, must be gotten rid of—and soon. After all, this *is* a war for freedom. Its logic must be straight in order for it to be successful. It is not logical to speak of freedom for Poland and forget Georgia. These things Negro writers must tell America. After all, it embarrasses us to see our white folks acting foolish.

"What Shall We Do about the South?"

Common Ground 3 (1943): 3–6

For a New Yorker of color, the South begins at Newark. A half hour by tube from the Hudson Terminal and one comes across street-corner hamburger stands that will not serve a hamburger to a Negro customer wishing to sit on a stool. For the same dime a white pays, a Negro must take his hamburger elsewhere in a paper bag and eat it, minus a plate, a napkin, and a glass of water. Jim Crow always means less for the one Jim Crowed and an unequal value for his money—no stool, no shelter, merely the hamburger, in Newark.

As the colored traveler goes further south by train, Jim Crow increases. Philadelphia is ninety minutes from Manhattan. There the all-colored grammar school begins, the separate education of the races that Talmadge of Georgia so highly approves. An hour or so further down the line is Baltimore, where segregation laws are written in the state and city codes. Another hour by train, Washington. There the conductor tells the Negro traveler to go into the Jim Crow coach behind the engine, usually half a baggage car, next to trunks and dogs.

That this change to complete Jim Crow happens at Washington is highly significant of the state of American democracy in relation to colored peoples today. Washington, as the capital of this nation, is one of the great centers of the Allied war effort toward the achievement of the Four Freedoms. Yet to a South-bound Negro citizen told at Washington to change into a segregated coach, the Four Freedoms have a hollow sound, like distant lies not meant to be the truth in the land of the Jim Crow car.

The train crosses the Potomac into Virginia, and from there on throughout the South life for the Negro, by state law and custom, is a hamburger in a sack without a plate, water, napkin, or stool—but at the same price as the whites pay—to be eaten apart from the others without shelter. The Negro can do little about this because the law is against him, he has no vote, the police are brutal, and the citizens think it is as it should be. For his seat in the half-coach of the crowded Jim Crow car, a colored man must pay the same fare as those who ride in the air-cooled coaches further back and are privileged to use the diner when they wish. For his hamburger in a sack served without courtesy the southern Negro must pay taxes but refrain from going to the polls, must patriotically accept conscription to work, fight, and perhaps die to regain or maintain freedom for people off in Europe or Australia when he hasn't it himself at home. To his ears most of the war speeches about freedom sound perfectly foolish, unreal, high-flown, and false. To many southern whites, too, it must all seem like playacting—the grand talk so nobly delivered, so poorly executed.

Liberals and persons of good will, North and South, including, no doubt, our President himself, are puzzled as to what on earth to do about the South—the poll tax South, the Jim Crow South—that so effectively and openly gives the lie to democracy. With the brazen frankness of Hitler's *Mein Kampf,* Dixie speaks through Talmadge, Rankin, Dixon, Arnall, and Mark Ethridge.[13]

In a public speech in Birmingham, Mr. Ethridge said, "All the armies of the world, both of the United States and the Axis, could not force upon the South an abandonment of racial segregation."[14] Governor Dixon of Alabama refused a government war contract offered Alabama State Prison because it contained an anti-discrimination clause which in his eyes was an "attempt to abolish segregation of races in the South. . . . We will not place ourselves in a position to be attacked by those who seek to foster their own pet social reforms," said he. In other words, Alabama will not reform. It is as bullheaded as England in India, and its Governor is not ashamed to say so.

As a proof of southern intolerance, almost daily the press reports some new occurrence of physical brutality against Negroes. Governor Talmadge was "too busy" to investigate when Roland Hayes and his wife were thrown into jail and the great tenor beaten on complaint of a shoe salesman over a dispute as to what seat in his shop a Negro should occupy when buying shoes. Nor did the Governor of Mississippi bother when Hugh Gloster, professor of English at Morehouse College, riding as an interstate passenger, was illegally ejected from a train in his state, beaten, arrested, and fined because, being in an overcrowded Jim Crow coach, he asked for a seat in an adjacent car which contained only two white passengers. Legally, the Jim Crow laws do not apply to interstate travel but the FBI has not yet got around to enforcing that Supreme Court ruling. Recently, en route from San Francisco to Oklahoma City, Fred Wright, a county probation officer of color, was beaten and forced into the Texas Jim Crow coach on a transcontinental train by order of the conductor, in defiance of federal law. A seventy-six-year-old clergyman, Dr. Jackson of Hartford, Connecticut, going into the South for the National Baptist Convention in September, was set upon by white passengers for merely passing through a white coach on the way to his own seat. There have been similar attacks upon colored soldiers in uniform on public carriers. One such attack resulted in death for the soldier, dragged from a bus and killed by civilian police. Every day now, Negro soldiers from the North, returning home on furlough from southern camps, report incident after incident of humiliating travel treatment below the Mason-Dixon line.

It seems obvious that the South does not yet know what this war is about.

As answer Number One to the question "What Shall We Do About the South?" I would suggest an immediate and intensive federally directed program of pro-democratic education, to be put into all schools of the South from the first grade to the universities. As a part of the war effort, this is urgently needed. The Spanish Loyalist Government had trench schools for its soldiers and night schools for civilians even in Madrid under siege. We are not yet under siege. We still have time (but not too much) to teach our people what we are fighting for, and to begin to apply these teachings to race relations at home. You see, it would be too bad for an emissary of color from one of the Latin American countries, say Cuba or Brazil, to arrive at Miami Airport and board a train for Washington, only to get beaten up and thrown off by white Southerners who do not yet realize how many colored allies we have—nor how badly we need them—and that it is inconsiderate and impolite to beat colored people, anyway. Education as to the real meaning of this war might help the South a little in this respect.

Because transportation is so symbolic of the whole racial problem in the South, the Number Two thing for us to do is evolve a way out of the Jim Crow car dilemma at once. Would a system of first, second, and third class coaches help? In Europe, formerly, if one did not wish to ride with peasants and tradespeople, one could pay a little more and solve that problem by having a first class coach almost entirely to himself. Most Negroes can hardly afford parlor car seats. Why not abolish Jim Crow entirely and let the whites who wish to do so ride in coaches where few Negroes have the funds to be? In any case, our Chinese, Latin American, and Russian allies are not going to think any too much of our democratic pronunciamentos as long as we keep compulsory Jim Crow cars on southern rails.

Since most people learn a little through education, albeit slowly, as Number Three I should suggest that the government draft all the leading Negro intellectuals, sociologists, writers, and concert singers, from Alain Locke of Oxford and W. E. B. Du Bois of Harvard to Dorothy Maynor and Paul Robeson of Carnegie Hall, and send them into the South to appear before white audiences, carrying messages of culture and democracy, thus offsetting the old stereotypes of the southern mind and the Hollywood movie, and explaining to the people, without dialect, what the war aims are about. With each, send on tour a liberal white

Southerner like Paul Green, Erskine Caldwell, Pearl Buck, or William Seabrook. And, of course, include soldiers to protect them.[15]

Number Four, as to the Army—draftees are in sore need of education on how to behave toward darker peoples. Just as a set of government suggestions has lately been issued to our soldiers on how to act in England, so a similar set should be given them on how to act in Alabama, Georgia, Texas, India, China, Africa, Brazil—wherever there are colored peoples. Not only printed words, but intensive training in the reasons for being decent to everybody. Classes in democracy and the war aims should be set up in every training camp in America and every unit of our military forces already abroad. These forces should be armed with understanding as well as armament.

I go on the premise that Southerners are reasonable people, but that they just simply do not know nowadays what they are doing, nor how bad their racial attitudes look to the rest of the civilized world. I know their politicians, their schools, and the Hollywood movies have done their best to uphold prevailing reactionary viewpoints. Heretofore nobody in America, really, except a few radicals, liberals, and a handful of true religionists, have cared much about either the Negroes or the South. Their sincere efforts to effect a change have been but a drop in a muddy bucket.

Basically, of course, the South needs universal suffrage, economic stabilization, a balanced diet, vitamins for children. But until those things are achieved, a few mild but helpful steps might be taken on a lesser front, to ameliorate—not solve—the Negro problem.

It might be pointed out to the South, for instance, that the old bugaboo of sex and social equality doesn't mean a thing. Nobody as a rule sleeps with or eats with or dances with or marries anybody else except by mutual consent. Millions of people in New York, Chicago, and Seattle go to the same polls and vote without ever cohabiting together. Why does the South think it would be otherwise with Negroes were they permitted to vote there? Or have a decent education? Or sit on a stool in a public place and eat a hamburger? Why they think simple civil rights would force a Southerner's daughter to marry a Negro in spite of herself, I have never been able to understand. It must be due to some lack somewhere in their schooling.

A federally sponsored educational program of racial decency could, furthermore, point out to its students that co-operation in labor would be to the advantage of all—rather than to the disadvantage of anyone, white or black. It could show quite clearly that a million unused colored hands barred from war industries might mean a million weapons lacking in the hands of our soldiers on some foreign front—and a million extra deaths—including southern white boys needlessly dying under Axis fire—because Governor Dixon of Alabama and others of like mentality need a little education. It might also be pointed out that when peace comes and the Southerners go to the peace table, if they take there with them the traditional Dixie racial attitudes, there is no possible way for them to aid in forming any peace at all that will last. China, India, Brazil and Free French Africa, Soviet Asia, and the whole Middle East will not believe a word they say.

Peace only to breed other wars is a sorry peace, one we must plan now to avoid. Not only in order to win the war but to create a peace along decent lines, we had best start *now* to educate the South. That education can not be left to well-meaning but numerically weak civilian organizations. Government itself should take over—and vigorously. After all, Washington is the place where the conductor comes through every Southbound train and says, "Colored people, change to the Jim Crow car ahead."

That car, in these days and times, has no business being "ahead." War's freedom train can hardly trail along with glory behind a Jim Crow coach. No matter how streamlined the other cars may be, that coach endangers all humanity's hopes for a peaceful tomorrow.

"Maker of the Blues," *Negro Digest* 1.3 (January 1943): 37–38

The other day, W. C. Handy was 69 years old. He is the dean of popular American Negro musicians, and the composer of the greatest American song written in our time—"The St. Louis Blues." For more than a quarter of a century, this song has been heard around the world everywhere, played by dance bands from Constantinople to Melbourne, Cape Town to Seattle. I heard it sung in Japanese by a popular star in Tokyo. It was often used by the orchestra at the smart Metropol hotel in Moscow when I went dancing there. I've heard Bessie Smith sing it, Bing Crosby croon it, Louis Armstrong beat it out.

Most people would think of a man nearing 70 as old. It is impossible to think of W. C. Handy as old. He is much more active today than many people 40 years his junior. He has the same kind of incredible energy that enables Mrs. Roosevelt to keep dates in San Antonio and Washington on the same day, then speak in Seattle 24 hours later.

W. C. Handy does two shows a night at the Diamond Horseshoe.[16] At two in the morning his car and chauffeur call for him and drive him to Harlem. At an hour when most people have had half their night's rest he is just getting to bed. But he's up bright and early listening to the radio shortly after eight the next morning, and ready for his morning's mail when his secretary comes at nine. He covers a heavy correspondence, answers dozens of phone calls, often receives interviewers or agents while still at breakfast, and with a full morning behind him, frequently reaches his Broadway office before noon. When the "Old Man" comes into the office things start humming.

Handy Brothers Music company is right on Broadway in the heart of the theatrical district, just across the street from the building that housed the once famous Cotton Club.[17] The offices occupy an entire corner suite overlooking the bright heart of Tin Pan Alley.

W. C. Handy says, "As long as there is a Broadway, I want the firm of Handy Brothers here, so that any Negro boy or girl coming to New York with his music under his arm will be sure of a place where he can get a sympathetic hearing."

And the "Old Man," as he is affectionately called around the office, means what he says. W. C. Handy is a "race man." He is proud of the Negro music that he has helped popularize and create. He feels that the potentialities of this great music are unlimited. He knows that some day it will be the basis for great ballets, great sonatas, and great new forms still unevolved. He knows that already the American Negro has given to the world a musical treasure beyond compare.

Normally, at night, other people have stopped their work and gone to bed. Not W. C. Handy. Often after dark, his apartment is humming with activity, typists are typing, secretaries are receiving dictation, the chauffeur is waiting for his orders, a couple of out-of-town visitors are trying to get a word in edgewise, and in the midst of it all, the "Old Man" sits down at the piano to demonstrate the new harmonies he has conceived for the arrangement of an old spiritual his firm is bringing out, or perhaps to indicate to the visitors the difference between the strictly counted beat of "white" music and the flowing but persuasively smooth rhythm of Negro music.

The Handy office, or apartment, when the "Old Man" is around is often like a scene from that highly dynamic play, *You Can't Take It With You*. Dozens of things are happening at once. At midnight, he speeds down Riverside Drive toward the Diamond Horseshoe for the last show. When the lights come up for the finale, the incredibly sweet notes of the "St. Louis Blues" flow from that golden trumpet.

When you hear W. C. Handy play it, after midnight at the Diamond Horseshoe in New York, you wouldn't believe that he had put in a long day of hard work since early morning. I tell you these things to show you that a mighty lot of energy, race pride, will-to-create, love of music and of all people—went into the making of the "St. Louis Blues." It is a great song and he is a great man.

"Is Hollywood Fair to Negroes?"
Negro Digest 1.6 (April 1943): 19–21

This is a very touchy subject with Negro actors.[18] I know a great many of them personally and like them, and like some of them much better as people than I do as actors—so I hope they don't get mad at me for what I am about to say. But the time has come for them to do better, particularly in Hollywood.

For a generation now, the Negro has been maligned, caricatured, and lied about on the American screen, and pictured to the whole world in theatres from Los Angeles to Bombay, Montreal to Cape Town as being nothing more than a funny-looking, dull-witted but comic servant. Even Hollywood knows that is not a true picture of American Negro life. Of course, we have in our group funny-looking, dull-witted, comic domestics—as have the Jews, the Irish, the Poles, and the just ordinary New England and old-stock white folks. But Hollywood does not people the screen exclusively with such characters when it comes to white folks.

Those roles, speaking by and large, are ALL they give us to do on the screen—yes sir, yes ma'am, come seven, come eleven, praise-de-Lawd, whaw - whaw - whaw, boss roles. To judge from the Hollywood screen, nobody would think there was an educated, well-groomed, self-respecting Negro in America—or that many colored servants speak perfect English and are not afraid of ghosts or their employers.

It is time now for the Negro actor to stop degrading the Negro people on the screen. With defense work running full blast, they can all get jobs elsewhere, if it is still a matter of bread and meat. Poverty used to be the old excuse. They used to say, "But we have to make a living."

Unfortunately, some colored actors continue to think of Hollywood only as a job. They do not seem to realize that the motion picture is and has always been one of the greatest propaganda and educational mediums in the world. And that millions of people take what they see on the screen to be an approximate representation of contemporary life in America—which is why so many otherwise uninformed people all over the earth think so disparagingly of the American Negro—because they see him on the screen—the only place they see him—always so stupidly portrayed—and portrayed by Negroes.

Some of our colored artists are very fine actors, and they do excellently by the miserable material Hollywood gives them. They are sometimes very bothered inside themselves at the roles assigned them. Others have a hard and cynical approach to their art. "Negroes have no money," they say. "They don't support us. White folks pay our salaries."

That certainly explains, but can never excuse, what they are doing to the Negro people. The Bundists and Fifth Columnists can very well say, "Hitler pays us. That is why we are betraying America." Money never meant decency.[19]

The best of our Negro actors who have been working in Hollywood for years have enough money now, or should have, to retire for the rest of their days. Living comfortably like ladies and gentlemen and owning their own lovely California homes, there is no longer any reason for them to keep on being domestic Uncle Toms for celluloid white folks and carrying to all the Allied Nations in these serious times Hollywood's false version of the Negro's inferiority.

There are great roles for Negro artists to play. Let Louise Beavers play Sojourner Truth or the life of that renowned poetess of George Washington's day, Phillis Wheatley. Let that fine actress Hattie McDaniel play Harriet Tubman in a sure-enough *Gone With The Wind* that shows how slavery was wiped out and how courageous Negro men and women helped to wipe it out. Let that great colored showman, Clarence Muse, play Colonel Charles Young or Crispus Attucks. Let Leigh Whipper play the late Dr. George Washington Carver or the Emperor Haile Selassie. Let superb Ethel Waters play Black Patti, the Marian Anderson of her day, beautiful in lace and spangles.[20] Let the glamorous Lena Horne play a lovely and heroic Negro war nurse in North Africa or the South Seas—for there are Negro nurses abroad, and good looking ones at that!

Why should Miss Horne, in her first important screen role, have to be a strumpet and a hussy? I presume, Hollywood thinks that the white world thinks that all Negro women are strumpets and hussies if they are pretty, comic servants if they are not so pretty—and Hollywood above all wants to be box-office, even though it betrays a race in the process.

But do the finest Negro actors in the world have to continue to help a prejudiced Hollywood make money at the expense of the decency and good-will of the Negro people? Couldn't Rochester give all those actors jobs in his defense factory making parachutes? Or do you suppose that in real life they are all stupid and lazy? Personally, I know that is not true. They are hard-working, talented men and women.

But when white folks see them in the movies, they think these Negro actors are portraying their REAL selves. That is what makes the fantasy of the screen so dangerously harmful to the colored people. And that is why it is time now, actors, for you-all to stop.

"The Case against Segregation,"
Negro Digest 1.9 (July 1943): 45–46

When I read about the signs up in Germany, "Aryans Only," that exclude Jews from restaurants and other public places, I think it is pretty bad. But I think it is equally bad when I see signs up in America separating Negroes from whites, or barring out Negroes altogether. And I do see them from New York to California.

I think the Negro is right in demanding an end to segregation in the armed forces of the United States. From the segregated regiment it is naturally no step at all to segregated tables for Negro and white officers, Jim Crow seats for Negroes in the post movies, colored and white toilets, and unscientific cans of Jim Crow blood via the Red Cross.

When the army sets the pattern, then with logic the railroads, private employers, and ordinary citizens can say, "To the Jim Crow with you, black boy. To the labor gang. To the segregated local union. Up the back stairs to the movies. You go to a Jim Crow army. Why shouldn't we segregate you in civilian life?"

That's one good reason why there should be no segregation in a democratic American army fighting to preserve and extend democracy. It sets a bad example for the rest of the country, and it doesn't fit the pattern of our war aims.

The Jim Crow car, and the Jim Crow seats in buses, are a disgrace to the American way of life and should be done away with. Substitute a system of first, second, and third class coaches, if need be, such as has long been customary in Europe—then if there are some people who simply cannot ride with poor Negroes, let them pay more to ride first class where they will probably find only a very few wealthy colored people like Chicago's Jones brothers. Or maybe Rochester.[21]

I agree with the Southern liberals that the Negro problem cannot be solved overnight. But certainly some of its most obnoxious features could be gotten rid of at once, and to nobody's detriment.

Shall those of us who are colored in America ask for half-democracy? And shall we compromise with the poll-tax, with the segregation, with the Jim Crow car, with the Southern senators who are not elected by the people's vote, with the politicians who speak of liberty for the whole world and forget us, with the cheatery of the sharecropping system of the South, with the cheatery of the unequal distribution of public movies and the poor schools, poor parks, poor public services that we get? Shall we pipe down on dishonesty, cruelty, stupidity, and insults?

Shall we dilute the Four Freedoms to the strength of near-beer? Shall we, who are the Negro people of America, have no great dreams? Shall we ask only for the half-freedoms that move nobody to action for the great freedoms that this war is supposed to be about?

Or shall we, with all other Americans of foresight and good will, seek to create a world where even Alabama will respect human decency?

"The Future of Black America,"
Negro Digest 2.1 (November 1943): 3–6

Quite simply, the future of the American Negro is the future of America itself. We are one out of every ten in the United States. Where America goes, we go. And, believe it or not, where we go, so goes America.

The American Negro is a barometer of American progress at the moment, not only on a national scale, but on a world scale.

In the midst of a war ostensibly for the preservation of freedom and democracy, it is absurd to proclaim the Four Freedoms as a world-ideal and deny those same freedoms by force to a large portion of our own population, particularly in the southern part of the United States where several millions of colored people are not yet permitted to vote, are denied skilled work in industry, and segregated into Jim Crow coaches when traveling.

How then may we solve this problem of obvious contradiction between democratic theory and undemocratic practice? If we do not solve it the people of the Allied countries, particularly those of Asia and Latin America, will not believe us when we say we follow democracy. The Axis, particularly Japan, will continue to use this contradiction as a strong psychological weapon against us.

It is easy to use the great words, freedom, liberty, democracy, loosely. Apparently it is not easy for the Anglo-Saxon peoples to put those words into practice regarding the colored peoples of the world. Generations of miseducation, of education for exploitation rather than cooperation, is partly to blame. In the United States the historical circumstances of slavery are not a century away, and a freedom granted the body but not the soul, a freedom without the ballot, with limited economic opportunities, and with definite curtailment (by custom and violence if need be) of normal human aspirations is, of course, also to blame.

How to overcome today these past errors of human relationship, and achieve a decent minimum of racial cooperation, is a problem of national importance now recognized by all liberals of all political parties from Roosevelt and Willkie to the Communists.[22] The reactionaries who ignore the problem, or who take cognizance of it only to apply to it the theories and actions of Hitler, are also those who are most anti-labor and anti-progressive in general, both in their local and global outlook. Those who take time out from war-production to foment race riots from Beaumont to Detroit obviously do not know what the war is about, or else they do not care.

They must be made to know and taught to care if victory is to come soon, and if there is to be a decent peace after the war. Therefore education, that old hope and remedy for human ills, is the first step toward racial unity. White Americans must be shown that colored Americans are not a danger to them but a potential reservoir of help and friendship, not a liability but an asset. The labor waste alone that discrimination in industry brings about is appalling. The mounting racial tension is disastrous and unnerving to morale.

Fifty years ago the cry was for education for the Negro people. Hampton, Tuskegee, Fisk, and Howard University appealed to the consciences and purses of liberal white Americans.

Today the need is for education along racial lines for whites rather than Negroes. And since it is a job of national scope, the government itself must take a hand in its achievement, just as the army is preparing millions of pamphlets on how our soldiers should behave in North Africa, Persia, in Australia, so the government must use the printing press, the radio, and the schools and colleges to educate the civilian masses for racial decency at home, lest the anti-Negro feeling that has been allowed to grow spread (it has already begun to spread) to Mexicans, Jews, and over the color and race line, to Catholics and other national minorities.

As a gesture of decency not only at home, but for its effect on our Chinese and Latin American allies, the Jim Crow car, and the denial of equal travel facilities to colored people—even to Latin Americans of darker skin arriving at Miami airport—must be abolished.

Negroes realize that it is not possible to solve overnight an ugly racial situation that has been allowed to drift from year to year, with only now and then an effective voice raised in protest.

Now, however, it becomes a matter of practical necessity that all the American people be concerned with these things. Ship building stopped at Mobile and Beaumont during the riots. Tank and plane production was greatly hindered in Detroit for almost a week. The Axis radio had a field day with its reports of the "democratic" killing of Negroes radioed to Africa, Latin America and the East where millions of colored people live.

Humanitarian interests aside, it does not make sense for a people fighting for the national survival of democratic ideals and the free way of life to continue to hamper their own struggle by condoning or protecting antiquated and vicious Jim Crow provisions as applied to one-tenth of their local population.

There are more Negroes in the United States than there are people in Canada, or in Norway or most of the Scandinavian countries taken individually, or in Australia. So large a body of people cannot be mistreated politically and economically without harming the entire war struggle of the United Nations, and without seriously damaging the prestige and good-will necessary to the establishment of a decent peace when this war is over.

Certainly a group of colored people who have produced within the last fifty years such outstanding citizens as Booker T. Washington who introduced the idea of industrial education to the world, as Dr. George Washington Carver in agricultural science and the chemistry of foods, as Dr. Hinton of Harvard University in the field of medicine, as Marian Anderson and Paul Robeson on the concert stage, as Ethel Waters and Canada Lee in the theatre, as Richard Wright and Countee Cullen in literature, as Rev. A. Clayton Powell in the church and Charles S. Johnson in the social sciences—not to speak of Joe Louis in the prize ring or Dorrie Miller at Pearl Harbor—surely such a people deserve more than the Jim Crow car and the *mores* of the Ku Klux Klan.[23]

Wendell Willkie and Pearl Buck are right when they say that tomorrow's world can have no place in it for narrow racial chauvinism.

Fortunately, for the Negro, there is no way of changing the world without beginning at home to put one's own house in order—as an example of what democracy in action can mean.

That is why I say the future of the American Negro is the future of America. We stand or fall together. If the minister is himself a sinner, it is very hard to bring others into the fold. Of course, armies will do a great deal, but a man convinced by force against his will remains unconvinced still. A peace that is a troubled peace becomes but an interlude for the future breeding of disastrous warfare. Surely civilized people can be taught that simple fact. For Americans the place to begin teaching it is at home.

"My America," *What the Negro Wants,* ed. Rayford W. Logan (Chapel Hill: University of North Carolina Press, 1944), 299–307

This is my land, America.[24] Naturally, I love it—it is home—and I am vitally concerned about its *mores,* its democracy, and its well-being. I try now to look at it with clear, unprejudiced eyes. My ancestry goes back at least four generations on American soil and, through Indian blood, many centuries more. My background and training are purely American—the schools of Kansas, Ohio, and the East. I am old stock as opposed to recent immigrant blood.

Yet many Americans who cannot speak English—so recent is their arrival on our shores—may travel about our country at will securing food, hotel, and rail accommodations wherever they wish to purchase them. *I may not.* These Americans, once naturalized, may vote in Mississippi or Texas, if they live there. *I may not.* They may work at whatever job their skills command. *But I may not.* They may purchase tickets for concerts, theatres, lectures wherever they are sold throughout the United States. *Often I may not.* They may repeat the Oath of Allegiance with its ringing phrase of "Liberty and justice for all," with a deep faith in its truth—as compared with the limitations and oppressions they have experienced in the Old World. I repeat the oath, too, but I know that the phrase about "liberty and justice" does not fully apply to me. I am an American—*but I am a colored American.*

I know that all these things I mention are not *all* true for *all* localities *all* over America. Jim Crowism varies in degree from North to South, from the mixed schools and free franchise of Michigan to the tumbledown colored schools and open terror at the polls of Georgia and Mississippi. All over America, however, against the Negro there has been an economic color line of such severity that since the Civil War we have been kept most effectively, as a racial group, in the lowest economic brackets. Statistics are not needed to prove this. Simply look around you on the Main Street of any American town or city. There are no colored clerks in any of the stores—although colored people spend their money there. There are practically never any colored street-car conductors or bus drivers—although these public carriers run over streets for which we pay taxes. There are no colored girls at the switchboards of the telephone company—but millions of Negroes have phones and pay their bills. Even in Harlem, nine times out of ten, the man who comes to collect your rent is white. Not even that job is given to a colored man by the great corporations owning New York real estate. From Boston to San Diego, the Negro suffers from job discrimination.

Yet America is a land where, in spite of its defects, I can write this article. Here the voice of democracy is still heard—Wallace, Willkie, Agar, Pearl Buck, Paul Robeson, Lillian Smith.[25] America is a land where the poll tax still holds in the South—but opposition to the poll tax grows daily. America is a land where lynchers are not yet caught—but Bundists are put in jail, and the majority opinion condemns the Klan. America is a land where the best of all democracies has been achieved for some people—but in Georgia, Roland Hayes, world-famous singer, is beaten for being colored and nobody is jailed—nor can Mr. Hayes vote in the State where he was born. Yet America is a country where Roland Hayes *can* come from a log cabin to wealth and fame—in spite of the segment that still wishes to maltreat him physically and spiritually, famous though he is.

This segment, the South, is not all of America. Unfortunately, however, the war, with its increased flow of white Southern workers to Northern cities, has caused the Jim Crow patterns of the South to spread *all* over America, aided and abetted by the United States Army. The Army, with its policy of segregated troops, has brought Jim Crow into communities where it was but little, if at all, in existence before Pearl Harbor. From Camp Custer in Michigan to Guadalcanal in the South Seas, the Army has put its stamp upon official Jim Crow, in imitation of the Southern states where laws separating Negroes and whites are as much a part of government as are Hitler's laws segregating Jews in Germany. Therefore, any consideration of the current problems of the Negro people in America must concern itself seriously with the question of what to do about the South.

The South opposes the Negro's right to vote, and this right is denied us in most Southern states. Without the vote a citizen has no means of protecting his constitutional rights. For Democracy to approach its full meaning, the Negro *all over* America must have the vote. The South opposes the Negro's right to work in industry. Witness the Mobile shipyard riots, the Detroit strikes fomented by Southern whites against the employment of colored people, the Baltimore strikes of white workers who objected to Negroes attending a welding school which would give them the skill to rate upgrading. For Democracy to achieve its meaning, the Negro like other citizens must have the right to work, to learn skilled trades, and to be upgraded.

The South opposes the civil rights of Negroes and their protection by law. Witness lynchings where no one is punished, witness the Jim Crow laws that deny the letter and spirit of the Constitution. For Democracy to have real meaning, the Negro must have the same civil rights as any other American citizen. These three simple principles of Democracy—the vote, the right to work, and the right to protection by law—the South opposes when it comes to me. Such procedure is dangerous for *all* America. That is why, in order to strengthen Democracy, further the war effort, and achieve the confidence of our colored allies, we must institute a greater measure of Democracy for the eight million colored people of the South. And we must educate the white Southerners to an understanding of such democracy, so they may comprehend that decency toward colored peoples will lose them nothing, but rather will increase their own respect and safety in the modern world.

I live on Manhattan Island. For a New Yorker of color, truthfully speaking, the South begins at Newark. A half hour by tube from the Hudson Terminal, one comes across street-corner hamburger stands that will not serve a hamburger to a Negro customer wishing to sit on a stool. For the same dime a white pays, a Negro must take his hamburger elsewhere in a paper bag and eat it, minus a plate, a napkin, and a glass of water. Sponsors of the theory of segregation claim that it can be made to mean equality. Practically, it never works out that way. Jim Crow always means less for the one Jim Crowed and an unequal value for his money—no stool, no shelter, merely the hamburger, in Newark.

As the colored traveller goes further South by train, Jim Crow increases. Philadelphia is ninety minutes from Manhattan. There the all-colored grammar school begins its separate education of the races that Talmadge of Georgia so highly approves. An hour or so further down the line is Baltimore where segregation laws are written in the state and city codes. Another hour by train, Washington. There the conductor tells the Negro traveller, be he soldier or civilian, to go into the Jim Crow coach behind the engine, usually half a baggage car, next to trunks and dogs.

That this change to complete Jim Crow happens at Washington is highly significant of the state of American democracy in relation to colored peoples today. Washington is the capital of our nation and one of the great centers of the Allied war effort toward the achievement of the Four Freedoms. To a south-bound Negro citizen told at Washington to change into a segregated coach the Four Freedoms have a hollow sound, like distant lies not meant to be the truth.

The train crosses the Potomac into Virginia, and from there on throughout the South life for the Negro, by state law and custom, is a hamburger in a sack without a plate, water, napkins or stool—but at the same price as the whites pay—to be eaten apart from the others without shelter. The Negro can do little about this because the law is against him, he has no vote, the police are brutal, and the citizens think such caste-democracy is as it should be.

For his seat in the half-coach of the crowded Jim Crow car, a colored man must pay the same fare as those who ride in the nice air-cooled coaches further back in the train, privileged to use the diner when they wish. For his hamburger in a sack served without courtesy the Southern Negro must pay taxes but refrain from going to the polls, and must patriotically accept conscription to work, fight, and perhaps die to regain or maintain freedom for people in Europe or Australia when he himself hasn't got it at home. Therefore, to his ears most of the war speeches about freedom on the radio sound perfectly foolish, unreal, high-flown, and false. To many Southern whites, too, this grand talk so nobly delivered, so poorly executed, must seem like play-acting.

Liberals and persons of good will, North and South, including, no doubt, our President himself, are puzzled as to what on earth to do about the South—the poll-tax South, the Jim Crow South—that so shamelessly gives the lie to Democracy. With the brazen frankness of Hitler's *Mein Kampf,* Dixie speaks through Talmadge, Rankin, Dixon, Arnall, and Mark Ethridge.

In a public speech in Birmingham, Mr. Ethridge says: "All the armies of the world, both of the United States and the Axis, could not force upon the South an abandonment of racial segregation." Governor Dixon of Alabama refused a government war contract offered Alabama State Prison because it contained an anti-discrimination clause which in his eyes was an "attempt to abolish segregation of races in the South." He said: "We will not place ourselves in a position to be attacked by those who seek to foster their own pet social reforms." In other words, Alabama will not reform. It is as bull-headed as England in India, and its governor is not ashamed to say so.

As proof of Southern intolerance, almost daily the press reports some new occurrence of physical brutality against Negroes. Former Governor Talmadge was "too busy" to investigate when Roland Hayes and his wife were thrown into jail, and the great tenor beaten, on complaint of a shoe salesman over a dispute as to what seat in his shop a Negro should occupy when buying shoes. Nor did the governor of Mississippi bother when Hugh Gloster, professor of English at Morehouse College, riding as an inter-state passenger, was illegally ejected from a train in his state, beaten, arrested, and fined because, being in an overcrowded Jim Crow coach, he asked for a seat in an adjacent car which contained only two white passengers.

Legally, the Jim Crow laws do not apply to inter-state travellers, but the FBI has not yet gotten around to enforcing that Supreme Court ruling. En route from San Francisco to Oklahoma City, Fred Wright, a county probate officer of color, was beaten and forced into the Texas Jim Crow coach on a transcontinental train by order of the conductor in defiance of federal law. A seventy-six-year-old clergyman, Dr. Jackson of Hartford, Connecticut, going South to attend the National Baptist Convention, was set upon by white passengers for merely passing through a white coach on the way to his own seat. There have been many similar attacks upon colored soldiers in uniform on public carriers. One such attack resulted in death for the soldier, dragged from a bus and killed by civilian police. Every day now Negro soldiers from the North, returning home on furlough from Southern camps, report incident after incident of humiliating travel treatment below the Mason-Dixon line.

It seems obvious that the South does not yet know what this war is all about. As answer Number One to the question, "What shall we do about the South?" I would suggest an immediate and intensive government-directed program of pro-democratic education, to be put into the schools of the South from the first grades of the grammar schools to the universities. As part of the war effort, this is urgently needed. The Spanish Loyalist Government had trench schools for its soldiers and night schools for its civilians even in Madrid under siege. America is not under siege yet. We still have time (but not too much) to teach our people what we are fighting for, and to begin to apply those teachings to race relations at home. You see, it would be too bad for an emissary of color from one of the Latin American countries, say Cuba or Brazil, to arrive at Miami Airport and board a train for Washington, only to get beaten up and thrown off by white Southerners who do not realize how many colored allies we have—nor how badly we need them—and that it is inconsiderate and rude to beat colored people, anyway.

Because transportation in the South is so symbolic of America's whole racial problem, the Number Two thing for us to do is study a way out of the Jim Crow car dilemma at once. Would a system of first, second, and third class coaches help? In Europe, formerly, if one did not wish to ride with peasants and tradespeople, one could always pay a little more and solve that problem by having a first class compartment almost entirely to oneself. Most Negroes can hardly afford parlor car seats. Why not abolish Jim Crow entirely and let the whites who wish to do so, ride in coaches where few Negroes have the funds to be? In any case, our Chinese, Latin American, and Russian allies are not going to think much of our democratic pronunciamentos as long we keep compulsory Jim Crow cars on Southern rails.

Since most people learn a little through education, albeit slowly, as Number Three, I would suggest that the government draft the leading Negro intellectuals, sociologists, writers, and concert singers from Alain Locke of Oxford and W. E. B. Du Bois of Harvard to Dorothy Maynor and Paul Robeson of Carnegie Hall and send them into the South to appear before white audiences, carrying messages of culture and democracy, thus off-setting the old stereotypes of the Southern mind and the Hollywood movie, and explaining to the people without dialect what the war aims are about. With each, send on tour a liberal white Southerner like Paul Green, Erskine Caldwell, Pearl Buck, Lillian Smith, or William Seabrook. And, of course, include soldiers to protect them from the fascist-minded among us.

Number Four, as to the Army—draftees are in sore need of education on how to behave toward darker peoples. Just as a set of government suggestions has been issued to our soldiers on how to act in England, so a similar set should be given them on how to act in Alabama, Georgia, Texas, Asia, Mexico, and Brazil—wherever there are colored peoples.

Not only printed words should be given them, but intensive training in the reasons for being decent to everybody. Classes in democracy and the war aims should be set up in every training camp in America and every unit of our military forces abroad. These forces should be armed with understanding as well as armament, prepared for friendship as well as killing.

I go on the premise that most Southerners are potentially reasonable people, but that they simply do not know nowadays what they are doing to America, or how badly their racial attitudes look toward the rest of the civilized world. I know their politicians, their schools, and the Hollywood movies have done their best to uphold prevailing reactionary viewpoints. Heretofore, nobody in America except a few rascals, liberals, and a handful of true religionists have cared much about either the Negroes or the South. Their sincere efforts to effect a change have been but a drop in a muddy bucket. Basically, the South needs universal suffrage, economic stabilization, a balanced diet and vitamins for children. But until those things are achieved, on a lesser front to ameliorate—not solve—the Negro problem (and to keep Southern prejudice from contaminating all of America) a few mild but helpful steps might be taken.

It might be pointed out to the South that the old bugaboo of sex and social equality doesn't mean a thing. Nobody as a rule sleeps with or eats with or dances with or marries anybody else except by mutual consent. Millions of people of various races in New York, Chicago, and Seattle go to the same polls and vote without ever co-habiting together. Why does the South think it would be otherwise with Negroes were they permitted to vote there? Or to have a decent education? Or to sit on a stool in a public place and eat a hamburger? Why they think simple rights would force a Southerner's daughter to marry a Negro in spite of herself, I have never been able to understand. It must be due to some lack of instruction somewhere in their schooling.

A government sponsored educational program of racial decency could, furthermore, point out to its students that cooperation in labor would be to the advantage of all—rather than to the disadvantage of anyone, white or black. It could show quite clearly that a million unused colored hands barred out of war industries might mean a million weapons lacking in the hands of our soldiers on some foreign front—therefore a million deaths—including Southern white boys needlessly dying under Axis fire—because Governor Dixon of Alabama and others of like mentality need a little education. It might also be pointed out that when peace comes and the Southerners go to the peace table, if they take there with them the traditional Dixie racial attitudes, there is no possible way for them to aid in forming any peace that will last. China, India, Brazil, Free French Africa, Soviet Asia and the whole Middle East will not believe a word they say.

Peace only to breed other wars is a sorry peace indeed, and one that we must plan now to avoid. Not only in order to win the war then, but to create peace along decent lines, we had best start *now* to educate the South—and all America—in racial decency. That education cannot be left to well-meaning but numerically weak civilian organizations. The government itself should take over—and vigorously. After all, Washington is the place where the conductor comes through every southbound train and tells colored people to change to the Jim Crow car ahead.

That car, in these days and times, has no business being "ahead" any longer. War's freedom train can hardly trail along with glory behind a Jim Crow coach. No matter how streamlined the other cars may be, that coach endangers all humanity's hopes for a peaceful tomorrow. The wheels of the Jim Crow car are about to come off and the walls are going to burst wide open. The wreckage of Democracy is likely to pile up behind that Jim Crow car, unless America learns that it is to its own self-interest to stop dealing with colored peoples in so antiquated a fashion. I do not like to see my land, America, remain provincial and unrealistic in its attitudes toward color. I hope the men and women of good will here of both races will find ways of changing conditions for the better.

Certainly it is not the Negro who is going to wreck our Democracy. (What we want is more of it, not less.) But Democracy is going to wreck itself if it continues to approach closer and closer to fascist methods in its dealings with Negro citizens—for such methods of oppression spread, affecting other whites, Jews, the foreign born, labor, Mexicans, Catholics, citizens of Oriental ancestry—and, in due time, they boomerang right back at the oppressor. Furthermore, American Negroes are now Democracy's current test for its dealings with the colored peoples of the whole world of whom there are many, many millions—*too many* to be kept indefinitely in the position of passengers in Jim Crow cars.

"White Folks Do the Funniest Things," *Common Ground* 4 (winter 1944): 42–46

Although Negroes laugh at many of the same things white Americans do, they also laugh for *different* reasons at different things.

Some incidents of Jim Crowism which I personally have experienced have amused me more than they have angered me—due, as nearly as I can analyze them, to their very absurdity. For instance, once I was driving south from New York to Richmond. An hour or so below Washington those of us in the car became thirsty and someone suggested stopping at a roadside refreshment hut we saw ahead. We knew we could not eat or drink inside—since there is "legal" Jim Crow in Virginia—but it was my intention to purchase a few bottles of soda and bring them out to the car.

When I went to the door and put my hand on the knob, it did not open, although I saw a man just inside. I pulled on the door again and discovered, to my amazement that the man was holding it. He shouted through the screen, "What do you want?"

I said, "I'd like some sodas."

He said, "You get 'em through the hole."

I said, "What hole?"

He said, "We got a hole cut for niggers on the side." And he continued frantically to hold the door as though I were a dangerous savage intent on murder. I went around the side of the little frame building—and there, sure enough, was a square hole cut in the wall through which colored people were served! I did not buy, but I had to laugh! Who could help it? Almost within the shadow of the Capitol of American democracy, a little two-by-four roadside shack had cut a hole in its wall through which to serve Negroes. A colored person could not even come in the door. That seemed to me so absurd as to belong in *Alice in Wonderland.*

Another time in Savannah, Georgia, I wanted to buy a copy of the Sunday *New York Times* and could find it nowhere in town except at the railroad station. In the colored Jim-Crow waiting room there was no newsstand, so I went outside on the sidewalk and around into the white waiting room where I bought the *Times* without incident. But, coming out of the station, just at the door, a white policeman stopped me and said, "You can't come in and out of this front door."

I said, "But there is no newsstand in the colored waiting room!"

He said, "I don't care nothing about that! You can't come in here."

"O.K.," I said, "I am going out now."

"You can't go out this door neither," said the cop.

Well, that puzzled me, as there was no other way out except into the train sheds. "I just came in that way," I said.

"Well, you can't go out that way," said the cop. "Niggers can't use that door."

"How do I get out then?" I asked.

"Only way I see," said the cop, seriously, "is for you to walk the tracks."

So, in order to get out of the Savannah station with the *New York Times,* I had to go through the train gates and follow the railroad tracks to the street crossing. I had never experienced anything so absurd before in my life. The seriousness of that cop and the utter stupidity of being at a door but not permitted to go *through* it, kept me laughing all day. I grew up in Kansas, so the absurdities of southern Jim Crow were new to me at that time and unbelievably quaint.

Once, when I was about eighteen, I was coming up from Mexico City to attend school in Cleveland. I went into the diner one evening as the train was heading north through Texas. I was seated alone when a white man came in and sat down opposite me. I looked across the table and saw that he was staring at me with a look of utter amazement. Suddenly he jumped up as though he had been shot and cried, "Why, you a nigger, ain't you?"—then fled from the dining car as though he had sat down in front of a lion by mistake. I am still laughing at the incident and I suppose the waiter, who saw it, is still laughing, too.

As many Negroes as there are in Texas, what is there about one at a table in a public dining car that can so startle a white man that he runs away wild-eyed without his meal? Certainly the comedy of Jim Crow in action often outweighs the tragedy of so pathetic a mind as that man possessed.

But by no means is everything funny about Jim Crow. Once I had to wait for hours before driving my car onto a ferry boat in Louisiana because, each trip, *all* the Negro cars had to wait until *all* the white people's cars drove onto the boat. By the time the ferry crossed the river and returned, more white cars had gathered, so, each time, for several trips, the white cars filled the boat. Since the Negro cars had to fall back to the very end of each newly formed line, we were continually left ashore. That was not funny. I was due to lecture at a colored college a hundred miles away that night and I wanted to get there on time. Jim Crow caused me to be late.

It is like that now, soldiers tell me, in regard to bus service for colored Army men at some southern camps. If the white soldiers fill the bus, the colored soldiers must wait for the next one. By the time another bus comes, enough white soldiers have gathered to fill it, too—so again the Negroes must wait. Thus it goes, until sometimes the colored soldiers never get to town at all that night. Their passes run out with them still waiting at the gates of the camp for space in a bus. That, of course, is not funny either. Soldiers writing home about these insane inequalities at democratic Army camps don't seem amused.

Of late, Negro humor has taken on a kind of macabre quality in relation to the race problem. When I speak of Negro humor, I do not mean it in a purely racial sense; what I do mean is that, due to environmental factors, namely segregation, Negro humor at this stage of American society has certain nuances that seem to be missing in white humor.

At the moment, some pretty grim stories, albeit told laughingly, are going the rounds. Some of the cartoons in the Negro press have this macabre quality, too. After the Detroit riots there was such a cartoon in *The People's Voice* of New York. It was funny. Lots of Negroes laughed, clipped it, and sent it to friends. But no white person, out of a dozen or more to whom I showed it, laughed.

This was the cartoon. Two little white boys are standing looking at one of the boys' father's collection of hunting trophies hanging on the wall of Papa's den—an elk head, a tiger head, a walrus. There among them, nicely mounted, is a human head—a Negro's. Proudly, the small son of the house explains, "Dad got *that* one in Detroit last week."

The late Robert Russa Moton, President of Tuskegee, world's largest Negro school, once told this story at a student assembly when I was present. Dr. Moten said that he had just come down from the North, and that he had taken a Pullman as far as Atlanta, Georgia. He said that as he stepped from the Pullman in the early morning in the Atlanta station, he suddenly heard a scream behind him. He turned, saw that a woman had caught her heel in the top step of the train and was falling forward. Naturally, his first impulse as a man was to reach out his arms and catch her—but when he looked up and saw that she was a white woman, he dropped his arms.

At this point in his story the student audience roared with laughter. Every one of those colored kids knew that for a black man to catch a white woman in his arms in Atlanta might mean a lynching party. Naturally, Dr. Moten dropped his arms! The woman landed head first on the concrete platform. At any rate, she did not have a chance to cry, "Rape." So Dr. Moten lived to tell the tale—which amused his audience no end. But somehow I could not laugh. It seemed to me one of the saddest stories in the world.

There is at the moment, a tale being told in Negro communities that seems well on its way to becoming a folk story. It is always told as being true, but within the month I have heard it in three varying versions, and as having occurred in both the North and South. The gist of it is this: Among those standing on a bus crowded with both white and colored there is a Southerner who cannot bear to see white folks stand and Negroes sit, so the Southerner says to a Negro in a nearby seat, "Hey you, black boy, get up and let me sit down."

The Negro rises and the white man takes his seat. Whereupon the Negro sits down on the white man's lap, presses a knife to his ribs, and says, "So you want to sit down, huh? So you make me get up? Well, now you're sitting down! And so am I! Say something! Go ahead! Say something!"

At this point, colored people, hearing the story, rock with laughter. Naturally, the white man with a knife in his ribs, says nothing, so the Negro rides to his destination on his lap! Thus justice triumphs, and everyone is tickled.

A new folk hero is developing among the Negro people. He is not a soldier hero on the war fronts of New Guinea or Italy. He is the man who fights back on the local front of American Jim Crow. New tales come into being about him every day. Some are true stories spread by word of mouth or printed in the Negro press. Some are obviously fantasies—like that of the black man on the white man's lap. Almost all are touched with the heart-stopping humor of Jim Crow—desperately and grotesquely funny.

The colored papers not long ago carried an item colored people read with laughter. It seems that on the Jim Crow cars in the South, crowded as they are, white conductors and news butchers often take up a whole pair of seats with their paraphernalia, to the exclusion of the passengers. Some colored soldiers who were standing in the crowded aisle put the magazines of the news butcher and the ticket box of the conductor on the floor and sat down in their seats. When the conductor came and saw what had happened, he ordered the soldiers out of the seats immediately. The soldiers would not rise. The conductor said, "All right, I'll put you bad niggers off the train." He reached for the cord. Whereupon the colored soldiers grabbed the conductor instead—and threw him off the speeding train into the night. This story amused the colored public no end.

I suppose environment creates varying nuances in regard to humor. Certainly there is nothing funny about a man being thrown off a speeding train in the middle of the night—not if he is a good man. But that particular conductor, in Negro eyes, was a devil—and everybody enjoys seeing a devil get his due. The devil-getting-his-due thinking is what conditions many Negro minds in regard to our current war with Japan. Negroes know that white people in Asia have had an attitude toward the Asiatics not unlike their general attitude toward colored people in America. That accounts for the deep belly laughter that greets such jokes as the following:

A distinguished Negro member of the Black Cabinet (whose function is to advise Washington on problems of color) was in session with a big official of the government during the days when Japan was beating back the British in Asia. That afternoon his colored office boy, unaware that he had a visitor, rushed in and shouted jubilantly, "Boss, we just took Singapore!"

Another joke of the same vintage concerns the white man who came to a Negro church in the South to speak for the Red Cross—which Negroes do not respect very much since that organization began segregating Negro blood in its blood bank. The white man made a most passionate speech about the evils of Hitler and Hirohito in the course of which he said, "Why, you know, these Japs are really trying to wipe us white folks off the face of the earth."

A dark and wrinkled old grandma in the amen corner who had known seventy years of Jim Crow said, "It's about time!"

These are the kind of anecdotes that currently amuse black America. New ones are being born by the minute. Their humor is based on the absurdity of white Americans giving freedom and democracy such a grandiose play, while still selling Negroes strawberry sodas through a hole, or threatening to throw black soldiers off a train for objecting to the outrageous conditions of the southern Jim Crow car, or putting our blood in separate cans a la Hitler at the Red Cross blood banks. Negroes think democracy's left hand apparently must not know what its right hand is doing.

When the daily papers recently published the news about the President signing a bill granting freedom to the Philippines, a colored man in front of a newsstand at 125th Street and 8th Avenue in Harlem held up his paper and laughed loudly.

"We ain't even got the Philippines," he said, "and here we are grantin' 'em freedom! White folks do the *funniest* things!"

That statement I would qualify thus: *Some* white folks do the funniest things! Personally, I know that not *all* white Americans practice Jim Crow at home and preach democracy abroad. But what puzzles me about those who do is their utter lack of humor concerning their own absurdities. I have read that Hitler has no sense of humor, either. Certainly, among Hitler's hunting trophies today are thousands of human heads, scattered across the world in the bloody mud of battle. I suppose the greatest killers cannot afford to laugh. Those most determined to Jim Crow me are grimly killing America.

"Down Under in Harlem," *New Republic* (March 27, 1944): 404–5

If you are white and are reading this vignette, don't take it for granted that all Harlem is a slum. It isn't. There are big apartment houses up on the hill, Sugar Hill, and up by City College—nice high-rent-houses with elevators and doormen, where Canada Lee lives, and W. C. Handy, and the George S. Schuylers, and the Walter Whites, where colored families send their babies to private kindergartens and their youngsters to Ethical Culture School. And, please, white people, don't think that all Negroes are the same. They aren't.

Last year's Harlem riots demonstrated this clearly. Most of the people on Sugar Hill were just as indignant about the riots as was Mayor LaGuardia. Some of them even said the riots put the Negro race back fifty years. But the people who live in the riot area don't make enough money really to afford the high rents and the high prices merchants and landlords charge in Harlem, and most of them are not acquainted personally—as are many Sugar Hillites—with liberals like Pearl Buck and John Haynes Holmes. They have not attended civic banquets at the Astor, or had luncheon with the emancipated movie stars at Sardi's. Indeed, the average Harlemite's impression of white folks, democracy and life in general is rather bad.[26]

Naturally, if you live on nice, tree-lined, quiet Convent Avenue, even though you are colored, it would never occur to you to riot and break windows. When some of the colored leaders whose names are often in the white newspapers came out of their elevator houses and down into Harlem during the riots, to urge, with the best intentions in the world, that the mobs stop breaking windows and go home, lots of the rioters did not even know who they were. And others of them said, "Boo-oo-o! Go home yourself."

It is, I should imagine, nice to be smart enough and lucky enough to be among Dr. Du Bois' "talented tenth" and be a race leader and go to the symphony concerts and live on that attractive rise of bluff and parkway along upper Edgecombe Avenue overlooking the Polo

Grounds, where the plumbing really works and the ceilings are high and airy. For just a few thousands a year one can live very well on Sugar Hill in a house with a white-tiled hall.[27]

But under the hill on Eighth Avenue, on Lenox, and on Fifth there are places like this—dark, unpleasant houses, with steep stairs and narrow halls, where the rooms are too small, the ceilings too low and the rents too high. There are apartments with a dozen names over each bell. The house is full of roomers. Papa and mama sleep in the living room, the kids in the dining room, lodgers in every alcove, and everything but the kitchen is rented out for sleeping. Cooking and meals are rotated in the kitchen.

In vast sections below the hill, neighborhood amusement centers after dark are gin mills, candy stores that sell King Kong (and maybe reefers), drug stores that sell geronimoes—dope tablets—to juveniles for pepping up cokes, pool halls where gambling is wide open and barbecue stands that book numbers.[28] Sometimes, even the grocery stores have their little side rackets without the law. White men, more often than Negroes, own these immoral places where kids as well as grown-ups come.

The kids and the grown-ups are not criminal or low by nature. Poverty, however, and frustration have made some of them too desperate to be decent. Some of them don't try any more. Slum-shocked, I reckon.

One Saturday night last winter, I went into a barbecue stand where the juke-box was loud and the air thick with smoke. At the tables there were mostly young folks—nice, not very pretty girls dressed in their best, with young men who had cleaned up after work. Some of the young men still wore their last spring's artificial camel's-hair coats—a top coat in winter with the snow outside—but they were trying to look nice, to be nice in the Harlem slums.

A half-dozen teen age boys came in and stood around listening to the records on the juke-box. Shortly, a quarrel began among them. Almost immediately knives were drawn and switch-blades flashed, and one youngster let a blackjack a foot long slide out of his sleeve.

The woman at the counter who served my sandwich said, "Somebody ought to call the cops." (As though cops could solve the problems of poverty and delinquency in Harlem.) The white proprietor behind the beer bar paid no attention to the turmoil. Short of murder or destruction, white proprietors in Harlem seldom mix in Negro squabbles—just as they never belong to neighborhood committees to improve conditions, either.

"I just don't want 'em to fight in here," the woman said, "that's all!"

The boys didn't fight. They simply milled around, showed their weapons, bluffed and cursed each other. But their language frightened some of the quiet, not-very-pretty girls at the tables with the young men in their thin near-camel's-hair coats, out on a Saturday night trying to look nice and have a nice quiet time.

Louis Jordan on the juke-box, loud.[29] Over the music the woman behind the counter said, "This time of night, all these young boys ought to be home."

"That's right," I said.

Home. A dozen names on the bell. Roomers all over the house. No place for a kid to bring his friends. Only the pool halls open, the candy stores that bootleg liquor, the barbecue stands where you can listen to the juke-box even if you're broke and don't want to buy anything, and the long Harlem streets outside dimmed out because Hitler might send his planes overhead some dark night.

Should the planes come, their bombs most certainly would be louder than the juke-boxes, and their flying fragments of metal sharper than the cheap steel of drug-store switch-blades in the hands of kids who have no homes where they can bring their friends. A piece of bomb can hit harder than a boy with a blackjack up his sleeve.

Hitler in Berlin. Bad kids in Harlem. Indignation in the Mayor's office. Also on Sugar Hill. Louis Jordan's records:

I'm gonna move . . .
. . . outskirts of town . . .

Barbecued ribs, a quarter. Sign:

DON'T ASK FOR CREDIT—HE'S DEAD!!!

Riots. Long discussions downtown about forming more committees to make more surveys for more reports for more detailed study by more politicians before taking action on conditions in Harlem.

Sign over the barbecue counter:

WE CAN'T PAY OUR BILLS WITH TRUST!
CAN YOU?

That sign, of course, is in reference to credit for sandwiches. It has nothing to do with the democratic system. It simply means that if you haven't got a quarter, you don't eat. There has been a sort of permanent scarcity of quarters in Harlem, so that sign might very well serve the committees as a motto for their surveys.

"Saved from the Dogs,"
Negro Digest 2.7 (March 1944): 17–19

The rich white woman in the mansion on the hill took an interest in him. All the other small town Negroes were envious, jealous—and glad. They were envious because she didn't take an interest in them, except to offer an occasional job cooking, cleaning, or chauffeuring for her. They were glad because one of their black boys from the Bottoms was getting a break.

The boy was talented. He could play a violin like nobody's business. He had even played with the local white amateur symphony orchestra, and with the musically better Jewish string ensemble. This black boy was smart! He played classical!

But it was too bad he never got very far after that nice rich white lady took such a kind interest in him. Of course, he went through music school in New York. Then his patron, and his parents, wanted him to go and teach down South somewhere. But he didn't want to go teach. He was young and talented. Handsome, too. So it seems he hung around New York hoping for a break in radio or concert—until he went to the dogs.

Now, the dogs have a way of running very fast. If you are not used to them, it is hard to keep up with them. The New York dogs outran our boy from the Bottoms. He was, after all, a small town boy who had never been to the dogs before.

He got to worrying about having to go down South and teach in a school to make a living when he wanted desperately to play with a Philharmonic, be another Kreisler, fill Carnegie Hall, and tour all over the world just playing on a violin, and not be buried in a provincial Negro school in a state where they lynch folks easy. But the concert bureaus, radio stations, and orchestras were not interested in a Negro violinist. So he got to worrying.

Somebody said, "Blow some gage, kid, and you'll dream you're on top of the world. You'll dream the sweetest music you ever heard, sweeter than any you could ever play from notes off paper, don't care how many schools you went to, sweet and frantic, Jackson! And mad! Blow some gage!"

The rich white lady had written through her secretary a year ago that now that he was educated, she couldn't extend his allowance any longer. His mother had written in pencil on tablet paper with lines that it was time for him to go to work. His girl friend who was going to Hunter College said she would marry him when he had a job. "Why, you might even be the Dean of a music school down South!"

But he didn't want to go down South. He had a new crowd of friends, not rats—but cats. Hepcats, hey-now boys and girls who never let responsibilities weigh down their pleasures. He soon met up with a new gal who didn't mean him good, either. But he liked her, so he didn't care, and they ran together.

I said, "Listen," when I saw him at the Braddock Bar one night. "You don't think this is how an artist like Kreisler got ahead in the world, do you, drinking and carrying on this way?"

He said, "No, but Kreisler is a German, and I am a Negro."

"Kreisler is no German," I said, "he's an Austrian."

"Anyhow, he never had to go teach school down South," he said.

"You must think the only place to become a good violinist is on a stage in front of a lot of people," I yelled over the noise of the juke box. "You could be a good violinist even in Georgia."

"I don't like Jim Crow," he shouted.

"Maybe you could play Jim Crow away," I contended.

"You talk like a rich white lady who don't know what Jim Crow is," he said.

"You are using color as an excuse not to do anything," I answered.

But I knew it wasn't as simple as all that even when I said it. And I knew that when you butt your head against the color bar, it sometimes knocks the senses out of you, throws you off balance, and makes you see the wrong kind of stars. That's what happened to this kid.

"Let's smoke some tea," he said.

"I'm crazy enough now," I answered, "without smoking tea."

"Then excuse me," he said. And went away.

The next time I saw him, he was thin as a rail. "I have been sick," he told me. "I had to give up smoking, drinking, also blowing my top. I'm going down South to teach."

"How's the girl friend?" I asked.

"I lost her."

"Which one?" I said.

"Both. Now, I'm going down and play prejudice away, as you once suggested. I am going to make such beautiful music that everybody who hears it will forget color and just hear music."

"Good for you," I said. "So you haven't gone to the dogs, after all?"
"No," he said, "I'm gone to Tennessee."

The next time I saw him, it was just his picture in a colored paper. Underneath, it read:

NEW DEAN OF THE MUSIC SCHOOL

And I thought, "Good for him!" Then my mind said, "That is no good for him. But, anyhow, doing what is no good for him is better than going to the dogs which was also no good for him." Then my mind said, "Shut up!" Which I did.

I did not think of him any more for a couple of years. The last time I saw his picture it was again in a colored paper and, underneath, it said he was dead. So I guess there was really nothing much in this world—that he could find—good for him. At any rate, he didn't go completely to the dogs.

"Solving the Race Problem: A State or Federal Issue?"
Negro Digest 2.6 (April 1944): 37–38

The race problem is a pressing *national* problem now—because we are fighting a war in which men are dying.[30] Those of us on the civilian front have no right to hold up war production and thus increase death on the battle-lines by walking out rather than work beside Negroes on the production lines.

Nor have we any right to undermine the morale of Negro soldiers by segregating them in our armed forces, and by continuing to Jim Crow them and their civilian brothers in public places, in war industries vital to the public welfare, and as workers or passengers on public conveyances.

An over-all Federal program protecting the rights of all minorities, and educating all Americans to that effect, should be evolved.

It took Executive Order 8802 to open war industries to colored workers.

It took Federal housing to clean up slums to some extent in poor Negro and white neighborhoods all over the nation.

It took the National Labor Relations Board to protect the bargaining rights of labor, white and Negro.

It took the National Youth Administration Act to break down existing community patterns in regard to work for Negro youths—formerly limited in many localities to employment as bootblacks, maids, and elevator boys.

The NYA gave them, often for the first time, a chance to learn and work at some form of skilled or semi-skilled labor heretofore denied them.

Some of our states have no intention of doing anything about racial decency.

Almost 14 million colored people should not be left to the shortsighted mercy of the same kind of "state's rights" that have acted so undemocratically in Congress of late, regarding the soldier vote.[31]

Some Congressmen have publicly declared that this vote is a matter of "white supremacy." "White supremacy" is one of Hitler's corner stones. It has not helped him much. Certainly, it is a liability to a democracy.

Democracy does not lose by *sharing* its privileges. It loses by denying them. In ratio to that denial, it approaches the very fascist patterns we are fighting against abroad.

"Greetings, Good Neighbors," LHP 482 (ca. 1945?)

Most of us in the United States know all too little about our Latin American neighbors to the South, about their culture and their ways of life.[32] Certain of our business men know something of them in terms of trade. The vast American public knows them only through the rhumba, the tango, and the samba. Up to very recently, the best ambassadors of the Americas to the South of us have been the musicians and the entertainers—the Xavier Cugats, the Elsa Houstons, and the Carmen Mirandas who have come to us bringing their incomparable songs and rhythms. From Cuba, Eusebia Cosmé came bringing to a limited audience an expert and dramatic reading of some of their poetry. In turn, to Latin America we have sent a few of our jazz bands, a few of our singers, and lately a few of our writers and movie stars. In both cases, no doubt, the musicians and the singers reach the widest popular audiences. Certainly, I do not mean to discount their value in terms of Good Neighborliness—music has a way of reaching the heart quicker than words—but now the time has come for a more exact, a more explicit form of communication, and a more comprehensive exchange of cultural values.

As an American of Negro blood, I, too, am deeply concerned with this exchange of cultural values. Marian Anderson and Edward Matthews of the concert stage have carried their art and our songs to our brothers to the South. In a more popular field, Josephine Baker, Etta Moten, and others from the American Negro theatre have visited them. John Kirby's band is about to go to Rio. These people are happy representatives of one phase of American Negro culture. But I would like to see, also, writers and scholars of color carrying to Latin America other phases of our activities—men like the sociologists, Dr. W. E. B. Du Bois and Charles S. Johnson; like the writers, Arna Bontemps and Richard Wright whose novel, *Native Son,* was a great success in both Brazil and the Argentine; editors like Elmer Carter of *Opportunity* magazine, Roy Wilkins of *The Crisis* and Carl Murphy, head of the great Negro newspaper, the *Baltimore Afro-American;* and popular and important leaders of Negro activity such as Mary McLeod Bethune, distinguished Negro woman of the National Youth Administration, and Walter White, secretary of the National Association for the Advancement of Colored People.[33]

In turn, we of Negro America would like to have the pleasure of welcoming here Nicolás Guillén, great Cuban Negro poet; of knowing better the brown-skin Diego Rivero, Mexican Indian painter, who once told me he had a Negro grandmother; and of receiving from Venezuela and Brazil, from Trinadad and Panama, many other dark-skinned representatives of the Latin cultures whose names are not known in this country.

Unfortunately, here in the United States life is still very much cut and dried in terms of color. We know that in the Americas to the South of us, where there are millions of people of Indian blood, and of Negro blood, the color and race lines are not so tightly drawn, nor so hard and fast. We never hear of lynchings there, nor of Jim Crow cars, nor of segregated divisions in the army and the navy, nor of a Red Cross that will take only white blood. Such stupidities, thank God, are not a prominent part of the Latin American set-ups—whatever their other defects, from the stand point of the American go-getters, may be. So the American Negro, under the pleasant Good Neighbor policies now being established, wishes to welcome to our United States *all* representatives of Latin American cultures whatever their racial strains or complexions may be.[34] We feel that they have much to give *all* Americans, whatever our complexions may be. We feel that our Latin American friends can teach us much in terms of tolerance and good will, in terms of live and let live, in terms of the full rhythm and joy of life that they know in the lands beneath the Southern Cross. We are glad that their statesmen, and their artists, and their men of letters are visiting us in increasing numbers these days. And also that their actors and film writers are coming to Hollywood, city of the silver screen—where Negroes and Indians and Orientals have been for so long but caricatures of themselves, fools, clowns, or villains. And, since motion pictures are certainly the most powerful medium of entertainment and propaganda in the world, we hope the writers and performers from Latin America will tell the Hollywoodians it doesn't really pay to always make *all* the heroes white and Nordic, and the villains, servants, or gigolos dark. Negroes, Orientals, Indians, and Latin Americans have their heroes, too.

Our friends from the great South American continent, and from the Caribbean, have much to teach us here in the United States. They bring quite as much to give us as we have to give them—if not more. In terms of race relations, certainly, they know better than we do, what it means to be good neighbors. Humbly, I hope, we will learn from them.

Over a period of years now, I have received many clippings from Latin American newspapers and magazines of various translations of a certain poem of mine published almost twenty years ago in *The Crisis*. That poem is called, "I, Too." It goes like this:

> I, too, sing America.
> I am the darker brother.
> They send me to eat in the kitchen
> When company comes.
> But I laugh, and eat well, and grow strong.
> Tomorrow, I'll be at the table
> When company comes.
> Nobody'll dare say to me,
> "Eat in the kitchen," then.
> Besides, they'll see how beautiful I am,
> And be ashamed.
> I, too, am America.

"My Most Humiliating Jim Crow Experience," *Negro Digest* 3.7 (May 1945): 33–34

It happened in Cleveland years ago when I was in high school, and the Great Migration of Negroes from the South during World War I was at its height. Jim Crow, new to Cleveland in most public places, was beginning to raise its ugly head.

Our high school French class had gone to see a matinee performance of the late great Sara Bernhardt, with her wooden leg, in Cleopatra's death scene, where the asp stings her in the bosom. The magic of Sara's famous golden voice still rings in my ears.

But of that afternoon, there is an even more vivid memory. Following the performance, with one of my white classmates, a Polish-American boy, I went across the street from the theatre into one of Cleveland's large cafeterias. Its self-service and low prices appealed to our schoolboy pocketbooks. Its long cases and counters and steam-tables loaded with appetizing food whetted our appetites. We took our trays and got in line. My white school-mate was just in front of me.

We passed around in front of the colorful green salads, the sweet, good looking desserts, the white and pink chocolate frosted cakes, the long steam table with its soups and vegetables and meats. Each of us selected our foods, and stopped with our trays before the cashier's desk. She rang up my friend's bill, he paid her, and passed on to seek a table.

But when the white woman looked at me and then down at my tray, I thought she would never stop striking the keys on the cash register. It rang and rang and rang. The amount it registered on the black and white tabs behind its glass strip became larger and larger. Finally the cashier pulled out a check and flung it on my tray. It was *Eight Dollars and Sixty-Five Cents!*

My friend's check had been only about forty-five or fifty cents. I had selected about the same amount of food. I looked in amazement at the cashier.

"Why is mine so much?" I asked.

"That is just what you will pay if you eat in here," said the cashier.

"But I don't have that much food," I said.

"That is what you will pay to eat it," said the cashier, her face growing more and more belligerent, her skin turning red and her eyes narrowing. I could see the hatred in her face.

"But it doesn't cost that much," I said.

"Pay your check—or else put your tray down and leave it," she shouted. "You are holding up the line. That's what it costs if you want to eat!"

I put my tray down and left it there in front of her. I had not run into anything like that before in Cleveland, but I knew it was because I was colored. I went up to the table where my white classmate was eating and said, "Come on, let's get out of here. They won't let me eat in this place."

He was astonished, and it took a long time to explain it to him, because he did not know that such things went on in this democratic land that his parents had travelled way across the sea to find. But neither one of us made any protest. We were only fifteen or sixteen, and we did not know what to say. He and I both were embarrassed.

Some years later a large group of Communists picketed that same restaurant and others like it in Cleveland. Negro and white workers together went in and insisted on service for all. In that way they broke down the color line and ended that kind of un-American Jim Crow in the downtown cafeterias in Cleveland. I do not believe such an incident would happen to a high school boy there today. At least, I hope not. Such things are harder to take when one is young.

"My Poems and Myself," LHP 735 (July 12, 1945)

I was elected class poet of our eighth grade graduation class in Lincoln, Illinois.[35] That was the beginning. Then all through Central High School in Cleveland, I wrote verses for our school magazine, and again was elected class poet at graduation. Thus my literary career began in school. At Cleveland's Central High during my time, there was a mixture of many racial groups, mostly poor pupils, so I learned early that poverty and its allied problems were not limited to Negroes. Many of my poems since then have dealt with the problems of all underprivileged people. But most of them have dealt with the memories, hopes, dreams, and aspirations of the fourteen million of my own people in our common country, America.

Basically, our dreams are the same as any one else's. But because of our unique history of slavery, then freedom limited by prejudices, but lighted by the teachings of democracy in the air all around us, our dreams take on an intensity and fervor all our own, as I have tried to express in my poem about a young Negro, "As I Grew Older." Sometimes, as in "The Weary Blues," a man can sublimate his troubles through song. Perhaps that is why American Negroes have given our country such beautiful music, from the spirituals and the blues, to the compositions of William Grant Still and Duke Ellington. One of America's greatest songs, known and loved all over the world and played on the air a thousand times a day, is W. C. Handy's *St. Louis Blues.*

I do not believe there were ever any beautiful "hate" poems. I think the dreams in my poems are basically everybody's dreams. But sometimes, on the surface, their complexion is colored by the shadows and the darkness of the race to which I belong. The darkness has its beauty, and the shadows have their troubles—but shadows disappear in the sun of understanding.

"America's Most Unique Newspaper," *Negro Digest* 3.12 (October 1945): 23–24

Wendell P. Dabney owns, edits, manages, runs, and writes all by himself Negro America's most unique newspaper. In fact, *The Union* is probably America's most unique newspaper in that it is entirely personal and, since Dabney is a personality, highly individual.

For one thing, it is the only newspaper that I have ever seen which constantly goes in for rhymed headlines. For instance, in reporting Dr. Julian Lewis on contraception, the heading was:

BIRTH CONTROL MAY AFFECT BODY AND SOUL

And calling attention to a feature article on the trucking firm of Mrs. George Brown, Scranton, Pennsylvania's leading Negro businesswoman, doing hauling for some 100 A. & P. stores, the head reads:

THE A. & P.
GAVE HER A CHANCE:
SHE PROVED HER GREATNESS
DESPITE COLOR OR PANTS.

The way in which the news is written up, too, is highly original and, from front page to back, world news to society, it has the Dabney touch, interspersed with editorial comment and opinion whenever he wishes. His own column of "Gossip and Reflections" often contains little gems of anecdote, bits of Negro history, and personal reminiscence, for Dabney has known just about all the great Negroes since the Civil War, and many who, if not great, were certainly colorful.

The walls of his two-room office in downtown Cincinnati are crowded with the signed photographs of just about all the folks whose names are in the Negro history books of our time—from those who have gone like Charles W. Chesnutt and Ada Overton Walker to those who still carry on valiantly like Emmett Scott and Walter White.[36] Paul Laurence Dunbar is there, and the young James Weldon Johnson. And Dabney's mind is full of stories of their youth and his own. Some of the stories will certainly never be in anybody's memoirs (not if the subject or their relatives can help it) so you have to visit Dabney to hear them.

He is going on eighty, and his paper, *The Union,* is going on forty, and both have become a kind of institution in Cincinnati. Dabney himself is widely known outside his own city, although his paper is not. Possibly his personal fame is due to the fact that he is a great conversationalist, and also because he was once one of America's finest banjo and guitar players. He has published several works on the guitar, as well as a number of songs of his own composition, including one from the days of the Spanish-American war, *You Will Miss the Colored Soldiers.*

On the evening that I visited Mr. Dabney, he took his guitar down from on top of the office piano and played me some of his own pieces. Then he took his banjo and showed me what banjo playing was in the days when it really was banjo playing. Then he got up and showed me the styles of clog dancing of 50 years ago, including a step that Bill Robinson himself said he had never seen. Then we got to talking about the old days of the Negro theatre and of the folks who made our race famous on the American stage.

The *Union*'s office contains not only the conventional desks and typewriters of newspaperdom, but a piano, guitars, mandolin-guitars and banjos, hundreds of photographs of great living people and people who still live because they were great, lithographs of Ethiopian princesses and African slaves, and three or four original Tanner and Duncanson oils hung in the midst of the other pictures, stacks of old magazines and newspapers, filing cases, and a couple of stoves—one for heat and the other for cooking lunch when the editor is too busy to leave the office, since he is owner, editor, secretary, and office boy all in one.

I only hope that when I am 80 I will have something of his vitality, zest for life, and earthy humor. One of Dabney's recent columns in his rhyming newspaper closes with this observation:

> A man will shake a hand.
> A dog will shake his tail.
> In such friendly greetings,
> Neither will ever fail.
> But if it's love
> They want to tell,
> A man's lip twitches for a kiss,
> The dog's nose itches for a smell.

"Simple and Me,"
Phylon 6.4 (winter 1945): 349–52

The character of My Simple-Minded Friend is really very simple. It is just myself talking to me. Or else me talking to myself. That has been going on for a number of years and, in my writing, has taken one form or another from poetry to prose, song lyrics to radio, newspaper columns to books.

I write for myself. I say to myself that is good, or that is not good, or I don't know how I feel about that, or I feel like this and like that both. In the *Chicago Defender* columns concerning My Simple Minded Friend, I have developed this inner discussion into two characters: the *this* being me, and the *that* being Simple, or vice versa.[37] We are both colored, American, and Harlemized. And we both possess that unity and race-consciousness characteristic of the American Negro as opposed to the West Indian or South American of color.

Some people are under the impression that My Simple-Minded Friend wears a zoot suit. He does not wear a zoot suit, in fact, he has never had a zoot suit on. But he knows a number of people who wear zoot suits. I know such persons, too.

Some people have written to My Simple Minded Friend and said that he is smarter than me—which I do not doubt—except that that would make me smarter than myself—which could also be true. Certain portions of everybody's brain function better than other portions, mine included.

Among my readers, there is an old lady who reads and remembers everything My Simple Minded Friend says and quotes it back at me with glee. She remembers practically nothing that I say in print—which would make Simple a better writer than me, if he wrote. But, fortunately, he does not write. He talks and I write.

It is a writer's job to put down, within limits, what people say and do and think in life. Of course, I am happy to re-create in Simple a certain stratum of Negro Society. Space limitations in my paper prevent me from giving Simple's friends and associates a greater play. The space limits for "Here to Yonder" in the *Chicago Defender* are one column of print—or three typewritten pages double-spaced. If I run over three pages, the editor is forced to cut something out. The *Chicago Defender* does not censor its columnists, but they cannot stretch their space, so when something is too long it must be cut. Where and what my editor cuts does not always make sense to me, although I reckon it does to him.

That is akin to what makes Simple interesting—the fact that what makes sense to one may not make sense to another. In life, as in art, the beginnings of drama lie in disagreement. As long as I let Simple disagree with me, we get along. Once I did not permit him to disagree and he did not say anything more for weeks. He refused to argue or converse with me. During that time, naturally, he did not appear in the *Chicago Defender.* He wanted to talk then about Paul Robeson—and I did not want to talk about Paul Robeson because I like Paul Robeson. It turned out Simple liked him, too, but not as Othello in *Othello.* Simple claimed that he did not like to see Paul Robeson slapping a nice white lady around, neither did he like to see him deceived and betrayed—because it looked like to Simple that Shakespeare was just making a fool out of the Negro and Simple does not like to see the Negro be a fool.

Of course, Simple knows he is a fool himself at times, but he does not like to see *the* Negro be a fool. To Simple, Paul Robeson is a very great Negro—so great as to practically be *the* Negro—and Simple does not like to see Shakespeare nor anyone else make a fool out of *the* Negro, on stage or off.

Of course, me, I know that Othello is not Paul Robeson—but the night that Simple saw the play, they looked one and the same to him. That is where art often puts it over on nature. That is also where Jim Crow puts it over on all of us. Some people really think Lena Horne would be a bad girl if she played a bad girl in *St. Louis Woman.* They cannot disconnect drama from reality, art from life. Their critical objectivity is limited by race and previous condition of servitude. Unfortunately, I am afraid Simple thinks like that, too. He does not always show good judgment. I have been trying to teach him, but when I try to teach him, he tries to teach me, and we get all mixed up. Sometimes we find that we have really been saying the *same* things back at each other when each of us thought he was saying something different. I am usually quite sure what *I* am saying is right, but Simple always thinks he has won the argument.

In one column the conversation runs as follows:

"Do you ever feel like you do not know where you are going?" asked my Simple Minded Friend.

"Sure," I said, "I feel that way almost all the time. I feel like the old folks who used to say, 'I will do so-and-so—*if I live and nothing happens.*' "

"But something is always liable to happen," said Simple.

"That is right," I said.

"Especially if you are colored," said Simple.

"You put it on too simple a basis," I said. "In this uncertain world, something can happen to anybody, colored or white, to keep you from getting where you want to go—sickness, death, accident, fire—anything."

"Um-hum," said Simple. "You can be robbed and mugged in the night —or choked."

"That's right," I said, "or you can get ptomaine poison from drinking King-Kong."

"Sure can," said Simple. "Or you can go crazy from worriation."

"Or you can lose your job," I said.

"Or else lose all your money on the horses every week."

"Or on the numbers," I said.

"Or on policy," said Simple.

"Or on Chinese lottery, if you live on the Coast."

"Or on poker or blackjack or pokino or tonk."

"You ain't mentioned skin," said Simple.

"I do not play skin," I said.

"It is a rugged game," said Simple. "If I had never learnt it, I might be rich today. But skin is a mere skimption to some of the things that can keep a man from going where he wants to go in life. For instance, if you was a porter, your train could wreck. Or if you was in the Merchant Marine, your boat could sink. Or if you was a aviator, you liable to run into the Empire State building—or even Abyssinia Baptist church. Oh, it's awful, man, what can happen to you in this life!"

"You talk like you have had a hard time in this world," I said. "Have any of those things ever happened to you?"

"What are you talking about?" yelled Simple. "*Everything* has happened to me! I have been cut, shot, stabbed and run over, hit by a car and tromped by a horse—but I am still here! I have also been robbed, fooled, deceived, two-timed, double-crossed, dealt seconds, and mighty near divorced—but I am still here!"

"You're a tough man," I said.

"I have been fired, laid off, and just last week given an indefinite vacation, also jim-crowed, segregated, barred-out, insulted, eliminated, called black, yellow, and a red, locked out, locked in, locked up, also left holding the bag! I have been caught in the rain, caught in raids, caught short with the rent, and caught with another man's wife! Oh, man! I have been caught—but I am still here!"

"Boy, you have suffered!" I said.

"Suffered!" yelled Simple. "My mama should have named me Job! I have been under-fed, under-paid, under-nourished, and everything but *undertaken!* I have been bit by dogs, cats, mice, rats, pol parrots and fleas, chiggers, bedbugs, grand-daddies, mosquitoes, and a gold-toothed woman!"

"Great day in the morning!" I said.

"That ain't all," said Simple. "In this life I have been abused, confused, misused, accused and false-arrested, tried, sentenced, paroled, beat, blackjacked, third-degreed and near about lynched."

"Anyhow, your health has been good," I said. "You look husky as a bear."

"Good health nothing!" yelled Simple. "I done had everything from flat feet to a flat head! Why, man, I was born with a croup! And since then I had

> small-pox, chicken-pox, whooping cough, measles, double pneumonia, appendicitis, athlete's foot, tonsillitis, arthritis, backache, and a strain—but I am still here! Jack, I am still here!"
>
> "Having survived all that," I said, "then what are you afraid of now?"
>
> "That I will die before my time," said Simple.

At any rate, Simple has to speak his mind. If I do not let him speak his mind, he gets mad. On such occasions, when I sit down to write my weekly column, I cannot write about Simple at all if he is mad, since he refuses to cooperate. Then I have to write about something else, such as Jim Crow in Asia, or Negro business, or Christmas books. I have to write all by myself at such times.

Simple is a very positive person at times with definite opinions, but more often he is negative. He knows quite well what he does *not* like. He genuinely does not like hang-overs, wives who are hard to get along with, card sharks, white folks who make fine speeches about liberty and freedom and democracy but who practice Jim Crow, neither does he like high hospital beds, a woman who drinks a man up at the bar then goes her way alone, robbers who rob poor people, irrational Southerners, or friends who will not lend him a couple of dollars on Monday—even if he did just get paid on Saturday. He is also dead set against Dixie's racial customs.

Simple once said to me, "Let the South secede from the rest of the United States, because I do not think it can be reformed. It is full of Hitlerites."

I disagreed and accused him of wanting to start the Civil War over again. We argued it out all up and down the right hand column of the *Defender*'s editorial page. Lately I was interested to read a similar suggestion in relation to the Army in New York's *PM* for October 24, 1945. It was made by one of the editors, white, and unrelated to Simple—unless, perhaps, they both have Indian blood.

In *PM,* John P. Lewis said:

> "Instead of segregating Negroes in the Army, why not segregate those of our white Southern military caste who hold to the fascist belief that one race is superior to another? . . . That would free the rest of the Army to operate as an Army should operate, on the basis of only one consideration: the ability and willingness of each individual soldier to do his job without regard to distinction of race and creed."

I have never heard anyone say that editor John P. Lewis is simple-minded, yet he talks like Simple, who happens to have that nickname.

Where he got it, I do not know. His real name is Jess Semple. He is also called, Hey, Jack, Jackson, What do you know, Joe, Daddy, and Daddy-o. He is a good scout and I like him very much. He is a solid buddy. He is also great, generous, regular, and will buy you a beer anytime. He is O.K. by me.

I once met a fellow who worked in a war plant. I asked him what he was making. He said, "Cranks."

I said, "What kind of cranks?"

He said, "Cranks! Cranks! Just Cranks!"

I said, "What do they crank?"

He said, "I do not know! I don't crank with those cranks. I just make 'em."

I lost track of that guy—but I remember him as a very straightforward kind of fellow. Simple is not unlike that, himself. If he doesn't know what he doesn't know, he just doesn't know. And that's that.

On the contrary, I am acquainted with some very smart people who do not know that they *don't* know what they don't know. That is what makes life complicated—since the smart people run the world. They are the ones who bank the banks that crank the cranks that start the tanks that haul the gas that fuels the planes that drop atom bombs on you and me. Those bombs can annihilate me, Simple, and you—not to speak of the human race.

I wish the smart people who run the world could realize that they don't know they *don't* know what they don't know. Don't you?

"It's About Time,"
LHP 555 (May 22, 1946)

It's about time some Negro writer wrote a *good* novel about Negroes who do *not* come to a bad end. With all of the millions of good, kind, decent, hard-working colored folks in America, it is about time some Negro writer picked out a good, decent family of colored folks to put into a novel.[38]

With all of the millions of colored people in America who never murder anybody, or rape or get raped or want to rape, who never lust after white bodies, or cringe before white stupidity, or Uncle Tom, or go crazy with race, or off-balance with frustration—with all the millions of normal human, lovable colored folks in the United States, it is about time some Negro writer put some of them into a book.

From the recent successful novels of Negro life, it would be hard for an outsider to tell that we have men or women in the race like those, for instance, who read *The New York Age,* who work steadily, send their children to school regularly, and live as do normal people anywhere—in spite of the color line—with no overpowering complexes driving them to manslaughter, rape, jail, evil, defeat, decay, or an untimely death.

How come the race that produced Phillis Wheatley, Crispus Attucks, Benjamin Banneker, Sojourner Truth, Frederick Douglass, James Weldon Johnson, Mary McLeod Bethune, Josephine Baker, Joe Louis, Lena Horne, Dr. Charles Drew, and Governor Hastie—also their fathers and mothers—how come the race that produced the current crop of wholesome young Negro students from Harvard to Howard to Xavier, or the fine lot of colored workers at Sperry's in Long Island or Ford's in Detroit or the airplane factories in Los Angeles—how come that race cannot produce one single clean fine upstanding triumphant Negro hero or heroine in current fiction?[39]

Of course, a writer has a right to write as he pleases, and of course there's the seamy side of life, and of course great art can (and often does) come out of the gutter. But it would be wonderful right now to have one new post-war Negro novel with lift and verve and triumph and glory in it instead of death, defeat, hopelessness, and the quicksand of utter futility.

If it were not a great novel—just a good novel—or even fair—it would be welcome! If the writing were not as fine as Hemingway's or Wright's or Katherine Ann Porter's—if it were only as good as the late Booth Tarkington or as Edna Ferber—that would be OK—if only the characters would stand up tall and not get completely beaten down in the end! Colored readers, too, need books to give the soul a lift once in a while. Are there no modern John Henrys? Are there no Harriet Tubmans today? For a real Negro hero in a Negro book—it's about time!

"Culture Via the Back Door,"
Negro Digest 5 (July 1946): 47–48

Art crosses color lines and gets around into many places where the creators of the art themselves may not be welcome.

Traveling through the prejudiced Middle West, I was struck by the large number of records by Negro bands—Duke Ellington, Lionel Hampton, Louis Jordan, Cab Calloway—on juke boxes in cafes where

Negroes are not served. The patrons enjoy the music, and the proprietors of the places make money from the records of Duke Ellington, but Mr. Ellington himself could not drink a cup of coffee or sit at the counter in many a Kansas or Missouri cafe where his music is played.

In Salt Lake City, Utah, the public and the press recently acclaimed the great singing of Dorothy Maynor, but Miss Maynor stayed in a Negro home, not a first-class hotel. After her concert, many of Dorothy Maynor's hearers gathered for refreshments, to "oh!" and "ah!" over her music, in cocktail rooms and supper clubs that would not serve the great Miss Maynor (or any less famous member of her race) even so much as a pretzel.

In Amarillo, Texas, recently I saw an ad in the local paper of Ann Petry's new Harlem novel *The Street*. It was not on the back page either. But Amarillo is strictly a Jim Crow town, and many Texas papers, so I am told, would not even carry news or photographs of local black men who died for their country in our late war. Art rates higher than life or death in Texas, I reckon, which hardly makes sense. But I guess it is a point in favor for art.

In Joplin, Missouri, a downtown shoe-shine parlor had a big poster in the window announcing my program of poems at the Bartlett School during Negro History Week. But the colored shine boy employed inside said he was not permitted to shine my shoes! My picture on a poster concerning my poetry was welcomed in the shop, but not my patronage.

In a city in the South a Negro radio group, whose singing of spirituals delights thousands over the air on Sunday mornings, must use the alley entrance and the freight elevator of the hotel where the radio station is located in order to reach their broadcasts. Their songs do not go out the back door by way of the alley to the air lanes, but the singers must come in that way with the ash cans and the freight.

Any Negro actor or artist who has toured the theatres or concert halls of this country can tell of hundreds of American cities that receive their art with applause, but will not give them a warm, decent place to sleep when the performance is over. Even some American army camps, enjoying Negro USO talent, have been most discourteous to the artists. The men applauded warmly in the post theatres but, in some cases, not even eating accommodations were offered visiting colored performers.

Members of Fletcher Henderson's orchestra reported recently having to sleep all night in a bus after playing an air base dance because the field had accommodations for whites only. Yet those same whites danced to and applauded their music!

Art must be like religion—both can cross physical color lines with ease, but neither seems to have much effect on most white people's hearts and souls—at least not in this rude American country of ours. Or can it be that most American white folks have no hearts and no souls? I am really puzzled about this, ours being a Christian country, but with so many people who are not Christ-like toward their darker brothers.

As for art—Richard Wright is widely read and cordially applauded at lectures. Millions listen to Marian Anderson at concerts and on the air. *Carmen Jones* with Muriel Smith as Carmen, plays for months across America. Everybody loves Duke Ellington. But on tour, in many cities that applaud these artists, in so far as public accommodations are concerned—hotels, restaurants, shine parlors, taxi service—Richard Wright, Marian Anderson, Muriel Smith, or Duke Ellington, might just as well be dogs.

In most American hotels a guest may bring his dog without difficulty —but not a Negro, not even a great Negro, not even the greatest singer in the world or the greatest master of modern music.

"Don't Be a Bottle-Battler," LHP 293 (November 1946)

For confirmed drunkards I have the greatest sympathy, and the greatest pity.[40] Habitual drunkenness is an expression of escape, a seeking for release. It can begin as, or become, a psychological illness. It ends always as a physical illness, a saturation of tissues, and an inner thirst that the liquids of health can no longer satisfy. But escape from the problems of life by way of the liquor bottle usually means a harder battle in the end than that of facing the harshest of ordinary problems.

When drinking becomes a habit, it is likely to become a *bad* habit—so the best thing to do is not to permit it to become a habit at all. Bad habits have a way of fighting back at you. Once a foothold has been established, they are very hard to get rid of. For those addicted to drink, but wishing to get over it, the battle of the bottle is no easy one. Long indulgence in alcohol has a way of weakening the character and addling the brain. Certainly, hard drinkers of hard liquor are frequently not in their right minds—as hospital and police records prove.

But nobody needs written records to realize that. One has only to observe the way a great many drunks carry on on Saturday nights in the public streets. Nobody with his senses about him would behave so absurdly, reeling and staggering, walking against traffic, quarreling, picking fights, and getting locked up. Sometimes public drunks are amusing, but more often they are pitiful and tragic—irresponsible clowns whose antics become stupid and repellent.

One night in Chicago I saw a patrol wagon pull up to a house. The police went inside to remove a crazy man who was breaking up his landlady's furniture. As they brought the man out, a passing drunk saw fit to interfere. The cops gave him a push and told him to keep on up the streets, but he paid them no mind. Instead, he turned around and began to berate the police. Whereupon the blue-coats seized the drunk and tossed him into the patrol wagon, too, and off he went—perhaps to the same padded cell as the insane person.

Another evening I saw a speeding car caught by the red light, suddenly stop short at a corner. As it stopped, all the doors flew open and everybody except the driver jumped out, running and yelling, "We're not gonna ride with you—drunk as you are!" Whereupon the driver himself jumped out and yelled, "I ain't even gonna ride with myself!" He, too, ran away, leaving his car empty in the midst of traffic.

When I was a merchant seaman, I saw fellows who were good friends when sober, break bottles over each other's heads when drunk—and then regret it after their senses returned. I once saw an inebriated sailor jump into a muddy African river just for fun—but it took several men to rescue him from the swirling current. On Broadway I once saw a famous man of the theatre who was so intoxicated that he had to be propped up on the stage for a performance. But the propping up could not go on week after week. Today he is no longer famous—not even prosperous.

If you don't want to be a has-been, or a never-will-be, don't become a bottle-battler! Once the drink habit gets you, it is a very hard battle to fight. That there is a kick in alcohol is right. It will kick you down hill—but hard! It will do you dirt if you give it a chance. You may love liquor—but liquor won't love you very long. Familiarity with that demon only breeds contempt. Liquor delights in bringing low all who love it not wisely—but too well.

"Memories of Christmas," LHP 671 (November 1, 1946)

My first memories of Christmas center in Kansas, which is the very center of our U.S.A.[41] Christmas trees, candles, cotton snow, and pot-bellied stoves are all mixed up in these early memories. The stove is there because my first Christmas trees always stood in the corner behind the pot-bellied stove. On account of the cotton snow, we had to be careful of the stove, and of the candles on the tree. If the stove got red-hot, or the candles fell down, the cotton snow might catch on fire. The idea of snow catching on fire intrigues me to this very day. Early in life I had a love of excitement, and I always rather hoped the snow would catch on fire, but it never did.

For poor children, Santa Claus seldom lives up to expectation. I never remember finding on Christmas morning *all* of the things I had asked Santa Claus to bring. But always I would find at least one of the hoped-for gifts, and the surprise and happiness of that one would make up for those lacking. The big presents would always be under the tree. But hope for the missing B-B gun or the long desired cowboy suit would not be downed until the very toe of each hanging stocking was also searched. But out of the stockings would usually come mostly oranges, nuts, and hard candies. Certainly, not even Santa Claus could get an air rifle in a stocking!

Christmas without presents must be a strange Christmas indeed for an American child. But as I grew older, I learned that there are children (even in this richest of all countries) whose parents and whose Santa Claus sometimes cannot afford presents. I was twenty-one before I knew a Christmas without presents. That year I was working in the merchant marine, and in early December we sailed out of New York harbor for Rotterdam. The boat had a new crew. Of the forty seamen aboard, none of us had ever met or worked together before. Christmas eve we were at anchor in a strange Dutch port whose dock fronts and gabled houses were covered with the same white snow I had known in Kansas. Rotterdam's canal lights gleamed with a frosty glow as a half dozen of us took a motor launch across the harbor to the main part of the city where we found a cozy bar. There we greeted the Christmas dawn in a warm glow of Holland gin. Back aboard ship the next day, we had chicken for Christmas dinner, but no tree, and none of the crew exchanged presents.

That was my only Christmas without giving or receiving something. Even in the Soviet Union, where I spent a Yuletide away down in the heart of Uzbekistan in Central Asia, there were presents. Some thirty or forty miles from Tashkent there was at that time a colony of American Negro cotton chemists and growers teaching the Asiatics how to raise cotton Alabama style. Among them was the late Colonel Young's son, and some others who had been teachers at Hampton and other of our Southern colleges. With their wives, they invited Bernard Powers, a Negro road engineer working in Tashkent, and myself, to spend the holidays with them.

When I left Moscow for Central Asia in November, the citizens of the Soviet capital said they envied me going to the warm part of the Soviet union for the winter. I pictured myself as basking in a kind of Florida sunshine while Moscow suffered their customary twenty below zero temperature. Well, to a Moscovite the climate of Tashkent may be warm—but to me it was just as cold as Topeka or Kansas City or Chicago. In Uzbekistan the snow was half way up to my knees by December and, although the mercury never hit zero, it did get mighty near there. But to a Russian, *that was warm!*

The day before Christmas, Powers and I hailed a passing sled, horse-drawn—that took the place of taxis in snow-covered Tashkent—and off we went to the railroad station. There was a line of country-bound travelers a block long outside waiting to purchase tickets. When we finally got on the train it was crowded to the doors and beyond. Polite as Soviet citizens are to foreigners, often making way for them to have seats in a crowded coach, these coaches were too crowded for anyone to even move to let us inside. Powers and I had to stand on the open platform between the coaches in the bitter cold.

As the train pulled out, it started to snow again. Before we had gone ten miles, all the human beings who were crowded together on these old-time open platforms between the cars were covered from head to toe with the driving snow, until we looked like snow-men ourselves. After a half hour of this, the snow with which we were coated began to turn to ice, fanned as it was by prairie winds and the speed of the moving train. First my face, then my hands, then my feet froze—and the cold finally penetrated to the very marrow of my bones. After a while, it did not matter any more. That sweet don't-care-ness that I have always heard comes with freezing to death, came over me. At last the train came to a station in the stormy wilderness. Some of the people in the coaches got off. But by then it did not matter whether I got inside the train or not. I was frozen stiff—and Powers and I both were so covered with snow that we could have passed for white in Mississippi.

Finally we reached the farm where the Negro agricultural experts lived. There was warmth and good-will, good food and presents—and a Christmas tree. But it took Powers and I all night to thaw out and finally really realize that Christmas had come. For Christmas dinner we had fried rabbit and wonderful hot biscuits that one of the colored wives made. There was pie, too! And it was just like being back home in Kansas although we were in the ancient land of Tamerlane and Genghis Khan and the Thousand and One Nights.

Other memorable Christmases for me in foreign lands have been the Yuletides of Mexico and of France. Paris has its charming features all the year round, but Christmas there—if you live with and know French people—has a heart-warming delight all its own.

In Mexico the holidays possess picturesque joys I have seen nowhere else. For nine days before Christmas there is a series of neighborhood parties each night from house to house known as "*las posadas.*" At the "*posadas*" each guest takes a candle and a procession is formed that goes from room to room and door to door around the patio of the house singing:

Humildes peregrinos,
Maria, Jésus, José . . .

as Mary, with child, and her husband, Joseph, walked centuries ago seeking shelter in Bethlehem so that the Child might be born. But no door opens, so the procession moves on. The old story of man's lack of interest in his brother is acted out each night.

But each night it all ends in happiness and feasting, dancing and a party—and after nine such nights comes Christmas! Perhaps it simply means—this symbolic "*posada*"—that after the hard days, the long months (maybe even the bitter years), there comes somehow to everyone the clean white snow, the sparkling tree, the gifts, and the new birth of friendship and life that is Christmas, holiday of the new-born Child.

"My Adventures as a Social Poet,"
Phylon 8.3 (1947): 205–12

Poets who write mostly about love, roses and moonlight, sunsets and snow, must lead a very quiet life. Seldom, I imagine, does their poetry get them into difficulties. Beauty and lyricism are really related to another world, to ivory towers, to your head in the clouds, feet floating off the earth.

Unfortunately, having been born poor—and also colored—in Missouri, I was stuck in the mud from the beginning. Try as I might to float off into the clouds, poverty and Jim Crow would grab me by the heels, and right back on earth I would land. A third floor furnished room is the nearest thing I have ever had to an ivory tower.

Some of my earliest poems were social poems in that they were about people's problems—whole groups of people's problems—rather than my own personal difficulties. Sometimes, though, certain aspects of my personal problems happened to be also common to many other people. And certainly, racially speaking, my own problems of adjustment to American life were the same as those of millions of other segregated Negroes. The moon belongs to everybody, but not this American earth of ours. That is perhaps why poems about the moon perturb no one, but poems about color and poverty do perturb many citizens. Social forces pull backwards or forwards, right or left, and social poems get caught in the pulling and hauling. Sometimes the poet himself gets pulled and hauled—even hauled off to jail.

I have never been in jail but I have been detained by the Japanese police in Tokyo and by the immigration authorities in Cuba—in custody, to put it politely—due, no doubt, to their interest in my written words. These authorities would hardly have detained me had I been a writer of the roses and moonlight school. I have never known the police of any country to show an interest in lyric poetry as such. But when poems stop talking about the moon and begin to mention poverty, trade unions, color lines, and colonies, somebody tells the police. The history of world literature has many examples of poets fleeing into exile to escape persecution, of poets in jail, even of poets killed like Placido or, more recently, Lorca in Spain.

My adventures as a social poet are mild indeed compared to the body-breaking, soul-searing experiences of poets in the recent fascist countries or of the resistance poets of the Nazi invaded lands during the war. For that reason, I can use so light a word as "adventure" in regard to my own skirmishes with reaction and censorship.

My adventures as a social poet began in a colored church in Atlantic City shortly after my first book, *The Weary Blues,* was published in 1926. I had been invited to come down to the shore from Lincoln University where I was a student, to give a program of my poems in the church. During the course of my program I read several of my poems in the form of the Negro folk songs, including some blues poems about hard luck and hard work. As I read I noticed a deacon approach the pulpit with a note which he placed on the rostrum beside me, but I did not stop to open the note until I had finished and had acknowledged the applause of a cordial audience. The note read, "Do not read any more blues in my pulpit." It was signed by the minister. That was my first experience with censorship.

The kind and generous woman who sponsored my writing for a few years after my college days did not come to the point quite so directly as did the minister who disliked blues. Perhaps, had it not been in the midst of the great depression of the late '20's and early '30's, the kind of poems that I am afraid helped to end her patronage might not have been written. But it was impossible for me to travel from hungry Harlem to the lovely homes on Park Avenue without feeling in my soul the great gulf between the very poor and the very rich in our society. In those days, on the way to visit this kind lady I would see the homeless sleeping in subways and the hungry begging in doorways on sleet-stung winter days. It was then that I wrote a poem called "An Ad for the Waldorf-Astoria," satirizing the slick-paper magazine advertisements of the opening of that de luxe hotel. Also I wrote:

Park Bench

I live on a park bench.
You, Park Avenue.
Hell of a distance
Between us two.

I beg a dime for dinner—
You got a butler and maid.
But I'm wakin' up!
Say, ain't you afraid

That I might, just maybe,
In a year or two,
Move on over
To Park Avenue?

In a little while I did not have a patron any more.

But that year I won a prize, the Harmon Gold Award for Literature, which consisted of a medal and four hundred dollars. With the four hundred dollars I went to Haiti. On the way I stopped in Cuba where I was cordially received by the writers and artists. I had written poems about the exploitation of Cuba by the sugar barons and I had translated many poems of Nicholás Guillén such as:

Cane

Negro
In the cane fields.
White man
Above the cane fields.
Earth
Beneath the cane fields.
Blood
That flows from us.

This was during the days of the dictatorial Machado regime.[42] Perhaps someone called his attention to these poems and translations because, when I came back from Haiti weeks later, I was not allowed to land in Cuba, but was detained by the immigration authorities at Santiago and put on an island until the American consul came, after three days, to get me off with the provision that I cross the country to Havana and leave Cuban soil at once.

That was my first time being put out of any place. But since that time I have been put out of or barred from quite a number of places, all because of my poetry—not the roses and moonlight poems (which I write, too) but because of poems about poverty, oppression, and segregation. Nine Negro boys in Alabama were on trial for their lives when I got back from Cuba and Haiti. The famous Scottsboro "rape" case was in full session. I visited those boys in the death house at Kilby Prison, and I wrote many poems about them. One of these poems was:

Christ in Alabama

Christ is a Nigger,
Beaten and black—
O, bare your back.

Mary is His Mother—
Mammy of the South,
Silence your mouth.

God's His Father—
White Master above,
Grant us your love.

Most holy bastard
Of the bleeding mouth:
Nigger Christ
On the cross of the South.

Contempo, a publication of some of the students at the University of North Carolina, published the poem on its front page on the very day that I was being presented in a program of my poems at the University in Chapel Hill. That evening there were police outside the building in which I spoke, and in the air the rising tension of race that is peculiar to the South. It had been rumored that some of the local citizenry were saying that I should be run out of town, and that one of the sheriffs agreed, saying, "Sure, he ought to be run out! It's bad enough to call Christ a *bastard.* But when he calls him a *nigger,* he's gone too far!"

The next morning a third of my fee was missing when I was handed my check. One of the departments of the university jointly sponsoring my program had refused to come through with its portion of the money. Nevertheless, I remember with pleasure the courtesy and kindness of many of the students and faculty at Chapel Hill and their lack of agreement with the anti-Negro elements of the town. There I began to learn at the University of North Carolina how hard it is to be a white liberal in the South.

It was not until I had been to Russia and around the world as a writer and journalist that censorship and opposition to my poems reached the point of completely preventing me from appearing in public programs on a few occasions. It happened first in Los Angeles shortly after my return from the Soviet Union. I was to have been one of several speakers on a memorial program to be held at the colored branch Y.M.C.A. for a young Negro journalist of the community. At the behest of white higher-ups, no doubt, some reactionary Negro politicians informed the Negro Y.M.C.A. that I was a Communist. The secretary of the Negro Branch Y then informed the committee of young people in charge of the memorial that they could have their program only if I did not appear.

I have never been a Communist, but I soon learned that anyone visiting the Soviet Union and speaking with favor of it upon returning is liable to be so labeled. Indeed when Mrs. Roosevelt, Walter White, and so Christian a lady as Mrs. Bethune who has never been in Moscow, are so labeled, I should hardly be surprised! I wasn't surprised. And the young people's committee informed the Y secretary that since the Y was a public community center which they helped to support, they saw no reason why it should censor their memorial program to the extent of eliminating any speaker.

Since I had been allotted but a few moments on the program, it was my intention simply to read this short poem of mine:

Dear lovely death
That taketh all things under wing,
Never to kill,
Only to change into some other thing
This suffering flesh—
To make it either more or less
But not again the same,
Dear lovely death,
Change is thy other name.

But the Negro branch Y, egged on by the reactionary politicians (whose incomes, incidentally, were allegedly derived largely from gambling houses and other underworld activities), informed the young people's committee that the police would be at the door to prevent my entering the Y on the afternoon of the scheduled program. So when the crowd gathered, the memorial was not held that Sunday. The young people simply informed the audience of the situation and said that the memorial would be postponed until a place could be found where all the participants could be heard. The program was held elsewhere a few Sundays later.

Somebody with malice aforethought (probably the Negro politicians of Uncle Tom vintage) gave the highly publicized California evangelist, Aimee Semple McPherson, a copy of a poem of mine, "Goodbye, Christ." This poem was one of my least successful efforts at poetic communication, in that many persons have misinterpreted it as an anti-Christian poem. I intended it to be just the opposite. Satirical, even ironic, in style, I meant it to be a poem against those whom I felt were misusing religion for worldly or profitable purposes. In the poem I mentioned Aimee Semple McPherson. This apparently made her angry. From her Angelus Temple pulpit she preached against me, saying, "There are many devils among us, but the most dangerous of all is the red devil. And now there comes among us a red devil *in a black skin*!"

She gathered her followers together and sent them to swoop down upon me one afternoon at an unsuspecting and innocent literary luncheon in Pasadena's Vista del Arroyo Hotel. Robert Nathan, I believe, was one of the speakers, along with a number of other authors.[43] I was to have five minutes on the program to read a few poems from my latest collection of folk verses, *Shakespeare in Harlem,* hardly a radical book.

When I arrived at the hotel by car from Los Angeles, I noticed quite a crowd in the streets where the traffic seemed to be tangled. So I got out some distance from the front of the hotel and walked through the grounds to the entrance, requesting my car to return at three o'clock. When I asked in the lobby for the location of the luncheon, I was told to wait until the desk clerk sent for the chairman, George Palmer Putnam. Mr. Putnam arrived with the manager, both visibly excited. They informed me that the followers of Aimee McPherson were vehemently picketing the hotel because of my appearance there. The manager added with an aggrieved look that he could not have such a commotion in front of his hotel. Either I would have to go or he would cancel the entire luncheon.

Mr. Putnam put it up to me. I said that rather than inconvenience several hundred guests and a half dozen authors, I would withdraw—except that I did not know where my car had gone, so would someone be kind enough to drive me to the station. Just then a doorman came in to inform the manager that traffic was completely blocked in front of the hotel. Frantically the manager rushed out. About that time a group of Foursquare Gospel members poured into the lobby in uniforms and armbands and surrounded me and George Palmer Putnam, demanding to know if we were Christians. Before I could say anything, Mr. Putnam lit into them angrily, saying it was none of their business and stating that under our Constitution a man could have any religion he chose, as well as freedom to express himself.

Just then an old gentleman about seventy-two who was one of the organizers of the literary luncheon came up, saying he had been asked to drive me to the station and get me out of there so they could start the luncheon. Shaking hands with Mr. Putnam, I accompanied the old gentleman to the street. There Aimee's sound truck had been backed across the roadway blocking all passage so that limousines, trucks, and taxis were tangled up in all directions. The sound truck was playing "God Bless America" while hundreds of pickets milled about with signs denouncing Langston Hughes—atheistic Red. Rich old ladies on the arms of their chauffeurs were trying to get through the crowd to the luncheon. Reporters were dashing about.

None of the people recognized me, but in the excitement the old gentleman could not find his car. Finally he hailed a taxi and nervously thrust a dollar into the driver's hand with the request that I be driven to the station. He asked to be excused himself in order to get back to the luncheon. Just as I reached out the door to shake hands in farewell, three large white ladies with banners rushed up to the cab. One of them screamed, "We don't shake hands with niggers where we come from!"

The thought came over me that the picketing might turn into a race riot, in which case I did not wish to be caught in a cab in a traffic jam alone. I did not turn loose the old gentleman's hand. Instead of shaking it in farewell, I simply pulled him into the taxi with me, saying, "I thought you were going to the station, too."

As the pickets snarled outside, I slammed the door. The driver started off, but we were caught in the traffic blocked by the sound truck lustily playing "God Bless America." The old gentleman trembled beside me, until finally we got clear of the mob. As we backed down a side street and turned to head for the station, the sirens of approaching police cars were heard in the distance.

Later I learned from the afternoon papers that the whole demonstration had been organized by Aimee McPherson's publicity man, and that when the police arrived he had been arrested for refusing to give up the keys to the sound truck stalled midway the street to block the traffic. This simply proved the point I had tried to make in the poem—that the church might as well bid Christ goodbye if his gospel were left in the hands of such people.

Four years later I was to be picketed again in Detroit by Gerald L. K. Smith's Mothers of America—for ever since the Foursquare Gospel demonstration in California, reactionary groups have copied, used and distributed this poem.[44] Always they have been groups like Smith's, never known to help the fight for democratic Negro rights in America, but rather to use their energies to foment riots such as that before Detroit's Sojourner Truth housing project where the Klan-minded tried to prevent colored citizens from occupying government homes built for them.

I have had one threatening communication signed *A Klansman*. And many scurrilous anonymous anti-Negro letters from persons whose writing did not always indicate illiteracy. On a few occasions, reactionary elements have forced liberal sponsors to cancel their plans to present me in a reading of my poems. I recall that in Gary, Indiana, some years ago the colored teachers were threatened with the loss of their jobs if I accepted their invitation to appear at one of the public schools. In another city a white high school principal, made apprehensive by a small group of reactionary parents, told me that he communicated with the F.B.I. at Washington to find out if I were a member of the Communist Party. Assured that I was not, with the approval of his school board, he presented me to his student body. To further fortify his respectability, that morning at assembly, he had invited all of the Negro ministers and civic leaders of the town to sit on the stage in a semi-circle behind me. To the students it must have looked like a kind of modern minstrel show as it was the first time any Negroes at all had been invited to their assembly.

So goes the life of a social poet. I am sure none of these things would ever have happened to me had I limited the subject matter of my poems to roses and moonlight. But, unfortunately, I was born poor—and colored—and almost all the prettiest roses I have seen have been in rich white people's yards—not in mine. That is why I cannot write exclusively about roses and moonlight—for sometimes in the moonlight my brothers see a fiery cross and a circle of Klansmen's hoods. Sometimes in the moonlight a dark body swings from a lynching tree—but for his funeral there are no roses.

"Atlanta: Its Negroes Have Most Culture but Some of the Worst Ghettoes in the World," *Ebony,* January 1948, pp. 19–24

Atlanta, G-A! Some say the G-A means Georgia. Others swear it means *God Awful.* At any rate, life from rags to riches exists among Atlanta Negroes, described as the "most cultured, yet most enslaved" group of colored people in America by Morehouse College President Benjamin E. Mays.[45]

Such centers of teeming colored activity as Decatur Street in Southeast Atlanta or the Pittsburgh section of the Southwest side reveal the "rags," termed by John Gunther in his *Inside U.S.A.* as a section that "out-ghettoes anything I ever saw in the European ghetto, even in Warsaw. . . . I blinked remembering this was not India."[46]

The riches are not so concentrated. However, good living and conspicuous wealth can be seen by driving out well-known Hunter Road, Simpson Road, the Boulevard or numerous other "exclusive" streets located in all four sections of Atlanta—for Atlanta has its "400" too. But in Atlanta they call it the "27."

The "27 Club" is made up of college presidents, prominent businessmen, professionals and other financially successful colored gentry. The club meets the 27th of each month at 27 minutes before or after the hour, closes on the same time schedule. The "27 Club" symbolizes culture at its zenith in Negro America.

The other side of Atlanta is a story of contrasts:

Negro-operated businesses exceed in number, variety and sales volume any other city in the country but there is not a single Negro policeman in Atlanta.

There are more Negro schools of higher learning in Atlanta than any other city but the colored public school student is taught 3½ hours a day compared to 6 hours for whites.

Colored Atlanta, with one Negro for every two whites, is a city of bold paradoxes. Example: the colored-owned bank, the Citizens Trust Company, closes annually on the birthday of Jefferson Davis, observing a legal holiday just as other Georgia banks do in honor of the slave-owning president of the Confederacy.

Business and Schools

In Atlanta, as in other Southern cities, social standing, based on color, family background—whether your ancestors were house slaves or field slaves—is on the way out. Occupation, income, and personal achievement are rapidly becoming the significant factors in determining one's "social class."

Atlanta's Negro income receivers run the gamut from $6 a week "flunkies" to millionaire businessmen. In 1940, 3.2 per cent of the colored income earners were professional persons. This compared favorably with other cities. But the majority of Negroes in Atlanta as in other cities are in the lower-paid occupations.

Number writers, "bookies," "gamers," and other such illegal occupations exist, but are not as conspicuous in Atlanta as in Northern metropolitan areas. In the professional class, Atlanta has a great many teachers, both public school and college, relatively few lawyers (only seven), but many successful businessmen.

At last count in 1944, there were 843 successful Negro businesses in Atlanta. Biggest is the Atlanta Life Insurance Company, a $15,000,000 concern that is the only Negro insurance firm appearing in Best's list of recommended companies. Atlanta Life has a half million policy-holders in nine states, a total of 55 offices.

Negroes in Atlanta have their own bank, the Citizens Trust Company, a chain of three drugstores. There are many restaurants. Typical is Mrs. James' Cafe, which serves delicious food in ordinary surroundings. Indeed, the quality of the cooking is such that the cafe owner, after many years of enjoying her own Southern cuisine, is now of such proportions that she can no longer get in and out of her own booths unassisted. And she cooks sitting on a stool, turning out wonderful steaks, chicken, and pan-fried oysters unequalled elsewhere.

As a center of Negro higher education, Atlanta is unequalled anywhere in the nation. Its seven colleges centered around Atlanta University are all top rate. But getting into college is a trial for the younger generation of 30,000 school children in public and high school. There is only one public kindergarten for Negro children in the whole city. Although more than a third of Atlanta's pupils are colored, there are only 13 schools for Negro children, 52 schools for whites. Negro schools have no assembly halls, no swimming pools, very poor library facilities. When assemblies are held for the whole student body, Negro high schools must hold them out of doors. Reason: of the tax funds for city education, for every $6 dollars allotted annually for each child, only $1 goes to educate each Negro youngster.

Through the Negro vote, a bond issue was passed last year which will give $3,000,000 for colored schools. Result: a new Negro high school to relieve the load on the one high school in town jammed with double and triple shifts in many grades.

Society and Slums

Society in Atlanta is not as pronounced or rigid in its dictates of "Who's Who" as Washington, D.C., or Charleston, S.C., but nevertheless there is a marked similarity in the structure of social life in the cities.

The old citizens think they are the elite, the chosen, and dare anyone to dispute it. They believe that longevity, coupled with culture and affluence, should count for more than any other combination. They resemble that old Knickerbocker set in New York City, into whose social sanctum sanctorum the *nouveau riche* were not permitted to set unhallowed feet.

But groups like the Twelve Club, the most exclusive women's society in town limited to 12 members and including pioneer Atlantans only, are running into trouble. The Twelve Club has not found enough pioneers to complete their roster. Result: many vacancies.

The newcomers laugh up their sleeves at the old citizens. "While the old settlers sit wrapped in the drapery of scorn and contempt for us, we are up and doing things," says an interloper. If it were not for the newcomers, to hear them tell it, there would be very little progressive activity among Atlanta's colored population.

Having fun is done mostly at home in small groups. There are several reasons for this. Negroes of equal intelligence, culture, and financial standing do not all care to mingle with one another socially. Another reason is that Atlanta is relatively barren of desirable night clubs. The Georgia law banning the sale of liquor in establishments other than liquor stores partly accounts for the lack of night spots. In the big city of Atlanta, one cannot legally buy a "single" or "double" of any intoxicating drink "across the bar." The two main night clubs are Butler's Paradise on the outskirts of town and the Zanzibar in the heart of Atlanta's Harlem. Both are maintained as private clubs with customers holding membership cards so that they can buy alcoholic drinks.

Housing in Atlanta presents a picture of glaring contrasts. Some of the worst housing to be found anywhere in America exists in Atlanta. On the other hand, some of the most beautiful and well-appointed Negro homes in the world are located in Georgia's capital city. There are a few very expensive homes, and a great number of more modest but attractive, comfortable, well-furnished single dwellings with spacious front and back lawns usually displaying red, white, or pink roses, fragrant magnolias, bougainvillea, hibiscus, and a variety of other lovely garden flowers.

At the more sordid end of the scale there are large areas of squalor, filth, broken-down shacks, outside toilets, overcrowding and congestion. "Air-conditioned" huts are numerous; large gaps in the roofs and all four sides of many homes make housing not much better than residence on a park bench. In many cases, rain during the night means that the husband, wife, and children huddle on a rocking chair in the only dry corner of the room.

Atlanta's pre-war housing condition was such that one out of every eight homes was without running water and one out of every four was without sanitary, inside flush toilets.

In these depressing areas of row after row of rickety, dirty brown or grey frame houses falling apart inside and out, tenanted by poor whites and Negroes competing desperately for living spaces, the Columbians' hoodlum movement took root. Since Negroes in Atlanta are increasing, they must, of necessity, push outward from their suffocating quarters. The whites are immovable because there is not available space into which they might move. When Negroes move into the run-down white areas, there is great racial tenseness. Newspaper reports of bombs under Negro homes in formerly all-white areas are not infrequent. That is why one sees porch lights on all night in front of some Negro homes.

The Columbians used this tenseness to exploit the poor white's fear of a Negro invasion of his already crowded living space. But the "hate" theme of the Columbians was distasteful to many whites. The *Atlanta Constitution* and the *Atlanta Journal,* the two local white dailies, blasted the organization in the news and editorial columns. With the leaders drawing prison terms, the movement is now dormant.

"Separate but Equal" a Sham

"Separate but equal accommodations" is the legal subterfuge by which Negroes in Atlanta are relegated to the role of second-class citizens. A person, defined by Georgia code 1932, chapter 34, section 312 and chapter 79, section 103, as a Negro, is separated from white persons in almost every aspect of life by Georgia law. The all too familiar pattern of Southern racial segregation is the trend of the times in Atlanta. Separate, and by no means equal, accommodations are maintained in all public places. That is, if accommodations are available at all.

Transportation is a main sore spot and potential tinderbox of flaring racial friction in Atlanta. It affects all person who find it necessary to ride the street cars. At any time a person of color on the street car is likely to feel a tap on the shoulder and look up to see a white thumb motioning him further to the rear. The rear begins where white folks end, however far back in the vehicle that may be.

"A pistol fired into a crowded street car at Spring and Marietta St., N.W., at 3:20 P.M., Saturday during a disturbance growing out of seating argument. . . . The victim, Lucy Pyron, 50, Negro, of 990 Ashby St., S.W., was admitted to Grady Hospital suffering from a bullet wound in the stomach. . . . Garrett, the chief material witness admitted that he had asked a Negro to move back, and that an argument had ensued." This excerpt from an article recently appearing on the front page of the *Atlanta Journal* shows what can and may happen to any colored person using Atlanta's public transportation.

Since the war streetcar conductors, acting under a vague Georgia law granting them police power, with right to carry weapons, have shot three Negro passengers, two mortally. In city police court, dominated politically by Georgia Power Company, all three conductors were promptly cleared of the murder charges. Well-to-do Negroes do not ride on public transportation, preferring the added expense of driving their own cars through heavy traffic, but these are small in minority and do not basically alter the problem.

"Jamaica," *Ebony,* November 1948, pp. 45–50

Why more American Negroes have not discovered easy-to-reach, inexpensive Jamaica as a perfect vacation spot is puzzling and paradoxical since our own U.S.A. affords so few warm-weather, prejudice-free resorts. Just eight hours from New York by plane via Miami (round trip fare including tax: $276), the West Indies island offers lots of sun all year round with an average temperature of 78 and attractive open-to-all accommodations at lower-than-U.S. prices.

At the Palisadoes Airport in Kingston, charming hostesses greet you as you land with a tall cold glass of rum punch—free! From then on it's jazz, joy, and jive—if that's what you want. On the other hand if rum makes you sleepy (and you are tired anyhow), it's quiet, rest and sun. In luxury hotels or simple guest houses near the island's wonderful beaches, both are available. You can "whoop it up" or take it easy, as you choose. Nobody will say you "nay" either way.

The Jamaicans are a most amiable people and they do not have any obvious color lines. At least, I didn't run into a color line and I was there for a month. For a pleasant vacation one needs a good place to rest, good food, and available fun when rest becomes boring. Jamaica offers these to visitors, plus an English-African charm all its own.

The cost of living in Jamaica, like in the States, has gone up but it is still possible to rent a nice guest house for as low as $15 a week. With the price of beef only 40 cents a pound and pork 20 cents a pound, you can get along on less than in New York or Chicago. A cook can be obtained for 15 shillings a week or approximately $3, making life really leisurely and inexpensive at the same time.

Hotel rates—that is, the best—run from $8 to $12 a day, including three excellent meals.

Biggest lure of Jamaica is its beaches. All around the island is the blue Caribbean with some of the finest winter bathing resorts on earth. For swimmers who do not like cold water, Jamaica is paradise. At some of the beaches—particularly near Kingston—the water is nice and warm all the time. At others, such as the famous Dunn's River Falls or Ocho Rios (Eight Rivers) where the sea is fed with fresh water falls only a few yards away, naturally the sea is cold and invigorating. You swim in the ocean, then shower the salt away under the nearby natural falls that cascade down from the hills.

Montego Bay is a world-famous bathing resort—and quite expensive during the season if you stay at one of the smart hotels (most luxurious is the Casa Blanca with rates running to $12 daily with meals). But there are always modestly priced guest houses. Lords and Ladies come from far-off England to lie on the white sands of Doctor's Cave where the sea is a clean clear green. Coral reefs keep the sharks away. Sometimes at night the water is phosphorescent and it seems as if you are swimming in light. By day there are glass-bottom boats to look down at the sea gardens and the strange brightly colored fish.

Most of the townspeople of Montego Bay swim at the Cornwall Bathing Club just outside the town and right next to Doctor's Cave. It is a cooperatively owned beach managed by a peach-colored little lady known as "Cookie" who makes strangers feel right at home. There are beach cabins and a bar (with a pretty brownskin barmaid) and tall palms to lean against when you get tired of lying on the sand. There is a young attendant named Martel who will take his bicycle and ride down the road for sandwiches in case you get hungry. And if you want to see some Olympic-style swimming, watch the boys and girls on that beach any Sunday afternoon—young folks who learned to swim when they learned to walk.

Since most of the planes from Miami stop at Montego Bay first, you need never go any farther if all you wish to do in Jamaica is swim. But if you wish to go farther, Kingston, the biggest city, is not the only interesting place to visit. There is Mandeville, a charming English style village up in the cool mountains. There is Port Antonio where Erroll Flynn has acquired an island and where you can go down the rapids of the Rio Grande River on bamboo rafts. Or for folks interested in folk lore, there is the Maroon Cockpit country that Katherine Dunham has written about in her *Journey to Accompong*. The Maroons live under separate peace treaty with the British [and] are the only people on the island who still hunt wild boar. Nearer Kingston there is old Spanish Town with its ancient Cathedral. And around the peninsula beyond the airport lies what is left of Port Royal, renowned in pirate days as the "wickedest city in the world," but now almost all sunken in the sea.

For a Jamaican vacation the same clothes one would wear at home in summer are suitable—or what folks use in Florida or Southern California the year around, with the accent on sportswear. Except in the mountains, Jamaica is warm all the time, hot along the coast, but the air is usually pleasantly tempered by breezes from the sea. Men should take plenty of sportshirts, women light dresses. For a tropical vacation, clothing should be light, cool, and comfortable, and as washable and wrinkle-proof as possible. Unless you are staying at the most fashionable and expensive winter hotels or guest houses, evening clothes are not a necessity for a man.

The Jamaicans seemed to me a friendly and hospitable folk, interested in America and Americans, and delighted to entertain visitors of their own color. Our leading Negro newspapers and magazines may be found in Kingston shops. The records on the juke boxes are mostly American, as are most of the movies in theaters, although lately very good English pictures are being shown, too. There are cool open air theaters. Most modern of Kingston's motion picture houses is the Carib, a beautiful theater, completely air-conditioned.

There are direct flights from Miami or New Orleans to Jamaica, or one may go via Havana or Camaguey, Cuba, with stop-over-privileges in the land of the rhumba. (But Havana's best hotels cater to white American tourists and would just as leave not have you around.) During the war it was well-nigh impossible to reach Jamaica by boat. However, services are being resumed again. Personally I prefer air travel since there is no segregation and my experiences in the past with British and American boats have been none too pleasant. But if you like a boat trip, and particularly if you are traveling with your family or a party of friends and won't be the lone representative of the race aboard, you may book passage from New Orleans on United Fruit freighters which leave weekly (fare is a little more than $100 one way).

Island English Is Charming

Jamaica is just different enough not to be confusing. Its customs and its food are not exactly like our own, yet they are not foreign to the point of disturbing strangeness. And one great advantage is that you don't have to learn a new language to get around, as you should if visiting Cuba or Haiti. The Jamaicans speak English with just enough accent and dialect to seem charming to uninitiated ears. The educated Jamaicans have an English accent while the peasants speak an intriguing kind of Afro-Creole-Cockney with little musical lilts to each word.

It's hard to completely understand the average person at first, but gradually the language grows on you. For instance, folks say things like "Him thump him down," instead of "He knocked him down." And in the evening everybody says, "Goodnight" as a form of greeting when you meet, as well as a form of "Goodbye" on departure. "Goodnight" does not necessarily mean that you have gone. It may mean that you have just arrived—a kind of "Howdy-do."

Nobody said "Goodnight" to me when I landed in Jamaica because I got there in the daytime. I left New York by plane on a chilly drizzly midnight, had breakfast the next day at the International Airport in Miami, and was in warm and sunny Kingston in time for luncheon. At Miami I ate in the dining room without incident, and had another late breakfast on the plane as we flew over Cuba. There was a brief stop at Montego Bay on the north shore of Jamaica, then along the coast we flew southeast and over the Blue Mountains to Kingston's Palisadoes Airport on a neck of land curving into the Caribbean sea.

All the immigration officials, the doctor, and the health nurse were colored, as were the courteous customs inspectors. Entrance formalities were quickly over. You must have been vaccinated to go to Jamaica, but you do not need a passport, only a round-trip ticket. There's no red tape.

Once in Jamaica, it is very easy to get around. The island is only 140 miles long and less than 50 miles wide, so no place is very far. There are good roads and motoring is a pleasure. A car may be hired by the day or week at reasonable rates. There is a railroad that crosses the island—all day from Kingston to Montego Bay. And a plane that makes the same trip in half an hour.

98% of Population Is Colored

Parked outside the air terminal is a fleet of big old-fashioned open Packards waiting to drive passengers into the city. Sharing the back seat of one with me were a radio writer and his wife from New York. With much blowing of horn to scatter goats and donkeys in the road, we curved around the peninsula and sped along the sea down the left-handed side of the harbor road to the capital.

Tall palms swayed gently in the breeze while the brilliant sun sparkled on the lacy fringes of little waves that licked the shore. Kingston is hidden in a grove of trees. The houses and buildings are all low, not a one in town over four stories except maybe a church steeple. The houses are wooden with wide verandas and the downtown buildings are often porticoed with covered sidewalks to protect shoppers from the sun. Some school classes are held on porches or in the yards.

Everywhere along the highway and in the city streets, *everybody* was colored. Some 98 per cent of the population is descended from African slaves. Not until we got to the very center of the town did I see any white people at all, and then not many. The radio writer and his wife remarked about the handsome tall dark traffic cops in blue trousers, white jackets, and white helmets, directing traffic with precise movements of arms and hands.

Suddenly our big old Packard turned off busy Harbour Street into the green landscaped entrance of the Myrtle Bank Hotel and stopped beneath its portico. On the low arched terrace various guests sat at little tables having cool afternoon drinks. Brownskin bellboys in immaculate white took our baggage.

The Myrtle Bank is one of the finest hotels in the West Indies, a big, busy, cosmopolitan place with extensive grounds on the waterfront so that half of its rooms overlook the bay where the sun rises out of the sea. Its guests may have breakfast (choice of five to seven kinds of fresh fruit—eat all you want) in little outdoor arbors in the garden. Courteous colored waiters come across the lawn with white table linen and gleaming silverware. Shortly you have before you buried in ice a whole pineapple, slices of paw paw and melon, and large sweet navel oranges as a preliminary to delicious coffee, piles of golden toast, and whatever main dish you may order.

Luncheon in the main dining room (where a coat is worn) or in the open air pavilion bar (where you may dine in a sports shirt) is preceded by an amazing variety of buffet *smorgasbord* to which you may help yourself. These appetizers range all the way from lobster to baked beans. The unwary may eat so much of the *smorgasbord* that there is no room for the main luncheon where, from a typical menu containing a variety of choices, you may select jellied consommé madrilene, panned veal chops with crushed pumpkin, yams, Blue Mountain Coffee, and guava ice cream. Dinner in the formal dining room in the evening is served in courses with a grave tuxedoed head waiter to show you to your table. You may have afternoon tea, too, if you wish. Meals are included on your bill which runs about $10.00 a day per person.

During the winter season there is dancing almost nightly in a kind of pavilion ballroom whose arches on three sides open onto the gardens. In the hotel bar labor leader Bustamente and local island celebrities are frequently seen. Across the gardens there is a large swimming pool where you may bathe in fresh water while just over the rail naked diving boys besport themselves in the salt but rather oily water of the bay. After swimming you may sit on the hotel pier (where there is another bar) and watch the ships go by with a cold rum punch at hand, or linger in a beach chair in the sun beside the pool.

Finds No Color Lines at All

In the days when the Myrtle Bank Hotel belonged to the United Fruit Company (an American firm, God help us!) they tell me that Negro guests were not particularly welcome and were put in attic rooms, if received at all. But now the hotel belongs to the Issa family (Syrians) and the color bar is broken. During my sojourn there a number of colored guests came and went including the Caribbean Beauty Queens from the various British islands, three of whom were a luscious brown. Everyday I saw colored diners, and on Sundays tan-skinned youngsters from the "better" families had a wonderful time in the pool.

In the restaurants and cabarets of Jamaica, I encountered no color lines at all, whites and Negroes dining and dancing together. In and near Kingston there are some lovely night clubs. The most attractive are a few miles outside the city where the breezes are cooler—Morgan's Cove, the Springfield, the Glass Bucket. Some of the clubs are Negro-owned and on weekends there are "native" shows at the Sugar Hill or the Midway Club high on Stoney Hill Road at Red Gal Ring. There's an excellent Jamaican M.C., Ben Bowers, who "came up" under Willie Bryant in New York and who sings all the latest American songs. And there's a highly amusing comedian named Rudolph who does comic female impersonations of unhep and unglamorous ladies—a kind of Jackie Mabley in reverse.[47] Chinese crooners and "coolie girl" singers often add to the entertainment.

The "coolie girls" (in the vernacular of the people) are those generally attractive daughters of the not uncommon Negro-Chinese-East Indian marriages of the Caribbean. Tan skinned or golden with lustrous hair and dreamy eyes, these young ladies usually cause West Indian gentlemen to turn around and look twice. It seems that girls mature early in the tropics and at sixteen they are quite ready to be kissed. Certainly the nightclubs of Kingston are alive with youth and beauty.

With a girl and a car you drive through the starry night perhaps to the Wickie Wackie on the open ocean seven miles from town. Surely this is one of the most romantic night clubs in the world—out of doors beside the sea beneath a grove of curving sea-grape trees. Here you dance on a little raised dance floor, or drink at the tiny thatched bar. When the late moon rises, if the mood strikes you, you leave your shoes under the table, take the girl's hand and run barefooted through the trees down to the sea and across the sand into the warm surf. In the golden moonlight with the lights and music of the club farther and farther away you wander down the beach. The night, the sand, the sea, and the stars.

If you are a man and want to see the "sporting life" of Kingston—the less respectable bars and clubs and verandas where the ladies of the evening lean—the safest way to do so is with a friend who knows the town, or a trusted chauffeur. Not that you are likely to be robbed, but you very well might be over-charged. Hanover Street is famous with the sailors. Its little bars and "salons" are full of willing young ladies from chocolate browns to peaches-and-creams. At each stop (in case you don't know) you are expected to buy a drink, after which it is quite all right to take in the atmosphere, then walk on, if you wish, a few steps to the next place. Just because a girl calls you "darling" you don't *have* to stay. But you need have no fear that the cops will raid the "joints" while you are there—they are legal in Jamaica.

Curried goat, Indian style, is the popular after-midnight dish with Jamaicans who have been out "having a ball." Highly seasoned and spiced with pepper, the Kingstonians say it is wonderful to keep from having a hangover the next morning. But the light Jamaica rum seldom leaves one with a hangover, anyhow. I ate many a plate of curried goat with rice just because it tasted good. Under ideal circumstances goat is eaten in the country at big curried goat feeds—not unlike our Southern barbecues. But not every tourist meets a country gentleman who will invite him to his farm. So the next best thing is to try it in town. And it need not always be eaten at night.

Colored Jockeys, Too

Certainly there are plenty of daytime activities in Jamaica of a diverting nature. There are all forms of sports, participating or spectator—cricket, baseball, tennis, cycling, yachting, fishing, hunting—even alligator shooting, horseback riding, and races. Kingston has one of the most beautiful racetracks in the Western Hemisphere—Knutsford Park—where colored jockeys ride. At night there are bicycle races, or trap shooting.

For the souvenir hunters the most attractive objects typically Jamaican seem to me the various colored baskets, bags, and hats woven from the native straw, withes, or jippi joppa palms. The native markets have fascinating displays where all shapes and sizes of patterned baskets may be purchased cheaply.

The Jamaicans are excellent wood carvers and cabinet makers. The island is rich in hardwoods, so if you are a lover of hand-made furniture or chests or cabinets built to order, there are skilled workmen awaiting your patronage. Visitors may bring back to the United States a hundred dollars worth of goods duty free—even cases of twenty year old rum, if you choose.

Although Jamaica has perpetual summer, in the towns there are almost no flies or mosquitoes. In the country snakes are just about unheard of—because the mongoose has eaten them up. Jamaica is a calm and beneficent island with few if any plagues. Certainly it is not plagued by Jim Crow, which is a very great blessing for colored vacationists. Lord Oliver once called it the "Blessed Isle." I agree—and bless it twice!

"Backstage," *Ebony,* March 1949, pp. 36–38

Backstage dressing rooms are hardly ever the glamorous satin-lined bandboxes shown in the movies. Small barren cubicles, they are usually hot in summer and cold in winter, often dingy and drab.

Most of the glamour of the theater is ON the stage, not BACK stage. Even stars usually get ready for a performance in cramped little spaces that would give many non-theatrical folks claustrophobia. Glaring lights, barren walls, a mirror and plain chairs are the rule—except in the movies where glamour not truth prevails.

Since theater people are a transient tribe, dressing rooms seldom take on the personalities of their occupants, except in the case of long-run plays. However, some performers keep with them certain identifying objects. Ethel Waters, for instance, always has in her dressing rooms, no matter how brief the engagement, a crucifix and a little statuette of the Virgin Mary. The comedienne, Miss Jackie "Mom" Mabley, keeps on her makeup table a colored picture of Christ surveying Jerusalem from a hilltop. She found it a number of years ago in a garbage can in Baltimore and has never been without it since. Many male performers away from home on long tours keep a photograph of wife or children near the mirror beneath the makeup lights.

To pass their time while out of sight of the audience there is usually a great deal of visiting back and forth between dressing rooms. And sometimes those who like to play cards keep a continuous game in progress during performances. Actors lay down their cards to go on the stage and pick them up again when they come off.

In theaters, as a rule, no visitors are permitted backstage during a show. But night clubs are not strict in this regard. Cabaret artists often keep their dressing rooms full of fans and friends.

Visitors often take possession of Lena Horne's dressing room. When Lena is not entertaining friends between shows, her chief relaxation is reading detective stories. Lena does not play cards very well, but sometimes friends try to teach her.

Some performers study or work in their dressing rooms. Erskine Hawkins writes music backstage. Ella Fitzgerald knits while her husband, Ray Brown, reads. Bill Kenny of the Ink Spots writes verses and lyrics.

"Church for the Deaf"
(coauthored with Whitman Sierra),
Ebony, May 1949, pp. 47–50

There is a church in Harlem where services from beginning to end are conducted in complete silence. Not a sound is heard. The sermon is preached in silence. The choir "sings" in silence. Only the eyes "hear," for the services are conducted entirely in the language of signs. It is St. Ann's Church for the Deaf.

Most of the parishioners of St. Ann's are deaf-mutes who neither hear nor speak. Of the 300 members on the church rolls about fifty are Negroes. On a typical Sunday as many as half the congregation may be colored. Negroes and whites sit side by side, moving their hands and fingers together in responsive readings, prayers, and hymns. There is no color line in either the religious or social activities of this church.

St. Ann's Church, although it is under the Protestant Episcopal Diocese, in non-sectarian. All may worship there. Its attractive high-ceilinged colonial interior looks not unlike any other modest church. Although no microphone is needed for their silent sermons, it is important that special spotlights be carefully trained on the pulpit so that no shadows obscure the moving fingers of the minister.

Another unobtrusive difference from the ordinary church is the white marble baptismal font. It has not printed words, but three hands carved into the marble whose fingers form in sign-language the word, "GOD." On the wall behind the altar there is a decoration most appropriate to the church, a painting of Christ healing a deaf-mute. Beneath is an inscription from the Book of St. Mark:

"And they bring unto him one that was deaf, and had an impediment in his speech; and they beseech him to put his hand upon him. And he took him aside from the multitude, and put his fingers into his ears, and he spit, and touched his tongue. And looking up to heaven, he sighed, and saith unto him, Ephphatha, that is, Be opened. And straight-way his ears were opened, and the string of his tongue was loosed, and he spake plain."

Pastor Is Main Link with Talking World

The St. Ann's Church for the Deaf is the oldest church of its kind in the United States, lacking only three years of being a full hundred years old. It grew out of a small Bible class for deaf-mutes organized in New York City in 1850 by Rev. Thomas Gallaudet, whose father before him had established at Hartford in 1816 the first school in America for the deaf.

St. Ann's began regular sign-language services in its first building in Greenwich Village in 1852. Forty-six years later, the congregation bought its present building in Harlem.

St. Ann's is the only "deaf" church in Manhattan, although there are several other deaf-mute missions, and some "hearing" churches conduct occasional services for the deaf, or have a sign-language assistant who translates the spoken sermon. But at St. Ann's the entire service is in the language of the hands.

At present, having lost their permanent minister, the church is seeking a pastor. Some of the members prefer a "hearing" minister, having also the facility of sign-language. They feel that for the social and business life of the church a "hearing" minister would be especially helpful, in that he would not have to write all his communications to the normal world. In helping to secure jobs for church members, for instance, much time would be saved if the pastor could use the telephone and talk personally with prospective employers.

The pastor ofttimes must help in transacting business and making personal contacts with the world of hearing. Although most deaf-mutes would normally lead happy, well-adjusted lives among their own circle of friends and society, it is when they are faced with the necessity of contacting hearing people for jobs or carrying out the most ordinary piece of business that they feel the pressure of their handicap.

Because the members of the parish board cannot "speak plain," the board room on the second floor of the church has an interesting seating arrangement. There is no table. Instead, ten chairs have been strategically grouped in a square facing each other so that every board member may clearly see the hands and faces of his colleagues as they transact the business of the church.

St. Ann's clubs and auxiliaries play an important role in the lives of its parishioners. Most deaf-mutes are, in a very real sense, socially isolated from normal hearing and speaking peoples, and out of a simple necessity for human companionship, the members of St. Ann's must turn to organizations like the Ladies' Auxiliary and the Men's Club to form a nucleus for their social life.

Mutes Resent Use of "Deaf and Dumb"

Deaf-mutes do not like the phrase, "deaf and dumb." They prefer "deaf-mute." The word "dumb" should never be used in reference to them since, they say, it is their hearing, not their intellect, which has been lost. The deaf have a great sense of humor and often tell jokes on themselves in reference to their lack of hearing—such as the story about a young man who thought for many years that the hymn *Onward, Christian Soldiers* was really *Awkward Christian Soldiers.*

The basis of the sign-language used in St. Ann's is believed to have been invented and perfected by Abbé de l'Eppée more than 180 years ago in France. Sign language consists not only of the language of the hands and fingers, but embraces facial expressions, and pantomime, and various manual gestures—all of which become codified for the experienced user. Finger spelling is reserved mostly for uncommon words, and the whole movement of the hand and arm has meaning. In the language of the deaf, the hand over the heart means "love." One hand up with the eyes raised means "God." The index finger of the right hand in the palm of the left—symbolizing the wounds in the hand of Christ—means "Jesus." And "C" for "church" is formed by the thumb and index finger of the right hand resting on the left. Raised palms together at the end of a prayer is "Amen."

Although there are many colored deaf-mutes, there are no Negro deaf-mute ministers or separate Negro deaf churches in the United States. Members of St. Ann's, both colored and white, come to Harlem not only from the five boroughs of New York and New Jersey, but from points as distant as Connecticut.

St. Ann's Church has a well-equipped stage where a yearly pageant is presented with scenery and costumes. Often popular plays are given, the scripts being adapted for sign-language, and the lighting being arranged so that no shadows ever fall on the players' hands. Facial and body pantomime is stressed and comedy situations are greatly enjoyed. The audiences appear to derive as much pleasure from their silent-language shows as do the spectators at a Broadway theatre from the spoken drama. A few years ago the students of Gallaudet College brought to New York what is believed to have been the first public performance on Broadway of a play in sign-language, *Arsenic and Old Lace*.

4

Essays, 1950–1959

"Curtain Time,"
LHP 277 (ca. 1950?)

With reference to the fact that there is no serious Negro musical or dramatic theatre in America, the Negro might well sing the refrain of the old song, "It's nobody's fault but mine."[1] The Negro minority of more than fourteen million people has no professional acting group in the United States such as the Abbey or the Gate in Ireland, the Habimah in Palestine, or the Old Vic in England. In truth, the American Negro has no professional theatre of his own at all.

Nevertheless, we are very much a part of the American entertainment world, although still in a limited and inhibited fashion. Our actors act, our singers sing, our dancers dance—but in the field of the commercial entertainment we almost always amuse under censorship, or under limitations which prevent a full realization of our potential talents.

There is a great deal of money to be made from commercial entertainment in the U.S.A. But American life is heavily afflicted with anti-Negro prejudices so, in order not to offend these prejudices, those who control entertainment for profit mould its forms insofar as colored actors and entertainers go. White Americans control commercial entertainment for *white* Americans. There will be no complete revelation of Negro talent in entertainment in Jim Crow America until some areas of it are controlled completely by Negroes, providing entertainment for their own racial group first, and only incidentally for others who may wish to enjoy it.

Even theatres such as the Apollo in Harlem catering to a Negro audience are controlled entirely by the whites who run them. That is no doubt why, unlike the social comedy of European or Latin countries, in the humor of the low comedians of theatres such as the Apollo there almost never creeps the slightest jibe at the *status quo* of Jim Crow under which the audience and the comedians themselves live. Negro comedians have a wealth of unused satirical material of an hilarious nature inherent in our pseudo-democratic race relations in America. But you would never know it at the Apollo where black comics limit themselves entirely to making fun of Negroes. They are afraid of not getting a return engagement at white-owned theatres if they make fun of white people. So they kid themselves about a ghost in a graveyard instead of kidding the Ku Klux Klan whose hoods and sheets are as absurd as the garb of a ghost. They are afraid of managers and booking agents, afraid they will get but few engagements in the North and none at all in the South.

The shadow of the South hangs heavily over the Negro in entertainment in the U.S.A. It is worse over Hollywood. It also rides the radio waves. It makes a "Mammy" or a "Carolina Moon" of popular songs. This shadow is perhaps least heavy over Broadway. But even on Broadway the producers of a play like *Mulatto* or *Deep Are the Roots* will think ruefully how the road tour, if there is one, must be limited to cities above the Mason-Dixon line.[2] For a serious Negro-white problem play, even Washington and Baltimore, only a few hours from New York, might have to be eliminated. And there will be no movie sale. So it is more profitable to produce a raceless, shootless comedy like *Anna Lucasta* purely for entertainment's sake, than to produce *On Whitman Avenue* or *On Trial* about restrictive covenants and housing. The all-Negro musical fantasy, *Cabin in the Sky,* could tour the South and even be sold to the movies. But for Duke Ellington's interracially cast *Beggar's Holiday,* there were no such chances. The South would not like *Beggar's Holiday.*

Show business is first and foremost a *business.* Often the art therein gets no further than the artist's heart. Still the American theatre has had some fine art groups—the Provincetown Players, for instance. The early Theatre Guild and the Group Theatre once greatly influenced the purely commercial Broadway theatre for the better. But Negro America has as yet had no such serious art groups attaining professional stature. In time we will have. Historically speaking, circumstances regarding our participation in the various fields of entertainment have been against us. In explanation, let us take a look at the past.

The Negro as a folk entertainer has always been accepted in America, but as a trained professional artist he has had a long hard way to go. It is one thing to listen to a black troubadour picking a guitar on a street corner and *maybe* drop a dime in his cap. But when you pay a dollar to see a picture, your prejudices as well as your risibilities must be tickled. The Negro began long ago tickling America's risibilities. In slavery he could hardly tickle anything else. It was fun listening to unorganized unprofessional Negro singing, hearing the absurd broken dialect spoken, watching the clog and buck and wing of slave dancers. It was so much fun that before the Civil War professional white entertainers borrowed these things from the Negro and made their famous and highly hilarious blackface minstrels. White actors even borrowed a comic version of the Negro's color—burnt cork. Eddie Cantor and the late Al Jolson only recently discarded it after many years. Amos and Andy still wear it on their tongues. In the movies there are some Negroes who do not have to wear it, it almost comes natural—so well do they take direction on the lot. Uncle Tom did not really die. He simply went to Hollywood.

Not all the slave songs were humorous. But it was the humorous ones that sold best, the minstrel men discovered. Not all the slave dancers were hilarious buck and wing. But in the early 1800's, who could sell the ache of the spirituals or the frenzy and terror of Congo Square and its drums? Not all things said in dialect were laughable. But the heartbreaking phrases had to wait until today for a dramatist like Theodore Ward to remember. They were not for the minstrel. Thus long ago in America the stereotype of the Negro as a humorous clown was born. That shadow of the South is still over the Negro in professional entertainment. A superb dancer like Bill Robinson told jokes shaming his people because he danced in that shadow.

Negro entertainers themselves in the 80's began to imitate the white minstrels—they began to imitate the imitators of themselves. They, too, sang "coon" songs that the Negro people did not like, but which the whites paid money to hear. From the first Negro "coon" of minstrel days to Stepin Fetchit on the screen there is a direct line. Therein lies the tragedy of the Negro in American entertainment. For money he became a stereotype *of his own white stereotype*—and for so *little* money. The white Al Jolsons and the Amoses and Andys made much more.

Fortunately there has been another and more truthful line from the folk art of the Negro past to the commercial entertainment of today. It, too, has had its humor, but it is the humor of the heart, not merely that of imitative tongues and burnt cork shadows. The vitality of Negro folk music from the slave songs to Broadway and the inventiveness of the Negro dance from the plantation to Katherine Dunham have been too great to be completely lost even when exploited most commercially. The Negro has influenced *all* American popular music and dancing.

The Broadway musical theatre from the minstrels to *Porgy and Bess* has been enriched by Negro rhythms, thematic material, and Negro singers and dancers. White composers and lyricists from Stephen Foster to George Gershwin have utilized Negro folk sources for their inspirations. Negro song writers, too, have wisely gone back to these sources. In the minstrel days one of the greatest of these was James Bland of *Carry Me Back to Old Virginny* fame.

Ragtime began as a folk art, became a conscious creation, turned into jazz, to swing, to be-bop, and took decisive hold on American popular music no matter what the composer's color. Given new vitality just before World War I by the folk blues and the personal creations of W. C. Handy in those forms, Negro syncopation became the popular music of America. James Reese Europe created a sensation with the first orchestral concert of syncopated music at Carnegie Hall in 1912. Now Duke Ellington has an annual concert there. And Negro bands, white bands, and mixed bands play syncopated rhythms all over the country, not only for dancing, but for listening. Negro rhythms have begun to affect symphonic composers.

In the theatre there have been many excellent Negro composers and lyricists. At the turn of the century Cole and Johnson wrote a series of beautiful operettas sung and danced by colored artists of national fame. Williams and Walker toured the country in *In Abyssinia* and *Bandana Land.* Will Marion Cook, Will Vodery, and Alex Rogers created songs that swept the U.S. up to the time of World War I. Then there came a lull in the activities of the Negro musical stage, until Sissle and Blake wrote *Shuffle Along* that was to begin the new Negro vogue in theatre, literature, and art of the 1920s. *Shuffle Along* was the show that shot Florence Mills to international stardom.

There followed happy entertainments like *The Chocolate Dandies, Runnin' Wild, Dixie to Broadway, Blackbirds, Hot Chocolates,* and *Rhapsody in Black* spotlighting such talents as Louis Armstrong, Adelaide Hall, Josephine Baker, Ethel Waters, and the comedians Miller and Lyles. The 1930's brought about another lull, particularly in the use of Negro creative talents. Musicals employing Negro casts were more and more often written by whites. Individual Negro performers were more and more spotted in otherwise all-white revues; as an example, Ethel Waters in *As Thousands Cheer.* The all-Negro musical gradually began to disappear from the Broadway scene. That old American depression custom regarding the Negro as "first to be fired and last to be hired" had found its way into the theatre, too. An occasional *Cabin in the Sky* or *Carmen Jones* written by non-Negro composers is a far cry from the days of the gloriously dark and full-throated richness of *In Dahomey* when the century began its series of Negro-created musicals.

For both the musical and dramatic actor of color, the Federal Theatre of the depression period was more than a gift from Roosevelt: it seemed like a gift from God. Not only did it bring forth food in a lean period, but it brought forth such real contributions to the art of the stage as

Chicago's *Swing Mikado;* the Los Angeles record-breaker directed by Clarence Muse, *Run Little Chillun;* and Harlem's *Macbeth,* beautifully played in which the young Orson Welles had a directorial hand. Chicago, through an excellent production of *Big White Fog,* brought to light a new Negro playwright of genuine talent, Theodore Ward.

Top authorities in the Federal Theatre, Hallie Flannigan and Elmer Rice, believed in no color line. For the first time in America, in a sustained manner, Negroes were able to create their own plays and musicals, act in them, and also gain experience in directing, scene painting, and the other technical aspects of the theatre which had hitherto been closed to them. With few previous exceptions, it was the Federal Theatre that dared cast Negro actors in non-Negro roles, not only on Broadway, but in its units elsewhere as well. The Federal Theatre broke down not only the old taboos against colored Americans as backstage technicians, but the bars against colored actors playing other than racial roles.

Ten years later the results were seen in the mixed dancing chorus of *On the Town,* the colored and white ensembles of *Finian's Rainbow,* and the complete integration of singers, dancers, and actors in the interracially written and interracially produced *Beggar's Holiday,* the Duke Ellington–John LaTouche novelty coproduced by Negro Perry Watkins and white John R. Sheppard, Jr. In the drama, an interracial producing team, Canada Lee and Mark Mervin, presented *On Whitman Avenue* with a mixed cast. In Gian-Carlo Menotti's *The Medium,* the gypsy boy was played by a Katherine Dunham dancer, Lee Coleman, who made love to a white girl. In the Arena revival *The Medium* was played by a Negro singer, Zelma Watson George.

The history of the Negro in America's spoken drama goes back more than a hundred years. Before the Civil War his problems provided themes for the serious stage, although his roles were acted by whites in blackface. Even Uncle Tom was *first* played by a white actor in 1852. *Uncle Tom's Cabin* shook the world then. Perhaps it shook some theatre taboos, too, for long before the play lost its popularity—and it had a popularity of fifty years—many Negro actors had essayed the leading role.

At least thirty years before *Uncle Tom's Cabin* hit the boards, there were Negro actors, and good ones, performing in New York City. As early as 1821 the African Free Players presented Shakespearean plays and produced a star in the person of James Hewlett as *Othello.* In the mid-1800's, from our own shores to England and the Continent went brown-skinned Ira Aldridge to become internationally famous in the same role, having for his Iago in London the great Edmund Kean.

Just as the old stock companies served as a training ground for many of the stars of stage and screen today, the colored stock company of the Pekin Theatre in Chicago so served for Negro actors. From that famous Negro theatre of the early 1900's came many competent performers, some still active today. Following the Pekin group came New York's Lafayette Players, successfully presenting for a number of years such Negro-acted versions of Broadway successes as *Within the Law* and *Madam X.*

In March, 1917, *Three Plays for a Negro Theatre* began a new era. These poetically written plays by Ridgely Torrence were about Negro life to be acted by Negroes. They were not great box office hits, but they paved the way for a play that was—Eugene O'Neill's *The Emperor Jones.* With this play in 1920, Charles Gilpin put the Provincetown Playhouse on the world map. The decade between *The Emperor Jones* and *The Green Pastures* brought many interesting dramas of Negro life to Broadway and uncovered some fine acting talents. Some of the plays were acted entirely by Negroes. Others had mixed casts. *Lulu Belle,* the Pulitzer Prize winner, *In Abraham's Bosom,* Paul Robeson in *All God's Chillun Got Wings,* and later, *Black Boy,* the musicals *Deep River* and *Show Boat,* and the dramatic *Porgy* that was to later become the musical *Porgy and Bess* enlivened Broadway.

Written by socially minded whites and aflame with protest against racial and class injustice, in the 1930's Paul Peters' *Stevedore* reached the stage at the downtown Theatre Union, and John Waxley's *They Shall Not Die* pled the cause of the Scottsboro boys uptown. My own *Mulatto* opened at the Vanderbilt and had a record long run for a drama written by a Negro playwright. Various Paul Green plays, Hall Johnson's music-drama *Run Little Chillun,* and Gertrude Stein's quaintly pretty *Four Saints in Three Acts* set to music by Virgil Thomson helped keep the public interest in the Negro at a high boxoffice pitch. Then came Ethel Waters, superb in *Mamba's Daughters* and later in *The Member of the Wedding.* She proved her versatility of range: from revue singer to dramatic actress, and also proved the value of a Negro star's name in lights over the marquee.

In the '40's appeared *Native Son, Jeb, Strange Fruit, Deep Are the Roots, Anna Lucasta,* the musicals *Carmen Jones* and *St. Louis Woman.* But unfortunately, there have been few good Negro playwrights, and these few have written but few plays. Lack of contact with living theatre, and lack of outlet for their plays, has contributed to this scarcity of colored playwrights. Broadway has not been cordial to the Negro dramatist.

The one consistently sympathetic outlet to the New Negro playwright during the past twenty years has been the Gilpin Players of Karamu House in Cleveland, Ohio. This settlement house acting group under the direction of Rowena Jelliffe is the nearest thing we have in America to a Negro dramatic theatre portraying racial life through drama and, whenever good scripts can be found, through drama *written by Negro writers.*

Other promising Negro little theatre groups have sprung up only to die after two or three seasons. Such was the Harlem Suitcase Theatre whose presentation of *Don't You Want to Be Free?* for 135 performances marks its only major achievement. The Negro Playwrights Company, attempting to operate in Harlem on a professional basis, closed after a short run of *Big White Fog*. In Chicago the Skyloft Players at Parkway Community House and the newer Negro Art Theatre have managed to survive several seasons.

The most active (but non-professional) producing group with a large membership was the American Negro Theatre in Harlem. The Broadway hit, *Anna Lucasta,* originated with this group, as did an excellent series of radio programs. But this group, while providing good training for actors, did little to stimulate the growth of a real Negro theatre or search out Negro playwrights of talent. The majority of its scripts were by non-Negro writers. And many were rehashes of old Broadway potboilers with themes far removed from the realities of Negro life. From these experimental groups, however, have come to Broadway fine and sensitive actors. Contrary to the popular misconceptions, Negro actors do not act simply with their "natural" talent. On the contrary, most of them have had experience or training before they get any good parts in the professional theatre. What the Negro actor needs most now is a reservoir of plays about his own people written from the Negro viewpoint.

As long as Negro life is a ghetto life, the plays for a true Negro theatre must be written from *within* the ghetto, not from without. As sincere as a Lillian Smith may be, or as skilled at the craft of theatre as are d'Usseau and Gow, the little nuances of racial life that give a Negro drama its individual glow cannot be known to them. Too often, too, in spite of himself, the white playwright unconsciously falls into stereotypes. But because it is seeking after truth, the dramatic theatre, more often than the musical, has managed to avoid the stereotype. The serious dramatic writer usually does not pander to popular prejudices or chauvinism.

Perhaps comedy is the pitfall of the musical theatre. In drama, problems tend to become universal, even though in racial guise. On the other hand, comedy is often provincial. Exaggerations of racial types, overstressing the peculiarities of regional speech and stereotyped conventions, frequently dominate comedy—especially that of the music hall.

Nevertheless, just as out of the serious theatre has come a Rose McClendon, a Robeson, or a Canada Lee, so from the minstrel-vaudeville-musical stage have come some very talented Negro comedians, despite the narrow vein of humor in which they were forced to work—Ernest Hogan, the great Bert Williams, Miller and Lyles, Dusty Fletcher of "Open The Door, Richard" fame, Pig Meat Markham, Jackie Mabley, and Eddie Green.

Since the end of World War I, colored comedians have devoted as much of their time to the night clubs, and more recently to radio, as to the stage or screen where opportunities for them are not so readily available as to white comics. Radio, and the night clubs too (the clubs even more than the former), have nourished such entertaining talents as the Mills Brothers, the Ink Spots, Ella Fitzgerald, Hazel Scott, Bill Bailey, Cab Calloway, Billie Holiday, Pearl Bailey, the late Fats Waller, and the King Cole Trio, also such folk singers as the great Bessie Smith, Lead Belly, Sister Tharpe, and Josh White. White entertainers haunt the clubs featuring Negro talent, pick up their mannerisms and tricks, and copy their dance steps to use later on stage and screen. Thus, the Negro artist has influenced the whole field of American popular entertainment.

Radio utilizes the colored singer, musicians, and comic sparingly, welcoming most often the musicians, although sometimes giving a semi-permanent welcome to such comics as Rochester, Eddie Green, Butterfly McQueen, Hattie McDaniel, and the shadows of Amos and Andy—as long as they do not wander too far from the stereotype. Singers from Maxine Sullivan to Marian Anderson are granted occasional fifteen minute sustaining shows or guest spots. (A notable exception was the King Cole Trio's commercial program.) But you must be white, usually, to have a long-term spot on radio. If the lips that sing are dark, you await an infrequent guest invitation. Whereas for the Negro actor, the American airwaves might as well originate in Borneo. (A recent exception is the entertaining addition to commercial radio, the "Beulah Show," starring Hattie McDaniel.) Juano Hernandez and a few other colored radio actors work more or less steadily, and not always are they limited to Negro roles. Sometimes they play Indians or some other type of "primitive." And sometimes, but still too infrequently, a Negro may be just an American on the air. But in the vastly popular "soap operas" Negroes are limited practically always to servant roles, if they are heard at all.

There are no radio serials on Negro family life, or of any interracial activity. There have been sustaining series of Negro dramatic programs—*New World A-Comin'* during the war, for example—and local station programs such as the *Chicago Defender's Democracy: U.S.A.* series in Chicago. Richard Durham and Robert Lucas are good script writers. There are a few Negro disc jockeys. But radio is still by and large a white man's world for actors and script writers, and entirely so for announcers, directors, and technicians.

Surprisingly enough, television is getting off on a somewhat more liberal foot than its cousin, radio, has yet shown. In its short life, various types of Negro artists from singers to dancers to actors—the Hall Johnson Choir, Pearl Primus, Gordon Heath as Lincoln—have appeared before its audio-visual apparatus. Let us hope the limitations of Hollywood do not affect the television screen, at least, not in the North.

Hollywood is the *bête noire.* It produces America's (and the world's) most popular art, and is one of the great industries. It is a mighty educational force, as well as a powerful force for mis-education. Hollywood is cognizant of its powers. Yet, shamelessly and to all the world, Hollywood has since its inception spread in exaggerated form every ugly ridiculous stereotype of the deep South's conception of Negro character. Until recently, it has given world audiences almost nothing else on film about colored people in the U.S.A. Hollywood's favorite Negro character is a grinning happy-go-lucky half-stupid servant, male or female, usually speaking broken English.

It is true that there are many Negro servants in America, but if the majority of them were of the Hollywood variety, they would not be employed long. Hollywood has distorted and made viciously laughable the role of black domestics in America. Hollywood has almost entirely ignored the fact that there are also in our country thousands of Negro mail carriers, for instance, or Negro policemen, Negro teachers, lawyers and other kinds of professional men, Negro government officials, models, streetcar conductors, insurance salesmen, and just plain housewives and husbands.

Hollywood has not and seemingly will not show the Negro simply as an American citizen. In recent serious films, such as *Host Boundaries* and *No Way Out,* he is a problem. In most others, merely a comic. The shadow of the South is Hollywood's excuse. The Southern box office, Southern censors, Southern exhibitors who cut out sequences of film showing Negroes in normal relationships with their fellow Americans, all prevent Hollywood from doing much about the Negro films—so says

Hollywood. According to Lena Horne, as interviewed by Allan Morrison, the Motion Picture Production Code "has ruled that Negroes and whites must not be portrayed on the screen as social equals."

Miss Horne, who is a notable exception to the servant stereotype, says that in fifteen film assignments, she was not permitted to speak a single line, but only to sing, except in the all-Negro film, *Stormy Weather.* Miss Hazel Scott, the pianist, in her film appearances has had to fight to keep the apron and bandanna from being a part of her costume. Hollywood finds it hard to think of Negroes in terms other than as servants—even when the picture is an all-Negro film.

Some of Hollywood's most effective films, cinematographically speaking, have been all-Negro films: *Hearts in Dixie, Hallelujah, Cabin in the Sky.* Colored actors, within the limitations of story and direction imposed upon them, have given remarkably fine performances, in spite of the fact that all-Negro casts are usually recruited from the stage without past movie experience. But among the few old veterans of Hollywood there are fine Negro actors and actresses, and they are certainly deserving of a little variety in roles once in a while. At the top of such a list stands Hattie McDaniel and Louise Beavers, the great performers of *Gone with the Wind* and *Imitation of Life* respectively, to mention only single performances. Clarence Muse and Leigh Whipper, Rex Ingram, and small, attractive Dorothy Dandridge are competent actors, but they have had few opportunities to perform. Whipper was great in *The Ox-Bow Incident* and as Haile Selassie in *Mission to Moscow,* but he has never had a role commensurate with his talents, nor is he likely to have in this day and generation.

Our recent war might have put an end to Hilter-like racism, but it did not put an end to segregation in Hollywood. Even radio with all its timidity is ahead of the films in its employment of Negro themes and actors. For every film like *In This Our Life, Bataan, Casablanca,* or *Bright Victory,* where a Negro character is pictured with some semblance of normality, there are a dozen in which he remains the dialect speaking clown. Because of its great influence on public thought, on the conditioning of children, and on world opinion, it would be hoped that Hollywood, out of common democratic decency, would overhaul its film presentations of American Negro citizens, Dixie or no Dixie. But as long as boxoffice dominates decency, I am afraid that Hollywood will continue to degrade Negroes.

Paul Robeson's only good pictures were made in England. Josephine Baker has starred in French films. *Poison* and *To Live in Peace* were made in Italy. Negro artists have been received abroad not only with audience acclaim and newspaper praise, but with personal and community courtesy as well. Louis Armstrong, Ellington, Calloway, and other colored bands and their leaders have enjoyed the hospitality of European countries. Teddy Weatherford was for many years until his death the favorite orchestra leader of Asia from China to India. In night club circles Bricktop was a success in Montmartre for a decade, as was Josephine Baker on the Parisian revue stage. Elizabeth Welch, Nora Holt, Jimmy Daniels, and many other colored entertainers have been hits outside the U.S.A.

As concert artists, of course, Marian Anderson, Roland Hayes, Dorothy Maynor, and Paul Robeson have been widely acclaimed. Ella Belle Davis, Aubrey Pankey, and Edward Matthews have been favorites in Latin countries, while Katherine Dunham and her dancers captivated three continents. Our country, in turn, has welcomed a few East Indian calypso entertainers, Moune, the Martinique *chanteuse,* and it also showed a limited appreciation for the African dancing of Asadata Dafora.

Abroad, colored performers live normally as human beings without discrimination, but at home Negro artists on tour will give them a place to sleep or even a place to eat. American hotels and restaurants will refuse service to a Duke Ellington, an Ethel Waters, a Marian Anderson, or a Lena Horne as quickly as they will to any other Negro. Touring orchestras have to live in busses or Pullman cars most of the time and often subsist on sandwiches out of a bag.

In plays, mixed casts are still taboo in the South. Constitution Hall in Washington still refuses its stage to Negro concert artists. Many Southern radio stations require Negro entertainers to use the back door or the freight elevator. In communities where racial prejudices are in full sway, the ordinary courtesy and politeness granted visiting white performers are denied to Negro performers. Hundreds of American newspapers in the South will not carry photographs of colored entertainers. (These same papers refuse to publish pictures of American Negro war heroes.) Against the entertainer of color in the United States the same Jim Crowisms that make life difficult for all Negroes operate. Since entertainers and actors must travel more than most people, these injustifiable restrictions become doubly difficult for them, often meaning that in a strange town they must search for hours for a place to eat, sleep, or even go to a lavatory.

In opera, Katharine Yarboro and Muriel Rahn have sung *Aida* in an otherwise white company. At the Civic Center in New York Todd

Duncan has sung more than one role. Camilla Williams has received an ovation in *Madame Butterfly.* But no Negro singers have been signed by the Metropolitan. The ranks in opera choruses and ballet companies have not been opened to colored aspirants as have some leading roles to stars. (But in regard to choristers, radio has been democratic.) Negroes themselves have no professional opera companies, just as they own no movie studios, control no radio chains, and have no theatres.

Where does the Negro stand today in entertainment? He stands on one leg, with the other tied behind him by Jim Crow. If he were standing flat on two feet with his head up, competing "in the American way" with other artists and entertainers for a chance to work and develop, Negro singers would be at the Metropolitan in big roles and little roles according to their abilities, they would be dancing in its ballet, someone like Dean Dixon could be directing in the pit, and William Grant Still's operas might be part of the Metropolitan's repertoire.

In the movies once in a while, along with other film biographies—from Pasteur to Al Jolson—there could be a biography of Mary McLeod Bethune with Hattie McDaniel in the leading role, or of Frederick Douglass with Leigh Whipper. And Lena Horne could talk as well as sing. And not every colored servant would have to drool, drawl, bow, grin and speak dialect endlessly.

If the Negro were standing solidly on his own two feet in the entertainment world, he would have a serious professional dramatic or musical theatre of his own in which plays by Negro and white playwrights about Negro life might be presented free from the limitations of the Broadway boxoffice, or where the music of Negro life might be heard without having to make it more "primitive" or more commercial, or sweeten up or tone down its lyrics for white audiences with preconceived notions.

The increasing integration of Negro performers in entertainment, aided by the Federal Theatre, *On the Town, The Medium,* and *Flahooley,* for example, would be even more pleasing if Negro spectators were not sent to the gallery in almost every American city outside of the Eastern states. The courageous stand of Actors Equity: no more plays for the National Theatre in Washington until discrimination is dropped, and the amazing crusade of Josephine Baker during her highly successful return to America, point to the coming of a better day for colored performers. Certainly, in the world of commercial entertainment, in spite of prejudice, the Negro stands farther ahead now than ever before. But he is still *farther behind* than anybody else in America.

"Some Practical Observations: A Colloquy," *Phylon* 11 (winter 1950): 307–11

Editors: Mr. Hughes, very few Negro writers in America have chosen, or have felt themselves able to choose, writing as their sole occupation as you have. What has being a Negro meant for you as a writer?

Hughes: Well, for one thing, I think it's pretty obvious that the bulk of my work stems directly from the life of the Negro in America. Since the major aims of my work have been to interpret and comment upon Negro life, and its relations to the problems of Democracy, a major satisfaction for me has been the assurance given me by my readers that I have succeeded in some measure—especially in those areas lightly touched upon, if at all, by the writers who preceded me.

Editors: You certainly must have been asked this next question before: From this vantage point, and as one of the major figures in the "Negro Renaissance," what would you say as to the value of the "Renaissance"? Is there any real truth in the suggestion advanced by some that the "Renaissance" was in certain respects actually a harmful thing for the Negro writer?

Hughes: My feeling would be that the "Renaissance" represented a positive value mainly. It certainly helped a great deal by focusing attention on Negro writers and on literature about Negroes for some six or eight years. It provided a springboard for young Negro writers and for those who wanted to write about Negroes. That impetus in many cases has continued into the present.

Now there may have been certain false values which tended at the time to be over-stressed—perhaps the primitivism and that business of the "color" of Negro life was overdone. But that kind of exaggeration is inevitable, and I doubt that any real harm was done. Those of us who were serious about writing weren't actually affected very much. We knew what we were doing and what we wanted to do. So we went ahead with our work, and whatever false emphasis there was didn't really disturb us.

Editors: You have behind you well over two decades of varied and substantial achievement. How would you say the general situation has changed for the Negro author in America since you began writing?

Hughes: Oh, in several ways, but the most striking change I would say has occurred in the magazine world. In the past twenty years—and in the case of some publications, in the past five years or so—the field of magazine writing has opened up considerably. For instance, when I first started writing, it was said that the *Saturday Evening Post* would not accept work written by Negroes. Whether or not the *Post* actually followed such a policy, it did seem to be true of certain other magazines. Yet in recent years the *Post* has run pieces by Zora Neale Hurston and Walter White, as well as some of my own work; and, in many major magazines articles and stories which take something other than the Octavus Roy Cohen line now appear frequently.

Editors: Would you say that this is one of the gains which may in part be attributed to the "Renaissance"?

Hughes: I think so—though, of course, there are other factors in the picture, including two which I think are often overlooked in accounting for the increased activity among Negro writers and the widening audience to which these writers may address themselves. But it can hardly be disputed that the "Renaissance" did a great deal to make possible a public willing to accept Negro problems and Negro art.

Editors: You spoke just now of two factors which tend to be overlooked. What are they?

Hughes: The first of these is the international fame which Negroes in fields other than literature have won in the last fifteen years or so. The world renown won by such diverse figures as Joe Louis, Marian Anderson, Duke Ellington, and Ralph Bunche has created greater interest abroad in the American Negro.[3] I think this has helped to bring about the present situation in which we find books by Negro writers in this country being translated into other languages and reaching an international audience.

Another factor which will, I believe, become increasingly important is the growth in the number of good Negro bookshops and efficient booksellers. Negroes operate at least four first-rate bookstores in New York; there is at least one such bookstore in Atlanta run by Negroes, and this is true of other cities. This, in my opinion, is one of the healthiest developments which could have occurred for the Negro writer and for the Negro reading public.

Editors: We are inclined to agree with you on that—though as difficult to analyze statistically as the influence of the labor and liberal movements in this country—the factors you cite must undoubtedly be recognized as gains for the Negro writer. Granted these and other gains and the access to a wider reading public, in which literary areas would you say Negroes have done the best work in recent years?

Hughes: In the novel and in poetry, I should think. We've had Wright, and Motley, and Ann Petry, and Yerby in the novel. And in addition to the older poets still writing there is a promising group coming along in Bruce McWright, Myron O'Higgins, Margaret Walker, and M. Carl Holman. And, of course, Gwendolyn Brooks, the Pulitzer poet. But here I'm thinking mainly of poets who haven't yet published books. There are three or four good young poets in this category, like Russell Atkins, whose work appeared in *The Poetry of the Negro*.[4]

And in fiction, among those who haven't yet brought out books, there is a really significant talent in Ralph Ellison.[5]

Editors: What about the theatre? You probably have done as much in the theatre as any other contemporary Negro writer. Why haven't there been more plays by Negro authors?

Hughes: We've had some plays, of course. There's Theodore Ward, whom you know of—though he hasn't had any real "success" yet. And George Norford, who had a comedy done by the Group Theatre last year.[6] We haven't made too much progress as writers in the theatre—mainly because it's pretty hard to have professional contacts. Such contacts are indispensable to success in modern playwriting and it's difficult to make headway when the opportunities for achieving the contacts are so limited.

Editors: The lag then, if we may call it that, in playwriting seems due to this difficulty in getting "inside"—a problem which does not seem to be restricted to Negro playwrights alone. The difference may be one of degree.

But are there any other points at which the Negro writer seems not to be making any significant contribution?

Hughes: Well, let me put it this way: it seems to me that there is a crying need for good literary criticism. I can't give the reasons for it, but our great deficiency is this dearth of really good critics. We have almost no books of literary criticism—certainly not recent, competently-done books.

And it's not just literary essays, and books of criticism which are lacking. There is a need for good journalistic articles and for non-fiction works in many fields. In history and in sociology the record is better than elsewhere. Frazier, John Hope Franklin, Cayton, Drake, and others, have done fine work here.[7] I hope to see more good writing in these and other fields.

Editors: The almost inevitable question in any discussion of this kind makes its appearance now: Are there any special problems which face the Negro writer here in America which the white writer is not likely to encounter?

Hughes: I think so. It's pretty clear by now, for example, that the Negro writer has to work especially hard to avoid the appearance of propaganda. Then there is the hypersensitivity arising from the Negro's situation in this country which causes him to take offense at certain realistic portrayals of Negro life.

Editors: There are those problems arising from his materials and his audience, then. But what of marketing problems? It has been suggested, for example, that Negro authors sometimes meet with special difficulties in selling manuscripts. It has even been charged that publishers have insisted on editing of the kind which was, in effect, censorship based on prejudice, or on the willingness to kowtow to the prejudiced reader in the interest of sales.

Hughes: That the Negro writer marketing the fruits of his talent meets with problems which the white writer does not face, I would agree. I would not agree that the field of book publishing is actually involved. Other experienced Negro writers would testify, I believe, that when a writer has done a good book, the publisher usually tends not to alter or limit it in any way—and certainly not with racial considerations in mind.

Editors: If the book publishers deserve a clean bill of health, then where does the Negro writer meet with his "special problems?"

Hughes: The real limitations are in the "tributary" fields where race is definitely a handicapping factor. Hollywood is the Number One example of this, using practically no Negroes as writers. Radio also is a very limited field for the author who happens to be a Negro. Television, while newer, seems no more likely to be hospitable to Negro writers.

All this means, of course, that unless he is fortunate enough to produce best-sellers the Negro who wishes to write must usually supplement his writing by some occupation which is generally not very closely related to writing. If Negro publications could be, or would be, more generous in the fees paid (or which they should pay) Negro writers, there would be an improvement in the quality of these publications and more Negro writers would be able to earn a living from writing, rather than from teaching and other activities. Failing that, the Negro writer turns in vain to the editorial staffs of other American magazines and of publishing houses. These almost never hire Negroes. Negro book reviewers—even for such publications as the *Times,* the *Herald-Tribune,* and the *Saturday Review of Literature*—are limited by the fact that they are usually given only books about Negroes or by Negroes to review.

Another important source of income for most authors—that of lecturing—is severely limited if the author happens to be a Negro. Only the most liberal women's clubs care to have Negro lecturers—so about seventy-five or eighty per cent of this field is closed. And you can count on your hands the white colleges in the southern and border states of this country which will invite Negroes to lecture.

Editors: What you have just said is good strong medicine. And it is certainly not with any desire to palliate it that we pose our final question: As you consider the Negro writer in the field of contemporary letters, what do you find most heartening?

Hughes: There are, as I think I have indicated by some of the things I said earlier, many encouraging aspects which were not present twenty, or ten, or even five years ago. The most heartening thing for me, however, is to see Negroes writing works in the general American field, rather than dwelling on Negro themes solely. Good writing can be done on almost any theme—and I have been pleased to see Motley, Yerby, Petry and Dorothy West presenting in their various ways non-Negro subjects. Dunbar, of course, and others, wrote so-called "white" stories, but until this particular period there have not been so many Negroes writing of characters not drawn from their own race.

Edna Ferber originally wrote stories of Jewish life, but she broadened her perspective and went on to write *So Big, Show Boat* and *Cimarron.* I think we are headed in the direction of similar and perhaps superior achievement.

"From the Blues to an Opera Libretto," *New York Times,* January 15, 1950, p. X9

As a child in Kansas City, I used to hear wandering musicians playing guitars and singing the blues on Independence Avenue. Some of my earliest attempts at verse-making were creating words in my own mind to the rhythms of the blues. As a child I did not put my words down. But some years later when I consciously began to write poetry, many of my poems followed musical rhythms of negro folk songs and jazz.

Most folk blues sing either of love or economics, and frequently both themes are interwoven in the same song.

In my first book there is a poem entitled, "Cross." Its mood is that of the blues, although its lyric form lacks the folk repetition. And, to the theme of love and economics a third theme is added, that of race:

My old man's a white old man
And my old mother's black.

If ever I cursed my white old man
I take my curses back.
If ever I cursed my black old mother
And wished she were in hell,
I'm sorry for that evil wish
And now I wish her well.
My old man died in a fine big house.
My ma died in a shack.
I wonder where I'm gonna die,
Being neither white nor black.

At Jasper Deeter's Hedgerow Theatre during the summer of 1929, just after my graduation from college, I used the theme of this poem as the basis for my first play, *Mulatto,* which Deeter intended to present with Rose McClendon.[8] That fall, however, Miss McClendon was engaged for a Paul Green play. So it was not until 1935 that she originated the role of the Negro mother in my drama.

The play was a tragedy of a son's love for his father that turned to murder, caused his mother's madness and his own suicide. Its conflict was motivated by the barrier of race between them. There were no melodies with the spoken words, but I thought of it even then as the possible basis for a musical drama.

It was not until William Grant Still asked me to write a libretto for him, that I began to work directly in terms of words and music. The result was *Troubled Island,* produced ten years later at the City Center.

One of the problems of poetry and music in our country, where the Government does not subsidize these arts, is that the economic returns from them may not cover the costs of time, paper, thought and typing. I know of no poets who live from their poetry. And very few serious musicians live from their compositions.

Teaching, lecturing, arranging and other activities that absorb many hours that might be devoted to creation, are necessary to keep body and soul together. Sometimes it is long after midnight, when the day's jobs are done, before a creative word or note may be put down. Still, such words and such notes do get put down. How? Why? It must be for sheer love of words and music, rhythm, rhyme and the glory of the finished song.

Naturally, poets and musicians hope some day to make enough to pay the rent from what they create. But someday is a far off thing. And if a windfall should arrive, the income-tax man comes along and takes most of that. There is something wrong with our tax laws as they relate to the creative artist—who may be years in achieving a single "commercial" production—and then never have a second one. But the law does not take all those years of struggle and debt into account.

That, however, has no immediate bearing on *The Barrier*, which the Columbia Theatre Associates are presenting this week on the Brander Matthews stage. This new opera, at the moment, is being done for love, not money. Singers have given up lucrative concert dates to appear in it. The director, Felix Brentano, has turned down other jobs to direct it. Willard Rhodes, its conductor, and all those connected with the production have, besides their daytime work, devoted many evening hours—until two and three in the morning—to its preparation. It must be love.[9]

About two years ago, when Jan Meyerowitz, the composer, after having set to music some of my poems, asked me for a libretto, the play *Mulatto* immediately came to mind. But I had sworn never to have anything more to do with non-commercial theatre, since lecturing and teaching, I had found, met the demands of the landlord so much better.

But Meyerowitz began to work on the music even before I had made up my mind to transpose the play into musical words. So persuasive were his melodies that I succumbed. When we drew up the collaboration agreement, my lawyer (who very kindly never accepts a penny) said, "What? Another opera!" And in his voice was not delight, but despair. I said, "But this will be a very exciting one."

Is it a far cry from blues to opera? It shouldn't be, not in America. George Gershwin came pretty near bridging the gap. Someday someone will. I would like to be the man to write that libretto.

"How to Be a Bad Writer (In Ten Easy Lessons)," *Harlem Quarterly* (spring 1950): 13–14

1. Use all the cliches possible, such as "He had a gleam in his eye," or "Her teeth were white as pearls."

2. If you are a Negro, try very hard to write with an eye dead on the white market—use modern stereotypes of older stereotypes—big burly Negroes, criminals, low-lifers, and prostitutes.

3. Put in a lot of profanity and as many pages as possible of near-pornography and you will be so modern you pre-date Pompei in your lonely crusade toward the best seller lists. By all means be misunderstood, unappreciated, and ahead of your time in print and out, then you can be felt-sorry-for by your own self, if not the public.

4. Never characterize characters. Just name them and then let them go for themselves. Let all of them talk the same way. If the reader hasn't imagination enough to make something out of cardboard cut-outs, shame on him!

5. Write about China, Greece, Tibet, or the Argentine pampas—any place you've never seen and know nothing about. Never write about anything you know, your home town, or your home folks, or yourself.

6. Have nothing to say, but use a great many words, particularly high-sounding words, to say it.

7. If a playwright, put into your script a lot of hand-waving and spirituals, preferably the ones everybody has heard a thousand times from Marian Anderson to the Golden Gates.[10]

8. If a poet, rhyme June with moon as often and in as many ways as possible. Also use *thee's* and *thou's* and *'tis* and *o'er,* and invert your sentences all the time. Never say, "The sun rose, bright and shining." But, rather, "Bright and shining rose the sun."

9. Pay no attention really to spelling or grammar or the neatness of the manuscript, and in writing letters, never sign your name so anyone can read it. A rapid scrawl will better indicate how important and how busy you are.

10. Drink as much liquor as possible and always write under the influence of alcohol. When you can't afford alcohol yourself, or even if you can, drink on your friends, fans, and the general public.

If you are white, there are many more things I can advise in order to be a bad writer, but since this piece is for colored writers, there are some things I know a Negro just will not do, not even for writing's sake, so there is no use mentioning them.

"Fooling Our White Folks,"
Negro Digest 8.6 (April 1950): 38–41

I never was one for pushing the phrase "social equality" to the nth degree. I concur with those persons, white or colored, who wish to reserve the right of inviting whom they choose into the house as friends, or as dinner guests. I do not believe civil rights should encroach on personal privacy or personal associations. But health, wealth, work, the ballot, the armed services, are another matter. Such things should be available to whites and Negroes alike in this American country.

But, because our American whites are stupid in so many ways, racially speaking, and because there are many things in this U.S.A. of ours which Negroes may achieve only by guile, I have great tolerance for persons of color who deliberately set out to fool our white folks. I remember the old slave story of the mistress who would not allow her house servants to have any biscuits. She was so particular on this point that she would cut the biscuits out herself and count them. But the cook went her one better. When the mistress left the kitchen, the cook would trim a narrow rim off every biscuit—with the result that the Negroes had in the end a pan of biscuits, too.

A great many Negroes in America are daily engaged in slyly trimming off the biscuits of race prejudice. Most Negroes feel that bigoted white persons deserve to be cheated and fooled since the way they behave toward us makes no moral sense at all. And many Negroes would be way behind the eight ball had they not devised surreptitious means of escape. For those who are able to do it, passing for white is, of course, the most common means of escaping color handicaps. Every large Negro section has many residents who pass for white by day, but come home to their various Harlems at night. I know dozens of colored whites in downtown offices or shops. But at night they are colored again.

Then there are those Negroes who go white permanently. This is perhaps a more precarious game than occupational passing during work hours only. Some break down under the strain and go native again or go to pieces. But hundreds of others pass blithely into the third and fourth generations—entirely losing their dusky horizons by intermarriage. There is one quite well-known Negro family in the East with an equally well-known brother out West who has been "white" for forty years, and whose children's children are "white"—now, no doubt, beyond recall. A famous Negro educator told me recently of having lost track of one of his most brilliant students, only to be asked to address a large and wealthy congregation in the Midwest and to find as pastor of this church his long lost colored graduate, now the "white" shepherd of a white flock. The educator was delighted at his former student's ministerial success in fooling our white folks.

The consensus of opinion among Negroes seems to be approval of those who can get by with it. Almost all of us know Negroes of light complexion who, during the war, were hustled through their draft boards so fast that they were unwittingly put into white units and did their service entirely without the humiliations of the military color bar. One young Negro of my acquaintance took his basic training in Mississippi in a white unit, lived with the white boys, went to all the local dances and parties, and had a wonderful time without the army or Rankin being any the wiser. He is back now in the Negro college from which the draft took him. The army policy being stupid anyway, all his family and friends applaud his having so thoroughly fooled our white folks in the deep South.

Negroes are even more pleased when persons of *obviously* colored complexion succeed in calling white America's bluff. Those young ladies who, in spite of golden or brown complexions, take foreign names and become Hollywood starlets, delight us. And the men who go to Mexico as colored and come back as Spanish to marry wealthy white debutantes gain a great deal of admiration from the bulk of the Negro race. Negroes feel it is good enough for Nordic debutantes to be thusly fooled. Besides, nothing is too good for those with nerve enough to take it. Anyhow, hasn't the army a strange way of classifying black Puerto Ricans as "white"—while quite white American Negroes are put down as "colored"? Simple, our white folks: so why not fool them?

When the Waldorf-Astoria first opened in New York, Negroes were not served in its main dining rooms. In a spirit of fun, a well-known Harlem journalist of definitely colored cast, put on a turban and went into the hotel. He was served with the utmost courtesy. During the war a fine Negro chemist, quite brownskin, applied for a position in a war plant and was given a blank to fill out. He truthfully put down his nationality as American, his race as Negro. He received a letter saying no openings were available, in spite of the fact that every day the firm advertised for chemists. He simply procured another blank. Instead of putting down Negro as his race, he wrote Puerto Rican—and was hired at once. Silly, our white folks!

Some Negroes make sport of them all the time. There is a very dark gentleman in a large Midwestern city where prejudice in public places is rampant, who delights in playing upon white gullibility. Being truly African in complexion, he does not pretend to pass for white. He can't. But since many of the restaurants and theatres are owned or managed by foreign-born Americans, or Jewish Americans, he simply passes for whatever the nationality of the management might be at the time. He will tell a Jewish theatre manager who wishes him to sit in the Negro section, "Do you not know that I am a black Hebrew?" Usually the man will be so taken aback that he will say no more. Such sport this patron enjoys more than the films.

He once went into a Greek restaurant at the edge of the Negro section, but which, nevertheless, had a custom of not serving Negroes. He was told he could not eat therein. He said, "but did you never hear of Socrates? He was a black Greek. Many noble Greeks of old were colored. I am descended from such ancient Greeks. What do you mean, *I*, a black Greek, cannot eat here?" He was served without further ado. Funny, our white folks—even those not yet Americanized! They, too, act right simple sometimes.

In the early days of the war, reading my poems at various U.S.O.'s in the South, one day between Nashville and Chattanooga I went into the buffet section of a parlor car coach for luncheon. The Filipino steward-waiter looked at me askance as I sat down. He made several trips into the kitchen before he finally came up to me and said, "The cook wants to see you." I said, "Please send the cook out here, then." He did. The cook was a Negro. The cook said, "That Filipino wants me to tell you that you can't eat in here, but I am not going to tell you no such thing. I am going to send your lunch out." He did. I ate.

Another time during the war, before they had those curtained-off tables for colored folk in Southern diners, passing through Alabama, I went to dinner and sat down in the very center of the car. The white steward leaned over and whispered politely in my ear, "Are you Negro or foreign, sir?" I said, "I'm just hungry!" The colored waiters laughed. He went away. And I was served. Sometimes a little nerve will put discrimination to rout. A dignified lady of color one day walked into a white apartment house elevator whose policy was not to take Negroes upstairs except on the servant's lift. The elevator man directed her, "Take the service car, please." She drew herself up to her full height and said, "How dare you?" He did not dare further. He took her up without a word to the white friends on whom she was calling.

A little daring with languages, too, will often go a long way. "*Dame un boletto Pullman to Chicago*," will get you a berth in Texas when often plain English, "Give me a Pullman ticket to Chicago," will not. Negroes do not always have to change color to fool our white folks. Just change tongues. Upon returning from Europe one summer, a mulatto lady I know decided to live downtown for the winter. So, using her French, she registered at a Fifth Avenue hotel that has never before nor since been known to house a Negro guest. But she stayed there several months before moving back to Harlem. A little, "*S'il vous plait*" did it. I once knew a West Indian Negro darker than I am who spent two weeks at the Beverly-Wilshire Hotel in the movie colony simply by registering as a Chinese from Hong Kong.

Our white folks are very easily fooled. Being so simple about race, why shouldn't they be? They have no business being prejudiced with so much democracy around. But since they are prejudiced, there's no harm in fooling the devil, is there? That old mistress in slavery time with plenty of dough, had no business denying her house servants a few biscuits. That they got them in the end served her right. Most colored folks think that as long as white folks remain foolish, prejudiced and racially selfish, they deserve to be fooled. No better for them!

"When I Worked for Dr. Woodson,"
Negro History Bulletin (May 1950): 188

In the mid-1920's when I worked for Dr. Woodson, he set an example in industry and stick-to-it-tiveness for his entire staff since he himself worked very hard.[11] He did everything from editing *The Journal of Negro History* to banking the furnace, writing books to wrapping books. One never got the idea that the boss would ask you to do anything that he would not do himself. His own working day extended from early morning to late at night. Those working with him seldom wished to keep the same pace. But he always saw that we had enough to do ahead to keep our own working hours entirely occupied.

One time Dr. Woodson went away on a trip which those of us in his office thought would take about a week. Instead, he came back on the third day and found us all in the shipping room playing cards. Nobody got fired. Instead, he requested our presence in his study—where he gave us a long and very serious talk on our responsibilities to our work, to history, and to the Negro race. And he predicted that neither we nor the race would get ahead playing cards during working hours.

My job was to open the office in the mornings, keep it clean, wrap and mail books, assist in answering the mail, read proofs, bank the furnace at night when Dr. Woodson was away, and do anything else that came to hand which the secretaries could not do—since they were girls. My most responsible job covering a period of several months was the arranging in alphabetical order of all the names in Dr. Woodson's compilation of the "Thirty Thousand Free Negro Heads of Families." It was like alphabetizing a phone book, and it had to be checked and double-checked, counted in manuscript and in proofs to be sure the final book was absolutely correct. I worked as carefully as I knew how, slowly, and for me it was good training in accuracy and methodicalness. Dr. Woodson complimented me for it in the end.

He was never one for small-talk or joking with his office staff. And sometimes when engaged in writing or research, he did not say much more than "Good morning," for days on end. But we all respected greatly and admired his ever-evident devotion to the work he was doing, the history he brought to life, and the racial cause he so well served. We often said, sometimes with envy, that if we could work that hard we might get somewhere someday, too. But none of us really wanted to work that hard and we wondered how Dr. Woodson did it. To that old saying about "how much devotion it takes to serve a cause" might be added, "and how much labor."

"Ten Ways to Use Poetry in Teaching," *CLA Journal* 7.2 (spring 1951): 273–79

It was Mary McLeod Bethune who, way back in the early 1930's, first set me to reading poetry to students. She asked, "Why don't you bring your poems to the young people of the South? So many artists and writers seem to forget us down here. We like culture, too."

With Mrs. Bethune's encouragement and the aid of the Rosenwald Fund, I got a Ford car and set out to carry poetry to the high schools and colleges of the South. My tour began at Hampton in October, and I intended to extend it as far as Mrs. Bethune's campus in Florida, ending my trip by Christmas. But bookings continued to come in. Shortly my commitments included Mississippi and Louisiana, Arkansas and Texas. And by spring my tour had extended all the way to Los Angeles, San Francisco, and Seattle, including the University of California at Berkeley. But mostly my audiences had been entirely Negro—Edward Waters College, Fort Valley and Albany, Georgia, Fisk, Alcorn, Piney Woods, Prairie View, as well as high schools, grammar schools, and consolidated country schools—with age groups ranging all the way from kindergarten to Meharry medical students.

Since then, for almost twenty years now I have been reading my poems to young people all over America. During the war I visited the high schools of Milwaukee for the National Conference of Christians and Jews. I spent a week in Philadelphia appearing at senior and junior high schools for the Philadelphia School Board. And, for the Common Council for American Unity, I read my poems at thirty high schools' assemblies in the New York–New Jersey area where there had never been a Negro assembly speaker before. In recent years I have been a Writer-in-Residence at Atlanta University and at the University of Chicago's Laboratory School working with young people through poetry. On these experiences I base the materials I shall discuss here.

Before considering ten ways to use poetry in teaching, let's investigate certain reasons for using poetry at all, as distinguished from other forms of literary art, in the classroom. There comes to mind immediately the fact that since many poems are brief, concise, and to the point—literary time-savers—often more can be done with a poem in a limited classroom period than with a story or an essay.

Poems employ rhythm, often rhyme. These two devices help greatly to fix in the mind what is being said. Long after school days are passed, a line or two, or a verse of poetry learned and loved will remain in the memory. As one of my poems for children states:

> To make words sing
> Is a wonderful thing—
> Because in a song
> Words last so long.

Therefore, new words learned in poetry are more apt to remain clear in the mind longer than the unusual word in prose. Poetry can be a vocabulary builder.

Poetry is rhythm—and, through rhythm, has its roots deep in the nature of the universe; the rhythms of the stars, the rhythm of the earth moving around the sun, of day, night, of the seasons, of the sowing and the harvest, of fecundity and birth. The rhythms of poetry give continuity and pattern to words, to thoughts, strengthening them, adding the qualities of permanence, and relating the written word to the vast rhythms of life.

Poetry can be used to bridge the often imagined gulf between literature and life. To achieve this, the contemporary poets and particularly the poets of one's own country are most useful—poets writing about things we live and know. Then there will be no time or language gulf between poetry and life. Starting with today as introduction it will be easier for students to take the road back to the great poets of other ages.

Poetry can be made an exciting game—a game of exploration to find, beneath the surface of words and phrase, the deeper moods and meanings at the heart of a poem. A poem is often the distilled essence of experience, the concentrated flavor of an emotion. Set the student to seeking its fully expanded meanings—and you will find that young people are often as intrigued as they would be with a riddle, a new crossword puzzle, or a quiz show.

Poetry can be used to stimulate students to start a mental search. At the Laboratory School of the University of Chicago, I found that teenagers were often more excited by the adventure of digging into the on-the-surface hard to grasp poems of E. E. Cummings, Gertrude Stein, or the esoteric young Negro poet, Russell Atkins, than they sometimes were in reading the simpler, easier-to-understand-immediately poets. Young people love the challenge of exploration and conjecture which much modern poetry offers.

Read for its sheer sensuous beauty poetry, from the Psalms to Countee Cullen, can be used to acquaint young people with the musical and esthetic value of words used carefully and precisely.

Lastly, poetry can be used as a steppingstone to the other literary arts—to the poetry-in-prose of all great writers, from Homer to Willard Motley. Now, for ten ways to use poetry in teaching: Given the broadest possible student base—young people from cultured homes, from uncultured homes, from big cities, from rural areas, with good reading habits or bad reading habits, mature or immature—everybody these days, unless deaf, listens to the radio, television, or jukebox. As a point of departure then for inculcating a taste for poetry one might begin with:

1. The Poetry of the Popular Song: Here there would be a wide area of immediate understanding. There is at least one good text available, the "Lyrics" of Oscar Hammerstein as published by Simon and Schuster, containing the words of the songs from *Oklahoma, Show Boat,* and *South Pacific.* And students can buy their own song-sheets on any newsstand for a dime. Questions for the teacher to raise: when is a song lyric a poem and when is it just a jingle? What gives *Bali Ha'i* a true lyrical quality as contrasted to a song like *Music, Music, Music,* which is mere rhyming? Why do the words of *The Tennessee Waltz* have a poetic quality? What makes W. C. Handy's *St. Louis Blues* a fine poem even without music? From the popular songs it is but a step to:

2. The Poetry of the Folk Songs—particularly those of America and the Negro people. Often the folk song tells a story, *John Henry, Casey Jones, Frankie and Johnnie,* and so they are doubly appealing to young people. Along with the folk songs there are:

3. Folk Verses—the anonymous poems of the people, often humorous and amusing. From the Negro people, to be found in Talley's book of folk rhymes are such gems as these:

> What a wonderful bird the frog are!
> When he sit he stand almost.
> When he hop he fly almost.
> He ain't got no sense hardly.
> He ain't got no tail hardly neither
> Where he sit almost.

Children often make up their own folk poems, chanting over and over their rhymes, which is no doubt the way many children's games were born. This brings us up to:

4. Choral Speech or the Verse Choir as a means of interesting young people in poetry. This group participation device has great possibilities. Particularly with the richness and clarity of the Negro voice, amazing results can be obtained. Many of the poems of Walt Whitman, with their long oratorical lines, lend themselves well to choral speech. And the poems of Paul Laurence Dunbar are often particularly lovely done with group voices. My own poem, "Freedom's Plow," has often been performed this way. Sometimes students are interested in hearing:

5. Recordings of Poets Reading Their Own Poems. The late James Weldon Johnson recorded his *God's Trombones.* Vachel Lindsay's *The Congo* is available, as well as the readings of Carl Sandburg and other distinguished American poets. I have made an album of some of my poems. And the Library of Congress has recorded many living American poets.

6. Having Students Select and Read Poems Aloud in Class, however, is more often more fun than listening to recordings. Let the class choose a theme a week, then find poems illustrating the theme—adventure, nature, love, morality, or death—whatever it may be. This method was used with interesting results at the Chicago Laboratory School, some students thereby discovering a compatible poet and reading most or all of his work afterwards at home.

7. The Poetry Quiz Party is also a competitive way of arousing interest in poetry—having each student read a poem aloud, not giving the author or the title or the national origin of the poem, then letting the class guess what country it is from, what form, what it is really about, and who wrote it. If, by then, the title is not yet known, let the members of the class give it a title of their own choosing—and see how near they come to the title given the poem by the author. There is also:

8. The Poetry Costume Party in which folks come dressed as "The Ancient Mariner," or "Hiawatha" and recite each his own poem—which gives an added incentive to the memorizing of poetry.

9. And for poetry in English, there is lastly, The Simple Custom of Reading It Aloud frequently to students, simply, plainly, and clearly, with understanding—but unless one is good at it, *not* with dramatics. Dramatics and "the faraway voice" sometimes alienate young people from poetry. The simpler poetry can be made, the better.

10. Finally, as an incentive toward the study of foreign languages, American poems in French or Spanish or German translations might be studied, with the original at hand. The Dudley Fitts *Anthology of Contemporary Latin-American Poetry,* with the Spanish on one page and the English on the other, is particularly good for this. Various editions of Federico García Lorca are published in this way, too, as are the Edna St. Vincent Millay translations of Baudelaire. For Negro students it is particularly interesting to see their own writers in another language. Almost all recent foreign anthologies of American or world poetry now contain some poems by our American Negro poets. Here is a recent Puerto Rican translation of a poem of my own as published in *Bayoan*:

Wonderful World

Wonderful bed—
That is nothing but bed—
With no question about its
Being bed.

Wonderful clock
That alarms promptly at eight,
Neither Democrat or Republican,
Titoist or Stalinist.

Wonderful light
That always turns on
Except when the bulb's burnt out.

Wonderful world
That is always world—
Come what may!

Mundo de Prodigios

Lecho maravilloso
no más que simple lecho,
sin la mínima duda
de ser tan sólo éso.

Reloi maravilloso,
punctual siempre a las ocho,
Republicano ni Democrata,
Stalinista o Titoísta.

Maravillosa luz
que siempre brilla aquí,
excepto que se funda la bujía.

Mundo maravilloso,
qua es siempre mundo,
¡no importa lo que pase!

In excellent English translations published in this country, one may find the poems of the Cuban Negro poet, Nicolás Guillén, in a volume called *Cuba Libre;* and the astonishing poems of the great Martinique Negro poet, Aimé Césaire, published with the French on one page and the English on the opposite in a beautiful edition by Brentano's under the title, *Memorandum on My Martinique.*

Here then are ten possible ways of using poetry in the teaching of our own or other languages. Any resourceful teacher can devise other, and perhaps even more exciting methods. My contention is that poetry will be liked, even loved, by students if presented to them in a fresh and contemporary fashion.

"Bright Chariots,"
Negro Digest 9 (April 1951): 59–62

Swing low, sweet chariot,
Coming for to carry me home!

So sang the lowly of a century ago.[12] But even way back yonder there were those who did not wait for that final chariot to ride sweetly. Then as now, if you had what it took to make the wheels go around, you could ride about in grand style. Even in ante-bellum days in the South, wealthy free Negroes were transported in elegance as great, if sometimes not greater, than wealthy whites. Long before the Civil War there were in New Orleans free Creoles of color and quadroon belles who rode down Canal Street in a coach-and-four—the equivalent then of a special built Cadillac today. Handsome surreys and handsome bays were the property of well-to-do colored folks as well as well-to-do whites.

Before the days of motor cars, in areas where there were bayous, rivers, or canals, water travel was not uncommon. Boats and barges were a convenient mode of private transportation. In the early 1800's a free Negro woman in Florida persuaded her mate, a wealthy white planter, to have built for her a palatial barge propelled by six black slaves at the oars. It had a silken canopy and was painted in gorgeous colors. Reclining among the cushions like a new-world Cleopatra, this beautiful ebony woman would ride regally up and down the Sewanee River in the cool of the evening to the envy and astonishment of all the whites along its banks. When their envy finally became too great for comfort, she persuaded her mate to book passage for her, the children, and himself to Santo Domingo where they settled down and where their descendants are among the leading families of that island today.

Just after the Civil War several of the Reconstruction congressmen of color drove from their Washington mansions to the Capitol in the handsomest rigs money could buy behind the finest horses available. Congressman John M. Langston possessed a sleek black rubber-tired carriage, drawn by two snow-white horses with a coachman at the reins. He lived in LeDroit Park near Howard University, whose Law School he founded. To get home he had to pass through a well-to-do white neighborhood whose inhabitants did not relish seeing a Negro ride in such style. Some of them put up a wooden barrier across the street to keep him from passing. Mr. Langston did not believe in barriers, so one day on the way home from the Halls of Congress he stopped at a hardware shop on Pennsylvania avenue and bought himself an axe. When his carriage reached the wooden barrier he got out, took his axe and chopped it down while the coachman held his gloves. From then on, without hindrance, he rode behind his snow-white horses through the street of Washington, the ebony spokes of his highly lacquered carriage wheels gleaming—such wheels being the nearest thing in those days to the contemporary elegance of white-walled tires.

When motor cars were first made, no sooner were they acquired by white folks than they were acquired by Negroes. Just who the first Negro in America to own an automobile was, I do not know. But old New Yorkers tell me Avery and Hart, a famous dancing team of the early 1900's, and Oscar Hammerstein, colored man-about-town, were among the first to be seen speeding up Broadway in long open cars, all occupants dressed in linen dusters to keep the rush of air from blowing their garments into disarray. One of the first Negro-owned cars on record to attract wide attention belonged to Jack Johnson, the heavyweight champion of the world. Jack, at one point in his career, was not satisfied to own an ordinary automobile, so legend says. He bought an armored car.

In the Golden Era of the 20's when the so-called "Negro Renaissance" of the theatre and the arts was in full bloom, money was free and the Harlem nightclubs packed with downtown whites, some very elegant chariots sped through Central Park from Lenox avenue to Broadway and back. One of them belonged to Aubrey Lyles of Miller and Lyles, the comedy stars of *Shuffle Along*. The Lyles car was as long as a Pullman. Its back seat opened up into a bed when its owner took to the road. And its decoration and accessories were all of pure white ivory. It was the kind of car that attracted a crowd whenever and wherever it was parked. It was frequently sighted near the famous tree of hope in front of the old Lafayette Theatre on Seventh avenue, with the Rhythm Club nearby where Bojangles and other greats of the theatrical and sporting world went for recreation. Always there would be a curious and admiring group of people about Lyles' chariot. Lyles himself was a very little fellow and he looked lost in so large and fine a car. But the car itself was most imposing. Lesser vehicles gave way before it when it took out, its horn sounding off. Historians call that era in American life the "Roaring Twenties." The horn on Lyles' car formed a part of its roar.

A few years later the great Negro actor and baritone, Jules Bledsoe, who originated the role of Joe in *Show Boat* and first sang *Ole Man River,* appeared on the streets of Harlem in a long black Rolls Royce, sleek and striking in its funereal simplicity, and obviously very expensive. But even more startling to the Harlemites of those days than the car, was the fact that Mr. Bledsoe had a white chauffeur in full uniform. Jules Bledsoe was very dark. With his great sense of humor, he explained to his friends that he had a *white* chauffeur so folks could better tell who was the chauffeur and who the owner of the car, otherwise there might be a mistake. But the envious and small-minded had another explanation that they whispered. They said the chauffeur went with the car of necessity, supplied by the firm, because the Rolls Royce people would not let anybody else drive it until the car was at least half paid for. Such a rumor, however, did not prevent Jules Bledsoe from emerging from his Broadway dressing room after a performance to settle his dark self among the soft cushions of the rear seat, and call through a speaking tube to his white chauffeur, "Home, James."

When *Rhapsody in Black* was playing with its wonderful cast including Ethel Waters, Valaida Snow, and the Berry Brothers, Miss Snow purchased a mauve-colored Mercedes Benz of a striking orchid tone.[13] She had her designer make for her an orchid suit trimmed in silver fox. Miss Snow had a pet monkey, so for the monkey, too, a suit was made and a little cap to match. Her chauffeur also had a specially designed uniform to set off the car. When the show went on the road, Valaida Snow toured in her mauve-orchid chariot, causing the natives of such places as Terre Haute, Indiana, to stand agape with wonder as, chauffeur at the wheel and monkey on shoulder, she would draw up to the door of the local colored rooming house in her gorgeous foreign-made car. As the softly purring motor went still and the chauffeur jumped out to open the door, the beautiful brownskin Miss Snow would rise and walk with dignity into the dingy third-rate kind of a hotel which was the only sort of lodging place where Negro performers touring the Middle West could stop in those days. Her chariot was a dream, but many other factors in the lives of touring artists of color were less glamorous. A monkey could stay at a white hotel, but not a colored star.

That was before the second World War for democracy. Things are a bit better now. When Lena Horne steps out of her new foreign-made car and into the lobby of almost any hotel in the larger cities of the North, she will be received with courtesy. The curious outside will ask: "Whose car is that?" "What make is it?" "From what country did it come?"

In this year of our Lord, 1951, the mode among celebrities of color seems to have turned more than ever to cars of foreign make. Domestic Packards and fish-tail Cadillacs no longer incite much comment, being far too numerous for notice in Harlem, Hollywood, and Chicago's South Side. For this reason, no doubt, Mr. Billy Eckstine, I hear, has recently purchased a silver-toned Jaguar of French make. Several English and a few Italian cars, too, are to be seen about Harlem these days. But Sugar Ray turned the tables by taking with him to Europe a brand new canary-yellow *U.S.A.* Cadillac that became the talk of Paris, leaving behind for secondary uses his eye-filling flamingo-red buggy which he still possesses.[14] His new and cheerful bird-colored chariot helped gild the foreign lily of this young fighter's reputation as one of the two greatest things America has produced since the War—these things being Sugar Ray and the Marshall Plan.

Griffith J. Davis, another patriot who has recently returned from photographing Haile Selassie in Abyssinia, did not bring back an African made car.[15] He has instead just purchased a satin-blue Henry J. whose name plate he changed to Griffith J.

And Eddie "Rochester" Anderson is having a special car built at a Culver City shop which is reportedly costing $12,000.

It's a far cry from the elegant horse-drawn carriages of ante-bellum days or the canopied barges of the Sewanee River to the colorful cars of today and the sleek white yachts of Dr. Marshall Ross or Binga Dismond—for Negroes have yachts, too, sailing nonchalantly up the Harlem River.[16]

In whatever style others ride, we ride. There are even those of us who have private planes. Several well-to-do Southern professional men of color possess them, taking to the air for a pleasure flight or a trip to Harlem at will. But I have not yet had the thrill of riding in any of these private planes, so I cannot tell you about them. I only know that now *our* bright chariots have wings, too, and some of us, anytime we wish, without waiting for heavenly chariots to swing low, may cleave the air. As soon as rockets to the moon are made, no doubt we will possess a few, probably better, longer, and brighter than most others. When estates on the moon become more fashionable than mansions in St. Albans, West Chesterfield, or Blueberry Hill, there will most certainly be Negroes (probably movie stars or public relations executives) who will step into their rocket planes and call to a uniformed pilot, "Home, James!" Elegantly taking off—out of this world.

"The Streets of Chicago,"
LHP 3684 (May 28, 1951)

Long before Carl Sandburg published his famous "Chicago Poems" in which he called that big brawling city "hog-butcher to the world," even before Hollywood's unending series of gangster movies laid in the Windy City, Chicago had a reputation for two-fisted toughness unequalled by any other city in the world.[17] Prohibition and the era of Al Capone further added to this rough and ready rep. A whole double generation of novelists from Dreiser to Farrell to Algren to Motley gave this factual truth fictional life.[18] Richard Wright's *Native Son* and Gwendolyn Brooks' *A Street in Bronzeville* continued the picture in indelible words, bringing the Negro South Side into the literary orbit of Chicago's mad vitality.

From the first week that I arrived in Chicago, I learned that it was a tough town. I was sixteen. We lived on Wabash Avenue just across the street from the Branch Y.M.C.A. The el trains roared past our back windows and, as loud as the el trains and more continuous, the sounds of State Street's balling and brawling kept up day and night. Being a youngster who always liked to explore on my own, my first Sunday in town I went out walking. Not knowing any better I continued across State Street, past Wentworth, and on into what was then a Polish neighborhood. I had gone only a few blocks when I was set upon by a group of white boys who tripped me up, knocked me down, and beat me thoroughly. Then they chased me all the way back to the Negro area.

That evening when my jaw began to swell, I was ashamed to tell my mother I had been bested in a fight. The next morning, with my face swollen even more, my mother took me to a doctor. He diagnosed the swelling as mumps, and treated me for that childhood disease. I never told him or my mother any better.

It was summertime and our windows opened on the alley and the elevated. Almost every night one could hear or see fights outside. At first I used to run to see what was going on, but after a few weeks, I became used to them, and sometimes would not even bother to look out the window. The great old comedian, Billy King, was at the Grand that summer during World War I, and up the street at the Monogram such amusing personalities as Stringbeans or the Whitman Sisters or Ma Rainey.[19] There were a half dozen movies nearby, too, mostly showing westerns. But the streets of Chicago were then, and have remained to this day, more interesting and exciting to me than any stage show or western shoot 'em-ups. Almost every time I have walked down a Chicago street, I have seen some sort of excitement, sometimes violent, sometimes humorous, sometimes a combination of both.

One night walking along 43rd Street near Prairie, I heard a woman screaming from a second floor window, against a background of furniture smashing, for somebody to get the police. Surprisingly soon, the patrol wagon arrived. The police went upstairs and brought down a heavy-set man who was, so the crowd learned, a roomer in the woman's apartment. He had, so she said, suddenly lost his mind and started breaking up all her furniture. Between two policemen, the man seemed mild enough as they led him to the wagon. About that time a drunk came along and got into the act. He began to berate the police who were white, for throwing a colored man into the patrol wagon.

The police told the drunk to go on home and mind his business. He insisted on presenting his viewpoint, whereupon a cop grabbed him by the scruff of the neck and threw him half way up the street. The drunk came back. A policeman whacked him across the seat with a billy club and told him again to go home. He would not go home, so they finally threw the drunk in the wagon, too. The patrol drove off to a nearby precinct house. I went into the corner cafe for a cup of coffee. Before I finished my coffee, I saw the patrol wagon return. They let the crazy man out and drove off. He went back upstairs. In a few moments, the same woman was screaming in the same window again, but this time nobody paid her any mind. Apparently, only the drunk stayed in jail.

At various times during my life, I have worked for newspapers, so maybe it is my nose for news that causes me to hurry toward a spot where I see that a crowd has gathered. One evening near 55th and Michigan I saw a large crowd so I stopped to ask what was going on. A lady courteously explained to me, "There's been a little accident upstairs. A man just killed his wife."

Another day on Calumet shots rang out in the hallway of an apartment house. People stopped to look. Windows flew open. Then all was quiet. A few bold souls ventured into the vestibule to see what had happened. When they came out they told us what it was about. Some fellow had lost his keys, so he simply shot the lock off his door.

Chicago is a great pistol town. On New Years Eve folks fire up and down the streets just for fun. And I have frequently seen guns drawn in bars and dance halls. One midnight in 55th Street I saw a man pull a gun on another in a liquor store. The other man was not fazed in the least. He said, "Aw, fellow, put that gun away. I'd be ashamed to be shot by a little old pistol like that. I got a switchblade that can reach further than your bullets." No blood was shed and both weapons eventually went back to their respective pockets and nobody seemed in the least disturbed. Chicago is a cool town.

You didn't have to be big to be tough, either. A classmate of mine was once interning at Provident Hospital and, on occasion, did evening duty in the emergency room. One Saturday night I was waiting for him to complete his duties when the police arrived with a fellow about the size of Joe Louis who had been cut to ribbons.

We looked. Inside the patrol sat a midget, unscratched, on his way to jail.

One zero winter night at 47th and the elevated a young man came running into the bar nearby with his overcoat in his hand and called for a drink to steady his nerves. He was as pale as I have ever seen a colored man become. As he gulped his drink, he explained to the bartender that a very pretty girl he had picked up had taken him to a room in a Prairie Avenue basement. While she went to the bathroom he had looked around for someplace to hang his overcoat. He noticed a curtain catty-cornered across one corner of the room, and believing it to be an improvised closet, thought to hang his coat there. He pulled the curtain aside—and behind it stood a fellow with a knife a foot long. Fortunately the door was open, so he got away before the man had a chance to rob him, coat in hand as he fled.

Not all the sights and sounds of Chicago streets have overtones of violence. There is really more fun than fighting, more mirth than murder. A blind beggar holding out his cup at 35th and Cottage Grove one sunny day seemed to have a great appreciation for women in spite of his sightlessness.

"Uh!" he said as a young woman passed. "That chick sure has got some fine hips."

"How can you tell?" I asked.

"I sense their vibrations," he said.

At East 51st Street and that great race track, South Parkway, the lights suddenly changed one night and, with a great screeching of brakes, a car came to an abrupt halt. Five or six people, in fact, everybody in the car jumped out except the driver. They scattered in all directions as one woman yelled back, "I ain't gonna ride with you. You're too drunk."

Half dazed, the driver watched his departing friends for a moment, shook his head and got out, too.

"You-all are right," he said. "I'm too drunk to even ride with myself."

He walked off and left his car standing empty in the middle of the street.

If you keep your ears open in Chicago you can sometimes hear very odd things. One night on Vincennes Avenue I heard a man tell a woman, "Baby, when I get you home, I'm gonna beat you till you cry—then love you till you laugh."

Another time a woman came to the door of a poolhall and called her husband to come out. He said, "Aw, honey, go ahead on home. Can't you see I'm in the middle of a game?"

Unwilling to take no for an answer, the woman proceeded to call him all the names in the book, from bad to worse, including mention of his mother. None of this disturbed him. The man calmly kept on shooting his game of black-ball. Finally, in an outburst of extreme impatience, the woman said, "All right then, if you won't come, you kiss my behind!"

This made the man mad. With cue stick upraised, he rushed toward her.

"What did you say?" he demanded.

"I said, kiss my behind."

"You know I don't allow no woman to tell me to kiss her behind," the man said. "Now you just told me to kiss yours, didn't you?"

He braced himself to bring the stick down on her head when she cooed softly, "I told you that—but," very coyly she added, "you don't *have* to do it."

"All right, then," the man said, returning to his eight-ball. "Get supper ready, honey. I'll be home in a few minutes, you mean little sugarlump, you."

So in Chicago from the North Side to the South Side, the Gold Coast to Bronzeville, the pendulum swings between toughness and tenderness, goodness and guns, fights and fun, up and down almost any of the Windy City's dirty but never dull streets.

"Jokes Negroes Tell on Themselves," *Negro Digest* 9 (June 1951): 21–25

They say once there was a Negro in Atlanta who had made up his mind to commit suicide, so one day he went down to the main street and took the freight elevator up to the top of the highest building in town, in fact, the highest skyscraper in Georgia. Negroes could not ride the passenger elevators, but he was so anxious to commit suicide that he did not let Jim Crow stand in his way. He rode as freight. Once at the top of the building, he took off his coat, drew a deep breath, approached the ledge and jumped off. He went hurtling through the air and was just about to hit the sidewalk when he saw a white woman come around the corner. He knew he had better not fall on that white woman, so he curved and went right on back up.

There was another Negro who one day came to a strange town in Mississippi where he had never been before. When he got off the bus he did not see any of the race around, so he asked a white man, "Where do the colored folks hang out here?"

The white man pointed at a great big tree in the public square and said, "Do you see that limb?"

Negroes in Arkansas, when you ask them what life is like in Tennessee, will tell you the white folks are so bad in Memphis that black folks can't even drink white milk. But if you ask Negroes in Tennessee what it is like in Arkansas, they will say, "Man, in that state you better not even put your black feet in no white shoes!"

There are innumerable variations on the use of the word *white* in the South. They say, for example (presumably in fun), that the reason Negroes eat so many black-eyed peas in Dixie, and in Louisiana so many red beans, is because for years after the Emancipation, colored people did not dare ask a storekeeper for white beans. Red beans or black-eyed peas, okay. But it was not until folks began using the term *navy beans,* that Negroes had the nerve to purchase white beans, too. In a Wylie Avenue hash-house one day I heard a Negro say to another one at the counter, "Here you are up North ordering white bean soup. Man, I know you are really free now." Everybody laughed.

Some of these types of jokes are even laid on animals. They say there was once a black cat in Mobile who decided to head for Chicago because he had always heard that up North there was no color line. Hardly had that cat gotten to Chicago than he met a white cat. Desirous of being shown about a bit,

The black cat said to the white cat,
"Let's go round the town."
But the white cat said to the black cat,
"You better set your black self down."

In some places, so another pleasantry goes, white folks are so mean they will not give a Negro the time of day. A colored man said to a white man, "What time is it, sir?"

The white man asked the Negro, "Do you play chess?"

The Negro said, "Yes, sir."

The white man said, "Then it's your time to move."

These, and hundreds of other jokes of a similar nature which Negroes tell on themselves, belong in the category of:

White is right,
Yellow mellow,
But black, get back!

Their humor is the humor of frustration and the laughter with which these sallies are greeted, for all its loudness, is a desperate laughter. White people often do not understand such humor at all. Negroes do, and such jokes told at appropriate moments amuse them no end.

Shortly after the big Detroit race riots, a cartoon appeared in a Negro newspaper that Harlemites thought highly, if wryly, hilarious.[20] But no white person to whom I have ever shown it even cracks a smile, let alone laughs aloud. The cartoon pictures a wall in a sportsman's den on which the heads of the game he has bagged are hung—a deer's head, an elk's head, a tiger's head. Among them, mounted like the others, is a Negro head. Two little white boys are looking at the head. One little boy, pointing at the Negro's head, tells the other youngster, "My daddy got that one in Detroit last week."

Most such jokes, however, are at the expense of the South. In Harlem they say a young mother-to-be, about to bear her first child, decided to go back down South to be with her mother when the great event came. Her young husband tried to keep her from going, pointing out to her that aside from having better hospital facilities, New York had no Jim Crow wards, and colored physicians could attend patients in the hospitals. In the South one often has to have a white doctor since many hospitals there will not permit Negro doctors to practice inside their walls. Still the expectant mother insisted on going home to mama.

The father in Harlem waited and waited for news of the birth of his child. No news came. The ninth month passed. The tenth month passed. Finally he phoned his wife and told her something must be wrong, to go to the hospital anyhow and be examined. She went. The white physician marvelled that her child had not yet come. Putting his earphones to his ears and baring her abdomen, he pressed his instrument against her flesh to listen for the prenatal heartbeats of the unborn child. Instead, what he heard, quite clearly and distinctly inside the body of the mother, was a Sugar Chile Robinson type of voice singing the blues:[21]

I won't be born down here!
I won't be born down here!
If you want to know
What it's all about—
As long as South is South,
I won't *come out!*
No, I won't be born down here!

He wasn't. She had to come on back to New York to have her baby. Harlemites swear that the colored child had plenty of sense.

A great many jokes with which Negroes regale each other, but seldom tell white folks, are hardly complimentary to racial intelligence. Jokes relating to tardiness are among them. Some such jokes even go so far as to blame the darkness of the race upon a lack of punctuality on that morning long ago in the dawn of creation when the Lord called upon mankind to wash in the River of Life. They say that everybody promptly went down to the water to wash—except the Negroes. The Negroes lingered and loitered along the way, dallied and played, and took their own good time getting down to the river. When they got there, the other folks had used up all the water and had emerged whiter than snow. In the river bed after so much washing, the Negroes found only a little mud. Into the mud they waded with their bare feet. Late, in their desperation, they bent down and put the palms of their hands in the mud, too. By that time, even the mud was used up. Therefore, to this day, nothing is light about Negroes except the palms of their hands and the soles of their feet. Late, always late.

Other jokes relate to behavior and how a Negro (in so far as these jokes go) will always snarl things up, even in heaven. They say the first time a Negro went to heaven, all the other angels became excited when they heard he was coming and had prepared a great welcome for him. Even Saint Peter and the Lord were moved at the prospect of greeting the first member of the darkest race into celestial glory. In honor of the occasion the Gates of Pearl were shining and the Streets of Gold had been polished until each cobblestone gleamed. But what did that Negro do?

That Negro was so excited when he first got his wings that he took off then and there at top speed and would not stop flying. He flew, and he flew, and he flew, and he flew. In his crown of gold and his snow white robes he lifted up his wings and flew like mad from the East to the West, from the North to the South up and down and all throughout the universe. He whizzed by the Golden Throne at 100 miles per hour, wings spread like a Constellation. He flew around God's footstool so fast the Cherubims thought he was greased lightening. He went past Saint Peter at such speed that he started a tailwind on the Golden Streets. Finally Saint Peter said, "Whoa!" But that Negro did not stop.

Peter sent a band of angels out to catch him but they could not get anywhere near that Negro. Gabriel blew his horn but he paid him no mind. He was a flying soul! He made wings do what wings had never been known to do before. He looped a loop in the sky, then he looped another loop, and tied a knot. That Negro was gone, solid gone! He scattered feathers all over heaven and stirred up such a gale that the Lord God himself stood up and cried, "Stop!"

When he stopped, that Negro skidded bang! into the Pearly Gates, broke one wing smack off, knocked his crown into eternity, snagged his robes wide open, and fell panting at the foot of the Throne.

Saint Peter just looked at him and said, "Just like a Negro!"

In the category of the bawdy joke there are hundreds illustrating the prevalent folk belief in the amorous prowess of the Negro male. Many such jokes cut across the color line in boastful fashion. They say a white man came home one cold winter night to find his golden blond wife on the living room divan deep in the loving arms of a great big dark Negro. Petrified, in his astonishment the white man forgot to close the front door. The icy winds rushed in. Thinking his wife was being raped, in a frenzy he cried, "Darling, what shall I do to this Negro?"

She sighed from the couch, "Just shut the door so he won't catch cold."

Even in hell, according to the joke makers, a Negro is hell. Since for so long Negroes had had such a hard time on earth, as compensation, up until the end of the Civil War all of them automatically went to heaven when they died. But after Lincoln signed the Emancipation Proclamation and things got a little easier for Negroes on this globe, the Lord decided to send a few colored folks to hell. The first Negro consigned to the Devil was a tall strapping man of color who in his day had been a great lover from St. Louis to the Gulf. Because his boudoir skills left him so little time for grace, the Lord said, "Send that Negro to hell." So Peter threw him out of heaven.

No sooner did the Negro set foot in hell than he grabbed the Devil's daughter and ruined her. Ten minutes later he enticed the Devil's wife behind a hot rock and ruined her. About this time the Devil's mother came along. The Negro grabbed her and ruined her. The Devil suddenly became aware of this mighty despoliation. Trembling for the first time since he had been ruler of hell, he fell to his knees and called on God for help, "Lord *please,* take this Negro out of here before he ruins me!"

Whether or not hell then began to draw the color line, the story does not say. But Negro jokes often draw a color line through their humor in such a fashion that only a Negro can appreciate them. Certain aspects of the humor of minority groups are often so inbred that they are not palatable for outside consumption. There are thousands of Jewish jokes that rarely reach the ears of Gentiles, and if they did they might be embarrassing to the ears of both groups. So it is with Negro humor—a part of it is intended only for Negroes. To others such jokes are seldom funny anyhow. The point is lost for often the nuances are too subtle for alien comprehension. A joke is not a joke when nobody laughs.

"The Wages of Sin Are Not Always Death," *Negro Digest* 9.12 (October 1951): 3–6

When I went back to my home town, Cleveland, during the depression I found that some of the brightest of my schoolmates had become bankers—number bankers. Certain colored fellow students of the 20's had turned into the black financiers of the 30's. Meanwhile I had written a half dozen books, acquired a literary reputation, and been around the world as a writer—but I had barely enough money to buy a ticket home from New York. These young men had Packards and Cadillacs, fine homes and servants. I had lived within the law. They lived outside the law—and well.

In many countries where I had been—Cuba, Mexico, France—it was not legally wrong to gamble. Lotteries, betting, and other forms of gambling are controlled there by the state, regulated by the police, and taxed for the benefit of the people. In our rather hypocritical setup, gambling is permitted by a state that winks its legal eye while legislators, city councilmen, and police collect graft. The people play but the public treasury is not paid. Gangsters and grafters here make the big money that in many other lands goes instead to the state. With us only pari-mutuel betting at the track is legal—which does not make too much sense. If it is legal to gamble at a track, why should it not be legal to do so it the corner, or at home, or wherever it is convenient?

I did not see any Negro tellers in the legal banks in Cleveland when I returned, nor colored bookkeepers or clerks. In fact, thousands of Negroes had no jobs at all there during the depression. But my former classmates who had become involved in numbers lived well. They told me quite frankly that between the color line and the economic slump, the only way they could figure out how to live decently was by getting into "the racket."

"The only way for a colored man to be a banker," they said, "is to bank numbers."

When I went on to Chicago and Detroit, I found that some of the brightest young Negroes there were involved in the digits that came from the stock exchange—but had for them nothing to do with stocks. And the tie-up between men in the numbers and men in politics was even more open in western cities than in Cleveland and New York. And there seemed to be even more Negroes making sizable incomes in the West from "the rackets" than in the East. In the 30's almost all had their homes paid for. In the 40's they had, many of them, acquired flourishing legitimate businesses "to absorb income taxes" and to furnish "a front." Some of these businesses were of the sort sorely needed in Negro communities—really good restaurants, really entertaining nightclubs with headline talent.

The more I looked upon the wages of sin, the more I saw those wages being turned into useful enterprises for the Negro public. One young Negro in numbers told me, "In this country they won't let us get into automobiles, steel, or any other phase of American big business. Where else or how else can a black man make the money we make—except in numbers? Folks like to play numbers. It is no crime to gamble two dollars, or $200, or $2000 at the track. Why should it be wrong for a poor man to risk a nickel or dime on a digit at home? The politicians and the police, who make the laws and are supposed to enforce the laws, don't care as long as they get their share. So what's wrong with it?"

It proved too lucrative—that is what became wrong with it. White racketeers moved in on Negro areas and took the big play away from Negro bankers in most cities. White politicians played ball with the white racketeers. Now almost everywhere the same racial forces that bar Negroes out of automobiles or steel, have reduced the black numbers men to small time operators. The same old cry echoes through the rackets in the Black Belts, "The white men don't want us to have a thing!"

But for a decade or more, Negroes did pretty well. From numbers in the 20's in New York, Casper Holstein is reputed to have made millions. Certainly he did many good things with his money. He built some of the first really modern apartment houses for Negro tenants in Harlem. He helped any number of young Negroes through college. He gave money for the Opportunity Literary Awards through the Urban League. The first poetry prize I ever received came from funds put up by Casper Holstein for the Opportunity Awards. In another time in a more democratic land Casper Holstein might have been a great legitimate financier and a patron of the opera like Otto Kahn or J. P. Morgan. But Holstein was colored.

According to authorities on the origins of great American fortunes, our famous white "robber barons" of the past did not always come by their wealth gently or ethically. One of the venerable names in American statesmanship, of distinguished family lineage, based an honorable career on inherited wealth alleged to have its roots in a great-grandparent's trading in opium between the Orient and the West. Another fabulous American fortune allegedly came from double dealing during the Civil War—selling munitions and supplies both to the Union and the Rebel

Armies. Not all the solid names today in Bradstreet and Dun, nor all the fashionable skirts that sweep through Society's Blue Book are free of the dirty mud of ill-gotten gains. But without much of their money American art and culture, from the Metropolitan Museum to the Metropolitan Opera House, would be poor indeed.

Some American Negroes whose incomes did not come from socially-approved sources have, nevertheless, sometimes used large portions of their monies for socially-worthy or culturally-valuable purposes. New Yorkers familiar with the theatre and concert field, during and after the "Negro Renaissance" of the 20's, can tell of several careers whose beginnings are rooted in the nickels and dimes of the numbers. It is no secret in Harlem that at least two very famous American musical stars were helped to study abroad and to gain eventual fame by relatives in the "what are you playing today" rackets. The wages of sin for them became song.

In a midwestern city for more than a decade now one of the most generous contributors to social and civic activities has been a Negro numbers banker. Hundreds of poor children have benefited by his contributions. Dozens of young artists, white and Negro, have been helped by this man without ever knowing who he is. Quietly anonymous in his benefactions, only a few people are aware that many of the nickels and dimes played in numbers in the Negro section of this city come back to the community in the form of summer camps for kids, art shows, dental supplies for settlement house clinics, or uniforms for playground baseball teams.

In another city where Negroes formerly had no decent hotels and where they were not welcome at the white hotels, numbers money financed new inns for colored travellers that compare well with any in the country for any race. In yet another city that I know of, a border town, among the most solid donors to the work of the leading social organizations in the Negro community from the Y.M.C.A. to the Urban League are the men who have made their money from numbers. Boys and girls who cannot swim in "white" pools in that city have a pool in which to swim. In a sense, here the wages of sin have on hot summer days given children the water of life.

Many such Robin Hood benefactions are not generally known to the public outside the immediate communities in which they take place. But when the income tax man clamps down, or the Crime Committees and grand juries start investigating, or the politicians suddenly become puritanical, then the papers may blaze a Negro numbers man's name across the headlines in an unsavory way. Naturally, he will get no credit for the good he may have done. Yet even in the rackets, as the Kefauver probe proved, no Negroes in America have been permitted to get far enough to be *really* important.[22] Nevertheless, many have made enough from figures in one way or other—policy, bolito, one figure or three—to ride fine, live fine, and contribute generously to the delight of social service fund raisers, community chests, and politicians.

When some poor but law-abiding young man sees these wealthy numbers bankers riding by on fine rubber, he might murmur, "The wages of sin are death." Although he could well add in bewilderment, "But it doesn't look like it."

"Do Big Negroes Keep Little Negroes Down?"

Negro Digest 9.13 (November 1951): 79–82

Freed not yet 90 years, and economically free not at all, the upper class Negro is still so closely related to the lower class Negro that it is sometimes hard to tell the difference. If, by upper class, we mean money, even the wealthiest Negro family usually has relatives, sometimes as close as brother or sister, mother or father, still working in service or for Mr. Pullman.[23] If, by upper class, we mean family tradition, some of our best families—with a legitimate name reaching back to free colored peoples in slavery time—have sons or daughters, grandsons or granddaughters whom the economics of life have forced into occupation of less than society status.

I know a peach-colored young lady of international social fame moving in the best circles here and abroad, twice wedded to men of means, whose father is still running on the railroad out of Chicago. From my viewpoint, this is nothing at all to be ashamed of, but rather to be proud of. However, certain elements of society would look down on this young woman were this fact generally known. As to family name, it is not rare at all to come across a Red Cap in a big city station whose people are among the first families of the South, racially speaking. But nobody can eat a family name—and there is nothing wrong about honest labor, bag-carrying or otherwise. I admire the Red Caps with the family names much more than I do those young men who, in order to keep up a front commensurate with their background, resort to sponging, pimping, gambling, or other shady ways of living.

Snobbism, social striving, pretensions, and looking down the nose at other people never appealed to me. I like all kinds of honest folks, in society or not. I don't object to people being in society if they want to be, and can afford it. Even the question of "can afford it" might be dropped from my discussion, since that is their business. People who have the nerve to go in for Society with a capital "S" without having Money with a capital "M" are, at least, to be admired for their gall. Some, unfortunately, seem to think that snobbism is related to *society.* That indicates ignorance.

In the days when folks thought I didn't amount to much, I was snubbed a few times. But those snubs amused more than they worried me. At the very beginning of my writing career I was invited to a society supper for Roland Hayes after one of his concerts. At the table, I was seated next to a lady who never said a word to me during the whole supper, talking instead always up the table in the direction of Mr. Hayes. The next day, however, when she learned that I was a writer who had just been awarded an important literary prize, she told the hostess she *would* have talked with me—had she known who I was. She even wrote me a note to this effect. I laughed. My feelings were not hurt. I only thought the lady unaccustomed to social conversation at a supper table.

My own experience has never led me to believe that the upper class Negro as a group is intent on keeping the lower class Negro down. But I have encountered, or known of, certain instances where *some* upper class Negroes have shown more snobbishness than intelligence in their attitudes or actions toward those they felt to be beneath them. Not too long ago in Harlem a visitor made the "mistake" of bringing a very dark girl to a party given by a professional man notorious for his intra-racial color prejudice. The young woman and her escort were made to feel so uncomfortable by their host that they left the party soon after it began. But a number of other guests were uncomfortable, too, for they repeated the boorishness of their host's attitude all over Harlem the day after. Not many Harlem socialites sympathize with a color line within the race. And certainly few sophisticated people believe in being so rude as to express such a prejudice, even if one has it.

The fact that there are in most cities some Negro clubs or social groups who do not admit outsiders to their private parties or closed formals need not necessarily mean that these groups are snobbish. Even the least pretentious and poorest neighborhood or church clubs resent strangers or unknown folks crashing their parties. People of every social level have the right to choose their associates. Why anyone would envy any group that privilege is beyond my understanding, especially when often the group that pretends to be the most exclusive will have in it members whose incomes are derived from businesses sometimes illegitimate enough to be without the law. Other members may make less income than an honest plumber or hairdresser. Social lines in some Negro groups are often based on standards as absurd as those among snobbish whites. But people have the right to be absurd if they wish. Rudeness and discourtesy are other matters.

If a person's car happens to be finer than someone else's, that still does not give the owner of the fine car the rude right of blowing dust in the other person's face. If one family possesses a mansion and another does not, the children of the mansion still should not be taught to high-hat the children of a poorer family. In this regard, upper class Negro manners (like white manners) can, no doubt, stand improvement. The true lady or gentleman never humiliates or low-rates others. Good manners and civility are the marks of real gentility everywhere in the world. Was it not George Washington who tipped his hat to a slave when he saw the Negro tipping his, saying he could permit no man to be more polite than himself? Nobility is as nobility does.

That there are in the Negro race persons of social standing too crude to be courteous to others cannot be denied. Some folks just do not have any raising. Also, no one can deny that some of us have an escape complex. Unfortunately, a minority of our professional people try to get as far away from the masses as they can in every way. Their offices may be in the heart of the Negro ghettoes (from whence come their incomes) but their homes are in the whitest suburbs money (and covenants) will permit them to live in. Their cars are expensive and showy. Their children go to private schools—if possible one that "has only a few Negroes" of which perhaps "our children are the first." When such people come to visit Chicago or New York, they wouldn't dream of stopping at the Grand or the Theresa. It's the Sherman or the Waldorf for them. Maybe they don't even visit the Southside or Harlem.

Me, I never miss them, and don't care where they stay. More power to them! But there are folks who say, since their money comes from the black working man, such people ought to stick a little more closely to that ordinary man, his problems, and his community. I think it would be nice if they did. On the other hand (since I consider myself a working man, too) I feel that we can get along damn well without them, if that's the way they feel.

But, from what little I know about them, I would say most of our upper class Negroes do *not* feel that way, and do not shun the problems of the race. I am acquainted with hundreds of our professional people in Negro communities across America who give a great deal of time and money to community betterment efforts, to the National Association for the Advancement of Colored People, the Urban League, the Y.M. or Y.W.C.A.'s, and other groups having branches in their cities. And when they come to New York they spend as much time in Harlem as they do on Broadway. Others devote themselves to private philanthropies that never get in the papers. I have known monied Negroes who have sent through school the son or daughter of a poorer relative or friend. I know others who regularly either finance entirely, or help to finance, scholarships at various colleges for young colored men and women. I know a number of race men and women who are most generous with help to artists and writers. One woman realtor in Harlem very seldom collected any rent from the poets and painters living in one of her houses during the Negro Renaissance—and she did not evict them, either.

Other colored professional men and women I know have been equally kind to poets and painters of my acquaintance who needed medical, dental, or legal service and could not pay. I can name at least a dozen colored headliners in music and the theatre—at the very top of their professions—whom I know to have given generously of both time and money to help younger Negroes make the grade in the concert or dramatic field. To name these people in print would only subject them to a flood of requests and letters they do not have time to answer, otherwise I would list a few of them here. But, at that, many of them being modest about their kindnesses, might not like being publicized in this regard. Most people do not do good for publicity, and theatre folks are no exception. Publicity for their *art,* yes, but they don't tell the press about their kindnesses all the time, unless it is the Cancer Fund or something of a public nature. The greater the artist, the bigger the heart.

I have heard folks make the blanket statement that "upper class Negroes don't care about the rest of us at all." If the word "some" were put in front of that statement, I would agree with it. *Some* big-shot white folks don't care about the rest of the white race. In neither instance is this lack of social interest desirable or right. But in the case of Negroes, my guess is that more upper class Negroes are socially and racially conscious of their obligations to the masses than a proportionate number of upper class whites are. Negroes *have* to be. The dark upper classes are *still* too close to the dark masses to get very far away from those at the bottom of the scale.

Doctor Big Dog from Virginia may stay at the Waldorf when he flies to New York. But Dr. Big Dog's first cousin, Joe Little Fice, visiting

Harlem on a cut-rate excursion from Richmond, will have to stretch his bankroll like rubber to even spend a couple of days in the Hotel Marietta whose rates are less than the Theresa's. And the grandpa from whom both Big Dog and Joe descended is still Mr. Charlie's yardman, raking leaves. Upper class Negroes haven't gotten far enough up the American ladder yet to keep anybody down, although some may look down their noses a few inches at those who do not possess Fishtails.

But all it takes to get a Fishtail is the first payment. And the numbers take care of that every day.

"The Negro Artist," *American Writer* (April 1953): 16–17

When the following statement—which two of our members, Langston Hughes and Sidney Kingsley, helped to draft was submitted to the Dramatists Guild Council, everyone present individually agreed with the important ideas it expresses.[24] *We felt, however, that the Council should not act on it as a body as we have always avoided any action which might be interpreted as an attempt to tell our members what they should write; but we are glad to bring this statement to the attention of our membership through the medium of* THE AMERICAN WRITER.

Moss Hart

STATEMENT OF COMMITTEE OF THE DRAMATISTS GUILD, LEAGUE OF NEW YORK THEATRES, AND ACTORS AND CHORUS EQUITY ASSOCIATIONS ON THE INTEGRATION AND EMPLOYMENT OF NEGRO PERFORMERS.

The theatre and all other expressions of American entertainment are today among the most powerful and influential media of communication and education. In a critical world period, when the democratic credo is under fire, it becomes increasingly important that the expanding role of our Negro citizens in the community of this nation be adequately portrayed in the entertainment arts.

The realities of the American scene today confirm the portrayal of the Negro as a more general part of the scheme of our society, for example, as postmen, policemen, clerks, secretaries, government workers, doctors, and teachers, without the necessity of emphasis on Race.

If writers, producers, directors, and casting agents would consider the Negro artist primarily as an artist, to be given consideration for casting in any roles which his ability permits, it would be a vitalizing force in the theatre. In the instances where this had been observed, there has been no violation of the naturalistic tradition of the theatre. On the contrary, realism has been more faithfully served, has advanced the interests of the theatre, and has actually lent increased variety and excitement to the presentations.

In the recent past, a well-intentioned but ill-directed sensitivity to this problem has worked inadvertently to the Negro artist. Apprehensive of doing injustice to the Negro citizens and offending humanity, writers and producers have tended to completely eliminate the Negro in comedy and servant roles. This policy, well-meant though it may be, is unrealistic and has seriously curtailed the employment of the Negro artist. While caricature and stereotype are always to be condemned, there is nothing inherently wrong in comedy or servant roles when they are part of an honest living presentation. However, when the Negro citizens are presented exclusively in such roles, an imbalance results, and their integration in American life is improperly set before the world.

We must correct this situation, not by eliminating the Negro artist, but by enlarging his scope and participation in all types of roles and in all forms of American entertainment—just as in American life, the Negro citizen's role now extends from the kitchen to the United Nations.

"My School Days in Lincoln, Illinois," LHP 736 (November 16, 1953)

It was 1916 in the Spring that I was graduated from the grammar school in Lincoln, Illinois, a town in Logan County.[25] It was then that I began my literary career, because it was as Class Poet that I wrote my very first poem. Up to that time I had never thought about being a poet and I was rather surprised at being elected Class Poet. In fact, I hadn't expected it. But I guess the youngsters in my class felt that I had some rhythm to give a poem. The teacher told us a poem had to have rhythm. And so suddenly a boy called out my name, Langston Hughes, and the whole class said, "Aye," unanimously—and that's the way I became a poet. Well, my Class Poem was about the longest poem that I've ever written. We had eight teachers in our school and I thought there should be one verse for each of our teachers. Then I thought, well, my class should have eight verses. So my first poem was sixteen verses long, just about the longest poem that I've ever written in my life. I think it got cut down a little before graduation. When I read it at graduation the class, the teachers, the parents, everybody seemed to like it. They applauded very loudly, and I was so pleased with all that applause that ever since that time I have just kept right on writing poetry.

We had three teachers, Ethel Welch, Laura Armstrong, and Frances Dyer. Those three teachers have had a very great influence on my life, particularly Ethel Welch. Miss Welch helped me and encouraged me and told me that she felt that I had some talent for writing and said that she liked my Class Poem, and indicated other poetry for me to read. And so, in a sense, I feel that I owe the beginning of my literary career to Ethel Welch. After I graduated from grammar school I went to Mexico for a year with my father, then to Central High School in Cleveland, and from there I went to Columbia University. I went to sea for a while. It wasn't until 1929 that I finally graduated from Lincoln University in Pennsylvania. By the time I came out of college I had written, or rather written and published, two books of poems, and my first novel, *Not Without Laughter*, was finished. Since that time I have published about fifteen books. It's been a long time ago—not too many books for that many years. But, anyway, my fifteen books, my poems, my whole literary career I owe in a sense to having been made the Class Poet in the grammar school in Lincoln, Illinois, because up to that time I had never thought about writing anything, never thought about being a writer, never tried to write a poem. And so my classmates and my teachers, Miss Welch, and Miss Armstrong, and Miss Dyer, started me out on a literary career which became my life's work, because now I make a living from writing. For about twenty years I have lived as a writer. And when I think back to my beginning as a writer, I think of Lincoln, Illinois.

"Old Lyric File Yields Show Song,"
Variety, October 19, 1954

The value of filing away lyric ideas for possible future use was clearly proven to me when I was doing the lyrics for the musical version of Elmer Rice's *Street Scene* (Adelphi Theatre, New York, January 9, 1947), score by Kurt Weill.

For some of the songs and arias as many as 20 or 30 lyrical versions were written, and then when the director, Charles Friedman, came to work with us about 6 months before the show went into rehearsal, some of the songs were again rewritten. To achieve a lyric for the one dance number planned for the show—a lyric that would at the same time carry on the story—posed a problem that for a time seemed almost incapable of solution. If Kurt Weill liked the lyrics I brought in for the number, Elmer Rice would not. If both of them thought a lyric satisfactory, Charles Friedman would find it not to his liking for staging purposes. Finally, after several weeks of work on the number and, lacking any further ideas myself, it occurred to me to look through my files of old lyric ideas and see what I might come across. I found in the files in almost perfect 32 bar form, a lyric called "Moon Faced, Starry Eyed," which I pulled out, copied, and took to my associates at the Playwright's office. Everybody said right away, "That's it!" Almost overnight, Kurt Weill set the lyrics to music, and everyone liked the result. It was one of the few songs in the show that did not require any changes later.

"Moon Faced, Starry Eyed" was sung and danced by Sheila Bond and Danny Daniels in the Broadway production, usually stopping the show; and was recorded by Benny Goodman and Johnny Mercer, Freddy Martin, Teddy Wilson, and a number of others, achieving more recordings than any other number in the show—an old lyric out of my old files, filed away several years before Rice and Weill ever thought of making a musical of *Street Scene.*

"Walt Whitman and the Negro," *Nocturne* 7 (spring 1955): 9

Louis Untermeyer in his preface to *Modern American Poetry* terms Walt Whitman "the Lincoln of our literature." Certainly, although not usually classified among the Abolitionist poets, there is as clear a call for Negro freedom and equality in Whitman's poetry as in that of Lowell or Whittier or Longfellow. Because of the deeply human or broadly universal qualities of Whitman's poems or passages about the Negro, his words possess, as of today, a lasting rather than merely an historical value. Very simply Whitman wrote:

> . . all the men ever
> born are also my brothers,
> and the women my sisters . . .

And these words might well be part of a United Nations speech today: "I say man shall not hold property in man, I say the least developed person on earth is just as important and sacred to himself or herself, as the most developed person is to himself or herself. I say where liberty draws not the blood out of slavery, there slavery draws the blood out of liberty . . . With one man or woman (no matter which one—I even pick out the lowest) with him or her I now illustrate the whole law; I say that every right, in politics or what-not, shall be eligible to that man or woman on the same terms as any."

Specifically, concerning Negro slavery in the American South, in "By Blue Ontario's Shore" Walt Whitman wrote, "Slavery—the murderous, treacherous conspiracy to raise it upon the ruins of all the rest, On and on, to grapple with it—Assassin! then your life or ours be the stake, and respite no more." In his great "Song of Myself" he pictures a wounded runaway slave, and himself becomes that runaway: "I am the hounded slave, I wince at the bite of the dogs . . . my gore drips . . . I fall on the weeds and stones . . . Agonies are one of my changes of garments. I do not ask the wounded person how he feels, I myself become the wounded person." And in another passage of the same poem, he aids a runaway who "staid with me a week before he was recuperated and pass'd North. I had him sit next me at table, my fire-lock lean'd in the corner." In "By the Roadside" Whitman wrote, "Not a grove of the murdered for freedom but grows seed for freedom, in its turn to bear seed which the winds carry afar and re-sow, and the rains and the snows nourish . . . Liberty, let others despair of you—I never despair of you."

Of two slaves at auction in "I Sing the Body Electric" Whitman writes: "A man's body at auction . . . Gentlemen, look on this wonder . . . This is not only one man, this the father of those who shall be fathers in their turns, in him the start of populous states and rich republics, of him countless immortal lives with countless embodiments and enjoyments. How do you know who shall come from the offspring of his offspring through the centuries? . . . A woman's body at auction . . . Have you ever loved the body of a woman? Have you ever loved the body of a man? Do you not see that these are exactly the same to all in all nations and times all over the earth?" Not only does Whitman make it very clear in his poems that he did not believe in slavery, but that he believed in human equality as well: "Whoever degrades another degrades me, and whatever is said or done returns at last to me . . . I give the sign of democracy. By God! I will accept nothing which all cannot have their counterpart of on the same terms." Whitman says, "I observe the slights and degradations cast by arrogant persons upon laborers, the poor, and upon Negroes, and the like," but for him the grass is "growing among black folks as among white," and as for himself, "Neither a servant nor a master I . . . I will be even with you and you shall be even with me."

The power to create human oneness Whitman ascribes to poetry in his "Song of the Answerer" where he writes: "The words of true poems give you more than poems, they give you to form for yourself poems, religions, politics, war, peace, behavior, histories, essays, daily life, and everything else. They balance ranks, colors, races, creeds, and the sexes . . . Whom they take they take into space to behold the birth of stars, to learn one of the meanings, to launch off with absolute faith, to sweep through the ceaseless rings and never be quiet again." These "ceaseless rings" of Walt Whitman's poems embrace us all and, in the clearest of terms, project the issues of today and the concepts upon which they must be solved. "Leaves of Grass" is as contemporary as tomorrow's newspaper.

"My Collaborator: Kurt Weill," LHP 729 (October 27, 1955)

Kurt Weill vas a great folk artist. I use *folk* in the sense of meaning one who could capture in his art the least common denominator uniting all humanity. He did it in Germany. He did it in France. And he did it in the United States of America. Kurt Weill was not French. He was not an American, except in the formal sense of naturalization papers. By nature definitely he was not American. But by nature, he was a human being and an artist. Being an artist, *in the true sense of the word,* he understood all human beings, and *all* their songs—for good songs are but the dream, the hopes, and the inner cries deep in the souls of all the peoples of the world. Kurt Weill did not scorn even the least of these songs—for he knew that the least might well be the most. Neither did he scorn their national forms and folk shapes. That is why he could write *The Protagonist* in Germany, *Maria Gallante* in France, and *Street Scene* in America, and each rang true.

For example, in preparing a very specific piece of Americana for *Street Scene,* the Negro blues near the beginning of the first act, Kurt Weill went with me to various Harlem cabarets and listened to numerous blues records—for musical form. The content which I supplied in words, he immediately recognized as a least common denominator for anybody and everybody. The result: *A Marble and a Star,* set to music in an American Negro national idiom—but which a German might sing, or anyone else, and without seeming affected or strange. Kurt Weill was an artist of the heart first, but also a great craftsman in order to give form in music to what he as an artist felt.

In preparing the *Children's Game* at the opening of Act One of *Street Scene,* that it might be as American as possible in form and content, we watched children at play in the New York streets—hours of watching—for they were not always playing singing games, so we had therefore to wait and watch. We went to a session of the Folklore Society devoted to children's games and learned a little, too, from what was said there. Elmer Rice, with his keen ear and great feeling for what the common people say and do, helped us with the lyrics of this sequence. And my own knowledge of the relation between the comic books and comic strips in the newspapers and their influence on children's lives in America, supplied some of the links between newspaper fantasy and playing reality—for Harold Teen and Superman of the comic strips have taken the place of Jack and the Beanstalk and the Fairy Princess in the lives of big city children in the United States today. Kurt Weill took the lyrics we produced and made of them a children's game so real that many people thought it was real—and so American that it has become so. That is why I know Kurt Weill was a folk artist—a universal folk artist. Had he immigrated to India instead of the United States of America, I believe he would have written wonderful Indian musical plays, and re-created realistic Indian children's games. Only the universal man and the universal artist could do this.

Some people contend that when Kurt Weill worked in the vein of popular theatre he became "commercial." I contend instead that he became universal. In New York had Weill written in the strict style and form of traditional opera, he would have had a very small audience—for opera in the United States is still regarded as "European" and has appeal to but a small group of music lovers outside the patrons of the Metropolitan. But by writing a "Broadway opera" such as *Street Scene* in a national idiom understood by the American people, Kurt Weill reached them, and stirred them to compassion, pity, and understanding of themselves as he could not have done had he not written in their own language. The purpose of art, in my opinion, is communication, the wider the better. Kurt Weill was a great musical communicator. He had something to say and he said it in the simplest and most direct terms, in the surface language of each country in which he lived, but in the universal language of that world beyond worlds to which all human souls are related. No man belongs to any one country *really.* You don't. I don't. Nobody does. And least of all (yet most of all) does the true artist. That is why Germany can claim Kurt Weill as German, France as French, American as American, and I as a Negro.

That I, an American Negro, should be chosen to write the lyrics of *Street Scene* did not seem odd or strange to Kurt Weill and Elmer Rice. They both wanted someone who understood the problems of the common people. Certainly Negroes understand these, for they are almost all common people. They wanted someone who wrote simply. I write simply because I myself am simple, and my people are not yet highly sophisticated nor greatly cultured. The characters in the original dramatic play of *Street Scene* are simple uncultured people. Weill wanted a poet. I am glad he considered me one. He wanted someone who knew city life. I grew up in Mexico City, Kansas City, Chicago, Cleveland, and New York—all big metropolitan centers. So when Mr. Weill and Mr. Rice asked me to consider doing the lyrics for *Street Scene,* I did not need to ask them why they thought of me for the task. I never did ask them. I knew.

We worked fourteen months on the show before it was ready for rehearsals. We worked several weeks on it after that, changing, testing, deleting, as we went along. The number that gave us all the most trouble was "Wrapped in a Ribbon and Tied in a Bow." To get this graduation song just right, natural, real, yet in theatrical form, took us a whole summer. Even then it was re-written twice after the show opened in Philadelphia, before it came to Broadway. Kurt Weill was a hardworking artist and a very careful craftsman who did not mind doing and re-doing a musical sequence over until music matched words, and words matched music, and the whole was just what it should be in terms of emotional expressiveness, character-true and situation-true, as well as communicative in theatrical terms. To get the graduation story just right in terms of all these requirements took all of us almost as much time as it did to work out an entire act of the rest of the show.

Two beautiful songs were discarded, "Italy in Technicolor" as Rose imagined that land might be from seeing it in motion pictures, and a "Horoscope Song" for one of the women to sing in her window. Otherwise, the show is intact as performed in New York, U.S.A. It is a very American show. But understood anywhere where ordinary people—like Mrs. Maurrant—who can never "believe that life was meant to be all dull and gray," and who "always will believe there'll be a brighter day."

"A Night at the Apollo," liner notes, LHP 804 (February 18, 1956)

The Apollo Theatre in Harlem is an institution—but nobody in Harlem would think of calling it that. It is generally referred to more precisely as "the old Apollo" and sometimes affectionately as the "jive joint." It has the noisiest audiences and the rudest ushers on the North American continent. But the noises are happy noises complimenting the usual happy goings-on on the stage. And the ushers, who are seldom prominent except on those occasions when numbered seats are sold—namely Saturday midnight and Wednesday amateur night performances—would claim, no doubt, that they have to be rude in order to cope at all with non-numerical minded patrons in relation to numbered seats. For at these performances, at first almost nobody sits where he or she is supposed to sit, so great arguments between ushers and patrons ensue, with much use of searchlights, since usually the patrons have dropped their ticket stubs on the floor as soon as they have taken the best seats their natural eyes can find. Late comers, at these often sold-out-in-advance shows, are likely never to get the seats they have paid for. But, by tipping an usher, one might even get better seats. And when the grade B movies go off, just before the theme for the stage show begins, an ice cream vendor comes up and down the aisles, and there's time for everybody to cool off.

Then a hidden orchestra softly begins to play, "I May Be Wrong but I Think You're Wonderful," the warm and familiar syncopated theme of the "old Apollo," and a kind of musical glow spreads over the house, all the way up from the lower floor where a liberal sprinkling of white faces gleam in the darkness to the balcony, and on up to the gallery which is 99½% pure Harlem and whose heart throbs with the music all the time it's playing. The Apollo is primarily a musical theatre and its entertainment is vaudeville built around a name band or smaller musical combination, and/or a singing star. A few times in the summer off season, when the Apollo has essayed drama, its box office has not done too well. I saw there once an excellent all-colored cast enliven *Tobacco Road* and the following week perform with effectiveness *Detective Story.* But the Harlem public did not flock to these revivals of Broadway fare in anywhere near the numbers that are drawn by Bonnemere, Sarah Vaughan or the Duke, not to mention the Count.[26] Perhaps, however, if Pigmeat Markham had been starred in *Tobacco Road* the theatre might have been filled, and if Jackie "Moms" Mabley had played the old cracker grandma, it probably would have been S.R.O. all summer.

Next to music, it is comedy that most delights an Apollo audience. In my opinion, some of the best comedians in America perform on the Apollo stage. They are little known elsewhere, but in a five-show day at the Apollo, these artists in humor clock up almost as many laughs as might some of the biggest Hollywood or TV clowns in a whole season. Miss Jackie Mabley, working on home ground with her own material, is one of the great female comics of our time, ranking quite easily with Bea Lillie or Imogene Coca. And to Harlemites Mr. Pigmeat Markham is undoubtedly as funny as any performer on two feet, not excluding Jimmy Durante. The late Dusty Fletcher of "Open the Door, Richard" fame was another Apollo favorite, as was Eddie Greene who went from Harlem to radio. Working straight without benefit of makeup, Willie Bryant and Nipsey Russell are among the funniest Masters of Ceremonies in the business. And Leonard Reed, currently managing the Apollo, is a great laugh-getter, too.[27] Unfortunately, for customers from outside the community, the nuances of some of the Apollo's funniest comedy is, on occasion, likely to be entirely *en famille,* and rather hard to explain to strangers without going to great lengths. But, mostly, it has the gusto and openness of the humor of unabashed burlesque without seeming off-color even when it is. For example, Jackie Mabley once said, "I've been reading in the papers about Mother England. There's a mother for you." It was five minutes before the show could continue.

Apollo audiences are discriminating. They know instinctively good jazz from bad, empty "progressive" music from intelligent "progressive" music, *low* low comedy from good low comedy—and they have been known to hoot a flat comedian or laugh a pretentious musician off the stage. For a new performer at the Apollo, the opening show can be a real test of nerves and ability. And even a veteran might think twice before signing a contract for a week there if it is to be a first appearance. Star billing without star ability has sometimes been fatal at the Apollo. Yet to the young and nervous, Apollo audiences are often very kind. The current vogue for quartettes has brought many a group of singing youngsters to the Apollo stage, and it is heartwarming sometimes to observe how an Apollo audience, with rhythmical handclapping or shouts of encouragement, will help four young singers who can't find the key to get together and swing into their number. Old time quartettes like the Ravens get an ovation, of course, and newcomers like the Heartbreakers sometimes get an ovation, too—maybe just because they are trying so hard, and the listeners recognize their potentialities.

It was an Apollo audience that first recognized the possibilities of Ella Fitzgerald at an amateur hour. This amateur hour now occurs every Wednesday night after the final professional show and may be observed on the same ticket. Sometimes an Apollo amateur hour can be almost as moving and exciting as a Spanish bull fight—except that in a bull fight not always does a matador get killed. But every amateur night at the Apollo, some one or more of the participants are "done away with" in plain sight, "killed"—literally shot—but fortunately with a blank cartridge. Those amateurs who do not make the grade, who are interrupted by laughter and whistles of impatience from the audience—which are really at heart a kindly warning to the aspirants not to hope further for a career on the tough professional stage—are shot by a clown who prances out from the wings to the syncopated music and points in rhythm a jive pistol at the untalented amateur and "blows him down." A few spectators claim to find this almost as cruel as some Americans do "the moment of decision" in the Spanish bullfight. And certainly the moment of the blank cartridge at the Apollo is a moment that changes many a young life. But some of the youthful singers or dancers or monologuists who manage to survive an Apollo amateur night go on to fame and fortune—as did Miss Fitzgerald and Sarah Vaughan. And others who are top prize winners sometimes receive a week's contract at the Apollo to try out their abilities for thirty shows.

On the Apollo stage the finest of American Negro talent has performed—and some excellent white talent, too, for the shows are not always entirely Negro. George Shearing, Tito Puente, and Gene Krupa are favorites there. But the record breakers have been bands like that of Lionel Hampton and Count Basie, and stars like Josephine Baker, Pearl Bailey, Sammy Davis, and Eartha Kitt who had the box office lines all the way to the corner. But although the big names appear there frequently, such stars do not hold forth each and every week at the Apollo. A more typical show (and sometimes in the over-all quite as entertaining as a bill with a big headliner might be) is the show recorded in this first album ever made at Harlem's most famous theatre—a show with a real Apollo veteran in it, Jackie Mabley; a new young comedian, George Kirby, whose tape impersonations are marvellous; the well-known tap-dancers who make "much music" with their feet, Coles & Atkins; and the quartette of appealing youngsters, the Heartbreakers. Also, for it does not happen all the time—as the marquee announces—THIS WEEK—GIRLS—a chorus line, the

Dyerettes.[28] And, to climax the evening, when this show was recorded, it was amateur night at the Apollo. So here are two shows for one! Sit back and relax, and listen to that theme song. . . . Feel a glow?

"Humor and the Negro Press," speech made at the Windy City Press Club Banquet, LHP 515 (January 10, 1957)

I am delighted to be invited to Chicago by the Windy City Press Club which is, I understand, an interracial club—but, from all I can gather, somewhat Negro orientated. I live in Harlem, and you can see from looking at me what my orientation is. I went to college in New York, and later to Lincoln University. I have been exposed to lots of literature in my time—but my favorite reading is the Negro press. Perhaps it should be the Iliad, the Odyssey, Shakespeare, or Tolstoy, but it isn't. It is the Negro press. Every week the Lord sends, if possible, in Harlem I buy the *Afro*, the *Courier*, the *Amsterdam News*, and, of course, the *Defender* for which I write—so I can read myself. Also I buy whatever local colored papers there are in whatever city I may be when traveling. Whenever I find myself in a town where the colored papers are not available—like Carmel, California, for instance—I feel on week-ends as though I were completely out of this world and have lost contact with my people. Abroad the two things that I miss most are American ice cream and Negro newspapers.

In my time I have been all around the world and I assure you there is nothing printed in the world like the American Negro press. It is unique, intriguing, exciting, exalting, low-down, and terrific. It is also tragic and terrible, brave, pathetic, funny, and full of tears. It's me and my papa and mama and Adam Powell and Hazel Scott and Daddy Grace and Rev. Martin Luther King, Eartha Kitt, and folks who are no blood relations of mine, but are brothers and sisters in skin.[29] It is also George S. Schuyler.

When I was a child, headlines in the colored papers used to scare the daylights out of me. I grew up in Kansas and for years I was afraid to go down South, thinking—as a result of the Negro press—that I might be lynched the minute I got off the train. Now the colored papers still help to keep me afraid of the Southern white folks. Even on the days when white folks do not do anything bad to me, I read in the papers about what they have just done to others. Democracy as recorded in the Negro press certainly has a woeful record.

However, up to date, America's traditional freedom of speech finds one of its strongest examples in the Negro press. There the Negro race says just about anything it wishes to say concerning white folks, and democracy, too. *The Black Dispatch* of Oklahoma City, edited by Roscoe Dungee, has some of the longest, strongest, and most unique editorials against prejudice in the world.

Humor in headlines is also a unique contribution of certain of our race papers. The *Baltimore Afro-American* and the *Los Angeles Tribune* are particularly blessed with impish souls in the editorial rooms. (In the case of the *Tribune* I suspect it is Almena Lomax who is the female Philip Wylie of Negro journalism.)[30] The leading editorial in the *Tribune*'s pre–Mother's Day issue once was, THE HAND THAT ROCKS THE CRADLE HAS THE WORLD ALL LOUSED UP. Easterners have not yet forgotten an *Afro-American* news headline some years ago: GROOM HONEYMOONS WITH BEST MAN. Since then, the *Afro* has inserted many more laughs into its heads and even more into its news coverage.

But Negro newspapers usually do not intend to be funny—and usually they are not. For a race with so great a sense of humor, however, as that of the Negro people, it is strange that we have no primarily humorous publications. Since we have in our race a number of excellent cartoonists—some unsurpassed in America—and since we have several good writers capable of creating fun on paper, a humorous Negro magazine should be a welcome addition to American cultural life and a happy success from the beginning. For cartoonists there are E. Simms Campbell, kingpin of *Esquire;* Ollie Harrington, creator of Bootsie; Mel Tapley of the *Amsterdam News;* and Mary Bell, an artist in Boston who could be a cartoonist if she wanted to be; plus a number of others.[31]

For writers of humor there is the inimitable Zora Neale Hurston who is one of the most amusing and aggravating female scribes living. There is Evelyn Cunningham, Nat Williams, Enoch Waters, and Ted Poston, also George S. Schuyler whose wry satire carries a punch as well as a laugh. There is Dan Burley, the Ring Lardner of the Negro race, and an old past master of Harlem jive talk. There is Arna Bontemps who has a rare sense of humor when he chooses to put his mind to it. And maybe Willie Bryant, Nipsey Russell, Jackie Mabley, or Timmie Rogers could dictate a bit of hot cha for publication now and then.[32]

The serious colored magazines like the *Crisis* or *Phylon* do not publish humor even if given to them *free*. These magazines evidently think the race problem is too deep for comic relief. Such earnestness is contrary to mass Negro thinking. Colored people are always laughing at some wry Jim Crow incident or absurd nuance of the color line. If Negroes took all the white world's daily boorishness to heart and wept over it as profoundly as our serious writers do, we would have been dead long ago.

Humor is a weapon, too, of no mean value against one's foes. In the Latin American countries, it is used socially. The humorous magazines there are often more dangerous to a crooked but ambitious politician than the most serious articles in the intellectual press. Think what colored people in the United States could do with a magazine devoted to satire and fun at the expense of the Dixiecrats! Since we have not been able to moralize them out of existence with indignant editorials, maybe we could laugh them to death with well-aimed ridicule.

The race problem in America is serious business, I admit. But must it *always* be written about seriously? So many weighty volumes, long dissertations, cheerless novels, sad tracts, and violent books have been written on race relations, that I would like to see some writers of both races write about integration, segregation, and the racial state of the nation with black tongue in white cheek—or vice versa. Sometimes I try. Simple, with his beer at the bar, helps me. The other day he said to me, "Listen, you know, with my wife's help—her name is Joyce—I have writ a poem."

"I know you are determined to read it to me," I said, "so go ahead."

"It is about that minister down in Montgomery who has committed a miracle," said Simple.

"What miracle?" I asked.

"Getting Negroes to stick together," said Simple.

"I presume you are speaking of Rev. King," I said.

"I am," said Simple, "and this is my poem. Listen fluently now! I have writ it like a letter, and it is addressed to the White Citizens Councillors of Alabama. And here it goes:

> Dear Citizens Councillors:
> In line of what my folks say in Montgomery,
> In line of what they're teaching about love,
> When I reach out my hand,
> Will *you* take it?
> Or will you try to cut it off
> And make a nub?

Since I found it in my heart to love you,
If I love you like I really could,
If I say, "Brother, I forgive you,"
I wonder, would it do *you* any good?

So long, *so long* a time
You've been calling me *all* kinds of names,
Pushing me down.
I been swimming with my head deep under water—
And you wished I would stay under till I drowned.

Well, I didn't! I'm still swimming!
Now, you're mad
Because I won't ride in the back end of your bus.
When I answer, "Anyhow, I'm gonna love you,"
Still and yet, *right now today,*
You want to make a fuss.

Listen, white folks!
In line with Reverend King in Montgomery—
Also, because the Bible says I must—
I'm gonna love you—
I say, I'm gonna love you!
I'll be DAMNED if I won't love you—OR BUST!

"Langston Hughes' Speech at the National Assembly of Authors and Dramatists Symposium: 'The Writer's Position in America,'" Alvin Theatre, New York City, May 7, 1957, *Mainstream* (July 1957): 46–48

Bruce Catton spoke today of the writer's chance to be heard.[33] My chance to be heard, as a Negro writer, is not so great as your chance if you are white. I once approached the Play Service of the Dramatists Guild as to the handling of some of my plays. *No,* was the answer, they would not know where to place plays about Negro life. I once sent one of my best known short stories, before it came out in book form, to one of our oldest and foremost American magazines. The story was about racial violence in the South. It came back to me with a very brief little note saying the editor did not believe his readers wished to read about such things. Another story of mine which did not concern race problems at all came back to me from one of our best known editors of anthologies of fiction with a letter praising the story but saying that he, the editor, could not tell if the characters were white or colored. Would I make them definitely Negro? Just a plain story about human beings from me was not up his alley, it seems. So before the word *man* I simply inserted *black,* and before the girl's name, the words *brown skin*—and the story was accepted. Only a mild form of racial bias. But now let us come to something more serious.

Censorship, the Black List: Negro writers, just by being black, have been on the blacklist all our lives. Do you know that there are libraries in our country that will not stock a book by a Negro writer, not even as a gift? There are towns where Negro newspapers and magazines cannot be sold—except surreptitiously. There are American magazines that have *never* published anything by Negroes. There are film studios that have never hired a Negro writer. Censorship for us begins at the color lines.

As to the tangential ways in which many white writers may make a living: I've already mentioned Hollywood. Not once in a blue moon does Hollywood send for a Negro writer, no matter how famous he may be. When you go into your publishers' offices, how many colored editors, readers, or even secretaries do you see? In the book review pages of our Sunday supplements and our magazines, how often do you see a Negro reviewer's name? And if you do, 9 times out of 10 the Negro reviewer will be given a book by another Negro to review—seldom if ever, *The Sea Around Us* or *Auntie Mame*—or *Compulsion*—and yet a reviewer of the calibre of Arna Bontemps or Ann Petry or J. Saunders Redding could review anybody's books, white or colored, interestingly. Take Lecturing: There are thousands and thousands of women's clubs and other organizations booking lecturers that have never had, and will not have, a Negro speaker—though he has written a best seller.

We have in America today about a dozen top flight, frequently published and really good Negro writers. Do you not think it strange that of that dozen, at least half of them live abroad, far away from their people, their problems, and the sources of their material: Richard Wright—*Native Son* in Paris; Chester Himes—*The Primitives* in Paris; James Baldwin—*Giovanni's Room* in Paris; William Demby—*Beetle Creek* in Rome; Frank Yerby—of the dozen best sellers, in Southern France; and Willard Motley—*Knock on Any Door* in Mexico. Why? Because the stones thrown at Autherine Lucy at the University of Alabama are thrown at them, too. Because the shadow of Montgomery and the bombs under Rev. King's house, shadow them and shatter them, too. Because the body of little Emmett Till drowned in a Mississippi river and no one brought to justice, haunts them, too. One of the writers I've mentioned, when last I saw him before he went abroad, said to me, "I don't want my children to grow up in the shadow of Jim Crow."[34]

And so let us end with children. And let us end with poetry—since somehow the planned poetry panel for which I was to have been a part did not materialize. So therefore, there has been no poetry in our National Assembly. Forgive me then, if I read a poem. It's about a child—a little colored child. I imagine her as being maybe six or seven years old. She grew up in the Deep South where our color lines are still legal. Then her family moved to a Northern or Western industrial city—one of those continual migrations of Negroes looking for a better town. There in this Northern city—maybe a place like Newark, New Jersey, or Omaha, Nebraska, or Oakland, California, the little girl goes one day to a carnival, and she sees the merry-go-round going around, and she wants to ride. But being a little colored child, and remembering the South, she doesn't know if she can ride or not. And if she can ride, where? So this is what she says:

Where is the Jim Crow section
On this merry-go-round,
Mister, cause I want to ride?
Down South where I come from
White and colored
Can't sit side by side.
Down South on the train
There's a Jim Crow car.
On the bus we're put in the back—
But there ain't no back
To a merry-go-round:
Where's the horse
For a kid that's black?

"How Real Is Make-Believe?"
LHP 511 (September 1957)

Jesse B. Semple and Joyce, the girl he loves, are the only characters—out of the many I have created in fiction—whom some readers seem to think are actually living, breathing contemporary human beings.[35] For some fifteen years now Jesse B. Semple, better known as Simple, has been speaking his mind on various subjects in my weekly column in the *Chicago Defender* and there Joyce often speaks her mind, too.

Meanwhile Simple has appeared as a character in three books, several theatre sketches, on musical revue, and now in *Simply Heavenly* at the Playhouse. But all of these were make-believe characterizations first on paper then in the theatre. Nevertheless the Simple of the typewriter has been taken for a real live man by unknown readers more than once, and over the years he has been sent a number of letters addressed directly, not to *me* as author, but to him.

A few autumns ago a fan in Tennessee, reading Simple's words on the delights of southern food, sent him a possum skinned and packed in dry ice. This created a problem for the author for, although I had eaten possum and liked it, I was acquainted with no one in Harlem who knew how to roast a possum. It took me several days to locate someone to cook the animal. But when it appeared on table, done to a turn and with sweet potatoes all around it, it was delicious and I, the writer, ate it. But one Christmas some presents arrived for Joyce which were of no use to me at all. A woman in Mississippi, having read about Joyce making lingerie for a girl friend about to get married (which I later converted into a scene in *Simply Heavenly*) made for Joyce herself a beautiful quilted boudoir bag and in it, all hand-sewn, she placed a pair of quilted slippers, a brassier, and a pair of panties edged with lace. For fear no one would believe me, these amazing gifts, along with the Christmas card bearing Joyce's name, I have saved to this very day, as well as a letter which the woman later wrote to Joyce about sewing.

I as a writer am, of course, flattered that my make-believe characters seem real to the people who write to them. I was even pleased with a letter from one reader of the *Chicago Defender* who said that she wished I would stop expressing my own opinions in the paper and let Simple do all the talking. She said she agreed with all Simple had to say, but did not like what I wrote at all! From this reader, I gather that she seems to think Simple can just walk away from my typewriter and stand on his own two feet all by himself. Maybe he can. Sometimes he acts like it. In fact, sometimes he does.

"You're Simple if You Want to Write a Play,"
LHP 3851 (September 25, 1957)

Usually after every venture of mine into the commercial theatre, I swear, *Never again!*[36] It is much simpler and easier to write a book and see it through the printer's than it is to write a play and follow it through production. A novel, a collection of short stories, or a book of poems is generally all one's *own* creation. What suggestions a sympathetic editor in a publisher's office may offer are usually few and of minor importance. But the suggestions which everyone offers who looks at a play script are generally many and major, requiring a great deal of time, trouble, and thought to consider. What it is about the manuscript of a play that causes almost any reader, from the very first page, to begin demanding changes, I will never know. But that is usually what happens to a playwright's work when it comes to readers, directors, producers, and even actors. All want something changed, and often a great many changes. Nobody is ever satisfied with a play as it is—except the author. And to most directors, the only good author is a dead author.

Directors can think of more ways of changing plays than an author ever thought possible, and producers are almost as bad. Although a playwright may think his third act wonderful, to a director it is never right. I think that is why some contemporary dramatists write plays in two acts, to avoid the customary hassle over the alleged defects of the third act. A dramatist may defend the ending of his play by swearing that it is true to life. But the powers that be in production will declare that life is not art, truth is not good theatre, and in any case what the author has dreamed up would never be box-office. The word "box-office" is the key word in the Broadway theatre. In fact, Broadway and box-office are practically synonymous. On Broadway, if there is no box-office, there will be no play for long.

That is one reason why, for my current stage venture, I sought the off-Broadway theatre. Many off-Broadway theatres do not even have a box-office. They just sell tickets across a table, or hand them out on a "contribution" basis. And the seating capacities of the houses are so limited that it makes not too much difference be they full or empty, since the production pay rolls are limited, too, and the over-all budget low. For my show, *Simply Heavenly,* I wanted an off-Broadway production where unhampered by high rents, union stage hands, and steep production costs, it might run long enough for me to enjoy it a half dozen times myself. I was happy to get such a production at the 85th Street Playhouse, a genial hall belonging to the Order of the True Sisters, whose resemblance to a theatre at all was purely coincidental, in truth, in name only. After forty-four performances the Fire Department came to the same conclusion, and closed us up. But by that time I had had a lot of fun with the play.

From the beginning I conceived *Simply Heavenly* as a two-act play, so that I would not have to argue with anybody over a third act. *Simply*

Heavenly never had a third act. And into the mouths of its various characters I put a number of fantasies, so that much of what is enclosed within the framework of its two acts may be called either *life* or *art,* as producer or director might prefer, thus avoiding arguments on that score. As to "good theatre" I learned long ago that lines or situations which produce audible laughs in a playhouse cause producers and directors to term them "good theatre." So I made the characters and situations in *Simply Heavenly* as amusing as I knew how. Fortunately, audiences in 85th Street laughed out loud, and often. By the time the two acts were over, they applauded as if they wanted more, and walked out smiling. Why have a third act?

It took *Simply Heavenly* about four years to get from its initial conception on paper to its final form on the stage. Along the way several producers and directors had their hands on the script at one time or another. Each man or woman who touched it had different ideas for changes, cuts, additions, or new scenes. For these eventualities I was fairly well prepared in front. Since the play was derived from my Simple books—*Simple Speaks His Mind* and *Simple Takes a Wife* with a bit of the latest one, *Simple Stakes a Claim* in it, too—I had plenty of material to dramatize. So I dramatized almost all the chapters in these books. So when a directorial personality did not like a scene, offering elaborate suggestions for a new bit, I could almost always go to my files and pull out an already dramatized sequence—since the Simple books cover a lot of ground—that would suit his fancy, and substitute it for the old scene, without losing character at all. I had fun letting the directors think I am a fast writer. I wrote *Simply Heavenly* for fun, so I saw no harm in having fun out of its production processes, as well.

Songs are the most fun. Originally a comedy without music, *Simply Heavenly* at one point in its evolution had twenty numbers. But then it would have lasted as long as *The Ice Man Cometh* so I eventually kept only the best songs. The others went back into the files, maybe for future Central European productions, where spectators eat between acts and like shows to be longer. My composer, David Martin, an excellent jazz piano player and a long-time worker in the vineyards of pop music and the blues, was an amiable tunesmith with whom to work. We enjoyed putting together "Let Me Take You for a Ride," "Did You Ever Hear the Blues," "When I'm in a Quiet Mood" and other songs in the show. And the syncopated march for Simple's "Dixie Day Dream" gave us lots of laughs in the composing of it. It still tickles me on the stage as General Simple leads his white Mississippi troops off into the rocking wings of the Playhouse in 48th Street where Local 802 now provides the show with a heavenly musical combination—Sticks Evans, Al Hall, Paul Webster and men like them whaling away.[37] And it all seems to add up to "box-office." The tickets to *Simply Heavenly* are no longer sold across a table as they were uptown. And I can stand on Broadway and look up to see the name of my show all lighted up. Lucky, I guess! Book writing is nice, peaceful, a quiet occupation. But I believe I'll write another show—even if I do tell young folks who want to be playwrights, "You must be simple."

"Children and Poetry," *The Langston Hughes Reader* (New York: George Braziller, 1958), 145–48

Children are not nearly so resistant to poetry as are grown-ups. In fact, small youngsters are not resistant at all. But in reading my poems to children from kindergarten to junior high school age, I sometimes think they might want to know *why* people write poetry. So I explain to them:

> If you put
> Your thoughts in rhyme
> They stay in folks' heads
> A longer time.

Since most people want others to remember what they say, poetry helps people to remember.

For instance, I say, "Does your mother ever send you to the store and you forget what she sent you after? Or you bring back the wrong thing? That often happened to me when I was a boy. But if my mother had told me in verse what she wanted, for example:

> Langston, go
> To the store, please,
> And bring me back
> A can of peas.

"I wouldn't have brought back a can of corn. *Please* and *peas* rhyme, which makes it easy to remember. Or if my mother had said:

> Sonny, kindly
> Do me a favor

And go get a bottle
Of vanilla flavor.

"Then I am sure I would not have gotten a bottle of vinegar. The word *flavor,* not simply *bottle,* would have stuck in my head because of its sound tag with *favor.* That is one reason why:

To make words sing
Is a wonderful thing—
Because in a song
Words last so long.

"Of course," I say, "there are other very good reasons for making rhymes or writing poetry. One is to share a beautiful or moving scene or experience that you have known. When I first saw the new high-arching bridges in San Francisco, one spanning the Golden Gate and the other leaping across the city's harbor, I made up a poem called, TRIP:

I went to San Francisco.
I saw the bridges high
Spun across the water
Like cobwebs in the sky.

"And when I saw the city all sparkling with lights at night—also remembering other cities like New York, Cincinnati, Chicago, Dallas, with tall cliff-like buildings—this is the song I wrote:

In the morning the city
Spreads its wings
Making a song
Of stone that sings.

In the evening the city
Goes to bed
Hanging lights
About its head.

"When the sun is hidden behind a sky of grey, soft and fluffy and dark, it seems as though the heavens had sort of wrapped up for bad weather, so it goes into rhyme like this:

The clouds weave a shawl
Of downy plaid

For the sky to put on
When the weather's bad.

"But here is a poem of much brighter cloth. All of us have seen gypsy women in gay, colorful clothes, wide skirts swinging as they stride. Maybe some of us have lived near a vacant lot where a gypsy family has stopped for a day or two to cook and wash. To see their vari-colored garments hanging on a line from tree to tree is a wonderful sight. I once tried to capture something of the gypsies in a poem:

Gypsies are picture-book people
Hanging picture-book clothes on a line.
The gypsies fill the vacant lots
With colors gay as wine.

The gypsies' skins are olive-dark,
The gypsies' eyes black fire.
The gypsies wear bright headcloths dyed
By some elfin dyer.

The gypsies wear gay glassy beads
Strung on silver threads
And walk as though forever
They've had suns about their heads.

"But poems need not always be about what one sees or thinks or feels oneself. During the war I was deeply moved by the plight of many poor people in Europe mistreated and enslaved by the Nazis suffering bombardments and hunger and cold. Some were fortunate enough to escape and get to the United States. There must have been great joy in their hearts when they saw our Statue of Liberty. And when those who are permitted to become citizens of our country take the Oath of Allegiance, they must feel a great emotion such as I have tried to capture in my poem, REFUGEE IN AMERICA:

There are words like *Freedom*
Sweet and wonderful to say.
On my heart-strings freedom sings
All day everyday.

There are words like *Liberty*
That almost make me cry.
If you had known what I knew
You would know why.

"To help us all remember what America is, and how its future belongs to all of us, recently I added two new lines to an old poem of mine—the last two lines to help us remember to walk together:

> We have tomorrow
> Bright before us
> Like a flame.
>
> Yesterday
> A night-gone thing,
> A sun-down name.
> And dawn-today
> Broad arch above
> The road we came.
>
> We march!
> Americans together,
> We march!

"The Fun of Being Black,"
The Langston Hughes Reader, 498–500

It is a shame to say it, but apparently mankind thrives on conflict. A nation is never so alert and alive as when it is a nation at war. Literature, science, and art may thrive on peace, but the ordinary human being seems to have a hell of a good time out of conflicts, whether they be wars, political battles, arguments, athletic contests, debates or just plain old free-for-alls.

Some of the world's most stirring songs are songs of conflict. One that belongs to France but is loved by the whole world is "La Marseillaise" which begins somewhat to this effect, "Let's go, sons of our country! The bloody flag of tyranny is raised against us." And then proceeds to unfurl some of the most stirring martial words in musical literature.

One of America's greatest songs is "The Battle Hymn of the Republic" which starts:

> Mine eyes have seen the glory
> Of the coming of the Lord . . . .
> He has loosed the fateful lightning
> Of His terrible swift sword . . . .

In other words, He is ready to fight.

One of our most venerable Christian hymns goes:

> Onward, Christian soldiers,
> Marching as to war. . . .

So I do not know why some folks (me included) are always lamenting the particular fact that we have a race conflict in America—because a great many people get a great deal of fun out of our contemporary white-Negro battles, not to speak of the jobs that are held as a result. Look at the number of Civil Rights lawyers who make a living and a reputation suing white folks, or fighting Jim Crow vote cases or teacher's salary inequalities right on up to the Supreme Court—and what a kick they get out of defeating some of our reactionary white folks. Look at the joy with which the NAACP attacks a segregation problem, or the delight with which the Urban League goes after factory owners who won't hire Negroes.

And did you ever hear Mary McLeod Bethune make a speech about Negro rights? Do you recall with what pride and joy she lifted her ample bosom to the enemy? And those of us who remember Roscoe Conkling Simmons, can never forget the vim, vigor, vitality—and pleasure—with which he lashed into the problems of the Negro race and, incidentally, tied them all up in the hold of that ship which is the Republican Party to which all else to him is the sea.[38]

Crusaders—off the public platform—are some of the happiest-looking people you could ever hope to meet, possibly because they are so sure of the ultimate triumph of their causes. Negroes in Georgia have told me that the late Eugene Talmadge was really a most amiable man if you met him at home—but he was a hellion in favor of white supremacy in public. That venerable old lady of Communism, Mother Bloor was in person as sweet and full of sunshine as she could be—yet she battled the capitalists tooth and nail for seventy years.[39] Individuals, like nations, seem to thrive on struggle. Look at Joe Louis, still as fat and sassy as he can be after all of his battles!

This racial struggle of ours in America has so many intricate and amusing angles that nobody taking an active part in it can ever be bored. It's very variety from North to South—from Boston where New England Negroes side with New England whites in opposing black southern migration, to Mobile on the Gulf where a Negro dare not oppose anybody—keeps the contest exciting. In the far West a Negro can sometimes eat in a Mexican restaurant but he cannot eat in a Chinese restaurant—so it is fun figuring out just where you can eat. In some towns a colored man can sit in the balcony of a theatre, but in others he has to sit in the last three rows on the left downstairs because the balcony is for whites who smoke. So, trying to see a movie in the United States can be for a Negro as intriguing as working a crossword puzzle.

Those of us engaged in this racial struggle in America are like knights on horseback—the Negroes on a white horse and the white folks on a black. Sometimes the race is terrific. But the feel of the wind in your hair as you ride toward democracy is really something! And the air smells so good!

"Jazz as Communication," *The Langston Hughes Reader,* 492–94

You can start anywhere—Jazz as Communication—since it's a circle, and you yourself are the dot in the middle. You, me. For example, I'll start with the Blues. I'm not a Southerner. I never worked on a levee. I hardly ever saw a cotton field except from the highway. But women behave the same on Park Avenue as they do on a levee: when you've got hold of one part of them the other part escapes you. That's the Blues!

Life is as hard on Broadway as it is in Blues-originating-land. The Brill Building Blues is just as hungry as the Mississippi Levee Blues. One communicates to the other, brother! Somebody is going to rise up and tell me that nothing that comes out of Tin Pan Alley is jazz. I disagree. Commercial, yes. But so was Storeyville, so was Basin Street. What do you think Tony Jackson and Jelly Roll Morton and King Oliver and Louis Armstrong were playing for?[40] Peanuts? No, money, even in Dixieland. They were communicating for money. For fun, too—because they had fun. But the money helped the fun along.

Now; To skip a half century, somebody is going to rise up and tell me Rock and Roll isn't jazz. First, two or three years ago, there were all these songs about too young to know—*but*. . . . The songs are right. You're never too young to know how bad it is to love and not have love come back to you. That's as basic as the Blues. And that's what Rock and Roll is—teenage *Heartbreak Hotel*—the old songs reduced to the lowest common denominator. The music goes way back to Blind Lemon and Leadbelly—Georgia Tom merging into the Gospel Songs—Ma Rainey, and the most primitive of the Blues.[41] It borrows their gut-bucket heartache. It goes back to the jubilees and stepped-up Spirituals—Sister Tharpe—and borrows their I'm-gonna-be-happy-anyhow-in-spite-of-this-world kind of hope. It goes back further and borrows the steady beat of the drums of Congo Square—that going-on beat—and the Marching Bands' loud and blatant *yes!!* Rock and roll puts them all together and makes a music so basic it's like the meat cleaver the butcher uses—before the cook uses the knife—before you use the sterling silver at the table on the meat that by then has been rolled up into a commercial filet mignon.

A few more years and Rock and Roll will no doubt be washed back half forgotten into the sea of jazz. Jazz is a great big sea. It washes up all kinds of fish and shells and spume and waves with a steady old beat, or off-beat. And Louis must be getting old if he thinks J. J. and Kai—and even Elvis—didn't come out of the same sea he came out of, too. Some water has chlorine in it and some doesn't. There're all kinds of water. There's salt water and Saratoga water and Vichy water, Quinine water and Pluto water—and Newport rain. And it's all water. Throw it all in the sea, and the sea'll keep on rolling along toward shore and crashing and booming back into itself again. The sun pulls the moon. The moon pulls the sea. They also pull jazz and me. Beyond Kai to Count to Lonnie to Texas Red, beyond June to Sarah to Billy to Bessie to Ma Rainey. And the Most is the It—the all of it.[42]

Jazz seeps into words—spelled out words. Nelson Algren is influenced by jazz. Ralph Ellison is, too. Sartre, too. Jacques Prévert. Most of the best writers today are. Look at the end of the *Ballad of the Sad Cafe*. Me as the public, *my* dot in the middle—it was fifty years ago, the first time I heard the Blues on Independence Avenue in Kansas City. Then State Street in Chicago. Then Harlem in the twenties with J. P. and J. C. Johnson and Fats and Willie the Lion and Nappy playing piano—with the Blues running all up and down the keyboard through the ragtime and the jazz.[43] House rent party cards. I wrote *The Weary Blues:*

> Downing a drowsy syncopated tune . . . . . . etc. . . . .

Shuffle Along was running then—the Sissle and Blake tunes. A little later *Runnin' Wild* and the Charleston and Fletcher and Duke and Cab. Jimmie Lunceford, Chick Webb, and Ella. Tiny Parham in Chicago. And at the end of the Depression times, what I heard at Minton's. A young music—coming out of young people. Billy—the male and female of them—both the Eckstein and the Holiday—and Dizzy and Tad and the

Monk.[44] Some of it came out in poems of mine in *Montage of a Dream Deferred* later. Jazz again putting itself into words.

But I wasn't the only one putting jazz into words. Better poets of the heart of jazz beat me to it. W. C. Handy a long time before. Benton Overstreet. Mule Bradford. Then Buddy DeSilva on the pop level. Ira Gershwin. By and by Dorothy Baker in the novel—to name only the most obvious—the ones with labels. I mean the ones you can spell out easy with a-b-c's—the word mongers—outside the music. But always the ones of the music were the best—Charlie Christian, for example, Bix, Louis, Joe Sullivan, Count.[45]

Now, to wind it all up, with you in the middle—jazz is only what you yourself get out of it. Louis's famous quote—or misquote probably—"Lady, if you have to ask what it is, you'll never know." Well, I wouldn't be so positive. The lady just might know—without being able to let loose the cry—to follow through—to light up before the fuse blows out. To me jazz is a montage of a dream deferred. A great big dream—yet to come—and always *yet*—to become ultimately and finally true. Maybe in the next seminar—for Saturday—Nat Hentoff and Billy Strayhorn and Tony Scott and the others on that panel will tell us about it—when they take up "The Future of Jazz." The Bird was looking for that future like mad. The Newborns, Chico, Dave, Gulda, Milt, Charlie Mingus.[46] That future is what you call pregnant. Potential papas and mamas of tomorrow's jazz are all known. But THE papa and THE mama—maybe both—are anonymous. But the child will communicate. Jazz is a heartbeat—its heartbeat is yours. You will tell me about its perspectives when you get ready.

"The Roots of Jazz," LHP (ca. 1958?)

Jazz is such happy music because it grew out of such great sadness.[47] Its rhythms of joy were born from the heartbeats of sorrow. In the early 18th Century, Congo Square in New Orleans was one of the saddest happy places in the world. It was there in this open dusty acreage that the slaves held their Sunday dances and all day long beat on their drums the rhythms of Africa. They made intricate wonderful happy music and shook their feet in gay abandon, until the sundown warning sent them back to the slave quarters. When dancing, many of them forgot their bondage. Yet the music itself, for all its gaiety, remembered Africa, the Middle Passage, whips, chains, the slave market, the lifetimes of work, past and to come, without pay and without freedom. So the rhythms of Congo Square became the first sad-happy rhythms that were to set the tempos of American jazz.

Then came the field hollers of the plantations, the work songs of the Levees and the southern roads, the spirituals and jubilees with their undertow of drums and their melodies of sorrow and hope, sadness and faith, darkness and dawn. And, as the years went on, the blues came into being with their mighty music of despair and laughter, of trouble and determination *to laugh* in spite of trouble:

When you see me laughin',
I'm laughin' to keep from cryin'. . . .

It is this combination of sadness and laughter that gives to jazz its unique quality, that roots its deep syncopations in the human soul, that keeps it from ever being a frivolous or meaningless music or merely entertainment, no matter how much it is played for fun. And jazz is fun music. Its spontaneous improvisations, its syncopations, its infectious rhythms are all tributes to the play spirit in men and women—the will to laugh and live. But behind the fun—in the beat of its drums, the cry of the trumpets or the wail of its sax—lie all the shadows of sorrow and suffering that were first woven into the distant origins of this wonderful music. Men and drums stolen from Africa, songs and drums held in the harshness of a new world, rhythms tangled in the tall cane, caught in the white bolls of the cotton, mired in the rice swamps, chained on the levees or in the heat of the Georgia roads, targets for the cross fire of the Civil War, crying in the poverty of Reconstruction:

How long, how long
Has that evenin' train been gone?
How long? How long? How long?

The lacy gaiety of ragtime, the rolling rumble of boogie woogie, the happy dignity of Dixieland bands playing for funerals, parades, dances, picnics, to the swing of swing, the satire of bebop, the heavy beat of rock-and-roll, and the cool sounds of a Charlie Mingus, there is in all this music something of the question, "How long, how long before men and women, races and nations, will learn to live together happily?" The cry and the question are ever present behind the gayest of jazz. It is this longing and this laughter combined that gives jazz its great basic human appeal and endows it with a kind of universality that causes it to be played and loved around the world. Jazz belongs to everybody now.

"Ten Thousand Beds,"
The Langston Hughes Reader, 489–91

Often I hear a person say, "I can't sleep in a strange bed." Such a person I regard with wonder and amazement, slightly tinged with envy. Wonder and amazement that such a small change as a strange bed would keep a person from sleeping, and envy that there are people who stay put so well that any bed other than their own upsets them. At a most conservative estimate, I figure I have slept in at least ten thousand strange beds.

As a child I was often boarded out, sent to stay with relatives, foster-relatives, or friends of the family. And my family itself was always moving, so quite early in life I got used to a variety of beds from the deep feather beds of the country to the studio couches of the town, from camp cots to my uncle's barber chair in Kansas City elongated to accommodate me. If strange beds had been given to upsetting me, I would have lost many a good night's sleep in my life. And there is nothing I like better than to sleep.

This year of our Lord, 1948, for example, I have slept in beds from Montreal, Canada, to New Orleans, Louisiana, from St. Petersburg, Florida, to Spokane, Washington, from Elizabeth City, North Carolina, to Los Angeles, California. Nowhere did I pass a sleepless night. Since January I have slept on trains in lower berths, upper berths, roomettes, and bedrooms, and on planes with the seat reclining flying over mountains and deserts. In anything moving, from cars to trains, boats to planes, I can sleep like a log. I can also sleep in movies, lectures, and theatres, not to speak of concerts, although I do not consider it polite to do so, and I try my best to stay awake.

Sometimes I hear a person say, "I always take a book to bed with me to read myself to sleep." How I envy such a person. I often wish that I could read for an hour or so at night in bed, but I usually go to sleep before I get to the bottom of a page. And it is a nuisance to have to wake up and close the book and put out the light.

I know many people who say they cannot drink coffee at night because it keeps them awake. Often I have wished that coffee would have such an effect on me. I have drunk several cups at times quite late at night, but sleep came down just the same. And once in bed, I did not even dream.

I have never had the need to count sheep. I have tried sometimes to see if I could count a hundred, but I never remember getting beyond thirty-six. I lost all interest in the sheep, being asleep.

Once, having undergone an experience that should have upset my nerves, a physician friend prescribed for me some sleeping pills. That night I said to myself, "If I wake up I will take a pill." So I placed the bottle beside the bed. But I did not wake up until noon the next day, so I never took the sleeping pills. I think I am the kind of fellow who needs pills to wake up rather than to go to sleep. The first night I was in Madrid during the Spanish Civil War, I slept through a Franco bombardment and did not even turn over.

Once in a hotel in the Middle West I was awakened by a loud altercation in the next room. A lady's boy friend was accusing her of infidelity with her dog. And one time in Samarkand, in Central Asia, in the early dawn some camels got to fighting and screaming among themselves just outside the window. Their unholy screeching aroused me before the master of the caravan subdued them. But as a rule I am not easily aroused. And I do not come to my senses immediately upon awakening. I have always admired those persons who can jump out of bed as bright as a dollar as soon as they open their eyes in the morning.

Some writers tell me they do their best writing by arising early and working three or four hours before breakfast. At five A.M. their minds are as clear as a bell. For them I have the greatest admiration. Also for persons like Edison, who can sleep only four or five hours a night, arising refreshed and full of creative powers, I have respect and admiration. Unfortunately, nature endowed me with quite a different constitution. Ten hours sleep suits me much better than five. And twelve hours really restores my soul. I consider it unfortunate that I am not able to get along very well with less than eight hours sleep. On the other hand, I suppose I am fortunate in being able to sleep in any bed, any time, any place anywhere. Ten thousand beds and not a sleepless night although I did wake up once when those folks quarrelled next door, and again when the camels fought outside my window before the caravan set out.

"Speak Well of the Dead," *Ebony,* October 1958, p. 30

Enormous sums of money go into the ground annually to cover the costs of fine funerals. And a part of a fine funeral is a *fine* sermon. To be "put away in style" is the major aim of many Negroes who expect to die. To be preached to heaven, rather than to hell is, of course, a respectable essential of any funeral. Many a minister is paid well to preach well over the late-lamented lying before him. Whether the deceased really lived decently on earth or not is beside the point. Funeral sermons are, in their finality, intended for the living, not the dead, intoned for the mourners rather than the mourned. But sometimes a sermon can go too far.

I once heard of a drunkard who never attended church, beat his wife, mistreated his children, betrayed young girls, cursed, fought, cheated, and died in debt. Nevertheless, when he was wheeled before the pulpit in a plush box the minister intoned, "This dear departed brother resting before us was a good husband, an ever-loving father, a generous provider, and a righteous man whose soul is winging today through celestial space and whose feet are treading the streets of gold." His widow, in bewilderment, turned around to a woman behind and asked, "Honey, am I at the *wrong* funeral?"

Ashes to ashes,
Dust to dust,
If whiskey don't get you,
Women must.

This happy verse which an old-time comedian once inserted into his singing of "I'll Be Glad When You're Dead, You Rascal You," expresses a sentiment seldom, if ever, uttered over the bodies of the numerous rogues and rascals who all over the U.S.A. daily go to their final rest. No minister would dream of frankly damning the damned. For the sake of the mourners, no matter how dark the deeds of the deceased may have been, over his bier some comforting words must be said. Besides, if truth were told in funeral pulpits, ministers in all likelihood would have a very hard time collecting their fees.

Once in a while pastors have been known to demur from any absolute commitment as to the earthly grace of the departed. A minister once preaching over the body of a notorious but good-hearted professional gambler looked mournfully down upon the casket and said, "Son, I cannot preach you, neither can I pray you, or sing you to heaven. Only God knows where *your* soul is gone."

But from the pew where the young underworldling's relatives were seated his mother spoke up and said, "Mama knows where his soul is gone. He's gone to glory!"

"If Mama knows, then that's where he must be," the minister said. "Bless God, Mother will meet him Over There! Amen!" Whereupon the congregation began to shout. His sermon was a success.

"Meeting Mother Over There" is a favorite theme of funereal orations —since it is always taken for granted that *all* mothers automatically go to heaven when they die. Even though some mothers may have been hell on wheels on earth, in death "Mother will be Over There." Yes, she will!

Another amiable funeral fiction is "He is not dead—he's only gone to sleep." Taking this literally, a recent Harlem widow, when she heard the minister describe her deceased husband as "only gone to sleep," cried, "Wake up, Papa! Darling, baby, wake up!" But Papa did not stir. Had he stirred, the church would have been empty in nothing flat.

Ministers are paid to speak well of the dead even when, in truth, there is actually nothing good to be said. But mourners need not go to such lengths of dissimulation in public. Nevertheless, they often do pretend that they think highly of the deceased, too. In Kansas City a man died who had not been living with his wife for several years. Indeed, he resided quite openly with another woman. Yet when he met his end, and the last rites were drawing to a close, his heavily veiled widow fell prostrate over the coffin, wailing, "Oh, Toby, why did you leave me? Husband, why do you have to go? Why did death take you away? Answer me, Toby, answer me!"

"Sister, death cannot break the bonds of love," intoned the minister. "Take comfort in the fact that this man loved you."

"That's a lie," hissed the "other woman" from the third pew back. "He loved *me*!"

Unruffled by this untoward interruption, the minister continued, "His heart was full of love, God knows, just *full* of love."

According to the social status of the family, the style of the church, and the popularity of the minister, rates for the preaching of a good funeral vary from five, ten and twenty dollars to a hundred, or even more in the case of wealthy or distinguished corpses. But rare indeed is the minister who does not expect some sort of fee for laying a soul to rest no matter how poor the soul may be.

There is a story current in Kentucky of a Louisville reverend who, in a most startling way, was tricked out of an expected payment. One of the pillars of his church, a pious deaconess and a fine fund raiser, had the misfortune to be tied to a husband given to frequent wandering and roaming. Sometimes he stayed away from home so long he was afraid to come back to his own fireside, yet return he always did—eventually.

Home was a comfortable place, the food good, and his wife, when she got over her anger, would provide well for him. But once, when the man had been gone an unduly long time, his wife swore she would not take him back again. Indeed, when he wrote her for money to return from a distant city, for once she did not send him a dime.

One day she got a wire from a mortician that he was dead. She screamed, cried, sobbed, and prepared to go at once to the town to get the body. She wired the undertaker who had sent the message, saying she would arrive there on the noon train the next day. Then, she thought, for comfort's sake she would take her pastor with her. On the train, as the widow dozed and dreamed of her now-lost husband, the pastor jotted down notes as to the sermon he would deliver after the body of the dead spouse of his favorite deaconess was shipped back home. When the train arrived at the distant station where they expected an unknown undertaker to meet them, with woebegone face the minister helped the black-veiled widow from the coach. Instead of a strange undertaker, however, who should stand there on the platform but her husband hale, hearty, and alive as could be! With an impish grin he greeted his startled wife, "Baby, I just wanted to find out if you loved me enough to come and get me. Now I see you do!"

The woman fainted. But the minister hollered, "You lowlife rascal! You gonna pay me for your funeral sermon I've already prepared!"

At funerals widows, no matter how bad their husbands have behaved while living, are given usually to tears. In spite of some very eloquent preaching, however, at one husband's funeral in a small New Jersey town, the widow did not cry. Although she was known to be a demonstrative woman, she sat through the services in silence. Pastor, pallbearers, relatives, and friends became worried concerning her pent-up emotions. Even at the very grave itself the bereaved showed no feeling—until the minister came to the lines, "Ashes to ashes and dust to dust," and began sprinkling upon the descending casket of her "beloved spouse" a few grains of earth. At this point the widow's true feeling burst forth. She threw back her veil, stooped down, and picked up the biggest boulder she could find in the freshly dug dirt. She reared back, lifted the stone above her head, and flung it full force into the grave. It struck the dead man's box with a mighty thud.

"Take that, you dirty so-and-so!" was her parting remark to her "loving" husband. "You no-good dog!"

Usually, however, mourners are pleased to have a soul "washed whiter than snow" while his mortal remains still rest above the ground. On the contrary, immediately after burial, attention frequently turns to the will or insurance money. When the last strains of "We Shall Gather at the River" have died away and (at really up-to-date funerals) the nurse has applied smelling salts to the noses of prostrate mourners so that they might rise and follow the casket down the aisle, everything is over but the dividing of the late lamented's worldly goods. Who inherited *what* becomes the burning question. It is well that pastors usually say nice things at funerals, for often in succeeding weeks relatives do not. In the end lawyers are paid larger fees than ministers to straighten out many a departed soul's affairs.

There are certain dangers for the clergy in preaching the funerals of unknowns, but shepherds of God are frequently called upon to say a few final words over persons they have never met. Once a young minister in Harlem was asked to conduct the services of one Vivian Cogley from the British islands of the Caribbean. In the West Indies Vivian is almost as common a name for a man as it is for a woman, so all the way through his sermon the young minister spoke of the gentle charms and womanly virtues of this fine soul now going to her glorious reward. Only after his sermon was over was the pastor informed, "Reverend, Vivian is not a female—he's a man."

New Orleans is famous for its funerals. So is Harlem. New Orleans has brass bands. Harlem has some of the preachingest ministers in the country. New Orleans buries many of its dead in the city in tombs above ground. Harlemites are not buried in Harlem at all, but are transported to Long Island to be put into the sod. When the late Papa Celestin, famous New Orleans trumpeter, died in 1954, so many people overflowed the church and crowded the streets outside that it took almost a half-hour for the pallbearers and police to get the casket through dense crowds to the hearse. Reverend Robert Hill preached a fine sermon over Papa, the Eureka Brass Band played "Just a Little While to Stay Here," and hundreds followed the cortege to the cemetery.

Louisiana's famous fraternal leader, Major Adolphe Osey, lay in state for five days. Since he belonged to more than twenty lodges, including the Odd Fellows and the Elks, his funeral at Fifth Baptist Church lasted for hours, and the resolutions of his numerous orders were filled with praises. As the services began one of several bands played, "I Am Coming to You," and at the grave an unusual touch was rendered in that taps were blown by a *lady* bugler.

Probably the most memorable New Orleans funeral of all was that of Johnny Metoyer who died in 1939. He was president of the Zulus, famous for their Mardi Gras parades. On a Sunday afternoon six thousand people surrounded the packed Mount Zion Baptist Church as within Reverend Duncan preached, Reverend Nash prayed, and a fourteen-piece brass band made music. On the way to Mount Olivet Cemetery dolefully the band played "Flee as a Bird to the Mountain." But on the way back to town, as is the custom with New Orleans funeral bands, the musicians burst into a lively tune and the "second line"—those following the band—pranced ecstatically along the way. In New Orleans they believe in giving everybody's funeral a happy ending.

Harlem has brass bands, too, that sometimes march at funerals. One such band, that of the Prince Hall Masons, played outside New York's Abyssinian Baptist Church as "de evenin' sun went down" for W. C. Handy. Of him the Reverend Adam Clayton Powell said, "When the last trumpet shall sound, Handy will blow the last blues." Twenty-five thousand people filled the church and surrounding streets that day. When Handy's cortege reached the bridge leading across the river out of Harlem, the band burst into "The St. Louis Blues." It was a fine funeral with the mayor of the City of New York among the honorary pallbearers.

Adam Powell, who preaches a great service, has conducted the final rites of such celebrities of the show world as the dancer Bill Robinson and the pianist Fats Waller. Formerly an assistant to Reverend Powell, but now possessing a church of his own, a runner-up for funeral fame in Harlem is the Reverend Willard Monroe. At Monumental Baptist Church many funerals are held. To be preached to glory by Reverend Monroe is to get there really in fine style. Sometimes Reverend Monroe takes a rose and, as he lets its gentle petals drop one by one on the casket of the deceased, he enumerates the lost soul's virtues. Sometimes he lets his own tears fall upon the bier as he talks. It was Reverend Monroe who preached the memorable funeral of the late George Woods, genial master of the Red Rooster, Seventh Avenue's popular bar and dining place. At the ceremonies Ethel Waters sang. A tape recording of this funeral, it is said, was later played back at the Red Rooster so that George's numerous Harlem friends who could not get into the crowded services might hear it as they sat at the bar.

Old Harlemites still talk about the burials of the comedian Bert Williams and of the cabaret owner Baron Wilkins. That of the star of *Shuffle Along* and *Blackbirds,* Florence Mills, lingers in many memories, too. The prettiest of chorus girls were flower bearers for Florence Mills and, as her procession went down Seventh Avenue, an airplane overhead released a flock of bluebirds in memory of her song, "I'm Just a Little Blackbird Looking for a Bluebird." Dickie Wells, dancer and loverman, also had a fine funeral.[48] And at the rites for the great jazz artist Charlie "Yardbird" Parker, Nat Hentoff, the jazz critic, gave a eulogy. Dizzy Gillespie was among the greats of syncopation, Negro and white, who were pallbearers. All of them wore formal clothes, and a group of interracial wives mourned for Yardbird. His funeral was integrated.

One of Harlem's most dramatic funerals was that of A'Lelia Walker, the stunning Amazon heiress of the Madam Walker beauty fortune.[49] When she died in 1931 a grand funeral was held. A giver of many fabulous parties in her lifetime, for her funeral—just as for her parties—handsome invitations were issued. In life A'Lelia Walker, a generous soul, had always sent out more invitations to her parties than her house was able to accommodate. The same thing happened at her funeral—a great many more invitations to friends were issued than the small but exclusive Seventh Avenue funeral parlor could provide space for. Long before the funeral hour the street in front of the undertaker's chapel was crowded. Its doors were not opened until the cortege arrived—and the cortege was late. When the procession came there were almost enough family mourners, attendants, flower girls, and honorary pallbearers in the parade to fill the mortuary, not counting the representatives of all the various Madam Walker beauty parlors throughout the country. After these had marched in there were still hundreds of friends, white and colored, outside waving engraved invitations aloft in the vain hope of entering.

There was a great crush at the doors, but some managed to get through. Inside, everybody was startled to see a man who looked just like De Lawd in *The Green Pastures* standing over the bier. It was Reverend A. Clayton Powell, the father of Adam Powell. With white hair and kind face, he stood motionless in the soft light behind the silver casket of A'Lelia Walker. Soft music played and the air was very solemn. When everyone was seated and the chapel became silent, De Lawd said, "The Four BonBons will now sing."

A night-club quartette that had often performed at A'Lelia Walker's parties arose and sang, "I'll See You Again," and they swung it slightly, as she would have liked it. It was a grand funeral, very much like a party. And in the course of the afternoon many fine words were spoken over her body.

To hear fine words over those no longer alive makes the living feel good. What else good can be done for a person who is gone? Relatives and friends often fail each other in life. In death, who would be helped by unpleasant words, even though they are true? No good cause would be served then by a sharp tongue. So why not speak well of the dead? Amen.

"Writers: Black and White,"

The American Negro Writer and His Roots: Selected Papers from the First Conference of Negro Writers, March 1959 (New York: American Society of African Culture, 1960), 41–45

Even to sell *bad* writing you have to be good.

There was a time when, if you were colored, you might sell bad writing a little easier than if you were white. But no more. The days of the Negro's passing as a writer and getting by purely because of his "negritude" are past.

Even pure Africans find it hard to get published in the U.S.A. You have to be a Nadine Gordimer or an Alan Paton.[50] For the general public, "the blacker the berry, the sweeter the juice" may be true in jazz, but not in prose. These days I would hate to be a Negro writer depending on race to get somewhere.

To create a market for your writing you have to be consistent, professional, a continuing writer—not just a one-article or a one-story or a one-book man. Those expert vendors, the literary agents, do not like to be bothered with a one-shot writer. No money in them. Agents like to help build a career, not light a flash in the pan. With one-shot writers, literary hucksters cannot pay their income taxes. Nor can publishers get their money back on what they lose on the first book. Even if you are a good writer, but *not* consistent, you probably will not get far. Color has nothing to do with writing as such. So I would say, in your mind don't be a *colored* writer even when dealing in racial material. Be a *writer* first. Like an egg: first, egg; then an Easter egg, the color applied.

To write about yourself, you should first be outside yourself—objective. To write well about Negroes, it might be wise, occasionally at least, to look at them with white eyes—then the better will you see how distinctive we are. Sometimes I think whites are more appreciative of our *uniqueness* than we are ourselves. The white "black" artists—dealing in Negro material—have certainly been financially more successful than any of us real Negroes have ever been. Who wrote the most famous "Negro" (in quotes) music? George Gershwin, who looked at Harlem from a downtown penthouse, while Duke Ellington still rode the "A" train. Who wrote the best selling plays and novels and thereby made money's mammy? White Eugene O'Neill, white Paul Green, white Lillian Smith, white Marc Connelly, and DuBose Heyward: *Emperor Jones, In Abraham's Bosom, Strange Fruit, Green Pastures, Porgy.*[51] Who originated the longest running Negro radio and TV show? The various white authors of the original AMOS AND ANDY scripts, not Negroes. Who wrote all those Negro and interracial pictures that have swept across the Hollywood screen from H*allelujah* to *Anna Lucasta,* from *Pinky* to *Porgy and Bess*? Not Negroes. Not you, not I, not any colored-body here.

Our eyes are not white enough to look at Negroes clearly in terms of popular commercial marketing. Not even white enough to see as Faulkner sees—through Mississippi-Nobel-Prize-winning-Broadway eyes in his play *Requiem for a Nun.* There his "nigger dope-fiend whore" of a mammy, Nancy Manningoe, "cullud," raises the curtain with three traditional "Yas, Lawd's," and when asked later by a white actor, "What would a person like you be doing in heaven?" humbly replies, "Ah kin work." Since Faulkner repeatedly calls Nancy "a nigger dope-fiend whore," all I can add is she is also a liar—because the *last* thing a Negro thinks of doing in heaven is working. Nancy knows better, even if Faulkner doesn't.

Nigger dope-fiend Nancy, Porgy's immoral Bess, Mamba's immoral daughter, street-walking Anna Lucasta, whorish Carmen Jones! Lawd, let me be a member of the wedding! "White folks Ah kin work!" In fact, yas, Lawd, I have to work because—

> You've done taken my blues and gone—
> Sure have! You sing 'em on Broadway,
> And you sing 'em in Hollywood Bowl.
> You mixed 'em up with symphonies,
> And you fixed 'em so they don't sound like me.
> Yep, you done taken my blues and gone!
> You also took my spirituals and gone.
> Now you've rocked-and-rolled 'em to death!
> You put me in *Macbeth,*
> In *Carmen Jones,* and *Anna Lucasta,*
> And all kinds of *Swing Mikados*
> And in everything but what's about me—
> But someday somebody'll
> Stand up and talk about me,

And write about me—
Black and beautiful—
And sing about me,
And put on plays about me!
I reckon it'll be me myself!
Yes, it'll be me.

Of course, it may be a long time before we finance big Broadway shows or a seven-million-dollar movie like *Porgy and Bess* on which, so far as I know, not a single Negro writer was employed. The *Encyclopaedia Britannica* declares *Porgy and Bess* "the greatest American musical drama ever written." The *Encyclopaedia Britannica* is white. White is right. So shoot the seven million! 7 come 11! Dice, gin, razors, knives, dope, watermelon, whores—7-11! Come 7!

Yet, surely Negro writing, even when commercial, need not be in terms of stereotypes. The interminable crap game at the beginning of *Porgy and Bess* is just because its authors could not see beyond the *surface* of Negro color. But the author of the original novel did see, with his white eyes, wonderful, hectic human qualities in the inhabitants of Catfish Row that made them come alive in his book, half alive on the stage, and I am sure, bigger than life on the screen. DuBose Heyward was a *writer* first, white second, and this you will have to be, too: *writer* first, *colored* second. That means losing nothing of your racial identity. It is just that in the great sense of the word, anytime, any place, good art transcends land, race, or nationality, and color drops away. If you are a good writer, in the end neither blackness nor whiteness makes a difference to readers.

Greek the writer of *Oedipus* might have been, but *Oedipus* shakes Booker T. Washington High School. Irish was Shaw, but he rocks Fisk University. Scottish was Bobby Burns, but kids like him at Tuskegee. The more regional or national an art is in its origins, the more universal it may become in the end. What could be more Spanish than *Don Quixote:* yet what is more universal? What more Italian than Dante? Or more English than Shakespeare? Advice to Negro writers; Step *outside yourself,* then look back—and you will see how human, yet how beautiful and black you are. How very black—even when you're integrated.

As to marketing, however, blackness seen through black eyes may be too black for wide white consumption—unless coupled with greatness or its approximation. What should a Negro writer do, then, in a land where we have no black literary magazines, no black publishers, no black producers, no black investors able to corral seven million dollars to finance a movie? Sell what writing you can, get a job teaching, and give the rest of your talent away. Or else try becoming a good *bad* writer or a black *white* writer, in which case you might, with luck, do as well as white *black* writers do. If you are good enough in a *bad* way, or colored enough in a *good* way, you stand a chance perhaps, maybe, of becoming *even* commercially successful. At any rate, I would say, keep writing. Practice will do you no harm.

Second, be not dismayed! Keep sending your work out, magazine after magazine, publisher after publisher. Collect rejection slips as some people collect stamps. When you achieve a publication or two, try to get a literary agent—who will seek to collect checks for you instead of rejection slips. See along the way how few editors or agents will ask what color you are physically if you have something good to sell. I would say very few or NONE. Basically they do not care about race, if what you write is readable, new, different, exciting, alive on the printed page. Almost nobody knows Frank Yerby is colored. Few think about Willard Motley's complexion. Although how you treat the materials of race may narrow your market, I do not believe your actual race will. Certainly racial or regional subject matter has its marketing limitations. Publishers want only so many Chinese books a year. The same is true of Negro books.

However, if you want a job as a free-lance writer in Hollywood, on radio, or in TV, that now is sometimes possible—in contrast to the years before the War. But in the entertainment field, regular full-time staff jobs are still not too easy to come by if you are colored. Positions are valuable in the U.S.A., so commercial white culture would rather allow a colored writer a book than a job, even fame rather than an ordinary, decent, dependable living. But if you are so constituted as to wish a dependable living, with luck you might possibly nowadays achieve that too, purely as a writer. I hope so—because *starving* writers are stereotypes. And a stereotype is the last thing a Negro wants to be.

But you can't be a member of the Beat Generation, the fashionable word at the moment in marketing, *unless* you starve a little. Yet who wants to be "beat"? Not Negroes. That is what this conference is all about—how *not* to be "beat." So don't worry about beatness. That is easy enough to come by. Instead, let your talent bloom! You say you are mired in manure? Manure fertilizes. As the old saying goes, "Where the finest roses bloom, there is always a lot of manure around."

Of course, to be highly successful in a white world—commercially successful—in writing or anything else, you really should *be* white. But until you get white, *write*.

5

Essays, 1960–1967

"Richard Wright's Last Guest,"
LHP 3445 (December 16, 1960)

When I saw Richard Wright at his apartment in Paris three days before he died, he did not look ill.[1] He looked perfectly all right—except that it appeared he was freshly laid out for dead. I had not seen Wright for many years. When I rang his doorbell, his charming teenage daughter, Julia, said, "Daddy is in the bedroom," and she escorted me there. The foot of the bed faced the door. Fully clothed in a gray suit and tie, but two-thirds covered by a quilt, Wright lay all dressed up flat on his back on the bed. The effect was startling—as if he were on a bier. I stopped short in the door. Without thinking, my words came out even before I greeted him. "Man," I said, "you look like you are ready to go to glory!"

We both laughed as Wright, while we shook hands, explained to me he was waiting for a car to come at any moment to take him to the hospital, that was why he already had his jacket and tie on. Periodically, he said, he needed routine treatments for an old stomach ailment he had picked up in Africa. He felt fine, he told me as he offered a cigarette, except that he had been unable to eat anything much for three days. The medicine he had taken, he grinned, upset him more than the ailment. As he talked, he seemed and looked very much like the young Dick Wright I had known in Chicago before he became famous—vigorous, questioning, very much alive, and with a big warm smile. He wanted to know the happenings in the states, especially, "How is Harlem these days? I'd like to see it again."

As we talked his doctor arrived with the car to take him to the hospital. Wright swung briskly out of bed and handed me the manuscript of a play he had adapted from the French, *Daddy Goodness,* which he asked me to bring to New York. He hoped, he said, some little theatre might be interested in it. Then with daughter Julia's help, he slipped into his topcoat, meanwhile apologizing to me for having to walk out on a guest. I left the house as he headed for the hospital. "But I'll write you soon," he said.

Three days later in London, I learned that Richard Wright was dead. I was his last visitor at home.

"An Adventure with Absinthe," LHP 7 (July 10, 1961)

Of all the hangovers in the world to suffer, the worst is an absinthe hangover. And of all the forms of drunkenness for the uninitiated, the weirdest is an absinthe drunk. Only once in my long life have I been intoxicated to the point of hilarious and utter irresponsibility. That was from absinthe. The memorable occasion took place in Cap Haitien on a Monday night when there was nothing better to do. It was a lazy night, with no congo dances or voodoo dances, no parties, not even a wake. No drums sounded anywhere within earshot. It was hot and very quiet in the dark streets of the Cape. The hotel bar was empty. It was too early to go to bed. I was bored, so I sought a cafe.

I have forgotten the name of the cafe, but it was a fairly large room with a long bar near the entrance and a dance floor at the back. This particular night there was nothing much happening there either, only a few pretty mulatto girls sitting around, looking lonesome. There was no orchestra so some of us there put coins in the juke box and danced a few dances with the girls, but the heat drenched us. We sat at the bar and ordered beers.

While I was sitting on a stool my eyes were attracted to the bright array of bottles on the mirrored shelves behind the bar. Whiskeys, gins, cordials, wines, and liquors of all sorts and colors enlivened the bar. Among the many bottles, I suddenly spotted one labelled *Absinthe*. From my youthful memories of French novels—tales of love and intrigue, affairs of passion and danger, in which the heroes, and ofttimes the heroines, too, drowned their frustrations in *absinthe*—phrases describing its cloudy charms came to mind, but I had never been in its presence before.

"Give me a drink of absinthe," I ordered the bartender.

He took the romantic bottle down, placed a tall glass in front of me and said, "Say when."

Never having taken absinthe before, I did not know when. I let him pour until the glass was perhaps a third full. Ice and water were added to the clear fluid, then it all began to change color as if in a genie's pot. The milk white cloudy fumes I had read about swirled upward smokily through the cool liquid. I took a sip. It tasted wonderfully mild, cold and delicious—almost like an ice cream soda. I drank it down. Smooth!

"Another one," I ordered. The bartender looked at me with a half smile as he took the bottle down and poured again. This I sipped slowly to savor and enjoy it longer. Its mellow licorice-sweet coolness soothed my pallet. After a third, I felt friendly and lively. My customary shyness disappeared. I began to laugh and talk and joke with everybody at the bar. Soon it seemed that in no time at all midnight had arrived. It was closing hour. The barman was gathering up bottles and glasses, and the girls retrieving fans and pocketbooks, making ready to leave.

I walked on air to the door. But when I got there, instead of leaving, it seemed to me enormously amusing to sit down on the floor in the doorway and make it difficult for anyone else to pass. So I sat down. I leaned back against the door jamb and put my feet high in front of me on the opposite jamb of the door. It tickled me no end seeing people trying to step over my upraised legs. I laughed fit to kill. All the while I knew just what I was doing. Fortunately, everyone else seemed in a good humor, too, so no one made a row about it. Finally someone got me up and out into the street. There I shook hands and jovially cried goodnight to everyone in sight. On the way to the hotel, I greeted late passersby as though they all were favorite cousins whom I had not seen for years. Their astonishment amused me greatly. I was in a world of euphoria.

Provincial Haitian hotels, like those in France, close up lock, stock, and barrel before midnight, so one has to ring, call, and shake the door to arouse a porter. Finally someone came, but at that moment it amused me to seek entrance to my second floor room by climbing the garden wall, clutching the balcony rail and pulling myself into my room. The garden wall was high so, jump as I might, each time my hands managed to reach the top, they slipped and I came down again. The hotel porter did not think this amusing. He tried to persuade me to come in by way of the door. He even pushed me toward the door, but I spread out my arms and legs, laughing all the while, and refused to be pushed in. Finally he took me by main force, carried me upstairs, and put me to bed.

This seemed an unfriendly act so I reviled him loudly. Several guests woke up, hearing the commotion, and came running to see what it was about. By then I had determined not to remain in bed, and said so vociferously. I wanted to go to the beach and swim, I said, even if it was two o'clock in the morning.

The beach—the only safe beach where sharks would not bite a man in half—was fully a mile away from town over a rocky hillside trail that, the assembled guests assured me, would be impossible to find in the dark of night. I arose from bed, nevertheless, and proceeded to get dressed. Weary of trying to cope with my determination, friends in the hotel gave up. So out I went alone, laughing down the road to what they predicted would be my certain doom—for between the town and the beach lay a cliff-like hill covered with brambles, with a tangle of underbrush in the deep gullies below. A narrow path, scarcely to be seen clearly even in daylight, led across this wild hillside. On the mile-off slope that descended to the sea, the path was rocky with loose boulders and ran near a steep ledge where a mis-step might send a person tumbling hundred of yards into the gulch below. Yet something of second-sight must have been mine because, without a mishap, I went over this rocky hillside in the pitch black darkness to arrive safely on the wide sands of the beach, how I don't remember. There I must have lain down by the water's edge to sleep.

The next thing I knew it was broad daylight with the sun high in the sky, blazing like fury. As I stood up on the sandy beach in the sun, the world began to go around and around, faster and faster. The sand felt like the unsteady deck of a ship rolling in a heavy swell, and the sky seemed at once both blazingly bright and scaldingly dark as I staggered blindly toward the hillside path leading to Cap Haitien. The mountain lurched and swayed as I made my uncertain way across its formidable hump. When I reeled down hill into town to sight the corner of my hotel, I was indeed thankful. Had there been another mile to go, dizziness, an ever mounting illness in my stomach, knees of rubber and feet of clay might have laid me low in the public highway.

Somehow I achieved my bed, and fell upon it, unable to rise for three days. The world went round and round like a top as wave after wave of nausea swept over me. The sickly sweet taste of *absinthe*—sweeter than any ice cream soda—I could not wash out of my mouth for weeks. At first my friends tried to laugh me out of it, but for me, it was no laughing matter. I turned my face to the wall and attempted to remember just what books had given me the idea that *absinthe* was a fascinating and romantic drink. It is bottled ether, insidious wormwood, and gall. My admonition: Never try it. But if you do, take the advice of old absinthe drinkers who told me later it is something one must become accustomed to in slow and *very* easy stages. As for me, absinthe? *Never again!* Not even a drop.

"Langston Hughes on Writing," *Overview* 2 (July 1961): 38–39

When I was a high school student, English teachers limited the study of literature pretty much to the "Old Masters"—Shakespeare, Wordsworth, Longfellow. But I was lucky. My English teacher at Central High Cleveland (Miss Ethel Weimer—I remember her well) liked the modern poetry of our own day and time. We read Sandburg, Millay, Masters, and other American poets who wrote of the things we knew about; we could identify their poetry with our lives. (It was in Miss Weimer's class that I began to take poetry seriously.)

Good literature that relates to the student's own life can be a powerful creative stimulus to a young person. But after the creative stimulus is quickened, there comes the harder job of learning (or teaching) how to write. I don't think schools need to set up special courses on writing. There's nothing wrong with "writing courses" as such, but good writing should be expected in *every* course. Creative expression doesn't belong solely to the English department. Students should be encouraged to express themselves well, and creatively, in *all* their work. Looking back, I can remember sociology and French teachers who stimulated me as much as anyone to express myself better. . . .

One of the faults in teaching English has been to encourage students to "write like" Poe or "like" Wordsworth. This, of course, is wrong. Those writers were great because they wrote like themselves and employed the forms and meters that were right for what *they* wanted to say at the time that they said it. There are no "correct" forms in writing; each person must choose his own. The aim of the teacher must be to stimulate the individual to create freely and individually—regardless of the great models of the past or present.

Actually, the younger the student, the easier it is for him to express himself. My experiences at the lab school at the University of Chicago proved this to me. The children were freest and most excited at the idea of expressing themselves, and so they expressed their thoughts in more exciting ways than older students did. They didn't imitate favorite models at that age simply because they didn't have any yet.

If children wait to start writing in high school they're apt be too inhibited to write freely. Their work will read like Housman or Millay or somebody else they've just read. If they don't start writing until college, they'll try to be young T. S. Eliots or Dylan Thomases.

I found this to be the case in a graduate creative writing class I taught for the English department at Atlanta University. Many of the students were so intrigued with the writers they admired that they couldn't shake loose from those styles. . . .

Encouraging creative expression in student writing is an art itself. Miss Weimer had it and she inspired a number of her students to go on to writing careers. She wasn't a writer herself—just an English teacher—but she had that rare gift of enthusiasm. She gave us a good deal of freedom in class and imparted the excitement of being able to express one's self. She was always sympathetic to our problems (personal ones, too, I remember, as well as literary) and constantly marvelled at the better things we did. She made us feel excited at having said something original at all!

This is as far as the teacher should try to go. She should encourage her students to the point that they can express themselves freely and genuinely, but she shouldn't try to make professional writers out of them. Instead, when a student comes along who shows real talent, the teacher should be able to spot it and direct him to professional guidance.

Guidance of this kind could be provided by a poet-in-residence or a professional writer on the faculty. This is the "living presence" which can be uniquely helpful to the young writer—if the man is carefully selected, vocal and friendly, and not too withdrawn (poets are often shy, non-verbal people). Possibly he should not be required to teach at all but just be "available" to students.

A poet-in-residence could be valuable for all grades, kindergarten on up. At the Chicago lab school I sat with kindergarteners who hadn't yet learned to read or write. They'd make up stories and I'd take them down and some of them turned out to be charming. Even in advanced seminars, the fact of my being poet-in-residence there stimulated a lot of writing activity, quite a bit of it good. . . .

Another thing that the teacher should be aware of is that the writer doesn't develop separately from other artists. All the arts are interrelated. I remember a number of students at Central High who were undecided then about which art form they should pursue. One girl concentrated on writing at that time but went on to become a fine graphic artist. There is no question but that her writing helped her discover how she really wanted to express herself in her life's work.

The school's function, then, is to provide the means for self-discovery through self-expression. Actually, the school can do more in this respect than any other agency in the community—including the family. The school is frequently the only place where young people *can* express themselves freely and creatively.

In that respect the schools can do one thing more: provide a publishing outlet. Every secondary school should have a magazine or paper in which students can see their own writing in print. This has the value of both criticism and encouragement. My first stories were printed in my high school magazine; just reading them there stimulated me to get them published elsewhere.

Creative writing, I must add, is not an easy way to make a living. But even if it were, schools should not think it is their responsibility to turn out batches of "creative writers" every year. I would like to think that the schools' responsibility is to train young people to express themselves genuinely so that they may communicate better with their fellow man.

"The Woes of a Writer,"
Authors Guild Bulletin (1962): 8

A sizable portion of the reading public must be very naive indeed regarding the income to be made from creative writing. Over the years I have gotten hundreds of letters from complete strangers asking me for large financial aid. Unknown correspondents have requested that I help send a son or daughter through college, that I aid in a sudden family emergency, that I underwrite the publication of a book or finance an artistic career, or simply that I cater to the urgent need for a loan for some purely personal reason, such as rent due or an unwanted pregnancy with which the correspondent is sure I will sympathize.

It is incredible what strangers will ask writers to do for them. I suppose movie stars see thousands of such letters. But, according to the motion picture magazines, the studios take care of fan mail for the stars. Writers have no studio staffs to read and answer letters. Our hearts are sometimes torn by what seem to be sincere and often pitiable requests—with which most of us have no means of complying.

Since I have been writing for the *New York Post,* my "please-help-me" mail has increased.[2] Because one's name appears in a major metropolitan paper, it seems taken for granted that the writer is making a million dollars a year. I think it wise to state here and now that I am not making, from all my sources of writing income put together, one per cent of that amount.

In recent years, since my Simple books, poetry and other work have been serialized in Africa, I've gotten hundreds of letters from various African countries beseeching aid of one sort or another. Many are from students who wish to come to the U.S. to study and who hope that I can offer them scholarships, or board and house them in New York.

Others (and some of these are heart-rending) are from men and women in apartheid countries wishing to escape, or who have gotten out to Tanganyika or some other half-way point to Europe, but are stranded and starving, and write urgently for plane fare to get to London or some place more civilized than their own benighted homes, or the tolerant but none too friendly cities in which they have found refuge.

I have tried sending small checks to the limit of my ability. But small checks really do no good, as subsequent letters from recipients reveal. I have tried referring student letters to foundations concerned with bringing young people to America for study. But the foundations are swamped with applications. To keep false hopes from being raised, lately I have been replying, to most unknown Africa correspondents requesting aid, in the vein of this letter I have written to a young South African stranded in a refugee camp in Dar-Es-Salaam and seeking the fare to England:

"I very much wish I could help you, but I cannot. I have nothing to help with. I get dozens of letters like yours from Africa making similar requests. The only wealthy Negro writers I know of are Frank Yerby, who has had numerous best-sellers, the late Richard Wright, who had two highly successful books, and perhaps now James Baldwin, whose latest novel, *Another Country,* is on the best-seller list. I have never had a best-seller, never had a motion picture sale, never had a hit play in the commercial sense. I make just about enough to pay my part-time secretary and my weekly expenses. Because my name is known abroad I am sorry many people seem to be under the impression that I must be rich. I am not. Sometimes I wonder how I am going to pay my monthly bills. All I can send you or offer you is my good wishes that all will turn out well with you, and that what you hope will be realized. This is the answer I am forced to send many others than just yourself. I wish it could be something more tangible."

To a writer who must make a living from writing, long letters can be very time-consuming. When letters are accompanied by thick manuscripts, they can become millstones around a writer's neck.

Many senders of unsolicited manuscripts are very impatient. If the manuscript is not returned with praise almost immediately, an angry note may come. The sender evidently thinks he or she is the only person who has posted you a manuscript that week or that month. The truth is that perhaps 20 unsolicited sheaves of poems, envelopes of short stories, or even whole novels have come in the mail that week from people one does not know at all. It would take an editorial staff to carefully consider them all, and the postage for returning them eventually becomes considerable.

I sometimes wish I were a movie star rather than a writer, with a big studio staff to open and answer my mail—that is, that portion of it that is not from my family, friends, or fans who do not want anything. The sad fact is that I have so little free time, and NO money, to give away. But maybe some day I will have a best seller, then I can make it up to everybody. It must be nice to be able to be generous with both time and money.

"Gospel Songs and Gospel Singing," LHP 479 (April 16, 1962)

The first thing that one should know about gospel songs is that they are *not* spirituals.[3] The spirituals are the old anonymous songs of the Negro people dating from the days of slavery. They are folk songs, and nobody knows who made them up. *Go Down, Moses,* or *Deep River,* or *All God's Chillun Got Wings* have no known individual authorship. On the other hand, gospel songs are composed songs. They are contemporary songs which borrow from the spirituals, from blues, and even from jazz. Therefore they have a folk flavor, but in the true sense, they are not folk songs. Most of them are written and copyrighted by men and women living today—Alex Bradford, Clara Ward, Jobe Huntley and others.[4]

Gospel singing, however, is *folk* singing rooted in the Negro masses, its style invented by the dark millions who make up the congregations where gospel songs are a part of the services. These songs originated in the humbler Negro churches, not in the established orthodox sects like the Methodist, Episcopalian, or Lutheran with their set hymns. Gospel singing is free-wheeling and free-swinging. The Holiness churches, the Sanctified churches and the independent sects where gospel singing predominates in the United States are now the last refuge of pure Negro folk singing.

The spirituals as a folk form have disappeared, and their singing has become arranged, standardized and concertized by Marian Anderson, the Robert Shaw Chorale, Harry Belafonte and other artists of the entertainment world. The blues have become the property of Hollywood and Broadway, commercial bands and night clubs. Only the gospel songs and gospel singers remain almost entirely in the hands of the Negro people, rooted in the mass Negro churches, the songs sung in uninhibited Negro fashion, not yet subjected to formal arrangements, rigid notation, or commercial gimmicks for the sake of record sales or radio commercials.

Gospel singers still sing as they feel like singing, varying and improvising at will, repeating as much and as long as they choose, allowing themselves at times to be entirely carried away by rhythm or words, or both. When singing in churches, often even professional gospel groups become so completely identified with their audiences that guest-singers and host-congregations become one in song and ecstasy, in foot-tapping and hand-clapping, in praise and thanksgiving. Gospel songs are in general happy songs, praise-songs, shouting songs, celebrating the greatness and glory of God and affirming His loving way with men. When gospel singers sing the old spirituals or transform traditional hymns, as they frequently do, they imbue them with a new leaping life, a fresh assurance that the promise of salvation is good, and an indication that even if hell is a yawning pit, its dangers may nevertheless be sung in happy fashion.

Thomas A. Dorsey of Chicago was the first great composer of gospel songs. In his youth more than a quarter of a century ago, Dorsey was the pianist-composer for the famous singer of the blues, Ma Rainey, teacher of Bessie Smith. When Dorsey became a religious man and began to write songs for the church, he carried over into his songs the flavor of the blues. Musicologists state that church music is usually a half century behind secular music. In gospel music there is no such lag. Although religious in mood and meaning, it is very much of today in its melodic flavors, its driving beat, its popular appeal, and its textual use of contemporary idioms.

Gospel music is music to be shouted to, to move to, and in which to become yourself a participant. Gospel singers often do a sort of religious dance (although the feet must never cross, for then it would become the devil's dance) in which they move energetically to the rhythms. Like Spanish flamenco, both gospel singing and gospel dancing have certain set patterns, but within these patterns a wild and wonderful ecstasy may develop, an ecstasy "out of this world." The thing to do when you hear gospel music is to let yourself go with it.

"South of Light Bulbs and Pomegranates (An Appreciation of Two Artists)," LHP (November 14, 1962)

Jacob Lawrence went to Africa 100 years after some sort of Centennial before it was after, and somewhere between the Federal Palace Hotel in Lagos a third from Lisbon betwixt Lourenço Marques bound by Emancipation yet els and leagues from Brazil, Lawrence met Malangatana.[5]

He said, "I see you put a clock in your panel."

Malangatana said, "I see you put an electric bulb with no shade on it in yours."

Jacob Lawrence said, "I did."

Malangatana said, "I put three dots on two breasts, and I put a breast on her belly."

Lawrence said, "In one picture you made her buttocks look like two breasts, and like a waterfall in profile in another."

Malangatana said, "Yes, I did."

Said Lawrence, "I see you got a cross and a window frame that crosses like a cross and maybe the window frame is a cross and I put a cross over three black heads on a white wall."

"I painted a cross between two breasts round as light bulbs," said Malangatana.

"Yes, you did," said Jacob Lawrence. "And you painted a clock in your story about the *Letter* but you only put three clocks but you had four panels, although the bottom of the chair in one looks like a clock and the window looks like a cross with three crossbars in the one that has no clock, and in the last one the clock you painted melts into a heart that says 3 o'clock."

"And it was 3 o'clock," says Malangatana.

"I know it," says Jacob Lawrence. "Everywhere it is O'clock with an *O* and a thing ' that means *of* all the time."

"That's right," said Malangatana. And the word became *said* because *says* had become what *was* after 3 o'clock. "One of your children has a 3 in her hand. And one of your men has a rope around his neck. And your cannon has a wheel."

"You put a nipple on one buttock and elsewhere higher cheeks of buttocks for two breasts up there."

"I did," said Malangatana.

"And maybe a nipple on the other buttock but I could not did not cannot see it."

"I do not know myself if it is there," said Malangatana.

"Certainly three of your women have bellies like breasts, and one like a melon."

"Woman's belly (*women's* bellies painted into one belly) shall give birth to me up there," said Malangatana of the Regedoria Magaia of Marracuene south of pomegranates and figs. Round as the light bulbs of Harlem breasts heads and wheels north of pomegranates south of girls and figs blacker than blackboards painted with the blackest paint.

"Two shades darker, two shades darker than Africa, two shades darker than Africa and me," says Malangatana.

2-3-4. Children: 2-3-4. On the last clock: 3. In the last hand: 4.

"So you paint panels, too."

"I do," says Jacob Lawrence.

"I do, too," says Valente Malangatana.

"I do, too," says Jacob Lawrence.

"I do, too."

"My Early Days in Harlem,"
Freedomways 3 (1963): 312–14

On a bright September morning in 1921, I came up out of the subway at 135th and Lenox into the beginnings of the Negro Renaissance. I headed for the Harlem Y.M.C.A. down the block, where so many new, young, dark, male arrivals in Harlem have spent early days. The next place I headed to that afternoon was the Harlem Branch Library just up the street. There, a warm and wonderful librarian, Miss Ernestine Rose, white, made newcomers feel welcome, as did her assistant in charge of the Schomburg Collection, Catherine Latimer, a luscious café au lait. That night I went to the Lincoln Theatre across Lenox Avenue where maybe one of the Smiths—Bessie, Clara, Trixie, or Mamie—was singing the blues. And as soon as I could, I made a beeline for *Shuffle Along,* the all-colored hit musical playing on 63rd Street in which Florence Mills came to fame.

I had come to New York to enter Columbia College as a freshman, but *really* why I had come to New York was to see Harlem. I found it hard a week or so later to tear myself away from Harlem when it came time to move up the hill to the dormitory at Columbia. That winter I spent as little time as possible on the campus. Instead, I spent as much time as I could in Harlem, and this I have done ever since. I was in love with Harlem long before I got there, and I still am in love with it. Everybody seemed to make me welcome. The sheer dark size of Harlem intrigued me. And the fact that at that time poets and writers like James Weldon Johnson and Jessie Fauset lived there, and Bert Williams, Duke Ellington, Ethel Waters, and Walter White, too, fascinated me. Had I been a rich young man, I would have bought a house in Harlem and built musical steps up to the front door, and installed chimes that at the press of a button played Ellington tunes.

After a winter at Columbia, I moved back down to Harlem. Everywhere I roomed, I had the good fortune to have lovely landladies. If I did not like a landlady's looks, I would not move in with her, maybe that is why. But at finding work in New York, my fortune was less than good. Finally, I went to sea—Africa, Europe—then a year in Paris working in a night club where the band was from Harlem. I was a dishwasher, later bus boy, listening every night to the music of Harlem transplanted to Montmartre. And I was on hand to welcome Bricktop when she came to sing for the first time in Europe, bringing with her news of Harlem.

When I came back to New York in 1925 the Negro Renaissance was in full swing. Countee Cullen was publishing his early poems, Aaron Douglas was painting, Zora Neale Hurston, Rudolph Fisher, Jean Toomer and Wallace Thurman were writing, Louis Armstrong was playing, Cora Le Redd was dancing, and the Savoy Ballroom was open with a specially built floor that rocked as the dancers swayed. Alain Locke was putting together *The New Negro.* Art took heart from Harlem creativity. Jazz filled the night air—but not everywhere—and people came from all around after dark to look upon our city within a city, Black Harlem. Had I not had to earn a living, I might have thought it even more wonderful than it was. But I could not eat the poems I wrote. Unlike the whites who came to spend their money in Harlem, only a few Harlemites seemed to live in even a modest degree of luxury. Most rode the subway downtown every morning to work or to look for work.

Downtown! I soon learned that it was seemingly impossible for black Harlem to live without white downtown. My youthful illusion that Harlem was a world unto itself did not last very long. It was not even an area that ran itself. The famous night clubs were owned by whites, as were the theatres. Almost all the stores were owned by whites, and many at that time did not even (in the very middle of Harlem) employ Negro clerks. The books of Harlem writers all had to be published downtown, if they were to be published at all. Downtown: *white.* Uptown: *black.* White downtown pulling all the strings in Harlem. Moe Gale, Moe Gale, Moe

Gale, Lew Leslie, Lew Leslie, Lew Leslie, Harper's, Knopf, *The Survey Graphic,* the Harmon Foundation, the racketeers who kidnapped Casper Holstein and began to take over the numbers for whites.[6] Negroes could not even play their own numbers with their *own* people. And almost all the policemen in Harlem were white. Negroes couldn't even get graft from *themselves* for themselves by themselves. Black Harlem really was in white face, economically speaking. So I wrote this poem:

Because my mouth
Is wide with laughter
And my throat
Is deep with song,
You do not think
I suffer after
I have held my pain
So long?

Because my mouth
Is wide with laughter,
You do not hear
My inner cry?
Because my feet
Are gay with dancing,
You do not know
I die?

Harlem, like a Picasso painting in his cubistic period. Harlem—Southern Harlem—the Carolinas, Georgia, Florida—looking for the Promised Land—dressed in rhythmic words, painted in bright pictures, dancing to jazz—and ending up in the subway at morning rush time—*headed downtown.* West Indian Harlem—warm rambunctious sassy remembering Marcus Garvey.[7] Haitian Harlem, Cuban Harlem, little pockets of tropical dreams in alien tongues. Magnet Harlem, pulling an Arthur Schomburg from Puerto Rico, pulling an Arna Bontemps all the way from California, a Nora Holt from way out West, an E. Simms Campbell from St. Louis, likewise a Josephine Baker, a Charles S. Johnson from Virginia, an A. Philip Randolph from Florida, a Roy Wilkins from Minnesota, an Alta Douglas from Kansas.[8] Melting pot Harlem—Harlem of honey and chocolate and caramel and rum and vinegar and lemon and lime and gall. Dusky dream Harlem rumbling into a nightmare tunnel where the subway from the Bronx keeps right on downtown, where the money from the nightclubs goes right on back downtown, where the jazz is drained to Broadway, whence Josephine goes to Paris, Robeson to London, Jean Toomer to a Quaker Meeting House, Garvey to the Atlanta Federal Penitentiary, and Wallace Thurman to his grave; but Duke Ellington to fame and fortune, Lena Horne to Broadway, and Buck Clayton to China.[9]

Before it was over—our New Negro Renaissance—poems became placards: DON'T BUY WHERE YOU CAN'T WORK! Adam Powell with a picket sign; me, too. BUY BLACK! Sufi long before the Black Muslims. FIRST TO BE FIRED, LAST TO BE HIRED! The Stock Market crash. The bank failures. Empty pockets. *God Bless the Child That's Got His Own.* Depression. Federal Theatre in Harlem, the making of Orson Welles. WPA, CCC, the Blue Eagle, Father Divine.[10] In the midst of the Depression I got a cable from Russia inviting me to work on a motion picture there. I went to Moscow. That was the end of the early days of Langston Hughes in Harlem.

"Gospel Singers: New Asset to American Theatre," *Dramatists Bulletin* 3.7 (April 1963): 1–2

Gospel singers are amazing people capable of making music drama from the simplest of material. They are not unlike Gypsy flamenco singers who can take hold of a line that says nothing more startling than "Love is a heartache" and, with that single line, make the air vibrate around them and the hair stand on your head. Like Gypsies, most Negro gospel singers have never studied a note of music in their lives. They have never had their voices placed and they have no idea that there is such a thing as "correct breathing." But maybe that is why their voices never seem to wear out. They can sing for days, weeks, and months on end, many hours a day, without giving it a thought.

"Because they do not give singing a thought, is why they can sing without worry," a trained musician once told me. "It is because gospel singers are so utterly relaxed when singing, and enjoy their own ecstasy so much, that problems of vocalizing never cross their minds. They jump octaves at will, breathe wherever they wish, and create improvisations that defy notation. They are folk singers in the truest sense. Their musicality comes naturally."

"Are you trying to say that all Negroes are natural born singers?" I asked, hardly thinking so intelligent a person would be guilty of that old cliche.

"Millions of Negroes are not gospel singers," countered my informant. And his last statement is true. There are many colored people, in fact, who loath gospel singing. They love Leontyne Price but look askance at Mahalia Jackson.

In contrast to a singer who follows a score, gospel artists take highly individual liberties with notes or text. I once heard Mahalia Jackson rehearsing a new song her accompanist kept playing over and over for her. Mahalia sang it differently each time. At one point Mildred Falls at the piano asked, "Why don't you sing it like you did the last time?"

"Because I don't want to," Miss Jackson said. And that was that.

Gospel pianists and organists have to be dexterous accompanists. They seldom have any music in front of them. And, if they do, they watch the singer, not the music. They are capable of never missing a beat, even when a singer skips a whole line, or chooses to suddenly repeat innumerable times a phrase usually sung only once. Since gospel singers are masters of drama, they delight at improvising on the moods of their audiences as well as on the music itself. Like the "ole" that eggs on the Spanish Gypsy, so audience response, handclappings and shouts egg on the gospel singer. Sometimes there is no telling what may happen to a gospel group when the audience gets with them. How long or how varied they may make the song they are attacking, only God and their accompanists can divine. The enormous driving power of their singing seems to come from outer space.

The traditional Negro ministers—those who do not read their sermons but intone or shout them—are at their best when backed by swinging gospel choirs. The singers have a sense of drama equal to that of the ministers. Intuitively they know just when to sneak in a hum or moan a song behind the minister's words to heighten a sermon's dramatic values or embellish a Bible tale he may be telling. In the days when unwritten words made vivid the religious mysteries, the first plays grew out of the churches. Today in the American Negro churches of the gospel faiths, one can sometimes hear what amounts to highly effective religious drama, spontaneous and different at every service.

In preparing my gospel song-play, *Black Nativity,* that is currently touring Europe, I visited a number of gospel temples in Harlem, usually arriving about ten at night when services were in full swing. I was never bored. Song and a sense of drama swirled around me. A mingling of ancient scripture and contemporary problems were projected with melodic intensity and rhythmic insistence. Every night I was drawn into the circle of oneness generated by the basic beat of the gospel tempo.

When *Black Nativity* began rehearsals, one of its singing groups, Marion Williams and her Stars of Faith, were appearing at the Apollo Theatre in Harlem.[11] Over a period of ten days, they did four and sometimes five shows a day. Meanwhile, they rehearsed downtown before and between their shows uptown. Hours of singing! Yet every morning at the first rehearsal downtown, they seemed as fresh as daisies. Immediately after they closed at the Apollo, *Black Nativity* opened just before Christmas, 1961, at the 41st Street Theatre. The Stars of Faith sang like lusty angels, and they have been singing loudly and strongly ever since—from New York to Spoleto to London to Brussels, Copenhagen and Rome. Hardly anyone in the company is ever hoarse or in bad voice. Their dramatic projection, after almost two years of telling the Nativity story, is still unimpaired. Gospel singers are amazing people. I think their tribe can become a new and stimulating asset in the American musical theatre.

"Problems of the Negro Writer: The Bread and Butter Side," *Saturday Review,* April 20, 1963, pp. 19–21

The Negro writer in America has all the problems any writer has, plus a few more.

I have been writing books for more than thirty years and have had the good fortune to be published by some of our major houses. During that time it has been my observation that publishers will bring out almost any book they believe is salable regardless of the race of the author. They will frequently even bring out a book they simply consider good. I doubt that a book by Willard Motley or Frank Yerby or James Baldwin would be turned down on account of the author's color. But if James Baldwin wrote six books a year and all six were about the Negro problem, I think perhaps some of them would be rejected—on the grounds of subject matter.

Just as a firm with two Japanese novels on their list might not wish to publish another in the same season, so prolific Negro authors who write exclusively about Negroes may find their acceptance limited. Shortly after his wonderful Negro story, "Health Card," in *Harper's* two decades ago, Frank Yerby decided he did not wish to be limited to racial subject matter. He extended his range. Result: a best-selling novel almost every year since then, plus numerous movie sales. However, until recently, novels by and about Negroes had almost no takers in Hollywood—a factor that helped to make publishers chary of such works unless they were sensational or of unusual quality.

Until 1962 there were no major publishers appealing directly to a Negro reading public. The Johnson Publishing Company, owners of *Ebony* and *Jet,* have not set up a branch specializing in books by and about colored people. The titles on their list are selling well, so that house would not turn down a good Negro book just because it already has a couple in its catalogue this season. Johnson knows how to reach the Negro market; through their widely selling magazines, the company has the necessary publicity and promotional facilities. White publishers, as a rule, do not have the same know-how and have not much cared. But bias is not involved.

Where prejudice operates most blatantly against the Negro author is in the areas peripheral to writing: Hollywood, radio and television, editorial staff positions, and lecturing. Take lecturing, a lucrative field for famous (or even fairly well-known) white writers. Because many women's clubs and forums booking lecturers have teas or receptions following the programs, nine times out of ten, Negro speakers are not invited. Teas are social events: Negroes are not wanted, not even as star names. Many college lyceum programs, too, are booked by not very broad-minded officials. Not only in the South, but in the West and Midwest as well, there are campuses that have never yet had a Negro novelist or poet as a speaker.

For a long time not a single major publishing house in the United States had on its staff any Negroes except occasional clerical workers. It is only in these ever more democratic days since the Second World War that even clerical help has been employed. But now in a few publishing houses in New York there is a handful of Negroes working in capacities above the level of ordinary office routine. In radio and television, however, there are so few Negroes who are not janitors that one hand might have enough fingers to count them. When an author of color sells a novel to Hollywood, if ever he does, he is seldom called to California to work on the script. Almost all well-paying jobs in the mass media are still reserved for whites, no matter how celebrated the Negro author may be.

Everybody knows it is hard to make a living from books alone. Most Negro writers have been teachers. That is as near to a position related to writing as they can get. But a white writer with only an unprofitable first novel to his credit can usually get a fairly high-salaried job in publishing, radio, or TV without half trying. Thus he can make enough money in a little while to compose his next novel. Most Negro writers have to create at night after correcting a hundred student papers.

Added to job difficulties, the Negro writer, of course, suffers from all the other prejudices color is heir to in our USA, depending on what part of the country he lives in or travels. In New York, a Negro going to a downtown cocktail party given for a white fellow-writer may be told by the apartment house doorman, no matter how well dressed the guest may be, "The servant's entrance is around the corner." Such occurrences seem incredible in Manhattan today, but they are not. In the South, on the other hand, nothing boorish is incredible.

Once on a lecture tour I had hardly crossed the Potomac into Virginia when I stopped my car to buy some sandwiches and Coca-Colas. I knew I, a Negro, could not eat sandwiches inside the little roadside lunchstand where I had parked, but I thought I could at least enter and buy some to take out to the car. When I went to open the screen door, a man held it shut. "We have a hole cut for you folks around on the side," he said through the screen. Out of curiosity, I went around to the side of the wooden building. Sure enough, there was a square hole cut there with a sign over it: COLORED. But this is a dissertation on the problems of Negro writers, not Negroes in general. Writers do have a few little special problems. Negroes however, have a great many more that are too omnipresent to be special.

"Eight to Two,"
Liaison 1.13 (May 4, 1963): 1–4

In the popular mind all over the world, wherever I have traveled, French women and black men have the reputation of being very great lovers. As skilled and desirable companions of passion, they are known from here to yonder. Their boudoir acclaim is international.

In both the underworld and the upper world, amorous esteem for the French female on the one hand and the black man on the other holds true. In fact, in some countries—including the American South—the sex prowess of the Negro male has become a folk legend, magnified beyond the possibility of physical truth. And from Shanghai to Cape Town the amorous charms of Gallic women are, among men, held to be of the highest. Folk-beliefs, no doubt, have made these charms seem greater than they are.

Catering to this world folk belief from Chicago to Conakry, Hamburg to Havana, the underworld of prostitution often attempts to palm off as

French, women who are no more French than an Eskimo is Italian. But for business reasons ladies of the evening often pretend to be direct from Paris, and their tariff is correspondingly raised to cover the extra charms with which *la française* is popularly endowed. For instance, in Mexico City, the "French" houses of ill fame have the highest prices.

In *The Road to Buenos Aires,* Albert Londres wrote of the popular desirability of the French *demimondaine* in South American cities, and of the traffic in women from Marseilles to the Latin American countries.[12] Londres also stated that these women often make enough money from their bodies in a year or two in the Argentine to return to France for life and settle down in bourgeois comfort as small business women or bar owners. That is, if they do not fall under the influence of the South American *créoles* whose dusky powers often induce these fair female *artistes* of love to give up their all, including the hard-earned cash they had meant to take back to Europe. Once they succumb to such creole lovers, it seems they are usually lost, and forget all about going home.

So far as I know, no black Don Juans or Casanovas have left written records of their amorous exploits for posterity to read. (They probably were too busy practicing the art to take time out to write about it.) But concerning at least two distinguished literary men of color, Pushkin in Tzarist Russia and Dumas in France, the chronicles of their times state that both gentlemen were great favorites with the women of Moscow and Paris, and their achievements in love as well as letters were mighty. The high society of their respective capitals accepted them as great lovers.

At the other end of the social ladder in the Middle Ages were the black page boys of Venice imported from Africa by Italian ladies of fashion. But, mere pages though they were and servants in caste, word has come down through the centuries that not only did these dusky lads run milady's errands, but frequently served milady in a much more intimate capacity—which helped to account for their great popularity with the mistresses of ducal palaces and doges' mansions. Not for nothing did these shining blackamoors wear silks and velvets and sometimes sport cords of gold about their necks.

During the American slave period, intrigues between mistresses and slaves were sometimes reported. And no wonder, because the strongest and most virile male Negroes were sometimes set apart particularly as breeders, bringing high prices on the Southern slave block. Of course, they were not supposed to breed with their master's womenfolk, but slip-ups did on occasion occur. Since some Negro breeders became quite famous—as blue-ribbon prize bulls are famous now—gentle ladies could hardly be expected not to be curious concerning them. This the novel, *Mandingo,* vividly reports.[13]

History records that Virginia, known as a slave raising state, bred Negroes so rapidly that an average of six thousand a year could be sold to other parts of the South. John Hope Franklin, in his excellent history, *From Slavery to Freedom,* states that slave breeding was a highly approved method of increasing agricultural capital. Concerning Negro babies, he quotes one planter as saying that "every one of them was worth two hundred dollars the moment it drew breath." Negro women of great fertility were worth considerable money to their masters, but black stud males were even more valuable on the slave market. That these sleek and healthy human studs should occasionally attract white women's glances is hardly against nature—although it was against the established mores of the South. If the truth were known, some stud Negroes were probably worth more to their mistresses than to their masters.

Discretion and the libel laws prevent discussion of contemporary swains of color who are famous in our own day and age as lovers. But there are those living in this year of our Lord who are known to have occupied positions of high estate in the hearts of internationally famous ladies of American or Continental society from whose snow-white hands have emanated gifts of great value. Almost anybody who moves in rich and sophisticated society in Paris, London, or New York can tell of various such cases concerning dark lovers and soignée ladies. However, because of our provincial color complexes in the United States, such alliances are discussed less openly here than abroad, and with more resentment than amusement.

J. A. Rogers, in his volumes on *Sex and Race,* has much to say about interracial love around the world in all countries and all ages. Many distinguished and serious writers on sex, including Havelock Ellis, comment on the extraordinary powers of the Negro male and his sustained capacity for physical dalliance. American Army statistics bear this out, if what I have been told at army prophylaxis centers is true.

During my tours of army camps and USO clubs in the World War II years as a newspaper columnist I was frequently shown throughout camp installations from motor pools to hospital operating rooms and VD control centers. At more than one camp I was told by attendants or physicians that prophylactic station records indicate greater sex activity per man among Negro soldiers than among whites, according to the tabulation of those men who registered for prophylaxis to prevent the development of disease following sexual contacts. Indeed, one source reported the over-all figures racially as being eight to two per month per man—eight rounds of love for the Negro male out of camp on pass or furlough, as compared to two rounds of love for the white male a month. This, of course, applied only to those reporting to military pro stations after contacts presumed to have been illicit or commercial.

Eight to two—reduced to the ratio of four to one—puts the Negro GI well in the lead as a more frequent physical love maker. This is on local soil. Unofficial word of mouth reports from overseas with each returning Negro unit after the War indicated that the world folk belief of Negro prowess in amours had been ably upheld by dark GI's from Burma to Rome, Melbourne to Marseilles. In years to come, the facts will gradually be embroidered into further legend, re-enforced, no doubt, by that summer of 1945 newspaper story of the weeping and wailing English girls at Bristol standing all night in the rain beyond the compound gates to bid farewell to their beloved chocolate soldiers about to sail for home.

That British farewell will probably become one of the stories of World War II that will go down through the ages—incidentally helping to immortalize the song, "Don't Fence Me In." That is the song the lassies sang to their Negro sweethearts behind the barbed wire of the embarkation camp. The dark soldiers, finally no longer able to stand being fenced in, tore the barbed wire down and rushed across the line to clasp the English lassies in their arms as rain and tears mingled with their kisses.

That old saying that "being born black is to be born behind the eight-ball" hardly applies to love—not when it's eight to two!

"Gospel Songs: From Kansas to Broadway," LHP 478 (October 1963)

Fifty years ago when I was a little boy in Kansas, there were only two colored churches in Lawrence, one Methodist and one Baptist.[14] No Negroes in those days dreamed of going to a white church there. The Methodist church was the quiet church and the Baptist was the shouting church. To the Methodist church went most of the school teachers and professional men and their wives. To the Baptist church went the Negroes who had never gotten through high school. The Baptist church had the loudest and best singing and the most soul stirring sermons. Baptist revivals (their songs the forerunners of gospel singing) could be heard for blocks. Although I was christened in the Methodist church, I liked the Baptist church best.

In Chicago where we moved in my teens, I first heard the music of the Holiness or Sanctified churches. I was entranced by their stepped up rhythms, tambourines, hand clapping, and uninhibited dynamics, rivalled only by Ma Rainey singing the blues at the old Monogram Theatre. I was mesmerized by the highly musical sermons screamed, shouted, and intoned from the pulpits by ministers just out of the South, come North to save souls. Some of them, I thought, easily could have been great actors. I was particularly entranced by one who, in depicting the climb of Christ to Cavalry, ascended first to the piano stool, then stepped on the keyboard and finally stood on top of the piano depicting Christ on Calvary. There he unfolded most movingly the story of the Crucifixion—and nobody laughed. The music and drama of these less formal Negro churches early took hold of me, moved me and thrilled me—so much so that to this day I do not really enjoy churches where ministers read their sermons from paper and choirs sing to the beat of a conductor's baton. Maybe that is why I so much like gospel singing.

I think I was the first newspaper columnist in America to write about Mahalia Jackson—after I had heard her one cold winter night in a little church on Indiana Avenue in Chicago when I had first begun to do articles for the *Chicago Defender.* I wrote about Chicago's Princess Stewart, too, and Norsalus McKezik who are also great gospel singers.[15] Years later it was my good fortune to have Princess Stewart as part of my gospel song-play, *Black Nativity,* and to find my opinion of her artistry reaffirmed by the music and drama critics wherever it played. Last winter Princess Stewart sang in Coventry Cathedral.

Gospel music began in the poorest of the poor Negro churches. The richer more genteel of churches would brook no shaking of tambourines nor shouting of the spirituals. They preferred the refined Dett or Burleigh arrangements, if they sang spirituals at all.[16] Many of their choir members could read music. In the poorer store front churches almost nobody read music, and the pianist or organist usually played by ear. Their spontaneous group arrangements always seemed more exciting to me than the arrangements bought in music stores. The congregations where there are no scores in front of the choirs never sing anything the same way twice. In their music there is infinite variety. I once heard Mahalia Jackson rehearsing a song with her pianist, Mildred Falls. Each time they went over the song Mahalia sang it differently. Finally her accompanist said, "Mahalia, why don't you sing it like you did last time?"

Miss Jackson said, "Because I don't want to, that's why." So she kept right on changing and embroidering on it that day, as she probably did even after it went into performance. From the mouths of true gospel singers, one never quite knows what will come out. That is what makes (and keeps) gospel singing exciting. When the spirit really moves a gospel singer, the songs can lift the hair off your head. Clara Ward has lately been lifting the hair off the heads of hardened gamblers in Las Vegas. Recently, Dorothy Drake, as yet undiscovered, shook the walls of the Variety Arts Studio just off Broadway when she auditioned for *Tambourines to Glory.* Perhaps when people hear Mrs. Drake in the show at the Little Theatre, she may not sing the same way on Tuesday night as she did on Monday (probably Clara Ward won't either), which is one reason folks may come back to the performance more than once. To hear the singers in *Black Nativity* in New York and London and Paris, some people came as many as fifteen or twenty times, and each time they claimed to find something wonderful and different in the singing of Marion Williams, her Stars of Faith, and Alex Bradford. Gospel singers, like flamenco people, recreate their songs anew every time they sing them.

In the formal sense, they do not rehearse songs. They absorb them. They never look at printed music. They listen to the melodies over and over. They hum them. They croon them, harmonize them without consciously harmonizing, weave one voice behind another, sit and rock and sing, or maybe stand and improvise and laugh and cry and love and enjoy a song together while they are learning it. Then in public performance, often someone in the group will do something no one thought of in rehearsals. But nobody is thrown off the track, and the song retains its overall entity. This is what the oldtime jazz musicians call "head arrangements" right out of themselves—or else from outer space. Like the best of jazz, much of gospel singing defies notation.

Gospel songs are composed songs, not spirituals. Gospel singing is built on the basic beat, and through much of it runs the melodic flavor of the blues. But gospel singers do not like to have their songs spoken of in terms of blues or jazz. Their lyrics are religious lyrics, their words often Biblical words. Not being musicologists, most of them do not know that throughout the ages religious music has eventually caught up with worldly music. But the process has usually been a long one. In the U.S.A., however (where things move faster than they do in the Old World), gospel songs today have not only caught up to but passed popular songs in adapting contemporary styles—so much so that popular music is now imitating gospel. Ray Charles is an example. Even Charlie Mingus.

I do not know when the Negro spirituals first came into the American theatre. But, in my time, I first heard them beautifully employed on stage in the Theatre Guild's production of the play *Porgy* in 1927. Later the Hall Johnson Choir formed a singing orchestra for *The Green Pastures* in which the spirituals were a musical curtain rising and falling between the scenes. Still later they were a part of the dramatic action in *Run, Little Chillun*. Gospel songs first reached the stage in my own *Black Nativity* (now on a national tour) where the Bible story is told largely in song. But *Nativity* is not a play in the theatre sense of the word. In *Tambourines to Glory*, however, gospel songs are an integral part of a dramatic action built around the actual church rituals through which the characters move. This then is, I believe, the first time gospel songs have been woven into a Broadway drama, as an actual part of the play itself. Jobe Huntley, himself a gospel singer, is the composer. His happy songs are real. The Little Theatre will soon be full of jubilation.

"Draft Ideas," LHP (December 3, 1964)

Politics in any country in the world is dangerous. For the poet, politics in any country in the world had better be disguised as poetry. Sartre could not do other than refuse the Prix Nobel, because he once made the mistake of being political.[17] Politics can be the graveyard of the poet. And only poetry can be his resurrection.

What is poetry? It is the human soul entire, squeezed like a lemon or a lime, drop by drop, into atomic words. The ethnic language does not matter. Ask Aimé Césaire. He knows. Perhaps not consciously—but in the soul of his writing, he knows. Of all of the poets of African blood, he most unconsciously knows. The Negritudinous Senghor,[18] the Caribbeanesque Guillén, the American me, are regional poets of genuine realities and authentic values. Césaire's "Cahier" takes all that we have, Senghor, Guillén and Hughes, and flings it at the moon, to make of it a space-ship of the dreams of all the dreamers in the world.

As a footnote I must add that, concerning Césaire, all I have said I deeply feel is for me true. Concerning politics, nothing I have said is true. A poet is a human being. Each human being must live within his time, with and for his people, and within the boundaries of his country. Therefore, how can a poet keep out of politics?

Hang yourself, poet, in your own words. Otherwise, you are dead.

"Hold Fast to Dreams,"
Lincoln University Bulletin 67.2 (1964): 1–8

Thank you very much indeed for your most warm and friendly welcome back to this campus where I got my education.[19] I am very proud and happy to be invited to be the speaker for the 50th anniversary of Beta Chapter, my Chapter, of Omega.[20] It is always a pleasure to come back to the campus and to see some of the old friends and teachers whom I knew here . . .

I'd say that college days are days not only for learning but for dreaming; for dreaming about what you would like to do with your lives, what you would like to make of yourself; for dreaming about the girl you would love to make your wife and about the home you would like to create; for dreaming about the career you would like to have and the good things you would like to do in the world, because I don't think anybody ever really dreams about doing bad things or ugly or uncreative things. And so I say:

Dreams

Hold fast to dreams
For if dreams die
Life is a broken-winged bird
That cannot fly.

Hold fast to dreams
For when dreams go
Life is a barren field
Frozen with snow.

Those of us who are colored have, of course, difficulties to overcome, obstacles in the way of our dreams, that most other Americans do not have. Much of my poetry has dealt with these difficulties, these problems, of the Negro people in America. I think it is interesting to contemplate the fact that we did not come here of our own free will; we were brought here, you know.

American Heartbreak

I am the American Heartbreak—
Rock on which Freedom
Stumps its toe—

The great mistake
That Jamestown
Made long ago.

Many Americans living in our contemporary society, if they were to think about it, would think it was a big mistake to have brought us here. But they are stuck with us and it is our determination certainly to stay here. Despite all the difficulties and hardships including 250 years or so of slavery, the Ku Klux Klan, the Reconstruction Period, and the Depression and all that, we are still here.

Still Here

I've been scarred and battered.
My hopes the wind done scattered.
Snow has friz me, sun has baked me.
   Looks like between 'em
   They done tried to make me
Stop laughin', stop lovin', stop livin'—
   But I don't care!
   I'm still here!

Well, we have carved out of all of our difficulties, a place for ourselves in America and we've stuck to our dreams and we continue to dream bigger and bigger dreams . . .

If you're familiar with my character, Simple, you might recognize some of his qualities in these poems:

Bad Luck Card

Cause you don't love me
Is awful, awful hard.
Gypsy done showed me
My bad luck card.

There ain't no good left
In this world for me.
Gypsy done tole me—
Unlucky as can be.

I don't know what
Po' weary me can do.
Gypsy says I'd kill myself
If I was you.

But you know, Negroes are not noted for committing suicide. This next poem is about the kind of resiliency and the determination to live that apply not only to love but to economics and racial hardships too:

Life Is Fine

I went down to the river,
I set down on the bank.
I tried to think but couldn't,
So I jumped in and sank.

I came up once and hollered!
I came up twice and cried!
If that water hadn't a-been so cold
I might've sunk and died.

But it was
Cold in that water!
It was cold!

I took the elevator
Sixteen floors above the ground.
I thought about my baby
And thought I would jump down.

I stood there and I hollered!
I stood there and I cried!
If it hadn't a-been so high
I might've jumped and died.

But it was
High up there!
It was high!

So since I'm still here livin',
I guess I will live on.
I could've died for love—
But for livin' I was born.

Though you may hear me holler,
And you may see me cry—
I'll be dogged, sweet baby,
If you gonna see me die.

Many of my poems, as most of you probably know, are semi-humorous poems. I try sometimes to treat real social problems in humorous terms.

I would like next to read to you two poems, twin poems I guess you might call them.

Many of our fellow white Americans do not realize that there are social and cultural divisions among the Negro people. They sometimes think that all of us are just alike, you know. They used to think that all of us could sing and dance and had a sense of rhythm. I think that was why the 8th grade class I entered late in Lincoln, Illinois, elected me class poet. The teacher used the word "rhythm," you know, in relation to poetry. Having no other nominations and seeing a little colored boy there, they must have thought I had rhythm to give a poem and to be class poet.

Well, of course, these general, across-the-board beliefs are not true. They're like most other generalizations.

We do, however, have economic and social division, but they don't very much affect our fight for Civil Rights. I think the American Negroes are about 90% united among themselves in the demand for complete equality and certainly everybody, almost everybody, who can afford to at all, poor or not poor, gives money to the Urban League or the NAACP, to CORE, or SCLC or the other organizations fighting for equality.[21] We not only give money; most of us try to help in other ways as well. There is, however, a certain kind of snobbishness that sometimes exists between those who own the big white Continental car and those who don't. And that is what these poems are about. The first is called *Low to High.*

How can you forget me?
But you do!
You said you was gonna take me
Up with you—
Now you've got your Cadillac,
you done forgot that you are black.
How can you forget me
When I'm you?

But you do.

How can you forget me,
fellow, say?
How can you low-rate me
this way?
You treat me like you damn well please,
Ignore me—though I pay your fees.
How can you forget me?

But you do.

Well, the answer is called *High to Low.*

God knows
We have our troubles, too—
One trouble is you:
You talk too loud,
look too black;
don't get anywhere,
and sometimes it seems
you don't even care.
The way you send your kids to school
stockings down,
(not Ethical Culture)
the way you shout out loud in church,
(not St. Phillips)
and the way you lounge on doorsteps
just as if you were down South,
(not at 409)
the way you clown—
the way, in other words,
you let me down—
me, trying to uphold the race
and you—
well, you can see,
we have our problems,
too, with you.

Another example of the attempt to use humor in relation to social problems is a poem about the right to vote, the very problem that is so acute now and so often in the newspapers in Mississippi and Alabama and parts of Georgia. It's amazing, I think, that in the greatest so-called democracy in the world, there should be large sections of our country where Americans who happen not to be white cannot vote, and where it is worth your life to try to vote. Well this young man wants to vote and he tells in his own words what happens to him. The poem is called *Ku-Klux:*

They took me out
To some lonesome place.
They said, "Do you believe
In the great white race?"

I said, "Mister,
To tell you the truth,

I'd believe in anything
If you'd just turn me loose."

The white man said, "Boy,
Can it be
You're a-standin' there
A-sassin' me?"

They hit me in the head
And knocked me down.
And then they kicked me
On the ground.

A klansman said, "Nigger,
Look me in the face—
And tell me you believe in
The great white race."

The poem of mine that is most often quoted, most widely translated, and most often anthologized by interracial groups working for a better democracy, is the poem called *Merry-go-round.* And I think maybe it is because this poem presents the race problem through the eyes of a child very simply that it has been so often quoted and used in a social way. When I wrote it I imagined a little girl, maybe six or seven years old, who had come up from the South with her family to live in an industrial town like Detroit; or Oakland, California; or Newark. In this northern town or western town one day this little girl goes to a carnival and she wants to ride, but, remembering the segregations of the South, she doesn't know if a colored child can ride a merry-go-round in the North or, if she can ride, she doesn't know where. So this is what she says:

Merry-Go-Round

Where is the Jim Crow section
On this merry-go-round,
Mister, 'cause I want to ride?
Down South where I come from
White and colored
Can't sit side by side.
Down South on the train
There's a Jim Crow car.
On the bus we're put in the back—
But there ain't no back

To a merry-go-round.
Where's the horse
For a kid that's black?

Well, all of us here today feel that our country is big enough and rich enough to have a horse for every kid, black or white, Jewish or Gentile, Catholic or Protestant, and, of course, it's up to us, and particularly to the young people, to find a horse for every kid.

I think the students today, on the whole, can be very proud of themselves, and the Negro students in particular can be proud because, out of the Negro student body in the last five or six years, have come some of the greatest, most effective leaders in our country.

That may sound strange, when you consider that some of these leaders are only 18 and 20 years old. But they have done things that some of the leaders who lived to be 80 years old have not done. One thing that the student freedom movement, initiated by the Negro students, has done is to begin to activate students all over America and to create a new social consciousness among them.

Ten or fifteen years ago the American students, most of them, had very little social consciousness, and registered very little effective social action. At Yale they were eating goldfish, you know; they were dancing the Lindy Hop all over the country. That was all right, anybody ought to have fun, but, unlike Latin-American students and unlike European students who overturn governments when they get angry, American students weren't overturning anything and certainly they weren't trying to overturn prejudice and bigotry. But now they are.

I have read my poems on many college campuses in recent years, at colleges like Antioch, where I found an increasing number of white students joining the Negro students, for example, and the University of California, where I found an increasing number of white students joining with Oriental students and Mexican students to create equal rights—not only for our young people but for all minorities in America. I think we can give ourselves credit for creating a new, social consciousness among the young people of our country.

I think I'd like to read you one or two of my more serious poems:

Democracy

Democracy will not come
Today, this year

  Nor ever
Through compromise and fear.

I have as much right
As the other fellow has
  To stand
On my two feet
And own the land.

I tire so of hearing people say,
Let things take their course.
Tomorrow is another day.
I do not need my freedom when I'm dead.
I cannot live on tomorrow's bread.

Freedom
Is a strong seed
Planted
In a great need.

I live here, too.
I want freedom
Just as you.

Well, by and large, our demands for freedom were, until about 50 years ago, confined mostly to speech-making, writing poems like I write, and petitioning and hoping that white America would do more than they had been doing about our common problems. But it didn't happen.

Only when we became active, when we entered suits in the Supreme Court, when we became more and more militant and students began to sit-in at lunch counters and to conduct freedom rides did real changes begin to come about. But real changes have come and are coming about. The situation is by no means hopeless; we have nothing to be pessimistic about. This is really an exciting period in which to live, a period in which, with great pushing, sometimes we move forward.

When I first began to read my poems at Fisk, Hampton, Dillard, and other college campuses in the South I couldn't get anything to eat in the dining cars. I would have to wait, if I got into the diner at all, until all the white people had finished. And then along came the War . . . and the diners in the South instituted a system, I am sure many of you remember this, of having two tables at one end of the dining car reserved for colored passengers. But they had curtains and when you sat down they would pull this curtain so the rest of the people didn't have to look at Negroes eating.

An amazing country we live in. Imagine people doing that kind of thing. Well, today the curtains have gone, entirely gone, because of the NAACP, the student demonstrations, and because of the increasing refusal of Negroes to sit at tables where they pull curtains.

Today when I go into the South to read my poems somewhere, I go into the dining room like anyone else and I must say that, in the last five or six years, I found no discrimination of any kind . . . So you see there have been changes made, but what little changes are these that you have to fight and die and sue and spend a half-million dollars to get a simple meal like anybody else who isn't colored can get.

I have the feeling that it is all quite wonderful to picket and freedom-ride, and to sit-in for hamburgers, for coffee and for the right to swim in a pool, but those things are not enough. And I think most of you will agree with me that there will have to be a big, basic, social change in our country before equality will really come to the minority groups, and the poor people of America.

Our problem is not simply one of color. Perhaps color is a minor problem. The major problem for us is the problem of poverty, of not having enough money to live decently, of not having a job that will give a family at least a minimum decent living. And those problems go far beyond color. We know that there are many, many white people in our country who don't have enough to eat, whose children go to school in tennis shoes, too, and who live in tenements. So the big social change must go far beyond the things that most of our Negro organizations seem to consider the major problem.

When the big problems are solved, we won't have to sit-in anywhere for hamburgers; we won't have to risk being killed to go to register or to drop a ballot in the box in the South. And I think the day is coming when those major problems too will be solved. I can't say when because sometimes it seems a long ways off and yet, step by step and little by little the color problem is reaching a partial solution. And the struggle for democratic equality is moving much more rapidly now than ever before. And of course we haven't fought alone—ever. That's another nice thing about this America of ours.

In concluding, I would like to read a very old poem of mine from among those written while I was a student at Lincoln, and I graduated, as you heard, in 1929—quite a long time ago. But they are still valid poems because this problem that I have been telling you about is not solved. Poems that are thirty years old, poems that I had felt would be obsolete and outdated by now, are still in my book and are still, I think, applicable.

I, too, sing America;

I'm the darker brother.
They send me
To eat in the kitchen
When company comes,
But I laugh,
And eat well
And grow strong.

Tomorrow
I'll sit at the table
When company comes.
Nobody'll dare
Say to me,
"Eat in the kitchen,"
Then.

Besides,
They'll see
How beautiful I am
And be ashamed.

I, too, am America.

In my opinion what America is and what it really can become is what our Lincoln University has been and is becoming to an increasing extent, as anyone can see by looking at this audience of people, not just brown people or white people, but people of all colors.

"Carl Van Vechten: An Appreciation,"
LHP 226 (January 8, 1965)

A sure sign of old age is when a man begins to disapprove of the young. At the age of 84, Carl Van Vechten had not yet grown old. His enthusiasm for youth in the arts, and his quest for new talent, remained until the end unabated in music, in theatre, in writing and in painting. His tastes continued as catholic as ever. Despite Carl Van Vechten's long known deep interest in the creativity of the Negro people, and the immense amount of time he devoted to Negro activities, his concerns were by no means limited to darker Americans. James Purdy is a recent example of Van Vechten discovery and interest from manuscript to final printed page. In music from blues to bop and beyond, from Yvette Guilbert to Mahalia Jackson, from the long ago Mary Garden to the contemporary Leontyne Price, from George Gershwin of the Twenties to Charlie Mingus of the Sixties, Carl Van Vechten kept a listening ear as to the grace notes, and a listening heart as to the meanings of the music of each generation—in spite of the fact that he gave up professional music criticism at the age of forty because, he said, "intellectual hardening of the arteries" made one unreceptive to innovations.[22] As subsequent enthusiasms indicated, however, he must have found this statement untrue during the decades that followed.

Almost always Carl Van Vechten was ahead of his times in so far as public taste and the cannons of publicity went. The times had to catch up with him. In 1924 when most "cultured" people ignored America's basic Negro music, Carl Van Vechten wrote, "Jazz may not be the last hope of American music, nor yet the best hope, but at present, I am convinced, it is its only hope." In 1942, when he founded the James Weldon Johnson Memorial Collection of Negro Arts and Letters at Yale University, he presented it his enormous collection of recordings, jazz and otherwise, by colored composers and artists, as well as his many letters and manuscripts from Negro writers, painters and theatre people. Dr. Charles Johnson, then president of Fisk University, termed Carl Van Vechten, "the first white American to interpret objectively, with deftness and charm, the external features of the American Negro in a new age and setting."

Deftness and charm were so much a part of Carl Van Vechten's articles and critiques hailing his various enthusiasms that some, accustomed to more ponderous academic criticism, felt that the Van Vechten personality consisted mostly of fanfare and fun. It did possess these attributes. But behind the fanfare lay genuine critical acumen, often of a highly prophetic nature. And humor, wit, and sophistication in the best sense gave yeast to all the fun Van Vechten found in writing and living. He might be called both a hedonist and a humanist. In New York, Hollywood and Paris, he had a wide circle of lively, intelligent and decorative friends, particularly in the arts. There were no ethnic or religious barriers to his friendships. For many years on June 17 the joint birthdays of James Weldon Johnson, Negro, Alfred A. Knopf, Jr., Jewish, and himself were celebrated together with the three colors of our flag—red, white and blue—on the cakes at dinner, presided over by his charming wife, Fania Marinoff.[23]

When, late in life, he became a serious photographer, Van Vechten photographed not only his friends, but hundreds of valued and celebrated personalities, to the extent of some 15,000 negatives. Steichen termed his photography "darned good."[24] On the shelves of the world's libraries, Van Vechten leaves, for the pleasure of future readers who will discover him, 7 novels, numerous critiques, essays and memoirs, and three charming books about cats. He established the Anna Marble Pollack Memorial Library of Books About Cats at Yale. Fisk University has the George Gershwin Memorial Collection of Music and Musical Literature, as well as his gift of the Florine Stettheimer Memorial Collection of Books About the Fine Arts. The New York Public Library possesses his personal papers, letters and manuscripts. And, of his long and happy sojourn among us, his friends possess a rainbow of memories.

"A Letter from America,"
BBC Radio broadcast, LHP 3403 (March 1965)

Europeans seem so conditioned by Western movies concerning cowboys and Indians on the one hand; and on the other, by newspaper and magazine photographs of violent race struggles—beaten Negroes, white constables, police dogs—that no wonder the moment a foreign visitor lands at New York, he expects to see along the banks of the Hudson, Redskins lurking in the shadows, or Negroes and whites clashing in Central Park. The unexciting truth is, that to see any Indians at all, he would have to go at least a thousand miles from Manhattan, or more—far beyond Chicago. And to observe police dogs in action against Negroes, Alabama would be the most likely locale—another thousand miles or more from New York. Cowboys and Indians are Western. The West does not begin until one gets at least to Kansas or Colorado, half way across the United States. And unless there is a Harlem Riot going on—(which doesn't happen every day) the race problem in the North can seldom be spotted with a casual eye. Even in the South where race issues are acute, the *WHITES ONLY* signs have almost all disappeared since the passage of the Civil Rights Bill.[25] On an ordinary day when no demonstrations are taking place, Birmingham, Alabama, looks as peaceful to the naked eye as Birmingham, England. Even the dynamite is hidden.

America (a name the United States has arrogated unto itself) is a vast and varied collection of states, each having its own manners, morals, local laws, and folk mores. Varied indeed. Yet in *many* aspects, the vast stretch of United States "from sea to shining sea" is monotonously uniform—the same endless asphalt highways, the same motels, the same coca cola, the same hot dogs, the same hamburgers. There is a woeful lack of regional cooking—except for the Negro influence on New Orleans gumbos and Creole jambala of the Mississippi Delta region. But there is throughout America a very *great variation* in race relations between blacks and whites. And this is what seems hard for the average foreign visitor to understand. There is as much difference in this regard between Massachusetts and Mississippi as there is between the colors black and white, or between silk and sackcloth.

You may have read recently about a young Negro in Idaho who, as a joke, joined the Ku Klux Klan by mail—and lived unharmed to tell the tale and to release to the press the news of his mischievous prank. Had a Negro joined the Klan by mail (or otherwise) in Georgia, he might have been lynched. No Negro has been beaten for ordering a hot dog in any California restaurant, yet hundreds have been beaten for doing the same thing in the South. Negroes and whites have always gone to school together in the New England states. But until recently, they have not attended the same schools in the South. It took a major Supreme Court edict, government intervention, and in some cases troops, to achieve even token integration in education in Dixie.

Southern Negroes, of course, are no longer chattel slaves, but they are slaves of subterranean or open terror. While in the subways of New York, gangs of young Negroes lately are given to terrorizing whites, all over the South gangs of young and old whites have long been given to terrorizing Negroes. That certain ugly aspects of the Southern race problem have lately begun to spread all over the United States, is one result of America's allowing the South to get away with violence and Jim Crowism for much too long a time. Now push has come to shove. A lot of young Negroes in the North have violence in mind, even though it is seldom put into action.

One good thing about America is that there is a great tradition of free speech for almost everybody, and in almost all localities except the hard core South. In the race situation, this has served as a safety valve against bigger and better explosions than were the 1964 riots in the North. Free speech for Negroes ranges from the comparatively mild words of the executive head of the National Association for the Advancement of Colored People, Roy Wilkins, to the Christian non-violent speeches of Martin Luther King, to the more provocative utterances of the late Malcolm X, and the oral and written words of James Baldwin, or LeRoi Jones, the current gadfly of *all* whites—right, left, liberal or otherwise. Jones advises the whole white world to drop dead. By and large, Negroes in the United States, even where they cannot vote, can at least talk freely, hold meetings, and march. Even though, as on the road from Selma to Montgomery, troops must be mustered to protect them, they *do* march.

Why troops in Alabama to protect a peaceful protest? Because the patterns of slave days—a hundred years after Emancipation—still exist there. Why for a long time, were racial problems more acute in *Southern* California than in Northern California? Because Southern California with its oil and industrial plants, drew thousands of white and black workers from Louisiana and Texas and other southern areas who brought their prejudices and problems with them. These folks did not migrate to Northern California in such vast numbers. When I lived in San Francisco, for example, racial discrimination scarcely existed in any serious degree, while a few hundred miles to the South in the same state, many public places—restaurants, theatres, bowling alleys—refused service to Negroes and Mexicans. Japanese, Chinese, and Filipino-Americans were also discriminated against in Southern California. There, during the war, Japanese-Americans, even third and fourth generation citizens born in America, were put into concentration camps. White German Americans were not so incarcerated. German prisoners of war could eat in Southern restaurants and dining cars, while American Negro soldiers guarding them could not. One of the contradictions of democracy!

Variations in patterns of race relations really vary to a confusing degree even in the North, from one state to another, one city to another, but worsening the further South one travels. In New York City, during my residence of more than a quarter of a century, I have encountered perhaps less than a half dozen incidents of color discrimination—and these of a very minor nature. New York is, I would say, like London, a not unpleasant city for people of color to live in. But just across the river from New York, in New Jersey less than a half hour away, Negroes may still encounter difficulties or downright refusal in some places of public service. Two hours further South by train, in Delaware or Maryland, in cities like Baltimore, deep South prejudices still prevail. An hour further on, in Washington, until a few years ago, Negroes could not attend any downtown theatres. Not only Negroes, but dark diplomats from the African and Asian countries today, find housing most difficult in our nation's capital. And a little thing like getting a haircut outside the Negro neighborhoods can become a major problem.

In Virginia, just across the Potomac from Washington, colored motorists may find food and lodging along the highways a serious problem. Once when I was motoring through Virginia on a lecture tour, on a warm autumn day I stopped at a roadside refreshment shop to purchase some cool bottles of soda to take out to the car. But when I went to open the screen door of the shack, the proprietor inside held the door so that it would not open. He said, "We got a hole cut around on the side where we serve niggers."

Under the Civil Rights Bill, Negro travellers theoretically are allowed to use the rest rooms at gas stations along the highways. But many toilet facilities are now kept locked. Negro motorists may buy gas, but station attendants often refuse to give them rest room keys, claiming the plumbing is out of order. There are some gas stations in the Deep South that will not even sell petrol to Negroes—and sometimes not even to whites if their cars bear Northern licence tags. Southerners lately are inclined to take most Northern whites as "nigger-lovers," therefore they may refuse them service, too.

To me, a Northern Negro, the ways of the South are puzzling indeed. In some cities anyone may ride in any taxi cab. In other cities, Negroes may not ride in white driven cabs; and white persons may not occupy Negro driven cabs. For example, a white and a Negro professor travelling together from, say a New York University to attend an educational seminar in, say Atlanta, may not ride together from the station to the seminar in the same taxi. Once in Texas I learned that in Houston I could ride from the airport into the city by official airport transportation. Forty miles away, in Dallas, Negroes were *not* permitted to ride in airport limousines. I had to telephone into the city for a colored taxi and wait an hour to get into town. Airlines claim that they are not responsible for ground transportation. The Negro singing-actress, Muriel Rahn, was once on a plane forced to make an emergency landing in an Alabama cotton field during a blinding snowstorm. The pilot telephoned into Huntsville for taxis to transport the passengers into town. However, none of the cabs would take Miss Rahn, the lone Negro passenger, who was left standing alone in the middle of an icy field. She had to take refuge in a black tenant farmer's cabin. When she finally got into the city, no hotel would house her for the night. Miss Rahn sued the airline, but without results. Just as a white person is almost never punished for a crime against a Negro in the South, so a Negro seldom wins a lawsuit against a white man or firm.

Such are the ways of the American South—not only strange, but contradictory from region to region.

There is an old saying to the effect that white Southerners love individual Negroes whom they know, but do not like Negroes in the mass at all. Certainly most Southerners oppose mass aspirations toward civic, social or political equality—Selma being a case in point—where even the basic democratic right of the ballot is not granted black citizens. But Negroes may vote freely in New York and Chicago, Detroit, San Francisco and Los Angeles—as the number of Negroes in national, state and municipal offices proves. Negroes in most large Northern cities work not only in industries, but in laboratories, offices, department stores, hospitals, and transportation facilities. While some unions, North and South, still hold to antiquated color bars, and the powerful Brotherhood of Locomotive Engineers may not have any Negro members, the most powerful entertainment union in the country, Actors Equity, has a Negro president, Frederick O'Neil; and A. Philip Randolph, a Negro, is vice-president of the American Federation of Labor.

Front doors are gradually opening to Negroes in many parts of America, but in Alabama and Mississippi, South Carolina and Georgia, even back doors are still closed. That is the American dilemma. The country is divided in its racial attitudes. Its major parties are divided in their racial attitudes. The Southern Democrats and the Northern are far from seeing eye to eye. The Republicans are even more divided and, at the moment cannot make up their minds at all what to do before the next presidential election rolls around. "To be or not to be" pro-Negro, that is the question. And how to square daily behavior with all those beautiful words about equality in the Constitution, the Bill of Rights, and the Supreme Court decisions? Certainly the Negro poses a mighty problem for America these days. It is too bad that that first slave ship in 1619 landed twenty *Negars* at Jamestown.

Maybe that ship should have been sunk.

"The Task of the Negro Writer as Artist,"
Negro Digest 14 (April 1965): 65, 75

Whatever a white writer may write in this America of ours, or whatever picture he may present, nobody says derogatorily of his presentation, "That is just like white folks." But whatever a Negro writer writes today is likely to be taken as representative of us all, *"Just like Negroes."* Therefore, it behooves Negro writers in our segregated society, not necessarily to put our *best* foot forward, but to try at least to put a *balanced* foot forward, so that we do not all appear to be living in a *Cool World* in *Another Country* in the *Crazy House of the Negro* in which the majority of *The Blacks* seem prone to little except the graffiti of *The Toilet* or the deathly behavior of a *Slow Dance on the Killing Ground.*[26] Pride, nobility, sacrifice and decency are qualities strangely lacking in some of the most talented outpourings by or about Negroes these days. The Negro image deserves objective well-rounded (rather than one-sided) treatment, particularly in the decade of a tremendous freedom movement in which all of us can take pride. The last thing Negroes need now are black imitators of neurotic white writers who themselves have nothing of which to be proud. We possess within ourselves a great reservoir of physical and spiritual strength to which poetry, fiction and the stage should give voice—Cambridge, Albany, Fort Royal, Selma, Jackson, Atlanta. There is today no lack within the Negro people of beauty, strength and power—world shaking power. If I were a young writer, I would try to put some of these qualities on paper and on stage. Contemporary white writers can perhaps afford to be utterly irresponsible in their moral and social viewpoints. Negro writers cannot. Ours is a social as well as a literary responsibility.

"*Ebony*'s Nativity: An Evaluation from Birth," *Ebony*, November 1965, pp. 40–46

I cannot say I was a mere stripling of a boy when *Ebony* was born—but I was twenty years *younger* than I am now. I cannot say I was any less race conscious in 1915 than I am today, but two decades ago I found less in the world to bolster my pride than we have now. An especially happy event in regard to race was the birth of *Ebony* in the autumn of 1945—a new young and handsome journalistic child of which to be proud.

I liked *Ebony* from its very beginning, and only a few times during its adolescent period did I get a bit put out with it—as often happens to parents with children, who, in the puberty years, are inclined to try even a saint's soul. There was a time about ten years ago when to me some of the articles and pictures in *Ebony* seemed on occasion in rather bad taste. I then complained to its editors that somebody on the staff seemed to be leading John H. Johnson's offspring (and mine by love and adoption) astray.[27] That period of occasional cheapness and puerility passed. Now on the threshold of maturity, and heading toward its twenty-first year, *Ebony* has developed into a hale, hearty, wholesome, intelligent and beautiful publication indeed, of which I think every American might be proud.

Today Negro America finds in *Ebony* an increasingly well rounded picture of itself in a handsome frame. The format is attractive, its layout eye catching, and its paper good. This latter fact is of great importance, lest our picture history crumble into dust within a few years. Many of the magazines of twenty years ago are now sear, yellow, dry and falling apart. Not so with the early editions of *Ebony* which I have managed to keep in spite of my travelling hither and yon. And the bound volumes I have seen preserved in libraries are in good shape.

From the start *Ebony* has had consistently eye-catching and interesting covers, racial as well as interracial, beginning with Rev. Ritchie's seven boys of the Children's Crusade on the first issue, followed by lovely Hilda Simms of *Anna Lucasta* fame on the second cover. Over the years almost every famous Negro from Josephine Baker to Thurgood Marshall has looked out at us from an *Ebony* cover, with the most beautiful and talented of women getting an especially handsome print job on the inside and outside of the magazine. The pert face and piquant figure of the inimitable Miss Eartha Kitt has appeared so often in *Ebony* that some folks think she owns the magazine. But I never objected to Miss Kitt, it being hard ever to see too much of that particular charmer. From Lena Horne and the late Dorothy Dandridge to the sepia toned international beauties Vera Lucia Couto dos Santos of Brazil and Monique Cartright of Haiti, *Ebony* covers have presented pulchritude par excellence.[28] High fashion model Janie Burdette in the briefest of bikinis to Helen Williams in winter coat; the Supremes all in red; sweet and simple Ruby Dee in plain and simple blouse against the background of her husky husband, actor-playwright Ossie Davis; blonde May Britt and family, its head being Sammy Davis Jr., domesticated. And the lustiest beauty of them all, Miss Pearl Bailey.

But not by any means have all of *Ebony*'s covers been devoted to pulchritude. Two covers that I remember well are the massed faces, Negro and white, of a portion of the crowd surging forward in the great March on Washington of 1963; and Pope Paul VI canonizing the Uganda Martyrs with the assistance of African Cardinal Laurian Rugambwa at a Pontifical Mass in St. Peters. If we had had no *Ebony,* we would not have such photographs in dramatic color piled on thousands of newsstands throughout the country for our white fellow citizens to see at a glance the new roles Negroes play in today's world. One picture is sometimes worth a million words, and much easier to take in quickly. Passersby who might never buy a copy of *Ebony* see these vividly effective photographs as they purchase their newspapers. On the few times that *Ebony* has departed from photographic covers, striking drawings have served to attract attention—the sharp black and white of the recent

"White Problem in America" issue, and the striking sketch of Frederick Douglass on the issue devoted to the 100th Anniversary of the Emancipation Proclamation, an occasion on which a whole magazine became a historical document that might well be printed between book covers.

The files of *Ebony* from its inception in 1945 to this 1965 issue could well serve as an overall history of the American Negro during the past twenty years—and on back beyond the Mayflower, since some articles have been devoted to past as well as contemporary happenings, such as Lerone Bennett's splendid pieces.[29] While the main emphasis has been on the presentation of the positive side of Negro achievement, *Ebony* has not hesitated to face the grim realities of such ugly episodes in American life as the Emmett Till lynching or the Birmingham brutalities and to present them in all their horror. The careless charge some critics have made that *Ebony* presents only successful Negroes, colorful sports and entertainment personalities and pretty fashion models is not true. Even if it were true, there has been such a need in Negro lives to see themselves pictured beautifully, to view on the printed page something other than slums, and to learn that at least some black men and women can be successful in this highly competitive world, that a magazine presenting *nothing* but the positive side would still be of value, even if the balance were a bit overboard. I do not feel that *Ebony* has gone overboard.

To "accent the positive" as *Ebony* has done, is to give Negro America a sorely needed psychic lift. Nowhere is this lift more in evidence today than in the advertisements of high calibre which it has attracted to its pages within the last decade. When *Ebony* first began publication, it had never occurred to most national manufacturers of commodities which millions of Negroes as well as whites buy, to place advertisements in Negro publications. When major firms did advertise in the Negro press, which was very seldom, it never crossed their minds to use Negro faces in the ads, or to picture black youngsters eating national brand cereals, or colored people riding in an automobile, be it Ford or Lincoln, or buying a soft drink for their children. Now in *Ebony* there are strikingly beautiful ads of Negroes doing all these things.

Look at the handsome young brownskin couple extolling the delights of Coca Cola in full page color, or the good-looking young Negro in the "Camel Time" ad, the stunning brown girl smoking a Newport, and those wholesome Negro families now pictured getting into sleek and shining cars. Twenty years ago, to expect to see such advertisements in a colored magazine would have been unthinkable. In the field of the American commercial, *Ebony* has been as much of a pioneer as was brownskin

Matt Henson when he became the first man to set foot on the North Pole.[30] That *Ebony* can now afford not only to have color covers, but feature articles *in color* inside the magazine, is due to its determined and dogged assault on the white battlements of Madison Avenue advertising. It was not easy to make "the walls come tumbling down." But they did. Result: now even the *New York Times, Life* and *The New Yorker* picture Negro models in ads—not of the once popular "ham what am" variety, either.

Five years after the birth of *Ebony,* its publisher presented a series of authenticated facts to the advertising agencies that helped open their eyes to the dollar value of the Negro market. Nine out of ten *Ebony* readers carried life insurance. Four out of ten *Ebony* readers owned cars. Two out of ten in 1950 possessed television sets, and the same percentage bought pianos. One out of four had graduated from college and were potential culture buyers. *Ebony* had its circulation authenticated by the Audit Bureau of Circulations, and its contents indexed in the Readers' Guide to Periodical Literature. The result is that today *Ebony*'s advertising is voluminous, the format of the ads most attractive and, if they were to be one hundred per cent visually believed, *all* Negro Americans are good looking. (Typical example, the charming *café au lait* couple at their lovely dining table advertising Simplicity patterns). To see ourselves presented so handsomely in commercial advertising (which now has spread to other national publications) is a great achievement on the positive side due, I believe, largely to *Ebony.*

In 1945, the year that *Ebony* was born, the world lay in shambles. Europe had been devastated by war. Hiroshima was in ruins. The atom bomb had been dropped. Most of Berlin was a mass of rubble. Hitler had committed suicide, Mussolini was hanged, and that year Franklin D. Roosevelt died. But World War II had ended with the Japanese surrender in September. Then at San Francisco the triumphant powers gathered to create the United Nations. Among those present at its beginnings were Dr. Ralph Bunche, Walter White of the NAACP, Mary McLeod Bethune of the National Council of Negro Women, and Dr. W. E. B. Du Bois. Negroes were as interested in the world of tomorrow as anybody else, and wanted to make it more than a mint of blood and sorrow. There had been only one lynching in the United States in 1945, but in other ways race prejudice was still rampant. And there was the perennial problem of Negroes and jobs. The very first issue of *Ebony* contained an article entitled, "60 Million Jobs, or Else," and another on "Catholics and Color."

On the surface in 1945, American life, of course, went on more or less as usual. *Amos and Andy* in dialect was the most popular show on radio. Ex-GI Joe Louis was anticipating his return bout with Billy Conn. Teen-age movie star Shirley Temple got married. Dizzy Gillespie and Billy Eckstine and Charlie Parker were giving birth to be-bop. Richard Wright's *Black Boy* appeared in the bookshops. Jackie Robinson became the first authenticated Negro signed for major league baseball. Adam Powell was elected to the House of Representatives. Segregation in the Navy ended. The Spingarn Medal was awarded to Thurgood Marshall, and Nat King Cole was singing *Straighten Up and Fly Right* which lots of Negroes took as being directed at white folks.[31] Certainly, Negroes were ripe for a change in the American status quo, and things were not changing fast enough for them. The war was over in Europe and Asia. Black soldiers would soon be coming home. Question—To the same old Jim Crow they had known before?

The Negro soldier had been to many lands, seen many peoples, and been treated with a dignity and sensibility, even by his foes, that was alien to him in his own country. The die cast, he could never return in spirit to racial complacency in America, and certainly not to the old days of Uncle Tom—even though Booker T. Washington was elected to the Hall of Fame in 1945. In fact, Uncle Tom was probably slain in Normandy, at Anzio or Iwo Jima, never to be resurrected again by the army of brave young black men returning to America with a new sense of freedom and purpose. The year *Ebony* was born marked not only the beginning of the Negro's broader horizon, but that of America itself. Our country could no longer stand alone in lofty isolation as it had tried to do before the war. The United States could no longer insulate itself from world problems. And, willingly or unwillingly, it had to start practicing what it preached in regard to liberty and freedom and democracy, both at home and abroad.

Though America was slow to realize it, the world was not entirely white. It was *predominantly* colored—and what is right for the white nations is not always right for the colored nations. Indeed, in 1945 America was being forced for the first time to carefully examine the values of human dignity proclaimed in its own constitution, and to begin practicing, however grudgingly, those ideals to which it had been giving lip service for generations. As to that world within a world of black Americans, new understandings had to be developed. At this crucial period, fortunately, along came *Ebony,* whose very name means *black,* to help America better understand ourselves and—itself.

"The Negro and American Entertainment," *The American Negro Reference Book,* ed. John P. Davis (Englewood Cliffs: Prentice-Hall, 1966), 826–49

"The Negro singers, as always, make opera credible. And, as always, they make music shine. They have a physical beauty of movement, natural distinction and grace. Musically they have rhythm, real resonance, excellent pitch, superb enunciation, and full understanding of the operatic convention. They never look bored or out-of-place on the stage or seem inappropriately cast for any musical style," so wrote in 1943 the distinguished composer and critic, Virgil Thomson, in commenting on the Broadway scene. Many before and since have confirmed his opinions.

The logs of slave ships crossing the Atlantic do not reveal African captives willingly singing for the pleasure of others during the long voyage under sail to the Americas. But in *A Journal of a Voyage Made in the Hannibal of London, Ann. 1693–1694* it is recorded, "We often at sea in the evening would let the slaves come up into the sun to air themselves, and make them jump and dance for an hour or two to our bagpipes, harp, and fiddle, by which exercise to preserve them in health." And *An Account of the Slave Trade on the Coast of Africa* published in England in 1788 states concerning captives during the Middle Passage, "Exercise being deemed necessary for the preservation of their health, they are sometimes obliged to dance, when the weather will permit their coming on deck. . . . The poor wretches are frequently compelled to sing also; but when they do so, their songs are generally, as may naturally be expected, melancholy lamentations of their exile from their native country." Those Africans who revolted with Cinque aboard the *Amistad* off Cuba and themselves brought their ship to Northern waters, reported during their trial for murder and piracy in New Haven in 1839 that sometimes on the decks of that runaway slaver men in chains chanted songs of Africa and black mothers in shackles crooned to their children.[32] On the shores of colonial America, very early records of life on the plantations and in the cities, as well, report whites as being entertained by the singing and dancing of their black chattels.

In the early eighteen hundreds in New Orleans on Sunday afternoons when the slaves were allowed a few hours of "freedom" to rest and play, the bamboula drums throbbed on Congo Square. There the whites often gathered to watch the blacks sing and dance in African fashion. Many of the newly imported slaves spoke neither French nor English, and their music was as yet uninfluenced by the European. There and then, say the chroniclers of jazz, the rhythms of Africa began to seep into America's musical heritage. Scarcely had the slaves set foot on our shores than their influence on American entertainment began.

Wealthy slave owners soon developed the habit of sending for their most musical slaves to sing and dance for them as they sat on their wide verandas of a summer evening. And some plantations permitted their more talented blacks to travel from plantation to plantation to entertain other wealthy masters and their guests. There were in these slave troops field hands who could crack jokes, others who shook the bones of spareribs or sheep in syncopated rhythms or played the comb or the banjo or the saw or the corn-stalk fiddle and could do the buck-and-wing or the *danse calinda.*

Slaves sometimes became name performers and their masters were in effect their booking agents. The following advertisement on behalf of Toler and Cook appeared on June 27, 1853, in the *Richmond Daily Enquirer:* "FOR HIRE, either for the remainder of the year, or by the month, week, or job, the celebrated musician and fiddler, GEORGE WALKER. All persons desiring the services of George are notified that they must contract for them with us, and in no case pay to him or any other person the amount of his hire, without a written order from us. George Walker is admitted, by common consent, to be the best leader of a band in all eastern and middle Virginia." And in his slave memoirs of life on a Louisiana cotton plantation in the mid-eighteen fifties, Solomon Northrup wrote, "My master often received letters, sometimes from a distance of ten miles, requesting him to send me to play at a ball of festival of the whites. He received his compensation, and usually I also returned with many picayunes jingling in my pockets . . . and secured the loudest and heartiest welcome of them all at the Christmas dance."[33]

The escaped slave, Frederick Douglass, in his *Life and Times,* wrote that on the plantations during the Christmas holidays, "fiddling, dancing, and 'jubilee beating' was carried on in all directions. This latter performance was strictly Southern. It supplied the place of the violin or other musical instruments and was played so easily that almost every farm had its juba beater. The performer improvised as he beat the instrument, marking the words as he sang so as to have them fall pat with the movement of his hands. Once in a while among a mass of nonsense and wild frolic, a sharp hit was given to the meanness of the slaveholders. Take the following example:

We raise de wheat,
Dey gib us de corn:
We bake de bread,
Dey gib us de crust.
We sif de meal,
Dey gib us de huss.
We peel de meat,
Dey gib us de skin—
And dat's de way
Dey take us in."

Thus were born, under the guise of entertainment, the first Negro protest songs. Others grew out of religious meetings and developed into such great ante-bellum spirituals as *Go Down, Moses, Oh, Freedom,* and *God's Gonna Cut You Down.* Using the spiritual as entertainment, seven singers born in slavery formed the major part of a group that comprised the Fisk Jubilee Singers who in 1871, eight years after Emancipation, began a concert tour of America and Europe that brought the spirituals to international attention. Since then these plantation songs have become world famous. The Negro as a factor in American entertainment stems from the plantation singer, dancer and jester who, in entertaining themselves, entertained their masters. Booker T. Washington in his *Up from Slavery* says that even after freedom came, when he went to Alabama in 1881 to found Tuskegee, the customs of slave Christmases still continued on the nearby plantations. Each night the field hands "usually had what they called a 'frolic.' "

At least one slave, Blind Tom, became nationally famous before Emancipation as a professional entertainer under the management of his master, Colonel Bethune. Tom became known as a concert headliner, booked as a moneymaking attraction long after slavery ended. Billed as the "MUSICAL PRODIGY—with wonder Powers as a Pianist," it was said that Tom could reproduce any piece of music, no matter how difficult, upon hearing it only once. It was also advertised that Tom could "perform with his back to the piano." Blind Tom had a highly successful run in New York City, appearing in Irving Place both matinees and nights in the Spring of 1868—and playing on a Steinway, no less.

Before the Civil War, as an outgrowth of the singing and dancing of plantation slaves, the nation's most popular form of entertainment, the all male blackface minstrels evolved. In these shows, white men imitated on stage the singing, dancing, speech and humor of the Southern blacks. Their sketches were often dramatized plantation stories. And popular

American performers have been borrowing from Negroes ever since. It was in 1830 in Cincinnati that the white minstrel, Dan Rice, saw a little black street urchin dancing to a ditty that went:

Step first upon yo' heel
An' den upon yo' toe,
An' ebry time you turns around
You jump Jim Crow.
Next fall upon yo' knees
Then jump up and bow low
An' ebry time you turn around
You jump Jim Crow.

Rice copied the song, learned the boy's dance steps, and made a fortune from them.[34]

The Virginia Minstrels headed by Dan Emmett, composer of *Dixie,* was the first of such attractions to perform in New York. It opened on the Bowery in 1843. For more than 50 years thereafter minstrels were in vogue all over the country and in Europe. They played in theatres where the Negro whom the performers imitated could not even buy a ticket, and on whose stages black men were not allowed to perform. The earliest wide spread discrimination against the Negro in the American theatre, both as spectator and performer, began with the minstrels. This is an irony, if there ever was one, in that the minstrels derived their entertainment values solely from Negroes—Negro rhythms, Negro dance steps, plantation melodies, and a bold faced blackface imitation of Negro speech and humor.

The white minstrel performers developed so broad a burlesque of what the general public took to be "Negro life" that their shows created a stereotyped concept of colored Americans which continues to this day. The sooty burnt cork makeup, the exaggeratedly wide lips, the gold teeth, the gaudy clothing, the loud jokes, the fantastic dialect, the watermelon and razor props, and the dice that continue right down to *Porgy and Bess,* became so much a part of commercial theatre in the United States that black performers themselves, in order to be successful, felt impelled to imitate these blackface whites. As a result, Bert Williams made himself twelve shades darker than he really was and spoke, in the *Ziegfeld Follies,* a dialect he never heard except from white performers. Later Miller and Lyles imitated Moran and Mack so well that the white actors who played Amos and Andy in turn imitated Miller and Lyles. Then Rochester imitated all of them put together.

These performers as well as white Al Jolson and black Stepin Fetchit, white Eddie Cantor and black Mantan Moreland, all stemmed from the minstrel tradition. For a long time, most Negro comedians felt that in order to be funny, they had to work under cork. Strangest paradox of all was Pigmeat Markham, one of the funniest and most popular of Negro comedians. For years on stage his makeup was burnt cork. When changing times after the Second World War forced him to stop blacking himself up, his audiences were amazed to discover that in reality Pigmeat was himself darker than the burnt cork he had been using. For neither rhyme nor reason, some Negro performers continued to perpetuate the minstrel stereotype long after the minstrel era was over.

On the positive side, however, the white blackface minstrels introduced to the American public the entertainment values inherent in Negro material—before Negroes themselves could appear on Jim Crow stages. When genuine *Negro* minstrels did make their appearance, they had a public waiting for them, and in some cases were welcomed into theatres where Negroes had not formerly played. In 1865 a Negro, Charles Hicks, organized *The Georgia Minstrels* which later came under white management and toured America and Europe. In 1882 this troupe became a part of *Callender's Consolidated Spectacular Colored Minstrels* and toured the United States, as did other Negro minstrel shows, the largest being the *Richards and Pringle Minstrels.* Comedians Sam Lucas and Billy Kersands, who could put a cup and saucer in his mouth, became famous Negro names in minstrelsy. But the Negro performer of those days whose work will live—because not only did he appear on stages at home and abroad but was a great song writer as well—is James Bland, composer of *In the Evening by the Moonlight* and *Carry Me Back to Old Virginny,* now the official song of the State of Virginia.

On the part of Negro performers, the first successful breakaway from all masculine blackface minstrels came in 1891 with the opening in Boston of *The Creole Show* which featured a singing and dancing chorus of sixteen beautiful girls. In 1893 this show played a full season at the Chicago World's Fair and toured for several years thereafter. During the Gay Nineties other successful Negro shows were *The South before the War, The Octoroons,* and *Oriental America.* The latter was the first all-Negro company to appear on Broadway, the first to include operatic selections among its musical numbers and to feature in its cast trained musicians such as J. Rosamond Johnson.[35] The success of these shows led at the turn of the century to the great era of Negro musical comedy in which not only performers but Negro composers and writers gained a foothold in the commercial theatre, and beauty became a part of the brownskin world of make believe.

Sissieretta Jones, a statuesque woman with a gorgeous voice, made such a hit in the Jubilee Spectacle at Madison Square Garden in the spring of 1892 that in the autumn she was invited to sing at the White House. Billed as Black Patti, Sissieretta Jones with her company of Troubadours toured for many years. Dora Dean, another beautiful woman of color, was such a gorgeous cakewalker that a song called *Dora Dean* was written about her and her dancing. Belle Davis, Ada Overton, Abbie Mitchell, all golden brown and talented, smartly dressed on stage and off, became the early leading ladies of the Negro theatre. Abbie Mitchell's career spanned more than a half century from star billing in turn of the century musicals to featured roles on Broadway in such contemporary dramas as Lillian Hellman's *The Little Foxes.* Still in her teens, Abbie Mitchell married the brilliant composer, Will Marion Cook, appeared in his *Clorindy,* the first ragtime musical, and later bore him a son, Mercer Cook, who became American ambassador to Senegal.

The Cakewalk was the first dance of Negro origin to sweep the country and become a ballroom favorite—as did other Negro steps much later—the Charleston, the Lindy Hop, the Jitterbug, and in our times the Twist. Derived from the plantation frolics, and popularized as a comic burlesque in the minstrels, the real charm of the Cakewalk with its high stepping grace did not reach the stage until Cook's *Clorindy: The Origin of the Cakewalk* (for that was its subtitle) was produced in 1898 at the Casino Roof in New York, with book and lyrics by Paul Laurence Dunbar. Performed by handsome couples, the women gorgeously gowned, and nobody in blackface, the dance was a joy. Williams and Walker first came to fame as exponents of the Cakewalk. And it was the Williams and Walker musicals that in the early nineteen hundreds had great success in the theatres. Their *Sons of Ham* played for two years. *In Dahomey* was a Broadway hit, repeated by a long run in London, with a command performance in 1903 at Buckingham Palace. In New York *Abyssinia* and *Bandana Land* followed, with Will Marion Cook and Will Vodery as composers, Alex Rogers, lyricist of *Nobody,* as librettist, and a largely all Negro staff in the production end of these popular musicals. In 1910 Bert Williams graduated to the *Ziegfeld Follies* and became Broadway's first Negro star in an otherwise all white show. His burnt cork comedy, which stemmed from the minstrel tradition, and his droll songs kept him a star until his death in 1922. Williams and Walker, Cole and Johnson (*The Shoofly Regiment, Red Moon*) and Will Marion Cook were the musical pioneers who first opened the doors of Broadway to Negro entertainment.

But on the dramatic stage it took almost a hundred years for colored actors to attain success anywhere near that of the singers, dancers and comics. It was not for lack of trying. On Bleecker Street in New York City from 1821 to 1832 a group of free Negroes with James Hewlett as leading man performed Shakespeare's *Othello, Richard the Third,* and other classics. The players were known as the African Company and their playhouse the African Grove—where, according to a chronicle of the times, the breeze had "free access through the crevices of the boards." White hoodlums who came to laugh and jeer eventually forced this earliest of Negro dramatic theatres to close, but not before it had posted a sign which read: WHITE PEOPLE DO NOT KNOW HOW TO BEHAVE THEMSELVES AT ENTERTAINMENT DESIGNED FOR LADIES AND GENTLEMEN.

Before the African Grove closed, among its supers who helped create the illusion of a crowd on stage was a youngster from the nearby African Free School whose name was Ira Aldridge. His love for serious drama eventually made young Ira one of the greatest Shakespearean actors of his day—but *not* in the United States. He came to fame in Europe where, among other classic roles in London, he played Othello to Edmund Kean's Iago, performed to acclaim in all the great capitals of the Continent, and never came home. When Theophile Gautier saw Ira Aldridge as King Lear in 1858 in a crowded Russian theatre, the French journalist wrote that so convincing was his performance in Caucasian makeup—silver locks, flowing white beard, sallow cheeks—that "Cordelia would never have suspected that her father was a Negro." After forty years of European successes, America's first international star of color died in Poland in 1867. Today at Stratford-on-Avon there is an Ira Aldridge Chair designated in his honor at the Shakespeare Memorial Theatre.

After the demise of the African Grove, it was over a half century before Negro dramatic actors had access to theatres of any permanency in which they might perform with regularity. In some sections of the country small stock companies sprang up which sometimes presented plays as well as musical entertainments. Such a company headed by Bob Cole became a permanent part of Worth's Museum in New York for several years, with a number of young Negro apprentices involved and, in the later days of the play's popularity, various companies of *Uncle Tom's Cabin* employed Negro actors, instead of whites blacked up, for the slave roles. But it was not until the formation by Lester Walton in 1914 of the Lafayette Stock Company in Harlem that the Negro performer found himself able to work for a full season in straight dramatic plays ranging from the classics to revivals of Broadway hits—sometimes tailored to the taste of colored audiences.[36] From the Harlem productions of *Othello, Madame X, The Count of Monte Cristo,* and *On Trial* presented with all-colored casts, a number of talented players eventually reached Broadway and Hollywood—Charles Gilpin, Evelyn Ellis, Frank Wilson, Edna Thomas and Clarence Muse among others. Muse, a very dark young man from Baltimore, became a great favorite with Harlem audiences. At the Lafayette he pulled a complete switch from the days of the minstrels. Instead of appearing in blackface in such plays as *Within the Law,* Clarence Muse appeared in whiteface, complete with blond toupee. A quarter of a century later in *The Duchess of Malfi,* the late Canada Lee played the brother to Elizabeth Bergner on Broadway in white makeup. The Lincoln Theatre in Harlem, the Pekin Theatre in Chicago, the Standard in Philadelphia and the Howard in Washington also had, from time to time, stock companies, often borrowing stars from the Lafayette, whose production standards were high.

The Harlem chronicler, James Weldon Johnson, terms April 5, 1917, the most important date in the history of the Negro in the American theatre. On that evening at the Garden Theatre in downtown New York there opened a bill of three one-act plays, *The Rider of Dreams, Granny Maumee* and *Simon the Cyrenian,* by the poet Ridgeley Torrence. There was entr'acte music by a singing orchestra of Clef Club members conducted by J. Rosamond Johnson. The show was a great success and its presentation marked "the first time anywhere in the United States for Negro actors in the dramatic theatre to command the serious attention of the critics and the general press and public." Three years later at the Provincetown Theatre in the Village, Eugene O'Neill's first hit, *The Emperor Jones,* with Charles Gilpin in the title role, opened. Gilpin was acclaimed one of the ten best actors of the year, Eugene O'Neill began his ascent to fame, and from that time on the Negro performer in serious drama became an accepted part of the national scene.

Paul Green's earliest and greatest successes were also with plays cast largely with Negroes, among them *In Abraham's Bosom,* a Pulitzer Prize winner in 1926, in which Rose McClendon, Jules Bledsoe and Abbie Mitchell were featured. Commercially the most successful plays concerned with Negro life were then all written by whites, but a number of them furnished excellent vehicles for colored actors to achieve outstanding performances. Notable presentations included O'Neill's *All God's Chillun Got Wings* with Paul Robeson in 1924, David Belasco's production of *Lulu Belle* that same year, Lawrence Stalling's *Deep River* in which Rose McClendon won nightly applause merely by her wordless descent of a winding staircase, Jim Tully's *Black Boy* with lovely Freddie Washington; and, finally the Theatre Guild's *Porgy* with Frank Wilson, Evelyn Ellis and Georgette Harvey. Rounding off a decade of almost continuous Broadway activity for Negroes came in 1930 *The Green Pastures* with Richard B. Harrison as De Lawd. This folk fantasy by Marc Connelly with a singing orchestra under Hall Johnson achieved one of the longest runs in Negro theatrical history. It opened at the end of a delightful decade of Harlem creativity in the arts known as the Negro Renaissance. But when the Depression came, things artistic went downhill for Negroes. Their decade of popularity ended with *Green Pastures*. There came lean years both in the theatre and elsewhere for black men and women.

The Negro playwright hardly entered the picture during the rich decade of the Twenties although it was a good era for white playwrights and black actors. There were Negro playwrights then, but they seldom got a hearing. With little chance even to see plays in many parts of the country because of Jim Crow, and with almost no chance to gain any technical knowledge of theatre craft, the black playwright had a hard row to hoe. In the old days his scripts seldom got from the typed page to even the amateur stage, but perhaps a church might sponsor a reading. The earliest known American Negro playwright, William Wells Brown, gave one-man readings of his own plays in churches. In those days almost all plays had double titles. Wells' first play completed about 1856 was called *Experience or How to Give a Northern Man a Backbone;* his second was *The Escape, or a Leap for Freedom,* and the library rather than the stage was their fate.

It was fifty years before any other Negro playwright attracted any attention whatsoever when in 1903 the poet, Joseph S. Cotter, Sr., of Louisville published a drama, *Caleb, the Degenerate,* concerned with the racial theories of Booker T. Washington. Some ten years later, Angelina Grimké wrote *Rachel* which the NAACP produced at the Neighborhood Theatre in New York. But, other than functioning as sketch writers and occasional librettists for musical shows, Negroes attempted little creative writings for the theatre and they found no market for what little they did if it was of a serious nature. The commercial center of the theatre, Broadway, in all its history up to 1966 has displayed the work of less than a dozen Negro playwrights. When Wallace Thurman wrote the play *Harlem* which opened on Broadway in 1929, it seemed feasible for production purposes to accept the co-authorship of his agent, William Jordan Rapp—so the program credit reads, HARLEM by Wallace Thurman and William Jordan Rapp. Other Negro playwrights and many popular song writers and composers have accepted the co-authorship of whites on their creative work in order to achieve publication or production, but ofttimes the Negro work is damaged rather than improved by what few white additions are added. The work may get published or produced though, which has often been a difficult thing for a Negro to achieve alone. It takes a great deal of black integrity to prefer anonymity to publication—even if with an unwelcome collaborator.

In the thirty-five years since Wallace Thurman's *Harlem* there have been ten Negro playwrights—only ten—produced on Broadway. In 1929 there was Garland Anderson's *Appearances;* in 1933 Hall Johnson's *Run, Little Chillun;* the following year *Brother Mose* (retitled *Meek Mose*) by Frank Wilson; in 1935 *Mulatto* by Langston Hughes; in 1941 Richard Wright's *Native Son;* in 1947 Theodore Ward's *Our Lan';* in 1953 *Take a Giant Step* by Louis Peterson; in 1954 *Mrs. Patterson* by Charles Sebree; in 1957 *Simply Heavenly* by Langston Hughes; Lorraine Hansberry's *Raisin in the Sun* in 1959; *Purlie Victorious* by Ossie Davis in 1961; in 1963 *Tambourines to Glory* by Langston Hughes; *Blues For Mister Charlie* by James Baldwin, and Lorraine Hansberry's *The Sign in Sidney Brunstein's Window* in 1964. Only Lorraine Hansberry and Langston Hughes have had more than one production on Broadway. Their plays (*Mulatto* in the first instance, and *Raisin in the Sun* a quarter of a century later) enjoyed the longest runs of any vehicles by Negro authors, each playing for over a year in New York followed by extensive cross country tours. Both plays have also been translated and performed abroad, and *Raisin in the Sun* became a Hollywood picture.

Some of the most interesting work by Negro playwrights has been produced off-Broadway. The Federal Theatre of the Thirties in Harlem did Rudolph Fisher's *Conjur Man Dies, Turpentine* by J. A. Smith and Peter Morrell, and in Chicago *Big White Fog* by Theodore Ward. The American Negro Theatre under Abram Hill's direction sent its *Anna Lucasta* from Harlem to Broadway, and in its uptown productions such talented young actors as Sidney Poitier, Harry Belafonte, and Hilda Simms gained experience. The record run for any play in Harlem is that of the Suitcase Theatre's *Don't You Want to Be Free?* by Langston Hughes which had 135 performances. Ruth Jett's production of the Alice Childress play *Just a Little Simple* had a considerable run at the Club Baron on Lenox Avenue in 1951, as did *A Medal for Willie* by William Branch.

The most hospitable theatre in New York to the Negro playwright has been the Greenwich Mews under the direction of Stella Holt, dean of off-Broadway producers. In 1954, Miss Holt presented Branch's drama on John Brown and Frederick Douglass, *In Splendid Error;* in 1955 a hilarious comedy by Alice Childress, *Trouble in Mind;* and in 1956 Loften Mitchell's moving *A Land Beyond the River* about integration in the South. In 1963 the Mews produced William Hairston's *Walk in Darkness;* and in 1964 *Jerico Jim Crow,* a freedom song-play by Langston Hughes, and in 1965 his *The Prodigal Son.*

Only the Karamu Theatre in Cleveland has been more active in presenting plays by or about Negroes than the Greenwich Mews. That is because Karamu, a settlement house project, has been at it for years. Founded by Russell and Rowena Jelliffe in 1916 and known then as the Gilpin Players, over the years Karamu has produced almost every play concerned with Negro life by a white or Negro author, including the world premieres of some, and the only performances to date of others. The plays of the young Nigerian Wole Soyinka were first done in America by Karamu. And years ago the earliest comedies of Langston Hughes were presented by the Gilpin Players on a ramshackle stage before the erection of the present million dollar Karamu House which contains a proscenium theatre, an arena theatre, a concert hall and facilities for a children's theatre. Recognized as one of the most important of America's tributary theatres, Karamu has given to Broadway some excellent performers—Mildred Smith, Frank Marriott, Zelma George, Isabel Cooley, Clayton Corbin, Leesa Foster; and on its resident roster it has one of the masters of Negro humor, Nolan Bell, now a mature comedian who grew up from childhood with Karamu and has performed in many of its dramas and musicals.

If the Negro performer had had to depend entirely on Broadway for sustenance over the years, he would have fared badly indeed. Fortunately, between the First World War and the Second, there existed for about twenty years a booking agency for Southern Negro Theatres, known as the Theatre Owners Booking Association—the T.O.B.A.—or TOBY as performers called it. It booked some Northern theatres, too, the Lincoln in New York, the Monogram and the Grand in Chicago, the Gibson in Philadelphia, and its circuit supplied work for hundreds of Negro entertainers whose offerings ranged from blackface comedy and blues to one-act plays, opera arias, adagio dancing and magic—for the Negro performers' talents were many and varied. There have been tumblers like the Crackerjacks, ventriloquists like Wee Johnny Woods, magicians like the

Great Gowongo, comics like Butterbeans and Susie, divas like Madame Fannie Wise, dancers like Eddie Rector, and of course great blues singers from Ma Rainey to Bessie Smith and the unforgettable Virginia Liston singing *The Titanic Blues.* Ethel Waters worked the T.O.B.A. circuit long before her name went up in lights at the Winter Garden in *As Thousands Cheer* or over the marquee of the Empire in *A Member of the Wedding.*

T.O.B.A. was essentially a vaudeville circuit, but it also booked entire companies such as Tutt's *Smarter Set,* S. J. Dudley and Company with his mule, and the famous Whitman Sisters. The Whitman Sisters, four singers and dancers who began as a church trio in Kansas, produced tabloid musicals of a very lively nature usually with two blackface comedians, a blues singer, a pretty leading lady and a high stepping chorus line. For several seasons their comedy team consisted of a tall lanky young man who did not wear burnt cork and a midget, Willie Bryant and Princess Wee Wee. T.O.B.A. was both a proving ground and a meal ticket for the Negro performer, as well as a source of living theatre to millions of Negroes barred from other playhouses. Touring Negro tent shows of a nature like that of Silas Green, the Florida Cotton Blossoms, and later Flournoy Miller's *The Smart Set* were profitable for many years—until television made its inroads on all live entertainment and black and white variety, indoors and out, went by the board. Popular favorites of big time vaudeville like the Mills Brothers, the Deep River Boys, and the Ink Spots turned almost entirely to night clubs, records, and spot appearances on radio or television for a livelihood, whereas Palace headliners like Bojangles, the late great dancer, and featured acts like Glenn and Jenkins, Moss and Frye and Hamtree Harrington sought refuge in revenues, cabarets, or foreign tours. Billy Banks went to Tokyo where he became a television favorite, the Nicolas Brothers to Mexico, South America, Paris, and Adelaide Hall to the London night clubs.

Night clubs from the Barbary Coast of San Francisco earthquake days to Harlem of the present have been lively showcases for Negro entertainers. By way of the Cotton Club (where she was a chorus girl) Lena Horne came to Broadway. By way of T.O.B.A. and the Harlem night clubs, Ethel Waters rose to fame. Duke Ellington, Cab Calloway, Fats Waller and Fletcher Henderson first attracted attention in Harlem cabarets before moving on to Broadway, Carnegie Hall and the world. During the Twenties, Smalls Paradise, Baron's, the Nest and later Minton's were midnight havens for Negro entertainers, a slew of Billies among them—Billie Holiday, Billie Daniels, Billie Eckstein, Billy Banks, Billy Mitchell. Minton's is credited as the birthplace of be-bop music. In more recent years, Smalls Paradise popularized the Madison and the Twist. For more than ten years the Club Baby Grand showcased Nipsey Russell, Harlem's favorite comedian and seemingly a permanent fixture there until his hilarious integration jokes caught the ear of downtown listeners and he moved on up a little higher to the Playboy Clubs and the national TV screens.

It is a long step from the dialect comedy of Bert Williams in grotesque makeup, oversized coat and funny shoes to the social satire of dapper young comics like Nipsey Russell or Dick Gregory, cool, well dressed and impudent. If the race problem got even a remote mention in the comedy routines of the T.O.B.A. vaudeville or night club performers in the old days, its mention would usually be in terms unintelligible to white listeners. Even at the Apollo Theatre in Harlem with a 90% Negro audience, race problems were seldom a part of the comedy monologue there. Jackie Moms Mabley alone of all the old comics might slip in a racial wallop once in a while. Racial references, I think, were discouraged by the white owners and managers of most of the theatres and night clubs where Negroes performed. In changing this concept, Nipsey Russell and the Supreme Court were pioneers. The school desegregation decrees of 1954 and the subsequent front page explosions placed the race problem so squarely in the news that for even a night club comic to ignore it would be difficult. Nipsey Russell in his routines had never been ignoring it. At the Baby Grand he had long had free rein and just the right audience for his satire—an audience that would roar with laughter at the mention of the words *Little Rock* if uttered with proper recognition of their absurdity.

"You nine Negro boys and girls about to enter Little Rock High School for the first time," said Nipsey Russell impersonating a big race leader, "must uphold the honor of the Negro people when you go into that white school. I do not want you young people to go in there all belligerent and ignorant—like they expect Negroes to be. No! Don't go in that school carrying bricks, knives, razors or guns. Go in there *civilized*—throwing atom bombs!"

Jackie Moms Mabley, the grandmother of all Negro comediennes, who once performed in blackface but now contents herself with toothlessness and a red wig, has invented a great Cindy Ella story about the little colored girl who was invited by magic to the senior ball at the University of Mississippi—but at the stroke of midnight was changed back into her original little black self. Its telling and its denouement is one of the funniest and saddest bits to be heard on the American stage.

Dick Gregory's entire night club act is composed of social material—something unheard of for a colored comedian a decade ago—and Godfrey Cambridge thoroughly ribs all forms of segregation in front of the most fashionable audiences in clubs where cover charges are high. The current crop of Negro comics, unlike Lenny Bruce and some other whites, have not as yet resorted to dirty words to add pungency to their comedy. Young Negro playwrights, in contrast to the comedians, are great users of graffiti. Perhaps influenced by *The Blacks* and the avant garde trend in Paris, London and New York, Adrienne Kennedy's *The Funnyhouse of a Negro,* LeRoi Jones' *Dutchman, the Toilet, the Slave,* and James Baldwin's *Blues for Mister Charlie*—all 1964 productions—abound in what used to be called profanity. If a black Lenny Bruce appears on the scene as a social comic, the freedom movement can go no farther.

That the Negro has a great forte for comedy and music cannot be denied. The playbills for 100 years prove it so—from the minstrel comics of the eighteen sixties to Ossie Davis and Pearl Bailey now; in song from Elizabeth Taylor Greenfield, known as the Black Swan in 1854 when she sang for Queen Victoria, to Leontyne Price whose recordings are now in many a Royal record collection.

Some of the sweetest voices in the world today are Negro voices—the liquid voice of Camilla Williams, the mighty yet gentle baritone of William Warfield, the cool fountain of sound of Mattiwilda Dobbs, of Adele Addison. (And there is always the memory of the incomparable Roland Hayes, still singing in concert at the age of 75; Marian Anderson announcing her farewell tour after a quarter of a century of great performances; and Dorothy Maynor whose *Depuis le Jour* was pure delight.) Younger singers of outstanding ability in concert and opera include Margaret Tynes, George Shirley, Grace Bumbry, Reri Grist, Betty Allen, Shirley Verrett, Martha Bowers, and Billie Lynn Daniels. La Scala, the Metropolitan and all the great opera houses of the world have opened their doors to American Negroes, beginning with the pioneers of the Twenties and Thirties, Lillian Evanti and Katerina Yarboro, divas who achieved success abroad.

The loudest singers in the world today in concert halls or out are gospel singers, products of the Negro church, and capable of raising at all times "a joyous noise unto the Lord." They are America's last uncontaminated source of pure folk singing. The most famous exponent of gospel singing is Mahalia Jackson. Not far behind are Clara Ward, the Davis Sisters, James Cleveland, Princess Stewart and the Caravans.

Alex Bradford and Marion Williams have taken gospel singing from off-Broadway to the Philharmonic, to Europe, Asia, and around the world in the song-play, *Black Nativity* by Langston Hughes. They sang in 1963 in Coventry Cathedral in England, and their television film of *Black Nativity* received the Catholic Dove Award at Cannes. Since the advent of Josephine Baker and the *Revue Negre* in 1926, no group of American Negro artists received such opening night acclaim in Paris as did the *Black Nativity* company at the Champs-Elysées, with the press hailing Marion Williams as a dynamic new star. It was in that same theatre that Josephine Baker made her Parisian debut some 35 years before.

Josephine Baker is the world's most famous international star. She has drawn capacity audiences in all the great cities of the world, singing as she does in several languages, and wearing the most expensively elegant wardrobes to be seen anywhere, especially designed for her by the great couturiers. That so beautiful and talented a woman happens to be colored, seems not to have affected her career adversely except for an interim period in her own homeland where, when she refused to accept segregation in New York or Miami Beach during appearances there, important columnists attacked her with false charges of radicalism—for which Miss Baker filed libel suits. Subsequent American appearances were highly successful, and Miss Baker's performance at 60 is as sparkling, as joyous and as heart warming as ever.

If one were to be asked to name the Twelve Great Personalities of the Negro entertainment field in the Twentieth Century regardless of categories, it would be impossible to omit Josephine Baker. Bert Williams, of course, would have to be included, as would Marian Anderson and Roland Hayes, Paul Robeson, Bojangles Bill Robinson, Rose McClendon, who could move an audience emotionally without saying a word, Jackie Moms Mabley who is one of the funniest women on earth, and Louis Armstrong, Sidney Poitier, Harry Belafonte, and Katherine Dunham. Certainly there are others that should be included. But a dozen is only 12. If a baker's dozen be allowed, the 13th would have to be Pearl Bailey. Or did somebody say Billie Holiday? Florence Mills? Bessie Smith? Ethel Waters? Canada Lee? Alvin Ailey? Lena Horne? Eartha Kitt? Except for Louis Armstrong as a singer, we are omitting entirely the field of jazz, pops, and folk—the great Ray Charles, Nina Simone, Lionel Hampton, Jackie Wilson, Chubby Checker, Odetta, Sonny Terry and Brownie McGhee—performing artists as well as jazzmen, personalities in the theatrical sense of the word as well as musicians—Duke Ellington, Charlie Mingus, Max Roach.

Creatively a most productive period for the Negro in the arts began in the Nineteen Twenties. It continued for a decade and was termed by literary commentators the Negro Renaissance, or the period of the New Negro. Its center was Harlem where poetry, prose and painting took a new lease on life, and in whose productivity the downtown white world vouchsafed a more than passing interest. For a few years Harlem was in vogue, and the Negro in the arts was fashionable. This happy period began with the success in 1921 of an infectious musical called *Shuffle Along*. Intended for Negro audiences it opened at the Howard Theatre in Washington, moved on to Philadelphia, then ended up in a rather out of the way New York playhouse, the 63rd Street Theatre off Broadway, where it suddenly became the talk of the town and ran for nearly two years. It was the kind of joyous little show that people liked to see again and again. It sparkled. It exuded good nature. Its songs were catchy, its comedy easy-going, its girls prancingly pretty, and the overall effect one of happy syncopated fun. The book for *Shuffle Along* was by Miller and Lyles who performed the comedy routines. The songs were by Sissle and Blake who sang most of them. They produced the show themselves on a shoestring.

This ebullient musical had some wonderful people in it—most of them quite unknown at the time—Josephine Baker at the end of the chorus line, Hall Johnson and William Grant Still in the orchestra, the diva-to-be, Katerina Yarboro among the singers, Trixie Smith shouting blues, and Florence Mills as the leading lady, substituting for Gertrude Saunders who after opening had gotten a better paying job in burlesque. Florence Mills became the star and *Shuffle Along* a milestone in Negro theatre. It created a vogue for Negro musicals that lasted until the Depression. By that time white writers had realized the profits inherent in Negro materials so they began to write shows especially for Negro casts. It then became difficult for colored writers to achieve commercial production. Lew Leslie's *Blackbirds* with a white score made Florence Mills—and in a later edition, Ethel Waters—Broadway headliners.

Following *Shuffle Along* came *Put and Take,* then *Liza,* then late in 1923 *Runnin' Wild* which introduced the Charleston, a foot-flinging hand-clapping dance that swept the world. Other lively all Negro shows within the next few years were *Africana, Dinah;* a second Miller and Lyles show, *Chocolate Dandies; Rang Tang, Hot Chocolates* with lyrics by Andy Razaf and music by Fats Waller; *Brown Buddies, Sugar Hill, Hot Rhythm, Fast and Furious* and *Rhapsody in Black* featuring Valaida Snow and the Berry Brothers. *The Plantation Revue* starred Florence

Mills who then went to London in *From Dover to Dixie* (the same show renamed) and returned in *Dixie to Broadway*. At the time of her death in 1927, Florence Mills was one of the most beloved of Broadway performers. "I'm just a little blackbird looking for a bluebird" became her theme song and, as her funeral cortege went through Harlem an airplane overhead released a flock of bluebirds.

The big all-Negro musicals after the Thirties were for two decades almost all written by whites—Jimmy McHugh and Dorothy Fields, Vernon Duke, John LaTouche, Rogers and Hammerstein and others. Their shows included, besides various editions of *Blackbirds, Swinging the Blues, Swinging the Dream, The Hot Mikado, Cabin in the Sky, Carmen Jones,* and *The House of Flowers*. Then *Shinbone Alley* with Eartha Kitt, *Jamaica* with Lena Horne, *Mr. Wonderful* and later *Golden Boy* both starring Sammy Davis, and previously *No Strings* with Diahann Carroll began a trend away from all-Negro casts toward integrated shows built around Negro stars. Duke Ellington's *Beggar's Holiday* was an early integrated musical starring Alfred Drake, with sets by Broadway's lone Negro designer Perry Watkins. It marked the Negro composer's return to Broadway after a considerable absence. A Negro lyricist, Langston Hughes, in 1947 wrote the songs for what was termed the "first Broadway opera," *Street Scene,* with a score by Kurt Weill and book by Elmer Rice. Three years later, with a Hughes libretto and music by Jan Meyerowitz, *The Barrier,* starring Lawrence Tibbett and Muriel Rahn, opened on Broadway.

In the integrated musical theatre, appearing with primarily white casts, Jules Bledsoe in New York and later Paul Robeson in London came to fame singing *Ole Man River* in *Show Boat*. Ethel Waters starred in *As Thousands Cheer,* and later in *At Home Abroad* with Bea Lillie. Juanita Hall sang the haunting *Bali Hai* in *South Pacific,* and was a leading performer in *Flower Drum Song*. Todd Duncan was featured in *Lost in the Stars;* Thelma Carpenter in *The Seven Lively Arts;* Dooley Wilson and Richard Huey in *Bloomer Girl;* William Dillard in *My Darlin' Aida;* Pearl Bailey in *Arms and the Girl,* and Mae Barnes in *By the Beautiful Sea*. The all-Negro cast in the Harold Arlen–Johnny Mercer musical, *St. Louis Woman,* with a book by Arna Bontemps and Countee Cullen from the former's novel, *God Sends Sunday,* again brought colored writers to Broadway, and gave Pearl Bailey her first big role. Another showcase for topnotch Negro talent was Virgil Thomson's *Four Saints in Three Acts* by Gertrude Stein, with Edward Matthews and a glorious group of singers. *Carmen Jones* first brought the current star of the Moral Rearmament movement, Muriel Smith, to fame. *Simply Heavenly* established Claudia McNeil. Negro performers had bit roles in *Finian's Rainbow* as well as being in the chorus. And from the late Nineteen Forties, Broadway musicals have increasingly included colored boys and girls in their singing and dancing choruses, and Negro musicians in the pit.

While musical integration was gaining a foothold on the Broadway scene, the dramatic stage only infrequently from time to time offered effective starring or featured roles to Negroes: Ethel Waters in *Mamba's Daughters* followed years later by *A Member of the Wedding;* Paul Robeson's triumphant *Othello;* Ruth Attaway in *You Can't Take It with You;* Canada Lee in *Native Son;* Jane White in *Strange Fruit* and later off-Broadway, *Once upon a Mattress* and *The Trojan Women;* Gordon Heath in *Deep Are the Roots;* Ellen Holly in *Too Late the Phalarope;* Abbie Mitchell in *On Whitman Avenue;* Zelma Watson George in a powerful wheelchair revival of *The Medium;* Earl Hyman in *Mister Johnson;* Eartha Kitt in *Jolly's Progress;* Conchita Rivera and Reri Grist in *West Side Story;* Lawrence Winters in *The Long Dream;* Billy Dee Williams in *The Cool World,* and Claudia McNeil in *Tiger, Tiger Burning Bright.* Since World War II, more and more Negro performers have been able to gain professional experience, theatrical discipline, and even earn a living at their craft. For a professional actor, certainly the stage should be his bread basket.

The biggest single bread basket for the Negro in the history of the American stage has been *Porgy and Bess.* If ever colored performers erect a monument to a musician outside their race, it should be to George Gershwin, the composer of that melodic perennial based on the play, *Porgy,* dramatized from the DuBose Heyward novel of the same name concerning life in Catfish Row. The musical version has been performed all over the now known world. The moon is yet to see it, but it will in time. *Porgy and Bess* possesses great theatricality. It entertains. Commercially, it is a well-woven theatre basket, as durable as baskets come, and filled with a variegated kettle of fish. Its charms are many. Its songs, the melodies derived from the folk blues and spirituals of the Negro people, are beautiful. There is prancing and dancing. Its argot is quaint. Its characters are colorful and broadly drawn. There are children in the show, a goat, and a marching band. It has almost everything capable of drawing money into the box office. In other words, it is a good show. And it has fed, over long periods of time in many cities and many countries, a great many Negro performers.

If it were not for the racial complications in American life, one might forego any further discussion of *Porgy and Bess,* and accept it simply as an excellent theatre piece, and a helpful dinner basket. Unfortunately, its basket has been a trap, a steel-toothed trap leaving its marks upon the wrists of the Negro people who reached therein to touch its fish. And the fish themselves are tainted with racism. Art aside, it is an axiom in the American theatre that the cheapest shows to stage are Negro shows. Their cast budgets are always the lowest of any. If a Negro show is a hit, a great deal of money may be made. The bulk of this money does not go to Negroes. They are seldom if ever in the top echelons of management or production. Financially, the whites get the caviar, the Negroes get the porgies. A porgy is a fish, and *Porgy and Bess* concerns fishermen and their women. The character, Porgy, is a cripple, an almost emasculated man. His Bess is a whore. The denizens (as the critics term them) of Catfish Row are child-like ignorant blackamoors given to dice, razors, and singing at the drop of a hat. In other words, they are stereotypes in (to sensitive Negroes) the worst sense of the word. The long shadow of the blackface minstrel coarsens the charm of *Porgy* and darkens its grace notes. Those notes themselves are lifted from the Negro people. Borrowed is a more polite word; "derived from" an acceptable phrase.

Hall Johnson in *Opportunity,* the journal of the National Urban League, wrote in his review of the original production:

> The informing spirit of Negro music is not to be caught and understood merely by listening to the tunes, and Mr. Gershwin's much publicized visits to Charleston for local color do not amount even to a matriculation in the preparatory school that he needed for his work. Nothing can be more misleading, especially to an alien musician, than a few visits to Negro revivals and funerals. Here one encounters the "outside" at its most external. The obvious sights and sounds are only the foam, which has no meaning without the beer. And here let it be said that it is not the color nor the aloofness of the white investigator which keeps him on the outside. It is the powerful tang and thrill of the "foam" which excites him prematurely and makes him rush away too soon—to write books and music on a subject of which he has not even begun to scratch the surface. . . . What we are to consider then is not a Negro opera by Gershwin, but Gershwin's idea of what a Negro opera should be. . . . Artistically, we darker Americans are in a most peculiar situation with regard to what we have to give the world. In our several hundred years of enforced isolation in this country we have had plenty of time and plenty of reason to sing each other songs and tell each other tales. These songs and stories have a hidden depth of meaning as well as a simple and sincere external beauty. But the same wall

> which forced them into existence has closed in tight upon their *meaning* and allows only their beauty to escape through the chinks. So that our folk culture is like the growth of some hardy yet exotic shrub whose fragrance never fails to delight discriminating nostrils even when there is no interest in the depths of its roots.

Following the long four year tour of *Porgy and Bess* throughout Europe and South America, initiated under State Department auspices, Paul Henry Lang in 1956 wrote in the *New York Herald Tribune:*[37]

> Foreign audiences are seldom aware that *Porgy* does not deal with the present. They do not know that the music is not genuine Negro art. . . . What they do believe is that this is the sad life of the oppressed Negro everywhere in America, a sordid life riddled with vice and crime in the black ghetto. While I was in Europe last summer, I had many heated discussions on the subject but could not explain away the "authenticity" of life as depicted in *Porgy*. . . . They cannot realize that the world of Catfish Row, created and set to music by white men, is a view from the outside focussed on the Negro only for their entertainment value and as a group apart rather than as members of society. *Porgy and Bess* is indeed an excellent show, but it is no American folk opera.

"Unfortunately, the people in other countries don't think they are acting. They think they are giving a realistic portrayal of actual Negro life," the composer, William Grant Still, said in *Tones and Overtones,* backing up his contention with quotations from overseas papers. A review in the Spanish music magazine *Ritmo* declared: "*Porgy* is a strong emotional document of the life of the Negro in North America depicting the humiliation and misery of his way of living, the violent sensuality and passion of his psychology, his crude and spontaneous reactions. All of this constitutes the substance and soul of the Negro, his character and his tragi-comic life amidst sordid surroundings." The *Australian Music News* called "the whole libretto typically Negro." Which caused Mr. Still to ask, "Is that the impression we would like to have foreigners get of us, of our life here in America?"

"The ignorant, happy-foot, lust-loving, crap shooting clown—Porgy has them all," wrote Negro journalist James Hicks. "The presentation of *Porgy* could not happen to any other race in America but the colored race. The Jewish People have their Anti-Defamation League which sees to it that the role of the 'Sheenie' no longer walks the American stage. Catholic groups each week police the theatres and movie houses and order death by boycott to any theatrical presentation which dares depict them in any other light but good."

In Negro America's largest newspaper, the *Pittsburgh Courier,* J. A. Rogers observed, "While this stereotype gives joy to whites, it is to thinking Negroes like the frogs in Aesop's fable. To the boys who were having so much fun throwing stones into a pond, the frogs said, 'What is fun to you, is *death* to us.' "

When Samuel Goldwyn was casting the motion picture version of *Porgy and Bess* in 1957, Harlem's *Amsterdam News* ran a front page story to the effect that actor Sidney Poitier turned down a $75,000 offer to play the leading role. It quoted him as saying, "As a Negro I have a certain sensitiveness, and as an artist I have certain responsibilities. Certain things I will play, but they must be constructive to my life as a Negro. *Porgy and Bess* is always played within a restricted range for the actor. There is simply one crap game too many in it." Praising Poitier editorially, the *Amsterdam News* declared, "We think this is a ringing answer to those who say that Negroes are not willing to pay for their self-respect and freedom. . . . The Negro race has been dignified by his creed." But less than a month later, the wire services from Hollywood transmitted to the world Samuel Goldwyn's announcement of acceptance by Sidney Poitier of the role of Porgy. The *Amsterdam News* never informed Harlemites as to just what happened, so they were left wondering if Goldwyn's price went up, or Poitier's pride went down. Yet nobody faulted him much. Negroes are familiar with baskets that are also traps.

Backstage one cold day that winter at Harlem's Apollo Theatre, some of the actors were discussing another high salaried Negro artist of the female gender who had also accepted a part in the Goldwyn opus, but who felt impelled for the record to register a protest. After seeing the script she imperiously told Mr. Goldwyn, "I demands you remove them *dats* and *dis-es* from my role."

To which Mr. Goldwyn is said to have replied, "Why not, darling? Just talk like you are—and everything'll be all right."

So, "I loves you, Porgy" and "Bess, you is ma woman now—you *is,* you *is,* you *is*!" reached the screen intact, dialect and all, as did, "Oh, Lawd, I'm on ma way!" And a Todd-AO Technicolor wide screen million dollar production of *Porgy and Bess* went out to the whole wide world singing, "I got plenty o' nuttin', an' nuttin's plenty fo' me." Fortunately, the junkie, Sporting Life, in the person of Sammy Davis, Jr., sang, "It ain't necessarily so."

RETURN OF A CLASSIC
Porgy and Bess Comes Home From Europe

headlined the *New York Times* in the lead article by Brooks Atkinson on the front page of its theatre section for March 15, 1953 when, after its tour abroad the Robert Breen production came home. "Now that *Porgy and Bess* has settled down in New York," wrote Mr. Atkinson, "the people who last September opposed the project of sending it abroad ought to feel ashamed of themselves. . . . In the realm of art, nothing matters so much as the quality of the art, which in the case of the Gershwin opera is magnificent. . . . The zeal for outward respectability is a sign of inner uncertainty, and it should not be resolved at the expense of people who know what they are doing." Brooks Atkinson could hardly be accused of ill will or insincerity. And zeal for outward respectability might well be a sign of inner uncertainty. But Mr. Atkinson himself would probably be filled with uncertainty had he been born colored, segregated most of his life, denied a job on the *Times* and even tickets to many American attractions, laughed at and ridiculed from minstrel days to the Ziegfeld Theatre, and then chided for not liking make-believe porgies in a Broadway basket—when you have had almost nothing but porgies all your life. Almost nothing but porgies—nothing but porgies, porgies, porgies.

Balance is what America has long needed in relation to the Negro and entertainment. There would be nothing greatly wrong with the U.S. State Department sponsoring *Porgy and Bess* abroad, if at the same time (or before or after) it also sent abroad other equally effective spectacles in which Negroes were not portrayed solely as childish darkies, crap shooters, dope addicts, ladies of little virtue, and quaint purveyors of "You *is,* you *is,* you *is.*" From the days of the minstrels a hundred years ago, through the half century of Hollywood movies with their Stepin Fetchits and Butterfly McQueens and the Amos and Andys of radio and television, right up to *The Cool World* with its juvenile delinquents, the "you is" school has by and large prevailed in white versions of Negro theatrics. It has, with few exceptions, planted its concept of the Negro on the minds of the world. Always servants or clowns—and not just clowns or servants, but *burlesques* of clowns and servants. Certainly there are servants in the world so why should they not be portrayed in pictures? The late Hattie McDaniel once said, when attacked for her Hollywood roles as a domestic, "It is better getting $7,000 a week playing a servant, than $7.00 a week *being* one." Being an artist of ability, Miss McDaniel was capable of humanizing even the burlesque concepts of Hollywood directors.

A standard form of direction for Negro actors playing chauffeur's roles in Hollywood, so an old time performer told me, ran something like this. Upon opening the car door for one's white employer in any film, the director would command: "Jump to ground . . . Remove cap . . . Open car door . . . Step back and bow . . . Come up smiling . . . Now bow again . . . Now straighten up and grin."

The darkest actors with the widest mouths and the whitest teeth were the ones who until recent years got the best bit parts in Hollywood. There have been some decent, even charming films about Negroes—the early *Hallelujah* and *Hearts in Dixie,* much later *Bright Road* based on Mary Elizabeth Vorman's lovely little story; Maidie Norman in *The Well;* James Edwards in *Home of the Brave;* the moving semi-documentary *The Quiet One;* Belafonte's *A Man Is Ten Feet Tall;* Sidney Poitier in *Lilies of the Fields;* and Bernie Hamilton in *One Potato, Two Potato* and also *Nothing but a Man*. And from Brazil via France came *Black Orpheus* with the beautiful American Negro star, Marpessa Dawn, who came to fame abroad.

In the theatre, one must note, ninety percent of the plays about Negroes drop their final curtain on defeat—usually death. A serious drama about Negroes simply cannot end happily it seems. From *Uncle Tom's Cabin* to *Blues for Mister Charlie,* if every Negro who has died impotent and defeated on stage were to be buried end to end, their assembled corpses would reach around the world. Shakespeare started it with *Othello*. LeRoi Jones continues it with *Dutchman* where a white floozie stabs an Ivy Leaguish colored boy in the belly and has his body thrown between two subway cars. The stereotype of the Negro drama is the unhappy ending—spiritually and physically defeated, lynched, dead—gotten rid of to the relief of the dramatist and the audience, in time for a late supper. O'Neill's *Emperor Jones,* stone cold dead in the jungle; *Mulatto's* young hero a suicide; *Native Son* on his way to the electric chair; *Mandingo,* mortally cold cocked; the young African in *Mister Johnson* begging the white man to shoot him rather than snatching the gun from the white man and firing a few shots himself; Fishbelly in Richard Wright's *The Long Dream* as dramatized by Ketti Frings should also have shot first—but no! Like the Indians in the old Westerns, Fish bites the dust instead of his white enemy; likewise Richard Henry in *Blues for Mister Charlie*. Being such a bad, bad man, one would have thought the militant Negro in the Baldwin play might have shot first. But on Broadway Negro characters do *not* shoot first. They merely get shot.

A white dramatist once, when asked why the black hero in his play did not kill his white adversary, replied, "Why, that wouldn't be tragic!" Maybe his attitude explains why so many of the "serious" plays about Negroes ring hollow. Somebody's concept of tragedy is askew. Warren Miller's sociological study of Harlem delinquents reached the stage with all the nuances explaining how the delinquents got that way gone by the wayside. In a letter to the *New York Herald Tribune* Ellen Holly wrote, "The Cool World is about as concerned with sociology as an exposé magazine is concerned with morality. Such magazines leer endlessly through keyholes then tack on a sanctimonious conclusion in a pretense of respectability. To reiterate that a jungle produces animals tells us nothing new and brings us no closer to understanding. It is merely an excuse to ogle at that jungle."[38] Ogling at the jungle, many Negroes feel, is about all Broadway drama in the past has been able to do in regard to Negro themes.

"The constant whine of knives being sharpened is the predominant sound of *The Cool World*. Indeed, by the end of the ninth scene at the Eugene O'Neill, what seems like the entire juvenile delinquent population of Harlem is hard at work honing machetes, switchblades and stolen kitchen utensils," wrote Walter Kerr in his review which termed it, a "distressingly dreary play about the street-corner jungle that turns schoolboys into heroin addicts, schoolgirls into dollar-and-a-half prostitutes, and a random assortment of the group into corpses."

"Somebody is trying to pin their own defeatism, their mind sickness and their death wishes on the Negro," wrote Arna Bontemps. "They haven't stopped to think that Negroes are too black and ugly for that stuff. Look at any of the Negro athletes on TV. They ain't fixin' to quit. Neither are those knotty-headed Africans around Lake Victoria and such places. Something *else* has got to give, not their skulls." In the U.S.A. if Negroes accepted defeat as fatalistically as their counterparts do on the Broadway stage, there would not be twenty million of them alive from Coast to Coast today. White Broadway by and large simply fails to reflect the Negro with any degree of basic truth no matter how famous the playwrights, how skilled the director, or who designs the sets.

Perhaps it is good that one hundred years after Emancipation integration is coming apace in the arts—that Leontyne Price now stars at the Metropolitan in Italian roles; that Lynn Hamilton plays the Queen in *Midsummer Night's Dream* in Manhattan parks; that Mabel Mercer is a favorite in East Side night spots; that Eartha Kitt not only performs in, but lives at the Plaza when she is in New York; that Frederick O'Neil is President of Actor's Equity; that Katherine Dunham choreographed *Aida* at the Met and *The Bible* in Rome; and Donald McKale and Talley Beatty direct non-Negro dances; that Anne Bancroft in Hollywood, in full sight of 80 million television viewers, kissed Sidney Poitier when he received his Academy Award as the Best Actor of the Year; that Lorraine Hansberry's *Sign in Sidney Brunstein's Window* is cast with white actors; that Diana Sands plays a non-racial role as the leading lady in *The Owl and the Pussy Cat;* that Negro director Lloyd Richards is chosen to direct all-white casts; that white folk singers are singing colored gospel songs; that the great Martha Graham company, once all white, has three leading Negro dancers; and Arthur Mitchell is one of the stars of the New York City Ballet.

The formerly all Negro Alvin Ailey Dance Theater took a white ballerina and a Japanese one with its company to Paris. The ballet people sail happily through the international air with no regard whatsoever for racial problems or stereotypes. Such is the glory of the modern dance. May the Broadway theatre eventually acquire a similar glory. The American Negro has given great joy to the fields of light entertainment. He can add great understanding to the areas of serious make-believe as well. All he needs is playwrights, plays, and a reevaluation of what constitutes tragedy.

"Segregated Integration," *The Book of Negro Humor,* ed. Langston Hughes

(New York: Dodd, Mead and Co., 1966), 251–65

Lost in the shuffle during the filibuster concerning the 1964 Civil Rights Bill in the Senate, and therefore probably not to be found in the *Congressional Record,* was this shouted remark from the floor by a southern senator, "Gentlemen, Ah believe in segregated integration, *not* integrated segregation."

Once when former President Eisenhower was laid up with a cold during the time of the Little Rock School crisis and the Sputnik moon rocket experiments, one of the Negro attendants at the White House was listening outside Ike's bedroom door as the doctors consulted within.[39] He heard them talking about the things that had been preying on Eisenhower's mind, namely, Sputnik and Little Rock. When the Negro attendant went down into the kitchen to get Ike's luncheon tray, the other colored help asked him what had caused the President's new upset.

"Just moons and coons," he informed them, "that's all, moons and coons."

One day in Georgia a poor, ignorant white man came to the polls to vote.

"I wish you'd oblige me by voting this ticket," said a bright Negro who was standing near the polls. He handed him a leaflet.

"What kind of a ticket is it?" asked the poor white man.

"Why," said the Negro, "you can see for yourself."

"But I can't read."

"What? Can't you read the ballot you have there in your hand and are about to vote?" asked the colored man.

"No, I can't read nothing a-tall."

"Well," said the colored man, "this ballot means that you are in favor of equal franchise to both white and colored citizens."

"It means to let the Negras vote?" asked the white man.

"Yes, sir."

"Why, Negras don't know enough to vote," said the white man.

For years in the South, according to Martin Luther King, the white segregationist has been saying the Negro is "satisfied." He has claimed "We get along beautifully with our Negroes because we understand them. We only have trouble when outside agitators come in and stir things up." Many expressed this point of view, knowing that it was a lie of majestic proportions. Others believed they were speaking the truth. For corroboration, they would tell you: "Why, I talked to my cook and she said . . ." or, "I discussed this frankly with the colored boy who works for us and I told him to express himself freely. He said . . ."

White people in the South may never fully know the extent to which Negroes defended themselves and protected their jobs—and in many cases their lives—by perfecting an air of ignorance and agreement. In days gone by no colored cook would have dared to tell her employer what he ought to know. She had to tell him what he wanted to hear. She knew that the penalty for speaking the truth could be the loss of her job.

During the Montgomery bus boycott a white family summoned their Negro cook and asked her if she supported the terrible things Negroes were doing, boycotting busses and demanding jobs.[40]

"Oh, no, ma'am. I won't have anything to do with that boycott thing," the cook said. "I am just going to stay away from them busses as long as trouble is going on."

On a bus in Mississippi a young white man asked an old colored woman to get up, move to the back, and give him her seat. Whereupon a young colored man asked: "If you and I were on the battle front, would you ask me to move back and let *you* have the front?"

A wealthy white Georgian who for many years had held a position of prominence on Wall Street returned to his small Georgia home town for a visit. He encountered an aged Negro friend, a boyhood playmate, selling pies about the streets.

Said the wealthy lawyer, "Well howdy do, Old Jim! All these many years since I've been away from here I've held a position of prominence and have accumulated wealth, and here you are still selling pies on the street. You have my sympathy!"

To which Old Jim replied, "To hell with your sympathy—buy a pie!"

It seems that a southern town decided to spend $85,000 on the improvement of its schools. When it came to allocating the money, it seemed that the school for white children needed a new roof, a new toilet, a new gymnasium, and, to make a long story short, the white school's need totaled up to exactly $85,000. The principal of the Negro school was so informed.

"Gentlemen," he said, "do you mean to tell me that it is going to take all of that $85,000 to fix up the white school so that white folks can get a decent education?"

Yes, the committee was sorry to say, it was. "Then take it, gentlemen, take it, 'cause if there's anything we Negroes need badly in this town it's educated white men."

When a Negro comes to apply to vote in Mississippi, the white registrar might ask him, "Boy, do you know the meaning of *delicut status quo rendum*?"

If by some miracle the Negro applicant answers this tongue-twister successfully, the registrar will say, "Boy, since you're so smart, tell me what's going to happen to you if you don't get the hell away from here?"

A Negro one day came to a strange town in Mississippi where he had never been before. When he got off the bus he did not see any of his race around, so he asked a white man, "Where do the colored folks hang out here?"

The white man pointed at a great big tree in the square and said, "You see that limb?"

In the same town a month or so later a mob was fixing to lynch a man when a very dignified old judge appeared. "Don't," he pleaded, "put a blot on this fair community by hasty action. The thing to do, friends," he insisted, "is to give the man a fair trial—then lynch him."

Years ago a tall gaunt Southerner who had been listening to Tuskegee's Booker T. Washington make an address in a Deep South town went up to the famous Negro educator and extended his hand. The two fists, black and white, clasped warmly.

"I think," said the son of Dixie with a tremolo in his voice, "you're the greatest man in America today."

"You're forgetting President Teddy Roosevelt," smiled Booker T.

"Oh, him!" sniffed the elongated one. "Why, I've had no use for Teddy ever since that day he insulted the South by having you dine at the White House."

When William Pickens, a South Carolina Negro who won his Phi Beta Kappa key at Yale, was teaching in Montgomery before becoming an official of the NAACP, the white educators of Alabama met in that city at the same time that the Negro teachers were meeting, and one by one were called on for speeches.[41] The first white educator began, "My friends, there isn't a man in the state of Alabama who has the love in his heart for the Negro race that I have! Ever since my old black mammy rocked me to sleep I have loved that kindly old black soul like another mother." So he went on. And one by one the others said the same thing, constantly strengthened.

Pickens was called on to reply for the Negroes. "Brethren," he began, "these gentlemen tell you the Negro race ought to love them because of their black mammies. If that is so, the Negro ought to love me *twice* as much. I had not only a black mammy—*but a black daddy, as well*!"

A German, an Englishman, a Frenchman, an American, and a Negro were once commissioned to write on the subject: *The Elephant*. The German spent ten years in research in the world's best libraries and in scientific experimentation and then produced a twenty-volume work entitled: *An Introduction to the Study of the Elephant*. The Englishman bought the latest hunting equipment, went to Africa, and after five years of hunting in the jungle produced a slick-paper, highly illustrated work, *How to*

Shoot the Elephant. The Frenchman spent one year in the Bibliothèque Nationale in Paris, and wrote a spicy little work on *The Love Life of the Elephant.* The American white man with high-pressure technique organized four or five committees, made a flying trip to Africa, took a quick survey of the situation, and brought out in six months a pamphlet entitled: *Bigger and Better Elephants.* The Negro simply retired to his home and wrote a letter to the *Times* on the subject: "The Elephant and the Race Problem."

During the Detroit race riots in 1943 the police stopped a car that was racing through the battle area. A white pillowcase was flying from the hood of the car for all to see. "What's that for?" a policeman asked the driver, who explained, "It's a white pillowcase to show I'm neutral."

The policeman quickly frisked the driver and discovered a pistol in his pocket. "Neutral, eh?" said the cop. "Then what's this gun for?"

"In case somebody don't believe it," said the driver.

Shortly after the Detroit race riots a little white boy was showing a companion about the rooms of his father's country house on the shores of Lake Michigan. In the den where his dad's hunting trophies were displayed the boy paused to point out the stuffed heads of game his parent had bagged—a deer's head, an elk's head, a tiger's head, and others. Hanging on the wall among them all, mounted like the rest, was a Negro's head. Said the little host boy, proudly pointing, "My daddy got that one in Detroit."

In Little Rock they say some colored children after their first day in a mixed school said to a white child on the way out:

> See you later,
> Integrator.

Whereupon the white child answered:

> Yes! When night comes,
> Chocolate chums.

A white man's white horse jumped a black man's fence and trampled down his garden several times. Finally the Negro complained to the white man. This made the white man angry so the white man grabbed his gun and jumped over the Negro's fence himself. But the Negro shot the white man first. Said the judge to the Negro, "Did you shoot this white man in self-defense?"

"No," said the Negro, "I shot him because he *jumped* my fence."

In some places in the South they say white folks are so mean they will not give a Negro the time of day. A colored man said to a white man, "What time is it, sir?"

The white man in return asked the Negro, "Do you play checkers?"

The Negro said, "Yes, Sir."

The white man said, "Then it's your *time* to move."

In Harlem they say a young mother-to-be, about to bear her first child, decided to go back to her childhood home down South to be with her mother when the great event came. Her young husband tried to keep her from going, pointing out to her that aside from having better hospital facilities New York had no Jim Crow wards, and colored physicians could attend their own patients in the hospitals. In the South, upon hospitalization, one often has to have a white doctor since many hospitals there will not permit Negro physicians to practice inside their walls. Still the expectant mother insisted on going home to Mama.

After she left the father in Harlem waited and waited for news of the birth of his child. No news came. The ninth month passed. The tenth month passed. Finally he phoned his wife, and she said she was still awaiting the child. The husband told her something must be wrong so go to the hospital anyhow and be examined. She went. The white physician marveled that her child had not yet come. Putting his earphones to his ears and baring her abdomen, he pressed his instrument against her flesh to listen for the prenatal heartbeats of the unborn. Instead, he was astonished by what he heard. Quite clearly and distinctly inside the body of the mother was a voice singing the blues:

> I won't be born down here! No, sir!
> I won't be born down here!
> If you want to know what it's all about—
> As long as South is South, I won't come out!
> No, I won't be born down here!

The mother had to come back to New York to have her baby. Harlemites swear that that black child had plenty of sense.

"Did you hear that Governor Faubus is going to divorce his wife?"[42]
"No, why?"
"Because he caught her looking at colored TV last night."

Said a northern white senator during the school integration crisis to a Dixiecrat senator whom he saw winking at a colored girl in the corridors of the Pentagon, "Why, I thought you didn't believe in integration."

"I don't," said the southerner. "You northerners never understand anything. I don't want to go to school with that girl—just to bed with her."

Nipsey Russell says that some years ago when he was called upon to make a speech to the nine Negro boys and girls about to enter Little Rock High School surrounded by hostile troops with bayonets and hostile mobs with brickbats, he stated at their pep meeting the night before, "Children, I want you to behave with the utmost of behavior tomorrow. Watch your P's and Q's. I don't want you in your actions upon entering that white high school to in any way justify what white folks delight in saying about us—namely, that we are savage, wild, uncouth, barbarian. Don't go into that school carrying knives, razors, or guns. No! Be civilized! *Go in there throwing atom bombs!*"

Battle of Little Rock

Anonymous mimeographed handbill circulated in some southern areas during the Little Rock school crisis, 1958.

'Twas the first of September
   And all through the South
Not a word could be heard
   From nobody's mouth.
The kiddies were ready
   For school the next day
When all hell broke loose
   Down Arkansas way.
Old Ike had give orders
   To mix up the schools,
But old Faubus said, *Hold it!*
   We ain't no fools.
If you know what's good
   You will stand back and listen,
'Cause we ain't gonna stand

For no nigger mixin'.
He hollered an order
Heard around the nation.
He called on the Guard
To halt integration.
The Guard came runnin'
And took up their stand
To uphold the right
Of the good old Southland.
Ike didn't like this
So he ran to the phone
And called up old Faubus
At his Arkansas home.
He said, *Meet me in Newport*
Tomorrow night,
'Cause the niggers and white
Folks are fixin' to fight.
Faubus agreed
And hopped on his plane
And left in a hurry
In a drizzling rain.
Faubus returned home,
But stuck to his rule,
Ain't no nigger comin'
To this here school.
So on came the troops
In numbers yet bigger
To make the white folks
Go to school with a nigger.
Old Faubus was brave
And made a gallant stand—
But he had to abide
By the law of the land.
Old Ike won the battle
For the time being.
But God help the niggers
When the troops start leaving.

Said one white man to another, "Do you want to join a brand-new organization?"

"What is it?"

"SPONGE," said his friend, "S.P.O.N.G.E.—the Society for the Prevention of Negroes Getting Everything."

Two neighbors were standing on the corner. One was a white man, the other wasn't. The first said, "I've got nothing but trouble. My house just burned down and I had no insurance. My wife just ran away with my best friend in *my* automobile, and there are still ten payments due on it. To cap it all, my doctor just told me that I have to go to the hospital and have a serious operation. I sure have tough luck."

The second man just looked at him and said, "What you kicking about? You white, ain't you?"

At the height of the integration crisis it was rumored that the distinguished Negro diva, Leontyne Price of the Metropolitan, as a guest one evening in a fashionable Park Avenue home, was asked if she would be so gracious as to sing a few songs.

"But," said the hostess, "please don't sing any of those subversive Negro spirituals the integrationists are using these days to overthrow our American way of life—just some good old-fashion lieder."

They say that the reason Negroes eat so many black-eyed peas in Mississippi, and in Louisiana so many red beans, is because for years after Emancipation colored people did not dare ask a storekeeper for *white* beans. Red beans or black-eyed peas, O.K. But it was not until folks began using the term *navy beans* that Negroes had the nerve to purchase white beans, too. In a Pittsburgh hash house one day a Negro customer said to another one at the counter, "Here you are up North ordering *white* bean soup. Man, I know you are really free now."

Recently a Negro in Virginia, in his quest for the higher things, made up his mind to join a white church. At the door the frock-coated ushers that Sunday suggested that the Negro return on a weekday and see the pastor in the church office. This the Negro did. The pastor, somewhat taken aback by a black Christian who wanted to worship in a white church, advised him to go home and pray. "Tell God all about it first," the minister counseled, "and see what He says. Then come back and tell me."

The Negro went home, fell on his knees, and told God the whole story. The next day he came to the pastor's study again.

"What did God say?" asked the white minister.

"God said," the Negro replied, "that if He was to come to earth Himself, He couldn't join your church. So He told me, 'Don't worry about it.'"

When Governor Faubus of Arkansas went to heaven and knocked on the pearly gates, a distinctly Negroid voice inquired, "Who dat?"
Faubus, taken aback, yelled, "Aw, just forget it!"

Knock! Knock!
Who's there?
Ahs.
Ahs who?
Ahs your new neighbor.
The Puerto Rican version of the same joke in New York is:
Knock! Knock!
Who's there?
Yo.
Yo who?
Yo' new neighbor.

Dick Gregory says he can't get too excited over the appointment of a Negro astronaut since the United States doesn't even have Negro commercial airline pilots yet. However, he says, "You've got to admit that this Negro astronaut business is a radical step, though. We've jumped over several steps in between, and this may make us the first group of people in history who has jumped direct from the back of the bus to the moon."

A middle aged Southern plantation owner lived openly with a pretty Negro girl until, partly out of jealousy and partly out of "race pride," his fellow planters complained, accusing him of believing in racial equality. "That's a damn lie," protested the plantation owner. "It's true I stay with that girl a plenty, but I'll be damned if I let her sit at the table with me!"

A Dixie Negro who had just died arrives at the Pearly Gate and is directed by Saint Peter toward a side entrance marked COLORED. "What's the matter with you-all up here?" the Negro demands. "Don't you know that down on earth times have changed? In Alabama where I'm from all the hot dog stands, schools and churches have been integrated. Why, speaking of churches, just a few minutes ago I was all dressed up on my way to church to be married to a white woman. Come to think of it, that's the last thing I remember!"

After Josephine Baker was refused service at the Stork Club, two bopsters from Harlem decided they would try their luck at the joint, but they were stopped by the headwaiter who looked at them and said, "All the tables are gone."

The bopsters answered, "That's just what we want, a *gone* table."

Two other bopsters from Lenox Avenue went down to the Stork Club dressed as Argentine gauchos in wide hats, baggy trousers, boots, and spurs. But they got no further than the sidewalk where the doorman informed them that only people with reservations were admitted.

The bopsters said, "No speak de Engleesh."

"Reservations *only*," shouted the doorman.

"No onderstan'," shrugged the bopsters.

"What language do you speak?" demanded the doorman.

"Spaneesh," said the bopster.

"Then speak some," commanded the doorman.

"*Adios*, Old Bilbo's ghost," said the bopsters.

In New York a somewhat inebriated Negro got on the Lenox Avenue subway at Times Square muttering to himself, "White folks, this is a great country. I love my country. Can't nobody lick us." All the white people in the subway car smiled complacently. At the next express stop, 72nd Street, the Negro, still muttering, said, "Yes, I say this is a great country. But sometimes I get to thinking. Yes, I do." At the next stop, 96th Street, he muttered, "A great country, I'm telling you, but I swear I worries about how you white folks behaves." When the subway train curved under the park and got to Harlem, at 125th and Lenox Avenue, the Negro rose to stagger off. At the door he said, "White folks, you-all better watch out! Them Africans, Chinese, and Egyptians is going to give you-all hell one of these days."

An aged white-haired Negro who had been around for about seventy-two winters, had never joined a church, but he went along with his wife once in a while. Now death was barking at his heels. Lying in bed, his fever like unto a flame and his breath coming in gasps, he felt himself slipping and told his wife to get a minister to pray for him. The faithful wife, a member of the Catholic Church, called in her priest. As the white priest entered, the dying man looked up, noted his color, and cried out in anguish: "I don't want him. I need a real preacher, honey. I'm dying."

When a nice old Negro lady heard there were no longer any color bars in the Washington, D.C., restaurants, she decided to test them. Putting on her best clothes, the old lady entered the dining room of a very plush establishment near the White House. She was treated with every courtesy, and both a waiter and the headwaiter hovered over her to take her order. She asked for pigtails and black-eyed peas.

"I am most sorry, madam," the headwaiter murmured politely, "but pigtails are not on our bill of fare."

"Then, son," said the old lady, "I'll take chitterlings, rutabagas, and corn bread."

Both men shook their heads. "So sorry, those dishes we do not have."

"Then I know you got ham hocks and collard greens," said the old lady.

"Regrettably, no," the waiters replied. "They are not on our menu."

The old lady rose with dignity. "Honey," she said, smiling, "I knowed you-all wasn't ready for integration."

"The Twenties: Harlem and Its Negritude," *African Forum* 1 (1966): 11–20

When Ralph Ellison came from Tuskegee to Harlem in 1936 and Richard Wright left Chicago the following year, I would say that those migrations marked the tail end of the Negro Renaissance. Dr. Alain Locke, the granddaddy of the New Negro, introduced me to the recently arrived Ralph Ellison in the lobby of the Young Men's Christian Association, and Ellison almost immediately expressed a desire to meet Richard Wright, who was coming briefly to New York for a week or so to attend a writers' conference. I introduced them. They became fast friends. Wright influenced Ellison in the nineteen-forties, as I had influenced Wright in the thirties, as Claude McKay and James Weldon Johnson influenced me in the twenties. But by the time the thirties came, the voltage of the Negro Renaissance of the twenties had nearly run its course. Ellison and Wright were about the last of the young pilgrims to come to Harlem seeking its sustenance. The chain of influences that had begun in Renaissance days ended in the thirties when the Great Depression drastically cut down on migrations, literary or otherwise.

Claude McKay had come to New York from Jamaica by way of Tuskegee before the Harlem Renaissance had properly begun, and soon thereafter he went to live in Europe, leaving the influence of his poetry behind him. McKay might be termed the first of the New Negroes, of whom Dr. W. E. B. Du Bois, Alain Locke, and James Weldon Johnson were the deans. During the decade of the Renaissance, James Weldon Johnson lived at the corner of 135th Street and Seventh Avenue, in the very middle of Harlem, in a house which, I believe, belonged to his father-in-law and in which his charming wife, Grace, presided over midnight gumbo suppers following their literary soirees. James Weldon helped a number of Negro writers. We all needed help, but in sustenance and encouragement, we needed the examples of others before us who had achieved publication and who had written well and who had projected the feeling that in Harlem good writing might be done and that in downtown New York it might be published. From McKay and Johnson to Richard Wright and Ellison ran the Renaissance connections, with various plugs, switches, and cutoffs between. But the voltage in one way or another came through to all of us.

I arrived in Harlem at the very beginning of this New Negro Renaissance, and I have been in Harlem off and on ever since. Richard Wright and Ralph Ellison came to Harlem several years after the Renaissance had begun to go into decline. By 1935 the Federal Writers Project of the Works Progress Administration (WPA) was in the process of taking over. It had already taken on Wright before he left Chicago, and soon it took on Ellison in New York. I believe it did them no harm. Certainly, regular checks helped them to survive gastronomically, even to loaf at times and to contemplate their souls. I was never able to enroll in the Federal Writers Project because I had had two small volumes of poems published and a novel, so the government presumed I was well off—not realizing that a writer cannot eat poems, even when handsomely bound by Alfred A. Knopf. All my relatives were registered in the WPA except me, so they looked down on me as if I did not want to work. Disillusioned and having no regular source of income, Federal or otherwise, I ceased looking for work, WPA or otherwise. I have not had a job since. On the Federal Project, Wright and Ellison worked at writing for the government and got paid. But I just wrote.

It was Harlem's Golden Era, that of the twenties. I was nineteen when I first came up out of the Lenox Avenue subway one bright September afternoon and looked around in the happy sunlight to see if I saw Duke Ellington on the corner of 135th Street, or Bessie Smith passing by, or Bojangles Bill Robinson in front of the Lincoln Theatre, or maybe Paul Robeson or Bert Williams walking down the avenue. Had I been able to recognize any of them, it would have been only because of pictures I had seen in newspapers or magazines. I had read all about them in the Middle West, where I had gone to school, and I had dreamed of maybe someday seeing them. I hoped, too, I might see in New York some of the famous colored writers and editors whose names were known around the country, like McKay and Johnson and Du Bois, or lesser knowns, like the young George S. Schuyler, Walter White of the National Association for the Advancement of Colored People, poet Jessie Fauset on the staff of *The Crisis,* or Eric Walrond from the West Indies. And I was sorry by the time I got to New York that Marcus Garvey was in prison and I could not hear him speak. But Ethel Waters was singing in Harlem night clubs, and downtown Sissle and Blake's sparkling *Shuffle Along* had just begun its long and happy run that kicked off a renaissance for the Negro in Broadway musicals.

Aaron Douglas from Kansas was beginning to paint his exotic silhouettes and Barthé from Louisiana to know the feel of clay soon to be molded into bronze.[43] Charles Gilpin had already created *The Emperor Jones* at the Provincetown Theatre, and Paul Robeson was making his concert debut in Greenwich Village. Hall Johnson was gathering together in Harlem the first of his famous choirs. Countee Cullen was publishing his sonnets, and Zora Neale Hurston was writing her earliest stories. Jean Toomer was sending from Washington the poetic sketches that later became his book *Cane.* Mamie, Bessie, and Clara Smith were recording the blues. And Duke Ellington and his "Jungle Band" were at the Kentucky Club and later at the Cotton Club, where Negro patrons were not welcome unless they were very rich, like A'Lelia Walker, or famous, like Bojangles. Cabarets like Edmond's, Baron's, Small's, Leroy's, and the Lido were jumping. And J. P. Johnson, Dan Burley, Fats Waller, and Nappy were playing house-rent piano. All those things were happening during the years when I first lived in Harlem and wrote:

Droning a drowsy syncopated tune,
Rocking back and forth to a mellow croon,
I heard a Negro play.
Down on Lenox Avenue the other night
By the pale dull pallor of an old gas light
He did a lazy sway . . .
To the tune of those Weary Blues . . .

That is the poem that gave the title to my first book, *The Weary Blues,* published in 1926, a year after Countee Cullen's *Color* appeared.

In 1922, Claude McKay's *Harlem Shadows* had come out. In 1923, *Cane* appeared and received accolades from the critics of the avant garde.

In 1924, Jessie Fauset's *There Is Confusion* was published, and Walter White's novel about a lynching, *The Fire in the Flint.* In 1925, Alain Locke's exciting anthology *The New Negro* appeared. The next year brought Eric Walrond's *Tropic Death* and Walter White's second novel, *Flight.* In 1927, Countee Cullen's *Ballad of the Brown Girl* and *Copper Sun* were published; also James Weldon Johnson's *God's Trombones* and my second volume of poems, *Fine Clothes to the Jew.*

A banner year for Harlem authors was 1928, the year when the Negro vogue in the arts might be said to have reached its peak. Five novels were published—*Dark Princes* by W. E. B. Du Bois; *Plum Bun,* by Jessie Fauset; *The Walls of Jericho,* by Rudolph Fisher; *Quicksand,* by Nella Larsen; and *Home to Harlem,* by Claude McKay. In the following year, that of the Wall Street crash, came another Nella Larsen novel, *Passing,* another by Claude McKay, *Banjo,* and the advent of Wallace Thurman with *The Blacker the Berry.* I published *Not Without Laughter* in 1930, just as the Depression set in, so my first novel did not sell very well. A year later, Arna Bontemps published his first novel, *God Sends Sunday,* a little novel of great charm that had very little sale. During the remainder of that decade, nothing much exciting happened, literarily speaking, except for the debut in 1934 of the long-burgeoning talent of one of the most sparkling of Negro writers, Zora Neale Hurston, who blossomed forth in the midst of the Depression with her novel *Jonah's Gourd Vine,* followed in 1935 by another novel, *Their Eyes Were Watching God.* Had Miss Hurston's books appeared a decade earlier, during the Renaissance, they might have been best sellers. But it was not until 1940 that a Negro writer achieved that status: Richard Wright's powerful *Native Son* burst like a bombshell on the American scene. It sold a half million copies and was translated around the world.

When Richard Wright first came to Harlem, he lived at the Douglas Hotel, near the corner of 150th Street and St. Nicholas Avenue. There, in a small paper-cluttered room, he worked at completing *Native Son,* which he had begun in Chicago. At the Douglas, Ralph Ellison visited him, as did I and another of his friends, the playwright Theodore Ward. After the success of his novel, Wright got married and moved to Brooklyn Heights—living in the same house, I believe, in which Carson McCullers lived—and Harlemites did not see much of him any more. In 1941, Wright published his poetically written *Twelve Million Black Voices,* a folk history of the Negro in America. That same year, written in collaboration with Paul Green, his play, *Native Son,* in which Canada Lee played the role of Bigger Thomas, was presented on Broadway. And in

1943 his autobiographical *Black Boy* became a Book-of-the-Month Club selection. Then it was that Richard Wright moved to Paris, bought a farm in Normandy, and never came home any more. In ensuing years, his literary output abroad, so critics contend, was nowhere near the high quality of the books he wrote while still in America. *The Outsider* (1953), *Savage Holiday* (1954), *The Color Curtain* (1956), *Pagan Spain* (1957), and *The Long Dream* (1958) were written in Europe. Richard Wright died in Paris in 1960.

Until he came out of the Mississippi badlands, bringing with him all its mud and violence and hatred, no Negro writer in America had had so large an audience. For several years the big bad "burly nigger" of the Chicago slums, Bigger Thomas, who Wright created in *Native Son,* was a conversation piece for readers everywhere. They took sides, pro and con, on so monstrous a symbol of hate in a black skin. Should or should not Negro writers create such baleful characters? At any rate, Wright acquired a very wide audience indeed. Twelve years after the publication of *Native Son,* in 1952, Ralph Ellison, through his fantastic novel *Invisible Man,* achieved a similar public at home and abroad. But he did not move away from Harlem. Ellison still lives there.

Of the most famous of the Negro Renaissance writers, most are dead. James Weldon Johnson was killed in an automobile wreck in 1938 on the way to New York from his Massachusetts home. Claude McKay, having once been a Communist, became a Catholic and died in 1948 in Chicago. In 1960, Zora Neale Hurston died in Florida and Jessie Fauset in Philadelphia. Dr. Du Bois died in Ghana in 1963. The big names of Harlem writing deserted their old stamping grounds as the years went by. Now almost the last of the living Renaissance writers, besides myself, is Arna Bontemps, long-time librarian at Fisk University in Nashville. I still live in Harlem.

Once I was invited to a downtown party that I was especially urged to attend because my host wanted a charming white lady from Georgia who had never met a Negro socially to meet one—in this case, me. When I was introduced to the lady, she said graciously, "Oh, I am so glad to meet you! When I was at Sweet Briar, I wrote a paper on four Negra poets, and *you* were one of them. Now, let me see! Who were the other three? Oh, yes, Claude McKay was one. What became of him?"

"He's dead," I said.

"Well now, another one—he wrote sermons in verse," she recalled.

"James Weldon Johnson," I said.

"That's right! What became of him?"

"He's dead," I said.

"Oh, my! Well now, that lyric poet with the pretty name."

"Countee Cullen?"

"Yes, where is he?"

"Dead, too," I said.

"My goodness!" cried the white woman from Georgia. "Are you the *only* Negra poet living?"

Cullen died at the age of forty-three. Among the most beautiful of his poems was "Heritage," which asked, "What is Africa to me?" Had the word *negritude* been in use in Harlem in the twenties, Cullen, as well as McKay, Johnson, Toomer, and I, might have been called poets of *negritude*—particularly Toomer of the "dusky cane-lipped throngs" with his "memories of kings and caravans, high-priests, an ostrich, and a juju man." In "Harlem Shadows," in 1922, McKay had written a poem about a Negro girl in which he presaged the images and sounds of the French-African poets a quarter of a century later:

Her voice was like the sound of blended flutes
Blown by black players upon a picnic day.
She sang and danced on gracefully and calm,
The light gauze hanging loose about her form;
To me she seemed a proudly-swaying palm
Grown livelier for passing through a storm.
Upon her swarthy neck black shiny curls
Luxuriant fell. . . .

A few years after McKay, Cullen sang:

You have not heard my love's dark throat,
Slow fluting like a reed. . . .

And in "Heritage" he asked:

What is Africa to me:
Copper sun or scarlet sea,
Jungle star or jungle track,
Strong bronzed men or regal black
Women from whose loins I sprang
When the birds of Eden sang?

In 1925, in a much translated poem, Waring Cuney wrote of the unsung loveliness of a Harlem girl:

She does not know her beauty.
She thinks her brown body has no glory.
If she could dance naked under palm trees
And see her image in the river
She would know.
But there are no palm trees on the street,
And dish water gives back no images.

This poem appeared in the first German anthology of American-Negro poetry, *Afrika Singt,* published in 1929 in Vienna and Leipzig. It also included my

I am a Negro,
Black as the night is black
Black as the depths of my Africa . . .

and also an excellent translation of my

I've known rivers. . . .
I bathed in the Euphrates when dawns were young.
I built my hut near the Congo and it lulled me to sleep.
I looked upon the Nile and raised the pyramids above it . . .
I've known rivers,
Ancient dusky rivers.
My soul has grown deep like the rivers.

In France as well as Germany, before the close of the Negro Renaissance, Harlem's poets were already being translated. Léopold Sédar Senghor of Senegal and Aimé Césaire of Martinique, the great poets of *negritude,* while still students at the Sorbonne, had read the Harlem poets and felt a bond between themselves and us. In faraway South Africa, Peter Abrahams, who became one of Africa's most distinguished authors, wrote in his autobiography, *Tell Freedom,* how, as a teenager at the Bantu Men's Social Center in Johannesburg, he discovered the Harlem poets of the twenties. There for the first time he read Du Bois, McKay, Georgia Douglass Johnson, Cullen, and myself. Years later when he became a writer, he recorded:

> I read every one of the books on the shelf marked *American Negro Literature.* I became a nationalist, a color nationalist through the writings of men and women who lived in a world away from me. To them I owe a great debt for crystallizing my vague yearnings to write and for showing me that the long dream was attainable.

The Harlem poets and novelists of the twenties became an influence in faraway Africa and the West Indies—an influence reflected till today in the literature of black men and women there. To us, *negritude* was an unknown word, but certainly pride of heritage and consciousness of race was ingrained in us. But because we were Harlemites of the balling and brawling "Roaring Twenties" of midnight cabarets and bootleg gin, Wallace Thurman called us jokingly "the niggerati." In his novel *Infants of the Spring,* Thurman captured the era perfectly as it related to its black bohemians. Now in the sixties, LeRoi Jones, Welton Smith, Calvin Hernton, David Henderson, and numerous young black writers do their balling and brawling downtown in Greenwich Village—integrated. But in the twenties we had so much fun and liked Harlem so well that we did not think about taking the long subway ride to the Village, where white artists and writers gathered. We let them come uptown to us.

409 Edgecombe, then the tallest apartment house on Sugar Hill, was a sort of party-giving center and in-and-out meeting place for Harlem writers and artists. Walter White and his beautiful *café au lait* wife, Gladys, lived on the top floor there and loved giving parties. The painter Aaron Douglas and his wife, Alta, lived there, too, and always had a bottle of ginger ale in the ice box for those who brought along refreshments. Elmer Anderson Carter, the editor of *Opportunity* who succeeded Charles S. Johnson, was on the floor above the Douglases, and actor Ivan Sharpe and Evie had a flat there, too, as did—although much later—the poet William Stanley Braithwaite, the composer Clarence Cameron White, and the Tea Cup Reader Madam Vanderbilt Smith.

Just down the hill in the Dunbar Apartments lived the famous Dr. Du Bois, the cartoonist E. Simms Campbell, and, nearby, Dan Burley, humorist, newspaperman, and boogiewoogie piano player, whose wife was a concert singer. Artists and writers were always running into each other on Sugar Hill and talking over their problems and wondering how they could get a Rosenwald Fellowship, a Guggenheim, or a grant from the Harmon Foundation. It was in the Aaron Douglas apartment, at 409 Edgecombe, that seven of us gathered one night and decided to found a magazine the better to express ourselves freely and independently—without interference from old heads, white or Negro—a magazine which we would support ourselves, although none of us had enough money on which to eat.

It was about that time that I wrote, "We younger Negro artists who create now intend to express our individual dark-skinned selves without fear or shame. If white people are pleased, we are glad. If they are not, it doesn't matter. . . . If colored people are pleased, we are glad. If they are not, their displeasure doesn't matter either." Various of my friends said, "Amen!" And we set out to publish *Fire,* a Negro quarterly of the arts to *épater le bourgeois,* to burn up a lot of the old stereotyped Uncle Tom ideas of the past, and to provide us with an outlet for publishing not existing in the hospitable but limited pages of *The Crisis* or *Opportunity.* Wallace Thurman would edit *Fire,* Aaron Douglas would be its artist and designer, and John P. Davis (who years later edited the enormous *American Negro Reference Book* for the Phelps Stokes Fund) would be the business manager. All seven of us—including artist and writer Bruce Nugent, poet Gwendolyn Bennett, novelist Zora Neale Hurston, and myself—were to be the editorial board, and each of us would put in fifty dollars to bring out the first issue. But not all of us had fifty dollars to put in, so Wallace Thurman, who had a job, assumed responsibility for the printer's bills.

He was years paying off the ensuing indebtedness. As to format, we got carried away with ourselves, and our taste proved extremely expensive. Only the best cream white paper would do on which to print our poems and stories. And only a rich crimson jacket on de luxe stock would show off well the Aaron Douglas cover design. Beautifully laid out, *Fire*'s one and only issue was handsome indeed—and the printer's bills enormous. How Thurman was able to persuade the printer to release the entire issue to us on so small an advance payment, I do not know. But he did. The downtown newspapers and white magazines (except for *The Bookman*) paid no attention to the advent of *Fire,* and we had no money for advertising. Bruce Nugent, jobless and at leisure at the time, was in charge of distribution and collections. Being hungry, Nugent usually ate up on the spot the meager amounts he collected from *Fire*'s very few sales. As we had hoped—even though it contained no four-letter words as do today's little magazines—the Negro bourgeoisie were shocked by *Fire.* The *Afro-American*'s literary reviewer wrote in high indignation, "I have just tossed the first issue of *Fire* into the fire." He claimed that in his poetry Cullen tried "his best to obscure the thought in superfluous sentences" and that I displayed my "usual ability to say nothing in many words," while Aaron Douglas was "permitted to spoil three perfectly good pages and a cover with . . . the meaningless grotesqueness of his creations." When the editorial board of *Fire* met again, we did not plan a new issue, but emptied our pockets to help poor Thurman whose wages were being garnished weekly because he had signed for the printer's bills.

Yet somehow we still managed to go dancing at the Savoy on Saturday nights or to Edmond's to hear Ethel Waters sing.

The Negro writers of the twenties, it seems (or perhaps it is only because I am looking back through a golden haze of memories), did not take themselves as seriously as did the writers of the thirties—the hungry era, when proletarian authors came into vogue; or as did those of the forties, who went from a depression through a great war; or those of the fifties, when integrationist tendencies of let-us-write-white developed; or of the sixties, when a vengeful James Baldwin called down upon America "the fire next time" and LeRoi Jones of the four-letter words advised all white folks, "Drop dead!" Negro literature began to acquire its share of angry young men.

Now almost nobody's writing has fun in it any more—not even *The Wig* by Charles Wright, which begins with high hilarity and ends with a red-hot steel rod jabbed into the penis of its smiling hero, who says, "I'm beginning to feel better already." But none of these contemporary Negro writers lives in Harlem, and none of them was even a gleam in their daddies' eyes when the Harlem Renaissance began, and their truculent *negritude* emblazoned in graffiti is designed to *épater* a much more blasé bourgeoisie than that which existed in the far-off days of comparative innocence when, on the printed page, not even Richard Wright's big burly Bigger Thomas dared say, "mother -------!"

"Black Writers in a Troubled World," LHP 3390 (March 26, 1966)

The consensus among many Negroes is that American society is falling to pieces, going to the dogs, stewing in its own iniquity, and bogged down in the gutters of Saigon.[44] The work of the most dynamic of the younger Negro writers confirms this. Certainly, in some ways, their books are about as near the gutter as—in their opinion—America seems to be. Negroes in general are seldom inclined to do anything halfway. What they do, when they do it, is usually done whole hog and with gusto. A few years ago the United States Supreme Court let down the bars to literary censorship in America and *Lady Chatterley's Lover* could be published unexpurgated. Thereafter, Henry Miller's *Tropic of Cancer* and William Burroughs' *Naked Lunch,* as well as Jean Genet were without hinderance publicly offered for sale on American bookstalls. LeRoi

Jones must then have said in effect, "Why not I?" and proceeded to out-do and out-sex in four-letter words any known white writer up to that date.

In the Jones play, *The Toilet,* every other word is a word that in times past would have made ordinary citizens blush, and which even today makes ladies stuff their fingers in their ears. Younger Negro writers like LeRoi Jones, Charles Wright in *The Wig,* and the poets of the Village excuse obscenities by saying that America is obscene, and that the only way to show this obscenity is by calling a spade a spade, especially a *white* spade. James Baldwin sends down the "fire next time" on white America, and LeRoi Jones says to whites in print and in speeches, "Drop dead!"

In the old days of slavery no doubt Negroes used to talk quite badly about whites "down at the big gate"—but never in the Big House. Nowadays, Negroes talk about whites badly *right in the middle of the whites' own parlors,* lecture halls and libraries. They "tell them off" in profane and no uncertain terms. But the funny thing is that many whites seem to love it—or did—until the Black Arts Theatre in Harlem, operated by Mr. Jones, began to bar whites from entering—even those ultra liberals who had donated money to the theatre, and had most highly acclaimed LeRoi as a writer. But finally, the whites began to get mad, really mad. Now white critics are united in proclaiming the decline and fall of LeRoi Jones. He has goaded them into howling and growling. But this, Jones has done deliberately, I gather, in the belief that by giving America the shock treatment, something might happen to so shake America up that life between the Atlantic and the Pacific might change—for triumphant blacks, at least, if not for the country itself which is, according to their theory, beyond salvation. The most talented of the young Negro writers have become America's prophets of doom, black ravens cawing over carrion.

Slightly older Negro writers now in their literary prime like Ralph Ellison (*Invisible Man*), John Killens (*And Then We Heard the Thunder*), Julian Mayfield (*The Grand Parade*), Paule Marshall (*Brown Girl, Brownstones*) and Alston Anderson (*All God's Children*), all call attention to America's racial defects but, having developed as novelists before Baldwin's *Another Country* popularized the word merde (more ugly in English than it is in French)—and preceding LeRoi Jones' *The System of Dante's Hell* by at least a decade—content themselves certainly with dire pictures of their country's dilemma but without finger-painting in excrement on America's lily white canvas. The much older writers of color dating from the Negro Renaissance days of the Twenties—those writers who preceded and up to Richard Wright, like Arna Bontemps (*Black Thunder*), Ann Petry (*The Street*), and myself (the Simple books, for example), as well as Richard Wright in *Native Son,* never dreamed of revealing the Negro people to themselves in terms of motherfuckers; or of shocking white readers with bad language rather than with bad facts.

The Negro writer in the United States has always had—has been *forced* to have in spite of himself—two audiences, one black, one white. And, as long has been America's dilemma, seldom "the twain shall meet." The fence between the two audiences is the color bar which in reality stretches around the world. Writers who feel they must straddle this fence, perforce acquire a split personality. Writers who do not care whether they straddle the fence of color or not, are usually the best writers, attempting at least to let their art leap the barriers of color, poverty, or whatever other roadblocks to artistic truth there may be. Unfortunately, some writers get artistic truth and financial success mixed up, get critical acclaim and personal integrity confused. Such are the dilemmas which the double audience creates. Which set of readers to please—the white, the black, or both at once?

The best writers are those who possess enough self-integrity to wish first and foremost to please themselves, *only* themselves, and nobody else. But this, when one is young and one's thinking is unclear—and one's ability to analyze this world about one is uncertain—is not easy. To some extent, African writers must have a similar problem—not in terms of race and color, but I would think, in terms of folk life in contrast to urban thinking, regional tongues against European, tribalism *or* educated-ism, the basic roots *or* the young branches. These things should not be problems—but I imagine they *might* be. Then there is the reading and publishing world outside of Africa. The very fact that all the major publishers of African writers are in Paris or London or New York, and the ultimate editors are white, is not unlike a similar problem that has long faced American Negro writers. Until the recent formation of the Johnson Publishing Company in Chicago (owners of *Ebony* and *Jet*), all the major publishers in the United States where Negro writers might get published were white. All the major literary magazines are white. All the major critics and setters of literary styles are white. No wonder one of our most prolific and popularly gifted writers, Frank Yerby (who once wrote deeply moving short stories of Negro life), went "white." For a long time now Yerby has published only highly successful "white" romances that sell year after year to Hollywood.

An even more gifted colored writer in the Twenties, Jean Toomer, author of a single highly acclaimed book, *Cane,* filled with the sadness and beauty of life in the black South, went "white" too, and never wrote anything else worthwhile. Just this year a talented Negro writer refused to grant permission for the use of a story in an anthology of Negro short stories because the writer did not wish to "be typed as a Negro writer," but in complexion this author could by no stretch of the imagination be called white. So one of the dilemmas of the black writer in America is how to keep from being white-ized. That some of the young writers are going to the other extreme and insisting on being blacker than black is to be understood. And that, in their angry frustration, they resort to the use of the dirtiest words in the language, is to be understood, too.

Now, the subject of the colloquium: What is the function and significance of African Negro art in the life of the people and for the people? This is where *négritude* comes into play. *Négritude,* as I have garnered from Senegal's distinguished poet, Léopold Sédar Senghor, has its roots deep in the beauty of the black people—in what the younger writers and musicians in America call "soul" which I would define in this way: *Soul* is a synthesis of the essence of Negro folk art redistilled—particularly the old music and its flavor, the ancient basic beat out of Africa, the folk rhymes and Ashanti stories—expressed in contemporary ways so definitely and emotionally colored with the old, that it gives a distinctly "Negro" flavor to today's music, painting or writing—or even to merely personal attitudes and daily conversation. *Soul* is contemporary Harlem's *négritude,* revealing to the Negro people and the world the beauty within themselves. I once tried to say this in a poem:

I've known rivers:
I've known rivers ancient as the world
and older than the flow
of human blood in human veins.

My soul has grown deep like the rivers.

I bathed in the Euphrates
when dawns were young.
I built my hut near the Congo
and it lulled me to sleep.
I looked upon the Nile
and raised the pyramids above it.
I heard the singing of the Mississippi
when Abe Lincoln went down to New Orleans,

and I've seen its muddy bosom
turn all golden in the sunset.

I've known rivers:
Ancient, dusky rivers.

My soul has grown deep like the rivers.

If one may ascribe a prime function to any creative writing, it is, I think, to affirm life, to yeah-say the excitement of living in relation to the vast rhythms of the universe of which we are a part, to untie the riddles of the gutter in order to closer tie the knot between man and God. As to Negro writing and writers, one of our aims, it seems to me, should be to gather the strengths of our people in Africa and the Americas into a tapestry of words as strong as the bronzes of Benin, the memories of Songhay and Mele, the war cry of Chaka, the beat of the blues, and the *Uhuru* of African freedom, and give it to the world with pride and love, and the kind of humanity and affection that Senghor put into his poem *To the American Negro Troops* when he said:

You bring the springtime of peace
And hope at the end of hope. . . .
Down flowing streets of joy, boys play with dreams.
Men dance in front of machines,
and, astonished, burst out singing.
The eyelashes of students
are sprinkled with rose petals.
Fruit ripens in the breast of virgins.
And the hips of women—oh, how sweet!—
handsomely grow heavy.
Oh, black brothers,
warriors whose mouths are singing flowers—
Delight of living when winter is over—
You I salute as messengers of peace!

That is Senghor. To this I affirm, how mighty it would be if the black writers of our troubled world became our messengers of peace. How wonderful it would be if:

Les hommes dansent devant leurs machines
et se surprennent à chanter.
Les paupières des écolières sont pétales de rose,
les fruits nurissent à la poitrine des vierges,

Et les hanches des femmes—oh, douceur—
généreusement s'alourdissent.
Frères noirs, guerriers dont la bouche
est fleur qui chante—
Oh! délice de vivre après l'hiver—
je vous salue comme des messagers de paix.

6

Forewords, Prefaces, and Introductions to Edited Volumes

"The Negro," introduction to *Hunger and Revolt: Cartoons by [Jacob] Burck* (New York: Daily Worker, 1935), 141–42

Today, as the Fourth of July, 1934, approached, the United Press sends out a release from Kokomo, Indiana, saying that, "The fiery cross blazed again today on the hill around which 100,000 Knights of the Ku Klux Klan met in 1923, summoning remnants of the hooded order for a new campaign . . . to rejuvenate the Klan 'for protection of the constitution of the United States.' "

Laugh that off!

And if you can laugh it off happily, then you can laugh happily, too, at the grim and ironic humor of Jacob Burck's cartoons.

Burck's powerful drawings, with their crooked judges peering out from behind the pillars of justice and their fat sheriffs carrying the ropes of the lynchers they whitewash, portray the America of today with a laughter that chokes the proletarian throat and makes the blood run to fists that must be increasingly, militantly clenched to fight the brazen terror that spreads and grows from Alabama to the Pacific, from New York to Texas.

This week in San Francisco, four men are arrested for their activities in connection with the stevedores' strike. Four visitors who go to see them in jail are also immediately placed under arrest as they leave the prison. Those who send telegrams of protest to the judge are ordered detained at once for contempt of court. The local secretary of the International Labor Defense, for merely sending a wire, is being held under ten thousand dollars bail.

Laugh that off!

All over America police clubs swing on the heads of workers who organize and strike for a decent living and a little rest and a little pursuit of happiness. All over America the Silver Shirts and the White Legion and the vigilantes and similar groups march and maneuver. All over America Negroes are facing new jim-crow bars in the N.R.A., C.C.C., S.E.R.A., and other government sponsored projects. Almost weekly a new lynching is reported.[1]

Legally and illegally lynched, beaten, starved, intimidated and jim-crowed, nevertheless, the Negro masses of America are stirring. (Ralph Graves did not die in vain.) The poor whites, beaten and starved as well, are stirring. (Mooney does not lie in jail in vain.) And the black and white masses slowly but surely will put their two strengths together, realizing they face a common foe.[2]

Some of Jacob Burck's cartoons picture the harsh realities of today, the wall of struggle; others foreshadow the marching power of the proletarian future. Let the capitalists, who pay for our oppression, laugh that future off, if they can.

"Foreword," *Aunt Sara's Wooden God,* by Mercedes Gilbert (New York: Christopher Publishing House, 1938), vii

Miss Mercedes Gilbert, who comes from Florida to Broadway as one of America's leading Negro actresses, returns again to the deep south for the scene of her first novel, *Aunt Sara's Wooden God*. This is an authentic every-day story of thousands of little families below the Mason-Dixon line, bound to the soil by poverty and blackness, but living their enclosed lives always in the hope that someday some one of them may escape the family group and go on to higher things. Their tragedy is that there is so small a foundation on which to base such a hope. The wooden god of Miss Gilbert's novel is a mulatto country boy, worshipped by his mother, but himself unable to fulfill the faith and belief she has in him, balked as he is by poverty, the color-line, and his own inner weaknesses born of conceit and fear. That he lives and dies a hero to Aunt Sara, although he tortures and hurts so many others, constitutes the ironic tragedy of this book filled with little pictures of the rural and small-town life of the South.

Those readers who enjoyed *Jonah's Gourd Vine* or *Ollie Miss* will find in *Aunt Sara's Wooden God* a kindred volume.

"The Ceaseless Rings of Walt Whitman," introduction to *I Hear the People Singing: Selected Poems of Walt Whitman* (New York: International Publishers, 1946), 7–10

Walt Whitman, greatest of American poets, was born on a farm owned by his father near West Hills, Long Island, New York, on the last day of May, 1819. He died in a tiny little old house of his own on Mickle Street in Camden, New Jersey, at the end of March, 1892. The span of his life ran from American slavery through the Civil War to American freedom and the approaching dawn of the twentieth century.

Whitman did not fight in the War Between the States. He hated war and killing, but he devoted much of his time to nursing and caring for the wounded, both Northern and Southern, white or Negro, Yankee or Rebel. At Culpeper, Virginia, a staging area, he saw enough of combat to sicken him against war. But on errands of mercy, he went out to the battlefields and into field hospitals. From his friends he solicited money to buy cookies, candies, ice cream, magazines, and papers for the wounded. He tended them, read to them, wrote letters home for those who could not write, and cheered them with stories. He helped those with leg injuries to learn to walk again.

In 1864, assisting a surgeon in an amputation, Walt Whitman was accidentally cut with a gangrenous scalpel. An infection set in which caused him health complications in later life. While carrying on this voluntary nursing among the wounded in and near Washington, Whitman held a job as a clerk in the Indian Office. The attacks of narrow-minded readers on his poetry caused him to lose this job. But, through the help of friends, he secured a place in the Attorney General's office. In the late night hours, he continued to write his poems of democracy, articles, and letters for the papers.

His position in the Indian Office was not the first that Whitman had lost because of his liberal views. He had been an editor of the Brooklyn *Eagle,* but was fired there in 1848 because he refused to support Governor Cass of Michigan who advocated the continuation of slavery. Whitman called people like Cass "Dough Faces," because of their condonance of Southern slavery. Whitman abhorred slave catchers and those who gave them aid or supported their political beliefs. In the New York *Evening Post,* Whitman wrote:

We are all docile dough-faces,
They knead us with the fist,
They, the dashing Southern Lords,
We labor as they list.
For them we speak—or hold our tongue,
For them we turn and twist.

There had been a half-dozen or so slaves on the ancestral Whitman farm, and young Walt had played with them as a child. Perhaps that is where he acquired his sympathy for the Negro people and his early belief that all men should be free—a belief that grew to embrace the peoples of the whole world, expressed over and over throughout his poems, encompassing not only America but the colonial peoples, the serfs of tsarist Russia, the suppressed classes everywhere.

In our own land, Walt Whitman lived intensely within the currents of his time, absorbed in the democratic strivings growing in America and taking root like wind-blown seeds in varied soils around the world. His physical self wandered from the Long Island countryside to the Brooklyn ferries and Broadway trolley cars, from urban foundries and shops to Mississippi river boats and the fields of battle during the Civil War. His spiritual self roamed the earth wherever the winds of freedom blow however faintly, keeping company with the foiled revolutionaries of Europe or the suppressed coolies of Asia.

Because the vast sweep of democracy is still incomplete even in America today, because revolutionaries seeking to break old fetters are still foiled in Europe and Asia, because the physical life of the Brooklyn ferries and the Broadway street cars and the Mississippi river banks and the still fresh battlefields of World War II continue to pulse with the same heartbeats of humanity as in Whitman's time, his poetry strikes us now with the same immediacy it must have awakened in its earliest readers in the 1850's.

The good gray poet of democracy is one of literature's great faith-holders in human freedom. Speaking simply for people everywhere and most of all for the believers in our basic American dream, he is constantly growing in stature as the twentieth century advances and edition after edition of his poems appears.

Walt Whitman wrote without the frills, furbelows, and decorations of conventional poetry, usually without rhyme or measured prettiness. Perhaps because of his simplicity, timid poetry lovers over the years have been frightened away from his *Leaves of Grass,* poems as firmly rooted and as brightly growing as the grass itself. Perhaps, too, because his all-embracing words lock arms with workers and farmers, Negroes and whites, Asiatics and Europeans, serfs, and free men, beaming democracy to all, many academic-minded intellectual isolationists in America have had little use for Whitman, and so have impeded his handclasp with today by keeping him imprisoned in silence on library shelves. Still his words leap from their pages and their spirit grows steadily stronger everywhere:

. . . I give the sign of democracy.
By God! I will accept nothing which all cannot have their counterpart of on the same terms . . .

So there is no keeping Whitman imprisoned in silence. He proclaims:

I ordain myself loosed of limits. . . .
Going where I list. . . .
Gently, but with undeniable will, divesting myself of the holds that would hold me.

One of the greatest "I" poets of all time, Whitman's "I" is not the "I" of the introspective versifiers who write always and only about themselves. Rather it is the cosmic "I" of all peoples who seek freedom, decency, and dignity, friendship and equality between individuals and races all over the world.

The best indication of the scope of Whitman's poems might be found in his own *Song of the Answerer* where he writes about poetry:

The words of true poems give you more than poems,
They give you to form for yourself poems, religions, politics, war, peace, behavior, histories, essays, daily life and everything else,
They balance ranks, colors, races, creeds, and the sexes. . . .
They bring none to his or her terminus or to be content and full,
Whom they take they take into space to behold the birth of stars, to learn one of the meanings,
To launch off with absolute faith, to sweep through the ceaseless rings and never be quiet again.

In this atomic age of ours, when the ceaseless rings are multiplied a millionfold, the Whitman spiral is upward and outward toward a freer, better life for all, not narrowing downward toward death and destruction. Singing the greatness of the individual, Whitman also sings the greatness of unity, cooperation, and understanding.

> *. . . all the men ever born are also my brothers, and the women my sisters. . . .*

As an after-thought he adds:

> *(I am large, I contain multitudes).*

Certainly, his poems contain us all. The reader cannot help but see his own better self therein.

"Concerning Nicolás Guillén," LHP 265 (September 29, 1948)

Not only is Nicolás Guillén the most famous Cuban poet, but he is one of the most widely read poets in Spanish today, his books circulating throughout all of Latin America.[3] He is the author of seven volumes of poetry, four of them published in Havana, one in Mexico, one in Spain, and his selected poems, *El Son Entero,* has just been published in a de luxe edition in Buenos Aires.

Because Guillén writes about the everyday problems of the people, often using the idioms and rhythms of the *rumbas* and *sones* in his verses, his poems are recited and sung by thousands of men and women who are far from "literary." Yet Nicolás Guillén is no Cuban Edgar Guest, for many distinguished critics have paid tribute to the literary values of his poetry, its diversity, music, warmth, passion, and power. His style varies from delicate lyrics and ultra-modern unrhymed poetry to singing Afro-Creole dialect verses, but his subject matter is almost always the problems, poverty, and folk-ways of his native Cuba. That this subject matter finds its counterpart in the other islands of the West Indies and in South America, no doubt accounts for the great popularity of Guillén today.

With Aimé Césaire of Martinique and A. J. Seymour of British Guiana, Nicolás Guillén is one of the most exciting of the many interesting poets of Negro blood now writing in the Caribbean area. This winter Anderson & Ritchie are publishing for the first time in English a collection of his poems under the title *Cuba Libre.*

"Preface" (with Arna Bontemps), *The Poetry of the Negro, 1746–1949* (Garden City, N.Y.: Doubleday & Co., 1949), vii–ix

The title of this volume has somewhat more reference to a theme and a point of view than to the racial identity of some of its contributors. But this does not mean it has none at all. A number of the poems were chosen because the writers belonged to the group which is defined in the United States as Negro, even though the sum of such inclusions may be smaller than the number of selections made on other grounds.

If the compilers had sought for a racial idiom in verse form among Negroes, they should have concerned themselves with the words of Negro spirituals, with folk rhymes, with blues, and other spontaneous lyrics. These song materials, no doubt, suggest a kind of poetry that is racially distinctive, that lies essentially outside the literary traditions of the language which it employs. But the present anthology consists of poems written within that tradition, by Negroes as well as others.

The common thread, of course, is the Negro's experience in the Western world. Where the author is a Negro, any comment on any subject is considered within this limit. Poems by others are included only when they touch the subject directly, except in the case of the Caribbean countries, where a departure from this principle seemed necessary in a few cases in order to make representative selections.

Another factor, too, blurred this logic a little. Racial distinctions vary from country to country. Any effort to apply the yardstick of the United States to the other Americas is likely to confuse more than it clarifies. No such attempt was made by the compilers. Moreover, in the predominantly Negro countries around the Caribbean, selections of representative poems were made sometimes without respect either to racial implications in the verses or to the identity of the poets. This point was explained to those contributors to whom it was not clear.

The arrangement of the poems was influenced by other considerations. In the major section, containing the work of Negro poets of the United States, a chronological order was followed, based on the date of the poet's birth, or the closest estimate that could be made of it. The poems in the other two sections follow sequences which seemed generally appropriate for reading purposes, the deciding element being sometimes historical, sometimes dramatic.

On the whole the aim was to assemble selections which would be at once representative of the Negro's own poetic expression and of the poetry he inspired others to write. The Long Island slave Jupiter Hammon's "An Evening Thought: Salvation by Christ, with Penitential Cries" (1760) was the first well-known literary work by a Negro published in the United States. Evidence of an earlier Negro poet has been found in references to a Lucy Terry, to whom a verse account of an Indian raid on Deerfield in 1746 is credited. But the original version of this literary work appears to have been lost. The one used by George A. Sheldon in his *Negro Slavery in Old Deerfield* and quoted in this volume is rather enigmatically described as "secondary."

Hammon was followed by Phillis Wheatley, a delicate girl who not only produced a larger amount of poetry but also won the attention of George Washington and Thomas Jefferson as well as a number of prominent people in London. Somewhat later another slave, who was permitted to hire himself out, found employment in the home of the president of the University of North Carolina and in this atmosphere composed poems that were published in Raleigh in 1829.

These articulate slaves belonged to a tradition of writers in bondage which goes back to Aesop and Terence. While Aesop's writing appears to have won him rewards of a sort, there is no sure indication that he succeeded in writing himself out of servitude. Terence did, however, and so did Phillis Wheatley of West Africa and Boston. Hammon became a pamphleteer for freedom, but his final years are obscure. George Moses Horton, the slave poet of North Carolina, waited for his deliverance till the Northern armies invaded the South.

Meanwhile in Louisiana free men of color became an important element of the population, gained wealth, sent their youth to Paris to study drama, music, and fencing, and to hobnob with the friends of Alexandre Dumas; to Rome to devote themselves to sculpture and singing. Many of these young people were not inclined to return to their native state, with its oppressive racial attitudes, but some were drawn again by the bittersweet allurements of home in New Orleans. Enough trained musicians came back, for example, to bring about the organization of a symphony orchestra of one hundred members among this group at one time. Their influence in literature was strong enough to produce an anthology of poetry in 1845. The volume was called *Les Cenelles,* and it contained verse by a dozen of the younger French-speaking poets among the free Negroes writing at that time, including Victor Séjour, who was later to become a popular playwright in Paris. Oddly, the members of this group had not been taught to link themselves personally with the condition of the slaves, and their poetry scarcely touched racial feeling.

So the traditions of Negro poetry derive from influences and sources as far apart as those that inspired Jupiter Hammon's "An Address to Negroes in the State of New York" (1787) and Horton's book of verse, *The Hope of Liberty,* on the one hand, and Phillis Wheatley's refined and tempered *Poems on Various Subjects, Religious and Moral* (1773) and *Les Cenelles* on the other. The lines from these to Dunbar and Braithwaite, to Hughes and Cullen and Donald Jeffrey Hayes, to Margaret Walker and Gwendolyn Brooks are not hard to draw.[4]

The Negro in Western civilization has been exposed to overwhelming historical and sociological pressures that are bound to be reflected in the verse he has written and inspired. The fact that he has used poetry as a form of expression has also brought him into contact with literary trends and influences. How one of these forces or the other has predominated and how the results may be weighed and appraised are among the questions to which the poetry itself contains answers.

"Foreword," *The Free Lance Magazine Anthology of Poetry,* LHP 539 (May 1952)

Words are the paper and string to package experience, to wrap up from the inside out the poet's concentric waves of contact with the living world. Each poet makes of words his own highly individualized wrappings for the segments of life he wishes to present. Sometimes the paper and string are more arresting than the contents of the package. Sometimes the poet creates a transparent wrapping revealing with great clarity and from all angles what is inside. Sometimes the word wrapping is clumsy and inept, and neither the inside nor the outside of the package is interesting. Sometimes the word wrapping contains nothing. But, regardless of quality or content, a poem reveals always the poet as person. Skilled or unskilled, wise or foolish, nobody can write a poem without revealing something of himself. Here are people. Here are poems. Here is revelation.

"Introduction," *The Japanese Anthology of Negro Poetry,* trans. Shozo Kojima, LHP 545 (May 20, 1952)

In the United States of America the Negro people are a group apart.[5] Less than a hundred years from slavery, they have been seeking for three hundred years for freedom and democracy in the real sense of the words. In 1619 the first slaves were landed at Jamestown, Virginia. In 1919 Negro soldiers marched home from World War I in separate segregated Negro units. A quarter of a century later, in World War II, they still fought in separate segregated units. A white United States senator this very year has just issued a statement saying that he fully believes today in Negroes remaining a separate segregated part of American life.

There are thousands of restaurants in the United States where a Negro cannot get a meal. There are hundreds of railroad stations in the South where a Negro must enter and leave by a side or a back door. There are many American communities where a Negro cannot live, or where a Negro dare not vote, although under the Constitution he is legally entitled to both privileges. A Negro must ride on the back seats of busses in the South, and in separate coaches on the trains unless travelling first class. In the capital of the United States, a Negro may attend only two dramatic theatres—a very recent concession—and no motion picture theatres except those in colored neighborhoods. Most of the hotels in Washington will not house Negro guests.

This American color complex extends to other darker peoples—the Indians, the Chinese, the Japanese, and the Filipinos—although they do not suffer all the indignities and inequalities visited upon native born citizens of African descent. But some restaurants will not serve Orientals, some hotels will not receive them, and some communities will not rent them a house. So American Negroes share with other peoples of color various aspects of the same problem. To some white Americans *all* colored people are in the same boat. More and more, Negro Americans understand that their problems are closely related to the problems of the darker South Africans, the brown and yellow nations of Asia, and all colored peoples around the world.

The poems in this anthology of American Negro poetry are poems born of the heartaches and problems of the folks on the far side of democracy's fence. Not all Negro poets write always of racial or social problems. Some write of love, roses, and moonlight—as do poets everywhere around the world. But back of the love, at the roots of the roses, and always beneath American moonlight, the Jim Crow trains run, the Ku Klux Klan dons its robes, Dixiecrats spout white supremacy, the American delegates at the United Nations hesitate to ratify the Universal Declaration of Human Rights, and Negro and white youths who insist on riding together in a Southern bus are arrested. And, in a land of riches, all Negro poets are poor.

Democracy has its great and wonderful aspects, and some of them are shared by all American citizens, black and white. But other very basic rights are still denied to citizens of color, even in this democratic age. Until these basic rights are shared by all men and women, Negro poetry in America will continue to be largely poetry of protest and struggle, of aspiration, determination, and confirmation of the universal longing for complete human rights. This longing is shared with the people of Japan to whom these poems are sent in friendship and in brotherhood.

"Introduction," *Uncle Tom's Cabin*, by Harriet Beecher Stowe (New York: Dodd, Mead & Company, 1952), n.p.

The first publisher of *Uncle Tom's Cabin* was so fearful of not making his money back from the book that he wanted Harriet Beecher Stowe to share half the expenses of publication, offering in return to give her half the income, if any. The author's husband, however, insisted on what he felt to be a more businesslike arrangement, a ten per cent royalty to his wife. Mrs. Stowe, happy to have her book published at all, since another publisher had unequivocally turned it down as being unlikely to sell, simply sighed, "I hope it will make enough so I may have a silk dress."

Two days after its publication in Boston on March 20, 1852, the entire first edition of 5,000 copies had been exhausted. Four months after publication Mrs. Stowe's royalties amounted to $10,000. Within a year 300,000 copies had been sold in America and 150,000 in England. Six months after the book's appearance, George L. Aiken's dramatization of *Uncle Tom's Cabin* opened in Troy and ran for 100 performances in that small town, moving on to New York City for 350 performances at the National Theatre. At one time as many as four companies were performing it simultaneously in New York, sometimes giving three shows a day, so great were the crowds. It continued to be presented by various companies throughout the country, as America's most popular play, each season for the next eighty years. Meanwhile the book, translated into every civilized language from Welch to Bengali, became the world's second best seller, outranked only by the Bible.

Uncle Tom's Cabin was the most cussed and discussed book of its time. Tolstoy termed it a great work of literature "flowing from love of God and man." George Sand was so moved by it that she voluntarily offered to write the introduction to its first French edition. Longfellow, Dickens,

Macaulay, Heine praised it. But others damned it as vicious propaganda, bad art, cheap melodrama, and factually a tissue of lies. The truth of the matter is that *Uncle Tom's Cabin* in 1852 was not merely a book. It was a flash, as Frederick Douglass put it, to "light a million camp fires in front of the embattled hosts of slavery." It was an appeal to the consciences of all free men to look upon bondage as a crime. It was a call to action as timely as a newly printed handbill or a newspaper headline. During the Civil War, when Abraham Lincoln met Harriet Beecher Stowe at the White House he said, "So this is the little lady who started this big war." No doubt he smiled, but Lincoln knew that thousands of men who had voted for him had read *Uncle Tom's Cabin,* and many a Union soldier must have remembered it as he marched, for the book was a moral battle cry.

But in addition *Uncle Tom's Cabin* also happened to be a good story, exciting in incident, sharp in characterization, and threaded with humor. That is why it still lives. No reader ever forgets Simon Legree, Little Eva, Miss Ophelia, Eliza, or Uncle Tom. And Topsy, who in cartoons and theatre later became a caricature, is in the book not only funny but human. Harriet Beecher Stowe, who had six children, created out of mother love her Eva, her Topsy, Eliza's baby, Harry, and the other unforgettable children in her book. And perhaps because her father, Lyman Beecher, was a Congregational minister and she had grown up on the Bible, her novel, as Carl Sandburg has described it, became in essence the story of a gentle black Christ who turned the other cheek, Uncle Tom, with Golgotha a place south of the Ohio River, a whipping post instead of the Cross, and a plantation as the background of the passion and the death. Once when asked how her book came into being, Harriet Beecher Stowe said, "God wrote it."

The book began in 1851 in a series of sketches in a paper called *The National Era.* With a baby to nurse, other children to attend, and a house to manage, Mrs. Stowe wrote by sheer determination. Her husband was Professor of Natural and Revealed Religion at Bowdoin College in Maine. They were poor. Her friends and neighbors looked askance upon a woman who aspired to any sort of career outside the home, who took sides in national controversies, or participated in political issues. Slavery was a political issue. But Harriet Beecher Stowe had grown up in Cincinnati where she had seen slavery at first hand just across the river in Kentucky. She had helped her brother, Henry Ward Beecher, edit a paper which was forbidden in some parts of the South. She had once aided a Negro woman to escape from a pursuing master. So she had already taken sides.

When she was almost forty she wrote a friend, "I feel now that the time is come when even a woman or a child who can speak a word for freedom and humanity is bound to speak. The Carthaginian women in the last peril of their state cut off their hair for bow-strings to give the defenders of their country, and such peril and shame as now hangs over this country is worse than Roman slavery. I hope every woman who can write will not be silent." So she began to write *Uncle Tom's Cabin.*

When the book appeared in England Queen Victoria wrote Mrs. Stowe a note of gratitude, and in London an overflow meeting of 5,000 persons greeted the author at Exeter Hall on her first trip abroad. But our American Ambassador, James Buchanan, frowned upon such anti-slavery demonstrations and did not consider Mrs. Stowe's appearance at the London meeting in the best interests of our country. At home Northern papers such as the New York *Journal of Commerce* and Southern papers like the *Alabama Planter* denounced the book. A free Negro in Maryland received ten years in prison for possessing it. A book dealer in Mobile was hounded from the city for selling it. When Mrs. Stowe and her husband returned to Brunswick, Maine, from Europe, they found hundreds of scurrilous and even obscene letters attacking both the book and its author. And one day Mrs. Stowe opened a package that came in the mails, and a black human ear tumbled out.

In 1853 Mrs. Stowe published *A Key to Uncle Tom's Cabin* documenting and giving sources for the material relating to the horrors of slavery in her book. But readers around the world and throughout the years have not needed this "Key" to understand her book, nor to be moved by it to laughter and to tears. The love and warmth and humanity that went into its writing keep it alive a century later from Bombay to Boston.

"Introduction," ***Selected poems of Gabriela Mistral*** (Bloomington: Indiana University Press, 1957), 9–12

She did not sign her poetry with her own name, Lucila Godoy y Alcayaga, because as a young teacher she feared, if it became known that she wrote such emotionally outspoken verses, she might lose her job. Instead she created for herself another name—taking from the archangel Gabriel her first name, and from a sea wind the second. When the poems that were quickly to make her famous, *Sonetos de la Muerte,* were published in 1914, they were signed Gabriela Mistral.

She was born in 1889 in the Chilean village of Vicuña on the River Elqui in a valley where the sweetest of grapes grow. She grew up in the little town of Montegrande where her father was a schoolmaster, and she in turn became a teacher in rural schools, sometimes walking miles into the country to meet her classes. Her father made up verses for village fiestas and, as a young woman, his daughter composed little poems for texts to help children learn to read. She met a young man, Romelio Ureta, with whom she fell in love, but they were never married. For reasons unrelated to their friendship, Ureta committed suicide. Out of love for him and of her desolation at his death came the first of a series of poems soon to be read throughout all Latin America. These included *Sonnets of Death, Prayer,* and the *Poem of the Son,* in whose stark beauty and intensity her personal tragedy "lost its private character and became a part of world literature. It was then that Lucila Godoy y Alcayaga became Gabriela Mistral."

As her renown as a poet grew, so grew her reputation as a teacher of children. The young woman who had no children of her own took her work as an educator very seriously, and explored what was for Chile and the times the most progressive methods of enlightening young minds—visual aids, extracts from great literature, games sometimes in place of books. At first in country schools and coastal villages, then in Santiago de Chile she became an influence in educational circles, and soon was given a government post in the Department of Education at the capital. A group of teachers brought about the publication of her first book—happily for us, in the United States. Federico de Onis, Professor of Spanish Literature at Columbia University in New York, one day gave a talk about her and a reading of a few of her poems. This so inspired his students—most of whom were (or intended to be) teachers of Spanish—that they wanted to lay hands on more of her work. Then they learned that as yet no volume of her poems had been printed. Gabriela Mistral's first book, *Desolacion,* was published by the Spanish Institute of Columbia University in 1922. It has since been reprinted in various editions in South America, each time containing more poems as well as revised versions of previous work, for Gabriela Mistral rewrote often.

In Madrid in 1924 *Ternura* was published. In Buenos Aires in 1938 appeared a third small volume, *Tala,* the proceeds of whose sale went to the relief of the Basque orphans of the Spanish Civil War. In 1954 *Lagar* appeared in Chile, and there that same year a new edition of *Desolacion* was printed. In 1950 in Santiago the *Poemas de las Madres* (included in *Desolacion*) had appeared separately in a beautiful limited edition with drawings by Andre Racz. By then in Spanish speaking countries Gabriela's name (and almost everyone in referring to the poet said simply *Gabriela*) had long been a household word. She had become one of the most popular poets of her tongue. Although her first publication was achieved in our country, in Continental Europe her poems were more widely translated than in England or the United States. Even after she was awarded the Nobel Prize for Literature, why so little of Gabriela was translated into English, I do not know. Much of her poetry is simple and direct in language, never high-flown or flowery, and much easier, I think, to translate than most poets writing in Spanish. Since her poetry is so intensely feminine, however, I hesitated to attempt translations myself, hoping that a woman would do so. None did, in terms of a book. So when Bernard Perry of the Indiana University Press requested that I do so, it intrigued me to try—for the simple reason that I liked the poems.

For the most part I have selected from the various books those poems relating to children, motherhood, and love, including the famous *Poem of the Son* and *Prayer* written during her period of complete desolation, after the man for whom she cared so greatly had died by his own hand.

I have no theories of translation. I simply try to transfer into English as much as I can of the literal content, emotion, and style of each poem. When I feel I can transfer only literal content, I do not attempt a translation. For that reason I have not translated the three *Sonetos de la Muerte*. They are very beautiful, but very difficult in their rhymed simplicity to put into an equivalent English form. To give their meaning without their word music would be to lose their meaning.

The music of Gabriela's poetry started around the world a decade or more before she left her native Chile in the early thirties to begin her own travels, first to Mexico, which had asked her assistance in the organization of rural schools and libraries, then to become Chile's delegate to the League of Nations Institute of Intellectual Cooperation. And in 1931 Gabriela Mistral came to the United States as an instructor in Spanish history and civilization at Middlebury and Barnard colleges. Later she represented her government in various diplomatic posts in South America and Europe, and was a member of the United Nations Subcommittee on the Status of Women. For two years, at President Aleman's invitation, she lived in Mexico as a "guest of the nation." She was Chilean Consul in Brazil, Portugal, at Nice, and Los Angeles. Then after a year as Consul at Naples, in 1953 Gabriela Mistral came again to the United States and settled down in a charming house in Roslyn Harbor, Long Island, where she lived until her death. For twenty years before her death, Gabriela had been honored as Chile's only "life consul"—so appointed by a special enactment of the Chilean Congress—her consulate designated to be "wherever she finds a suitable climate for her health and a pleasant atmosphere to pursue her studies." In the end she chose Roslyn Harbor.

Early in the new year of 1957 Gabriela Mistral died. When the news reached Chile, President Ibañez decreed three days of national mourning. In the United Nations she was eulogized. And the press of the world paid her tribute. In an article at the center of a full page devoted to her memory in *The New York Times Book Review,* Mildred Adams wrote, "Gabriela's clarity and precision, her passion and that characteristic which can only be called her nobility of soul are accepted as ideals. She will not quickly vanish from the literary consciousness of those who value the Spanish tongue." And in *El Diario de Nueva York* Ramon Sender said, "There are poets who hide behind their verses. Others give themselves from their first poem, and so it was with Gabriela Mistral."

"Introduction," *Bootsie and Others: A Selection of Cartoons by Ollie Harrington* (New York: Dodd, Mead & Company, 1958), n.p.

Ollie Harrington was born on February 14, 1912, in New York City. Harlem soon became his stomping ground. Out of Harlem evolved a cartoon character called Bootsie, who has appeared for some twenty years now in the *Pittsburgh Courier,* America's largest Negro newspaper. With its various regional editions, the *Courier* has a big national circulation, so Bootsie's rather rugged adventures are widely known from coast to coast. Harrington has long been Negro America's favorite cartoonist.

The trials and tribulations of Bootsie and his friends are typical of the trials and tribulations of the average Negro from Lenox Avenue in Harlem or Hastings Street in Detroit to Central Avenue in Los Angeles or Rampart in New Orleans—woman problems, pocketbook problems, landlady problems, and race problems are the same. And fat little Bootsie, with his surprised little eyes, is always staring problems in the face. For example, at the top of a ski run whose slope is precipitous, Bootsie says, "I'm willin' to do anything to help the race to advance, but tell me . . . Do Doctor Bunche do foolishness like this?"

As a social satirist in the field of race relations, Ollie Harrington is unsurpassed. Visually funny almost always, situation-wise, his pictures frequently have the quality of the blues. Behind their humor often lurks the sadness of "When you see me laughin', I'm laughin' to keep from cryin'." Example: Bootsie and companion treed by a bear, yet blaming their situation on that old scapegoat, race: "I'm durned sure gonna contact the NAACP. . . . White folks has engineered this whole thing." Or two children looking at a robin in a tenement house window: "Do you reckon Uncle Bootsie was lying when he said spring comes three weeks earlier over 'cross town where the white folks live?" Shortly after the Detroit race riots of World War II, there appeared a Harrington cartoon which many whites found too bitter for laughter. It depicted a little white boy showing a small friend his father's hunting trophies. Mounted on display on the wall of the den among the moose, tiger, and walrus heads, hung the head of a Negro. The caption read, "Dad got that one in Detroit last week."

The Supreme Court decision outlawing segregation in public schools and the ensuing problems such as Little Rock continue to produce a series of highly satirical Harrington cartoons, like the one in this book of two colored kids, protected by ground troops, parachuting to school: "No, I ain't scared. But you gotta admit, this is a hell of a way to get an education!" Or little Luther seated forlornly in the middle of a road while the generals with tanks and infantry plan their maneuvers to get him past a mob at the school house door.

One of my favorite cartoons depicts the dilemma of the colored baseball fans, all of whom rooted for the Dodgers and *against* all Dodger opponents when Jackie Robinson was the first Negro to play on a Major League team. But now that all the major teams have colored players, "a pore soul can't hardly root against nobody."

In every Harrington cartoon there is an intriguing wealth of background detail, adding to the overall humor of the picture's total impact. Brother Bootsie is alone in his room on Thanksgiving. A milk bottle on the window ledge, a crooked shade, a stringless shoe under the bed, a bare electric bulb, highlight a gleeful landlady at the door inviting him to eat just as a reminder that she—with her no-rent-paying roomer—hasn't much to be thankful for. The Harrington animals are wonderful, too—a skinny sad-happy little hound sitting around in a picture for no real reason, a tiger cat on a stool, a droll elk's head.

A careful craftsman, an excellent artist, with a little of Daumier and a lot of Hogarth—although not really very much like either, being too full of laughter—Ollie Harrington is uniquely Harrington, and Bootsie of Harlem is out of this world.[6]

"Introduction," *Pudd'nhead Wilson,* by Mark Twain (New York: Bantam, 1959), vii–xiii

Mark Twain's ironic little novel, *Pudd'nhead Wilson,* is laid on the banks of the Mississippi in the first half of the 1800s. It concerns itself with, among other things, the use of fingerprinting to solve the mystery of a murder. But *Pudd'nhead Wilson* is not a mystery novel. The reader knows from the beginning who committed the murder and has more than an inkling of how it will be solved. The circumstances of the denouement, however, posed in its time great novelty, for fingerprinting had not then come into official use in crime detection in the United States. Even a man who fooled around with it as a hobby was thought to be a simpleton, a puddenhead. Such was the reputation acquired by Wilson, the young would-be lawyer in the Missouri frontier town of Dawson's Landing. But Wilson eventually made his detractors appear as puddenheads themselves.

Although introduced early, it is not until near the end of the book that Wilson becomes a major figure in the tale. The novel is rather the story of another young man's mistaken identity—a young man who thinks he is white but is in reality colored; who is heir to wealth without knowing his claim is false; who lives as a freeman, but is legally a slave; and who, when he learns the true facts about himself, comes to ruin not through the temporarily shattering knowledge of his physical status, but because of weaknesses common to white or colored, slave or free. The young man thinks his name is Thomas à Becket Driscoll, but it is really Valet de Chambre—a name used for twenty-three years by another who is held as a slave in his stead, but who, unknown to himself, is white—and therefore legally free.

Pudd'nhead Wilson is the man, who, in the end, sets things to rights. But for whom? Seemingly for the spectators only, not for the principals involved, for by that time to them right is wrong, wrong is right, and happiness has gone by the board. The slave system has taken its toll of all three concerned—mother, mammy, ward and child—for the mother and mammy, Roxana, matriarch and slave, are one. Roxy is a puppet whose at first successful deceits cause her to think herself a free agent. She is undone at the climax by the former laughing stock of the town, Pudd'nhead Wilson, whose long interest in the little swirls at the ends of the fingers finally pays off.

Years before he published *Pudd'nhead Wilson* Mark Twain had been hailed as America's greatest humorist. From *The Celebrated Jumping*

Frog of Calaveras County in 1865 to *The Adventures of Huckleberry Finn* in 1884, most of his fiction—and his spoken words on the lecture platform—had been sure sources of laughter. But in this work of his middle years (Twain was 59) he did not write a humorous novel. Except for a few hilarious village scenes, and a phonetic description of a baby's tantrums, the out-loud laughs to be found in *Tom Sawyer* or *Huckleberry Finn* are not a part of *Pudd'nhead.* In this book the basic theme is slavery, seriously treated, and its main thread concerns the absurdity of man-made differentials, whether of caste or "race." The word *race* might properly be placed in quotes for both of Mark Twain's central Negroes are largely white in blood and physiognomy, slaves only by circumstance, and each only "by a fiction of law and custom, a Negro." The white boy who is mistakenly raised as a slave in the end finds himself "rich and free, but in a most embarrassing situation. He could neither read nor write, and his speech was the basest dialect of the Negro quarter. His gait, his attitudes, his gestures, his bearing, his laugh—all were vulgar and uncouth; his manners were the manners of a slave. Money and fine clothes could not mend these defects or cover them up, they only made them the more glaring and pathetic. The poor fellow could not endure the terrors of the white man's parlour, and felt at home and at peace nowhere but in the kitchen."

On the other hand, the young dandy who thought his name was Thomas à Becket, studied at Yale. He then came home to Dawson's Landing bedecked in Eastern finery to lord it over black and white alike. As Pudd'nhead Wilson, who had the habit of penning little musings beneath the dates in his calendar, wrote, "Training is everything. The peach was once a bitter almond; cauliflower is nothing but cabbage with a college education." It took a foreigner with no regard for frontier aristocracy of Old Virginia lineage to kick Thomas à Becket right square in his sit-downer at a public meeting. In the ensuing free-for-all that breaks out, the hall is set afire. Here the sparkle of Twain's traditional humor bursts into hilarious flame, too, as the members of the nearby fire department—"who never stirred officially in unofficial costume"—donned their uniforms to drench the hall with enough water to "annihilate forty times as much fire as there was there; for a village fire company does not often get a chance to show off." Twain wryly concludes, "Citizens of that village . . . did not insure against fire, they insured against the fire-company."

Against fire and water in the slave states there was insurance, but none against the devious dangers of slavery itself. Not even a fine old gentleman like Judge Driscoll "of the best blood of the Old Dominion" could find insurance against the self-protective schemes of his brother's bond servant, Roxy, who did not like being a slave, but was willing to be one for her son's sake. Roxy was also willing to commit a grievous sin for her son's sake, palliating her conscience a little by saying, "white folks has done it." With "an unfair show in the battle of life," as Twain puts it, Roxy, as an "heir of two centuries of unatoned insult and outrage," is yet not of an evil nature. Her crimes grow out of the greater crimes of the slave system. "The man in whose favor no laws of property exist," Thomas Jefferson wrote in his *Notes on Virginia,* "feels himself less bound to respect those made in favor of others."

Roxy's fear of eventually receiving the same punishment as that threatened other servants for the thieving of a few dollars from their master, Percy Driscoll, was enough to start a chain of thought in her mind that led eventually to disaster. Even though her master was "a fairly humane man towards slaves and other animals," was he not a thief himself? Certainly he was, to one in bondage, "the man who daily robbed him of an inestimable treasury—his liberty." Out of the structure of slave society itself is fashioned a noose of doom. In *Pudd'nhead Wilson* Mark Twain wrote what at a later period might have been called in the finest sense of the term, "a novel of social significance." Had Twain been a contemporary of Harriet Beecher Stowe, and this novel published before the War between the States, it might have been a minor *Uncle Tom's Cabin.* Twain minces no words in describing the unfortunate effects of slavery upon the behavior of both Negroes and whites, even upon children. The little master, Thomas, and the little slave, Chambers, were both born on the same day and grew up together. But even in "babyhood Tom cuffed and banged and scratched Chambers unrebuked, and Chambers early learned that between meekly bearing it and resenting it, the advantage all lay with the former policy. The few times his persecutions had moved him beyond control and made him fight back had cost him . . . three such convincing canings from the man who was his father and didn't know it, that he took Tom's cruelties in all humility after that, and made no more experiments. Outside of the house the two boys were together all through their boyhood. . . . Tom staked him with marbles to play 'keeps' with, and then took all the winnings away from him. In the winter season Chambers was on hand, in Tom's worn-out clothes . . . to drag a sled up the hill for Tom, warmly clad, to ride down on; but he never got a ride himself. He built snow men and snow fortifications under Tom's directions. He was Tom's patient target when Tom wanted to do some snowballing, but the target couldn't fire back. Chambers carried Tom's skates to the river and strapped them on him, then trotted around after him on the ice, so as to be on hand when wanted; but he wasn't ever asked to try the skates himself."

Mark Twain, in his presentation of Negroes as human beings, stands head and shoulders above the other Southern writers of his times, even such distinguished ones as Joel Chandler Harris, F. Hopkins Smith, and Thomas Nelson Page.[7] It was a period when most writers who included Negro characters in their work at all, were given to presenting the slave as ignorant and happy, the freed men of color as ignorant and miserable, and all Negroes as either comic servants on the one hand or dangerous brutes on the other. That Mark Twain's characters in *Pudd'nhead Wilson* fall into none of these categories is a tribute to his discernment. And that he makes them neither heroes nor villains is a tribute to his understanding of human character. "Color is only skin deep." In this novel Twain shows how more than anything else environment shapes the man. Yet in his day behavioristic psychology was in its infancy. Likewise, the science of fingerprinting. In 1894 *Pudd'nhead Wilson* was a "modern" novel indeed. And it still may be so classified.

Although knowledge of fingerprinting dates back some two thousand years, and fingerprints are found as signatures on ancient Chinese tablets and Babylonian records, it was not until 1880 that the first treatise on the possible use of fingerprinting in criminal identification appeared in English. And it was sixteen years later (two years after the appearance of *Pudd'nhead Wilson*) before the International Association of Chiefs of Police meeting in Chicago in 1896 decided to set up a Bureau of Criminal Identification and, as a part of its program, study ways and means whereby fingerprinting might supplement or perhaps supplant the Bertillon system of bodily measurements as a means of identifying criminals. So Mark Twain was well ahead of the international keepers of law and order when he devoted several pages in his novel to a description of how fingerprints might be used for the positive identification of a criminal who has neglected to put on gloves before committing a crime.

"Every human being," Twain has Pudd'nhead Wilson inform the court, "carries with him from his cradle to his grave certain physical marks which do not change their character, and by which he can always be identified—and that without shade of doubt or question. These marks are his signature, his physiological autograph, so to speak, and this autograph cannot be counterfeited, nor can he disguise it or hide it away, nor can it become illegible by the wear and the mutations of time. . . .

This autograph consists of the delicate lines or corrugations with which Nature marks the insides of the hands and the soles of the feet. If you will look at the balls of your fingers—you that have very sharp eyesight—you will observe that these dainty curving lines lie close together, like those that indicate the borders of oceans in maps, and that they form various clearly defined patterns, such as arches, circles, long curves, whorls, etc., and that these patterns differ on the different fingers."

Curiously enough, as modern as *Pudd'nhead Wilson* is, its format is that of an old-fashioned melodrama, as if its structure were borrowed from the plays performed on the riverboat theatres of that period. Perhaps deliberately, Twain selected this popular formula in which to tell a very serious story. Moving from climax to climax, every chapter ends with a teaser that makes the reader wonder what is coming next while, as in Greek tragedy, the fates keep closing in on the central protagonists. And here the fates have no regard whatsoever for color lines. It is this treatment of race that makes *Pudd'nhead Wilson* as contemporary as Little Rock, and Mark Twain as modern as Faulkner, although Twain died when Faulkner was in knee pants.

The first motion picture was made in the year in which Twain wrote *Pudd'nhead Wilson*. As if looking ahead to the heyday of this medium, the author begins his story with a sweeping panorama of the river and Dawson's Landing, then briefly poses by name the cast of characters against it. Thereafter, he continues his tale in a series of visualizations, most of them growing logically one from another, but some quite coincidentally. A common dictum in Hollywood is, "Simply picture it on the screen, and the audience will believe it—because *there it is.*" The advent of two handsome Italian twins in Dawson's Landing is pictured so vividly that the reader believes the men are there, and only briefly wonders *why*—although these two fellows immediately begin to figure prominently in the frightful march of events leading toward the novel's climax. But, to tell the truth, we do not need to know exactly why these ebullient twins came to Dawson's Landing. And they do brighten up the story considerably.

Additional, and what seem at first to be extraneous flashes of amusing brilliance in the novel (and at other times sober or ironic comment) are the excerpts that serve as chapter headings from *Pudd'nhead Wilson's Calendar.* "Few things are harder to put up with than the annoyance of a good example." And another: "It is often the case that the man who can't tell a lie thinks he is the best judge of one." And an observation that would have almost surely, had there been a McCarthy Committee in Twain's day, caused the author to be subpoenaed before it: "*October 12—The Discovery*—It was wonderful to find America, but it would have been more wonderful to miss it." And a final admonition that might almost be Mark Twain himself concerned with the tight and astringent style of this smallest of his novels: "As to the Adjective: when in doubt, strike it out." *Pudd'nhead Wilson* marches along much too rapidly to be bothered with a plethora of adjectives.

"Introduction," *An African Treasury: Articles, Essays, Stories, and Poems by Black Africans,* ed. Langston Hughes (New York: Crown Publishers, 1960), ix–xiv

This is a very personal treasury—a selection gathered from several thousands of pages of writing by Africans of color that I have read during the past six years. Most of it was in manuscript, some in newspapers and magazines, and most of it had never been published in the United States.

My interest in native African writing began when I was asked by the editors of *Drum,* a Johannesburg magazine for nonwhite readers, to become one of the judges of a short story contest for indigenous South African writers. Some of the work that came to me contained pages which moved, surprised, and quite delighted me. I determined to see how much more writing of interest was being produced by black Africans.

To correspondents and to fans of my own work in Africa—where over the years my poems have been published and my "Simple" stories serialized—I wrote for the addresses of native writers. To Prime Minister Azikiwe's chain of newspapers in Nigeria I sent a letter asking for contributions to a proposed anthology.[8] My request was reprinted in numerous papers in other parts of Africa. Within a few weeks I began to receive floods of material from all over English-speaking Africa. Much that came was in longhand, often very hard to read. But nothing that arrived was completely lacking in interest. Even in the most amateurish writing, sometimes a line, a paragraph, even a whole page would come alive, achieve a character of its own, or make vivid some element of folk culture—only to bog down on the next page as the inexperienced writer continued his earnest attempt at communication.

To communicate in words is not always easy, especially when those words must be put down on paper. To communicate from one land to another, one culture to another, particularly when the language is not one's own native tongue but acquired—as English and French are for some of these writers—presents its problems, too. Amos Tutuola, born in the Nigerian jungle, has had very little schooling; he earns his living working in metals. But Abioseh Nicol of Sierra Leone is a graduate of Cambridge and a practicing physician. Matei Markwei of Ghana, well in his thirties, is still studying for a college degree. But Wole Soyinka took honors in his youth at the University of Leeds. Peter Kumalo is a dock worker on the wharfs of Cape Province. But Benibengor Blay is a member of parliament at Accra; and Léopold Sédar Senghor, deputy from Senegal, has long held a seat in the National Assembly at Paris.[9] Each of these writers, however varied their backgrounds, has the capacity for communicating in words—a capacity that comes from (I venture to say) innate talent. During the past decade there have been hundreds of books by white writers, but perhaps it remains for colored writers such as these, native to the soil, to tell us most faithfully what Africa is like today.

This collection in no way attempts to be comprehensive or all-embracing. There remains in my files of rejected material much worthy writing, which in some cases breaks my heart to return. There are excellent short stories that I feel are in some ways too special for American readers unfamiliar with the African scene. There are factual pieces of interest which will soon date—considering the rapidity of change in Africa. There are poems whose images are so native as to be obscure to people who have never been to Africa. And there are scholarly pieces whose interest would be confined mostly to academic readers, political experts or students of ethnic customs.

This volume is but a small sampling of the great variety of writing talents to be found in Black Africa today. Quite frankly, I have chosen to assemble here only those pieces which I enjoyed most and which I hope others will find entertaining, moving, possibly instructive, but above all readable. For me creative writing's first function is readability.

I hope, too, that this *Treasury* enables the reader to share the joy I find in African usages of the King's English, which often can be described as nothing short of intriguing. Amos Tutuola especially delights me. In writing him some five years ago, I suggested he send me a number of his stories for consideration. In due time, a *single* manuscript arrived in longhand, full of strange language structures. But his accompanying note was grammatical, brief and to the point. It said: "About sending several stories, when you send money I will send more." Another less businesslike young writer, however, advised me that he had had for weeks after receiving my letter, "a wide imagination and sweet thoughts." (He deluged me with manuscripts.) While a third, apologizing for sending his poems in his own hand, wrote: "But I hope soon to exploit the art of typewriting for the happy sake of the musical rhythms it produces when man beats the machine." Eventually he did learn to beat the machine, for his recent manuscripts arrived typewritten.

No collection of African material, no matter how personal its selection, can fail to reflect the massive conflicts going on today. That Africa is a changing continent, everybody knows, for the press and radio remind us of this continually. Entire countries change names, and it is difficult to keep maps—such as the fairly recent one provided elsewhere in the book—up to date. When I first began to gather this material, the term *négritude*—currently popular with African writers, especially poets influenced by Senghor—had not come into common use. But there was in most of the writing that reached me, an accent of Africanness—blackness, if you will—not unlike the racial consciousness found in the work of American Negro writers a quarter of a century ago. The Harlem writers of that period, however, had to search for their folk roots. The African writer has these roots right at hand. He is no outside observer. His tribal marks are sometimes still on his very skin. And, although some of the writers here assembled are colored—in the mixed-blood sense in which this term is used abroad—they are all Negro in the sense in which the word *Negro* is used in America.

Many of the problems, particularly those of the South Africans, are closely related to the problems of Afro-Americans, and their reactions are similar. The incident of *The Bench* could well happen in Alabama, but those of *New Life at Kyerefaso* and *Law of the Grazing Fields* could take place only in Africa. And only an African would be as conscious of *négritude* as Francis Ernest Kobina Parkes when he writes:

Give me black souls,
Let them be black
Or chocolate brown
Or make them the
Color of dust—
Dustlike,
Browner than sand.
But if you can
Please keep them black.

Through most of the writing that came to me out of Africa—from Senegal in the north, Kenya in the east, to Cape Town in the south—there runs a pride of race which the long years of colonialism could not erase. This pride extends to a deep appreciation and understanding of folk life which mission schooling or European education did not diminish. For those who studied in Europe, perhaps distance only made the bush—the great jungle heart of Africa—seem fonder. Abioseh Nicol writes upon returning from a long sojourn in England:

> *Go for bush—inside the bush*
> *You will find your hidden heart,*
> *Your mute ancestral spirit.*
>
> *And so I went*
> *Dancing on my way.*

Evident in most African writing, of course, is a pride in country, which underlies everything that is thought and spoken south of the Sahara today. It is an *African* pride, with a character all its own, which owes allegiance neither to West nor East but to its newly emerging self. Thus does Ezekiel Mphahlele remark, in his impassioned—and frankly opinionated—on-the-scene report of the historic Accra Conference of peoples from all over Africa: "Dr. Nkrumah spots the Tunisian ambassador in London . . . what an electric smile of recognition as the Premier waves his hand. So spontaneous. As Tom Mboya later ushers him on to the rostrum, with his arm round the Premier . . . I realize all the more that this is Africa—an Africa with a totally different sense of convention from that of the West."[10]

It is healthy pride, without apology, and its expression ranges from the almost primitive evocation of a tribesman's love for his tribe—Onyenaekeya Udeagu's *Ibos as They Are*—to Peter Abrahams' polished writings. Abrahams' exciting piece, *The Blacks,* brilliantly illuminates the dilemma of Africa's intellectual elite such as Ghana's Premier Nkrumah and the celebrated Jomo Kenyatta who, as this is written, still remains in custody for the part he played in the Mau Mau uprisings.[11] These men realize that Africa's task, indeed its mission, is to work out a fusion between tribal custom and modern ways.

Perhaps the phrase that best sums up this swelling pride and fierce insistence on individual identity is "African personality." It is a phrase much used in writings coming out of Africa today. It finds expression in the ironic humor of Todd Matshikiza's monthly column "With the Lid Off" in *Drum.* It is expressed in Can Themba's nostalgic reminiscences of the shebeens of Sophiatown, which may remind American readers of the late John McNulty's pieces in *The New Yorker* about his favorite Third

Avenue bars. It bursts forth in the bitterness toward the ousted colonial powers expressed in one portion of Abioseh Nicol's lovely lyric, *Return to West Africa,* and in the challenge posed by the Europeans who decide to stay on as future citizens—recently termed by Tanganyika's Julius Nyerere, "the new tribes," as against Africa's indigenous tribes. It cries through protest pieces such as *Why I Ran Away,* Phyllis Ntantala's moving *Widows of the Reserves* and J. Koyinde Vaughan's challenging *Africa and the Cinema.*[12] While it is a personality necessarily—and happily—as varied as the people of Africa, it is founded on a common bond, a common yearning that may best be described by the stirring, concluding response at the Accra Conference: *Mayibuye, Afrika!* Freely translated, that means "Long live Africa!" But the literal translation comes much closer: "Come back, Africa!"

"Is it really necessary for us to justify our demand for freedom?" asks Tom Mboya, Kenya's young and dynamic political leader. "If so, to whom are we accountable and by what and whose standards are we to be judged?" So speaks the voice of New Africa. What white writers think of the once Dark Continent we long have known. These pages tell what black writers think.

"Introduction," ***Poems for a Mixed-Up World,*** **by Andy Razaf,** LHP 548 (March 15, 1961)

Given to the poets of our planet are certain happy privileges not possessed by everyone.[13] Among these privileges are those of putting into concise form men's innermost hopes, dreams, and emotions; also of helping reveal man to himself; and of sometimes, too, acting as a sort of social historian of the writer's time and place, interpreting for others the real meaning of the living forces around us.

There are many kinds of poets—social poets like Walt Whitman, nature poets like Wordsworth, lyric poets like Housman, intellectual poets like Pound, humorous ones like Ogden Nash or bitter-sweet like Dorothy Parker, folk poets like Sterling Brown, and poet-philosophers like Emerson. Not all poets wrestle with the innermost turmoils of the soul, or deal in vast social canvasses. Some are regional. Some are very personal like Emily Dickinson. And some, while no less individual, are so close to the common man that it is his coloration that gives meaning to the words the poet puts down.

Andy Razaf is close to the common man. His verses express that man's thoughts, observations and aspirations. But they go beyond that and (like the singers behind the soloist in a gospel church) "they bear him up"—in that they give him aid and comfort—support him "on every leaning side." Andy Razaf is a philosopher-poet. His poems seek to give a positive meaning to life, to engender courage, to stimulate assurance, to add to the sunshine of a sunny day. Others seek to stimulate thought, especially regarding this race problem of ours in a democracy that professes equality but falls short in its practice. And others, highly humorous, seek through laughter to put over a message.

Andy Razaf has a talent for the concise line, the clever turn of phrase which comes, no doubt, from his many years of competence in the entertainment field and that of the popular song. Leading composers have set his lilting lyrics to music for more than a quarter of a century. Andy's songs have delighted millions. May his poems reach an equally wide audience.

A man with a warm personality and a big bright smile, Andy has carried this personality and this smile over into his work. Now, even though he has been bedridden in his California home for the past decade, Andy's poems, his smile and his courage—which is great in the light of his current afflictions—shine forth for you now in this friendly and uncomplicated yet deeply philosophical book of a man who—in spite of Broadway fame—is still "one of the common folks." He writes:

Give me your hand, my brother,
I don't care who you may be;
Regardless of color, class or creed,
It does not matter to me.

For all of us are kindred
Who walk this earthly sod;
Depending on one another,
All made in the image of God.

"Foreword," *Poems from Black Africa*, ed. Langston Hughes (Bloomington: Indiana University Press, 1963), 11–15

Usually poets have their fingers on the emotional pulse of their peoples, of their homelands. Traditionally, poets are lyric historians. From the days of the bards and troubadours, the songs of the poets have been not only songs, but often *records* of the most moving events, the deepest thoughts and most profound emotional currents of their times. To understand Africa today, it is wise to listen to what its poets say—those who put their songs down on paper as well as those who only speak or sing them. Perhaps it is more profitable to know how people *feel* than it is to know what they think. Certainly the poetry of contemporary Africa indicates its emotional climate. That climate is one of hope and of faith in a future that is coming more and more into the control of the peoples of Africa themselves.

But the best of the black poets writing today in English or French in Africa South of the Sahara are not so much propagandists for African nationalism, as they are spokesmen for variations of *négritude*—a word the French-speaking writers have coined to express a pride in and a love of the African heritage, physically, spiritually and culturally. The most interesting nonwhite poets of contemporary Africa are modernists in style, in contrast to the older writers of colonial days who were influenced by Victorian models or by the classical French poets taught in the missionary schools. Contemporary young African intellectuals, some of whom have but lately come home from Cambridge or the Sorbonne, are not unlike young writers elsewhere. They have read Auden and Spender and Eliot, Mauriac, Jacques Prevert and perhaps Brecht. Lagos, Accra or Dakar are no longer weeks away from Europe. In fact, from the heart of Africa to Paris or London by jet is now only a matter of hours. Not that all African writers have traveled abroad. But the bookshops in Africa's major cities today are fairly well stocked. Even American books make their way to the West Coast and the Union of South Africa. Then there is the BBC—the African networks of the British Broadcasting Company beaming from London cultural programs of high calibre and using much more poetry than the American airwaves ever dream of committing to the microphones. Many young African writers today augment their incomes by writing for BBC, which pays not badly for both poetry and prose.

Whatever their influences may be, local or foreign, there are sensitive and exciting poets in Black Africa now. Abioseh Nicol in Sierra Leone, Kobina Parkes in Ghana, Gabriel Okara in Nigeria, Sédar-Senghor of Senegal, Ezekiel Mphahlele of South Africa to name men who have produced more than simply an occasional magazine or newspaper verse. These poets represent their countries well on the printed page, and all of them have lately been published abroad as well as at home. The poetry of Abioseh Nicol is quietly moving and deeply personal; that of Kobina Parkes kaleidoscopically vivid and almost tribal in its imagery; while Okara's is sensitive and strange and semi-mystic to the Western reader. In the work of Dennis Osadebay and Michael Dei-Anang the poet and pamphleteer meet to cry aloud for African freedom, while in Senghor's poems of *négritude* French sophistication and the tall drums of Senegal lock arms.[14]

In general the French African poets, and particularly Senghor, tend toward creating Whitmanesque catalogues of fruits, rivers, trees and the other physical attributes of their land, and vie with one another in evoking the strength of black bodies, the dignity of black motherhood, the beauty of black maidens. From Senghor's *Femme Noire:*

> Naked woman, dark woman,
> Ripe fruit with firm flesh,
> Sombre ecstasy of dark red wine,
> Mouth which makes mine lyrical. . . .

The French poets of color create mosaics of blackness against the palm trees within a large and (to non-Africans) exotic framework of cultural nationalism, seldom tending toward miniatures, seldom reducing their subject matter to the framework of oneself. Black poets writing in English-speaking Africa, on the other hand, seem somewhat less concerned with color, personal or in landscape, and are more centered in self rather than race, their *I* less the *I* equivalent to *We* of the French poets. But the best poetry of both French and English expression bears the stamp of the African personality, and most of its emotional aura might be included within the term *négritude*—that "anti-racist racism," as Sartre called it, of black Africa's concentration on the rediscovery of self, a turning within for values to live by, rather than a striking outward in revenge for past wrongs. "Me fait songer à Orphée allant réclamer Eurydice à Pluton," wrote Sartre in his famous introduction to Senghor's anthology of French African poetry.

In a paper on African literature delivered at the First International Congress of Africanists at the University of Ghana, Ezekiel Mphahlele confirms that in general, "English and French writing move along different tracks, particularly in the realm of poetry. The Nigerian poet talks about things as they affect him personally and immediately. He is not protesting or trying to vindicate his blackness. The French-speaking poet, however, particularly of the *négritude* school, uses broad symbols in which immediacy of individual experience is not the important thing. These are symbols of Africa, of blackness, of what is regarded by the poet as African traits which are expected to be a unifying force—not only for the indigenous people of the continent but for the Negro world in general."

The American Negro poet Samuel Allen (Paul Vesey) writing on *négritude* says, "It represents in one sense the Negro African poet's endeavor to recover for his race a normal self-pride, a confidence in himself shattered for centuries when the enslaver suddenly loomed in the village pathway; to recover a world in which he once again could have a sense of unashamed identity and an unsubordinate role. . . . *Négritude* includes the characteristic impulses, traits and habits which may be considered more markedly Negro African than white or European. It is thus something which the poet possesses in the wells of his being and simultaneously something which he is seeking to recover, to make manifest; and again it is a subjective disposition which is affirmed and which objectivizes itself in the poem."

Most of the poems of Léopold Sédar-Senghor are colored by the blackness of Africa. The titles of his various works indicate as much: *Chants d'Ombres, Masque Negre, Hosties Noires, A l'Appel de la Race de Saba,* among others. He sings of the glories of blackness, of Africa's past trials and tribulations and of its future glories. Concerning his style, really that of a chant, Senghor writes, "I insist that the poem is perfect only when it becomes a song: words and music at once. It is time to stop the decay of the modern world and especially the decay of poetry. Poetry must find its way back to its origins, to the times when it was sung and danced. As it was in Greece, above all in the Egypt of the Pharaohs. And as it is still today in black Africa."

Certainly many indigenous poets in contemporary Africa, whether writing in the *lingua franca* of English or French, are still close enough to tribal life to know the names of the old non-Christian gods, the *orisha,* to hear in their ears the great mass chants of ancient rituals or the jolly rhymes of village feasts. Oral poetry is very much a part of daily living in tribal Africa where art and life have not yet parted company. The bulk of Africa's poetry is still that which is only spoken or sung. Most of it is not yet transcribed or translated into European tongues, and much of it is closely related to music, the rhythms of percussion and the dance, and is concerned with community rituals and the traditional gods worshipped by non-Christian or non-Moslem peoples.

Since oral poetry is highly regional, often with allusions and overtones obscure beyond tribal limits, much traditional verse is almost untranslatable. Then, too, like the Chinese, many tribal tongues utilize tone and pitch as well as mere words in communication. One example is the Yoruba of Nigeria. With them the same word pronounced in one tone may have quite a different meaning in another tone or inflection. There have been many adequate translations into English of African folk tales, the story line remaining intact. To translate folk poetry is, however, a much more formidable task. Ulli Beier of the University College at Ibadan is one of the few Europeans doing extensive work in this field. It is a privilege to include in this book some of Beier's translations from the Yoruba.

There will no doubt arise in the New Africa creative writers who will soon combine in poetry the written word and the oral traditionals of the bush as excitingly as Amos Tutuola of *The Palm Wine Drunkard* has combined English prose and tribal lore in fiction. Certainly this integration of indigenous elements can be beautifully done in poetry, as Nicolás Guillén of Cuba has proven in his poems of *ñañigo* and his use of the rhythms of *sones.* Written poetry in Africa today is moving away from the bench of the missionary school to walk abroad beneath the cocoa palms and listen for inspiration to the native songs in many tongues. Soon African poetry will capture the essence of these songs and recreate them on paper. Meanwhile, it walks with grace and already is beginning to achieve an individuality quite its own.

"Foreword," *Freedom School Poetry* (Atlanta: Student Nonviolent Coordinating Committee, 1965), n.p.

Goodmorning, Poetry!
Poetry, how-do-you-do?
I'm worrying along—
So I come to worry you.

To modify a line from an old blues, this means that poetry possesses the power of worriation. Poetry can both delight and disturb. It can interest folks. It can upset folks. Poetry can convey both pleasure and pain. And poetry can make people think. If poetry makes people think, it might make them think constructive thoughts, even thoughts about how to change themselves, their town and their state for the better. Some poems, like many of the great verses in the Bible, can make people think about changing all mankind, even the whole world. Poems, like prayers, possess power.

So goodmorning, Poetry!
Poetry, how-do-you-do!
I'm writing a poem
To see if it takes on you.

"Introduction," *Up from Slavery,* by Booker T. Washington (New York: Dodd, Mead & Co., 1965), v–x

Booker T. Washington was the Roy Wilkins, James Farmer and Martin Luther King of his day rolled into one. His period of prominence on the national scene dates roughly from 1895 to the time of his death in 1915 at the age of 57. Washington was in many ways a distinguished personality, provincially wise, astute, and certainly diplomatic. His life was devoted to one main effort: the building of the Tuskegee Normal and Industrial Institute as a vocational education center in the heart of the ante-bellum South. He had a one-track mind, in that all his other activities as the greatest Negro celebrity of his day concerned basically his school. He knew in his heart that most men can do only one thing well. His one thing was Tuskegee.

He was called "the leader of his people" and so billed on the national scene. But the mantle of his leadership was bestowed upon him by white America. To Negroes Booker T. Washington was for a quarter of a century a famous man, a distinguished speaker, often a front page celebrity, but never in any sense their leader in the way that Martin Luther King became a leader, inspiring hope, passion and intense devotion in a wide following. For Negroes, what Mr. Washington inspired was respect in many, mixed admiration in some, skepticism in others, and downright hatred in certain segments of the black population that refused to consider his oratorical and tactical compromises in the racial field the better part of wisdom.

"This man, whatever good he may do, has injured and is injuring the race more than he can aid it by his school," said William Monroe Trotter of Boston, and with him many others agreed. "Let us hope that Booker T. Washington will remain mouth-closed at Tuskegee."[15]

On them, Washington's comment was, "I think they misunderstood southern conditions. . . . If they had been through my experience, I do not think they would express the views that they do."

Historical and contemporary judgments affirm that Washington was in reality "a great accommodator." But to create Tuskegee in Alabama in that era he could hardly have been otherwise. He *did* create Tuskegee—a splendid achievement—but, in so doing, was in turn almost forced to create of himself an image of national leadership. But in time, he grew to like this image and eventually to take advantage of it, so his enemies claimed, for the exercise of power itself. As a bridge between the white and colored peoples of the United States, he sought and gained more often than not the favors of the white power structure from which came the endowments supporting Tuskegee. And before he died, the white millionaire, Andrew Carnegie, gave him and his family an income for life.

Booker T. Washington's enemies said that he was a man who could always be counted upon to produce the right thing at the right time to suit the right people. Some told a rather frivolous story to illustrate his adroitness in the role of accommodator. A distinguished Negro bishop known to be liberal in moral attitudes and a lover of good bourbon, once fainted during a long hot graduation ceremony on the Tuskegee grounds. When the good bishop came to under a clump of shade trees, he whispered to the attentive Dr. Washington, "Booker, I need a spot of bourbon."

It was a known fact that intoxicating liquors were not permitted at Tuskegee, and the sight of a whiskey bottle on the campus was unknown. But Dr. Washington disappeared into his study and quickly returned with what those surrounding the bishop clearly saw was a medicine bottle. Its contents were poured into a glass and stirred with a spoon. The bishop drank and was promptly revived. In truth the medicine bottle contained a double swig of the best Kentucky bond. Among the bindings on Booker T.'s bookshelf, the story ran, was one that contained a decanter. In this era of racial and religious intolerance in a Bible Belt controlled by Christian Klansmen it was wise, Booker thought, that all things between the covers of books did not meet the public eye.

The South and its Negroes at the end of Reconstruction, needed a man like Booker T. Washington. ONWARD AND UPWARD was the slogan on one of the popular Booker T. Washington calendars. A glowing photograph of Dr. Washington adorned the top center crowning a pathway to the sunup which freed Negroes marched with the humble tools of agriculture and simple industry in hand—hoes, mallets, axes, and hammers—while amiable and approving whites looked on from the sidelines. Everybody seemed happy. At the top was the word PROGRESS.

This calendar decorated numerous Negro homes, barber shops, pool halls, and juke joints, but many Afro-Americans who looked upon it did not believe its message. In Alabama itself there were too many night riders in Klan hoods, too many closed ballot boxes, and too much fear. But Washington felt that these unpleasant problems would be solved gradually. "It is at the bottom of life we must begin and not the top. Nor should we permit our grievances to overshadow our opportunities . . . The wisest among my race understand that the agitation of questions of social equality is the extremest folly." As to voting rights, they would be "a natural slow growth," therefore the Negro should "deport himself modestly in regard to political claims." The South should not be forced "to do something which it did not want to do," Washington contended, since there were "peculiar conditions that justify the protection of the ballot in many of the states, for a while at least, either by an educational test, a property test, or by both combined."

No less a personage than President Theodore Roosevelt agreed with Booker T.'s theories, and termed him shortly after his death as having been "the most useful, as well as the most distinguished member of his race in the world," and praised his influence as having tended "to remove the friction and trouble that inevitably come throughout the South at this time in any Negro district where the Negroes turn for their advancement primarily to political life." Thirty years after Washington's death, in *The South Old and New,* Francis Butler Simkins extolled his go-slow program and his tactic of not asking anything of the white South that could not then be freely given. "Washington proposed a program that was genuinely American," wrote Dr. Simkins. His "patient attitude secured for him the good will of Northern and Southern whites. Washington emphasized the material and moral advantages that would benefit both races through a dedication to mutual interests and he won favor with the upper classes by advising blacks not to join labor unions." It was his famous Cotton States Exposition address at Atlanta in 1895 that finally endeared Washington to millions of whites for all time when he said at this segregated fair, "In all things that are purely social we shall be as separate as the fingers, yet one as the hand in all things essential to mutual progress."

A young New England black man, William Edward Burghardt Du Bois, a scholar in the social sciences with a Harvard and European background, did not believe a word of this. Du Bois, then teaching at Atlanta University, began early in his career to cross swords with Dr. Washington. He disputed the thesis that it was possible to instill in black men self respect without at the same time instilling in them the need for complete equal rights, civil, social, and political. A voteless man, no matter how well skilled he might become in agriculture, blacksmithing or tailoring as taught at Tuskegee, would remain a powerless man. Furthermore, said Dr. Du Bois, skilled hands without a skilled mind could hardly cope intelligently with the problems of living. Washington's insistence on the values of industrial and vocational education at the expense of book-learning, so Du Bois felt, defeated his own purpose. Where, for example, in years to come would Washington get his teachers to staff Tuskegee? Hardly from institutions that taught little except the trades. And if, through Washington's influence, most of America's educational philanthropy were to be channeled into industrial institutions, what of liberal arts colleges for Negroes like Lincoln, Fisk, and Atlanta University?

"We shall hardly induce black men to believe that if their stomachs be full, it matters little about their brains," wrote Dr. Du Bois in *The Souls of Black Folk* published in 1903. "Washington distinctly asks that black people give up, at least for the present, three things—

First, political power

Second, insistence on civil rights

Third, higher education of Negro youth and concentrate all their energies on industrial education, the accumulation of wealth, and the conciliation of the South." But during the years of Washington's continuing influence on the national scene, Du Bois wrote, there occurred with ever increasing speed—

"1. The disfranchisement of the Negro.
2. The legal creation of a distinct status of civil inferiority for the Negro.
3. The steady withdrawal of aid from institutions for the higher training of the Negro."

In opposition to Washington's then widely accepted program, Du Bois (who was later to become the leading editorial mouthpiece of the then as yet unformed National Association for the Advancement of Colored People) declared, "Negroes must insist continually, in season and out of season, that voting is necessary to modern manhood, that color discrimination is barbarism, and that black boys need education as well as white boys."

A half century later, during the decade following the historic Supreme Court decrees of 1954 concerning Negro education, these problems with which Du Bois concerned himself exploded into even greater problems from Washington, D.C., itself to Selma, Alabama, only a stone's throw from Tuskegee. Booker Washington's great Institute had become a success, but his program of racial compromise in the South had completely and clearly failed. In 1965 the students of Tuskegee itself were picketing the Alabama State Capitol at Montgomery on behalf of the simple right to vote, a right denied even so great an American genius as Dr. George Washington Carver during his long years of invaluable service to the South at Tuskegee.

Born a slave on a Virginia plantation, growing to manhood during the South's savage Reconstruction, building a school for the underprivileged in a state where to ask for privilege was to court lynching, no wonder Booker T. Washington said, "When your head is in the lion's mouth, use your hand to pet him." In an essay on Washington's *Up from Slavery,* which Rebecca Chalmers Barton terms "a story of his life which would conform to the white demand for safe and sane Negroes," Mrs. Barton says of its author, "That he might sometimes have had his tongue in his cheek about some aspects of the fine white world seems likely, but he was too disciplined to show it."

Even after he became a world famous figure who had dined at the White House and visited Queen Victoria, when he came home Booker T. Washington still rode in the Jim Crow cars of the South. Perhaps this indicated his identity with the Negroes of the plantation country for whom he built his Tuskegee and of whom he said, "No race can prosper till it learns that there is as much dignity in tilling a field as in writing a poem." In all his speeches and writings (including the moving first half of *Up from Slavery)* I find no record of Booker Washington ever advising a Negro not to write a poem. For that I thank him. And I hope that someday a great black poet will write a great poem about this man who lived his life with his head in the lion's mouth—perhaps even with tongue most tragically in cheek. His story of himself, as half-seen by himself, is one of America's most revealing books. Its dissimulation is part of its truth.

"Three Men of Peace," introduction to *The Peacemakers [Die Friedensmacher],* by Rolf Italiaander, LHP 544 (March 18, 1965)

It is good that Rolf Italiaander has chosen to bring together in a single volume the exciting life stories of three of the most distinguished men of African descent in the world, each of them recipients of the Nobel Peace

Prize.[16] Ralph Bunch, the first man of Negro blood to be awarded the Nobel Prize for Peace, gained this award by his adroitness in handling most unpeaceful situations, in lands far from his own homeland, and without the use of force.

Ralph Bunche himself is a gentle, scholarly and mild mannered man. When one reads about him travelling to the troubled spots of the world on behalf of peace in the role of trouble-shooter for the United Nations, imagination pictures him as a tough hard-hitting and perhaps even loud talking negotiator. Not at all, although certainly he is persuasive. Maybe his persuasive powers lie in the fact that he is gentle, learned, mild of manner and of speech, possessing a quiet likable, easy-going charm.

In the United States Ralph Bunch is termed a *Negro,* but that does not mean he is dark in the literal meaning of the word which stems from the Spanish, *black.* In complexion, Dr. Bunche is as golden as an Oriental, more Indonesian in appearance than American, and the tone of his speech is far from typically U.S.A. so, aside from accident of birth, perhaps his true nationality today might be termed international.

Bunche was born in 1904 in the auto town of Detroit. He was both an athlete and a debater in secondary school. He then became a scholarship student at the University of California in Los Angeles. There in 1927 he was graduated *summa cum laude,* valedictorian, and Phi Beta Kappa, with five medals for excellence in his studies. He continued his academic pursuits with further studies at Harvard University where in 1928 he received a Master's degree in political science. He taught at Howard University in Washington, was co-director of the Institute of Race Relations at Swarthmore College, and later became an assistant to Gunnar Myrdal in the preparation of his monumental study of black-white relations in the United States, "An American Dilemma."[17]

In 1944 Dr. Bunche became Associate Chief of the Division of Dependent States in the State Department, and at San Francisco he was an advisor on the drafting of the first charter of the United Nations. In 1947 he was Acting-Mediator of the United Nations Special Committee in the Holy Land to negotiate peace between the Arabs and the Jews. He received the Nobel Peace Prize in 1950.

Ralph Bunche has said that he has great faith in the kind of world the United Nations is seeking to bring about, namely, "a world at peace; a world in which there is full respect for human rights and fundamental freedoms for all without distinction as to race, sex, language, or religion; a world in which all men shall walk together as equals and with dignity." These are simple, strong yet gentle words from a strong yet gentle man.

Just as Ralph Bunche sought to bring peace on the international front, so Albert John Luthuli of South Africa and Martin Luther King of the United States have sought to bring peace between the peoples within the borders of their own lands.[18] Rolf Italiaander knows not only the African world, but through his trips to the United States, he also knows well the problems of the American Negro. He has lectured at a number of Negro universities and has met not only the black leaders but hundreds of their followers. It is most important that three of the most prominent men of African descent be introduced to the world as the peace makers they are in these troubled times. Rolf Italiaander is well equipped to bring them to greater and more personalized public attention.

"200 Years of Afro-American Poetry," LHP 2931 (October 8, 1965)

Poets and versifiers of African descent have been publishing poetry on American shores since the year 1746 when a slave woman named Lucy Terry penned a rhymed description of an Indian attack on the town of Deerfield, Massachusetts, a quarter of a century before the revolt of the New England colonies against Britain.[19] And it was a Negro woman, Phillis Wheatley, who in one of her poems applied the oft quoted phrase "First in Peace" to General George Washington before he became the first President of the United States. From his rebel field encampment the General sent the young poetess a note which read in part, "If you should ever come to Cambridge or near headquarters, I shall be happy to see a person so favored by the Muses, and to whom Nature has been so liberal and beneficent in her dispensations. I am with great respect, Your Obedient Humble Servant, George Washington."

Born in Senegal, Phillis Wheatley fortunately had been purchased at the age of seven or eight by a kindly master and mistress who took a fancy to the little black girl offered for sale on the decks of a slave ship in Boston Harbor. Of course, the tiny African spoke no English, and nobody knew her name, so she was given her master's name, Wheatley, and her mistress, who called her Phillis, taught her to read and write. In her teens, the black youngster began to write poetry. Before Phillis was twenty, she was well known throughout the New England colonies for her poems. She wrote herself to freedom, modeling her verses after those of Milton, Dryden, and Alexander Pope (as was the fashion of her times) and, as a representative of colonial culture, Phillis Wheatley was sent to England where her book, *Poems on Various Subjects, Religious and*

Moral, was printed in London in 1773. It was the first bound volume of poems by an Afro-American to appear in print.

Previously, a Long Island slave, Jupiter Hammon, had published broadsides as early as 1760. But it was more than fifty years before another actual book by a Negro poet was published. Then in 1829 George Moses Horton issued *The Hope of Liberty* while still in bondage in North Carolina. Later other volumes followed, but Horton's books never sold enough copies, as he had hoped they might, to buy his freedom. Perhaps this was because Freedom was often the subject of his poems, and such a subject was no more pleasing to white southerners a hundred years ago than it is today in this century of Mississippi madness. Horton had to wait until the end of the Civil War to become a free man. Once liberated, he continued to protest in writing concerning the sad fate of the black man on American shores, in slavery or out. Almost all Negro poets—except the French speaking Louisiana Creoles—wrote plaints against slavery. The best of the black anti-slavery poets was a free woman in Baltimore, Frances E. W. Harper, whose books are said to have sold more than fifty thousand copies.[20] Hers was distinctly a poetry of protest, as has been most Negro poetry for two hundred years—which has limited its appreciation in America to a comparatively small circle of readers.

The first Negro poet whose work had a wide appeal for the white public was Paul Laurence Dunbar, born in Ohio in 1872 of parents who had been slaves. His mother could not read or write so, after Paul acquired some book learning in school, he began to teach his mother. But fortunately, the little boy did not erase from his mother's tongue the quaint broken speech of the slave period. Her plantation dialect, and that of other elderly negroes who had known bondage in the Deep South, injected the folk flavor in much of Dunbar's poetry. The charm and humor of this now almost unreadable slave English gave unique color to his work. Unfortunately, this idiomatic flavor is well nigh impossible to translate into European tongues—or even to put successfully into contemporary English—just as Chaucer or Shakespeare's original language loses much of its patina when transcribed into modern speech. Paul Laurence Dunbar was Negro America's first major (albeit minor) poet. A half century after his death, some of his poems are still read and recited by the Negro people, and some like *Li'l' Gal* have been made into charming songs.

Oh, de weathah it is balmy an' de breeze
  is sighin' low,
    Li'l' Gal,

An' de mockin' bird is singin' in de locus'
by de do',
Li'l' gal,
Dere's a hummin' an' a bummin' in de
lan' f'om eas' to wes',
I's a-sighin' fo' you, honey, an' I nevah
know no res',
Fu' dey's lots o' trouble brewin' an'
a-stewin' in my breas',
Li'l' gal . . . .

Dunbar died in 1906 at an early age. But a contemporary, James Weldon Johnson, lived much longer and wrote both poetry and prose of quality. Mr. Johnson simplified the folk speech of the semi-illiterate Negroes of their generation and, in his transcriptions of the prayers, chants and sermons of black preachers which he put into poetry (without the mis-spellings of literal dialect), achieved in *God's Trombones* a folk synthesis of genuine beauty. The poems from this volume are enjoyed on radio, television and in the theatre today. They are a blend of the regional idioms of the Negro South and the sonorous rhythms of the Bible from which the black religionists drew their inspiration. There is in *God's Trombones* no attempt at the exaggerated speech of the blackface minstrels which white performers put into the mouths of stage Negroes for so many burlesque years.

James Weldon Johnson, in his preface to *God's Trombones,* expresses well the problems of the American Negro poet who wishes to preserve in his work racial tones and color, but desires an instrument of greater range than illiterate speech. Mr. Johnson wrote, "What the colored poet in the United States needs to do is something like what Synge did for the Irish; he needs to find a form that will express the racial spirit by symbols from within, rather than by symbols from without—such as the mere mutilation of spelling and pronunciation." This transition in language from the quaintness of dialect to the preservation of Negro idioms and flavor in straight English, set a style which, since the publication of *God's Trombones* in 1927, many other Negro poets including Sterling Brown and myself have followed. In my poems in the manner of the blues and spirituals, I have attempted to inject a sense of racial color and rhythms into the broader framework of the American language. Brown has done likewise in his book *Southern Road.*

Whatever the forms Negro poetry has taken in the last century, ranging from conventional English couplets and quatrains to free verse, from light lyrics to the well knit sonnet, from the blues and the spirituals to the highly personalized beatnik concepts of some of the younger black poets in Greenwich Village or San Francisco, the subject matter of Negro poetry East, West, North or South has remained more or less constant—the problems of freedom in a white dominated society. Most Negro poets a hundred years ago, and most Negro poets today are protest poets. When Claude McKay (1889–1948) came out of the Caribbean to the United States to publish in 1922 his *Harlem Shadows* containing many excellent sonnets, the poem therein to attain lasting fame and great popularity was his most militant sonnet, *If We Must Die*. This poem was a protest against the monstrous barbarity of the race riots which plagued America in the second decade of our century, and its advice to fight back struck a responsive chord in Negroes:

If we must die, let it not be like hogs
Hunted and penned in an inglorious spot,
While round us bark the mad and hungry dogs,
Making their mock at our accursed lot.
If we must die, O let us nobly die,
So that our precious blood may not be shed
In vain; Then even the monsters we defy
Shall be constrained to honor us though dead!
O kinsmen! We must meet the common foe!
Though far outnumbered let us show us brave,
and for their thousand blows deal one death blow!
What though before us lies the open grave?
Like men we'll face the murderous, cowardly pack,
Pressed to the wall, dying, but fighting back!

When Countee Cullen in 1925 published *Color*, a volume of lyric poetry, his poem *Incident* about a little white boy in Baltimore who insultingly called another little boy *nigger* soon became and still is the most quoted of Cullen's poems:

Once riding in old Baltimore,
Heart-filled, head-filled with glee,
I saw a Baltimorean
Keep looking straight at me.

Now I was eight and very small,
And he was no whit bigger,
And so I smiled, but he poked out
His tongue, and called me, *nigger*.

I saw the whole of Baltimore
From May until December.
Of all the things that happened there
That's all that I remember.

Written in the Nineteen Twenties during the period of Harlem's "Negro Renaissance" Waring Cuney's *No Images,* about the proscribed beauty of a brown girl has, of all his work, been the most widely reprinted.[21]

She does not know
Her beauty,
She thinks her brown body
Has no glory

If she could dance naked,
Under palm trees
And see her image in the river
She would know.

But there are no palm trees
On the street,
And dish water
Gives back no images.

Directly concerned with the race problem, my own poem, *I, Too,* written in 1920 when I was eighteen years old, has over the years been translated into many languages and is still being reprinted in anthologies around the world.

I, too, sing America.

I am the darker brother.
They send me to eat in the kitchen
When company comes,
But I laugh,
And eat well,
And grow strong.

Tomorrow,
I'll sit at the table
When company comes.
Nobody'll dare
Say to me,

"Eat in the kitchen,"
Then.
Besides,
They'll see how beautiful I am
And be ashamed—

I, too, am America.

The desire to be an integral part of the life of the country whose soil the Negro people have inhabited for three hundred years is a majority desire. The Black muslims who wish a separate state, and the African Nationalists who advocate a return to the ancestral homeland, are the exceptions—and a small part only of twenty-two million colored Americans. In any case, over the years, the basic and most pertinent subject matter of Negro poetry has been *not* love, roses, moonlight, or death or sorrow in the abstract, but race, color, and the emotional problems related thereunto in a land that treats its black citizens, including poets, like pariahs. Only a very few Negro writers have been able to escape the impact on their lives of this white shadow across America.

It would seem to me then only fitting and proper—if art is to be an intensification or enlargement of life, or to give adequate comment on what living is like in the poet's own time—that Negro art be largely protest art. Our time today is the time of color from Selma to Saigon, and of the heartaches and heartbreaks of racial conflict from Cape Town to Chicago. A poet may try to hide in the bosom of Ezra Pound as much as he wishes, but the realities of conflict are inescapable. The color problem is a drag on the whole world, not just on Negro poetry.

The only Pulitzer Prize winning poet of color, Gwendolyn Brooks, has written that Negro poets "are twice-tried. They have to write poetry, and they have to remember that they are Negroes. Often they wish that they could solve the Negro question once and for all, and go on from such success to the composition of textured sonnets or buoyant villanelles about the transience of a raindrop, or the gold stuff of the sun." But, she continues, "The raindrop may seem to them to represent racial tears—and those might seem indeed other than transient. The golden sun might remind them that they are burning."

The most famous contemporary protest writer, James Baldwin, himself a poet in prose, was at the beginning of his career inclined toward "non-propaganda" writing, coupling an essay of his in *Perspectives USA* 2, 1952, denouncing *Uncle Tom's Cabin* with one by Richard Gibson denouncing what might be termed the *négritude* of American Negro literature.[22] Both pieces were published together under the heading, "Two Protests Against Protest." Today, fifteen years later, no black writer writes stronger protest literature than Baldwin. The weight of the Negro problem has caused him to out-Tom *Uncle Tom's Cabin*. I imagine some of the young Negro poets of the *avant garde* schools today who insist on writing non-racially very well might, after a few more years of Ku Klux Klan headlines, become ardent—or even chauvinistic—racialists themselves, especially should they happen to be visiting Harlem during a night of riots, or feel a white cop's club against their poetic heads. My point is not that all young poets should perforce write racially if they are black. It is simply that in America it is almost impossible for Negro poets not to do so.

Among the most interesting young Negro poets writing today are the exciting LeRoi Jones (also a playwright of no mean ability), Julia Fields (who was in Birmingham at the height of its racial disturbances), Julian Bond (of the Student Non-violent Committee), and David Henderson (only twenty-one, of Greenwich Village), all of whom are most intense in their poetic fervor against injustice.[23] "The Negro in Western civilization has been exposed to overwhelming historical and sociological pressures that are bound to be reflected in the verse he has written and inspired," wrote Arna Bontemps, which he balances by saying, "The fact that he has used poetry as a form of expression has also brought him into contact with literary trends and influences. How one of these forces or the other has predominated, and how the results may be weighed and appraised are among the questions to which the poetry itself contains answers." In the Annual Poetry Issue of the *Negro Digest* (September, 1965) there is a poem by Dudley Randall of Detroit,[24] "Black Poet, White Critic," which ends with a question that is also in its inverse way an answer:

A critic advises
Not to write on controversial topics
Like freedom or murder,
But to treat universal themes
And timeless symbols
Like the white unicorn.

A *white* unicorn?

Does it believe in integration?

And why not a *black* unicorn?

"A Note on Humor," ***The Book of Negro Humor,*** **ed. Langston Hughes** (New York: Dodd, Mead and Co., 1966), vii

Humor is laughing at what you haven't got when you ought to have it. Of course, you laugh by proxy. You're really laughing at the other guy's lacks, not your own. That's what makes it funny—the fact that you don't know you are laughing at yourself. Humor is when the joke is on you but hits the other fellow first—before it boomerangs. Humor is what you wish in your secret heart were not funny, but it is, and you must laugh. Humor is your own unconscious therapy.

What does this book mean? Simply that humor can be like faraway thunder or winter lightning, but seldom like a dropped brick or the roar of Niagara Falls. Humor maintains its distance while at the same time keeping you company so long as you are capable of meeting it halfway. Humor does not force itself on you (in fact, cannot) because it has none of the qualities of a bad joke, none of the vulgarity of the wisecrack, or the pushiness of the gag. Humor is a forgotten "Good morning" remembered tomorrow, a lent dime returned in a needy time, a gesture from across the room better than a handshake, a friend who looks like a stranger but isn't because you realize you have known him all your life. Humor is your own smile surprising you in your mirror. But, like the child Onyx, in one of the anecdotes in this book, its name is derived from the fact that the arrival is so "*on*-expected." Like a welcome summer rain, humor may suddenly cleanse and cool the earth, the air, and you.

"Introduction," ***The Best Short Stories by Negro Writers: An Anthology from 1899 to the Present,*** **ed. Langston Hughes** (Boston: Little, Brown and Co., 1967), ix–xiii

Just as many Americans believe, solely from having seen *La Dolce Vita* on the screen, that Rome is one vast seraglio teeming with orgiastic vices, so many also think, from having seen *The Cool World,* that all Negroes are primitive, dirty and dangerous. White persons of the older generation add to their contemporary concepts the ancient stereotypes lazy, grinning and illiterate, drawn from memories of Stepin Fetchit, Rochester and Amos and Andy. Art (and some motion pictures may be classified as art) molds the thoughts, opinions and concepts of millions of people, even before the age of reason. On one of my recent lecture tours, I was the house guest of a charming white professorial couple on a very advanced Midwestern campus of the caliber of Kenyon or Antioch. At dinner my first evening there, I was inwardly amused and not unduly surprised when the ten-year-old daughter of the house asked me (across the table), "Mr. Langston Hughes, can you teach me to shoot dice?"

Her embarrassed parents blushed deeply. "Darling, why do you ask such a thing of Mr. Hughes?"

"I see colored people all the time shooting dice in the TV movies," the child said.

I laughed. "At night they revive a lot of very old pictures, and they show a lot of old-time colored actors like Sunshine Sammy and Nicodemus and Mantan Moreland.[25] But Negroes don't *always* shoot craps in real life and many have never even seen a pair of dice. Still, there's no harm in your learning. So if your daddy has a pair of dice, after dinner I can show you what I learned when I was in the Merchant Marine. Then if you ever go to Las Vegas—where white people shoot dice all night—you will know. Dice is a very old game, mentioned in the Bible—played by King Ahasuerus and his court. And today there's a very fashionable gambling casino at Monte Carlo where high society shoots dice."

I was talking very fast to try to keep the little girl from becoming more embroiled with her embarrassed parents: "Why did you ask such a question?" I knew why. The old stereotypes of the blackface minstrels and of Hollywood descend even unto the third and fourth generations.

Because he did not wish to be associated with similar racial stereotypes of his time, in the 1880's, the first outstanding Negro writer of fiction in the United States, Charles Waddell Chesnutt, wrote as a white man for a number of years, without revealing his ethnic identity. By hiding his color, he did not run the risk of having his material turned down by editors because of race. But after twelve years of his literary "passing," a publication called the *Critic* discovered his background and in a biographical note revealed Chesnutt as an author who "faces the problems of the race to which he in part belongs." Being very fair—about the complexion of Congressman Adam Clayton Powell—with only a small percentage of black blood in his family tree, Chesnutt was what anthropologists term a "voluntary" Negro. The same might be said of Jean Toomer. Shortly after the publication of *Cane,* he moved outside the social confines of the Negro world to live in Taos, Carmel and finally Bucks County.

Like Chesnutt, the successful contemporary novelist Frank Yerby, author of *The Foxes of Harrow* and a dozen other best-selling romances, revealed recently to a reporter, "I did tell my publishers at one time not to identify me as a Negro." Yerby's vast reading public today is on the whole quite unaware of his race. But the white people in the Georgia town where he was born know. When the motion picture made from *The Foxes of Harrow* had its highly publicized premiere in Augusta, Yerby's relatives were relegated to the Negro section of the theater. Such are the strictures of race in America even against an author whose books are translated around the world and whose earnings from writing total well over a million dollars. For almost twenty years Yerby has lived abroad where such prejudices seldom are in evidence and racial indignities such as those revealed in his early story, "Health Card," are unheard of. "I love my country," Yerby is quoted as saying. But, "Unfortunately, my country doesn't love me enough to let me live in it."

"One of the inalienable rights is that of the pursuit of happiness," Yerby says. In this anthology the themes of many of the stories concern the search for that right and how Negroes may work out the problems of their lives in order to find a modicum of happiness in America. There are drama, comedy and tragedy to be found in this fiction—so near to fact—as put down by the best of the Negro writers since 1887, when Chesnutt published his initial story in the *Atlantic Monthly.* His "The Goophered Grapevine" marked the first fiction to be published by a Negro in that highly conservative magazine. Since that time a few Negro authors have become world famous—Richard Wright, Ralph Ellison, James Baldwin. (Their stories are published here.) But none has become really rich, except Frank Yerby who, after "Health Card," put the race problem on the shelf in favor of more commercial themes. His historical romances have wonderful moviesque titles like *The Golden Hawk* and *The Saracen Blade,* but there are no noble black faces among their characters when brought to the screen. Black faces seldom sell in Hollywood.

Twenty years after publication, Ralph Ellison's *Invisible Man,* a major American novel, has not yet been filmed, and Hollywood would not touch Richard Wright's famous *Native Son.* In all its years of activity Hollywood has never made a major motion picture which portrayed with sympathy our foremost American dilemma—jampacked with drama—the Negro problem. So far as I know, exciting though many of these tales in this anthology are, only one has been filmed by Hollywood: Mary Elizabeth Vroman's charming "See How They Run" under the title of

Bright Road. But this story is not concerned with racial problems and so offends nobody.

Ted Poston's Hopkinsonville tales or the stories of Zora Neale Hurston, Alice Childress or Lindsay Patterson would make delightful motion-picture, television, or radio comedies, much more human and real than Amos and Andy. (Alice Childress's off-Broadway comedy, *Trouble in Mind,* seemed to me as funny as *Born Yesterday.*) But Hollywood has not touched their work, nor have any other mass media to date. For screen-searing drama, John A. Williams's story, "Son in the Afternoon" (included here), could scarcely be surpassed. But unless times have changed greatly, Hollywood is not likely to buy it for screen treatment.

Since most Negro writers from Chesnutt to LeRoi Jones have found it hard to make a literary living, or to derive from other labor sufficient funds to sustain creative leisure, their individual output has of necessity often been limited in quantity, and sometimes in depth and quality as well—since Negroes seldom have time to loaf and invite their souls. When a man or woman must teach all day in a crowded school, or type in an office, or write news stories, read proofs and help edit a newspaper, creative prose does not always flow brilliantly or freely at night, or during that early morning hour torn from sleep before leaving for work. Yet some people ask, "Why aren't there more Negro writers?" Or, "Why doesn't Owen Dodson produce more books?"[26] Or how come So-and-So takes so long to complete his second novel? I can tell you why. So-and-So hasn't got the money. Unlike most promising white writers, he has never sold a single word to motion pictures, television, or radio. He has never been asked to write a single well-paying soap commercial. He is not in touch with the peripheral sources of literary income that enable others more fortunate to take a year off to go somewhere and write.

Fortunately, however, in recent years a foundation has occasionally rescued a talented black writer from the subway crush of his low-salaried job. And once in a while, one finds a patron. Writing is a time-taking task, and the living is not easy. I am in favor of national subsidies, as exist in Europe. State aid never seemed to impede good writing overseas. I do not believe it would hurt good writers here. It could hardly hurt black writers, who, so far, have had not anyone at all to subvert them. For the first national grant of a large and sizable sum, I nominate one of our solid and long esteemed writers, Arna Bontemps, who has been teaching all his literary life and who deserves release for the full flowering of his considerable talents—hitherto recognized by discriminating readers but unrecognized by money. Or if it must be a young talent as first choice for a subsidy, then why not the astounding Miss Alice Walker? Neither you nor I have ever read a story like "To Hell with Dying" before. At least, I do not think you have.

The stories in this book range geographically from South to North, East to West, from America's Panama Canal Zone to our Chicago Loop and, in point of time, from the Reconstruction through the Harlem Renaissance, the Depression, the Second World War, the period of James Baldwin's blues in De Gaulle's Paris, to the contemporary moment of Charles Wright's "A New Day." In fiction as in life Negroes get around. They have been covering varied grounds for a considerable time via the written word. Here they reveal their thoughts, their emotions, directions and indirections over three quarters of a century—from Chesnutt and Dunbar, Wright, Ellison and Williams, to the new young writers of the sixties, Lindsay Patterson, Robert Boles, and Alice Walker; from the fright and violence of the Deep South to the tinkle of iced drinks at an interracial party in Boston; from the twisted face of a black sharecropper to the spotlighted smile of a Harlem dancer, from tragedy to comedy, laughter to tears, these stories, culled from the best of Negro writing over the years, indicate how varied, complex and exciting is the milieu in which black folk live in America.

Just as once, so the saying goes, the sun never set on the British Empire (because it extended around the world), so today the sun is always rising somewhere on books by American Negro writers whose works in English and in translations are being read around the world. Wright, Ellison, Baldwin, Himes, Hughes and Yerby have all been translated into at least a dozen major languages and are to be found in the libraries and bookshops of most of the earth's large cities. Today in Japanese, French, German, Italian and Polish universities, among others, students are writing theses and working toward doctorates in various phases of Negro literature. Negro authors are beginning to reap their sunrise harvest.

7

Reviews

"Twelve Millions," review of *Black America*, by Scott Nearing, *Book League Monthly* 2.2 (June 1929): 174–76

There are in the United States today, if statistics do not lie, some twelve million Negroes. The population of the Argentine is not so large, nor that of Holland, nor that of Sweden. Eight million of these dark Americans live in the South. In Georgia alone there are more than a million colored people. In Mississippi 52.2 per cent of the population is Negro. In South Carolina the percentage is 51.4 of the population.

How do they live—these blacks in a country controlled by whites? Nearly two million engage in agriculture; others are in industrial plants doing the heaviest work; others are porters, house-servants, washerwomen, day-laborers, bell-boys; and, in comparison to the masses, there is a handful of professional men, artists, and teachers. But do you ever see a black clerk in a store, a colored girl stenographer in an office, a brown cashier in a bank, a Negro street car conductor, or a dark-faced member of the president's cabinet? Not hardly! Practically speaking, all the decent jobs, little or big, important or unimportant, in this country are closed to Negroes. They must make their living almost always at the hardest, dirtiest, lowest paid, and most undesirable labor to be found. They cannot expect advancement. They cannot expect high wages. They cannot even be sure of their jobs. Large hotels in Atlantic City that have been employing colored waiters for years recently discharged them because white people needed the work. In times of industrial depression Negroes are the first to be fired, and the last to be hired again. When the whites walk out, of course, they are used as strike-breakers. But many labor unions deny colored people admittance to their ranks so that they cannot work in certain industries except at times of strike.

In the South the average farm wage is just over $35 a month without board. In three states it is less than $30 a month. Many Negroes, working under the share crop system in which the landlord is the bookkeeper, crop salesman, and storekeeper, probably receive even less than $30. In the North the Negro in industry is often not paid as much as the whites for the same type of work and, as a rule, his wages, if they advance at all, advance at a much slower rate. In the teaching profession this is what happens to him: in Lexington, Kentucky, the minimum for white high school teachers is $1,400; the maximum for colored high school teachers is $1,200. Thus the highest paid Negro teacher in that city receives less than the lowest paid white teacher. Such a wage condition for Negroes is not rare.

Behind so harsh an economic color line, it is little wonder then that the Negro masses live badly or that their death rate is high. Because black men earn so little, most Negro mothers must work, so children are frequently badly cared for and the home life is broken. In the cities Negroes usually live in the oldest and most disreputable quarters while the rents they pay are often as high as 50 per cent more than the rents paid by the white people for similar accommodations. They are frequently forced into segregated black belts, overcrowded and dirty, with little attention from the city's street cleaning or garbage collecting departments. There the youngsters grow up under the worst conditions.

In many parts of the country Negro children attend what are known as separate schools. Accommodations in these schools are almost invariably poorer than those found in the white schools. And in many districts of the South where the greater number of Negroes live, there are no schools at all for Negroes! For the education of each white child in Alabama every year the state spends less than $27. For the education of each Negro child the state spends less than $4. Some of the other Southern states do worse. None of them do much better. Where there are separate schools in the North they are usually very much overcrowded and often they are housed in old buildings which the whites have vacated.

Scott Nearing tells you of this in *Black America.* Aided by the latest statistics, by photographs, and by excerpts from social service reports he states simply and clearly, without emotionalism, the position of the Negro in the United States. The white man owns the land on which he works; the white man controls the industries in which he works; the white man's state directs his education, and often directs it poorly; the white man's politics govern him without allowing him, in the South, even a vote. Socially, too, the Negro is an outcast; refused food in public restaurants, Jim-Crowed on the Southern railroads, given the top gallery or the back rows at the theatres if he is admitted at all, served without courtesy in the shops, denied membership in the Y. M. C. A. or the Y. W. C. A. unless there are black branches, and compelled to have his own churches, and sometimes his own burial grounds. In South Carolina his life is endangered by the mob; in New York he is segregated; in Boston he is not wanted at Harvard; in California as a citizen he has fewer privileges than an Oriental unnaturalized. Continually from birth to death the taunt of being a Negro is forced upon him.

And yet he lives! In Mr. Nearing's book more than a hundred and fifty amazing photographs show him living. They picture Negroes at work in fields and factories, at play, at school, or merely walking on the streets. They show the conditions of Negro housing both rural and urban, and how the back alleys of South Chicago look. (And almost how they smell.) There are included also thirteen actual photographs of lynchings. Four are of a burning at Waco, Texas; and one is of four Negroes hung to the same tree. They are lovely examples of modern barbarism, almost unbelievable in their ugliness. But is it not almost unbelievable, too, that twelve million people should live in an American democracy under a caste system as pernicious in its effects, and as tightly unyielding in its way, as any in India? Yet Scott Nearing with his statistics, his pictures, his excerpts from social service reports, and his own simple comments in *Black America* makes you feel the terrible realness of it all. Mr. Nearing is a white man, but I, being a Negro, will swear that he has not lied.

"A Fine New Poet," review of *A Street in Bronzeville*, by Gwendolyn Brooks, LHP 3418 (September 1945)

I do not consider myself a good critic since often I cannot analyze clearly why I like or dislike a book. However, in the case of Gwendolyn Brooks' first volume of poems, *A Street in Bronzeville*, several reasons why I find it enormously to my liking immediately come to mind.

First, I think it is her great simplicity—I know what every one of her poems is about at a single reading. Second, I think it is her picture-power—I see the places and the people she writes about. Third, it is no doubt because of my own sense of identity with her subject matter—me, a Negro, dweller in furnished rooms and kitchenettes, a product of the black belts of our big Middle Western industrial cities, Kansas City, Chicago, Cleveland.

Gwendolyn Brooks lives in and writes about Chicago. Her people are the people of Richard Wright's *Twelve Million Black Voices* caught in those kitchenettes with the innumerable names of tenants above the doorbells and the single bath on each floor confusing dreams with the exigencies of the body:

We wonder. But not well! Not for a minute!
Since Number Five is out of the bathroom now,
We think of lukewarm water, hope to get in it.

There was once a wonderful colored poet, Fenton Johnson, who wrote deeply and movingly about the Chicago South Side of thirty years ago.[1] Now another wonderful poet comes forward there to express that dark and teeming city within a city, scented by the stockyards and hemmed in by restricted covenants. But the people of *A Street in Bronzeville* could be the people of any Negro section of any of our great cities—the basic poor people, I mean, not the lucky exceptions (Dr., Rev., Ph.D., Hon.) who live well and become names or titles, not masses, climbing up out of kitchenettes to West Chesterfield and the middle classes.

Someday they will find their poet, too, the Negro middle classes, but right now, Gwendolyn Brooks writes about De Witt Williams who was

Born in Alabama.
Bred in Illinois.
He was nothing but a
Plain black boy.

And about the domestic, Hattie Scott, and Mrs. Martin's disappointing son, Booker T., and the handsomely zooted Smith cat, and Moe Belle Jackson serving grits, and the hairdresser's on a Saturday night, and the sparse Sundays of

Promise piled over and betrayed.

Her poem about another plain black boy, Dorrie Miller (who has become a symbol of war-time struggle against prejudice within and enemies without), indicates that the artistry of Gwendolyn Brooks is not limited by locale or restricted covenants. This *Negro Hero* poses powerfully and poetically one of the gravest problems of our democracy, now a problem all the way from Chicago to the South Pacific. The streets of Bronzeville run both ways around the world to all the camps and bases of our new imperialism. Everywhere dark men and women hope the years to come will *not* be promises "piled over and betrayed" nor sparse Sundays in areas of restricted covenants. Poets often say these things better than politicians. Gwendolyn Brooks speaks very well indeed.

"Chicago's South Side Comes Alive," review of *47th Street,* by Frank Marshall Davis, LHP 3422 (August 9, 1948)

Chicago's vast Negro South Side has given to American poetry within my time such fine poets as Fenton Johnson, Margaret Walker, Gwendolyn Brooks, and such distinguished Negro prose writers as Richard Wright and Willard Motley.[2] Big city area of drama and struggle, the end of a dark hegira from South to North, hemmed in by restrictive covenants, the home of steel and stockyard workers, numbers bankers, headline theatre names and shoeshine boys, "little" Negroes and "big" Negroes, the South Side is rich in challenging, provocative human material for the writer.

In his exciting new book of poems, *47th Street,* Frank Marshall Davis focuses a sharp creative eye upon the hopes and dreams, frustrations and defeats, intimate longings and great ambitions of the kitchenette dwellers and mansion house roomers of Chicago's enormous Black Belt. The title poem is a kind of verbal ticker-tape tour of the street that cuts through the heart of this dark city. Sound trucks, crusaders, pawnshops, numbers, street corner loungers and striving professional men, Jews, draftees, proud women and slatterns, all the character and color, conflict and comedy of this colored and colorful street find expression in the first poem in this straightforward, simple, readable, and occasionally powerful and heart-tugging book.

Frank Marshall Davis is not a sweet poet, and seldom a lyrical poet. (In this book the city lyrics of "Four Glimpses of Night" are a delightful exception.) But the subject matter of his poems is hardly lyric material. It is more the material of epic and dramatic poetry. Mr. Davis handles it in a dramatic way. The book's only fault, in an otherwise consistently fine volume, is when the drama spills over into oratory and direct statement, rather than maintaining the emotional moods and understatements of poetry. But evidently the poet, angry, troubled and disturbed by the needless stupidities of our society, sometimes wishes to speak his mind in the plainest and most direct way. Frequently he does so.

But when his poems are poetry, they are powerful. And Frank Marshall Davis possesses a kind of sardonic humor that I know of in no other poet of our race in America. This bitter biting thought-provoking humor is most evident in such poems as "Snapshots of the Cotton South" where he writes of the absurd contradictions and pretensions of segregation. This poem contains a wryly humorous parodying of a children's round (like "Three Blind Mice" but without rhyme) wherein he traces the course of a case of venereal disease back and forth across racial lines. In another section of the same poem, he comments upon the waste of public funds in maintaining the separate Jim Crow system in a region where:

Care must be taken
By public official
Not to make jails too strong
And thus inconvenience
The hungry lynchers.

"Chicago Skyscrapers" whose

Heaven will be
Merely another high floor
Barked by a uniformed boy
On an express elevator . . .

and his "Tenement Room" full of the "visual cries" of poverty, are among the most effective poems in the book. And this marvelous bit of imagery from "I Have Talked with Death" is a poem in itself:

Death's palm met mine.
The moon bounced against my window pane
Like a tossed white ball;
Stars rattled
Like popping corn in a covered pan;
The sky exploded
Like a pricked balloon
As I shook his ancient hand.

But, although here and there these Frank Marshall Davis poems are studded with lines beautiful in themselves, they are not the sort of poetry to be savored line by line. To gather the full cumulative effect of his poems, each of them should be read as a whole. Then sometimes their over-all punishment and power produces an emotional ache not unlike, I imagine, the physical effects of lasting twelve rounds with Joe Louis might be. Certainly *47th Street,* in its beautiful format by the Decker Press, is a book every lover of Negro literature should own.

"Name, Race, and Gift in Common," review of *The Resurrection,* by Jonathan Henderson Brooks, and *Annie Allen,* by Gwendolyn Brooks, LHP 3419 (November 14, 1949)

Jonathan Brooks, leaving a thin sheaf of unpublished poems, died in 1945, the year that Gwendolyn Brooks published her first book, *A Street in Bronzeville.* They were not related and had nothing in common save their last names, their race, and a gift for poetry. Jonathan Brooks was born, lived, and died in Mississippi. Gwendolyn Brooks was born in Kansas and lives in Chicago. One poet is rural and Deep South, the other urban and North. Their poems reflect these differences.

With the love of one poet for another, Henry Dalton, white, of Corinth, Mississippi, has assembled and brought to publication twenty-three of the poems of Jonathan Henderson Brooks under the title *The Resurrection and Other Poems.* Concerning this slender volume, Hodding Carter, another Mississippian, says, that this Negro poet "sings with a gentle mysticism and poignant imagery of an unbounded world, a world of faith that can 'measure great Gibraltar by a butterfly.' " Certainly Jonathan Brooks possessed deep religion, expressed in the simple loveliness of the musical word. His poems sing, yet say directly what they choose to say, as in this excerpt from "The Missionary," a fine tribute to one sincere white teacher and, through him, to many who have devoted their lives to education in the segregated Negro schools of the South:

> *Not as a priest and a pedagogue,*
> Espousing the cause of the underdog
> *But he came to us as a next-door neighbor*
> *And offered his life, a spring day's labor.*

Lovely and lyrical in quality are most of the poems in Brooks' small posthumous volume. Among my favorites are, "Song for a Love That Is Dead" and "My Angel," with its touching humor of the angel who wrestles with the poet's burden of sin. And "She Said," picturing a mother receiving news of a son's death in action, is one of the most beautiful American poems of the last War.

Quite different from Jonathan Brooks and much more modern in style are the poems in *Annie Allen,* the second book by Gwendolyn Brooks whose first, *A Street in Bronzeville,* received wide critical attention. Miss Brooks is a very accomplished poet indeed, often boiling her lines down to the sparest expression of the greatest meaning, sometimes almost to a kind of word-shorthand that defies immediate grasp. Less simple and direct than the poems in her initial volume, those in *Annie Allen* give, upon careful reading, as much interest and emotional impact. The book is a mood story in varying poetic forms of a girl's growth from childhood to the age of love, marriage, and motherhood.

There are sharp pictures of neighborhoods, relatives, friends, illnesses and deaths; of big city slums, cafes, and beauty shops. To me the third section containing about half the poems in the book, "The Womanhood," is its most effective. The qualms, the longings, the love of a poor mother for her child is here most movingly expressed:

> *The little lifting helplessness, the queer*
> *Whimper-whine; whose unridiculous*
> Lost softness softly makes a trap for us.

And from another poem:

> *Life for my child is simple, and is good.*
> He knows his wish. . . .
> *Like kicking over a chair or throwing blocks out of a window*
> Or tipping over an ice box pan. . . .
> But he has never been afraid to reach.
> His lesions are legion.
> But reaching is his rule.

The people and the poems in Gwendolyn Brooks' book are alive, reaching, and very much of today.

"Two Modern Poets," review of *Poems, 1928–1948,* by Edouard Roditi, and *The Wind of Time,* by Rolfe Humphries, LHP 3432 (1949)

Outstanding among present-day poetic voices are Edouard Roditi and Rolfe Humphries.[3] Both have exquisitely sensitive minds; nice distinctions in both the outer and inner worlds come naturally to their attention; their experience has been wide and varied; moreover, they have unusual ability to integrate experience into words. Both of these poets have a fine sense of melody and form—exemplified especially effectively in the modern images of Roditi's "Cassandra's Dream":

> But our planet is perhaps a parachute-trooper
> Dropped in the Universe, behind the lines
> Of eternity, with incendiary bombs to spread
> Terror and confusion in systems of order
> Where all who are whole will soon be studied
> As fossils from a lost age, missing links to prove
> The existence of hypothetical monsters, Trojan
> Horses or Political Termites, both extinct.

and in Humphries' "Test Paper":

> What do we really praise? Oh, Life and Time,
> (With capitals), books that Fadiman commends,
> The chromium bars, the streamlined cars and trains,
> The music played for music's newest friends. . . .
>
> Last question. (On your honor.) What do we all
> Praise, absolutely in this day and age?
> Re-read the question: answer thoughtfully;
> *Write nothing on this portion of the page.*

Poems: 1928–1948 and *The Wind of Time* are built upon an intelligent principle—that the enjoyment of poetry comes from a critical understanding of that poetry. Though Messrs. Roditi's and Humphries' purpose is simply to define their relation to life or to express their view of it, the reader is expected to follow where the poets lead, occasionally by abstruse allusions through various fields of learning. That is characteristic of modern poetry. The reader must exert himself, get rid of the habit of reading for surface melody, for surface meanings, for "traditional" effects, if he is to read modern poetry today.

Mr. Humphries is a genuine lyric craftsmen. In him especially we see that poetry is emotionalized experience. Like Mr. Roditi, he is chiefly preoccupied with the mystery men call Death, with Beauty becoming dust, with Love and its ways with men, and with man's eternal warfare with the demons of the mind. Yet, again like Mr. Roditi, he is mindful of the color of the flower, even in the most out-of-the-way cranny of the wall; he is unable to forget the branch that somehow has fallen from a tree and now lies broken and crushed in the snow.

Max Eastman has written against the extremes of obscurity and security in contemporary verse. Wilbert Snow has pointed out that " . . . Poetry was made for nobler ends. It should open doors into the houses of life. It should restore man's faith in himself and his species. It should unchain the heavy weight of heavy hours and light new sparks in the ashes of mankind." Edouard Roditi and Rolfe Humphries, then, have done us a splendid service, for their poems possess that humanness which modern verse is often said to lack.

"Fine Goings-On in Saint-Marc," review of *The Pencil of God,* by Pierre Marcelin and Philippe Thoby-Marcelin, translated from the French by Leonard Thomas, *New York Times Book Review,* February 4, 1951, p. 5

Writing with a hard pencil in thin strokes, the Marcelin brothers of Haiti, in the third of their short novels to be published in the United States, deal in the macabre materials of illicit sex and unhappy voodoo as they eventually affect a large portion of the population of Saint-Marc. This is a charming Caribbean seacoast town which had, when I was last there, one of the loveliest flower-strewn beaches I have ever seen. Little did I suspect that this sleepy Haitian village might harbor such goings-on as are revealed in "The Pencil of God."

The Marcelins make their tormented little tale of desire and guilt come to life in a surface kind of way, in terms of passion and conjure, without the reader ever getting to know any of the characters very well or really caring about anyone.

Though fate and the furies are leading characters, the writing has, particularly in the earlier chapters of the book, tongue-in-cheek quality. This seems out of keeping with the kind of story being told, as though rather quaint puppets are being described instead of human beings. Like pretty scenes in a smart musical revue, "against a background of waves gleaming like knives of steel, he saw again the full mouth, the small breasts, firm and upright, all the ebony of the face," the love affair of middle-aged married Diogene with a 16-year-old girl is told with frequent humor and the lightness of a Ronald Firbank.

A child is born, the lovers come to no good end and the whole town is upset, voodooized, and frightened. Illness, death and terror move through the final pages of the book without bringing tears. Its tragic ending is completely convincing, but not at all moving.

The story travels fast, is never dull, but the people are almost like comic-book figures. You know *who* they are but you never know *them,* except as you might know rather exotic neighbors from occasionally seeing them out the window or gossiping about them with servants. Not having read the brothers Marcelin in the original French, I cannot say what subtle overtones their writing might reveal at the source.

It may be entirely unjust to the translator to wonder whether some desirable qualities are lost in this very readable English version. Still, when it is said of the leading character who is knee-deep in tragedy, "Diogene, who was already seething, blew his top," the reader doesn't know whether the authors are laughing at him or not, or whether they are betrayed by translation. The story is too sad to be kidded in any language, even when told as a voodoo quickie.

"Satchmo," review of *The Trumpeter's Tale, the Story of Young Louis Armstrong,* by Jeanette Eaton, *New York Times Book Review,* February 27, 1955, p. 32

With appreciation of America's own music, jazz, at an all-time high not only in the land of its birth but around the world, the publication of Jeanette Eaton's life of Louis Armstrong is timely indeed. Born in New Orleans, the very cradle of jazz, Louis Armstrong grew up with it, and as that happy music spread up the Mississippi River northward to Chicago and on to New York, young Louis and his cornet went with it. In warm and human terms, Jeanette Eaton tells not only the story of a great musician but of the art that he helped to develop. As Louis, in his childhood, becomes aware of the elements that compose jazz, the reader hears through his ears the old spirituals, blues, and ragtime of the deep South and learns how these gradually crystallized into a new music.

"The Trumpeter's Tale" is an accurate tribute to the great part Negroes played in the creation of America's favorite music. Elton Fax has given the book excellent illustrations. An ideal way to read this book is with a pile of Armstrong's records at hand, so one can hear the pieces

Louis has played as one reads. But with or without records, the book is a pleasure.

"From Harlem to Paris," review of *Notes of a Native Son,* by James Baldwin, *New York Times Book Review,* February 26, 1956, p. 26

I think that one definition of the great artist might be the creator who projects the biggest dream in terms of the least person. There is something in Cervantes or Shakespeare, Beethoven or Rembrandt or Louis Armstrong that millions can understand. The American native son who signs his name James Baldwin is quite a ways off from fitting such a definition of a great artist in writing, but he is not as far off as many another writer who deals in picture captions or journalese in the hope of capturing and retaining a wide public. James Baldwin writes down to nobody, and he is trying very hard to write up to himself. As an essayist he is thought-provoking, tantalizing, irritating, abusing and amusing. And he uses words as the sea uses waves, to flow and beat, advance and retreat, rise and take a bow in disappearing.

In *Notes of a Native Son,* James Baldwin surveys in pungent commentary certain phases of the contemporary scene as they relate to the citizenry of the United States, particularly Negroes. Harlem, the protest novel, bigoted religion, the Negro press and the student milieu of Paris are all examined in black and white, with alternate shutters clicking for hours of reading interest. When the young man who wrote this book comes to a point where he can look at life purely as himself, and for himself, the color of his skin mattering not at all, when, as in his own words, he finds "his birthright as a man no less than his birthright as a black man," America and the world might well have a major contemporary commentator.

Few American writers handle words more effectively in the essay form than James Baldwin. To my way of thinking, he is much better at provoking thought in the essay than he is in arousing emotion in fiction. I much prefer *Notes of a Native Son* to his novel, *Go Tell It on the Mountain,* where the surface excellence and poetry of his writing did not seem to me to suit the earthiness of his subject-matter. In his essays, words and material suit each other. The thought becomes poetry, and the poetry illuminates the thought.

What James Baldwin thinks of the protest novel from *Uncle Tom's Cabin* to Richard Wright, of the motion picture *Carmen Jones,* of relationships between Jews and Negroes, and of problems of American minorities in general is herein graphically and rhythmically set forth. And the title chapter concerning his father's burial the day after the Harlem riots, heading for the cemetery through broken streets—"To smash something is the ghetto's chronic need"—is superb. That Baldwin's viewpoints are half American, half Afro-American, incompletely fused, is a hurdle which Baldwin himself realizes he still has to surmount. When he does, there will be a straight-from-the-shoulder writer, writing about the troubled problems of this troubled earth with an illuminating intensity that should influence for the better all who ponder on the things books say.

"A Boxcar of a Book," review of *The Big Boxcar,* by Alfred Maund, LHP 3428 (October 14, 1957)

The Big Boxcar is the kind of book about the Deep South that makes me as a reader wonder why anyone who can get away would live there at all when there are other large areas of the world to which a person might migrate.[4] Alfred Maund's little novel, streaked with brutal beauty, has a coarse and colorful intensity about its portrayal of certain segments of Negro life and Negro-white relationships in the South that compel following its half dozen men and women to the end of their train ride through Alabama. The seven human beings in the box car each tell their stories as the freight rattles toward Birmingham. And when it gets to Birmingham an heroic and horrifying assignation takes place beside the tracks as a group of white cops, bent on searching the train, linger instead to watch. The police have just killed one of the riders. But the couple on the ground prevent them from spotting the other four as the train pulls out toward Atlanta.

In the course of telling their stories about life behind the American 8-ball, the uglier aspects of the manners and mores of existence behind the cotton curtain pass in parade—and a sad and sorry parade it is indeed. That it leaves any human pride or dignity in its wake is a part of the miracle of the toughness of the human soul and body. But of it all, says one of the characters so strongly etched in Mr. Maund's book, "He saw that what a person did because he had to didn't have direct connection with his pride; if his pride could make something of it and keep it alive, it didn't matter what he did."

"Lord, Please Let That Number Be 417," review of *The Hit,* by Julian Mayfield, *New York Herald Tribune Book Review,* October 29, 1957, p. 12

In Julian Mayfield's novel *The Hit* for a large number of Harlemites the Godot of their daily life is a numbers banker named John Lewis of whom one of the characters says, "John Lewis never really comes." The chances in the numbers game are a thousand to one against the player. Yet masses of New Yorkers, white and colored, gamble on numbers every day, and it has become a multi-million dollar business. This popular lottery is cheaper to play than the horses, easier and far less time-taking than cards, roulette, or dice. One may gamble from a penny up, and on three numbers the returns are 600 to 1. The handful of people who hit are just enough to keep myriads more playing every day in the hope of winning. But for most Godot never comes. And for some, even when they have won, the banker fails to turn over the cash. But the lure of a hit in this dream world of luck keeps hope alive for many in the midst of poverty, boredom, and frustration. In Julian Mayfield's novel, after a whole life-time of hoping, Hubert Cooley finally hits for a large sum of money. The banker, however, does not have the money to pay the bet. John Lewis does not come.

A powerful little novel whose action is all concentrated on the day when 417 comes out, *The Hit* concerns what happens to a mother and father, their son, and a girl on that day. Against the backdrop of Harlem, vividly pictured in simple straightforward prose, the characters come alive and their stories seem real and very sad. Julian Mayfield writes well, at times poetically, and occasionally with high humor, as in a passage describing why Cadillac cars are held in such great respect among Negroes. There is an unforgettable vignette of a malingering soldier in a hospital bed as remembered by Cooley's son.

As a fictional exploration into a comparatively new field of subject matter—the numbers game—*The Hit* is a first novel of unusual interest, treating as it does one phase of "that most solid and persistent of all American phenomena—the dream." Concerning the numbers, as early afternoon approaches in Harlem and the time draws near for the announcing of the first digit, Mayfield writes, " . . . the great dream machine was wound tight. The nickels were in the slots and the players waited. Only a turn of the handle was needed to set the whole thing in motion . . . Oh, Lord, please let that number be 316 today. You know my life ain't been easy, with three mouths to feed and that man of mine done snuck away . . . Lord, let that number come 316 . . . A girl needs nice things . . . dresses, slips, a handbag . . . Just can't seem to make enough to keep up. But if I can hit 212 today . . . How a man can work so hard and never have any money I just don't know. There's the television set to be paid, the refrigerator, the furniture . . . the gas and the electricity and the telephone. I could take care of these things if 530 was to jump out . . ." As a montage of the dream that almost never comes true—and even if it does, Godot isn't there—*The Hit* is a highly readable and dramatic novel.

"The Boy Who Was Afraid to Go Home," review of *The Long Night,* by Julian Mayfield, *New York Herald Tribune Book Review,* October 26, 1958, p. 16

Steely is a ten-year-old boy whose youthful father talks better than he behaves. The father has deserted his wife and three children, so Steely becomes the man of the family. Steely belongs to a gang in East Harlem known as the Comanche Raiders and his proudest possession is his gang-land jacket with the name of his club on the back. He has earned the money to buy this himself so he wears it proudly. While his mother is at work, Steely has to be a baby sitter but, absorbed in dreams and comic books, he does not do well at his task, although he means well. Steely meant well too when his mother trusted him to collect $27 she had won on the numbers. But bigger boys took the money away from him in the street.

The Long Night concerns Steely's dusk-to-dawn search for some method of getting his hands on $27 again because without it he is afraid to go home. For the little boy it becomes an incredibly long and brutal night in which he runs "head-on into a simple but basic truth: that money is hard to come by and it is certainly not to be had for the mere asking. Good friends are reluctant to lend it, and it is not to be found on the street. It is most scarce when the need is greatest. If you don't have it you must get it, because happiness is impossible without it."

Steely seeks loans that he is willing to work out, but no one will advance the child so much money. He snatches a purse, only to find that it is almost empty. He steals a bicycle that is taken from him by a member of a rival gang. For his mother's sake (she had planned to buy shoes for the children with this lost money, and maybe a pair of stockings for herself) Steely is on the verge of getting into the car of a pervert who trails him. But when he asks for $27, he sees in the man's eyes that the man will not give him that much money.

In the later hours of the night when the bars close, Steely sees a drunk who has passed out in a doorway. He thinks he can rob him. But the drunk turns out to be some one Steely loves very much. His final encounter brings to a dubiously happy ending Julian Mayfield's touching little novel. But the author knows—and I think Steely does too—that there are no really happy endings readily available to little boys of poor families whose fathers have wandered away and who live in a fist-hard gangland world in the slums of our great cities. *The Long Night* is gentler and more poetic than many other such novels in its unfolding of a story that has been told before and each time in the telling is too grim for tears.

"When Bigotry Invaded a Chicago Suburb," review of *Trumbull Park,* by Frank London Brown, *New York Herald Tribune,* July 5, 1959

Just as *Uncle Tom's Cabin* was a broadside against slavery, so *Trumbull Park* is quite frankly a protest novel. Like *Uncle Tom's Cabin* it is, within the framework of its intentions, a very good book. Its intentions are to expose in no uncertain terms the bigoted mobs, and that segment of the police in sympathy with such mobs, who attempt to prevent Negro citizens from taking advantage of public financed housing in some urban communities today. From shouted insults to window-shattering bricks, from silent intimidation to exploding bombs, Frank London Brown's novel paints a picture of community terror almost unbelievable in a civilized city. But there *is* a real Trumbull Park. Brown lived in Trumbull Park. And from his harassed sojourn as a Negro in this troubled Chicago housing project, he emerged with a fictional account of its days and nights of racial tension that is almost documentary. Its account is substantiated by the on-the-spot reports of eyewitness newsmen writing for not only the Negro press but the national press as well.

Some people have said *Trumbull Park* is not true, that it could not possibly be true to conditions in any Northern city, that even as fiction it is exaggerated. My feeling is just the opposite. The book is probably less than true, although it is vivid with anger and hate and violence. It is very hard to put on paper with full truth exactly what deep and frightful damage overt and active prejudice can do to men, women and children. In *Trumbull Park* it is a young husband, a young wife, and their children, colored, who are for a very long while at the mercy of a white mob, old and young, children and adults. It is a bitter siege. How, in the end, determination and decency seem about to triumph, is the theme of this story, unfolded in terms of characters who are terribly alive and real. Simply as a story regardless of its social values, *Trumbull Park* should hold any reader's attention. It tells its tale well. Its protagonists are people first, though—as in life—they are also problems.

Just as there are novels that deal with the problems of divorce, or the problems of sex, or the problems of Madison Avenue's public relations, so long as there is a race problem fiction about the problems of race has a reason for being. Race happens to be, in the broadest sense, a social problem. From Chicago to the Congo color takes up a great deal of newspaper space these days, and occupies the time and attention of a great many governmental officials from the national down to the village level.

Frank London Brown's book concerns the Martin family and other colored tenants who have moved into Trumbull Park in the face of hostile mobs and threatened bombs. It is the Martins' first makeshift supper in their new home. "We hadn't put the curtains up yet, and all we had was the shade pulled down, but the moon was bright, and I could see the policemen in the moonlight, through the crack between the shade and the window. Lots of policemen, walking back and forth in no kind of order—not in single file, not two by two—just walking, walking. Helen got quiet in the kitchen. Luella and Dianne were asleep on the mattress on the floor. I could hear the cops walking outside my window, feet hitting heavy on the sidewalk. I looked in the kitchen because Helen was so still in there. . . . She looked at me, then looked away at the floor. 'What are you looking at?' I asked. . . . She got one of those fake smiles when I asked her that.

" 'I'm waiting to see what's going to happen.'

" 'You're waiting for the bomb?'

" 'I'm waiting to see what happens.'

" 'Well, what else are you waiting for, if you're not waiting for the bomb? That's what the man said was going to happen.'

"'Okay, okay, then! So I'm waiting for the bomb,' Helen said. 'Now, come on, let's eat.'"

And the Martins sit down to eat. While they are eating a bomb explodes. From then on the tension mounts through their long weeks of troubled residence, yet the Martins stick it out. *Trumbull Park* is a big book, but it moves rapidly through its more than 400 pages to a stirring close. It has what might be called—in terms of courage triumphant—a happy ending.

"A Mighty Engaging Soldier He Is, Too," review of *Jigger Whitchet's War*, by Avery E. Kolb, *New York Herald Tribune Book Review*, August 30, 1959, p. 4

It is good to read a book with a happy ending—especially when it is a book about Negroes, whose problems in fiction so often get them down. Not only does *Jigger Whitchet's War* have a happy ending, but it is a happy little book all the way through. Often, in fact, it is hilariously happy, without ever resorting to burlesque or caricature to create its fun. Its humor is mostly gentle, wistful and warm, then suddenly as funny as funny can be.

The hero of Avery Kolb's first novel is a little colored soldier whose adventures in transit and in Europe during the late war might seem incredible if he were not just the kind of person to whom in real life incredible adventures happen. A dusky cousin of the Chaplin of silent film days, likable little Jigger bungles in and out of the most amazing situations, and has what seems at first to be the worst luck, but always—like a cat with nine lives—he lands on his feet. In the end, he lands not only on his feet, but far ahead of all the other cats. His peregrinations are highly entertaining. Sometimes, too, in this book a moment of movement involving its hero is so beautifully described—like the invasion troops marching to the sea—that the poetry of its passing will be hard to forget.

Genial Jigger, like his Mississippi-born author (who must have been an officer in charge of Negro troops overseas) is from the deep South. But of the lethargy that seems to possess many characters in southern novels, Jigger has no part. He is a live wire whose youthful energy has him charging through the English countryside in borrowed jeeps, getting lost behind the enemy lines in France and saving a whole village from starvation, causing an entire detachment of Nazi troops to surrender to him, and finally taking French leave in high spirits to see Paris.

Nothing much gets Jigger down except pomposity and meanness. But in the sweetest and most ingenuous of ways, Jigger gets the best of official stuffiness and plain human cussedness in those around him.

The book is full of laughable little surprises which, if revealed in a review, might take away from the reader some of its ingratiating charm. Jigger is certainly one of the most endearing heroes I have come across in recent fiction. In Avery Kolb's delightful book he becomes the darling of an English family, then of a whole French village, then of a most beautiful lady with a handsome income in a fabulous house in Paris. As the final page is turned, it looks as if they both will live happily ever afterward. Certainly you hope so. *Jigger Whitchet's War* is the kind of book that makes you wish everybody in the world could have as much fun as does the warm-hearted little guy who lights its pages.

Review of *A Touch of Innocence,* by Katherine Dunham, LHP 3423 (October 19, 1959)

The American Midwest of rabbit hunts in autumn, of leaden skies and bitter cold in winter, of lady's-slippers and May apples and young dandelion greens in spring, is the backdrop for Katherine Dunham's story of her childhood and turbulent adolescence before she set out to make her own way in the world. It is an absorbing family chronicle written with a gift for physical detail sometimes too real for comfort. The biting winds of the Illinois prairies can actually be felt; the humid steam and the scent of cleaning fluids in her father's pressing shop can be felt in the nostrils; the sudden blow from the palm of his hand on a child's face can be felt by the reader, too; and the shouts of his anger sometimes seem to make the pages of this book tremble as did the girl who suffered his irrationalities. From its rather leisurely beginning *A Touch of Innocence* gradually grows into a series of family conflicts that are almost unbearable.

They are hardly bearable because Miss Dunham makes the people she writes about as real as your next door neighbors. And they are likable people. If one did not care about them from the very first pages, what happened to them in the rest of the book would not matter. But in quietly graphic prose the growing girl, the slightly older brother, the ambitious father and the kind stepmother are pictured in such human terms that when their lives get tied into harder and harder knots beyond their undoing, one can only continue to read helplessly as doom closes in upon the household. When the girl "turned to the closet to lift her one suitcase from its shelf" and goes away to the big city and the "great wide world opened before her" the book ends. But if one did not know that eventually Katherine Dunham became a world famous dancer, it would be difficult to call this a happy ending.

I have seen Miss Dunham dance many times. She dances very well indeed. I think she writes equally well, but in a quite different way. Her dancing and choreography have theatricality and glamor. Her writing has the quality of the shoeing of a horse, which "she found unpleasant: Lady Fern's foot would draw sharply up as the hot iron touched her thick cuticle. . . . yellow smoke would rise. . . . the nails were hammered in." But I have not mentioned the sudden flashes of humor in this book. There is Grandma, victim of Victorian modesty, who swears her husband never saw her nude. "Twenty-six years and three days, and thirteen children! And never once, mind you, did Ed Poindexter ever see me *even in a nightshirt*." And there is poetry, too, as on a certain night during her first visit to St. Louis when there "began a possession by the blues . . . deeper than prayer and closer to the meaning of life than anything else . . . something people are supposed to know about and don't look at, or knew a long time ago and lost."

Review of *The World of Carl Sandburg*, Henry Miller's Theater, September 14, 1960, LHP 3433 (September 14, 1960)

The World of Carl Sandburg, which opened tonight at Henry Miller's Theatre, is a sort of staged commentary by Norman Corwin on the work of Sandburg—primarily his poetry—recited and sometimes performed by Bette Davis, Leif Erickson, and singer-guitarist Clark Allen.[5] As an opener and for musical interludes between sections of poetry, prose, and jokes, Mr. Allen contributes a few folk songs, plus a spiritual or two. The whole is rather like a dressed-up forum or round-table discussion of Sandburg's poetry on a college lecture series—except that it is theatrically lighted and, during intermission, Miss Davis and Mr. Erickson change clothes.

Bette Davis' flexible voice and Leif Erickson's flair for the dramatic nuances underlying Sandburg's very simple poetry keep the first half of the program from becoming a bit on the sleepy side, for here the poetry is mostly that of mood or thought. The second half the performers bring gloriously alive through a series of dramatic monologues, humorously folksy jokes, and tiny little provocations like that of a child speaking of global conflicts: "Someday somebody'll give a war, and nobody will come."

Leif Erickson spoke of being in Babylon on a Saturday night and nobody knew where the woman he once loved had gone. And in a pale spotlight, in crystal earrings and long white gloves, Miss Davis made very beautiful one of Sandburg's loveliest lyrics, "Monkey of Stars." Then, near the end of the evening, draped in a white feathered boa over a stunning blue gown, Bette Davis gave a bitterly moving impersonation of a Negro kept woman speaking from her grave concerning how she had gotten ahead in the world. At the end of this unpublished poem, "Elizabeth Umpstead," Miss Davis received an ovation. *The World of Carl Sandburg* is an off-beat evening for a Broadway theatre, but an attractive one for lovers of poetry, and lovers of the grand old man who is the dean of American poets.

Review of *ANANSE: The Web of Life in West Africa,* by John Biggers, LHP 3417 (June 4, 1962)

A simple, brief and charming introduction, really a visualization in words of an Aframerican artist's travels in West Africa, precedes almost a hundred vivid drawings of people and places the artist observed in Dahomey, Togo, Ghana and Nigeria on an extensive trip sponsored by UNESCO. John Biggers made his safari into Africa not in search of animals but of people and, remembering his own ancestral history, he felt in a sense as if he were coming home after three hundred years. From Houston, Texas, to the Gulf of Guinea he made his way with pad and crayon, a keen eye and a sympathetic heart. He returned to the United States with a superb portfolio of drawings full of the strength in labor, the zest in buying and selling, the rhythm in movement and the laughter in living of the basic folk who constitute the backbone of today's new Africa.

Ananse: The Web of Life in West Africa is a handsome volume and the people in it are handsome, too, black and comely, the women carrying their babies tied on their backs in "a warm, soft, syncopated cradle." On their heads both men and women carry every property from a graven image to a hundred pound fish. And on feast days they dance, play drums, and jubilate their gods. In gorgeous *kenti* cloths, patterned cottons, or naked as Adam and Eve, John Biggers found the peoples of Black Africa fascinating subjects, and he has so put them down on paper for us now.

"A Lovable Book," review of *When Found, Make a Verse Of,* by Helen Bevington, LHP 3415 (September 1966)

One rarely comes across a book that has both guts and charm, but this one has: *When Found, Make a Verse Of* by Helen Bevington. It came out a few years ago. The people who discovered it then loved it, and those who never saw it missed a lot. Its dusk jacket, vermillion red with a black spine, simple white lettering at the very top, and in the upper corner a small medallion, is seductive to the eye, enticing to further exploration. Once open, each piece in the book is short enough to lead quickly to the next piece without strain, and the contents are varied and jolly enough, or dramatic enough, to keep you reading on—and then on—turning pages and still reading when you ought to put out the light and go to sleep.

Lest the title be misleading, let me assure you it is not a book of poetry. It is rather a collection of the liveliest and oddest and most exciting chosen items from memory and memoirs that you can possibly imagine, and about them Helen Bevington sometimes makes verses. For lack of a better phrase, it might be called a personal anthology, with the collector's wise and witty comments upon her many inclusions that range from *Snakes in Emerson's Journal* to *Praisegod Barebones,* and the tale of an elderly British naval officer who was a bird watcher and who invited her up to his room at dawn to show her "a perfectly splendid tit." *When Found, Make a Verse Of* is a highly personal yet unselfconcious book, like meeting a personality who does not act like "a personality," but rather like a welcome conversationalist whose conversations are fascinating even after long acquaintance. It is a going-back-to-book to open almost anywhere for sheer pleasure and read something over again—vivid vignettes and sparkling comments in clean clear type with air between the lines, on very good paper—a pleasure to both mind and eye, yes. Really a lovable book.

8

Brief Tributes, Letters to the Editor, Miscellaneous Pieces

"American Art or Negro Art?" [letter to the editor concerning George Schuyler's "The Negro-Art Hokum"], *Nation,* August 18, 1926, p. 151

To the Editor of the Nation:

Sir: For Mr. Schuyler to say that "the Negro masses . . . are no different from the white masses" in America seems to me obviously absurd. Fundamentally, perhaps, all peoples are the same. But as long as the Negro remains a segregated group in this country he must reflect certain racial and environmental differences which are his own. The very fact that Negroes do straighten their hair and try to forget their racial background makes them different from white people. If they were exactly like the dominant class they would not have to try so hard to imitate them. Again it seems quite as absurd to say that spirituals and blues are not Negro as it is to say that cowboy songs are not cowboy songs or that the folk ballads of Scotland do not belong to Scotland. The spirituals and blues are American, certainly, but they are also very much American Negro. And if one can say that some of my poems have no racial distinctiveness about them or that "Cane" is not Negro one can say with equal truth that "Nize Baby" is purely American.

From an economic and sociological viewpoint it may be entirely desirable that the Negro become as much like his white American brother as possible. Surely colored people want all the opportunities and advantages that anyone else possesses here in our country. But until America has completely absorbed the Negro and until segregation and racial self-consciousness have entirely disappeared, the true work of art from the Negro artist is bound, if it have any color and distinctiveness at all, to reflect his racial background and his racial environment.

[Letter to the editor concerning *Fine Clothes to the Jew* and Carl Van Vechten], *Crisis* 35.9 (September 1928): 302

Mr. Allison Davis, in his recent article, *Our Negro "Intellectuals,"* makes the following assertion:[1]

"I think that the severest charge one can make against Mr. Van Vechten is that he misdirected a genuine poet, who gave promise of a power and technique exceptional in any poetry,—Mr. Hughes . . . in *Fine Clothes to the Jew,* which Mr. Van Vechten undoubtedly *did* influence, is the real proof of his having finally misdirected Mr. Hughes."

This, to all my available knowledge on the subject, is quite untrue. I do not know what facts Mr. Davis himself may possess as to how, where, or when I have been misdirected by Mr. Van Vechten, but since I happen to be the person who wrote the material comprising *Fine Clothes to the Jew,* I would like herewith to state and declare that many of the poems in said book were written before I made the acquaintance of Mr. Van Vechten, as the files of *The Crisis* will prove; before the appearance of *The Weary Blues* containing his preface; and before ever he had commented in any way on my work. (See *The Crisis* for June, 1922, August, 1923, several issues in 1925; also the *Buccaneer* for May, 1925.) Those poems which were written after my acquaintance with Mr. Van Vechten were certainly not about him, not requested by him, not misdirected by him, some of them not liked by him nor, so far as I know, do they in any way bear his poetic influence.

My second book is what I personally desired it to be and if the poems which it contains are low-down, jazzy, cabaret-ish, sensational, and utterly uncouth in the eyes of Mr. Davis the fault is mine,—not Mr. Van Vechten's. I do not resent Mr. Davis' criticism of my work and I know very well that a great many persons agree with him,—nay, go even farther in believing that all of my verses are tainted with the evils of utter blackness. To such people my poems are as the proverbial red rag to the bull. To say the least they seem quite distasteful to them and evidently not the kind of reading diet on which they should feed, but I am not hurt about it. I have never pretended to be keeping a literary grazing pasture with food to suit all breeds of cattle. However, for the sake of truth, I cannot allow Mr. Davis' rather extravagant misstatement of fact to go unanswered, therefore this letter offering a correction.

"Greetings to Soviet Workers" [letter to the editor], *New Masses* 6 (December 1930–1931): 23

Not Without Laughter, the first novel by Langston Hughes, parts of which first appeared in *New Masses* a few months ago, has been published recently in this country and is now being issued in several foreign translations.

In Soviet Russia, the book is being published by the State Publishing Company "Land and Factory." On request, the following greetings were sent by the author to Soviet readers, to be included in the first edition:

"All over the world Negroes are robbed, and poor. In the name of their misery I salute the Russian people. I send my greetings to the great Soviet ideal, to its true realization in your own land, and to its sunrise hope for the downtrodden and oppressed everywhere on earth."

"A Letter from Haiti" [letter to the editor], *New Masses* 7 (July 1931–1932): 9

"Haiti is a hot, tropical little country, all mountains and sea; a lot of marines, mulatto politicians, and a world of black people without shoes—who catch hell.

"The Citadel, twenty miles away on a mountain top, is a splendid lovely monument to the genius of a black king—Christophe. Stronger, vaster, and more beautiful than you could possibly imagine . . . it stands in futile ruin now, the iron cannon rusting, the bronze one turning green, the great passages and deep stairways alive with bats, while the planes of the United States Marines hum daily overhead. . . ."

"An Appeal for Jacques Roumain," [letter to the editor], *New Republic,* December 12, 1934, p. 130

SIR: Jacques Roumain, poet and novelist of color, and the finest living Haitian writer, has just been sentenced at Port-au-Prince, Haiti, to two years in jail for circulating there a French magazine of Negro liberation called *Cri des Nègres.* Jacques Roumain is a young man of excellent European education who formerly occupied a high post in the Haitian government and is greatly respected by intellectuals as an outstanding man of letters. He is one of the very few upper-class Haitians who understands and sympathizes with the plight of the oppressed peasants of his island home and who has attempted to write about and to remedy the pitiful conditions of 90 percent of the Haitian people exploited by the big coffee monopolies and by the manipulations of foreign finance in the hands of the National City Bank of New York.

As a fellow writer of color, I call upon all writers and artists of whatever race who believe in the freedom of words and of the human spirit, to protest immediately to the President of Haiti and to the nearest Haitian Consulate the uncalled for and unmerited sentence to prison of Jacques Roumain, one of the few, and by far the most talented, of the literary men of Haiti.

"If I Were White" [letter to the editor?], *Northwest Enterprise,* March 24, 1948, p. 1

If I were white I would not have the nerve to loudly proclaim myself 100 per cent American and a noble champion of democracy in a town where a Negro child cannot use a public swimming pool on a hot day or eat a dish of ice cream in a downtown confectionery. I would not red-bait a great Negro singer, and at the same time race-hate a small black boy or girl. I would be ashamed to do that, if I were white.

But then I would be ashamed to be a great Secretary of State in Washington defending the right to vote three thousand miles away in the Balkans but not saying a word about the right to vote for thousands of black citizens in his own home state.[2] Maybe it is because our BIG white folks set such strange examples, that our little white folks in Georgia and Illinois act so badly. Anyway, I would be ashamed.

"A Reader's Writer" [brief tribute to Ernest Hemingway], *Mark Twain Journal* 11.4 (summer 1962): 19

Ernest Hemingway was a highly readable writer, one whose stories lost no time in communicating themselves from the printed page to the reader, from dialogue on paper to dialogue sounding in one's own ears and carrying his tales forward as if the characters were alive and *right there* in person. The immediacy of Hemingway's reality conveys itself with more than deliberate speed and with an impact few other writers so quickly and so compactly achieve. Some commentators said years ago that Hemingway was a writer's writer. He turned out to be a reader's writer as well.

"Du Bois: A Part of Me,"
Freedomways 5 (winter 1965): 11

So many thousands of my generation were uplifted and inspired by the written and spoken words of Dr. W. E. B. Du Bois that for me to say I was so inspired would hardly be unusual. My earliest memories of written words are of those of Du Bois and the Bible. My maternal grandmother in Kansas, the last surviving widow of John Brown's Raid, read to me as a child from both the Bible and *The Crisis.* And one of the first books I read on my own was *The Souls of Black Folk.* Years later, my earliest poems were accepted for publication by *The Crisis* under the editorship of Dr. Du Bois. It seems as if, one way or another, I knew Dr. Du Bois all my life. Through his work, he became a part of my life.

Notes

Note: Proper names that might not be familiar to readers are annotated upon their first appearance in the volume; readers are encouraged to consult the index for subsequent references.

Essays, 1921–1929

"The Fascination of Cities"

1. Bert Williams (1874–1922) and George Walker (1873–1911) teamed up in San Francisco in the 1890s. Billing themselves as "The Two Real Coons," they were among the better known performers in the blackface minstrel shows popular in the nineteenth and early twentieth centuries.

2. Mabel, Alberta, Essie, and Alice Whitman formed one of the most successful African American vaudeville troupes, helping to foster the careers of celebrity dancers, singers, and musicians such as Luther Bill "Bojangles" Robinson (1878–1949), Ethel Waters (1896–1977), and Count Basie (1904–1984).

3. Hughes is likely referring to the Chicago race riot of 1919, one of the most severe in a series of riots throughout the United States during the "Red Summer" following World War I. On July 27 an African American boy drowned in Lake Michigan after being stoned by a white man who was indignant that the boy had been swimming in a racially restricted area. Police refused to arrest the man, and soon angry crowds gathered on the beach. The violence that ensued as rumors about the incident spread throughout Chicago lasted nearly two weeks, resulting in numerous deaths, injuries, and African American families left homeless. See William M. Tuttle Jr., *Race Riot: Chicago in the Red Summer of 1919* (1970; Urbana and Chicago: University of Illinois Press, 1996).

4. Hughes met Sonia, "a Russian émigré dancer," when he was searching for inexpensive lodging in Montmartre. The two shared a room in a rundown hotel until, as Arnold Rampersad notes in his biography, "she lifted several hundred francs from a drunken Swede" and soon thereafter "left Hughes and Paris to return to her child and the dance." See Rampersad, *Life,* 1:84–86. Hughes's telling of his encounter with Sonia can be found in the first volume of his autobiography, *The Big Sea* (1940).

The French can be translated as: "It is very big, this Paris. . . . Can you see Notre Dame over there, and the [Eiffel] Tower?"

5. "It is very beautiful. . . . Yes, it is very beautiful."

6. Dante Alighieri (1265–1321), Italian poet best known for *The Divine Comedy;* François Villon (1431–1463?), French poet who was banished from Paris for killing a man; Jean Baptiste Poquelin Molière (1622–1673), French playwright and actor; Adrienne Lecouvreur (1692–1730), French actress; Heinrich Heine (1797–1856), German poet; Charles Baudelaire (1821–1867), French poet and critic; Oscar Wilde (1854–1900), Irish novelist, playwright, and wit; Sarah Bernhardt (1844–1923), French actress and playwright whose real name was Rosine Bernard.

7. "Let's go. . . . Yes, let's go."

"The Negro Artist and the Racial Mountain"

8. Hughes is likely referring to Countee Cullen (1903–1946), a classically trained African American writer whose poems largely adhered to European traditions of form and meter.

9. Raquel Meller (1888–1962), popular Spanish singer and actress; Clara Smith (1895–1935), African American blues singer who incorporated vaudeville and comedy routines into her shows, which often contained risqué sexual references.

10. Charles Waddell Chesnutt (1858–1932), prolific African American writer best known for his conjure tales and his novels of social purpose dealing with the psychological and social costs of the color line; Paul Laurence Dunbar (1872–1906), African American poet, novelist, and short story writer, was both praised and chastised for his dialect poems, which some critics felt reinforced popular stereotypes of a romanticized Old South.

11. Hughes is referring to what is now known as the Harlem Renaissance, a sociocultural movement of the 1920s that witnessed a florescence of African American literary, musical, and visual arts. During this period many whites, fascinated with African American art and culture, made trips to Harlem to experience its exciting nightlife.

12. Charles Gilpin (1878–1930) became the first African American to be widely recognized as a serious actor when he played the title role in Eugene O'Neill's *The Emperor Jones* in the early 1920s.

13. Hughes is likely referring to himself in this anecdote.

14. With its blend of short fiction, poetry, and arcane line sketches, *Cane,* published in 1923, is considered one of the most stylistically

sophisticated works of the Harlem Renaissance, but it offended some critics with its frank representations of sexuality and racial violence. Jean Toomer (1894–1967) considered *Cane* a swan song, a final meditation on his own conflicted relationship with African America and the rural South. After its publication, Toomer refused to be classified as a *black* writer. Paul Robeson (1898–1976), renowned African American singer, actor, and advocate for global human rights.

15. Winold Reiss (1888–1953), German artist whose portraits of African Americans were featured in Alain Locke's Harlem Renaissance anthology, *The New Negro* (see note 21, below).

16. Bessie Smith (1894–1937), the "Empress of the Blues," made over eighty recordings during her short career; Rudolph Fisher (1897–1934), was a leading African American novelist, short story writer, and essayist during the Harlem Renaissance; Aaron Douglas (1898–1979), once referred to as the "Dean of African American painters," was encouraged by Winold Reiss to incorporate African motifs into his art.

"These Bad New Negroes: A Critique on Critics"

17. Hughes wrote this essay at the request of the *Pittsburgh Courier* while he was a student at Lincoln University in Pennsylvania. The manuscript is inscribed to Carl Van Vechten (1880–1964), writer, photographer, patron of African American art, and a personal friend of Hughes's.

18. John Mercer Langston (1829–1897) was the son of a black woman and a white Virginia plantation owner. Active in the antislavery movement, he went on to become a Howard University law professor, the U.S. minister to Haiti, and a legislator in the House of Representatives.

19. Hughes describes this incident in *The Big Sea*.

20. In Fisher's story "The City of Refuge," published in the *Atlantic Monthly* in 1925, a black protagonist fleeing the South after killing a white man seeks refuge in Harlem.

21. Alain Locke (1886–1954), an African American professor of philosophy at Howard University, was commissioned in 1924 to design and edit a special Harlem issue of the popular *Survey Graphic* magazine. From this issue, published in March 1925, Locke created *The New Negro,* an anthology featuring artwork, essays, fiction, and poetry by some of the most exciting artists and intellectuals of the Harlem Renaissance. Winold Reiss's sketches of "Harlem Types" in this issue were introduced as "a graphic interpretation of Negro life, freshly conceived after its own patterns. Concretely in his portrait sketches, abstractly in his symbolic

designs, he has aimed to portray the soul and spirit of a people." Eric Walrond (1898–1966) was born in British Guiana and became a noted short fiction writer, journalist, and editor during the Harlem Renaissance; Zora Neale Hurston (1891–1960) was a master of the short story, but the work that fully reflected her adeptness at blending African American folk vernacular with poetic lyricism was her 1937 masterpiece, *Their Eyes Were Watching God;* John F. Matheus (1887–1983), African American educator, short story writer, and playwright.

22. Smalls' Paradise, a popular Harlem nightclub where an integrated clientele was served by waiters on roller skates. See David Levering Lewis, *When Harlem Was in Vogue* (1981; New York: Penguin, 1997), 106.

23. Hughes's second book of poems, *Fine Clothes to the Jew* (1927), was referred to by J. A. Rogers as "about as fine a collection of piffling trash as is to be found under the covers of any book." See "Langston Hughes' Book of Poems 'Trash': Noted Race Critic Attacks Pandering to White Man's Twisted Notion of What Race Authors Would Write," *Pittsburgh Courier,* February 12, 1927, sec. 2, p. 4.

24. *Porgy,* the basis for George Gershwin's opera *Porgy and Bess,* is the best known work of DuBose Heyward (1885–1940), a white writer who attempted a realistic portrait of an African American community in South Carolina.

25. "Red Silk Stockings" was included in *Fine Clothes to the Jew* (1927).

26. Memphis's Beale Street, Harlem's Lenox Avenue, and Chicago's State Street are streets rich in African American culture.

27. James Weldon Johnson (1871–1938), African American songwriter, poet, novelist, journalist, and autobiographer; Dorothy Scarborough (1878–1935), American novelist, short story writer, folk song anthologist; H. O. Osgood (1879–1927), American jazz writer.

28. Alice Dunbar Nelson (1875–1935), African American poet, fiction writer, and journalist; Nannie Burroughs (1883–1961), American educator and journalist.

29. Wallace Thurman (1902–1934), African American novelist, editor, poet, playwright, and literary critic; Edward Silvera, African American poet.

"Our Wonderful Society: Washington"

30. "Ofay" is a generally disparaging term for a white person.

31. Georgia Douglass Johnson (1880–1966), one of the most beloved woman poets of the Harlem Renaissance, whose home in Washington, D.C., was the site of frequent gatherings of literati.

Essays, 1930–1939

"A Cuban Sculptor"

1. Hughes met Teodoro Ramos Blanco during a brief trip to Cuba in 1931. A visit to Blanco's studio, a frequent gathering place of radicals, may have served in part as inspiration for Hughes's story "Little Old Spy" (1934), in which the protagonist is followed through the streets of Havana by a government spy. See Rampersad, *Life,* 1:204.

2. Sojourner Truth (ca. 1797–1883), a former slave, was an itinerant preacher, abolitionist, and early feminist; Frederick Douglass (1818–1895), author of the most influential slave narrative of his era, was also an orator, journalist, editor, and statesman; Booker T. Washington (1856–1915) endured slavery to become a renowned educator, autobiographer, and race leader.

"Negro Art and Claude McKay"

3. "If We Must Die" (1919) advocates pride, honor, physical bravery, and defiance in battle, even against overwhelming odds.

"Books and the Negro Child"

4. Hughes is referring to Pedro Alonzo Nino, a navigator of Christopher Columbus's flagship, *Santa Maria.* Crispus Attucks (ca. 1723–1770), believed to be a runaway slave, was a leader of the American patriots fired upon by British troops in the "Boston Massacre" of 1770. The first to fall, he was thus one of the first men to lose their lives for the cause of American independence. Benjamin Banneker (1731–1806), African American astronomer, mathematician, inventor, and social critic best known for his annual Farmer's Almanac, a copy of which he sent to President Thomas Jefferson in protest of Jefferson's contradictory rhetoric and practices concerning human equality and slavery.

5. Topsy, a stereotypically drawn black character in Harriet Beecher Stowe's *Uncle Tom's Cabin* (1852). Sambo, perpetually grinning, dancing, and making mischief, is the adult male equivalent of the pickaninny stereotype on which Stowe's Topsy was based.

6. John W. Vandercook (1902–1963), American author; Elizabeth Ross Haynes (1883–1953), African American social welfare reformer, politician, and author; Arthur Huff Fauset (1899–1983), African American

civil rights activist, educator, folklorist, and author; Mary White Ovington (1865–1951), American social activist, founding member of the NAACP, and author.

7. The Julius Rosenwald Fund, named after the American philanthropist Julius Rosenwald (1862–1932), was founded in 1917 to improve rural education, particularly in the South, and to develop leadership among black and white southerners through fellowships.

"White Shadows in a Black Land"

8. Toussaint L'Ouverture (ca. 1744–1803), Haitian patriot and martyr, was leader of the late-eighteenth-century black rebellion to liberate the slaves; Jean Jacques Dessalines (ca. 1758–1806) served under Toussaint L'Ouverture and later became emperor of Haiti; Henri Christophe (1767–1820), who aided Toussaint L'Ouverture in the liberation of Haiti and was army chief under Dessalines, was later elected president of the republic.

"Claude McKay: The Best"

9. This previously unpublished draft of an article is presumably part of an unfinished long essay or book entitled "American Negro Writers."

10. Dissatisfied with America's racist climate, McKay left the United States in November 1922 for the Soviet Union, where he remained for six months. He then spent a decade living in Europe and Africa, until poor health and poverty compelled his return to the United States in 1934.

11. Max Eastman (1883–1969), Floyd Dell (1887–1969), and Mike Gold (1894–1967) were American authors and editors associated with the radical left.

12. The Scottish poet Robert Burns (1759–1796) often wrote in dialect.

13. Founded in 1881 by Booker T. Washington, the Tuskegee Institute emphasized a practical course of study over a liberal arts education.

14. Hughes is referring to what has become known as the "Red Summer," a period in which race riots broke out in cities all over the country.

15. Harry Hibbard Kemp (1883–1960) was known as the "tramp poet" for his unconventional lifestyle.

16. Arturo Giovannitti (1884–1959), radical poet and IWW organizer.

"Moscow and Me"

17. G.P.U. is an acronym for the Russian words for the State Political Directorate, or the secret police.

18. *Tovarish,* comrade.

19. Besides Hughes, Dorothy West (1907–1998), African American novelist, journalist, and short story writer, was the only individual in the American group mentioned who would become well known for her artistic accomplishments; Vsevolod Meyerhold (1874–1940?) was a Russian theatrical director and producer.

20. *Udarnik,* member of a shock brigade.

"Negroes Speak of War"

21. Robert Russa Moton (1867–1940), an educator and race leader, succeeded Booker T. Washington as president of Tuskegee Institute in 1915.

22. Hughes is referring to a sheriff from Tuscaloosa, Alabama, who in 1933 allowed a white mob to lynch two black teenagers accused of murder. Sheriff Shamblin was in the process of moving the youths to a jail in Birmingham when they were met by the mob.

23. NRA refers to the National Recovery Administration, the administrative bureau established under President Franklin Delano Roosevelt's administration to address issues of industrial recovery and unemployment

"Negroes in Moscow: In a Land Where There Is No Jim Crow"

24. Pushkin used his great-grandfather's experience in the court of Peter the Great in an unfinished historical novella, *The Negro of Peter the Great.*

25. Ira Frederick Aldridge (1807–1867).

26. Hughes is referring to the October 1917 Revolution in which the Bolsheviks overthrew the tsarist government in Russia.

27. Roland Hayes (1887–1976), a famous tenor, was one of the first African American singers to achieve an international reputation.

28. *Komsomolka,* member of the Young Communist League.

29. *Georgia Nigger* (1932), a work of fiction by journalist John L. Spivak (1897–1981), is credited with helping to curtail the chain-gang system in the South.

30. Hall Johnson (1887–1970), African American choral conductor and composer whose arrangements of spirituals were popularized by Roland Hayes and Marian Anderson.

A Negro Looks at Soviet Central Asia

31. The text of this long essay is based on Hughes's own copy of the pamphlet published in Moscow, which is housed in the Langston Hughes Papers at Yale University's Beinecke Rare Book and Manuscript Library. Hughes made some revisions on the published pamphlet itself, which he later incorporated into three essays based on chapters 1, 2, and 4, respectively: "Going South in Russia," *Crisis* (June 1934): 162–63; "White Gold in Soviet Asia," *New Masses* 12 (August 7, 1934): 14–15; and "Minority Peoples in Two Worlds," *New Masses* 14.7 (February 12, 1935): 18–20. To avoid repetitiveness in this volume, these essays are not included. In those instances in which the revisions made in them change the original substance of Hughes's ideas, a note explaining the nature of the revision has been provided.

In the essay "Going South in Russia," Hughes specified in this first sentence: "To an American Negro living in the *northern part of the* United States . . ." (italics added).

32. In "Going South in Russia," Hughes substituted "sleeping car" for "International car."

33. Hughes alternately spells the name "Meschrabpom" in essays regarding the Soviet Union.

34. Hughes deleted this and the previous sentence in "Going South in Russia." The union to which Hughes refers is likely the Brotherhood of Sleeping Car Porters, organized in 1925 by Asa Philip Randolph (1889–1979), African American writer, editor, and labor leader.

35. *Kolkhozes,* collective farms.

36. In "Going South in Russia," Hughes added this additional sentence: "There we were met by a workers' delegation including brown Asiatics, fair-skinned Russians, and an American Negro engineer, Bernard Powers, from Howard University, now helping to build roads across Asia."

37. In the essay "White Gold in Soviet Asia," Hughes follows this sentence with: "The natives call it 'white gold.' "

38. Hughes deleted this and the preceding two sentences from "White Gold in Soviet Asia."

39. *Telpeks,* traditional Turkmen hats made of wool.

40. *Chainiks,* tea kettles.

41. Hughes deleted this anecdote about the two little boys from "White Gold in Soviet Asia."

42. *Sovkhoz,* a state-owned farm paying wages to the workers.

43. Aleksandr Feodorovich Kerensky (1881–1970), premier of Russia until the Bolshevik Revolution of October 1917.

44. *Paranjas,* heavy horsehair veils.

45. Vladimir Vladimirovich Mayakovsky (1893–1930), the chief poet of the Russian revolution.

46. Henry Louis Mencken (1880–1956), American editor, author, and critic.

47. Juliette Derricotte (1897–1931), in addition to serving as dean of women at Fisk, was a renowned speaker on issues relating to black colleges and education.

48. MOPR was an international organization that provided aid to revolutionaries.

49. Inaugurated by Joseph Stalin in 1928, the first Five-Year Plan was designed to industrialize the Soviet Union and facilitate the collectivization of farms.

50. Hughes is referring to Communist children's organizations created to teach pure revolutionary consciousness.

51. *Chai-khana,* a central Asian teahouse.

52. Hughes is perhaps misusing *subbotniks* here. The term refers to workers who labored voluntarily on Saturdays for the good of the collective.

53. Anatoli Vasilyevich Lunacharsky (1875–1933), Russian revolutionary, dramatist, and critic who advocated the creation of a new proletarian literature.

54. Nicola Sacco and Bartolomeo Vanzetti were executed in the United States on August 22, 1927, for the murder of two men in Massachusetts. The executions were criticized worldwide by liberals who believed that Sacco and Vanzetti, both acknowledged anarchists, were victims of antiradical hysteria.

"The Vigilantes Knock at My Door"

55. In September 1933 Hughes accepted an invitation from his friend, Noël Sullivan, to live for a time at Sullivan's vacation home in Carmel-by-the-Sea, California. While there, he wrote this draft of an article

concerning his involvement in the International Longshoremen's Association strike that began on May 9, 1934.

56. Angelo J. Rossi, mayor of San Francisco; Frank Finley Merriam (1865–1955), governor of California from 1934 to 1939; Frances Perkins (1882–1965), U.S. secretary of labor from 1933 to 1945.

57. Heywood Broun (1888–1939), American newspaper columnist, critic, and unsuccessful Socialist Party candidate for congress.

"The Soviet Theater in Central Asia"

58. The second Five-Year Plan (1933–1937) was a continuation and expansion of the first Five-Year Plan launched by Joseph Stalin in 1928.

"Tamara Khanum: Soviet Asia's Greatest Dancer"

59. This essay contains material from section 5 of *A Negro Looks at Soviet Central Asia*. Hughes includes enough new material here, however, to warrant the inclusion of both versions.

"To Negro Writers"

60. "To Negro Writers" is a transcript of a speech Hughes prepared for the first American Writers' Congress, a gathering of radical writers held in New York City in April 1935. Hughes was in Mexico at the time and asked that the speech be delivered in absentia.

61. Cordie Cheek, a seventeen-year-old African American youth, was lynched in 1933 by a Tennessee mob for the alleged assault of a white girl.

"Farewell to Mahomet"

62. Anna Louise Strong (1885–1970), American journalist and author; *Red Star in Samarkand* was published in 1929.

"Pictures More Than Pictures: The Work of Manuel Bravo and Cartier-Bresson"

63. While living in Mexico in 1935, Hughes roomed with Henri Cartier-Bresson (1908–), a French photographer and photojournalist. Cartier-Bresson asked Hughes to write an introduction for the brochure

of a photography exhibit shared with Manuel Alvarez Bravo (1902–), a Mexican photographer (see Rampersad, *Life,* 1:303–4).

"Just Traveling"

64. Hughes published this essay in the Carmel *Pine Cone* (May 2, 1941). The text used here, however, is Hughes's file copy (ca. 1935).

65. Hughes is actually referring to the University of Kansas in Lawrence. Kansas State University is located in Manhattan.

66. Hughes is perhaps referring to *Scènes de la vie de Bohème,* a romantic account of struggling artists and writers by the French poet and novelist Henry Murger (1822–1861).

67. Florence Embry Jones (?–1932), the African American singer and hostess for whom Chez Florence was named; Ada "Bricktop" Smith (1894–1984), an African American singer and entrepreneur, purchased Le Grand Duc and transformed it into Bricktop's, a nightclub that attracted celebrities, writers, and artists from Europe and America.

68. Juliet's tomb, a monument claimed to represent a factual foundation for William Shakespeare's *Romeo and Juliet,* is located within the ex-convent of San Francesco al Corso in Verona. Hughes mistakenly locates the monument in Milan.

"The Paris of the Tourists"

69. Hughes spent two weeks in Paris before traveling to Spain in late July 1937 as a war correspondent for the Baltimore *Afro-American.* This undated draft of an article was likely written during this two-week period.

"Negroes and Pushkin"

70. Hughes's file copy is inscribed, "Written especially for IZVESTIA."

71. Juan Latino (1518–1607?), a black African ex-slave, was a professor of Latin grammar and the first person of sub-Saharan African descent to publish a book of poems in a Western language; Antar, an Afro-Arabian slave by birth who lived toward the end of the sixth century, became a renowned poet, storyteller, and tribal chief.

72. Formerly known as the Karamu Players, the black theater group founded by Rowena Jelliffe (1892–1992) and Russell Jelliffe (1891–1980) was named after Charles S. Gilpin (1878–1930), a renowned African American actor who preceded Paul Robeson in the leading role in Eugene O'Neill's play *The Emperor Jones.*

"The Alliance of Antifascist Intellectuals, Madrid"

73. The text used here is Hughes's file copy. He later published this speech under the title "Madrid's House of Culture," *Volunteer for Liberty* 1.19 (October 18, 1937): 3, 6.

74. Hughes is referring to paintings by Joaquín Sorolla y Bastida (1863–1923), a Spanish painter, and Domenicos Theotocopoulos, known as El Greco (ca. 1541–1614), a Greek painter who lived in Spain.

75. Hughes is referring to the revolts against the liberal Popular Front, led by Francisco Franco (1892–1975) and other Rightists, that precipitated the Spanish Civil War.

76. Miguel Primo de Rivera (1870–1930), Spanish general and dictator who rose to power when he staged a coup in September 1923 against the Cortes, the representative assembly in Spain.

77. José Bergamín (1895–?), Spanish poet and prose writer; Rafael Alberti (1902–1999), Spanish poet; María Teresa León (1903–1988), Spanish writer and feminist; Ludwig Renn (1889–1979), German writer and soldier; Egon Erwin Kisch (1885–1948), Czech journalist; Jef Last (1898–1972), Dutch writer; Pablo de la Torriente (1901–1936), Cuban writer; Francisco Pérez Mateo (1903–1936), Spanish sculptor; Gerda Taro (1910–1937), German photographer.

78. Louis Aragon (1897–1982), French novelist and editor.

79. Gustav Regler (1898–1963), German writer.

80. Ramón Sender (1902–1982), Spanish novelist, journalist, and dramatist; Rafael Dieste (1899–?), Spanish playwright; Arthur Schnitzler (1862–1931), Austrian dramatist and novelist; Miguel Prieto, Spanish director and producer.

"Hughes Bombed in Spain"

81. This is the first in a series of thirteen essays Hughes wrote for the Baltimore *Afro-American* during the Spanish Civil War.

"Hughes Finds Moors Being Used as Pawns by Fascists in Spain"

82. William Grant Still (1895–1978), African American composer with whom Hughes collaborated on the opera *Troubled Island* (1941); Mary Church Terrell (1863–1954), renowned educator, civil rights activist, first president of the National Association of Colored Women, and founding member of the NAACP.

83. Benjamin E. Mays (1895–1984), African American clergyman who was dean of the Howard University School of Religion and later president of Morehouse College; J. A. Hamlett, African American bishop of the Christian Methodist Episcopal Church; Willis Jefferson King (1886–1976), African American Methodist bishop, college professor, writer, and president of Gammon Theological Seminary; Reverdy C. Ransom (1861–195?), African American bishop of the African Methodist Episcopal Church, civil rights activist, and editor; L. W. Kyles, African American bishop of the AME Zion Church.

"'Organ Grinder's Swing' Heard above Gunfire in Spain"

84. Jimmie Lunceford (1902–1947), African American bandleader.

85. Nina Mae McKinney (1909–1967), one of the most successful African American actors of the 1920s and 1930s.

86. William B. Seabrook (1887–1945), author of a number of sensational books on Africa, the Caribbean, and the Middle East; Julia Peterkin (1880–1961), American winner of the 1928 Pulitzer Prize for Literature, wrote about African American and southern culture; Paul Morand (1888–1976), French novelist.

87. Walter White (1893–1955), African American novelist, essayist, civil rights leader, and executive secretary of the NAACP.

88. Jesse Owens (1913–1980), African American track star who broke numerous world records at the 1936 Olympic games in Berlin.

89. The boxer Jack Johnson (1878–1946) became the world's first African American heavyweight champion.

90. "Il Duce" (the leader) was a popular name for Mussolini.

"Madrid Getting Used to Bombs; It's Food Shortage That Hurts"

91. The Congress of Industrial Organizations (CIO) was founded by the American labor leader, John L. Lewis, in 1935. In 1955 the CIO merged with the American Federation of Labor to form the AFL-CIO, a voluntary federation of American labor unions.

"N.Y. Nurse Weds Irish Fighter in Spain's War"

92. Martha Gellhorn (1908–1998), American writer and journalist, was one of the first female war correspondents. She was married to Ernest Hemingway from 1940 to 1945.

"Milt Herndon Died Trying to Rescue Wounded Pal"

93. Angelo Herndon (1913–), an African American labor leader and Communist party recruiter, was sentenced to twenty years in prison under an antiquated Georgia slave law that prohibited insurrectionist activities.

"Laughter in Madrid"

94. Alejo Carpentier (1904–1980), renowned Cuban poet, novelist, and musicologist committed to revolutionary politics.

95. Emilio Mola (1887–1937), the Spanish general next in command to Franco during the Spanish Civil War, led the nationalist conspiracy in July 1936 against the republic.

Essays, 1940–1949

"Concerning 'Goodbye, Christ'"

1. Octavus Roy Cohen (1891–1959), a regular contributor to the *Saturday Evening Post* best known for the stereotypically drawn black characters of his dialect fiction.

"Ancient Contemporaries in the Forest Theatre"

2. Hughes published this essay in the Carmel *Pine Cone* (June 27, 1941). The text used here, however, is Hughes's undated file copy.

3. Hughes is referring to the Australian soldiers who died while attempting to stem the German invasion of Greece in 1941.

"Songs Called the Blues"

4. Mamie Smith (1883–1946), an African American vaudeville and cabaret performer, was the first vocalist to record a blues song; Georgia White (1903?–1980?), one of the most prolific female blues singers in terms of recordings, was promoted in the late 1930s and early 1940s as "The World's Greatest Blues Singer"; Midge Williams (1908–?), who began her professional singing career in 1927, toured the Far East, was resident singer at a club in Shanghai, and worked on her own radio series in

California before singing with Louis Armstrong's band in the late 1930s and early 1940s; Louis "Satchmo" Armstrong (1900–1971), one of the most creative innovators in the history of jazz, is known for his technical brilliance on the trumpet as well as for his pioneering singing style; Lonnie Johnson (1889–1970), a singer, guitarist, and violin player, recorded blues under his own name but also teamed up with jazz musicians such as Duke Ellington and Louis Armstrong; Jimmy Rushing (1903–1972), a violin player, pianist, and singer, toured with Walter Page's Blue Devils and Bennie Moton's Kansas City Orchestra before joining Count Basie's orchestra in 1935; Huddie "Leadbelly" Ledbetter (1888–1949) was a guitarist, bluesman, folksinger, and composer whose songs often carried political messages.

"Negro Writers and the War"

5. Hughes wrote this essay for a special edition of the *Chicago Defender* (September 26, 1942); he published a briefer version under the title "Devils in Dixie and Naziland" in *Negro Digest* (November 1942). The text used here is Hughes's file copy.

6. In response to A. Philip Randolph's organization of the March on Washington Movement, President Roosevelt issued Executive Order 8802 on June 25, 1941, which prohibited discrimination in the defense industry and in government and led to the establishment of the President's Committee on Fair Employment Practices (FEPC).

7. Eugene Talmadge (1884–1946) generated a good deal of criticism during his second term as governor of Georgia (1941–1943) when he dismissed several educators in the state university system for advocating racial equality in the schools; John Elliot Rankin (1882–1960), a vocal leader of the southern Democratic Party, opposed legislation that favored African Americans, immigrants, and labor unions; Frank Murray Dixon (1892–1965), a Democratic governor of Alabama from 1939 to 1943, was a conservative advocate of states' rights and became a key figure in the Dixiecrat Party, a faction of the Democratic Party opposed to the main party's civil rights platform.

8. Henry Agard Wallace (1888–1965), vice president of the United States from 1941 to 1945, was outspoken in his denouncement of discrimination against African Americans, though his actions as a politician were not always consonant with his rhetoric; Pearl Buck (1892–1973), an American author whose novels won both a Pulitzer Prize and a Nobel Prize, was also outspoken against discrimination and bigotry.

9. The Gestapo was one part of the secret state police in Hitler's Germany that oversaw the concentration and extermination camps and perpetrated the crimes of the Nazi authorities during World War II.

10. Roland Hayes (1887–1976), the first black man to receive wide acclaim for his singing both in the United States and abroad, was brutally beaten in 1942 by a white shoe store clerk in Georgia, his home state.

11. Sterling Brown (1901–1989), African American poet, critic, anthologist, and teacher whose writings were heavily influenced by African American folklore and other elements of the vernacular tradition; Margaret Walker (1915–1998), African American poet, novelist, essayist, and teacher best known for her collection of poems, *For My People* (1942), and her novel of slave life, *Jubilee* (1966).

12. In a 1941 message to Congress, President Franklin Delano Roosevelt stated that freedom of speech and expression, freedom of worship, freedom from want, and freedom from fear should be enjoyed by people worldwide.

"What Shall We Do about the South?"

13. Hughes is perhaps referring to Ellis Gibbs Arnall (1907–1992), a southern politician who defeated Eugene Talmadge and served as governor of Georgia from 1943 to 1947. During his tenure, Arnall abolished the poll tax, which had long been a barrier to African American voting.

14. Mark Ethridge (1896–1981), a southern white liberal and the first chairman of the Fair Employment Practices Committee (FEPC), made the statement to which Hughes refers to alleviate southern fears of social integration.

15. Dorothy Maynor (1910–1996), renowned soprano and founder of the Harlem School of the Arts at St. James Presbyterian Church, became the first African American to serve on the Metropolitan Opera's board of directors; Paul Green (1894–1981), American dramatist, novelist, and humanitarian known for his plays depicting issues of race and class in the agrarian South; Erskine Caldwell (1903–1987), American novelist and short story writer whose fiction focused on life in the rural South.

"Maker of the Blues"

16. Billy Rose's Diamond Horseshoe, located in the basement of the Paramount Hotel on 46th Street, was one of New York's leading night clubs.

17. Located in Harlem and owned by a gangster, the Cotton Club was one of New York's premier nightclubs in the 1920s, attracting performers such as Cab Calloway, Duke Ellington, and Ethel Waters while maintaining a "whites only" policy for its clientele.

"Is Hollywood Fair to Negroes?"

18. This essay is Hughes's contribution to a "round table" discussion sponsored by *Negro Digest* in which a number of writers were asked, "Is Hollywood fair to Negroes?" Hughes's answer is a firm "no."

19. The Bundists were an organization of pro-Nazi German Americans; "Fifth Columnists" are secret sympathizers who engage in espionage or sabotage within a nation's borders to further an invading enemy's military and political aims.

20. Louise Beavers (1902–1962), African American actress; Phillis Wheatley (ca. 1753–1784), the first African American to publish a book; Hattie McDaniel (1895–1952), the first African American to win an Oscar, for her portrayal of Mammy in *Gone with the Wind;* Clarence Muse (1889–1979), American film actor, director, writer, and composer; Colonel Charles Young (1864–1922), African American military leader, linguist, and educator; Leigh Whipper (1876–1975), founder of the Negro Actor's Guild and the first African American member of the Actor's Equity Association; George Washington Carver (1864?-1943), although born into slavery, once free obtained an education and became a renowned agricultural chemist and director of the Department of Agricultural Research at Tuskegee Institute; Haile Selassie (1892–1975), emperor of Ethiopia from 1930 to 1974; Sissieretta Jones (1868–1933), African American classical and opera singer who was compared to the Italian soprano Adelina Patti and subsequently dubbed "Black Patti."

"The Case against Segregation"

21. Eddie "Rochester" Anderson (1905–1977), the African American actor who played Rochester on the *Jack Benny Show.*

"The Future of Black America"

22. Wendell Lewis Willkie (1892–1944), American industrialist, political leader, and author who argued in his book *One World* (1943) that

the American attitude toward African Americans was largely imperialistic and impeded the war effort.

23. William Augustus Hinton (1883–1959), a renowned bacteriologist and pathologist who did pioneering research on syphilis, was the first African American professor to join the faculty of Harvard University. Canada Lee (1907–1952) gave up a boxing career to pursue acting on Broadway and in Hollywood; his successful career was cut short when he died from a heart attack after being blacklisted for refusing to testify before the House Un-American Activities Committee in the early 1950s. Adam Clayton Powell Jr. (1908–1972) was an African American politician and clergyman elected to the U.S. Congress in 1945. Joe Louis (1914–1981), an American boxer, became the world heavyweight champion at age twenty-three and lost only three bouts in his long career. Dorris "Dorie" Miller (1919–1944), a mess attendant in the U.S. Navy, overcame racial restrictions in the military and became a hero when he manned a machine gun during the Japanese attack on Pearl Harbor in 1941.

"My America"

24. A briefer version originally appeared in *Journal of Educational Psychology* (February 1943): 334–36.

25. Lillian Smith (1897–1966), American writer and social worker best known for *Strange Fruit*, a novel that explores the relationship between a black woman and a white man.

"Down Under in Harlem"

26. The Harlem riots of 1943, in which 6 African Americans were killed and more than 180 injured, were a manifestation of tensions between Harlemites and the police that peaked when a white police officer shot a young African American male attempting to defend his mother, who had been arrested. Henry Fiorello LaGuardia (1882–1947), during his tenure as mayor of New York City from 1934 to 1945, focused on beautifying the city, reducing political corruption, and improving health and sanitary conditions; John Haynes Holmes (1879–1964), American clergyman and one of the founders of the National Association for the Advancement of Colored People and the American Civil Liberties Union.

27. In his 1903 essay entitled "The Talented Tenth," Du Bois argued

that the exceptional 10 percent of the black race would lead and uplift the masses.

28. "King Kong" is slang for barbiturate sleeping pills (it is also a term used to describe a major heroin habit); "geronimoes" refer to alcoholic beverages mixed with barbiturates.

29. Louis Jordan (1908–1975), African American saxophonist, singer, songwriter and bandleader.

"Solving the Race Problem: A State or Federal Issue?"

30. This essay is Hughes's contribution to a "round table" discussion sponsored by *Negro Digest* in which a number of writers were asked a question regarding racial issues in the United States. Hughes believes that racial conflict in the United States is a federal problem.

31. Hughes is perhaps referring to those in Congress who opposed the Green-Lucas bill—proposed in December 1943 to create a federal "war ballot commission" to ensure the voting rights of soldiers—on the grounds that the bill violated states' rights to all powers not specifically granted by the Constitution. Opponents of the bill feared that it would lead to the reelection of Franklin D. Roosevelt.

"Greetings, Good Neighbors"

32. Hughes's undated file copy is inscribed, "Radio talk? (I reckon)."

33. Etta Moten, singer and actress, the first black woman to perform at the White House; John Kirby (1908–1952), double bass player and bandleader; Elmer Carter (1890–1973), prominent African American editor of the Urban League's official journal, *Opportunity*, and the first chairman of the New York State Commission against Discrimination; Roy Wilkins (1901–1981), American civil rights leader who succeeded W. E. B. Du Bois as editor of *Crisis* magazine and later served as executive director of the NAACP; Carl Murphy (1889–1967), American journalist, publisher, civil rights leader, and educator.

34. President Franklin D. Roosevelt's efforts to improve relations with Latin America were known as the Good Neighbor Policy.

"My Poems and Myself"

35. Hughes's file copy is inscribed, "For the Burnett-Slatkin High School Anthology."

"America's Most Unique Newspaper"

36. Aida Overton Walker (1870–1914), African American dancer and actress; Emmett Scott (1873–1957), African American biographer and historian.

"Simple and Me"

37. Hughes began writing a regular column for the *Chicago Defender* in 1942. His first Simple column appeared on February 13, 1943.

"It's About Time"

38. Hughes's file copy is inscribed, "Especially for the *New York Age.*"

39. Charles Drew (1904–1950), African American surgeon and physician whose research on blood plasma led to his concept of the blood bank; William Henry Hastie (1904–1976), educator, judge, and the first African American governor of the Virgin Islands.

"Don't Be a Bottle-Battler"

40. Hughes's file copy is inscribed, "Written especially for the MESSAGE, Southern Publishing Association, Nashville, Tenn., November 4, 1946."

"Memories of Christmas"

41. Hughes's file copy is inscribed, "Written especially for *Circuit Magazine.*" Hughes later included this essay in *The Langston Hughes Reader* (1958).

"My Adventures as a Social Poet"

42. Gerardo Machado (1871–1939) was president of Cuba from 1925 to 1933.

43. Robert Nathan (1894–1985), American novelist and poet.

44. Gerald L. K. Smith (1898–1976) was the bigoted leader of the far-right America First Party.

"Atlanta: Its Negroes Have Most Culture but Some of the Worst Ghettoes in the World"

45. Benjamin E. Mays (1895–1984), noted minister, educator, counselor, civil rights activist, and author.

46. John Gunther (1901–1970), American author and journalist.

"Jamaica"

47. Willie Bryant (1908–1964), African American bandleader, singer, actor, and disc jockey; Jackie "Moms" Mabley (1894–1975), African American comedienne and singer.

Essays, 1950–1959

"Curtain Time"

1. Hughes's file copy is inscribed, "Written especially for *Where the Negro Stands Today*." The book, which was to be edited by Sylvestre C. Watkins, was apparently never published. Readers interested in African American theater and in more information on the many figures mentioned by Hughes in this essay are encouraged to consult Doris E. Abramson, *Negro Playwrights in the American Theatre, 1925–1959* (New York: Columbia University Press, 1969); William L. Andrews, Frances Smith Foster, and Trudier Harris, eds., *The Oxford Companion to African American Literature* (New York: Oxford University Press, 1997); Harry J. Elam Jr. and David Krasner, eds., *African-American Performance and Theater History: A Critical Reader* (New York: Oxford University Press, 2001); Rena Fraden, *Blueprints for a Black Federal Theatre, 1935–1939* (New York: Cambridge University Press, 1994); Bernard L. Peterson, *Profiles of African American Stage Performers and Theatre People, 1816–1960* (Westport, Conn.: Greenwood Press, 2001); Leslie C. Sanders, *The Development of Black Theater in America: From Shadows to Selves* (Baton Rouge: Louisiana State University Press, 1988).

2. Hughes's *Mulatto* (1935), which concerns miscegenation and the South, became the longest running Broadway play written by an African American until Lorraine Hansberry's *A Raisin in the Sun* (1959). *Deep Are the Roots* (1945), coauthored by Arnaud d'Usseau and James Gow,

focuses on an African American war hero who returns to his home in the deeply prejudiced South.

"Some Practical Observations: A Colloquy"

3. Ralph Bunche (1903–1971), American scholar, diplomat, and humanitarian, was awarded the Nobel Peace Prize in 1950 for his work in negotiating four peace agreements that ended the 1948–1949 Arab-Israeli War.

4. Willard Motley (1909–1965), African American novelist, journalist, diarist, and essayist; Frank Yerby (1916–1991), African American historical novelist and short story writer; Myron O'Higgins (1918–), African American poet; M. Carl Holman (1919–1988), African American poet, educator, and editor; Gwendolyn Brooks (1917–2000), African American poet, novelist, and writer of children's literature; Russell Atkins (1926–), African American poet, composer, theorist, and editor.

5. Ralph Ellison (1914–1994), African American novelist, essayist, short story writer, and musician.

6. George Norford, African American editor and television producer.

7. E. Franklin Frazier (1894–1962), African American sociologist whose work focused on the African American family and the black bourgeoisie; John Hope Franklin (1915–), African American historian and educator; Horace Cayton (1903–1970), African American sociologist whose work centered on African American urban life; St. Clair Drake (1911–), African American author of sociological and historical studies of African American life.

"From the Blues to an Opera Libretto"

8. Jasper Deeter, African American actor and director.

9. James Brander Matthews (1852–1929), American author and professor of drama at Columbia University; Felix Brentano, American educator and theater director; Willard Rhodes, American ethnomusicologist.

"How to Be a Bad Writer (In Ten Easy Lessons)"

10. Hughes is perhaps referring to the Golden Gate Quartet, an a cappella group composed of William Langford (first tenor), Willie Johnson (baritone), Henry Owens (second tenor), and Orlandus Wilson (bass).

"When I Worked for Dr. Woodson"

11. Carter G. Woodson (1875–1950), an African American editor and historian, founded the *Journal of Negro History* in 1916 and began Negro History Week (which evolved into Black History Month) in 1926.

"Bright Chariots"

12. Hughes later published this essay under the title "Sweet Chariots of This World" in *The Langston Hughes Reader* (1958) and *The Book of Negro Humor* (1966).

13. Valaida Snow (1903–1956), African American stage and film actress, singer, dancer, and trumpet player.

14. Billy Eckstine (1914–1993), American jazz singer; Sugar Ray refers, of course, to Sugar Ray Robinson (1920–1989), the world welterweight champion who also won the middleweight title on several occasions.

15. Griffith J. Davis (1923–1993), African American photographer.

16. Henry Binga Dismond (1891–1956), an African American radiologist, was made a Chevalier of the National Order of Honor and Merit by the republic of Haiti for his work following the massacre of Haitians by Dominican troops in 1937; no information could be located on Dr. Marshall Ross.

"The Streets of Chicago"

17. Hughes's file copy is inscribed, "Written especially for the *Negro Digest.*"

18. James Thomas Ferrell (1904–1979), American novelist, essayist, and short story writer; Nelson Algren (1909–1981), American novelist and author of numerous personal sketches.

19. Gertrude "Ma" Rainey (1886–1939), African American blues singer; Billy King, producer, writer, and minstrel comedian popular in the early twentieth century; "Stringbeans" may refer to Ethel Waters, known as "Sweet Mama Stringbean."

"Jokes Negroes Tell on Themselves"

20. The riots to which Hughes refers began on June 20, 1943, and resulted in the deaths of twenty-five black residents and nine white residents.

21. Sugar Chile Robinson (1940–), an African American boogie-woogie singer from Detroit, was only nine years old when his "Numbers Boogie" became a national hit in 1949.

"The Wages of Sin Are Not Always Death"

22. In 1951, Carey Estes Kefauver (1903–1963), a U.S. senator from Tennessee (1949–63), spearheaded an investigation of organized crime that led to increased law-enforcement activities against gangsters.

"Do Big Negroes Keep Little Negroes Down?"

23. "Working for Mr. Pullman" is a colloquial phrase pertaining to service on the railroad sleeping cars developed by George Mortimer Pullman (1831–1897).

"The Negro Artist"

24. Sidney Kingsley (1906–1995), American dramatist and Hollywood script writer.

"My School Days in Lincoln, Illinois"

25. Hughes's file copy is inscribed, "As tape recorded for the Illinois Education Association Central Division, Centennial."

"A Night at the Apollo"

26. Eddie Bonnemere, American jazz musician and bandleader.

27. Beatrice "Bea" Lillie (1894–1989), Canadian actress, singer, and comedian; Eddie Greene (1901–1950), magician, blackface dancer, and singer; Willie Bryant (1908–1964), American singer and bandleader; Leonard Reed, American dancer, comedian, songwriter, choreographer, bandleader, and director.

28. George Kirby (1925–1995), American comedian, nightclub performer, and actor; Honi Coles and Cholly Atkins, an American tap-dancing duo, toured with such bands as those of Count Basie, Cab Calloway, Lionel Hampton, and Billy Eckstine; the Dyerettes were an African American female dance and acrobatic troupe.

"Humor and the Negro Press"

29. Charles Manuel "Sweet Daddy" Grace (1881–1960), Portuguese evangelist and founder of the United House of Prayer for All People.

30. Almena Lomax (1918–), journalist and editor of the *Los Angeles Tribune* from 1940 to 1960; Philip Wylie, American journalist and fiction writer.

31. E. Simms Campbell (1908–1971), African American cartoonist whose drawings of "pin-up girls" made him one of the most renowned illustrators in the country; Oliver W. "Ollie" Harrington (1912–1995), African American political cartoonist and social satirist; Mel Tapley, African American cartoonist.

32. Evelyn Cunningham, African American reporter, columnist, editor, and patron of the arts; Nat D. Williams, African American educator and journalist; Enoch Waters, African American journalist and editor; Ted Poston (1906–1974), considered the dean of African American journalists during the civil rights movement; Dan Burley, the author of the *Original Handbook of Harlem Jive* (1944); Timmie Rogers, American blues singer.

"Langston Hughes' Speech at National Assembly of Authors and Dramatists Symposium: 'The Writer's Position in America' "

33. Bruce Catton (1899–1978), American historian.

34. Chester Himes (1909–1984), African American novelist best known for his naturalist and detective fiction; James Baldwin (1924–1987), African American novelist, essayist, playwright, scriptwriter, director, and filmmaker; William Demby (1922–), African American novelist, journalist, and actor. Autherine Lucy (1928–) was expelled from the University of Alabama in 1956 after rioting broke out in response to the state being ordered to admit black applicants. Fourteen-year-old Emmett Till was abducted and killed in 1955 after it was alleged he had whistled at a white woman in Mississippi. The NAACP immediately labeled the case a lynching, but despite organized protests that became a rallying point for the Civil Rights Movement, an all-white jury acquitted the men responsible for the boy's death.

"How Real Is Make-Believe?"

35. Hughes's file copy is inscribed, "Written Especially for the *Simply Heavenly* Playbill."

"You're Simple if You Want to Write a Play"

36. Hughes's file copy is inscribed, "Written for the Dorothy Killgalen column, sent to Dave Lipsky, September 25, 1957."

37. Sticks Evans, American percussionist; Alfred Wesley "Al" Hall (1915–1988), American double bass player; Paul Webster (1909–1966), American trumpet player.

"The Fun of Being Black"

38. Roscoe Conkling Simmons (1881–1951), African American politician and orator.

39. Ella "Mother" Bloor (1862–1951), American author and radical organizer who served as chairperson of the Communist Party's women's commission.

"Jazz as Communication"

40. Tony Jackson (1876–1921), American ragtime pianist and blues singer; Ferdinand Joseph "Jelly Roll" Morton (1885–1941) began playing piano in New Orleans's Storyville at the age of seventeen and was regarded by many as the first great jazz composer; Joseph "King" Oliver (1885–1938), popular ragtime performer with roots in New Orleans.

41. Blind Lemon Jefferson (1897–1929), early American pioneer of the blues; Thomas "Georgia Tom" Dorsey (1899–1993), African American blues singer, gospel songwriter, and pianist.

42. James Louis "J. J." Johnson (1924–), an American trombonist and composer, and Kai Winding (1922–1983), a Danish American trombonist, formed the popular group Jay and Kai in 1954; Lonnie Johnson (1889–1970), American guitarist and jazz singer.

43. Jacques Prévert (1900–1977), French poet; James Price "J. P." Johnson (1894–1955), American ragtime and blues pianist and composer; J. C. Johnson (1896–1981), jazz pianist and songwriter; Willie "The Lion" Smith (1897–1973), American jazz pianist and composer; Hilton Napoleon "Nappy" Lamare (1907–1988), American guitarist, banjoist, composer, and singer.

44. Chick Webb (1909–1939), American drummer and bandleader; Hartzell Strathdene "Tiny" Parham (1900–1943), Canadian American pianist, organist, and bandleader; John Birks "Dizzy" Gillespie (1917–1993), American trumpeter and bandleader; Thelonius Monk (1917–1982), American jazz pianist and composer.

45. W. Benton Overstreet, American songwriter; Perry "Mule" Bradford (1893–1970), American pianist, songwriter, singer, and producer; Buddy DeSilva, American songwriter; Dorothy Baker (1907–1968), jazz writer best known for *Young Man with a Horn,* a novel about the life of Leon "Bix" Beiderbecke; Charlie Christian (1916–1942), American guitarist; Joe Sullivan (1906–1971), American pianist and composer.

46. Nathan Irving "Nat" Hentoff (1925–), American writer and jazz historian; Billy Strayhorn (1915–1967), American composer, arranger, and pianist; Tony Scott (1921–), American clarinetist and saxophonist; Charlie "Bird" Parker (1920–1955), American alto saxophonist and one of the most influential soloists in jazz; Friedrich Gulda (1930–), Austrian pianist, flutist, baritone saxophonist, singer, and composer; Charlie Mingus (1922–1979), American double bass player, pianist, composer, and bandleader.

"The Roots of Jazz"

47. Hughes's undated file copy is inscribed, "For the Stratford Souvenir Program." Arnold Rampersad notes that Hughes read with a group of jazz musicians on July 22 and 23, 1958, at the Stratford, Ontario, Shakespeare festival (see Rampersad, *Life,* 2:285). "The Roots of Jazz" was likely written for this program.

"Speak Well of the Dead"

48. Dickie Wells (1907–1985), American trombonist.

49. Sarah Breedlove McWilliams "Madam C. J." Walker (1867–1919), African American entrepreneur and patron of civil rights organizations who made a fortune with her process for straightening hair.

"Writers: Black and White"

50. Nadine Gordimer (1923–), Nobel Prize–winning South African writer whose early works were deeply critical of the system of apartheid in South Africa; Alan Paton (1903–1988), South African novelist whose writing focused on the struggle to end the oppression of blacks in South Africa.

51. Marc Connelly (1890–1981), American dramatist best known for his Pulitzer Prize–winning play *The Green Pastures* (1930), which explores the religious lives of southern blacks.

Essays, 1960–1967

"Richard Wright's Last Guest"

1. Hughes's file copy is inscribed, "Written especially for *Ebony* on request."

"The Woes of a Writer"

2. Hughes began writing a regular column for the *New York Post* in 1962.

"Gospel Songs and Gospel Singing"

3. Hughes's file copy is inscribed, "*Final* revised copy for Spoleto program." Spoleto, Italy, was the location of the 1962 Festival of Two Worlds, a drama festival that included Hughes's own *Black Nativity.*

4. Alex Bradford, African American gospel singer, songwriter, choir director, promoter, and record producer; Clara Ward (1924–1973), African American gospel singer and songwriter; Jobe Huntley, African American songwriter.

"South of Light Bulbs and Pomegranates (An Appreciation of Two Artists)"

5. On his file copy for this odd little piece, Hughes indicated that a copy had been sent to the American Society for African Culture (AMSAC) newsletter. Jacob Lawrence (1917–2000), African American artist and educator best known for his series of paintings documenting the Great Migration and his mosaic mural for the New York subway system; Lourenço Marques was the original name of Maputo, the capital of Mazambique; Valente Malangatana (1936–), African painter and poet.

"My Early Days in Harlem"

6. Moe Gale, American music producer and manager of the Savoy Ballroom; Lew Leslie, American music promoter; the Harmon Foundation, which supported the work of outstanding blacks in business, farming, race relations, education, religious service, music, and science, was started by William E. Harmon (1862–1928), American philanthropist; Casper Holstein (1876–?), African American businessman, racketeer, and patron of the arts.

7. Marcus Garvey (1887–1940), Jamaican American social activist, journalist, and proponent of black nationalism.

8. Alta Douglas (d. 1959), the wife of artist Aaron Douglas, was a friend to many African American artists and writers during the Harlem Renaissance.

9. Wilbur Dorsey "Buck" Clayton (1911–1991), African American trumpeter and musical arranger.

10. *WPA* and *CCC* refer to the Works Progress Administration and the Civilian Conservation Corps, programs established as part of President Franklin Delano Roosevelt's New Deal; George "Father Divine" Baker (1882–1965), African American religious leader and founder of the Peace Mission movement. The Blue Eagle was the symbol for the National Recovery Administration (NRA).

"Gospel Singers: New Asset to American Theatre"

11. The African American gospel singer Marion Williams was the first vocalist to receive a "genius" award from the MacArthur Foundation.

"Eight to Two"

12. Albert Londres (1884–1932), French journalist.

13. *Mandingo* (1958), a novel by Kyle Onstott (1886–?), concerns the issue of miscegenation.

"Gospel Songs: From Kansas to Broadway"

14. Hughes's file copy is inscribed, "Written for Nat Dorfman, 'Tambourines,' N.Y. Herald Tribune."

15. Princess Stewart, an African American gospel singer, was known as the "Grand Lady of Gospel."

16. Nathaniel Robert Dett (1882–1943), American composer who drew from the African American folk tradition for his music; Harry Thacker Burleigh (1866–1949), American composer and singer who also arranged African American spirituals.

"Draft Ideas"

17. Sartre declined the 1964 Nobel Prize for Literature on the grounds that the prize was merely a political tool of a corrupt society.

18. Léopold Sédar Senghor (1906–), African statesman and poet, was president of the republic of Senegal from 1960–1980.

"Hold Fast to Dreams"

19. The text is a transcription of a program Hughes presented at Lincoln University in Pennsylvania on April 5, 1964.

20. Hughes is referring to Omega Psi Phi Fraternity.

21. The National Urban League was founded in 1910 to help end racial segregation and discrimination in the United States through volunteer service in areas such as employment, housing, and education; the National Association for the Advancement of Colored People (NAACP) was founded in 1910 to help end racial segregation, discrimination, and violence through litigation and nonviolent protest; the Congress of Racial Equality (CORE) was founded in 1942 to promote better race relations through nonviolent direct action; the Southern Christian Leadership Conference (SCLC) was founded in 1957 by Dr. Martin Luther King Jr. and others to promote social, political, and economic justice through nonviolent direct action.

"Carl Van Vechten: An Appreciation"

22. James Purdy (1923–), American novelist and playwright; Yvette Guilbert (1868–1944), French singer and performer; Mary Garden (1874–1967), Scottish-American soprano.

23. Fania Marinoff, silent film actress.

24. Edward Steichen (1879–1973), American photographer.

"A Letter from America"

25. Hughes is referring to the Civil Rights Act of 1964, which prohibited discrimination on the basis of color, race, sex, religion, or national origin in employment and places of public accommodation covered by interstate commerce.

"The Task of the Negro Writer as Artist"

26. Hughes is referring to Warren Miller's novel *The Cool World* (1959), James Baldwin's novel *Another Country* (1962), Jean Genet's play *The Blacks* (1958), LeRoi Jones's/Amiri Baraka's play *The Toilet* (1964), and William Hanley's play *Slow Dance on the Killing Ground* (1964). In his reference to *Crazy House of the Negro,* Hughes may have meant Adrienne Kennedy's play *The Funny House of a Negro* (1962).

"*Ebony*'s Nativity: An Evaluation from Birth"

27. John H. Johnson, African American founder, publisher chairman, and chief executive officer of Johnson Publishing Company.

28. Vera Lucia Couto dos Santos, as crowned Miss Brazil, was the first black woman to become a finalist in a major international beauty pageant.

29. Lerone Bennett (1928–), American social historian, columnist, essayist, and civil rights advocate.

30. Matthew Alexander Henson (1867–1955), African American explorer recognized as one of the discoverers of the North Pole.

31. The Spingarn Medal is the highest award bestowed by the NAACP.

"The Negro and American Entertainment"

32. Sengbe Pieh (1815–?), an African farmer and captive slave, was renamed Joseph Cinque by Spanish slave traders in 1839. John Quincy Adams, moved by the bravery of Cinque and his comrades, argued their case in front of the Supreme Court.

33. Solomon Northup (1808–1863), a free-born African American, was kidnapped and enslaved in the deep South, an experience he recounted in *Twelve Years a Slave* (1853).

34. Thomas Rice, a white man, developed a song-and-dance routine by impersonating the movements of an elderly slave.

35. J. Rosamond Johnson (1873–1954), the brother of James Weldon Johnson, was a vaudeville performer and songwriter.

36. Lester Walton (1882–1965), African American journalist, diplomat, civic leader, and theater manager.

37. Paul Henry Lang (1901–1991), renowned musicologist and music critic.

38. Ellen Holly, African American actress and autobiographer.

"Segregated Integration"

39. The "Little Rock School crisis" refers to the nine black students who, guarded by federal troops, integrated all-white Little Rock Central High School in Little Rock, Arkansas, on September 25, 1957.

40. The Montgomery bus boycott of 1955 was organized by Dr. Martin Luther King Jr. in protest of the city's segregated public bus system. In 1956, a federal court ordered Montgomery to desegregate its buses.

41. William Pickens (1881–1954), African American orator, journalist, essayist, and autobiographer.

42. Orval E. Faubus (1910–1994), governor of Arkansas from 1955 to 1967, defied a federal court order to integrate Little Rock Central High School by calling in the Arkansas National Guard to prevent black students from entering the school.

"The Twenties: Harlem and Its Negritude"

43. Richmond Barthé (1901–1989), African American sculptor renowned for his busts of performers such as Katharine Cornell, Sir Laurence Olivier, and Paul Robeson.

"Black Writers in a Troubled World"

44. Hughes's file copy is inscribed, "Written especially for the Colloquium at Dakar."

Forewords, Prefaces, and Introductions to Edited Volumes

"The Negro," introduction to *Hunger and Revolt: Cartoons by [Jacob] Burck*

1. The Silver Shirts, an American Nazi group, openly supported Hitler during the 1930s; the State Emergency Relief Administration (SERA), like the Civilian Conservation Corps and the National Recovery Administration, was part of Roosevelt's New Deal.

2. Thomas J. Mooney (1883–1942), an American labor agitator, was sentenced to death in 1916 for bombing a parade in California. His sentence was later commuted to life imprisonment, and in 1939 the governor of California pardoned him.

"Concerning Nicolás Guillén"

3. Hughes intended this piece as an introduction to *Cuba Libre,* a collection of Guillén's poems that he cotranslated with Ben Frederic Carruthers (Los Angeles: Anderson and Ritchie, 1948). Hughes's file copy is inscribed, "For the *Crisis.*"

"Preface" (with Arna Bontemps), *The Poetry of the Negro, 1746–1949*

4. Donald Jeffrey Hayes (1904–1991), a little-known African American poet, was a contemporary of the Harlem Renaissance writers.

"Introduction," *The Japanese Anthology of Negro Poetry*

5. Hughes's file copy is inscribed, "Written especially for the *Japanese Anthology of Negro Poetry* as translated by Shozo Kojima."

"Introduction," *Bootsie and Others: A Selection of Cartoons by Ollie Harrington*

6. Honoré Daumier (1808–1879), French caricaturist, painter, and sculptor; William Hogarth (1697–1764), English painter, satirist, and engraver.

"Introduction," *Pudd'nhead Wilson,* by Mark Twain

7. Joel Chandler Harris (1848–1908), American short story writer and humorist best known for his Uncle Remus tales; Francis Hopkinson Smith (1838–1915), American engineer, artist, and writer; Thomas Nelson Page (1853–1922), American author and ambassador to Italy.

"Introduction," *An African Treasury: Articles, Essays, Stories, and Poems by Black Africans,* ed. Langston Hughes

8. Benjamin Nnamdi Azikiwe (1904–1996), Nigerian statesman, publisher, and intellectual, held the premiership of Eastern Nigeria from 1954 to 1959 and became the first president of the Republic of Nigeria in 1963.

9. Amos Tutuola (1920–1997), Nigerian novelist best known for his first novel, *The Palm-Wine Drinkard* (1952); Abioseh Nicol (1924–), African physician, research scientist, fiction writer, and historian; Matei Markwei, Ghanaian poet, studied theology at Yale University; Peter Kumalo (1929–), South African poet and dockworker.

10. Ezekiel Mphahlele (1919–), South African writer, activist, and professor; the first Accra Conference (1958) brought together African

leaders to discuss the political future of Africa; Kwame Nkrumah (1909–1972), African political leader, prime minister, and president of Ghana; Thomas Joseph Mboya (1930–1969), Kenyan political leader who was elected president of the Accra Conference.

11. The Mau Mau, a secret insurgent organization, was composed of revolutionaries who mounted a rebellion in Kenya when the white minority resisted black participation in government. Jomo Kenyatta (1893?–1978), African political leader and first president of Kenya, and other nationalists were imprisoned, and many of the leaders of Mau Mau were hunted down by British troops and killed.

12. Todd Matshikiza (?–1968), South African writer, composer, and pianist; Can Themba (1924–1968), South African poet, essayist, and fiction writer; Julius Nyerere (ca. 1922–1999), African political leader, educator, and the first president of Tanzania; Phyllis Ntantala (ca. 1920–), South African activist, poet, essayist, and autobiographer.

"Introduction," *Poems for a Mixed-Up World,* by Andy Razaf

13. Apparently *Poems for a Mixed-Up World* was never published. Andrea Razafkeriefo, known as Andy Razaf (1895?–1973) was an African American songwriter, pianist, and poet.

"Foreword," *Poems from Black Africa,* ed. Langston Hughes

14. Gabriel Okara (1921–), Nigerian poet and novelist; Dennis Osadebay, Nigerian poet and autobiographer; Michael Dei-Anang, Ghanaian poet and autobiographer.

"Introduction," *Up from Slavery,* by Booker T. Washington

15. William Monroe Trotter (1872–1934), African American newspaper editor and civil rights organizer.

"Three Men of Peace," introduction to *The Peacemakers [Die Friedensmacher],* by Rolf Italiaander

16. Hughes's file copy is inscribed, "For Rolf Italiaander." Italiaander (1913–1993) was a prolific author and editor.

17. Gunnar Myrdal (1898–1987), Swedish author, economist, sociologist, and public official.

18. Albert John Luthuli (1898?–1967), South African political leader, activist, and autobiographer.

"200 Years of Afro-American Poetry"

19. Hughes intended this piece as an introduction to Jean Wagner's *Anthologie de la Poésie Negro-Américaine,* which was translated as *Black Poets of the United States: From Paul Laurence Dunbar to Langston Hughes* (Urbana: University of Illinois Press, 1973). The poem to which Hughes refers is "Bars Fight," by the African American writer Lucy Terry (ca. 1730–1821).

20. Jupiter Hammon (1711–ca. 1806), the first published African American writer, was a poet, essayist, and preacher; George Moses Horton (ca. 1797–ca. 1883), the first African American to use verse to protest slavery; Frances Ellen Watkins Harper (1825–1911), African American novelist, poet, essayist, and orator.

21. William Waring Cuney (1906–1976), one of the lesser-known poets of the Harlem Renaissance.

22. Richard Gibson, African American journalist.

23. Julia Fields (1938–), African American poet, short story writer, teacher, and dramatist; Julian Bond (1940–), African American activist, historian, and educator; David Henderson, African American poet and biographer.

24. Dudley Randall (1914–2000), African American poet, publisher, and editor.

"Introduction," *The Best Short Stories by Negro Writers: An Anthology from 1899 to the Present,* ed. Langston Hughes

25. Frederick Ernest "Sunshine Sammy" Morrison (1912–1989), African American child actor on the popular *Our Gang* series; Horace Winfred "Nicodemus" Stewart (1910–2000), African American actor, comedian, and founder of the Ebony Showcase Theater; Mantan Moreland (1901–1973), African American actor and comedian.

26. Owen Dodson (1914–1983), African American poet, novelist, and playwright.

Reviews

"A Fine New Poet," review of *A Street in Bronzeville,* by Gwendolyn Brooks

1. Fenton Johnson (1888–1958), African American poet, essayist, short fiction writer, and educator.

"Chicago's South Side Comes Alive," review of *47th Street,* by Frank Marshall Davis

2. Hughes's file copy is inscribed, "Written especially for the Associated Negro Press."

"Two Modern Poets," review of *Poems, 1928–1948,* by Edouard Roditi, and *The Wind of Time,* by Rolfe Humphries

3. Hughes's file copy is undated. Notes in the Beinecke Library's finding aid for Hughes's manuscripts suggest that the review was published in *Voices* in 1949. The editor was unsuccessful in locating this publication.

"A Boxcar of a Book," review of *The Big Boxcar,* by Alfred Maund

4. Hughes's file copy is inscribed, "Sent to Anne Braden Sou. Conf. Paper."

Review of *The World of Carl Sandburg*

5. Hughes's file copy is inscribed, "As Reviewed on the Air—WNEW —at 11:10, September 14, 1960."

Brief Tributes, Letters to the Editor, Miscellaneous Pieces

[Letter to the editor concerning *Fine Clothes to the Jew* and Carl Van Vechten]

1. Allison Davis (1902–1983), African American psychologist, educator, and essayist.

"If I Were White"

2. Hughes is likely referring to George Catlett Marshall (1880–1959), American general who was named secretary of state by President Truman in 1947 and that same year developed the Marshall Plan to promote postwar economic recovery in Europe, for which he was awarded the Nobel Peace Prize in 1953.

Index of Titles

Index